Song Sheets to Software, Third Edition

A Guide to Print Music, Software, Instructional Media, and Web Sites for Musicians

Elizabeth C. Axford

The Scarecrow Press, Inc.
Lanham, Maryland • Toronto • Plymouth, UK
2009

SCARECROW PRESS, INC.

Published in the United States of America
by Scarecrow Press, Inc.
A wholly owned subsidiary of The Rowman & Littlefield Publishing Group, Inc.
4501 Forbes Boulevard, Suite 200, Lanham, Maryland 20706
www.scarecrowpress.com

Estover Road
Plymouth PL6 7PY
United Kingdom

British Library Cataloguing in Publication Information Available

Library of Congress Cataloging-in-Publication Data

Library of Congress Cataloging-in-Publication Data

Axford, Elizabeth C., 1958–
  Song sheets to software : a guide to print music, software, instructional media, and web sites for musicians / Elizabeth C. Axford. —
3rd ed.
      p. cm.
  Includes bibliographical references (p.   ).
  ISBN-13: 978-0-8108-6725-3 (pbk.: alk. paper)
  ISBN-10: 0-8108-6725-7 (pbk.: alk. paper)
  ISBN-13: 978-0-8108-6726-0 (ebook)
  ISBN-10: 0-8108-6726-5 (ebook)
  1. Music—Computer network resources. I. Title.
  ML74.7.A94 2009
  780.26—dc22

2008047125

Dedication

This book is lovingly dedicated to my family, friends, colleagues, and students, without whom, I wouldn't be here.

Acknowledgements

I would like to thank my immediate family for their love and support, including my parents, Dr. Roy A. Axford and Anne R. Axford, my brothers, Dr. Roy A. Axford, Jr., and Dr. Trevor C. C. Axford, my sisters-in-law, Cyndi Axford and Sarah Axford, my nephews, Noah and Charlie Axford, and my nieces, Madison and Mackenzie Axford. Thanks for always loving, always supporting, and always believing in me.

Thanks to my editor at Scarecrow Press, Renée Camus, for understanding my vision. Thanks to all my friends and colleagues, the hundreds of songwriters and musicians I have known and worked with through the years, and the hundreds of students whom I have been blessed to meet and teach. You inspire me more than you'll ever know.

Thanks to my extended family, my godparents, Fleur and Jay Chandler, my great uncle and aunt, Howard and Muriel Paulson, Dorothy S. Donaldson, Carol and Bob Crumbaker, Susan Richards, and Sharon Parker.

In loving memory of my grandparents, Captain Charles and Lillemor Rasmussen, Charlotte D. Axford and Roy A. Paulson, my great uncles and aunts, Alan Donaldson, Kermit and Helen S. Donaldson, George and Rebecca T. Donaldson, Peg Chandler, and my aunt Betty Meier.

Contents

Introduction, 1

1—Song Sheets Yesterday and Today, 3
A Brief History of Printed Music, 3
Early American Religious, Folk, and Popular Music
  in Print, 4
Composer Profile: Stephen Foster, 9
Vaudeville, 12
Tin Pan Alley, 12
Tin Pan Alley Composers, 13
Popular Song Sheets without Lyrics, 14
Composer Profile: Scott Joplin, 15
Popular Song Sheets with Lyrics, 18
Song Sheet Cover Art and Artists, 21
Songs in Musicals, Silent Films, Talkies, Radio, and
  Records, 22
Collecting Song Sheets, 24
The Print Music Business Today, 26
Digital Sheet Music, 27
Print Music and Music Book Publishers—Digital
  Sheet Music—Historical Sheet Music, Song,
  Lyric, Hymn, and Orchestral Score Online
  Collections Web Sites, 29

**2—Print Music Royalties—Copyright Laws—
  Formats and Terms, 39**
Print Music Royalties, 39
Copyright Laws, 40
Print Music Formats, 44
Print Music and Copyright Terms, 51
Copyright, Legal, and Tax Information—Performing
  and Mechanical Rights—Government Grants
  Web Sites, 55

**3—Children's Music Software, Instructional
  Media and Web Sites, 59**
Children's Music Web Sites, 67

**4—Music Theory Fundamentals—Ear Training
  and Aural Skills Software, Instructional
  Media and Web Sites, 71**
Music Theory Fundamentals—Ear Training and
  Aural Skills Web Sites, 77

**5—Music Appreciation—Music History and
  Composers—Music Education Software,
  Instructional Media and Web Sites, 79**
Music Appreciation Web Sites, 85
Artist Web Sites, 85
Ballet—Ballroom and Modern Dance Web Sites, 85
Classical Music and Composers Web Sites, 86
Holiday Music Web Sites, 87
Music Education—Instructional Media Web Sites, 88
Music History Web Sites, 91

**6—Country—Folk—Traditional and World
  Music Software, Instructional Media and
  Web Sites, 93**
Country Music—Cowboy Songs—Line Dancing—
  Western Swing Web Sites, 98
Folk and Traditional Music and Instruments—Folk
  Dancing—Bluegrass Web Sites, 99
Latin and Caribbean Music Web Sites, 100
World Music—International—Ethnomusicology Web
  Sites, 101

**7—Jazz—Blues—Ragtime—New Age—Rock and
  Popular Music Software, Instructional Media
  and Web Sites, 105**
Jazz—Blues—Swing Web Sites, 109
Music and Health—Healing Music—Recovery Music
  Web Sites, 111
New Age and Ambient Music Web Sites, 111
Popular Music and Culture—Fashion—Dance
  Music—Techno—Electronica—Rock 'n' Roll—
  Oldies—Punk—Heavy Metal Web Sites, 112

R&B—Rap—Hip-Hop and Soul Web Sites, 114
Ragtime Web Sites, 114

8—Piano—Keyboard—Organ Software,
    Instructional Media and Web Sites, 117
Piano—Keyboard—Organ Web Sites, 125

9—Guitar and Bass Software, Instructional Media
    and Web Sites, 129
Guitar and Bass Web Sites, 141

10—Drums and Percussion Software,
    Instructional Media and Web Sites, 145
Drums and Percussion Web Sites, 149

11—Vocal—Choral—Opera and Musical Theater
    Software, Instructional Media and Web Sites,
    151
Musical Theater Web Sites, 158
Religious and Gospel Music—Inspirational Web
    Sites, 159
Vocal Music—Choral and Opera—Singing Web
    Sites, 160

12—Band and Orchestra—Patriotic Music—
    Classroom and Studio Management Software,
    Instructional Media and Web Sites, 163
Brass and Woodwind Instruments Web Sites, 168
Patriotic Music—Marches and Marching Bands Web
    Sites, 169
Stringed Instruments—Violin—Viola—Cello—
    Bass—Harp Web Sites, 170

13—Songwriting—Accompanying—Music
    Industry Software, Instructional Media and
    Web Sites, 173
Booking—Touring—Gigging—Clubs and Venues
    Web Sites, 177
Conferences and Showcases—Festivals and Fairs
    Web Sites, 179
Songwriting—Songwriting Contests and Camps—
    Tip Sheets Web Sites, 181

14—Composition—Scoring—Notation—Film, TV,
    and Video Game Music Software,
    Instructional Media and Web Sites, 187
Film and Television Music—Tip Sheets Web Sites,
    195
Music Video Games and Video Game Music Web
    Sites, 199

15—Digital Audio Recording and Editing—MIDI
    Sequencing—Plug-Ins—Sampled Sounds and
    Loops—Virtual Instruments—Software
    Synthesizers—CD Burning Software,
    Instructional Media and Web Sites, 201
Digital Audio Recording and MIDI—Computer
    Music Software and Electronics Web Sites, 229
Record Label Web Sites, 236
Recording Web Sites, 237

16—Music on the Internet, 241
Music Magazines—E-Zines—Webzines—
    Newspaper Web Sites, 241
Music on the Internet—Legal MP3s and Ringtones—
    MP3 Software and Hardware—Mobile
    Providers—Streaming Audio and Video Web
    Sites, 243
Music Resources—Directories—Portals Web Sites,
    246
Music Retailer Web Sites, 247
Musical E-Greetings—Singing Telegrams Web Sites,
    249
Networking—Blogs—Chat—Forums—Career
    Information—Indie Music Promotion Web Sites,
    250
Radio—Internet Radio—Television Web Sites, 255
Search Engine Web Sites, 257

Bibliography, 259

About the Author, 266

CD-ROM Contents:
A—Z Tech Talk
Chapters 1—16 Live Links
Sample Scores

Introduction

They say, "The third time is a charm." After researching and writing the third edition of this book, I finally feel truly connected to the information in it. Admittedly, it has been a daunting task gathering all this information and organizing it each time. However, this time, not only have I used many more of the software programs and web sites listed, but I feel I understand how to use them well enough to explain them to others.

The addition of the CD-ROM in this third edition will make it easier to search through the Tech Talk section using the "find" feature in the .pdf file. Also, there are now many sample scores, left blank simply to show the format and instrumentation for each. The Live Links included on the CD-ROM are some representative examples from each chapter of web sites worth visiting. A "thank you" goes out to all those who granted permission to include their live web links on the CD-ROM.

As stated in the two previous editions, the purpose of this book is to help sift through the maze of music software brochures and catalogs currently available, providing an easy-to-use sample listing of products. Hundreds of music software programs, CD-ROMs, instructional DVDs, and book/audio CD sets are listed and organized by category in the appropriate chapter, then alphabetically.

The manufacturer company Web site, if available, appears in parentheses immediately following the product title. The annotations list product features as well as system specifications (SYSTEM SPECS). It is important to check these before purchasing to make sure the product is compatible with the computer platform and/or operating system being used.

Some products are available for Windows only or for Macintosh only. Some are sold in platform specific versions although they are available for both operating systems. Hybrid CD-ROMs work on both Macintosh and Windows computers. Some programs and upgrades are available online as downloads.

Version numbers and years, which may be included in the software title, are not necessarily included here. Please consult the manufacturer's Web site for the latest version of a music software program and/or any available upgrades.

If no company or manufacturer Web site is listed, either the company is no longer in business or there is no active URL, but copies of the program are still available through distributors, online retailers, and/or site-licensed multimedia labs or libraries. No product endorsements are intended, and any choice of purchase is left to the discretion of the consumer.

Included in this edition of *Song Sheets to Software* are music-related software programs, CD-ROMs, instructional DVDs, and instructional Book/Audio CD sets which can be used currently on most computers. While music performance and documentary DVDs can offer valuable insights, there are simply too many available to mention all of them here. Similarly, there are by now many Book/Audio CD sets available for practice and self-instruction, too voluminous to mention all of them here. The best way to stay current on available titles is to frequently visit the Web sites of the companies who offer these formats, and/or the online retailers who sell them.

The music software programs listed here include those for scoring and notation, composition and songwriting, professional or home studio recording, sequencing applications, MIDI and digital audio recording and editing, CD burning, multimedia, MIDI file libraries, sample sounds and loops, software synthesizers, plug-ins, and MP3-related software. Many of these programs overlap in function.

There are also many programs listed for computer-assisted instruction (CAI), including children's music, music theory fundamentals, ear training and aural skills, rhythm skills, music appreciation, music history, composers, jazz, blues and rock, piano, guitar, vocal, drums, traditional instruments, band and orchestra, and choir and studio management.

The products listed are available online from the manufacturers directly, in music or school libraries, in multimedia labs, at computer software trade shows, and through online and offline computer product retailers and catalogs. Not surprisingly, new titles will appear as this book is being printed, and some may go out of print. This third edition attempts to include only those titles currently in print.

To stay current on new music software products, it is a good idea to consult music trade and recording magazines, attend music industry conferences, and to regularly browse the Internet.

By searching on the Internet under "music software" at any of the major search engine sites, many related Web sites could be accessed. Many noncommercial titles are available as downloadable freeware, shareware, or demo ware. The best way to stay current on new titles, new versions, and upgrades is to visit the music software Web sites often.

Product support, company e-mail addresses, phone numbers, and street addresses can be accessed from their respective Web sites. In many cases, products can be ordered and/or downloaded from the software company's Web site. Some music software retailers offer discounts when purchasing several titles at once, or "bundles," which may or may not include related hardware items such as keyboards or MIDI interfaces. Discounts are frequently given to teachers and to educational and religious institutions. It is a good idea to inquire about these. When purchasing a single software title as an individual for private use, one will usually pay the retail list price, possibly at a discount, depending on the retailer.

Working with music software programs, CD-ROMs, Instructional DVDs, and Book/Audio CD sets is a creative and effective way to improve musicianship skills and general knowledge about music. Many music instructors use these resources in their private studios as well as in teaching labs and multimedia centers. Some students purchase their own copies for home use. There is no reason why an individual couldn't obtain the titles that interest him or her, begin learning on their own, and consult a music instructor or software consultant when necessary.

The Web sites listed in these chapters are all music related, or are in some way of practical use to musicians. They are organized by category, then alphabetically. Most of the URLs *(Uniform Resource Locators)* or *Web addresses* begin with http://, meaning *hypertext transfer protocol*. This is the protocol by which computers exchange information on the *World Wide Web,* or www.

There are many three-letter codes or suffixes used in the United States to indicate the type of server or domain: .com = commercial, .edu = educational, .gov = government, .net = network, .org = nonprofit organization, and .mil = military. Other suffixes include .mobi, .eu, .us.com, .info, .co.uk, .cn, .biz, .de, .la, .us, .bz, .tv, and .am. Web addresses outside the United States may have a two-letter code at the end of the server location, such as .uk (United Kingdom) or .au (Australia).

A *home page* is the starting point on a Web site, which is often composed of many Web pages. A home page usually includes a table of contents, logos, photos, and links to other pages on the Web site. Most of the Web sites included in this chapter have information about the company, product, or organization, bios, a description of services, goals, or projects, answers to frequently asked questions or *FAQs*, images, graphics, sound, video, contact information, and/or links to related Web sites on the Internet.

Search engines, also known as *Web searchers* and *search directories*, are a great help in finding information on the Web. By choosing a category or subject heading, or submitting a word or descriptive phrase, one can locate any type of information. The search engine retrieves lists of related hypertext links. Because these lists can often be very long, it is important to sift through them, deleting unwanted, outdated, or unnecessary links.

Some search engines help to narrow or refine a search, and some will eliminate duplicate site listings. Setting *bookmarks* or *favorites* saves the trouble of typing in the URL each time a Web site is accessed, making it possible to quickly find and click on to frequently visited sites.

In trying to locate music-related Web sites of interest and of value, a lot of sifting was done before choosing those listed in the chapters that follow. Although some Web sites could be listed under more than one category, each one is listed only once, under what was believed to be the most appropriate category. As with music software programs, URLs are subject to change and discontinuation. As this book is being printed, new Web sites will appear, and some will expire. If any topic of interest, such as a particular artist or composer, is not listed here, simply "Google" it, or do a search on any of the available search engines. It is important to regularly use a search engine to find the most current information available.

Happy Web surfing!

1
Song Sheets Yesterday and Today

A Brief History of Printed Music

The musical content of *print music* or *sheet music* has changed along with the history of music itself. Printed music has evolved from the time of the early Catholic monks, the scribes and Gregorian Chant, to its present-day form. Sheet music is a generic term, covering many types of published music, including classical, popular, educational, instrumental, and vocal editions.

If not for the preservation of music through the print medium, centuries of music by the great composers and songwriters could not be performed and listened to today. We would not be able to re-create the great masterpieces of the Medieval, Renaissance, Baroque, Classical, and Romantic eras. We would not know the great songs of Stephen Foster and the Tin Pan Alley composers. We would know nothing of early vocal and keyboard music, symphonies and string quartets, operas and ballets. Before recordings, printed music was the only form of communication, documentation, and reproduction available to composers, musicians, musicologists, and consumers. Print music notation remains an important form of communication among musicians today for computer applications such as graphic music scoring, sequencer editing, and instrument instruction.

Gutenberg developed printing by movable type in the 1450s. Before this, handwritten music manuscripts sold throughout Europe and did so well into the nineteenth century. During this time, more printed music sold than handwritten manuscripts. Music printing developed more slowly than that of literary

works as it was more complicated and involved more symbols than the letters of the alphabet.

In the fifteenth century, chant and one-line musical examples in texts were the only music printed by movable type. The staff lines were printed first, then the notes were added. Sometimes this process was done in reverse, with the staff lines being added last. Double impressions were done by first printing the lines and then the notes. A German gradual from around 1473 is the earliest known book of printed music.

Printing from blocks of wood or metal was used into the first half of the sixteenth century, and in some isolated cases, up to the nineteenth century. This system was used for the ninth edition of the *Bay Psalm Book* (1698), the earliest example of music printed in North America. The previous editions did not contain any music.

The first printed mensural music was Ottaviano Petrucci's *Odhecaton* (1501), in choir-book format, in Venice, Italy. The printing was done in three impressions, the first being the staves, next the text, and then the notes. John Rastell was the first to use printing from one impression in London. Pierre Attaingnant, starting in 1527-1528, later developed this process. Printers in France, Italy, Germany, and Belgium used this system, where the note head, stem, and staff lines were combined as a single type unit, for part books for the next 200 years.

In 1752, music from movable type was first printed in America. In the 1750s, J. G. I. Breakup further developed the process whereby the music was formed from a type font made up of note heads, stems, and flags, each attached to staff lines. As music became more complex in florid melodies, keyboard chords, and opera scores, movable type was no longer a suitable process for printing music.

Engraving, where the music notation is drawn with a steel point on a copper plate, or punched onto a pewter plate, came to be the preferred system. Engraving was first used for music printing in the sixteenth century, gradually spreading over Europe in the seventeenth century. Venice was the main center for printed music in the sixteenth century.

Engraving was more common than typography by 1700, with the main music printing centers being Amsterdam, London, and Paris. Vienna became the main printing center later in the eighteenth century. The nineteenth century saw an increased market for printed music, leading to the establishment of music publishers and music stores.

Alois Senefelder invented *lithography* in 1796. It was fully developed by 1850. This chemical process made it possible for music to be written on paper as the preparation for plates. Engraving is still used for the preparation of camera-ready copy.

Most all of today's printing is done by the offset process, using photographic plates prepared from copy from engravings, music typewriters, transfers, composer's manuscripts and, more recently, music notation computer software. The use of computer scoring programs for preparing music notation for the printing process increased considerably during the 1980s and 1990s. The improved features of the programs and the quality of the graphics, along with the use of laser printers, have made it possible for smaller print music publishers to develop and produce their own line of products. Many of the larger print companies have greatly expanded their catalogs with the increased popularity and accessibility of electronic keyboards, multimedia teaching and learning aids, CDs, DVDs, and CD-ROMs.

The physical format of printed sheet music has more or less remained constant. This includes *single sheets* printed on one or both sides, *folios* with one sheet folded in half to form four pages, folios with a loose half-sheet inserted to form six pages, double-folios consisting of an inner folio inserted within the fold of an outer folio to make eight pages, and double-folios with a loose half-sheet inserted within the fold of an inner folio to produce ten pages. Print music formats and terms are defined further in chapter 2.

The term *song sheet* refers to popular songs, including words and music. Songwriters, musicians, scholars, collectors, dealers, and hobbyists alike are interested in the history of song sheets. Many collectors of print music do not read music and are as interested in the artwork on the covers as they are in the music itself. Noted print music artists have often been overlooked except by collectors, many of whom frame and display sheet music with attractive covers.

Collections may include song sheets with unique and artistic cover designs, or photographs of singers and entertainers, musicals, movies, images from World War I, World War II, pre-1900, and other categories.

Early American Religious, Folk, and Popular Music in Print

Religious Music

The earliest examples of printed music in colonial America included books of psalms, hymns, and spiritual songs from England. These included *The Book of Psalmes: Englished Both in Prose and Metre* (1612) by Henry Ainsworth (1570-1623), the *Sternhold and Hopkins* Psalter (1549, 1553, over 600 different editions from 1562 to 1828), *The Whole Booke of Psalms* (1621, 1667), and *The Whole Booke of Psalms Faithfully Translated into English Metre*, later titled the *Bay Psalm Book* (seventy editions from 1638 to 1773), the first book of any kind to be printed in British North America, with the ninth edition being the first to include printed music.

Other early American publications of note included *An Introduction to the Singing of Psalm-Tunes* (1721) by the Rev. John Tufts (1689-1750), *The Grounds and Rules of Musick Explained* (1721) by Rev. Thomas Walter (1696-1725), *Youth's Entertaining Amusement* (1754) by William Dawson, *Urania* (1761) by James Lyon, *Collection of the Best Psalm Tunes* (1764) and *Sixteen Anthems* (1766) by Josiah Flagg, *Royal Melody Complete* (1767) by William Tans'ur (1706-1783), and the *Universal Psalmodist* (1769) by Aaron Williams (1731-1776). The publications of the 1760s added more than 300 tunes to those already printed in the colonies, quadrupling the tune repertory. Some of the new psalm tunes appeared in more complex musical styles than the three- and four-part harmonies printed before the mid-1700s.

British publications of note were *New Versions of the Psalms of David, Fitted to the Tunes Used in Churches* (1696-1828) by Nahum Tate (1652-1715) and Nicholas Brady (1659-1726), and *The Psalms of David Imitated* (1719) and *Hymns and Spiritual Songs* (1707) by Isaac Watts (1674-1748).

The latter publication by Watts was the first collection of original, non-biblical devotional texts used in public worship in British and American Protestant churches, and was very well received. This led to the singing of more hymns and spiritual songs in both public and private worship into the eighteenth century. Watts believed that the texts sung for public worship should not be restricted to psalms and biblical canticles, as many did not have to do with the New Testament or the present circumstances of Christians.

Late in 1770, *The New-England Psalm-Singer: or, American Chorister*, the work of William Billings, was published by Benjamin Edes and John Gill in Boston. At this point in history, no more than a dozen musical compositions by native-born Americans had appeared in print. The Billings collection had 126 original pieces, marking its place in the history of American music publication. The original composition of psalms, hymns, and anthems had taken root in America. Thousands of these pieces would be written in the coming decades, establishing the first native school of American composition.

Billings's second collection was the *Singing Master's Assistant*, published in Boston in 1778. It contained seventy-one pieces and had four editions. *Music in Miniature* (1779) was his third book and was a tune supplement for congregational singing. This collection contained seventy-four pieces, of which thirty-one were new tunes he had written, thirty-two were previously published, and eleven were from other composers. *The Psalm-Singer's Amusement* was published by Billings in Boston in 1781 for experienced choirs as opposed to congregational singing or singing-school instruction, with long, complex compositions. *The Suffolk Harmony* (1786) included thirty-two psalm and hymn texts in homophonic settings. Billings's last publication was the *Continental Harmony* in 1794, financially supported by anonymous friends and those who admired him. In early 1782, of the 264 musical compositions published by American-born writers, 226 of them were by Billings. Of the 200 anthems published in America by 1810, over a quarter were by Billings.

Billings became widely known, and two of his pieces were published in England, the first compositions by an American-born composer to be published abroad. Billings did not see any money from his pieces published in collections compiled by others due to the absence of effective copyright legislation. It was not until 1790 that the first comprehensive federal copyright bill came into place.

Other tune books of the period included *Gentleman and Lady's Musical Companion* (1774) by John Strickney (1744-1827) and *Select Harmony* (1779) by Andrew Law. In the 1780s, tune books abounded. Hundreds of them were published through the first decade of the nineteenth century. These included eclectic anthologies such as *Laus Deo, or the Worcester Collection of Sacred Harmony* published by Isaiah Thomas in 1786. This was the first collection to be printed in America from movable type rather than engraved plates. Similar books included the *Chorister's Companion* (1782) by Simeon Jocelyn and Amos Doolittle, *Select Harmony* (1783) by Timothy and Samuel Green, and the *Federal Harmony* (1784). Daniel Read (1757-1836) was the

first American after Billings to publish a collection of his own compositions titled the *American Singing Book* in 1785.

Other tune books from the time following the American Revolution that featured compositions by the compiler included *The New American Melody* by Jacob French (1789), *American Harmony* by Oliver Holden (1792), *Rural Harmony* by Jacob Kimball (1793), *The Psalmodist's Companion* by Jacob French (1793), *The Harmony of Maine* by Belcher (1794), *The Responsary* by Amos Bull (1795), *New England Harmonist* by Stephen Jenks (1800), *New England Harmony* by Timothy Swan (1801), *The Christian Harmony* by Jeremiah Ingalls (1805), and *Harmonia Americana* (1791) and *Columbian Repository of Sacred Harmony* (1803) by Samuel Holyoke (1762-1820).

The most successful American hymn writer of the nineteenth century was Lowell Mason (1792-1872). In 1821, his famous compilation the *Boston Handel and Haydn Society Collection of Church Music* was published. Even after his death, *The Hymnal of the Methodist Episcopal Church*, published in 1878, contained sixty-eight of his original hymns, along with twenty-two arrangements of tunes by other writers. *The Methodist Hymnal*, published in 1935, contained thirty-two of his original hymns.

Early American Music Education

Mason played an important role in American music education and believed that children should be taught to read music as they were taught how to read. His first book written for children was *Juvenile Psalmist; or, the Child's Introduction to Sacred Music* (1829). Mason was appointed the superintendent of music in the Boston public schools in September of 1838. Boston was the first town in America where music became part of the regular curriculum for children. Other music books for children by Mason included *Musical Exercises for Singing Schools* (1838) and *The Boston School Song Book* (1840).

Later publications by Mason included *The Boston Academy's Collection of Church Music* (1835-1863, twelve editions), *The Boston Academy's Collection of Choruses* (1836), *The Boston Glee Book* (1838), and *The Song-Garden* (1864), the first graded, progressively arranged series of school music books. The market was expanding for instructional music books due greatly to Mason's support of general music literacy. Between 1841 and 1860, *Carmina Sacra* sold over 500,000 copies in thirteen editions. He had become very wealthy by the middle of the century, and was the first American to earn a fortune from music.

William B. Bradury (1816-1868) followed in Mason's footsteps, publishing sixty books for the music education of young children and church choirs between 1841 and 1867. These included *The Young Choir, The Sunday School Choir, The Shawn, The Jubilee,* and *The Devotional Hymn and Tune Book.* Like Mason, Bradbury combined adaptations of European pieces with his own compositions. Over two million copies of Bradbury's publications sold, including 250,000 copies of *The Jubilee.* Mason and Bradbury believed strongly that universal musical literacy was the way to improve the art in America.

Shape Notes

The first collection designed for singing schools used outside of New England was *The Easy Instructor* by William Little and William Smith in 1801. This book utilized a new system of notation called "shape" notes. Shape notes followed the four-syllable solmization system, where the octave was divided into two groups of three notes each, with the seventh note of the scale standing alone. This system was fixed visually by shape-note notation. This proved to be an effective teaching tool among the nonliterate, semiliterate, and newly literate people of the South and West. Many of these collections preserved the pieces sung in the camp meetings of the various populist religious movements of the late 1700s and early 1800s in America.

The Easy Instructor and other early shape-note books contained a New England repertory. By the 1820s, collections represented other parts of the country. These included *Repository of Sacred Music, Part Second* by John Wyeth (1813), *Patterson's Church Music* by Robert Patterson (1813), *Kentucky Harmony* by Ananias Davisson (1815), the *Kentucky Harmony* by Samuel L. Metcalf (1817), and *Missouri Harmony* by Allen D. Carden (1820). These collections came to be called folk hymns or white spirituals, frequently using pentatonic tunes and melodies similar to the ballads, songs, and fiddle and banjo pieces of the region. For pedagogical reasons, the composers drew on the indigenous melodic tradition of the people with whom they lived and worked, writing and arranging in a unique harmonic style. This included few triads and many parallel fifths, unisons, and octaves reflecting oral tradition polyphony and was an American innovation.

Important shape-note collections in the Deep South included *The Southern Harmony* by William Walker (1935), which is said to have sold over 600,000 copies by the time of the Civil War. This collection was used in singing schools, church congregations, and social gatherings. It contained hymns, spiritual songs, and anthems by New England composers of the late 1700s and early 1800s, folk hymns found in early shape-note collections, and new pieces, many written or arranged by Walker, in the melodic style of Anglo-Celtic oral-tradition music.

The most successful shape-note book, and most widely dispersed of the 1800s, was *The Sacred Harp* by Benjamin Franklin White (1800-1879), published in 1844, with revised and expanded editions in 1850, 1859, and 1869. *Sacred Harp* singing continued into the twentieth century, with two new editions printed in 1911, one of which was called the *Original Sacred Harp.* Other such collections were *The Hesperian Harp,* compiled by William Hauser in 1848, and *The Social Harp,* compiled by John G. McCurry in 1855. Shape-note music continued with the melodic style of the tunes from oral tradition becoming fixed in musical notation. Still, many learned this music by rote.

Folk Music

Important collections of oral tradition folk songs and ballads printed in America included a five-volume set containing 305 ballads titled *The English and Scottish Popular Ballads* (1882-1898) by Francis James Child (1825-1896), *Folk Songs from Somerset* (five volumes, 1905-1909), and *English Folk Songs* (1920) and *English Folk Songs from the Southern Appalachians* (1917 with 323 tunes, 1932 with 968 tunes) by Cecil J. Sharp (1859-1924). Though brought to America in their original form by immigrants from the Old World, many of these British folk tunes and texts were altered in the course of their oral transmission. Child's collections did not include the British broadsides, which could be traced to an individual, versus folk songs, which were transmitted by oral tradition, although more than likely conceived by an individual initially. American ballads and songs are those that originated in the United States and are of American character both in text and music, sung by adults and children.

Country dances brought over from England became popular in America. The first collection of dance figures published in the United States was by John Griffith, titled *A Collection of the Newest and Most Fashionable Country Dances and Cotillions* (1788). Thirty similar collections were published in America by 1800. Many publications of the nineteenth century contained both fiddle tunes and dance figures, including *Howe's Complete Ball-Room Hand-Book* (1858) and, also by Elias Howe, *The Musician's Omnibus* (1861).

Popular Music

Popular song was the first music to achieve a typically American character, representing a new style that combined several different national or ethnic styles. The first popular songs performed in America were from England. They were printed and sold as sheet music beginning in the 1780s, arranged for voice and keyboard accompaniment, and usually sung by amateurs for amusement in their parlors. At the turn of the century, Irish and Scottish songs became very popular, many of which were found in *The Irish Melodies* of Thomas Moore (1779-1852), published in Dublin and London from 1807 to 1834. These included *The Last Rose of Summer, Believe Me If All Those Endearing Young Charms* and *The Minstrel Boy.* A collection by Robert Burns (1759-1796) titled *Scots Musical Museum* appeared between 1787 and 1803, and included *Auld Lang Syne, Coming thru the Rye, John Anderson, My Jo,* and *Scots What Hae wi' Wallace Bled.*

Popular in the 1820s, 1830s, and 1840s were songs from operas such as *Away with Melancholy* by Mozart from *The Magic Flute.* Music publishers found a large market for songs based on Italian operatic airs and arias up to the middle part of the nineteenth century. Also popular in America was the German lied. Favorite sheet music items translated into English included songs by Franz Schubert, Franz Abt, and Friedrich Wilhelm Kücken.

Other British songwriters influenced the American market, including Sir Henry Bishop (1786-1855) who wrote *Home Sweet Home.* This was the most popular song of the nineteenth century in the English language, which sold over 100,000 copies in America a year after it was published in 1823 and several million copies before the end of the century. Many of his other songs were successful as well.

John Braham (1774-1856) wrote the most popular duet of the century, *All's Well,* from his opera *The English Fleet in 1342.* Samuel Lover (1797-1868) was the most successful Irish songwriter following Thomas Moore and wrote *Rory O'More* and *The Low-back'd Car.* The son of a German musician, Charles Edward Horn (1786-1849) wrote hundreds of songs, including *Cherry Ripe* and *I've Been Roaming.* The best female songwriter of the century was Claribel-Charlotte Alington Barbard (1830-1869), who wrote *I Cannot Sing the Old Songs, Take Back the Heart,* and *Come Back to Erin.*

During the nineteenth century, living standards improved, and many homes could afford both a piano and sheet music and had family members who could sing and play the piano. Many songs were written with the intention of being performed in the home and were arranged with the limitations of amateurs in mind, using simpler vocal lines and piano accompaniments. Publishers also made simpler arrangements of pieces written for professional singers available.

The first person in America to write songs for voice and keyboard was Francis Hopkinson (1737-1791). His *Seven Songs for Harpsichord* was published in Philadelphia in 1788. In a letter to Thomas Jefferson, Hopkinson described himself as an author who composes from his heart rather than from his head. Benjamin Carr (1768-1831) came from London to America in 1793, publishing sixty songs, including some he had written as well as arrangements of traditional songs. His most successful song was *The Little Sailor Boy* (1798), which had the widest distribution of any song in America prior to 1800.

Other immigrant songwriters were James Hewitt, Alexander Reinagle, George K. Jackson, Raynor Taylor, and Charles Gilfert. *The Wounded Hussar* (1800) by Hewitt was one of the most popular songs from 1800 to 1810, dealing with the tragedies of war.

Early American Songwriters

The first important songwriting movement in the United States was centered in New England. Musicians living in and around Massachusetts wrote songs for keyboard and voice following the American Revolution. Forty of these were published in *Massachusetts Magazine,* some were printed in periodicals, and others appeared as separate items of sheet music. Many of these songs were included in *The American Musical Miscellany,* published in Northampton in 1798, and other anthologies. These songs were derived from English pleasure garden and comic opera pieces and had limited distribution.

Oliver Shaw (1779-1848) was the first songwriter born in America to achieve national recognition and spent most of his life in Providence, Rhode Island. Although he became blind early in life, he was a successful organist, singer, teacher, choirmaster, and composer. His most successful songs were *Mary's Tears* (1812), *All Things Bright and Fair Are Thine* (1817), and *There's Nothing True but Heav'n* (1816), which went through six editions in a decade and earned Shaw $1,500 in royalties. Shaw was versed in classical music, and his pieces reflect the balanced, diatonic, symmetrical melodies and harmonies of the simpler works by the great composers of the 1700s.

Great commercial success was achieved by John Hill Hewitt (1801-1890) with the publication of his composition *The Minstrel's Return'd from the War* in 1825. A simple diatonic tune in strophic form with a three-chord keyboard accompaniment, the song was very much in the style of the day. The song remained in print for over half a century and sold all over the country. Its success was a surprise to Hewitt and his brother James, who published the first edition. Because they had failed to obtain a copyright, any publisher could print it without paying a fee or royalties, resulting in a loss of more than $10,000 to the Hewitts.

All of Hewitt's songs were well written, though some were more commercially successful than others. His songs showed the influence of several national schools imported to America. His greatest hit was *Farewell, Since We Must Part* in 1829, reflecting the English style. Other influences included the comic opera style, Italian opera, Swiss and Austrian mountain songs, and the black minstrel songs. Hewitt skillfully assimilated these different national elements into his distinctly American songs, creating new sounding pieces and not imitations. His most popular songs included *Girls Beware* (1832), *Ah! Fondly I Remember* (1837), *The Alpine Horn* (1843), *Eulalie, Mary, Now the Seas Divide Us* (1840), and *All Quiet along the Potomac* (1862). Because the income from his songs was not enough to support his family, Hewitt made a living as a journalist and teacher.

Another songwriter creating characteristically American songs was Henry Russell (1812-1901), the most important and successful songwriter before Stephen Foster. Russell performed his own songs, accompanied himself on the piano, and handled his own business affairs, including advances and publicity. He strove for an emotional response from his audience. One of his most famous songs was *Woodman, Spare That Tree*. Tens of thousands of Americans attended his concerts and purchased copies of his songs. He helped to shape indigenous American song and greatly influenced the next generation of American songwriters.

Early American Sheet Music Publishers

The publishing of sheet music in the United States was well established by the early nineteenth century. In 1800, there were several professional music publishers in Philadelphia. By 1820, there were publishers in southern cities as well. Most of the music produced during this time was of English and Irish origin. Not until the 1830s did American songwriters begin to achieve international success.

Engraved plates were used to print most music. Some music was published using *lithography* in the 1820s, but this was not very common until the 1840s. The development of *chromolithography* made it economically possible to do illustrated title pages. Both engraved and lithographed music continued being issued during this period.

During the Civil War, Confederate imprints were lithographed. These processes required less equipment and materials, including metal, which was in high demand for the war and in short supply for civilians. After the Civil War, there was a large increase in music publishing activity. The *stereotype process* made it possible for publishers to issue large numbers of music for consumption by the masses. This period in popular music history is known as the *Age of Parlor Music*.

Music publishers came to realize the commercial value of printing advertising on the blank pages of sheet music during the rise of parlor music in the 1860s. Entire catalogs of songs and music were printed on the back or inside front covers of publications. By the end of the nineteenth century, lists of songs with melodies or complete pages for the user to "try over on your piano" became standard. Manufacturing companies issued sheet music to advertise their products. During World War I, publishers promoted the war effort by using the margins of the music for slogans.

The *music publishing industry* in the United States was started by entrepreneurship. Before New York City became music publishing's headquarters in the late 1800s, many small music publishers sprang up around the country. For many, music publishing was not their only career. They may have been a local person who owned a printing press. This same printer who printed books, posters, stationery, and advertisements would be asked by local musicians to print sheet music copies of their songs and compositions.

The printer would often make an agreement with the composer whereby the composer and the publisher would share *royalties* based on the number of copies sold. This arrangement would later evolve into the *song contract*. The printer might sell copies of the sheet music in his printed goods store and at the local music store.

Traveling salesmen were hired to sell sheet music throughout a region on a commission basis, along with clothes and household goods. The salesmen would carry sheet music samples as part of his product line and sell the sheet music to the local music store or five-and-ten-cent store. There were some salesmen who could actually play the songs they carried in their cases of sheet music on the piano.

Some of these salesmen became entrepreneurs and set up their own publishing companies. They wrote and published their own songs or acquired new songs from songwriters whose sheet music they had sold previously. These new publishers might look for new songwriters to sign to publishing agreements. Some paid a printer to print their sheet music, and others acquired their own printing presses. In the mid-nineteenth century, publishers issued sacred and secular songs, lieder, opera excerpts, waltzes, marches, and etudes, all from the same catalog.

As folk music has survived through oral tradition, popular music has been promoted as published sheet music, recordings, or performances. One of the main venues for popular song during the early to mid-nineteenth century was the *traveling minstrel show*. The *minstrel song* became the first American genre and was rooted in English comic opera. Created by white Americans, the characters portrayed were black Americans. The music was not related to that of African Americans at the time. Tunes were sung in broken English and were simple, diatonic or pentatonic, with dancelike tempos, supposedly reflecting a primitive music. Music publishers issued many of the popular minstrel show songs in sheet music editions, including *Coal Black Rose, Jim along Josey,* and *Long Tail Blue.* Many of the song texts portrayed black people as illiterate, comical, subhuman beings. Some tunes were borrowed or adapted from traditional Anglo-American pieces, with the accompanying instruments playing in a traditional, nonharmonic style. The most famous traveling minstrel troupes were the Virginia Minstrels and Christy's Minstrels, whose first performance was in the 1840s in Albany, New York, moving to New York City in 1846.

In the 1840s, Stephen Foster combined the European American and African American folk traditions. He composed hundreds of songs, including *Oh! Susanna, Camptown Races,* and *The Old Folks at Home.* Stephen Foster is the father of American popular song and was America's first internationally renowned songwriter.

Composer Profile: Stephen Foster

Stephen Collins Foster was born on July 4, 1826, in Lawrenceville, Pennsylvania, now part of Pittsburgh. That particular Fourth of July marked the fiftieth anniversary of the Declaration of Independence as well as the deaths of the second and third presidents of the United States, John Adams and Thomas Jefferson. Stephen Foster was born the tenth of eleven children but remained the youngest of the family when his younger brother died in infancy.

Foster's very American birth date coincides with his important role in creating songs very near to indigenous American folk songs. The songs brought by ancestors from all over the world were representative of the cultures of their native lands. Although they may have emerged differently, they were still recognizable and not particularly American. The only race that developed a folk-song literature in America was the one which was brought here against its will and brutally exploited: the African American. The African American spirituals and Stephen Foster's songs have sometimes been confused as to authorship. Both politically and commercially, the Fosters were prominent people in western Pennsylvania. Stephen was different from the other members of his family. He was a dreamer and loved music. He could pick out tunes on the piano and learned to play the flute and violin. He began to compose as a teen-

ager. Although his parents noticed his talent, they did little to train him in music.

The other family members enjoyed music but felt it should not occupy too much of Stephen's time. They believed there was more important work to be done in their own pioneer community, which was beginning to flourish. Stephen promised upon entering boarding school that he would limit his music to a pleasant pastime, not paying any attention to it until after eight o'clock in the evening. Stephen's father wrote in 1841 that his son's leisure hours were all devoted to music, for which he possessed a strange talent.

In 1841, the Foster family moved to Allegheny, Pennsylvania. During the five years that he lived there, Stephen wrote many of his first songs. Stephen's father, William Barclay Foster, became the mayor of Allegheny. During this time, Stephen visited his brother, Morrison, in Youngstown. Morrison went to New Orleans and visited the towns and cities along the Ohio and the Mississippi Rivers. He brought home with him many tales of Southern life. When the two brothers returned to Allegheny, they went many places together, often borrowing from each other and trading between themselves.

Stephen was becoming more and more absorbed in his music. Those who knew him recalled that he was beginning to write songs. His first song published was issued in December of 1844, when he was eighteen, probably written when he was sixteen. He wrote only the music to a poem by George P. Morris, *Open Thy Lattice, Love.* It appeared in a supplement to the *New Mirror* (1843-1844), a Saturday paper edited in New York by Morris and Nathaniel P. Willis.

The song was issued by George Willig of Philadelphia as a two-page song, without a title page, with a heading on the first page listing Stephen's name as "L. C. Foster." The publisher had failed to print Stephen's name correctly on his very first song!

Starting in 1845, a club of young men met twice a week at the Fosters' home. They were known as "The Knights of the S. T. [Square Table]." The club meetings were secret and marked by formal, semiburlesque rituals. Each of the five members had a fraternal name and was described in a poem written by Stephen, dated May 6, 1845, "The Five Nice Young Men." Along with the writing of personal poems, the most important outgrowth of these meetings was that the group practiced songs. When they had learned all the current popular pieces, Stephen would try writing songs for them.

Stephen first wrote *Lou'siana Belle* for the group. They liked it so well, and he was encouraged to write *Old Uncle Ned* for another meeting. His sister, Ann Eliza, claimed later that *Oh! Susanna* was also composed for the club. This type of setting was an early model of the songwriting workshops and open-mics popular around the United States today.

After trying to make Stephen conform to an accepted and conventional pattern, including trying to get him appointed to West Point, his family decided to send him to Cincinnati. His brother Dunning would teach him how to do the bookkeeping for his commission business. At the age of twenty, Stephen sailed down the Ohio River on one of the riverboats he would immortalize in song. He was much more interested in the singing of the black deckhands than adding columns of figures, which he proceeded to do for over three years.

Stephen lived in Cincinnati from the fall of 1846 until early 1850. He was a good bookkeeper and was left in the office with Dunning's partner when Dunning enlisted in the army during the Mexican War. He was primarily interested in writing music and verses, however, and spent much of his spare time getting acquainted with the minstrel performers who might perform his songs in public.

The type of songs Stephen wrote at this time are indicative of the prominent influence that affected his early creative efforts. He thought the songs of the current minstrel shows to be crude and vulgar but, nevertheless, representing something definitely American. While this was a medium that influenced and affected Foster profoundly, he himself completely reformed it.

Some of the minstrel singers Foster encountered were unscrupulous and took his manuscript copies (which he had given them to perform) to publishers, who, in no time, issued pirated editions.

When he found a publisher to issue *Oh! Susanna* and *Old Uncle Ned*, other firms had already published these songs. It is still uncertain who first printed *Oh! Susanna* and *Old Uncle Ned* and where some of the manuscripts came from.

Because Foster was generous with manuscript copies and because common law copyright protecting the author of a manuscript until publication was apparently not established, the first to present a work at a district copyright office was allowed to take out a copyright.

Of the twenty editions printed of *Oh! Susanna*, some were printed from the manuscript copies Stephen had given to minstrel performers, and others were from transcriptions by those who had heard the song and written out their own versions. This can be seen in the musical and poetic differences between the many editions printed in southern New York, Massachusetts, Maryland, Kentucky, and eastern Pennsylvania.

Foster was credited for authorship on some of the editions of his early songs, but, on most of them, there was no mention of his name.

It is probable that the pirated editions show the variety of uses to which the song *Oh! Susanna* was immediately put: minstrel shows, in some collections of *Negro Songs* as the *Susanna Polka,* and in numerous arrangements with *Easy Variations for the Piano Forte.*

Oh! Susanna is an example of Foster's comic, Ethiopian songs. It was first performed in public at Andrews' Ice Cream Saloon in Pittsburgh on September 11, 1847.

While in Cincinnati, Stephen came in touch with W. C. Peters, a music publisher Stephen's family knew in Pittsburgh. He gave to Peters a number of songs, including *Oh! Susanna,* for either $100.00 or as an outright gift. Foster had no royalty interest, and Peters made a fortune from his early songs. Foster gained only the fame he needed to establish himself as a songwriter.

Oh! Susanna was an overnight hit and was sung by the forty-niners on their way to California. Most of the minstrel troupes sang it at every performance. From this success, two other publishers, Firth, Pond & Co. in New York and F. D. Benteen in Baltimore, offered royalty contracts to Stephen, agreeing to pay him two cents for every copy of his songs sold by them. Stephen returned to his family in Allegheny, able to prove to them he could make a living as a songwriter. On July 22, 1850, Stephen married Jane McDowell, daughter of a Pittsburgh physician. They honeymooned in New York and Baltimore, then went to live with the Foster family in Allegheny.

Foster published eleven songs during the first six months of 1850, including *Camptown Races,* issued by Benteen. He composed his finest songs during the first six years of his married life. These included: *Old Folks at Home,* 1851; *Massa's in de Cold Ground,* 1852; *My Old Kentucky Home* and *Old Dog Tray,* 1853; *Jeanie with the Light Brown Hair,* 1854; *Come Where My Heart Lies Dreaming,* 1855; and *Gentle Annie,* 1856.

Jeanie with the Light Brown Hair was written for his wife during their separation in 1854. It is an example of Foster's poetic songs and ballads. Due to Stephen's temperament, and Mrs. Foster's possible lack of interest in his songwriting, hoping to make him more of a businessman, their marriage was often strained. They were separated several times, and in the later year, Jane left him when he could no longer support her. He loved his wife and daughter, Marion, dearly and never showed an interest in another woman. He very much wanted them to be happy and enjoy their lives.

In 1851, Foster began to establish transactions on a business basis with E. P. Christy of the famous Christy's Minstrels. He offered Christy the opportunity to be the first performing troupe to perform his songs prior to their being issued by the publisher for a fee of $10.00 on such songs as *Massa's in de Cold Ground* (July 7, 1852) and *Old Dog Tray* (1853) and $15.00 for *Old Folks at Home* (October 1, 1851) and *Farewell My Lilly Dear* (December 13, 1851). Once issued, these songs were announced on the cover as being sung by the Christy Minstrels. Christy had his name alone put on *Ellen Bayne*. These songs were issued by Firth, Pond & Co. In the case of *Old Folks at Home*, entered for copyright by Firth, Pond & Co. on August 26, 1851, the title page deposited October 1, 1851, stated:

OLD FOLKS AT HOME
Ethiopian Melody
as sung by
Christy's Minstrels
Written and Composed by
E. P. Christy

There is no record of any reply from Christy to Stephen's letter of May 25, 1852, in which he asked to receive credit on the title page of his published songs.

Future printings of *Old Folks at Home* continued to list Christy's name as author and composer. When the copyright was renewed by Stephen's widow and daughter, future editions bore his name, beginning in 1879. It is believed that the extra $5.00 Christy paid Foster for the privilege of first performing his songs and having his name appear as a performer of the songs further included being named as author and composer.

The money Foster received from Christy for the privilege of introducing his songs was all Stephen is known to have received for what today is called a performing right. Stephen's income would have been far greater than it was if the copyright laws of the 1850s provided that public performance of a song for profit was the exclusive right of the copyright owner.

Had there been organizations such as ASCAP, BMI, or SESAC to assert this right and collect for him, Stephen would have made much more money from the public performance of his songs.

Though they were not supposed to advertise *Old Folks at Home* as being written by Foster, his publishers were quick to capitalize on his increasing fame. It finally came out that he was the actual composer of *Old Folks at Home* in the February 19, 1853, issue of the *Musical World*, under "Answers to Correspondence."

Foster had a comfortable income from the contracts signed with his publishers. In just over six years, he earned $9,596.96 from Firth, Pond & Co. and $461.85 from Benteen. An annual income just under $2,000.00 was adequate in the 1850s for living comfortably. It did not, however, constitute wealth or anything near what songwriters today would earn with works equal in popularity to those of Stephen Foster.

The Fosters spent a little more than he earned every year, and his accounting books clearly show debts to his landlords and tailors and money borrowed from his brothers Morrison and William. He continued to draw advances from his publishers. Financial matters reached a crisis level in 1857. Stephen drew a list of what each song had earned and what he estimated each one would bring him in the future. He calculated the thirty-six songs on royalty with Firth, Pond & Co. were worth $2,786.77. He negotiated with them to sell his future rights to those songs for the estimated amount.

They settled with him for about two-thirds of the amount for which he asked. He received $1,500.00 in cash and notes and canceled the amount of $372.28 overdrawn on his previous royalty account. The total sum was $1,872.28. He sold to Benteen for $200.00 the future rights to sixteen songs that had previously earned $461.85. The following year, a new contract was negotiated with Firth, Pond & Co. He was to compose exclusively for them for two-and-a-half years. He would receive a 10 percent royalty on the retail price of his songs and an advance of $100.00 on each song he wrote—up to twelve per year. This was a better contract than his previous one, but he had already passed his creative peak.

Foster published sixteen songs in the two-and-a-half years of the agreement, earning only $700.00 in royalties. He was again overdrawn at the publishers by nearly $1,400.00 by July of 1860. Once more he sold his future rights to Firth, Pond & Co. for $1,600.00. The overdraft was deducted, and Stephen was paid $203.36.

With this money Stephen moved his family to New York to be in closer touch with publishers and minstrel performers. Firth, Pond & Co. offered him a salary of $800.00 for writing twelve songs a year. The Philadelphia publisher Lee & Walker offered him $400.00 for six songs. His income was guaranteed at $1,200.00 a year. Upon arriving in New York, Stephen presented to Firth, Pond & Co. *Old Black Joe*. It proved to be only a momentary flash of his former genius. Though he turned out over a hundred songs during his last four years, they were not the quality of his previous work. He collaborated more often with lyric writers as he no longer wrote the words himself.

The salary contracts did not last long, and Stephen began selling songs to other publishers for cash. They were not especially particular about the material as they were glad to have songs bearing his name in their catalog. Stephen spent the cash as soon as he was paid, much of it on liquor. He had become an incurable alcoholic. After trying to help cure him of his habit, and talk him into leaving the strain and tension of New York, Stephen's wife, Jane, finally left him and moved away to live with her sister. Stephen's brother Morrison spent time with him during the last few years and tried to help him. Stephen stayed in New York after being invited to move to Cleveland with Morrison. He stayed in New York with his friends who would not try to reform him.

Stephen had an accident while living alone in a lodging house in January of 1864. He was ill and suffering from a fever, possibly tuberculosis. He fell and cut his neck near the jugular vein. He was taken to Bellevue Hospital, where he fainted on the third day and never again regained consciousness. He died on January 13, 1864, at 2:30 in the afternoon. Morrison and Jane took his body back to Pittsburgh, where it was placed in the family plot in the Allegheny Cemetery.

Vaudeville

The music industry flourished in the latter half of the nineteenth century, mostly through the sale of sheet music, pianos, and organs. Many of the most successful songs of this period were created for and performed in the minstrel shows. Publishers relied on performers to promote their songs, even more as the minstrel tradition evolved into American vaudeville.

Vaudeville was made up of variety shows featuring entertainers, singers, opera singers, soft-shoe dancers, comedians, comedy teams, contortionists, and animal acts. Vaudeville theaters appeared in cities all over the country. By mid-1869, the first American transcontinental railway was completed. Tens of thousands of miles of railroad tracks were put into place during the next two decades. Entertainers originating in New York City could now travel across the United States and perform in theaters and music halls in most of the country's major cities. This traveling variety show, vaudeville, gave music publishers a constant supply of performers needing new material.

New York City was a busy center for American vaudeville with many theaters, barrooms and dance halls, booking agents, and the industry trade paper the *New York Clipper* located in the district between West 14th and 30th Streets. By 1890, music publishers had also started to locate here, mainly on West 26th, 27th, and 28th Streets. Since this was where the entertainers were, and because they frequently traveled around the country performing songs before large audiences of prospective sheet music buyers, it made sense for the music publishers to be located in the same neighborhood. This area came to be known as Tin Pan Alley. As the theater district moved farther uptown to Broadway, the music publishers also moved to be near the performers and songwriters of the stage. The term *Tin Pan Alley* came to refer to the entire American music industry in the first part of the twentieth century.

Tin Pan Alley

Sheet music continued to be issued in large numbers in the twentieth century, centering on the area of Manhattan known as Tin Pan Alley. Tin Pan Alley refers to 28th Street between 5th and Broadway in New York City. The name comes from the sound made by many songs being played at the same time through open windows, in different keys on poorly tuned pianos. A newspaper reporter by the name of Monroe Rosenfeld is said to have been responsible for the name. Although he did not use the phrase "Tin Pan Alley" in his *New York Herald* article on the publishing houses in the district, he referred to the area as the "Alley" and the noise they collectively created as being "not unlike the sound of tin pans banging together."

Tin Pan Alley gained momentum with the coming of the American industrial revolution, and marked the golden age of the piano in the songwriting world. Musically uneducated tunesmiths fed the fledgling New York publishing houses. During this period, copyright laws were not enforced, and plagiarism was common. The American Society of Composers, Authors, and Publishers (ASCAP) would not be formed for another thirty years. Many songs were sold for very little money, and their success provided the finances needed for the small publishing companies to survive. Songwriters who were tired of selling their hit songs for such small fees eventually became their own publishers.

Tin Pan Alley's most important publishing companies included T. B. Harms, Irving Berlin, Shapiro & Bernstein, M. Witmark & Sons, F. A. Mills, Leo Feist, Inc., Harry Von Tilzer Music Publishing Company, and Jerome H. Remick & Company. Many hit songs came from these publishers, and sheet music became so popular it was issued as supplements to Sunday newspapers.

Some of these music publishing companies were started by the sheet music salesmen who had become publishers. Each of these companies had an office with one or more rooms and a piano. Songwriters were hired to sit in the rooms during the day and write new songs at the piano. Songs were continually needed, and there was a lot of competition. Musicians and lyricists collaborated all along Tin Pan Alley to come up with new song material. When the Tin Pan Alley songwriter or songwriting team had finished a new song, the publisher would go out and try to convince an entertainer to perform it in his or her act. This process, originating in Tin Pan Alley, was known as *song plugging*.

In the early days of song plugging, there were no set rules. The song plugger could be either the publisher himself or a singer hired to persuade the entertainer, the more famous, the better, to perform the number. Once an agreement was reached between the publisher and the entertainer, the publisher would print sheet music of the song. The entertainer's picture would often appear on the cover of the sheet music. This was done both to flatter them and to ensure that the performer would continue using the song in his or her act.

The sheet music was distributed to wholesalers, also known as *jobbers,* throughout the country, with the expectation of orders from retailers. Performers would travel the vaudeville circuit on the train routes throughout the United States, having been booked by Tin Pan Alley booking agents. After performing in a city, the local music store and other stores that sold sheet music would receive requests for copies of the new song that had been performed the night before.

During the 1800s, pianos had become a primary source of entertainment in the home. Sheet music was in high demand. This is hard to imagine in today's world of recorded music, where virtually any genre of music can be purchased and listened to, involving no effort to read music or play an instrument on the part of the consumer. During the Tin Pan Alley era, it was the number of copies of sheet music sold that determined whether or not a song was a *hit,* not record sales or a song's position on the charts.

Sheet music sales rose considerably during this period, and the music publishers profited. Millions of copies of sheet music had been sold by 1910. The most popular songs sold as many as a million copies each *in sheet music!*

Charles K. Harris's *After the Ball* was the first popular song to sell a million sheet music copies in 1893. By 1903, it had sold over ten million copies. During the gay nineties and the early 1900s, sentimental Victorian ballads and clever novelty songs were in vogue. *In the Shade of the Old Apple Tree* and *Little Annie Rooney* were the biggest sellers of this period. Comic songs like George M. Cohan's *So Long Mary* from the musical play *Forty-Five Minutes from Broadway* were also popular.

The advent of the recording industry and the birth of commercial jazz and blues caused a decline in the popularity of the sentimental ballads. Tin Pan Alley came to draw on a variety of new sources, including African American artists and rural American yodelers.

The main source of popular music in America from 1900 through the late 1940s was the Broadway stage. From the Broadway shows came many hit songs by such great songwriters as George and Ira Gershwin, Jerome Kern, Richard Rodgers, Oscar Hammerstein II, Lorenz Hart, and Harold Arlen.

The player piano, the phonograph, radio, and motion pictures gradually brought an end to Tin Pan Alley. As sound became synchronized with film in 1926, the demand for music to accompany the silent films was high. Publishing companies were bought out by the film tycoons and transplanted within the movie companies themselves. Tin Pan Alley came to serve the movie, record, and radio industries.

Tin Pan Alley Composers

Sheet music collectors often collect by composer, searching for representative works of an individual or team of composers. Tin Pan Alley composers who wrote both words and music included Paul Dresser, George M. Cohan, James Thornton, Charles K. Harris, Irving Berlin, Walter Donaldson, and Cole Porter. Irving Berlin occasionally collaborated with others. Walter Donaldson often worked with lyricists. Early Tin Pan Alley composers included Henry Dacre, Paul Dresser, Ed Harrigan and David Braham, Charles K. Harris, Harry Kennedy, Ed Marks and Joe Stern, Kerry (F. A.) Mills, Monroe Rosenfeld, William J. Scanlan, Joseph P. Skelly, and Jim Thornton.

Middle Tin Pan Alley composers were Ernest R. Ball, Irving Berlin, Will J. Cobb and Gus Edwards, George M. Cohan, Raymond Egan and Richard Whiting, Victor Herbert, Ballard MacDonald and Harry Carroll, Edward Madden and Theodore Morse, Andrew Sterling and Harry Von Tilzer, Albert Von Tilzer, Harry Williams, and Egbert Van Alstyne.

Late Tin Pan Alley composers were Irving Berlin, Buddy De Sylva, Lew Brown and Ray Henderson, Walter Donaldson, Al Dubin and Harry Warren, Dorothy Fields and Jimmy McHugh, Ira Gershwin and George Gershwin, Jerome Kern, Sam Lewis and Joe Young, Cole Porter, and Richard Rogers and Lorenz Hart.

Music was one of the first professions open to African Americans. *Oh, Dem Golden Slippers* (1870), *Carry Me Back to Old Virginny* (1878), and *In the Evening by the Moonlight* (1879) were written by James A. Bland, one of the first African American composers and influenced by the works of Stephen Foster. Other African American composers include William C. Handy, father of the blues, and Scott Joplin, ragtime master.

Jazz great Duke Ellington wrote *It Don't Mean a Thing, If It Ain't Got That Swing* in 1932, along with many other standard popular jazz tunes. Edward Kennedy composed *Don't Get around Much Anymore* (lyric by Bob Russell) in 1942.

The most active women composers of Tin Pan Alley prior to 1920 were Hattie Starr, the first successful woman composer, Charlotte Blake, Beth Slater Whitson, and Carrie Jacobs-Bond. Dozens of women who occasionally wrote songs included Nora Bayes, May Irwin, Anita Owen, Clare Kummer, Minnie Iris, Dorothy Fields, Mabel Wayne, and Beth Slater Whitson.

Popular Song Sheets without Lyrics

Popular song sheets without lyrics included cakewalks, rags, fox-trots, the hesitation waltz, Indian intermezzos or ballads, marches, and blues. Also included were dance styles such as the tango. Following are some examples of "music only" popular song sheets.

Cakewalks

Cakewalks were popular in the 1880s and 1890s. The best performing couple of this exaggerated strut received a cake as a prize, thus the name. Occasionally, lyrics were included. Examples of cakewalks include *After the Cakewalk* by Nathaniel Dett (1900), *At a Georgia Camp Meeting* by Kerry Mills (1897), and *Golliwog's Cakewalk* by Claude Debussey (1908), written for piano and using syncopated rhythms. The cakewalk was associated with ragtime rhythm. Although ragtime rhythm was established prior to 1896, the cakewalks were the first to be published in this rhythm.

Rags

From the cakewalk, ragtime developed into a dance craze that captured the nation unlike any other, reaching its peak in 1913. The ballroom idols of the day were the Irene and Vernon Castle and Maurice Mouvet and Florence Walton dance teams. Ragtime rhythm typically includes a syncopated melody played alongside a steady bass beat. Begun in brothels and honky-tonks, ragtime was not originally accepted by the upper class. People came to love the syncopated melodies with the compelling beat.

The most famous ragtime master is Scott Joplin, who composed and performed ragtime piano tunes.

Other ragtime composers included James Scott, Joseph F. Lamb, Tom Turpin, Ben Harney, George Botsford, Charles L. Johnson, and Eubie Blake. Hundreds and hundreds of rags were written by scores of writers. Most rags did not have lyrics. The first rag to be published was *Mississippi River* by William Krell in 1897. Rags lead all other categories in song sheet collecting. Some examples of ragtime titles include *Fuss and Feathers, Chills and Fever, Barbed Wire, Holy Moses,* and *Coal Smoke. Alexander's Ragtime Band* by Irving Berlin is not a rag, although he contributed greatly to ragtime music.

Fox-trots

At the peak of the Tin Pan Alley era, the nation was obsessed with new dance creations. Tin Pan Alley composers complied to the demand. The fox-trot was the successor to the rags. Some examples of fox-trot titles are *Frisky, Dr. Brown, Tiddledy Winks, Reuben, Cruel Papa,* and *Tickle Toes.* Fox-trot composers included Lucky Roberts, Chris Smith, Joe Jordon, and Charles L. Johnson.

Hesitations (Boston)

The waltz was once considered to be suggestive and indecent but later earned a position of respectability. By the late 1800s, many people had lost interest in the 3/4 waltz time rhythm. With the coming of the automobile, telephone, and telegraph was a new American rhythm. The new century had little in common with the old country-originated waltz, giving way to the fox-trots, one-steps, and two-steps. To keep the waltz from fading into obscurity, a modified step called the *hesitation* or *Boston* was born. Hesitations were written for the dance idols of the day. The *Lame Duck* hesitation was written for Irene and Vernon Castle. The *Maurice* hesitation was composed for Maurice Mouvet of the Mouvet and Florence Walton dance team. Unlike the rags and fox-trots, these waltzes were not given humorous titles. Examples of hesitation titles include *Waltz Elaine, Waltz Brune, Old Fashioned Roses, Love Thoughts, Yes and No Valse,* and *Valse June.* The covers were designed respectably, artistically, and with humor.

Indian Intermezzos and Ballads

In 1903 *Navajo* by Williams and Van Alstyne received national attention. *Silver Heels, Red Wing, Fawneyes, Morning Star, Red Man, Anona, Golden Arrow, Iola, Moon Bird,* and others were published as Indian intermezzos, or short, independent instrumental musical compositions. Lyrics were added to the more popular ones, and the songs became ballads. Because of their popularity, songwriters and publishers produced many Indian songs, calling them intermezzos. The Indian category is a popular field of collecting. The Indian song sheet covers are very attractive, especially the ones of Indian maidens. Other examples of Indian intermezzos and ballads include *Hiawatha* by Neil Moret (1902), *Indian Love Call* by Harbach, Oscar Hammerstein II, and Rudolph Friml (1924), *Kachina-Hopi Girl's Dance* by Albert Van Sand and Arthur Green (1914), and *Oh! That Navajo Rag* by Williams and Van Alstyne (1911).

Marches

Marches were written for every event, including inaugurals, expositions, political campaigns, and wars. John Philip Sousa, the "March King," composed over 150 marches, including the *Washington Post March, The Stars and Stripes Forever, Semper Fidelis,* and *Liberty Bell.* Many march composers were part of the Tin Pan Alley scene. E. T. Paull, Harry J. Lincoln, J. S. Jamecnik, Paul Lincke, and George Rosey (G. M. Rosenberg) are some of the better known march composers. After the turn of the century, march music was published with colorful covers encompassing a variety of subjects, including photographs of presidents and current events.

The Blues

W. C. Handy's 1911 publication of *The Memphis Blues* helped to credit him as the "Father of the Blues." Sorrows were expressed by singing the blues, a twelve-bar refrain with flatted thirds and sevenths. Duke Ellington, Jelly Roll Morton, and Fats Waller all contributed to the blues. Many non-blues songs had a blues title due to their popularity, and Tin Pan Alley profited.

The blues remained popular well into the post-Tin Pan Alley era. Blues singers Gertrude "Ma" Rainey and Bessie Smith became famous for their singing of Tin Pan Alley blues songs. Several blues styles evolved from primitive blues. Tin Pan Alley blues songs numbered in the hundreds.

Dances

To appeal to a variety of tastes in dance styles, it was common among publishers to advertise a song as being suitable for several different dance rhythms. *Tangomania* is a typical example as it could be a one-step, two-step, or tango. Usually the dance step named in the title, regardless of any other dances mentioned, is considered the correct classification. The dance mentioned first would take priority. Other dances included the turkey trot, kangaroo dip, fish walk, Texas Tommy, snake, crab step, grizzly bear, airplane dip, and the waltzes, either syncopated or hesitated. Examples of one- or two-steps were *Cannon Ball* by Joseph C. Northrop (1905), *Captain Betty* by Lionel Baxter (1914), *Cup Hunters* by Julius

Lenzberg (1915), *Fu* by George P. Howard (1919), *Great Snakes!* by Ernest Reeves (1911), *Melody Maids* by W. Leon Ames (1914), *Ole Virginny* by J. S. Zamecnik (1916), *Pepperpot* by Harold Iver (1913), *Pink Poodle* by Charles L. Johnson (1914), *Silhouette One Step* by Harold Bien (1914), *Thanks for the Lobster* by Clarence Jones (1914), *Tsin Tsin Ta Tao* by D. Onivas (1914), and *Yo San* by Al W. Brown (1914). Examples of tangos were *El Irrisistible* by Egbert Van Alstyne (1914), *Everybody Tango* by Paul Pratt (1914), *Pass the Pickles* by Grace LeBoy (1913), *Tangomania* by Egbert Van Alstyne (1914), and *Tom Tom* by Rosardios Furnari (1914).

Composer Profile: Scott Joplin

The "Ragtime Master" Scott Joplin was born November 24, 1868, in Texarkana, Texas. His mother, Florence Givens Joplin, was from Kentucky and had been free from birth. His father, Giles Joplin, was an ex-slave from North Carolina. Slavery ended only five years before Scott Joplin was born. The Joplin family led a very musical home life. The father was a violin player, having performed as a dance musician while he was a slave, and the mother sang and played the banjo. Scott had three brothers and two sisters. The two younger brothers, Will and Robert, both sang. Will also played the guitar and Robert composed. The older brother, Monroe, and sisters Myrtle and Ossie were also musical. Scott played the guitar and bugle when he was very young. He discovered a piano at a neighbor's house when he was seven and loved playing it. His musical talents soon became obvious to both his father and the neighbors. Giles Joplin managed to scrape together enough money to buy a secondhand square piano. Scott was at the piano day and night.

The ten-year-old Joplin became known through the black community as a remarkable improviser, and rumors spread to the white community about his talent. A German music teacher who had heard him play offered him free piano lessons. He also taught him sight-reading, the principles of harmony, classical music and composers, and introduced him to the famous operas. Although his first benefactor's name is unknown, Joplin never forgot him, and in his later years he sent his old, poor, and ailing teacher money. Scott Joplin's mother Florence died when he was a young adolescent. Friction developed between Scott and his father over learning a trade. This resulted in his leaving home in 1882 when he was about fourteen. His younger brothers Will and Robert followed him a little later. This move brought Scott into the subworld of the American honky-tonk and red-light districts where piano players, both black and white, were in demand. He traveled from Texas to Louisiana and all over the Mississippi Valley states of Missouri, Arkansas, and Kansas.

This region was "the cradle of ragtime. He was now in a different school: adult education for a child. He met hundreds of mainly self-taught musicians and singers, and heard popular music, light classical music, and folk music, old and new, black and white, respectable and not-so-respectable. It would be a prime source of melodic inspiration for the rest of his life. . . . It was a hurrying, exciting world of music, wine, and contraband love, a terrain not cosmopolitan, but still frontier. Its real music was not Strauss nor Waldteufel nor, even, our own Gottschalk. Nor was it the lugubrious teary ballads of the New York Rialto. It was a heady new music called RAGTIME, a dance-song alembicated from the native air, an intoxicant bubbling with the spirit of a wholly American time and place. . . . For a young man marked out to become the greatest composer of this new music, this folk-conservatory was far more valuable than a real conservatory could have been at that moment. It was a world where for the very first time in America black and white musicians were meeting as equals, competing, trading, and borrowing from the musical traditions of their two different races."[1]

Ragtime composition was prominent during the first two decades of the twentieth century. The first ragtime publication was William Krell's *Mississippi Rag* in 1897. This was followed by Tom Turpin's *Harlem Rag* the same year. By 1899 to 1900, many published compositions with the title "rag" started to appear. The ragtime style was extremely simple and light the first five years. More serious or "high class" rags came out toward the end of the first decade.

The leading composers of ragtime were Scott Joplin, James Scott, Joseph Lamb, Artie Matthews, and Tom Turpin. After 1910, ragtime became a national rage. The major ragtime composers published through the teens, with a few rags published in the early 1920s. By 1925, ragtime composition slowed down considerably due to the commercial exploitation of Tin Pan Alley, giving way to the Jazz Era. There are a limited number of rags recorded "straight." Ragtime was preserved primarily through the printed page and piano rolls, not recordings.

Scott Joplin became ragtime's special master as it began to take shape in the early to mid-1890s. At the age of seventeen, he arrived in St. Louis just as it was all beginning in 1885. The Mississippi was still a great trade and travel river and was heavy with traffic. The wealth on the river on St. Louis generated one of the most wide open "districts" in the country. The sound of syncopated pianos filled the saloons and cafes, pool halls, and parlors of the ill-famed Chestnut and Market Streets. "Jig piano," as ragtime was first called, was everywhere. Ragtime would come of age during the next eight years, centering mainly in St. Louis and Sedalia, Missouri.

Scott Joplin lived in St. Louis from 1885 to 1893, supporting himself by playing in the local honky-tonks. He then moved to Chicago, seeking work there in the clubs, bars, and honky-tonks that sprang up around the 1893 World's Columbian Exposition. Following this, he settled in Sedalia, Missouri, for a brief period, where he played second cornet in the Queen City Concert Band.

He spent the next two years touring with a vocal group he had formed called The Texas Medley Quartet, which included his two younger brothers Will and Robert. During this phase, Joplin began writing his own compositions. He published some of them, namely a pair of waltz songs and three piano pieces. In 1896, his vocal group dissolved and he returned to Sedalia.

This move marked a crucial turning point in Scott Joplin's career. He decided to attend an educational institution for blacks, George Smith College, sponsored by the Methodist Church. There he worked at translating the characteristic ragtime rhythms into musical notation and continued to refine his creative imagination. He composed his first rag, *The Maple Leaf Rag*, and immortalized a club in Sedalia by that name. The Maple Leaf Club became a favorite in Sedalia due to Joplin's piece, attracting the best pianists from all over to play there. Despite this fame, Joplin had difficulty getting the piece published. Both a local firm and a St. Louis publishing house that had bought his original rags turned it down. A break finally came for him in 1899 when a local Sedalia music dealer named Joseph Stark heard *The Maple Leaf Rag* and decided to publish it. This produced instant nationwide success for both Joplin and Stark.

With his newly acquired fortune resulting from *The Maple Leaf Rag*, Stack moved to St. Louis and established an expanded publishing firm. Joplin, newly married, soon followed him there. The two men developed a close relationship despite their differences of age and color. Prosperous from his royalties, Joplin was able to retire from the ragtime world of piano playing, buy a large house, and focus on teaching and composing. He continued to compose rags, and in 1902 brought out *Rag Time Dance*, a folk ballet based on material he had written three years earlier. Not long after this, his first ragtime opera, *A Guest of Honor*, appeared. Neither of these efforts met with much success, and the score to *A Guest of Honor* was subsequently lost and never found.

Personal problems started to afflict Joplin. His baby daughter died a few months after birth, and strained relations with his wife led to a separation.

She had no interest in music. After their breakup, Joplin moved back to Chicago briefly, then to St. Louis and on to New York, all within a year. He again hit the entertainment circuit, performing in hotels and rooming houses, attempting to sell his new compositions. Joplin sold his pieces to many different publishers over the years and published some himself as well. He remarried happily in 1909, after his first wife had died, and settled into a house on West 41st Street. He later moved uptown to Harlem. He began devoting most of his time to a new opera, *Treemonisha.*

The original production of *Treemonisha* received only one performance during Joplin's lifetime, in Harlem in 1915. Lacking in scenery, costumes, lighting, and orchestral backing, the production was unconvincing. The audience, including potential backers, walked out. This dealt a terrible blow to Joplin's spirit. His health began to fail, and in the fall of 1916, he was taken to Manhattan State Hospital. He still composed occasionally but never recovered. He died in the hospital on April 1, 1917, at the age of forty-nine from complications due to syphilis.

In Joplin's later years, from 1909 on, he was moving toward more varied and interesting structures, almost toward classical forms. This probably was not deliberate or conscious but inevitable. For example, *Magnetic Rag* points toward the sonata form, and *Euphonic Sounds,* the rondo. In ragtime, form was the servant of substance.

As stated by Gunther Schuller: "It has become increasingly clear that 'form' need not be a confining mold into which tonal materials are poured, but rather that the forming process can be directly related to the musical material employed in a specific instance. In other words, form evolved *out* of the material itself and is not imposed upon it. We must learn to think of form as a verb rather than a noun."[2]

Ragtime differs from jazz and other related music because it is a body of written compositions. Where jazz is improvised or arranged music, and in some cases recordings are the only permanent illustration, ragtime is printed music for the piano. This reflects a difference in the orientation of the music. In jazz, the creative process, whether written arrangements or improvisations, involves what is done with the melody and harmony.

In ragtime, the creative process involves the writing of the whole piece in all its parts, both horizontal and vertical. In this sense, ragtime is more oriented toward concert music than jazz. Ragtime is formal music, originally composed for the piano. It consists of three or four sections, each with its own melody. Improvisation and variation were not often found in classic ragtime, although they did occur in

some performances around the turn of the century. Many early Dixieland jazz pieces, with several sections and themes, owe their structures to ragtime.

In ragtime form, the elements of scale, key, and harmony, as well as the instrument itself, came from the "white side." The essential catalytic polyrhythms came from the "black side," going back to earlier Afro-American music and its retentions from African music of the duple and triple polyrhythms. Ragtime added syncopations to the cakewalk rhythm. This was "ragged" time.

The late cakewalk = ONE two THREE four. Ragtime = ONE and a TWO and a THREE and FOUR. Rhythmically, ragtime is characterized by its right-hand rhythmic phrases.

These typical rhythmic phrases are found in all published rags. Sixteenth-note runs stopping on a syncopated beat are common. The left hand is normally in a supporting role "oom-pah" pattern of alternating single notes and chords. The left hand rarely engaged in syncopation.

"James Scott's frequent left-hand syncopation always knows its place—that is, it is inserted in the eighth or sixteenth or perhaps seventh and eighth measures of a strain, where it will not interfere with the orthodox ragtime momentum. This rhythmic phrasing is virtually never more complicated. It is of the essence of ragtime style that it can be trusted not to throw in less regular rhythmic patterns. One of the surest giveaways of Jelly's (Morton) *jazz,* not ragtime, posture is his hitting the left hand a sixteenth note early. This can be seen in his 'transformation' of the *Maple Leaf Rag* and *Original Rags* by Scott Joplin. No rag written would dream of such a blatant New Orleans crudity. Many of the revivalists fail to get an appropriate rag sound because of left-hand syncopation alone."[3]

Ragtime's conventional form includes the organization of the whole strain, usually sixteen bars divided into four equal parts. Many strains are organized as ABAC—"B" being a semi-cadence and "C" a full cadence. This organization of tunes carried over into jazz. There are few exceptions to the rule in ragtime, and even fewer in jazz, once the early New Orleans stage was over because of the requirements of improvisation.

Most ragtime compositions are organized on the basis of four strains, either ABCD or ABACD, and less often, ABACDC. In most cases, a repeat will be indicated for all strains, except the return of a strain. Of the thirty-nine Joplin rags, including the collaborations, twenty-seven are ABACD.

Joplin's rags are considered the archetype of the music and are unusually fixed until his later experimental period. In all of Joplin's literature, only two rags, *Euphonic Sounds* and *Palm Leaf Rag,* have rags, *Euphonic Sounds* and *Palm Leaf Rag*, have less than four themes. Only his first and last rags have more.

Several approaches were used to develop the four-strain structure into a coherent whole. The "A" theme will usually be a straightforward statement, complete in itself, acting as a home base. The "A" theme gives the rag its individuality. The "B" theme is lighter, with a less filled-in treatment. It may begin with an unaccompanied right hand on the dominant. The "B" theme melodic line often has a tendency to soar, so that the effect of returning to "A" reinforces the home base feeling. This is further emphasized by leading off theme "A" with a tonic chord and theme "B" with a dominant chord. In *Chrysanthemum*, the "B" strain modulates to the dominant key. In his *Strenuous Life*, he modulates to the dominant chord of the dominant key.

The final two strains function to extend the development of the rag. Where the "B" strain is lighter, strain "C" is slightly darker, often modulating down a fifth in the lower register of the treble. Rhythmically, the "C" strain may have a kind of subdued excitement, which is released in the "D" strain. The "D" strain sometimes returns to the original tonic, as in *Maple Leaf Rag*, but it usually remains in the new key, the subdominant. The "D" strain often has more of a riff quality than the other strains and is generally more relaxed.

Ragtime harmony is based mostly on standard tonic-dominant changes. Extensive use of the common change tonic to submediant to supertonic to dominant back to tonic can be found. Tonic to subdominant is also used. Often, the final four bars will be IV - IV minor - I - VI - II - V - I. In the middle of a strain, the harmony will often move to the mediant minor, then to the dominant, returning to the second half of the strain. These harmonies are similar to those used in early jazz.

Harmonically speaking, everything found in early jazz is found in ragtime, except early jazz placed far more emphasis on the standard blues chorus and internal harmonies appropriate to that series of chord changes. Jazz did not require more complex harmonic resources until well into the 1920s.

One of Joplin's most famous pieces is continually played today by piano players of all levels and ages, *The Entertainer*. It first appeared in 1902, and was dedicated to James Brown and His Mandolin Club. Wandering string groups called "serenaders" performed at this time. These groups included guitars, mandolins, fiddles, and string bass. They played ragtime, waltzes, and popular ballads in the streets and would join with the piano player when invited indoors. *The Entertainer* was popular among these groups.

A quote from his article "Notes on Boogie Woogie" by William Russell in the *HRS Rag* could perhaps also describe the evolution of ragtime and other popular musical forms:

"An amateur is not to be regarded however with condescension. A perusal of the history of music and other arts shows that many important creative innovations have been due to the amateur. Usually in art a new style has its inceptions with the people, and not with cultivated performers."[4]

And if you're considering playing some of Scott Joplin's rags, remember the composer's request:

"Notice! Don't play this piece fast. It is never right to play 'ragtime' fast." (From the scores.)

Popular Song Sheets with Lyrics

Among the many popular song sheets that included lyrics, the following topics were found:

Alcohol and Prohibition

The subject of alcohol was popular among Tin Pan Alley songwriters and publishers, both pro and con. Many songs were associated with "the bottle." Some examples include *Budweiser's a Friend of Mine* by Bryan and Furth (1907), *Glorious Beer, Beer, Glorious Beer* by Leggett and Goodwin (1895), *Ida, Sweet as Apple Cider* by Eddie Leonard (1903), *I'm on the Water Wagon Now* by West and Bratton (1903), *Little Brown Jug* by Eastburn, *Prohibition Blues* by Ring Lardner and Nora Bayes (1919), and *What'll We Do on a Saturday Night When the Town Goes Dry* by Bert Kalmar and Harry Ruby (1919).

Blackface

Blackface songs, a result of the presence of African Americans and slavery in the American South, developed from the minstrel shows into a respected musical style in the late Victorian period through the Tin Pan Alley songwriters. Many of the song titles used the word "coon," which by today's standards is politically incorrect, and some of the caricatures on the covers appear as exaggerated stereotypes. Still, these songs are a part of American musical culture. Blackface songs were very popular from 1890 to 1910. Some examples include *Ain't Dat a Shame* by John Queen and Walter Wilson (1901), *All Coons Look Alike to Me* by Ernest Hogan (1896), *New Coon in Town* by Paul Allen (1883), *Rufus, Rastus, Johnson, Brown (What You Gonna Do When de Rent Comes Around?)* by Andrew Sterling and Harry Von Tilzer (1905), and *The Sound of Chicken Frying, Dat's Music to Me* by Chris Smith (1907).

Children

Although not many Tin Pan Alley songs were written about children, those that were had endearing melodies and tender lyrics. Both the song sheet covers and titles were beautiful. Mammy lullabies were very popular. The most famous children's song was *School Days* by Edwards and Cobb (1907). Other examples include *Hush Little Baby, Don't You Cry* by Rosenfeld (1884), *Little Puff of Smoke, Goodnight* by White and Lardner (1909), *Baby Shoes* by Joe Goodwin and Ed Rose (1916), *Sonny Boy* by De-Sylva, Brown, and Henderson (1928), *Ten Little Fingers and Ten Little Toes* by Ira Shuster and Ed G. Nelson (1921), *There's No More Buster Brown* by Harry Breen and James Conlin (1908), and *Toyland* by Glen MacDonough and Victor Herbert (1903).

Clothing

The most frequently referred to item of clothing in Tin Pan Alley songs was the "hat," fashioned after the popular Gibson girl hairdos of 1890 to 1910. Mention was also made of pinafores, sunbonnets, bustles, bloomers, peg-bottom trousers, derbies, and raccoon coats. In the field of fashion, Tin Pan Alley perpetuated whatever Paris dictated.

Examples of clothing songs include *Bandanna Days* by Noble Sissler and Eubie Blake (1921), *Bell Bottom Trousers* by Moe Joffe (1943), *Bloomer Girl* by Arlen and Harburg (1944), *Button Up Your Overcoat* by DeSylva, Brown, and Henderson (1928), *Get on Your Sneak Shoes Children* by Gussie L. Davis (1898), *The Gingham Girl* by Fleeson and Albert Von Tilzer, *Keep Your Skirts Down, Maryanne* by King, Sterling, and Henderson (1925), *The Lady in Red* by Dixon and Wrubel (1935), *Let a Smile Be Your Umbrella* by Irving Kahal and Francis Wheeler (1927), *One, Two, Button Your Shoe* by John Burke and Arthur Johnson (1936), *Top Hat, White Tie and Tails* by Irving Berlin (1935), *Where Did You Get That Hat?* by Joseph J. Sullivan (1886), and *Who Threw the Overalls in Mrs. Murphy's Chowder?* by George L. Geifer (1899).

Current Events

Headlines fueled the songs of Tin Pan Alley, including political themes, campaigns, new laws, inaugurals, dedications to political figures or entertainers, expositions, festivals, fairs, roundups, catastrophes, and famous news celebrities. The association of a hit song with a singing or movie star helped to advertise the song. When a photograph of the star appeared on the song sheet cover, it helped to promote the star. Dedication of songs by songwriters was a show of friendship, admiration, or appreciation. "This song is respectfully dedicated to" often appeared near the top border of the song sheet cover, elsewhere on the cover, or on the inside title page. Examples include *Goodbye Teddy Roosevelt, Meet Me in St. Louis* (1904 World's Fair), *Lewis and Clark Exposition March* (1905, Portland, Oregon), *Panama Canal March and Two-Step* (1914), *The Wreck of the Titanic* (1912), and *Little Colonel*, dedicated to Shirley Temple (1935).

Dixie

"Dixie" geographically includes the entire area south of the Mason-Dixon Line. Hundreds of songs of the Southland, with or without the word "Dixie" in the title, were written during the Tin Pan Alley era. These include *I Want to Be in Dixie* by Berlin and Snyder (1912), *Rockabye Your Baby with a Dixie Melody* by Jerome and Schwartz (1918), and *There's a Lump of Sugar Down in Dixieland* by Bryan, Yellen, and Gumble (1918).

Feminine Names

During the Tin Pan Alley era, "Rose" was the most frequently used female name in a song title. It was a very fashionable name at the time and was conducive to rhyming. Other female names such as "Edna" and "Gertrude" were also popular but were much harder to rhyme. Songs with feminine names in the title were usually love songs written by men and were sometimes humorous. Female rebellion against Victorianism came with the 1920s. Women wore bobbed hair, shorter skirts, rolled-down stockings, and smoked cigarettes, all symbols of freedom. The "vamp" was a sex symbol capable of getting her wishes and leaving a trail of broken hearts. The lyrics of these songs give an interesting insight into this rebellious time. Many girls' portraits were used on song sheet covers, and many were very beautifully done. Girls' names frequently used in Tin Pan Alley songs were Rose, Mary, Katie, Sue, Kitty, Maggie, Sally, and Marie. Other female names included Hannah, Bessie, Lulu, Liza, Jane, Ida, Irene, Peggy, Polly, Lessie, Rebecca, Rosalie, Ruby, and Sandy.

Flowers, Nature, and Animals

The rose, symbolic of love, is found more often than any other flower in flower-related Tin Pan Alley songs. Daisies and violets are the next two most popular. Many song sheet covers show flowers, in particular, the linens. Many dance steps were associated with animals, as the song sheets suggest. These included the grizzly bear, fox-trot, bunny hug, kangaroo hop, and tiger rag, among others. Examples of flowers, nature, and animal songs include *And the Green Grass Grew All Around* by William Jerome and Henry Von Tilzer (1912), *Cherry Blossoms* by Emma I. Hart (1907), *Down among the Sugar Cane* by Cecil Mack and Chris Smith (1908), *Who's Afraid of the Big Bad Wolf?* by Frank E. Churchill and Ann Ronell (1933), *Be My Little Baby Bumblebee* by Stanley Murphy and H. T. Marshall (1912), *When the Mocking Birds Are Singing in the Wildwood* by Lamb and Blake (1905), and *When the Red Red Robin Goes Bob Bob Bobbin' Along* by Harry Woods (1926).

Food and Beverages

Gratification from food was a subject of Tin Pan Alley songs. Examples include *Big Rock Candy Mountain, Blueberry Hill* by Stock, Lewis, and V. Rose (1940), *A Cup of Coffee, a Sandwich, and You* by Billy Rose, Al Dubin, and Joe Meyer (1925), *I'm Putting All My Eggs in One Basket* by Irving Berlin (1935), *Life Is Just a Bowl of Cherries* by Brown and Henderson (1931), *On the Good Ship Lollipop* by Sydney Clare and Richard Whiting (1934), *Oyster, a Cloister, and You* by Richard Connels (1925), *Tea for Two* by Harback, Ceasar, and Youmans (1925), *Yes, We Have No Bananas* by F. Silver and Irving Cohen (1923).

Locations

Songs about locations include Ireland, Hawaii, states, cities, rivers (e.g., the Mississippi River), Broadway, the South, Heaven, and other locations. For almost every state and major city, there is a song title containing its name. Rivers, mountains, and streets were all sources of sentimentality. Two well-known examples of location songs include Paul Dresser's *Banks of the Wabash* and James Bland's *Carry Me Back to Old Virginny*, which became Virginia's official state song in 1956. Other examples include *For Freedom and Ireland* by Woodward and Mack (1900), *Blue Hawaii* by Leo Robins and Ralph Rainger (1937), *California and You* by Leslie and Puck (1914), *Chicago* by Fred Fisher (1922), *Moonlight on the Colorado* by Billy Moll and Robert King, *Give My Regards to Broadway* by George M. Cohan (1904), and *Cheyenne* by Harry Williams and Egbert Van Alstyne (1906).

Mother

Sentimental feelings having to do with a mother dying or honoring her moral attributes while living were written about in hundreds of "Mother" songs throughout the Tin Pan Alley era. These songs were done so often it sometimes became necessary to remember that mother also divorced, smoked, drank, and even had a sense of humor. Examples of "Mother" songs include *Always Keep a Smile for Mother* by Converse (1884), *Handful of Earth from Mother's Grave* by Joseph Murphy (1883), *I Want a Girl Just Like the Girl That Married Dear Old Dad* by Will Dillon and Harry Von Tilzer (1911), *Ireland Must Be Heaven for My Mother Came from There* by

McCarthy, H. Johnson, and Fisher (1916), *Mother's Prayer* by Arnstein and Gilbert (1932), *Stories Mother Told* by Frank J. Gurney (1895), *There's Nothing Will Forgive Like a Mother* by Cooper and Wege Farth (1891), and *You've Got Your Mother's Big Blue Eyes* by Irving Berlin (1913).

Novelty Songs

As sentimental songs were the mainstay of Tin Pan Alley, novelty and comical songs helped to break the monotony, developing in the twenties and thirties as signs of the times. Extra verses were added to many novelty songs such as *It Ain't Gonna Rain No Mo'*, with at least a dozen or two extra verses. Novelty songs included *The Grass Is Always Greener* by Egan and Whiting (1924), *He Used to Be a Farmer but He's a Big Town Slicker Now* by Sterling and Harry Von Tilzer (1919), *Nobody Else Can Love Me Like My Old Tomato Can* by Downs and Baskette (1923), and *Yes, We Have No Bananas* by Silver and Cohn (1923).

Sports and Games

Although our society is very sports oriented, there were few sports-related Tin Pan Alley songs. Most had to do with horse racing and polo or college fight songs and a few about games. Examples include *Take Me Out to the Ball Game* by Jack Norworth and Albert Von Tilzer (1908), *The Gliders-Skating Waltz* by William Schroeder (1916), and *Checkers* by Edgar Allen and Leo Edwards (1919).

Tearjerkers

Tin Pan Alley songwriters and publishers composed many tragic stories set to music. Some examples include Paul Dresser's *The Convict and the Bird* (1888), *Don't Tell Her That You Saw Me* (1896), *I Wonder Where She Is Tonight* (1899), *Just Tell Them That You Saw Me* (1895), *The Letter That Never Came* (1886), *The Outcast Unknown* (1887), and *The Pardon That Came Too Late* (1891). Songs by Ed Marks and Joe Stern include *Break the News to Mother Gently* (1892), *Don't Wear Your Heart on Your Sleeve* (1901), *His Last Thoughts Were of You* (1894), *The Little Lost Child* (1894), *My Mother Was a Lady* (1896), and *The Old Postmaster* (1900). One more example is Charles K. Harris's *After the Ball* (1892).

Transportation and Communication

Tin Pan Alley made songs about transportation and communication legendary. These songs included the railroad, the automobile, the steamboat, the telephone and telegraph, the United States Postal Department, airborne transportation, walking, the bicycle, the covered wagon, sleigh rides, trolley rides, buggies, rolling chairs, and newspapers. Railroad songs lent themselves to the hypnotic rhythm of the train's engine moving along the track, such as *Shuffle off to Buffalo, Wabash Cannonball,* and *Casey Jones.* Any new invention became the subject of a song, such as *I'll Build a Subway to Your Heart,* coinciding with the building of the New York subway system. Many songs about the telephone were written at the time of its invention. Songs about walking included *Walking My Baby Back Home, Let's Take an Old-Fashioned Walk,* and *Let's Take a Walk around the Block.* The bicycle became a national pastime in the 1890s. Henry Dacre wrote *Daisy Belle,* also known as *A Bicycle Built for Two.* Postcards and the U.S. mail were other popular Tin Pan Alley song topics, reflected in songs such as *The Postcard Girl* (1908) and those dealing with letters or the United States Postal Department.

War Songs

Tin Pan Alley produced its share of war songs, some pro, some con. With World War I came many songs and emotions, including *Don't Take My Darling Boy Away* and *America, Here's My Boy,* depending on the current political view. War songs were comical, tragic, and patriotic. During World War I, in order to save paper, the old large-sized song sheets gave way to the present standard size. During the war, songs were printed in four sizes, including large, standard, small, and miniature for the armed forces. Of the hundreds of songs published during World War I, *Over There* by George M. Cohan (1918) was the most popular. Issued under three different covers, Norman Rockwell's portrayal of soldiers singing by a campfire is considered the most dramatic and unique.

Other examples include *Gee! What a Wonderful Time We'll Have When the Boys Come Home* by Mary Earl (1917), *Good-by Ma, Good-by Pa* by Herschell and Walker (1918), *Goodbye, Broadway, Hello, France* by Reisner, Davis, and Baskette (1917), *Hello, Central, Give Me No Man's Land* by Lewis, Young, and Schwartz (1918), *I'd Like to See the Kaiser with a Lily in His Hand* by Leslie, Johnson, and Frisch (1918), *Joan of Arc, They Are Calling You* by Bryan, Weston, and Wells (1917), *Just Like Washington Crossed the Delaware, General Pershing Will Cross the Rhine* by Johnson and Meyer (1918), and *Liberty Bell, It's Time to Ring Again* by Goodman and Mohr (1917).

Song Sheet Cover Art and Artists

Song sheets are collected as much for their covers as for the music itself. Digital collections of historical sheet music, available online and listed in the web site section of this chapter, allow anyone the opportunity to view these incredible works of art on the Internet. Sheet music covers by Norman Rockwell were very popular, and not many were issued. *Over There, Little Grey Mother of Mine, Down Where the Lilies Grow,* and the later *Lady Bird Cha Cha Cha* are the four known ones. The scarcity, along with Rockwell's popularity as the *Saturday Evening Post* artist, explains their high value.

Well-known illustrators Archie Gunn, Hamilton King, and James Montgomery Flagg also appeared as song sheet cover artists, and they, too, are rarities. Archie Gunn illustrated the cover of *The American Girl March* by Victor Herbert in the Sunday supplement to the *Examiner.* Hamilton King illustrated the cover of *Peggy O'Neil.* James Montgomery Flagg did the cover of George M. Cohan's *Father of the Land We Love.*

Almost half of all the song sheet covers were unsigned and included many outstanding and artistic covers. The signatures of over 150 different artists are found on large and standard song sheets. These should not be confused with celebrity autographs. Other notable cover artists and photographers include Alpeda, Starmer, J. V. R., Albert Barbelle, Andre Petakacs, Pfeiffer, John Frew, Frederick S. Manning, R. S., Carter/Myers/Pryor, and Gene Buck. Starmer, Barbelle, and R. S. contributed the most on both large- and standard-size song sheets.

A new breed of artists emerged in the 1920s with a strong feeling for Art Deco. J. V. R. contributed greatly to this style, creating and signing many striking covers. The signatures of Art Deco artists Wohlman, Perret, Griffith, Leff, Pud, and Lane varied little and can be found easily.

E. T. Paull, composer of marches, arranger, and, later, publisher, produced extremely popular and brilliant five-color lithographed song sheet covers, executed by the A. Hoen Lithograph Company. His songs were advertised on the back side of a standard 1922 reissue as "thirty-seven magnificently lithographed songs by E. T. Paull Publishing Company." All but six of the songs were marches. Almost all were solely Paull compositions, although he collaborated with others on twelve of them. In these cases, he was probably the arranger, as in *Midnight Fire Alarm,* where Harry J. Lincoln wrote the music and Paull the arrangement. Though his covers are more prevalent than Norman Rockwell's, they are considered in the scarce category, often found dirty and torn due to their popularity.

Art Deco (1910 to 1935)

The artistic elements of Art Deco included flower garlands, fruit baskets, popular trees, fountains, nudes, geometric designs, masked harlequins, jesters, clowns, long-legged beautiful women in billowy skirts, deer, flowers, greyhounds, streamlined human figures in exaggerated positions, Cubism, and Egyptian, American Indian, Mexican, and African influences. As Art Nouveau was a revolution against traditional art, Art Deco revolted against its predecessor, Art Nouveau.

Between 1910 and 1920, cover artists such as Starmer, Pfeiffer, R. S., DeTakacs, and Frew played an active role in the development of Art Deco. By the 1920s, new names appeared on Art Deco song sheet covers, including C. E. Millard, Wohlman, G. Kraus, Perret, Politzer, and Griffith. Art Deco is well represented on song sheet covers, both large and standard size. Examples of Art Deco covers in large size include *Cabaret Rag* by Pfeiffer, *The Kangaroo Hop* by F. E. Looney, and *Tiddle-de-Winks* by Starmer. Covers in standard size include *Let Me Call You Sweetheart* by Mary Kidder, *Secondhand Rose* by Wohlman, and *You Said Something When You Said Dixie* by Wohlman.

Cartoonists

Covers by prominent Art Deco era cartoonists such as Opper, Billy DeBeck, Clare Victor, Dwiggins, Swinnerton, Gaar Williams, Paul Fung, George McManus, and Harold Gray are rare. A few examples are *Barney Google* by DeBeck, *Little Orphan Annie* by Harold Gray, and *Seattle Town* by Paul Fung from the comic strip *Dumb Dora*.

Linens

Linens were issued in both large and standard size on a superior quality white, small pebbled surface with a matte finish, distinguishing them from other song sheets. Flowers and landscapes were often found on linen cover designs. Carrie Jacobs-Bond & Sons and Sam Fox Publishing Co. used linens to print sheet music. Linen cover samples include *Basket of Roses* by Fred G. Albers (1913) in the large size, and in the standard size, *Lazy River* by Carrie Jacobs-Bond (1923).

Sunday Supplements

From 1895 to 1908, before microphones, promoters tried to popularize a song by issuing supplemental song sheets in the Sunday newspaper. These Sunday supplements were issued on low-quality paper. Over the years, many became yellowed and brittle. The covers were often drawn by cartoonists on the staff of the newspaper with which they were issued. A popular Sunday supplement artist was H. B. Eddy. Sunday supplement songs were frequently composed for the newspapers as a good source for musical stars and musical shows. Sunday supplement

song cover samples include *American Girl March* by Archie Gunn and *I Caught You Making Eyes at Me* by H. B. Eddy.

Advertising Song Sheets

The Garland Stove Company was the first to use the song sheet as an advertising medium in 1889. The cover was a black-and-white lithograph. Soon to follow was the Bromo Seltzer Company, which used 171 song selections to promote their product, mostly standards and hymns. These were distributed to local pharmacies throughout the country. Anyone could submit a two-cent stamp and a Bromo Seltzer wrapper, and in return select and receive two songs. A prime example of an advertising song sheet was a colored lithograph by Gugler Company, *Wait for the Wagon*, published by the Studebaker Brothers. Free copies were distributed in 1884 for the new year. The cover showed the four Studebaker Brothers, Adams County, Pennsylvania, where they were born, and a horse-drawn wagon of folks celebrating New Year's. On the back side was printed a four-verse parody of *Wait for the Wagon* titled *A Carol of the Studebaker Wagon*, with information promoting it. In 1941, a free song sheet titled *Honeymoon for Three* advertised the new Chevrolet, the third party being the new car. *Miss Samantha Johnson's Wedding Day* was covered the most by advertisers. Twenty different advertisers used every available border space. In some instances, parts of the music were blocked. Advertising song sheets published by the companies themselves, or expressly for the companies, are hard to find. Using song sheets as a promotional scheme was quite successful and continued throughout the Tin Pan Alley era and later. More advertising song sheet samples include *Cable March and Two Step* by the Cable Piano Company (1903), *Song of the Great Big Baked Potato* by the Northern Pacific Railroad (before 1918), and *Way Down upon the Suwannee River* by the Southern Railway System (1921).

Cowboy and Action Westerns

The fascinating wild west was depicted in some song sheet covers, including the colorful action westerns reminiscent of Russell and Remington. Western song sheet covers include *Cheyenne*, *In the Land of the Buffalo*, and *Santa Fe Song* by Starmer.

Songs in Musicals, Silent Films, Talkies, Radio, and Records

Musicals

The earliest form of American entertainment, the minstrel shows, originated in the 1840s. By the 1880s, variety shows took over, followed by operettas, vaudeville, the follies, revues, scandals, and others, evolving into Broadway musicals. These musical entertainment forms became interwoven with Tin Pan Alley. Each contributed to the continuation of the show and its songs.

Musicals were advertised on the covers of song sheets. Samples of musical shows advertised on pre-1920 song sheets include George M. Cohan's *Hello Broadway* and Victor Herbert operettas, including *Naughty Marietta*. *The Ziegfeld Follies*, which ran from 1907 until 1943, was one of the most famous musical shows. Irving Berlin's *Music Box Revues* ran from 1921 to 1924. Other famous shows included George White's *Scandals*, the *Greenwich Village Follies*, Jack Norworth's *Odds and Ends*, the *Hippodrome Shows*, Earl Carroll's *Vanities*, Schubert's *Passing Shows*, the *Wintergarden Shows*, and the *Broadway Brevities*. Major producers of the period included Daniel Arthur, Richard Carle, Charles Dillingham, Lew Fields, Joe Hertig, Klaw and Erlander, George W. Lederer, Oliver Morosco, August Pitou, Henry Savage, Mort Singer, and Whitney.

Before radios and phonographs, minstrel shows, stage shows, and vaudeville were the only avenues of song plugging available to music publishers. Not unlike today, the association of a song with a star performer ensured its success. Every publisher or song plugger used any means available to convince a star to include a song in his or her repertoire. This included anything from giving expensive gifts such as jewelry to giving up a percentage of the song's royalties. This was "payola" in its early stages.

Songs and singers were dependent on each other for survival. Songs were made successful by a star performer's rendition, and singers became successful by introducing great songs. "Sung with great success by," "prominently featured by," "introduced and sung by the phenomenal," "triumphantly featured by," and "sung with tremendous success by" were phrases used along with a star's photograph on song sheet covers from the late 1800s through the early 1900s.

Blackface songs were the end result of the minstrel shows and were very popular at this time. Blackface song entertainers overwhelmed audiences with the power of their throaty tenor voices. In the minstrel shows, a carryover from the Civil War, the entire cast consisted of male members who personified the popular caricature of the African American in song and dance. They frequently worked in pairs, such as Primrose and West. The culmination of this impersonation came in the early 1900s with the legendary performer Al Jolson. Stars who were successful prior to and after the age of movies, phonograph, and radio included Al Jolson (*Bring Along Your Dancing Shoes*) and Sophie Tucker (*Darktown Strutters' Ball*).

Songs of the Silent Films

In 1895, Ed Marks came up with the idea, with the help of an electrician, to photograph actors and actresses in subsequent portrayals of episodes from his tearjerker song *Little Lost Child*, co-written with Joe Stern. These photographs were placed on slides and projected through a lantern onto a screen as the song was being sung. This was an instant success, and the lantern slide and *Little Lost Child* became synonymous. The silent movie and the theme song followed, as did the synchronization of musical score and film and, later, the *talkies*.

In 1926, Warner Brothers purchased a device called the *Vitaphone*, which synchronized a wax sound recording with a film projector. That same year, Warner Brothers produced the movie *Don Juan* with a musical score. Al Jolson sang the songs in *The Jazz Singer* in 1927. The first all-talking film, *Lights of New York*, was produced in 1928 by the Warner Brothers Vitaphone process. William Fox used a similar device called *Movietone*. Silent movie theme song covers advertised the movie from which they came. The film stars were normally shown on the cover as well as the film company and the producer. These songs were often dedicated to the stars by the songwriters.

The first movie theme song to gain national popularity was *Mickey* from Mack Sennett's 1918 film of the same name, starring Mabel Normand. This song was issued in three different sizes, with the star Mabel Normand in three different cover poses. The large- and small-sized song sheets were published in 1918. The standard-sized one was issued in 1919. A second standard-sized publication with Mabel Normand in yet another pose was also published, making four total distinct song sheet covers.

Some song sheets were definitely designated as a theme song or introduced in a motion picture and are collected as such. Other silent film song sheets are collected by the stars pictured on the covers. These covers often stated that the photograph was reproduced by permission of the film company with which the star was affiliated. Any song sheet marked *Vitaphone* or *Movietone* came from a movie that at least had partial sound. By 1930, there were no more silent films; however, Charlie Chaplin produced two such films at a later date.

Songs of the Talkies, Radio, and Records

In the post-silent screen era, radios and phonographs were becoming popular among the American people. The piano was almost completely ignored, and the player piano came to be considered out of style. Not only did pianos take up a lot of space, but a person had to work at learning how to play it. Turning a radio knob or phonograph crank was much easier and could produce many sounds at once from all over the world. "Successfully featured by" was still used on song sheet covers during the 1920s, in combination with a star and the song, but was soon replaced by "introduced by" or "as featured in."

Eventually, it was hard to distinguish if a song sheet cover star was associated with radio, film, or a record. Some stars were popular in all three mediums, including Al Jolson, Eddie Cantor, and Sophie Tucker. The movie performers took over the song sheet covers, providing a gallery of collectible stars. Along with individual performers, famous bandleaders or entire bands were being featured on the covers of song sheets.

Because they were instrumental in making so many popular hit songs, the most sought-after covers are those featuring Al Jolson, Charlie Chaplin, Shirley Temple, and Eddie Cantor. There are many covers featuring Al Jolson, Rudy Vallee, Bing Crosby, Sophie Tucker, and Ruth Etting. Bing Crosby, Shirley Temple, and Kate Smith were part of the Tin Pan Alley era early in their careers, but their greatest popularity was achieved later. Individual songs were often issued with several different stars on the covers. For example, *Bye, Bye, Blackbird* was issued with four separate covers, all identical, except for the star photographs of Gus Edwards, Frank Richardson, Olive O'Niel, or the Angelus Sisters.

Tin Pan Alley's cut off date is usually considered to be the early 1930s. Shirley Temple was born on April 23, 1928, and her first movie was produced in 1932. In 1928, Walt Disney produced his first animated cartoon, *Plane Crazy*, marking the beginning of the Disney dynasty. From the 1933 Walt Disney film *Three Little Pigs* came the first song written for an animated cartoon, *Who's Afraid of the Big Bad Wolf?*

Song sheets associated with Walt Disney and Shirley Temple are among the most sought after of those published in the post-Tin Pan Alley era, along with those issued during World War II. News, political, and exposition songs have also been popular with collectors. The post-Tin Pan Alley song sheet covers show many star celebrities from radio, records, and film.

Collecting Song Sheets

Song sheets are most valuable when they're in mint condition. If the sheet music has been damaged or reduced in size, the monetary value goes down. Sheet music is best kept in unsealed plastic bags, allowing it to breathe. The paper used for song sheets before 1900 and for the Sunday supplements was easily perishable, and requires extra care.

When determining the value of a song sheet, the following criteria are considered: age, composer's popularity, performer(s), scarcity, cover artist, category, early or late issue, condition, and identical songs with different covers or performed by different stars. Individual songs were sometimes issued under several different covers, and the same cover design may have been used for different performing artists. The best resource for current prices is *The Sheet Music Reference and Price Guide* by Anna Marie Guiheen and Marie-Reine A. Pafik. Songs are cross-referenced alphabetically by cover artists, performers, composers, and by miscellaneous categories. Many pictures of actual sheet music covers are included.

Using mint condition as the standard from which to work, the following guidelines should be followed when determining the value of a song sheet. Mint condition means near music store condition, with the absence of names, smears, tears, or frays and are valued at 100 percent.

If there is a music store stamp, but the condition is otherwise mint, the value is 90 percent of the mint condition value. If the owner's name appears in ink, but the condition is otherwise very good, the value is 75 percent. A sheet with carefully trimmed edges but otherwise very good condition is valued at 65 percent. Sheets with a separated cover but otherwise in very good condition are worth 55 percent. Dog-eared or slightly frayed sheets are worth 50 percent. Torn, somewhat smeared, or badly frayed sheets are worth 25 percent. Dirty, badly torn, or incomplete sheets are valued at 10 percent.

Song sheet covers show America's character and history. Those who collect song sheets do so both for the music and for the cover design. The collector may have an interest in certain composers, stage shows, theme music from the silent movies, Walt Disney, the various dances and rhythms of the era, locations, communications, political issues, news songs, sad songs, songs about mother, or novelty songs. Those who collect by cover may do so for the cover artists, Art Deco designs, advertising song sheets, or favorite categories. Song sheets are sometimes collected as a part of other antique collections.

Song sheets are seldom in mint condition as they were used frequently when the song was in vogue. The majority of music published prior to 1900 had covers decorated with black-and-white engravings. The pre-1900 black-and-white engravings consisted of fine lines. The name of the engraving or lithograph company was ordinarily placed somewhere near the bottom of the song sheet.

There are two basic sheet music sizes. Prior to 1917, with a few exceptions, all music was published in the large 13- x 10-inch size. From 1920 onward, all music was published in the standard 12- x 9-inch size. Dimensions in both instances could vary as much as an inch. The transition period from 1917 to 1919 was during World War I. As in any war, resources were needed for the war effort. This included paper. During this time, music was published in four different sizes, those being large, standard, small, and miniature. The small 10- x 7-inch was to help further the war effort. A miniature version 4- x 5-inch was distributed free to those in the armed services.

Because all popular music was published in the standard size from 1920 on, it is possible to date a late or early issue of a song sheet by its size, especially if the first release was prior to 1917. The first issue of *In My Merry Oldsmobile* was in 1905 and was large sized. A revival of the song reissued after 1926 was in the standard size.

"Now try this over on your piano" was a stock phrase used extensively by publishers to advertise current song issues, which were printed on the back cover or on the inside of the front cover. These current song samples had their copyright dates listed just below a printed line of the song.

First release issues are often difficult to determine. Copyright transfers can be a clue. William C. Handy's *Memphis Blues* was first published by Handy, but the copyright was later transferred to Theron C. Bennett and then again to Joe Morris Publishing Company. W. C. Handy's original publication is subsequently classified as a rare imprint.

First release songs or imprints, like first edition books, are highly valued. Whatever the reason for the copyright transfer, it is often the one and only clue to a first release. At the bottom of the title page, that being the first page of song, the copyright date of the song appears. This normally indicates the publication date of the song. If the copyright has been transferred, the original owner's date of copyright is listed first. Below this is listed the new copyright owner and date.

Successful marches, intermezzos, and waltzes prompted publishing companies to call in lyricists, changing the musical compositions into singable ballads, and thus requiring recopyrighting in the new form. Occasionally, songs were sold to another company, which would supply the lyrics and publish the song as a ballad. This also required a copyright transfer. Songwriters would sometimes publish their own songs either because they were unable to interest a publisher or because they wished to reap the profits. If a song achieved any degree of success, publishing companies eagerly sought a copyright transfer.

Identifying the date of a song sheet publication can be difficult. There has been more interest in the printing and publishing of music in the eighteenth and early nineteenth centuries than in the publications from 1825 to the Civil War. Copyright dates are not universal in the publications before the enactment of the first U.S. copyright law in 1871.

Because music was engraved on plates, publishers often kept the plates in storage for long periods of time, printing new copies as the stock ran low. They would sometimes sell plates to other publishers who may not have bothered changing the original copyright information on the plates. A plate number can sometimes be used to identify an approximate date of publication, but that depends on how much is known about the engravers or publishers.

Care and Repair

One of the difficulties of caring for sheet music collections is that music was intended to be used, and people did just that. The sheet music may have been stored on a music rack or in a piano bench, but it was usually played or sung and, therefore, came to show signs of wear and tear. Some pieces survived better than others.

Much of the music printed from engraved plates in the nineteenth century is in fairly good condition because the paper was usually made of rags rather than wood pulp and was a little thicker than paper used for other purposes. Music printed on cheap paper made of wood pulp becomes very brittle in a short period of time.

To preserve sheet music items, they are often placed in acid-free folders, in acid-free boxes with low light conditions, in climate-controlled stacks. Albums are a good place for storage and easy viewing of song sheets, consisting of plastic envelopes sized to fit the music. Before filing, framing, or inserting into an album, it is a good idea to go over a song sheet with a soft, dry cloth to remove dirt.

Attempting to remove an ink signature by erasure or ink eradicator will only leave a white area. Watercolors can sometimes be used effectively to color the white worn or creased areas noticeable on the darker covers. A pencil signature can be carefully removed with a gum or rubber eraser. Tape carefully applied can be used to repair torn song sheets.

Many song sheets had an insert sheet. If this is missing, the value decreases, and the pages are no longer numbered consecutively. Missing inserts can be combined with incomplete copies. Before the 1920s, nearly all pianos came with a stool. Sheet music cabinets rather than benches were used for storing sheet music.

After the 1920s, pianos came with benches that could accommodate standard-sized sheet music. If a new piano was purchased, the borders of large size song sheets were sometimes cut off with scissors, leaving the music intact. Cut-down song sheets show cut off designs and lettering on the covers and were usually not cut straight.

The large size song sheets were generally considered more attractive than the standard size covers for several reasons. Pre-1920 era artists used the entire color spectrum, with no preference for any particular color. The 1920 or 1930 era frequently used orange-blue, orange-green, orange-black, and orange-purple combinations. As the movie and record industries emerged, portraits of singers and movie stars were placed wherever they would gain exposure, including song sheet covers.

Song sheets came to serve the movie and record industry, and thus the decline in artistic covers. This was true somewhat in the pre-1920 era when vaudeville, minstrels, and stage shows were sometimes advertised on sheet music covers. But the trend became more common in the 1920s and 1930s. Simplicity of life in the 1930s was reflected in the sterile quality of interior design. This could also be seen in song sheet cover designs.

Framed song sheets complement any room and decor, and the decorating possibilities are endless. Simple frames matching or coordinating with a color in the cover art itself work best. Song sheets can be framed in pairs or sets, and may thematically compliment a room.

Song sheets have sentimental as well as monetary value and can hold a special meaning in the heart of the collector.

The Print Music Business Today

The music publishing industry was greatly affected by the new technology of the early twentieth century. Initially, the U.S. Copyright Act, on which publishing principles are based, was not keeping up with the rapid growth of technology, not unlike the situation today with Internet technology. Before the U.S. Copyright Act of 1909, there was confusion as to what should be owed to publishers by the piano roll manufacturers. The new law established that the publisher would receive two cents for each of his songs appearing on a piano roll or recording manufactured by these quickly growing American industries.

Beginning in the 1920s, recordings and radio had become important new forms of entertainment in the home. Many vaudeville entertainers had become radio stars. Publishers wanted the new radio stars to perform their songs on the radio, with the anticipation of greatly increased sheet music sales. Still more profits could be made from record sales of their songs sung by the stars.

Before the end of the 1920s, the addition of sound to film was another technological advancement creating major changes in the world of Tin Pan Alley. On October 6, 1927, the first movie musical, *The Jazz Singer*, starring Al Jolson, opened. This was the first film to use songs and moving pictures on the big screen, and it was a hit at the box office. This success caused Hollywood to turn to Broadway, and Broadway to Hollywood.

Many stars and songwriters, now in demand by Hollywood studios, headed for California. Motion picture companies began purchasing entire publishing companies from the original owners. Sheet music became a less important part of the music industry as sound recordings became prominent after World War II. By the early 1950s, many publishers started to *job out* the printing portion of their business to companies that specialized in printing sheet music for many different publishers, including song folios, band, orchestra, and choral arrangements. This new practice led to today's *print publishers*.

Print publishers own few or no copyrights, with the exception of original material composed for teaching method books or choral productions, and the copyrights on their particular arrangements of popular or public domain songs. They print and distribute music on behalf of the publishers that hold the copyrights on the music material printed, and share in the income earned from the print sales. Very few music publishers today have their own print departments. The print business today is a much smaller part of the music industry than it was in earlier times, but it remains an important one.

By the time of Elvis Presley in the 1950s, the songwriters who had been an important part of Tin Pan Alley were writing primarily for Broadway and film, or had been replaced by younger songwriters whose songs were those with which newer audiences identified. Very few songwriters of Tin Pan Alley's heyday made the transition to rock music. Older songwriters who adapted to the new styles of popular music in the 1950s survived in the music industry. New York still had many music publishers, the new ones of which specialized in rock and pop music.

By the early 1960s, the music publishing industry followed the youthful dance crazes that were popular all over the country. The Hollywood film industry did so as well. Many publishers moved into the recording industry, signing acts to record songs composed by the publisher's staff writers. The new independent record/publishing companies achieved much success.

In 1964, the Beatles brought their songs to America, written by them. American publishers were not ready for this. Unlike Elvis Presley who needed songwriters, popular music acts of the middle 1960s began to write their own material.

Many publishers tried to convince the self-contained acts that it was still necessary to sign over their publishing rights to properly promote and administer their songs. Not knowing how they were going to get their songs recorded, publishers signed the artists who had recording contracts and got the publishing rights to all the songs on their albums. Many well-known acts signed away the publisher's share to publishers who did little more than profit from their work.

Many of the self-contained acts began to realize the importance of publishing. They set up in-house publishing companies with the help of entertainment attorneys and managers, consisting of song catalogs written and recorded by them. When recordings were sold, instead of paying the publishing royalties to an outside publisher, the record company paid them to the publishing company owned by the act.

Many of the jobs that used to be the publisher's now belonged to the record company. In the Tin Pan Alley era, it was the publishing company's job to print, distribute, and promote sheet music. When recordings came to dominate home entertainment after World War II, it became the record company's responsibility to press, distribute, and promote records. As a result of this, if a self-contained act wanted to sign a recording contract with a label, the act also had to sign a publishing agreement with the label's in-house publishing company. This is how many record companies became owners of the important popular music publishing catalogs of the 1950s through the 1970s. Similar deals are made less frequently today. Usually record labels will ask for only a percentage of the publishing as opposed to all of it.

The music publishing industry is very much alive today in New York City and Los Angeles. Publishers resembling those of Tin Pan Alley, with staff writers and song pluggers who take their songs to artists and producers on a daily basis in an effort to get them recorded, are found today on Music Row in Nashville, Tennessee. Other publishing and recording centers in the United States include Miami, Seattle, Minneapolis, Chicago, Memphis, Philadelphia, Boston, and Muscle Shoals, Alabama. There are other regions throughout the United States where publishers and print music publishers do business. For the songwriter who does not perform, there are still many performers who do not write and need new songs.

Music publishers today may offer developmental deals to up and coming artists/songwriters who perform. Rather than signing a songwriter to compose songs for others to record, many publishers look for singer/songwriters or self-contained acts that the publisher can take into the recording studio, walk away with a polished demo or master recording, and shop to a major record label. The publisher gets all or part of the publishing rights to the songs written by the artist in exchange for paying for the demo and production costs and helping to secure the record deal.

By becoming involved in producing self-contained artists, many music publishers have survived in an industry that is constantly changing.

In recent years, music publishers have begun buying in and selling out. At one point in time, music publishing was an industry of several dozen major companies, each of which owned thousands of copyrights, and hundreds of smaller companies, each of which owned one to several hundred copyrights. The Hollywood film industry started buying up publishing companies in the early part of the twentieth century because it was an easy way to acquire many readily available songs.

Since that time, the number of publishing companies has risen and fallen considerably. While new companies are constantly emerging, new and old companies are being bought and incorporated into larger ones. The 1980s and 1990s, and into the new millennium, saw an unprecedented amount of buying and selling among music publishers. Songwriters and their songs have become part of huge catalogs, often with little priority being given to their work among thousands of other copyrights.

While performing artists, with rare exceptions, tend to come and go, great songs stand the test of time. In earlier days, they were marketed as sheet music. Today, music publishers have many ways to market songs, resulting in many different sources of income. While copyright laws and technology continue to change, it is still the music publisher that owns, promotes, and administers songs. Chapter 2 discusses the print music business today, including royalties, copyright laws, formats, and terms. It also includes web sites relating to these issues.

Digital Sheet Music

Digital sheet music is a relatively new technology. It allows for the distribution of high quality, low cost sheet music that can be created and arranged according to the users' preferences, also known as custom sheet music or sheet music by request. As with digital audio music, digital sheet music can be instantly downloaded from the Internet and printed.

Digital sheet music can be created from already printed sheet music by a scanner as digital photocopies. The quality is limited by image resolution and by the quality of the original document. Purely digital sheet music is created from scratch on a computer using music software graphic notation programs such as Finale or Sibelius, and many others listed in chapter 14.

Digital sheet music was a major turn in the printed music market. Millions of users browsing the Internet are able to find the sheet music they are looking for by typing its title in a browser search bar. Web sites distributing this kind of sheet music have Advanced Search tools that offer the opportunity to browse and find sheet music matching a specific title, composer, arranger, instrumentation, level of difficulty, etc. Once the user finds the right sheet music, they can then download the music and print it.

Most digital sheet music websites offer the opportunity to transpose the piece or the piece is already arranged in different keys. Musicians downloading sheet music, usually in PDF file format, can also choose to download the MIDI or MP3 audio file that goes along with it. Those downloading digital sheet music can benefit from personalized sheet music, according to their musical taste, price preference, transposition requirements, and with audio files to help their musical performance or study.

Various plug-ins can help display the digital sheet music files according to their published format. While PDF file format is the most common, some websites utilize different plug-ins to allow users to view and play the sheet music before purchase and to transpose it in real-time. An example is the Sibelius Scorch plug-in, as well as the Finale Viewer, and the musicRAIN2.0 software. Usually free of charge, these programs are helpful to users and website owners for the management of digital sheet music archives. They are user-friendly and speed up sheet music downloads for printing.

Digital sheet music, as a media for distribution of sheet music in digital format, started to form with the use of the Internet, around 1994-1995. Personal websites started creating sheet music in digital format in order to distribute personal compositions or classical music in public domain to their Internet audience.

At the beginning of 1998, the first digital sheet music store appeared on the Internet, SheetMusicDirect.com. It was the first site distributing popular sheet music in digital file format. Virtualsheetmusic.com was the first site offering high quality, pure digital classical sheet music together with custom arrangements and transcriptions tailored for any instrument and ensemble by user request. More sites emerged expanding the available digital sheet music repertoire. In 1999, more digital sheet music commercial sites were introduced such as MusicNotes.com and SheetMusicScore.com along with free and subscription websites such as Sheetmusicarchive.net, Musicaviva.com, and many others. In 2004, the first fully personalized digital sheet music service, rfkharris.com, appeared on the Internet, where the user could make any demands of their sheet music.

Today, many titles of printed sheet music can be found in digital format for instant download on the Internet. Technology is expanding digital sheet music

interactivity and enjoyment with the aid of devices such as Sibelius Scorch, allowing for MIDI playback, instrument changes and transposition and music tablets introduced by Free Hand Freehandmusic.com, allowing musicians to download music and store it into devices that allow for playing instantly and directly without any printing. These tablets are fairly expensive and are aimed primarily at the professional musician. Also available is a software program called MusicReader that runs on laptops. Vivaldistudio.com offers downloadable software for creating and reading interactive digital sheet music.

There are different viewers and formats used by the companies offering digital sheet music. All require the user to download software. SheetMusicScore.com is testing a new beta viewer that will no longer require that the user download and install software as both PCs and Macs will instantly display the sheet music using a viewer based on flash technology.

Digital printable sheet music has its limitations. It is best when used for short pieces of music. Printing digital sheet music on card stock can help to give it a longer shelf life and prevent it from tearing easily or flying off a music stand. It is less practical for large-scale works because most printers still print on one side of the paper only. Even though two-sided printing may be possible, it can be very time consuming, and a large score can have hundreds of pages. Paper size is also restricting.

For some smaller specialty sheet music publishers, downloadable digital sheet music is an excellent alternative to the expense of printing and storing inventory. Although many small publishers set high standards of editing and presentation, the easy availability of this technology to self-publishers and amateur composers means that some of the digital sheet music available on the Internet may be of questionable quality.

Like any other digital media, digital sheet music faces the issue of copyright management. Custom file formats displayed with special software can allow the user to print just one copy of music or allow printing only a specific number of copies.

Print Music and Music Book Publishers—Digital Sheet Music—Historical Sheet Music, Song, Lyric, Hymn, and Orchestral Score Online Collections Web Sites

19th Century American Sheet Music Digitization Project www.lib.unc.edu/music/eam/index.html University of North Carolina at Chapel Hill; listed by title, composer and series.

African-American Sheet Music memory.loc.gov/ammem/award97/rpbhtml From Brown University; 1305 pieces.

Alfred Publishing www.alfred.com Sheet music for all instruments; piano methods; guitar; band; DVDs; music software; popular songbooks; workshops.

America Singing: Nineteenth-Century Song Sheets http://lcweb2.loc.gov/ammem/amsshtml/ Collection of single printed sheets with lyrics and no music; from the 1850s to the 1870s; scanned images of the original sheet with lyrics; a unique perspective on the political, social, and economic life of the time, especially during the Civil War; searchable by keywords, titles, names, and publishers.

American Antiquarian Society www.americanantiquarian.org/ Collection of Sheet Music consists of about 60,000 pieces of instrumental, vocal, secular, and religious music by both American and foreign composers that were printed through 1880.

Ames Hymn Collection http://users.stargate.net/~bmames/hymnsjs.htm Brian M. Ames provides lyrics and sound files.

Annotated Grateful Dead Lyrics http://arts.ucsc.edu/gdead/agdl/ By David Dodd, librarian and co-author of *The Grateful Dead and the Deadheads: An Annotated Bibliography*.

Arnold Schoenberg Center www.schoenberg.at/ In German; resource for Schoenberg; Library and Archive; scores, manuscripts, teaching materials.

Arsis Press www.instantWeb.com~arsis Publisher of concert and sacred music by women composers.

Association of American Publishers www.publishers.org Home page; copyright information for books and text.

Audio Publishers Association (APA) www.audiopub.org Non-profit representing audio publishers, audiobooks, and spoken audio.

Bach Cantatas www.cs.ualberta.ca/~wfb/bach.html Walter F. Bischof provides access to the texts of all Bach cantatas, as well as oratorios, passions, masses, and motets; all texts are in the original language; most are in German, some are in Latin, and some in Italian and in Greek.

Bagaduce Music Lending Library www.bagaducemusic.org/ Located in Blue Hill, Maine; library's mission is to collect, preserve and lend printed music, and to provide music education programs; national resource center for choral, instrumental, vocal and keyboard music, both popular and classical, and for teaching and reference materials; Online Catalog.

Band Music from the Civil War Era http://memory.loc.gov/ammem/cwmhtml/cwmhome.html Library of Congress online collection; scores, recordings, photographs, and essays; over 700 musical compositions; eight full-score modern editions; nineteen recorded examples of brass band music in performance.

Base De Données Sur La Musique Vocale De La Renaissance Française http://arenai.free.fr/Database.htm Database of vocal music of the French Renaissance.

Bella C. Landauer Collection of Aeronautical Sheet Music www.sil.si.edu/ondisplay/Music/index.htm Smithsonian Institution Libraries collection is organized by category.

Berklee Press www.berkleepress.com Publications of interest to musicians; Books, Books with Audio CDs, and Instructional DVDs; online catalog.

Biblioteca Nacional de Portugal (National Library of Portugal) and Biblioteca Nacional Digital (Digital Library) www.bn.pt/ High resolution images of musical scores or Música impressa; a musical score manuscript by João Domingos Bontempo, Quinteto para piano e cordas; Porbase is the online catalog.

Bibliothèque Nationale Du Québec www.banq.qc.ca/portal/dt/accueil.jsp?bnq_resolution=mode_1024 Livres et partitions musicales with musique imprimée or sheet music.

Bob Dylan Songs www.bobdylan.com/#/songs Searchable database; lyrics and audio samples of every track on every album; includes a catalog of albums and an alphabetical or chronological list of songs.

Bodleian Library Broadside Ballads www.bodley.ox.ac.uk/ballads/ Over 30,000 ballads; search by title, first line, subject, author, performer, and publisher; single catalog along; scanned image of each ballad sheet; each record of a broadside with a musical score has a MIDI file.

Boosey & Hawkes, Inc. www.boosey.com or www.ny.boosey.com International music publisher; manufacturer of acoustic instruments;

twentieth-century music; commitment to performance and music education.

British Columbia Sheet Music
www.library.ubc.ca/music/bcmusic/default.htm
Collection.

Burt & Company Discount Music Supply
www.Burtnco.com Sheet music distributor.

C. F. Peters www.cfpeters-ny.com Print music publisher; classical editions.

California Sheet Music Project
www.sims.berkeley.edu/~mkduggan/neh.html
Virtual library of 2,000 pieces of sheet music published in California between 1852 and 1900.

Canadian Publishers' Council www.pubcouncil.ca
Guide to Canadian publishers; index.

Cantaria www.chivalry.com/cantaria/ Bardic song archive of lyrics for over 250 songs, most with accompanying sound clips; title and first line index; library of traditional and contemporary folk songs, mostly from Ireland, Scotland, and England; intended to be an educational tool.

Carl Fischer www.carlfischer.com New publications; retail stores; submitting a manuscript.

CD Sheet Music www.cdsheetmusic.com Collections of printable piano works on CD-ROM.

Ceolas: TuneIndex www.ceolas.org/tunes/TuneIndex/
Search James Stewart's master index of hundreds of Celtic tunebooks; over 55,000 entries; links to other notation sites.

Chansons d'Amour
http://base.kb.dk/pls/hsk_web/hsk_vis.forside?p_hs_loebenr=27&p_navtype=rel&p_lang=eng
French-Burgundian repertory of chansons from the late 15th century; contains texts and notes of thirty-three three-voiced songs; from the Royal Library in Copenhagen collection of E-manuscripts.

Chansons Françaises www.geocities.com/foursov/
By Mickaël Foursov, Minneapolis, Minnesota.

Charles Dumont & Son, Inc. www.dumontmusic.com
Distributor of print music.

Cherry Lane Music Group www.cherrylane.com
Publisher of songs; songbooks.

Chicago Jazz Archive www.lib.uchicago.edu/e/su/cja/
University of Chicago.

Chopin Online Catalog www.gwpstudies.net/chopin-catalog/ Descriptive catalog of a collection of early editions of the works of Frédéric Chopin; University of Chicago Library.

Choral Public Domain Library
www.cpdl.org/wiki/index.php/Main_Page Over 8716 scores, many with sound files.

Classical Guitar Music
http://ezzahir.esmartweb.com/ Scores by Dionisio Aguado, Fernando Sor, Matteo Carcassi, Napoleon Cost, Mauro Giuliani, Luigi Legnani,
Heitor Villa-Lobos, Barrios Mangore, Francisco Tarrega, Andres Segovia, and Antonia Cano.

College Music Society www.music.org/cgi-bin/showpage.pl Consortium of college, conservatory, university and independent musicians and scholars interested in all disciplines of music; searchable Directory of Music Faculties in Colleges and Universities, U.S. and Canada.

Copy Us www.copy-us.com Internet music publishing; sheet music by contemporary composers.

Cowpie Song Corral
www.roughstock.com/cowpie/songs/ Country music lyrics listed by artist; search engine.

Crucible of Empire: The Spanish American War
www.pbs.org/crucible/ PBS; popular songs from the Spanish-American War era in the Sheet Music Gallery.

Cyber Hymnal www.cyberhymnal.org/ Over 2,600 Christian hymns and Gospel songs from many denominations; lyrics, sound, background information, photos, links, MIDI and score downloads.

Demiq Music www.demiq.com Sheet music publisher of choral, instrumental, opera, orchestral classics, and unique new works.

Det Kongelige Bibliotek (The Royal Library) Copenhagen www.kb.dk/da/index.html E-scores and sheet music including Chansons d'Amour The Copenhagen Chansonnier with song list.

Digital Archive of Popular American Sheet Music
http://digital.library.ucla.edu/apam/ Collection.

Digital Scores from the Collections of the Eda Kuhn Loeb Music Library
http://hcl.harvard.edu/libraries/loebmusic/collections/digital.html Harvard University Library; thousands of pages of scanned images of rare and unique musical scores drawing on Harvard's extensive collections of first and early editions of Bach family composers, Mozart, and multiple versions of 19th-century opera.

Digital Tradition Folk Song Database
www.mudcat.org/threads.cfm Developed by Dick Greenhaus and friends; hosted at the Mudcat Café; magazine dedicated to blues and folk music; searchable index contains lyrics and music for over 9000 songs; Title List; links.

Digitales Liederbuch
www.strusel007.de/liederbuch/byauthor.html
German site provides song texts some with guitar chords; author and title index.

Directory of Music Publishers
www.mpa.org/agency/pal.html Large list of music publishers; links.

Disc-O-Logue
www.collectionscanada.gc.ca/discologue/index-e.html National Library of Canada; catalog of

French-language popular music recordings available in Canada published between 1962 and 1979, developed from the archive maintained by Louise Lamothe; card catalogue of 90,000 song titles maintained until 1985 has been automated; Search Page allows user to search by title, composer, performer, format, label, issue number, or all fields; Searching Guide provides database insights, searching tips, sample searches and Best Sellers; Top 50 Charts provide lists from 1963 to 1966; Encyclopedia of Music in Canada has info on songs.

Discount Sheet Music www.netstoreusa.com/music/ Detailed listing of 300,000 titles.

Dorothy Starr Sheet Music Collection http://sflib1.sfpl.org:84/ Special collection of the San Francisco Public Library; over 300,000 pieces of music for choir and ensemble, opera scores, children's music, popular, folk, and art songs; database for over 10,000 popular songs.

Duke University Sheet Music Index http://library.duke.edu/digitalcollections/smi/ Completed index will provide access to approximately 20,000 sheet music items in the Rare Book, Manuscript, and Special Collections Library of Duke University; bulk of the collection is from about 1830 to 1930; includes material selected for the American Memory Project; most music was published in the United States; significant number of English, German, and Viennese items; more Viennese publications from the Weinmann Collection are in the Duke Online Catalog; sample of lyrics has been transcribed and is available in the American Song Lyrics database; Sheet Music Sampler.

E. Azalia Hackley Collection www.thehackley.org/ Over 600 pieces of 19th and 20th century sheet music published between 1799 and 1922; first archive to document the contributions of African-Americans to the performing arts; Detroit Public Library.

Edwin A. Fleisher Collection of Orchestral Music http://libwww.freelibrary.org/collections/collectionDetail.cfm?id=14 Located at the Free Library of Philadelphia; world's largest lending library of orchestral performance material; over 21,000 titles and growing; houses virtually the entire standard repertoire; many rare and out-of-print works available for lending around the world.

eGigVision www.egigvision.com Sheet music management software; store sheet music to a database; view scores on LCD, laptop, or tablet PC; import music from notation software programs; create playlists; organize songs; Windows.

Electronic Hymnal www.ehymnal.com/ Hymns online.

EMI www.emimusicpub.com Music publisher.

Encore Music Publishers www.encoremupub.com Publishers of music for brass, woodwind, strings ensembles, and the tuba.

European American Music Distributors www.eamdc.com European American Music Distributors Corp. based in Miami, FL.

Evaluation of Web Access to Historical Sheet Music Collections and Music-Related Iconography http://firstmonday.org/issues/issue10_10/wheeler/index.html Maurice B. Wheeler, Mary Jo Venetis.

Film Score Rundowns www.filmscorerundowns.net/ Cue-by-cue musical analysis by Bill Wrobel of classic film and TV scores.

Finale www.finalemusic.com Professional music notation and composition software; Finale Viewer for digital sheet music.

Five Centuries of Scottish Music http://ahds.ac.uk/performingarts/collections/five-centuries.htm Arts and Humanities Data Service.

Florida Sheet Music Collection www.lib.usf.edu/spccoll/guide/f/fsmusic/ Spans late 19th and entire 20th century; indexed alphabetically by title; University of South Florida Library Special Collections Department; includes the NationsBank African-American Musical Heritage Collection, a collection of nearly 10,000 pieces of sheet music documenting the contributions of African-Americans to the nation's musical heritage at the University of South Florida Tampa Campus Library; provides composer, names of individuals who contributed, title, publisher, and dates; browse by title or names of individuals who contributed.

Folk Music of England, Scotland, Ireland, Wales and America www.contemplator.com/folk.html Lesley Nelson's collection of MIDI tunes, lyrics, information, historical background, and tune related links.

Frances G. Spencer Collection - American Sheet Music http://contentdm.baylor.edu/cdm4/index_01amp.php?CISOROOT=/01amp Baylor University; approximately 30,000 titles.

Free Scores www.free-scores.com Directory.

Free Sheet Music from Johan Tufvesson www.lysator.liu.se/~tuben/scores/ From the 17th and 18th century.

Free Sheet Music Guide www.freesheetmusicguide.com Guide to free online sheet music.

Free Sheet Music on the Internet www.freesheetmusicguide.com/ Links by genre.

Free Sheet Music www.freesheetmusic.net Sheet music search; downloads.

FreeHand Music www.freehandmusic.com Download over 98,000 digital music scores already formatted for FreeHand Systems.

FreeHand Systems www.freehandsystems.com MusicPad Pro Plus digital music notebook; store entire music library; scan music library into a computer and convert; zoom in and zoom out while writing; add or erase rehearsal marks and notations; easy-to-read personal on-screen color notes; extensive library of notation symbols; text annotation via a virtual keyboard; half-page turn option for look-ahead viewing in portrait mode; two-page display in landscape mode; remote easy page turning; audio player for MIDI; Solero viewer; search.

G. Henle USA, Inc. www.henle.de/ Urtext Editions; Musicological Editions; classical music.

G. Schirmer, Inc. www.schirmer.com Print publisher of classical music; famous yellow/gold covers; member of the Music Sales Group; details about composers; catalog listings; premiers; links.

German Music Database www.cory.de/music/_gmdyes.html Lyrics.

GIA Publications www.giamusic.com Major publisher of sacred choral music, hymnals, sacred music recordings, and music education materials.

Gilbert and Sullivan Archive http://diamond.boisestate.edu/gas/ Over 120 librettos in the Opera Index; MIDI and RealAudio files; searchable database of librettos, festival schedules, plot summaries, images, song scores, and newsletter articles; links to other sites; created and maintained by Jim Farron and Alex Feldman.

Goldband Recording Corporation www.lib.unc.edu/mss/sfc1/goldband/ Photographs, sound recordings and biographical essays in the Southern Folklife Collection, Manuscripts Department at the Univ. of North Carolina at Chapel Hill.

Green Label Music www.greenlabelmusic.com Buy music in the Green Label format.

Hal Leonard www.halleonard.com Large print music publisher and distributor; all instruments; DVDs; digital downloads; piano method; songbooks.

Heritage Music Press www.lorenz.com MIDI accompaniment disks; piano methods.

Historic American Sheet Music http://library.duke.edu/digitalcollections/hasm/ Digital images of over 16,000 pages of sheet music from 3042 pieces published in the United States between 1850 and 1920; project of the Digital Scriptorium, Rare Book, Manuscript, and Special Collections Library, Duke University.

Historic American Sheet Music mem-ory.loc.gov/ammem/award97/ncdhtml/hasmhome.html Includes 3,042 pieces of sheet music published in America between 1850 and 1920; selected from the collections at Duke University.

Historic American Sheet Music scriptorium.lib.duke.edu/sheetmusic/ Rare book, manuscript, special collections; Duke University.

Hoagy Carmichael Collection www.dlib.indiana.edu/collections/hoagy/index.html Project of the Indiana University Digital Library Program to catalog, digitize, and preserve every item in Indiana University's extensive collection of materials pertaining to the life and career of the master songwriter Hoagy Carmichael (1899-1981); sheet music, over 500 lyric sheets, a selection of sound files, photographs, correspondence, and supplemental research material.

Home Concert Xtreme www.timewarptech.com Follow sheet music on screen; synchronized accompaniment.

HymnSite www.hymnsite.com/ MIDI hymn and psalm tunes from the 1989 edition of the United Methodist Hymnal and the Standard Psalm Tune Book compiled by Henry E. Dibdin in 1851.

Independent Book Publishers Association (formerly PMA) www.pma-online.org Largest nonprofit trade association representing independent publishers of books, audio, video, and CDs; monthly newsletter; resource directory; promotional campaigns.

International Lyrics Server www.songtext.net/index.htm Lyrics to more than 62,000 songs; database of over 130,000 songs.

J. W. Pepper Music Network www.jwpepper.com Sheet music and music books; music software products; music teaching tools; music distributor specializing in music performance materials for schools, churches, community musical organizations, and home music enjoyment.

Jewish Song Database www.zemerl.com/ Jewish song lyrics.

Kalmus www.kalmus.com Source for all titles currently or formerly published by Kalmus; full orchestral and operatic catalog; scores, chamber and solo titles of the Kalmus Classic Edition.

Keffer Collection of Sheet Music, ca. 1790-1895 www.library.upenn.edu/collections/rbm/keffer/ From the University of Pennsylvania Library Center for Electronic Text and Image.

Kjos, Inc. www.kjos.com Piano instruction materials; band literature.

Koala Music Products www.learntoplaymusic.com Progressive; 10 Easy Lessons; Australian; teaching materials for piano, guitar, and other instruments; CDs; DVDs.

Ladyslipper Music by Women www.ladyslipper.org Publishes a comprehensive catalog of music by women featuring over 1,500 titles; indie label.

Leader in Lieder http://ingeb.org/ German site; lyrics for 18,000 folksongs and hymns; some MIDI files.

Lester S. Levy Collection of Sheet Music http://levysheetmusic.mse.jhu.edu/ Part of Special Collections at the Milton S. Eisenhower Library of The Johns Hopkins University; comprised of popular American music spanning the period 1780 to 1960; over 26,000 pieces of music in the Levy Collection are indexed on this site; images of the cover and music are available for pieces of music over seventy-five years old.

Liben Music Publishers www.liben.com Contemporary orchestral and chamber music; Double Bass music and recordings.

Library of Congress Catalogs http://catalog.loc.gov/ Search online.

Lib-Web-Cats www.librarytechnology.org/libwebcats/ Library Web Pages, Online Catalogs, and System Profiles; links to online catalogs in over 4,700 libraries worldwide; online library catalogs cab provide useful information on sheet music; use Library of Congress subject headings such as Popular Music United States Texts; Songs, English United States Texts; Musicals Excerpts Librettos; Popular Instrumental Music; Folk Songs; Dance Music; Vocal Music; Piano Music; Bugle Music; Marches (Piano); Cantatas, Secular Scores; Masses Vocal Scores, etc.; other access points for library catalogs include Library Catalogs Around the World, Libweb: Library Servers via WWW, National Library Catalogues Worldwide, National Libraries of Europe, and LibDex: the Library Index.

Lied and Song Texts Page www.recmusic.org/lieder/ Extensive archive of texts to Kunstlieder and art songs of many different languages; designed and maintained by Emily Ezus; search by Composer, Poet, Language, First Line, and Title.

Listen.com http://blog.listen.com/ Find music from more than 120,000 artists

Loeb Music Library Harvard University http://hcl.harvard.edu/libraries/#loebmusic The Internet Resources for Music Scholars has a good collection of links to sheet music.

Lutheran Hymnal www.lutheran-hymnal.com/ MP3, lyrics, and sheet music.

Lyrics Library http://tinpan.fortunecity.com/blondie/313/ Collection of links to Lyrics web sites.

Lyrics Search Engine http://lyrics.astraweb.com/ Find lyrics.

Lyrics World www.lyricsworld.com/ Search engine.

LyricSearch.net http://lyricsearch.net/ Search engine.

Mel Bay Publications, Inc. www.melbay.com Print music for all instruments; CDs; DVDs; method books, especially for guitar and folk instruments.

Mississippi State University Charles H. Templeton, Sr. Sheet Music Collection http://library.msstate.edu/content/templates/?a=1 496&z=359 Over 5,000 pieces of music.

MIT Lewis Music Library Sheet Music Collection http://libraries.mit.edu/music/sheetmusic/index.h tml The collection, entitled Inventions of Note, contains approximately seventy-five pieces of sheet music consisting of popular songs and piano compositions that portray technologies as revealed through song texts and/or cover art.

MIT Libraries libraries.mit.edu/music/sheetmusic/ Sheet music collection.

Mix Books www.mixbooks.com Large selection of music books on current topics.

Music Books Plus www.musicbooksplus.com Online music bookstore.

Music for the Nation: American Sheet Music memory.loc.gov/ammem/smhtml/smhome.html American sheet music by author, subject, or title.

Music for the Nation: American Sheet Music, 1870-1885 http://memory.loc.gov/ammem/smhtml/smhome. html Library of Congress site consists of tens of thousands of pieces of sheet music registered for copyright during the post-Civil War era; included are popular songs, piano music, sacred music, secular choral music, solo instrumental music, method books and instructional materials, and music for band and orchestra; search by keyword or browse index of authors, subjects, and titles.

Music in the Public Domain www.pdinfo.com/ Alphabetical list of more than 3,000 songs now in the public domain in the United States.

Music Library Association www.musiclibraryassoc.org/ A Guide to Copyright for Music Librarians, Sheet Music Cataloging Guidelines, Sheet Music Collections, and Useful Resources Online; Sheet Music Information; provides links to Libraries and archives with significant holdings of Sheet Music; other music cataloging sites include Princeton's Music Cataloging and Music Cataloging at Yale.

Music Notes www.musicnotes.com Digital sheet music; download and print; music books; classical, piano, guitar, and instrumental; enhanced CDs and DVDs with sheet music.

Music Publishers' Association www.mpa.org Resources; information; links; directories.

Music Room www.musicroom.com Sheet music available online.

Music Sales Corporation UK www.musicsales.co.uk Popular titles for guitar, piano, keyboard, and organ; online Internet Music Shop.

Music Sales Corporation www.musicsales.com AMSCO; Omnibus Press; Jam Trax; Yorktown Music Press; Oak Publications; Passantino Manuscript Papers; Ashley Music.

Music Scores Library www.score-on-line.com/freescores.php Online resource.

Music Students www.musicstudents.com Sheet music online.

Musica International Database www.musicanet.org/ Searchable database of choral repertoire.

Musica Viva www.musicaviva.com Free downloads.

Musicals.Net http://musicals.net/ Searchable site; songlists, lyrics, links, and synopsis for over eighty popular musicals.

MusicRain http://musicrain.us/ Online interactive sheet music viewer.

MusicReader www.musicreader.com Software that makes reading music easy and convenient; digital music stand software.

Music-Scores.com www.music-scores.com Free classical sheet music; book and CD recommendations; free music scores and MIDI files; free classical sheet music downloads.

Mutopia Project www.mutopiaproject.org/ Public domain music; download for free as Postscript and PDF files at both A4 and Letter paper sizes; Lilypond's own LY file format; audio previews available as MIDI files; composers include T. Arbeau, J.S. Bach, A. Banchieri, L. van Beethoven, M. Carcassi, F. Carulli, M. Clementi, J. Dowland, G. Giordiano, S. Joplin, L. Milan, W. A. Mozart, N. Paganini, C. Saint-Saens, E. Satie, and F. Schubert.

My Sheet Music www.mysheetmusic.com Free and "pay and play" music.

National Music Publishers' Association (NMPA) www.nmpa.org Information about music publishing, licensing requirements, copyright laws, editorial standards; correct use of printed music.

Nederlands Muziek Instituut www.nederlandsmuziekinstituut.nl/ Provides access to records for sheet music and books through Publiekscatalogus KB or Catalog of the Nederlands Muziekinstituut.

New York Public Library www.nypl.org/ The American Music Center's historic Collection of more than 60,000 scores and recordings of works by American composers has been transferred to the New York Public Library for the Performing Arts; The New York Public Music Division collection is searchable via CATNYP: Research Libraries Online Catalog; there is also a Library for the Performing Arts at Lincoln Center.

New York Sheet Music Society www.nysms.org/ Established in 1980; began with a small, dedicated group of collectors.

Nissimo www.nissimo.com Free classical sheet music; view; print.

Old and Gold www.oldandgold.com/plus.html Sheet music; songbooks; guitar tabs; records; over a quarter million titles; order online.

OperaGlass http://opera.stanford.edu/main.html Opera information; Libretti and Opera Librettists.

Organ Sheet Music Collection www.carnegielibrary.org/research/music/resourceguides/organmusic.html Collection of over 1300 individual pieces of sheet music owned by the Carnegie Library of Pittsburgh.

Oxford University Press www.oup-usa.org Catalog of thousands of titles including performance fields.

Peachpit Press www.peachpit.com Publisher of books on computer technology.

Peermusic www.peermusic.com Music publisher.

Peter, Paul & Mary www.peterpaulandmary.com/ Official site maintained by Noel Paul Stookey; lyrics to all recorded songs, organized by album.

Piano Press www.pianopress.com Sheet music for piano students and music teachers; world music repertoire guide; seasonal collections; songbooks and CDs; digital downloads; PPCPCP program.

Piano Street www.pianostreet.com Piano sheet music to download.

Pianopedia www.pianopedia.com/ Eric Brisson's database; 892 composers; 50 countries, 5433 works, 15558 movements or excerpts.

Popular Songs Library www.danmansmusic.com/songs2.htm From Music Lessons Television Network.

Print Music Online www.printmusiconline.com Print music; sheet music; band methods; DVDs.

Printed Music Worldwide www.printed-music.com Subscription directory for producers of printed classical music.

Professional Music Institute, LLC www.promusicbooks.com/ Rare and hard-to-find printed music; easy and intermediate piano; tab guitar; B-flat instruments; Music of the Stars; vocal songbooks.

Project Runeberg http://runeberg.org/ Swedish digital text project offers sheet music. Public-Domain Opera Libretti and Other Vocal Texts.

Publishers Weekly www.publishersweekly.com Online version of the international news magazine for book publishing and bookselling news.

Retail Print Music Dealers Association www.printmusic.org Membership; convention; newsletter; copyright information; directory.

Richard Harris www.rfkharris.com Personalized sheet music to download.

Roni Music www.ronimusic.com *Amazing Slow Downer;* intended for musicians wanting to slow down music without changing the pitch.

Sam DeVincent Collection of American Sheet Music www.indiana.edu/~liblilly/collections-sheetmusic.shtml Lilly Library collection at the University of Indiana; approximately 24,000 pieces of sheet music, songbooks, and folios.

Sam DeVincent Collection of Illustrated American Sheet Music http://americanhistory.si.edu/archives/d5300.htm American Music Collections at the Smithsonian National Museum of American History.

Santorella Publications www.santopub.com Print publisher; teachers aid products; piano; accordion; guitar; bass guitar; acoustic strings; Roy Clark; wind instruments; bagpipe; recorder; harmonica; orchestral strings; drums; Christmas.

Scarecrow Press, Inc. www.scarecrowpress.com Since 1950; large catalog of scholarly music titles; music reference books; academic trade.

Schott Music www.schott-music.com Publisher of modern classical pieces; composer pages; concert diary; news; sound clips.

Schubertline www.schubertline.co.uk/home.htm Online score service for singers.

Score Online www.score-on-line.com Sheet music online.

Seventh String Software www.seventhstring.demon.co.uk *Transcribe* software to help transcribe recorded music; ability to slow down the music without changing its pitch; shareware for Windows or Macintosh.

Shawnee Press www.shawneepress.com Music print publisher.

Sheet Music Service www.sheetmusicservice.com Sheet music retailer.

Sheet Music about Lincoln, Emancipation, and the Civil War from the Stern Collection http://lcweb2.loc.gov/ammem/scsmhtml/scsmhome.html Library of Congress; more than two hundred sheet-music compositions representing Lincoln and the war; reflected in popular music.

Sheet Music Archive www.sheetmusicarchive.net Download public domain classical sheet music.

Sheet Music Catalog www.sheetmusiccatalog.com Online retailer; browse by artist.

Sheet Music Center for Collector's of Vintage Popular Sheet Music www.sheetmusiccenter.com Buy, sell, and trade old sheet music.

Sheet Music Collections www.lib.duke.edu/music/sheetmusic/ Collections of sheet music with public access either through a Web page or online catalog.

Sheet Music Consortium http://digital.library.ucla.edu/sheetmusic/ UC Los Angeles, Indiana University, Johns Hopkins University, and Duke University.

Sheet Music Digital www.sheetmusicdigital.com/ Download sheet music; public domain library; copyrighted digital sheet music.

Sheet Music Direct www.sheetmusicdirect.com Browse sheet music titles; download and print out for a fee; thousands of titles in many notation styles and formats; legally licensed.

Sheet Music from Canada's Past www.collectionscanada.gc.ca/4/1/index-e.html Sheet music published before Confederation (1867) and during the era of the First World War (1914-1920); selected from the historical collection of the National Library of Canada.

Sheet Music Logistics www.sheetmusiclogistics.com Web management programs for music retailers.

Sheet Music Online www.sheetmusic1.com Free downloads of public domain piano music; emphasis on music education resources.

Sheet Music Online www.sheetmusiconline.net Free sheet music; sheet music search; downloads.

Sheet Music Plus www.sheetmusicplus.com Sheet music super store.

SheetMusicScore.com www.sheetmusicscore.com Digital sheet music downloads.

Sibelius www.sibelius.com Professional music notation and composition software; educational software; Scorch plug-in for digital sheet music.

SongDex.net www.songdex.net/index.cfm Directory of standard popular music in America; sheet music covers; links.

Southern Music Company www.southernmusic.com Established in 1937; distributor of sheet music, music books, and more for over 500 publishers; has published over 5,000 educational works.

Stadtbücherei Stuttgart: Musikbücherei www.stuttgart.de/stadtbuecherei/bvs/ausgabe.php?sid=36 Collection of music links in German.

Stanton's Sheet Music Online www.stantons.com Online retailer.

Statens Musikbibliotek (Music Library of Sweden) www.muslib.se/ The Boije Collection consists of guitar music from the early 19th century.

Templeton Music Collection http://library.msstate.edu/content/templates/?a=1496&z=359 Mississippi State University Libraries; sheet music collection.

The Dancing Master, 1651-1728: An Illustrated Compendium by Robert M. Keller www.izaak.unh.edu/nhltmd/indexes/dancingmaster/ Published by John Playford in London in 1651; contained the figures and tunes for 105 English country dances; other editions followed;

1,053 unique dances and their music; database searchable by edition or title.

The FJH Music Company, Inc. www.fjhmusic.com Ft. Lauderdale-based educational print music publisher; publisher of pedagogical materials for piano and other instruments; Nancy and Randall Faber.

The Frederick Harris Music Company, Ltd. www.frederickharrismusic.com Canadian-based print publisher of pedagogical materials for piano, guitar, violin, flute, voice, music theory, music history, and composition.

The Historic American Sheet Music Project scriptorium.lib.duke.edu/sheetmusic Access to digital images of 3,042 pieces of sheet music published in America between 1850 and 1920.

The Music on the Home Front: Canadian Sheet Music of the First World War www.collectionscanada.gc.ca/gramophone/index -e.html Searchable database that offers covers and bibliographical information for nearly 400 pieces of sheet music published in Canada between 1914 and 1920.

Theodore Presser Company www.presser.com Music publisher serving musicians, music educators, and music dealers since 1783; classical editions.

Trillenium Music Company & Tunbridge Music www.trillmusic.com On-line catalog of sheet music; located in Vermont's Green Mountains.

UNC—Chapel Hill Music Library www.lib.unc.edu/music/eam.html Nineteenth-century American sheet music.

Union Songs http://unionsong.com/ More than 610 songs and poems; over 250 authors; rebel songs, slave songs, songs of freedom, work songs, songs of dissent, songs of struggle, protest songs, liberation songs, labor songs, workers songs, industrial folk songs, environmental songs, songs of equality, peace songs.

University of Colorado at Boulder Music Library Digital Sheet Music Collection http://ucblibraries.colorado.edu/music/smp/index .html Approximately 150,000 items including examples from the late 18th through the 20th centuries; provides access to digital versions of some of the categories of sheet music within the physical collections; sheet music digitized originally published between 1890 and 1922.

University of Illinois, Urbana-Champaign, Online U.S. Sheet Music Database http://www.library.uiuc.edu/mux/about/collectio ns/specialcollections/uiucsheetmusic.html Collection contains about 100,000 titles of popular music as well as some classical from the early 19th century through the 1980s.

University of North Carolina-Chapel Hill Music Library 19th-Century American Sheet Music Digitization Project www.lib.unc.edu/music/eam/index.html Fifty-seven volumes, approximately 2250 titles, of sheet music have been indexed; contents of thirty-two of these volumes, approximately 1200 pieces, have been fully scanned and are available on this site; Alphabetical Index by Composer and a list of Volumes Indexed.

University of North Texas Libraries Digital Collections: Music www.digital.library.unt.edu/browse/department/ music/ Virtual Music Rare Book Room; Willis Conover Collection.

University of North Texas www.library.unt.edu/music/special-collections/lully/ Includes almost thirty rare 17th and 18th-century scores of operas and ballets by the 17th-century French composer Jean-Baptiste Lully and his sons; access to titles in the collection.

University of Tennessee, Knoxville, Song Index www.lib.utk.edu/music/songdb/ Publicly available database providing access to citations for about 50,000 songs in more than 1,400 published song anthologies owned by the George F. DeVine Music Library at the University of Tennessee, Knoxville.

Useful Addresses: Music Publishers www.cmc.ie/addresses/publishers.html Listing of music publisher addresses.

Variations www.dlib.indiana.edu/variations/ Online Musical Scores for Opera Literature, Song Literature and Symphonic Literature; project of the Indiana University Digital Library Program.

Victorian Popular Music www.collectbritain.co.uk/collections/vicmusic/ British Library collection consists of illustrated sheet music for 188 songs and piano pieces.

Vintage Sheet Music Storefront members.aol.com/vinsheets Vintage sheet music.

Virtual Sheet Music www.virtualsheetmusic.com Classical sheet music downloads.

Vivaldi Studio www.vivaldistudio.com Music Notation Software; Music Scanning Software; Digital Interactive Sheet Music.

Warner Chappell www.warnerchappell.com International publisher.

When U.S. Works Pass into the Public Domain www.unc.edu/~unclng/public-d.htm Lolly Gassaway of the University of North Carolina, Chapel Hill; only music copyrighted before 1923 can be guaranteed to be copyright free.

Women Song Composers: A Listing of Songs Published in the United States and England, ca. 1890-1930
http://musdra.ucdavis.edu/people/reynolds/Women_Songs_Home.html Includes title, composer, publisher, date and city of publication, and the existence of an accompaniment other than piano; created by Christopher Reynolds, Department of Music, University of California, Davis.

Writer's Digest Books www.writersdigest.com Books on songwriting; general writing books.

Footnotes

1. Rudi Blesh, "Scott Joplin: Black American Classicist," in *Scott Joplin Collected Piano Works* (Miami, FL: Warner Bros./CPP/Belwin, 1971), 15.

2. Gunther Schuller, "The Future of Form in Jazz" in *Saturday Review*, January 12, 1957, 62.

3. Guy Waterman, "Ragtime," in *Jazz*, ed. by Nat Hentoff and Albert McCarthy (New York: Rinehart, 1959), 47-48.

4. William Russell, "Notes on Boogie Woogie," in *Frontiers of Jazz*, ed. by Ralph de Toledano (New York: Ungar, 1962), 64.

Print Music Royalties

Before the invention of the phonograph, music publishers earned the majority of their income from the sale of printed music. Over one hundred songs sold over one million copies of *sheet music* from 1900 to 1910. Today, music publishers exploit songs in many different ways, including recordings, music videos, music for movies and television, music for the Internet and video games, music for the theater, and commercials for radio and television.

The demand for sheet music fell substantially with the coming of these new media. Today, *music print publishers* deal primarily in printed music. Many also offer instructional media in the form of audio CDs, cassettes, videos, DVDs, and CD-ROMs. Only a few major music print publishers are in operation, often acting as distributors for the smaller ones. A list of music print publisher Web sites can be found in chapter 4 under "Music, Print Music, and Music Book Publishers."

The print department of a publishing company will be in-house only if the publishing company is large. Very few publishers today have their own print departments. Instead, the copyright-owning publishing companies farm out their print work to print publishers who specialize in printing sheet music, folios, band and choral arrangements, and any other printed editions of songs. Whether the print department is in-house or not, it is the job of the copyright-owning publishing company to authorize the printing of music. It is the job of the print department or print publisher to account to the royalty department the amount of printed music that has been sold.

Print royalties are earned from the sale of printed editions of songs. This was the original source of income for music publishers and songwriters in the early days of music publishing. Although print royalties are not usually as great as mechanical, synchronization, and performance royalties, printed editions of songs are still an important part of music publishing.

Print publishers must acquire the rights to create printed editions of songs. They attempt to make exclusive deals with copyright-owning publishers. Exclusive deals give the print publisher the right to create printed editions of all the songs in the publisher's catalog for a given length of time. For song publishers, the major points of negotiation for agreements with print music companies include the advance, the royalties, and the term.

One print publisher may own the print rights of a large number of copyright-owning publishers at one time. The rights the print publisher acquires can include the rights to print sheet music, folios, and arrangements for bands, orchestras, and choirs. The print publisher usually pays an advance to the copyright-owning publisher in exchange for these rights. A percentage of royalties the print publisher earns from sales of the printed editions is then paid to the publisher.

It is the publisher's responsibility to see that, once a song has become successful, it is made available in printed editions and is properly distributed. This includes use of the song in sheet music, songbooks, folios, marching band or choral arrangements. Of the different types of printed editions available, sheet music is the most frequently published.

Songwriters earn a percentage of the retail-selling price of each copy of sheet music sold, depending on the print royalty agreement in the songwriter contract. Payment for use of a song in songbooks and folios is either a one-time fixed sum or a percentage of the retail-selling price of editions sold containing the song. The royalties from print music are usually split between the music publisher and the songwriter fifty-fifty, but some deals may vary. It is possible for a songwriter to discuss with the print publisher directly appropriate uses for a song in various print formats, deriving more income from the song in its printed versions.

Copyright Laws

Copyright law moral rights are of European origin, historically Roman, and reflect an early appreciation of the fact that the work of an artist is inseparable from the artist's soul. The work is an extension and representation of the person who created it, reflecting their inner spirit and vision, and projecting the artist's personality. The *Statute of Anne* was a 1709 British law recognized as the first true copyright law anywhere in the world. Copyright is a form of protection provided by the laws of the United States to the authors of "original works of authorship," including literary, dramatic, musical, artistic, and certain other intellectual works. This protection is available for both published and unpublished works.

A copyright gives the owner the exclusive right to reproduce, distribute, perform, display, or license his or her work. The copyright owner also has the exclusive right to produce or license derivatives of his or her work. A work must be original and in a concrete "medium of expression" to be covered by copyright law. Under the current law, works are covered whether or not there is a copyright notice and whether or not the work is registered.

United States Copyright Law

The U.S. Copyright Act is federal legislation enacted by Congress to protect the writings of authors under its constitutional grant of authority. The federal agency in charge of administering the act is the Copyright Office of the Library of Congress. Evolving technology has led to many changes in the meaning and interpretation of the word "writings." The copyright act now includes architectural design, software, the graphic arts, motion pictures, sound recordings, and Internet technology. Copyrighted works on the Internet include music, news stories, software, novels, screenplays, graphics, pictures, and e-mail. Copyright law protects the majority of the items on the Internet.

The first United States copyright act was the Copyright Act of 1790, granting copyright protection for books, maps, and charts. The first United States copyright act to grant copyright protection for musical works was the Copyright Act of 1831. The Copyright Act of 1909 called for a general revision of copyright law in the United States. It was the first law to recognize the *mechanical right*, originally licensed by publishers for works used in *piano rolls*, the first widely accepted means of recording songs. The 1909 law also helped to strengthen the *performance right*.

To prevent any one manufacturer of piano rolls from monopolizing the industry with the only recording of a popular song, Congress enacted the Compulsory Mechanical License in the Copyright Act of 1909. This law stated that once a copyright owner had recorded a song for public distribution, or had given permission to someone else to record the song, anyone could record that song as long as they followed certain procedures, including paying a royalty of two cents per recording to the copyright owner. The copyright owner, therefore, controlled the first recording of a work, but anyone willing to pay the two-cent mechanical royalty to the copyright owner could record the song.

As the phonograph came to replace piano rolls in the first half of the twentieth century, and recordings started to sell in the millions, music publishers gladly accepted the two cent per recording mechanical royalty, half of which went to the composer. Music publishers and songwriters made millions of dollars by the 1950s and 1960s at the fixed mechanical royalty rate of two cents per recording. The mechanical royalty rate remained the same until the new Copyright Act of 1976.

On October 19, 1976, President Gerald R. Ford signed into law a new and long overdue revision of United States copyright legislation. Copyright Revision Bill S.22 became Public Law 94-553 and was the first completely new copyright law since 1909. Congress took twenty-one years to approve the modern copyright law, which began revision in 1955. Provisions of the new statute became effective January 1, 1978, superseding the Copyright Act of 1909, which remained in force until the new enactment took effect.

Most of the elements of the Compulsory Mechanical License of the 1909 act were retained in the Act of 1976, with "mechanicals" referring to all recorded media, including vinyl records, tapes, CDs, music boxes, and MIDI disks played only in audio format. The mechanical royalty rate was raised from two cents to two and three-quarter cents or one-half cent per minute of playing time, whichever was greater. The Copyright Royalty Tribunal, a panel established to review royalty rates on compulsory licenses, would periodically review the rate.

Although this panel no longer exists, increases in compulsory royalties have been revised under the jurisdiction of the copyright office and continue to be subject to revision. This involves negotiation between copyright owners and users and requires approval of the copyright office. The mechanical royalty rate from 2004 through 2005 is 8.5 cents per recording and is the maximum rate allowed by statute.

Occasionally lower mechanical rates are negotiated between copyright owners and record companies, especially in the commercial music industry. MIDI disks with computer codes other than audio, for example, those that can print scores, and CD-ROMs that contain visual images, are not covered by the Compulsory Mechanical License, and a separate fee must be negotiated between the copyright owner and the producer of the MIDI disk or CD-ROM.

The 1976 law established a single national system of statutory protection for all copyrightable works, whether published or unpublished. Common law, which gave a work protection under the common laws of the various states before it was published, was superseded by the single national system effective January 1, 1978.

Notice of Copyright

The new law does call for published copies of music to contain the notice of copyright; however, omission or errors in the notice of copyright do not immediately result in the copyright becoming public domain. The copyright notice on any tangible work, be it printed or recorded, should include (1) the symbol, either the letter "C" in a circle "©," the word "Copyright," or the abbreviation "Copy," (2) the first year of publication of the work, and (3) the name of the copyright owner of the work, or its abbreviation; in the case of compilations or derivative works using previously published material, the date of first publication may be used and/or the new date; examples: Copyright 2001 Elizabeth C. Axford; © 2001, 1992 Piano Press. A copyright notice should appear on all copies of a piece of music, even if it has not been registered with the U.S. Copyright Office.

Duration of Copyright

By the Copyright Act of 1976 and the subsequent Copyright Term Extension Act passed in 1998, the duration of copyright provides for the following terms: (1) works published before 1923 are in the public domain; (2) works published between 1923 and 1963 have an initial term of twenty-eight years and must be renewed for an additional sixty-seven-year term for a total of ninety-five years; (3) works published between 1964 and 1977 have an initial twenty-eight-year term plus an automatic sixty-seven-year second term for a total of ninety-five years; (4) works published after 1977 have a term of the life of the author plus seventy years, or in the case of works with multiple authors, seventy years after the death of the last surviving author.

Fair Use

There are limited exceptions to the exclusive rights of copyright owners for certain types of "Fair Use." These include such use by reproduction in copies or phonorecords or by any other means for purposes such as criticism, comment, news reporting, teaching, scholarship, or research and are not considered an infringement of copyright.

There are four factors, which are used in determining a Fair Use. These include (1) the purpose and character of the use, including whether such use is of a commercial nature or is for nonprofit educational purposes; (2) the nature of the copyrighted work; (3) the amount and substantiality of the portion used in relation to the copyrighted work as a whole; and (4) the effect of the use upon the potential market for or value of the copyrighted work. The fact that a work is unpublished does not influence a finding of Fair Use if it is made by considering all the above factors.

This first factor takes into account the following three subfactors: (1) commercial nature or nonprofit educational purposes; (2) preamble purposes, including criticism, comment, news reporting, teaching, scholarship, or research; and (3) degree of transformation.

The second factor acknowledges the fact that some works are more deserving of copyright protection than others and attempts to determine where the work is in the spectrum of worthiness of copyright protection.

The third factor looks at the amount and substantiality of the copying in relation to the copyrighted work as a whole. The critical determination is whether the quality and value of the materials used are reasonable in relation to the purpose of copying and is not a pure ratio test. The quantity, as well as the quality and importance, of the copied material must be considered.

The fourth factor considers the extent of harm to the market or potential market of the original work caused by the infringement, taking into account harm to the original, as well as harm to derivative works.

Photocopying of Print Music

Regarding the photocopying of print music, the Fair Use guidelines include (1) emergency copying to replace purchased copies which for any reason are not available for an imminent performance, provided purchased replacement copies shall be substituted in due course and (2) for academic purposes other than performance, single or multiple copies of excerpts of works may be made, provided that the excerpts do not comprise a part of the whole which would constitute a performable unit such as a section, movement, or aria, but in no case more than 10 percent of the whole work; the number of copies shall not exceed one copy per pupil.

Under the Fair Use guidelines, the following are expressly prohibited: (1) copying to create or replace or substitute for anthologies, compilations, or collective works; (2) copying of or from works intended to be "consumable" in the course of study or teaching such as workbooks, exercises, standardized tests and answer sheets, and like material; (3) copying for the purposes of performance except for emergency copying to replace purchased copies as outlined in (1) of the Fair Uses; (4) copying for the purpose of substituting for the purchase of music, except as in Fair Uses (1) and (2); and (5) copying without inclusion of the copyright notice which appears on the printed copy.

It is important to note that copyright protection is not related to the print status of a piece of music. Permission must be granted for copying a piece of out-of-print music. Photocopying a piece of out-of-print music is as much an infringement of copyright as copying one that is in print. Check the copyright notice for the date and subsequent duration of copyright on any piece of music that is out of print.

Other uses requiring permission from the publisher include photocopying works from collections, extra parts for bands, or choral or speaking parts for musicals. Most contests prohibit the use of photocopies and require that an original copy of the music be provided to the judges.

Public Domain

Public domain is the repository of all works that for any reason are not protected by copyright and are free for all to use without permission. Works in the public domain include items that by their very nature are not eligible for copyright protection such as ideas, facts, titles, names, short phrases, and blank forms.

The public domain contains all works which previously had copyright protection but which subsequently lost that protection. An example includes all works published before January 1, 1978, that did not contain a valid copyright notice. Owners of works published between 1978 and March 1, 1989, that did not contain a valid copyright notice were given a five-year grace period in which to correct the problem before their work was placed into the public domain.

The public domain contains all works for which the statutory copyright period has expired. Any work

published before 1964 in which the copyright owner failed to renew the copyright is considered public domain. Copyrightable works may enter the public domain if the copyright owner grants the work to the public domain.

Some aspects of a piece of music may be protected by copyright, while other parts are in the public domain. For example, although a piece of music and its lyrics may be in the public domain, a specific recording of the music may be protected by copyright. Anyone wishing to use that recording would be required to get a master recording license from the holder of the recording rights.

Furthermore, some parts of a piece of music, for example, the melody, may be in the public domain, while other parts, say the lyrics, may be protected by copyright. The rights to a specific recording may be held by someone different from the holder of the rights to the music, lyrics, or arrangements.

Performing Rights Organizations

ASCAP, BMI, and SESAC are licensing organizations that collect performance royalties (radio airplay, TV broadcasts, etc.) through licensing fees, which are then distributed to the organizations' members, including artists, songwriters, lyricists, and composers. More detailed information on these organizations can be found at their respective Web sites.

ASCAP, BMI, and SESAC are excellent resources for identifying the copyright holder for any given piece of music, or of a particular recording of a piece of music. These organizations have Web sites with searchable databases, making it possible to find the rights holders to any piece of music in question.

Compulsory Mechanical License

Artists may record a *cover version* of any song through a compulsory mechanical license. A compulsory mechanical license is authorized by copyright law and issued by the Copyright Office. This license can be secured without the permission of the copyright owner and allows the licensee certain use rights of copyrighted material. All compulsory licenses, however, have many conditions, restrictions, fee payment requirements, and liabilities inherent to their use that are defined by copyright law. Information on procedures that must be followed to obtain such a license may be received from the Copyright Office or its Web site.

Who Can Claim a Copyright

(1) The author of the work; (2) Anyone to whom the author has assigned his or her rights of ownership to the copyright; (3) In the cases of a work made for hire, the employer rather than the employee, or creator, is regarded as the author and can claim copyright.

Only those authorized people are permitted to sign the copyright application form.

Copyright Registration and Forms

Copyright registration is a legal formality intended to make a public record of the basic facts of any given copyright. Although registration is not required for protection, the copyright law provides several advantages to encourage copyright owners to register their work.

Registration establishes a public record of the copyright claim. Before an infringement suit may be filed in court, registration is necessary. If made before or within five years of publication, registration will establish evidence in court of the validity of the copyright and of the facts stated in the certificate. If registration is made within three months after publication of the work or prior to an infringement of the work, statutory damages and attorney's fees will be available to the copyright owner in court actions.

Otherwise, only an award of actual damages and profits is available to the copyright owner. Copyright registration allows the owners of the copyright to record the registration with the U.S. Customs Service for protection against the importation of infringing copies.

The Copyright Office supplies various application forms for copyright registration. *Form PA* is for works in the performing arts, including published and unpublished musical works, any accompanying music, motion pictures, and other visual works. This form does not cover sound recordings. *Form SR* is for sound recordings and includes published songs. *Form TX* is for nondramatic literary works, including all types of published and unpublished works. The form covers lyric books and also poems that may be used as lyrics. *Form RE* is for renewal registrations. *Form CA* is for correction of an error in a copyright registration or to amplify the information given in a registration. Most applications for copyright will be made on Form PA, and are then issued a PA copyright number. These forms may be obtained for free by writing: Copyright Office, Library of Congress, Washington, D.C. 20559-6000 or call (202) 707-3000, or visit the Web site.

To register a work for copyright, send the following in the same package to the Register of Copyrights, Copyright Office, Library of Congress, Washington, D.C. 20559-6000: (1) a properly completed application form; (2) a nonrefundable filing fee for each application; (3) a complete recording (cassette, CD, etc.) of the work or a lead sheet or complete score; (4) a complete lyric sheet, if applicable.

Prior to 1978, songwriters had to submit lead sheets of their work for copyright registration. Because many songwriters could not notate music, this requirement was changed in the Copyright Act of 1976 to allow recordings such as demo tapes to be used instead. It is important to keep a copy of any submission, as the one submitted to the Copyright Office will not be returned.

For the copyright registration of musical works, the new law allows for one complete copy or recording of an unpublished work to be submitted. For a published work, two complete copies or recordings of the best edition of the work must be submitted.

More than one song per application may be registered as a "collection" under a single title. This is an economical means to protect two or more songs under the same copyright registration number. If there is interest in a particular song by a publishing, production, or recording company, it is best to register it separately.

Assignment of Copyright

This states that the writer assigns or transfers the copyright ownership of a musical composition to a publisher. Under copyright law, this may be done in full or in part. Exclusive rights, that is, rights that may be exercised only by a single person or company in copyright, are divisible.

Copyright Infringement of Musical Compositions

A copyright registration certificate does not guarantee originality of a song. It is evidence of the approximate date of a song's creation. This information and registration certificate is necessary in order to file a lawsuit against an alleged infringer of a composition in federal court. A lawsuit in federal court as opposed to state court provides for stipulated damages and in some circumstances for tripling those damages.

Before January 1, 1978, an original work that had not been published was protected under the common law without requiring the filing of a copyright claim. In the event an infringement occurred regarding an unregistered composition, one would bring a lawsuit in the state court under common law. To prove plagiarism or copyright infringement, one had to prove substantial similarity between the songs and that the alleged copier had access to the song.

Copyright infringement cases involving musical works deal initially with similarity. Substantial similarity between two compositions brings up the possibility of an infringement.

Despite the popular misconception, there is no rigid standard for the exact number of duplicate bars that will constitute an infringement. If substantial similarity is found, then the element of "access" must be considered to determine if the alleged copier had access to the song. Access may include anything from hearing a song played on the radio to seeing a written lead sheet of the song.

The Audio Home Recording Act of 1992

This act allows for the digital copying of copyrighted music. It is generally acceptable to make one copy of copyrighted music, provided it is for personal use and not for distribution to others. Fees are built into the sales of all blank digital media and digital recorders, which are collected and distributed to copyright holders. The act requires a built-in fee of 3 percent to be added to all blank digital tapes and of 2 percent to be added to all digital recording devices. The fees are collected and distributed to copyright holders, including record companies, publishers, performers, and songwriters. Included in the act was the requirement of the inclusion of a Serial Copy Management System (SCMS) circuit to be included in all digital recorders. The circuit allows users to make copies of copyrighted works but not to make second-generation copies, or copies of copies.

The Digital Performance Rights in Sound Recording Act of 1995

This act gives copyright owners of sound recordings the exclusive right, with some limitations, to perform the recording publicly by means of a digital audio transmission. This act extends the provision for compulsory mechanical licenses to include downloadable music.

The Digital Millennium Copyright Act of 1998

This act states that without permission from a song's owner, it is illegal to make copyrighted music available online for unlimited distribution. This law also puts specific limitations on the length of public broadcasts, the types of song and artist announcements, and the frequency and sequence of songs played.

The Copyright Royalty and Distribution Reform Act of 2004

The law makes extensive changes to the procedural framework for adjudicating royalty rates for compulsory licenses under the Copyright Act. Compulsory licenses facilitate many copyright-related activities, including digital transmissions of sound recordings in webcasting. The previous ad hoc three-member Copyright Arbitration Royalty Panel is replaced by standing Copyright Royalty Judges appointed for six-year terms.

The Copyright Royalty Board Mechanical Rate Terms Decision of 2008

New mechanical rate terms for physical products, such as CDs, permanent downloads, such as iTunes, and ringtones, were announced in October, 2008. Songwriters and music publishers will be paid a rate of 9.1 cents for digital downloads. The CRB judges also ruled that the rate for physical products will remain at 9.1 cents. Each will be subject to an overtime rate. The CRB judges also established for the first time a rate of 24 cents for each ringtone subject to the Section 115 mechanical license. Music publishers will have the right to seek a 1.5 percent late fee, calculated monthly. The announcement was the culmination of a trial that began in January 2008, and marked the first time the Board had established mechanical royalty rates for songs distributed digitally. The Board also adopted the terms of an historic industry settlement on rates for two other types of services, interactive streaming and limited downloads. The National Music Publishers Association, along with Nashville Songwriters Association International, and the Songwriters Guild of America represented the music publishers and songwriters in the trial.

U.S. Copyright Office Web Site

Visit the U.S. Copyright Office web site at www.copyright.gov for information on the following: Copyright Basics, Frequently Asked Questions (FAQ), Current Fees, Taking the Mystery Out of Copyright, Search Copyright Records, Registrations and Documents, Notices of Restored Copyrights, Online Service Providers, Vessel Hull Designs, Publications, Circulars and Brochures, Forms, Factsheets, Reports and Studies, Licensing, Compulsory and Statutory Licenses, Preregistration, How to Register a Work, How to Record a Document, Law and Policy, Copyright Law, Federal Register Notices, Current Legislation, Regulations, Mandatory Deposit, Rulemaking, Related Links, Patents and Trademarks, and the Copyright Royalty Board.

Print Music Formats

With the exception of music that is in the public domain, print music publishers must license the rights to print, package, and distribute music from the song publishers, copyright owners, or their publishing administrators. Printed music falls into three main categories: *classical*, *popular*, and *educational*.

Classical Print Music

Modern classical sheet music may come in different formats. If a piece is composed for just one instrument or voice such as a piano or an a cappella song, the whole work may be written or printed as one piece of sheet music. If an instrumental piece is intended to be performed by more than one person, each performer will usually have a separate piece of sheet music, called a part, to play from. This is especially the case in the publication of works requiring more than four or so performers, though invariably a full score is published as well. The sung parts in a vocal work are not usually issued separately, although this was historically the case before music printing made sheet music widely available.

Sheet music can be issued as individual pieces or works, for example a popular song or a Beethoven sonata, in collections, for example works by one or several composers, as pieces performed by a given artist, etc. When the separate instrumental and vocal parts of a musical work are printed together, the resulting sheet music is called a score.

Conventionally, a score consists of musical notation with each instrumental or vocal part in vertical alignment, meaning that concurrent events in the notation for each part are orthographically arranged. The term score has also been used to refer to sheet music written for only one performer. The distinction between score and part applies when there is more than one part needed for performance.

Scores come in various formats, as follows. A full score is a large book showing the music of all instruments and voices in a composition lined up in a fixed order. It is large enough for a conductor to be able to read it while directing rehearsals and performances. A miniature score is like a full score but much reduced in size. It is too small for practical use but handy for studying a piece of music, whether for a large ensemble or a solo performer. A miniature score may contain some introductory remarks. A study score is sometimes the same size as, and often indistinguishable from, a miniature score, except in name. Some study scores are octavo size and are thus somewhere between full and miniature score sizes. A study score, especially when part of an anthology for academic study, may include extra comments about the music and markings for learning purposes.

A piano score or piano reduction is a more or less literal transcription for piano of a piece intended for many performing parts, especially orchestral works. This can include purely instrumental sections within large vocal works. Such arrangements are made for either piano solo with two hands, or piano duet with one or two pianos, four hands. As with vocal score, it takes considerable skill to reduce an orchestral score to such smaller forces because the reduction needs to be not only playable on the keyboard but also thorough enough in its presentation of the intended harmonies, textures, figurations, etc. Sometimes markings are included to show which instruments are playing at given points.

While piano scores are usually not meant for performance outside of study and pleasure, ballets get

the most practical benefit from piano scores because with one or two pianists they allow unlimited rehearsal before the orchestra is absolutely needed. They can also be used to train beginning conductors. Piano scores of operas do not include separate staves for the vocal parts, but they may add the sung text and stage directions above the music.

A vocal score or piano-vocal score is a reduction of the full score of a vocal work, for example opera, musical, oratorio, cantata, etc., to show the vocal parts, solo and choral, on their staves and the orchestral parts in a piano reduction, usually for two hands, underneath the vocal parts. The purely orchestral sections of the score are also reduced for piano. If a portion of the work is a cappella, a piano reduction of the vocal parts is often added to aid in rehearsal as with a cappella religious sheet music.

While not meant for performance, vocal scores serve as a convenient way for vocal soloists and choristers to learn the music and rehearse separately from the instrumental ensemble. The vocal score of a musical typically does not include the spoken dialogue, except for cues. The related choral score contains the choral parts with no accompaniment.

The comparable organ score exists as well, usually in association with church music for voices and orchestra, such as arrangements of Handel's Messiah. It is like the piano-vocal score in that it includes staves for the vocal parts and reduces the orchestral parts to be performed by one person. Unlike the vocal score, the organ score is sometimes intended by the arranger to substitute for the orchestra in performance if necessary. A collection of songs from a given musical is usually printed under the label vocal selections. This is different from the vocal score from the same show in that it does not present the complete music, and the piano accompaniment usually is simplified and includes the melody line.

A short score is a reduction of a work for many instruments to just a few staves. Rather than composing directly in full score, many composers work out some type of short score while they are composing and later expand the complete orchestration. An opera, for instance, may be written first in a short score, and then in full score, and then reduced to a vocal score for rehearsal. Short scores are often not published. They may be more common for some performance venues, for example band, than in others.

A lead sheet specifies only the melody, lyrics, and harmony, using one staff with chord symbols placed above and lyrics below. It is commonly used in popular music to capture the essential elements of song without specifying how the song should be arranged or performed. A chord chart or chart contains little or no melodic information at all but provides detailed harmonic and rhythmic information. This is the most common kind of written music used by professional session musicians playing jazz or other forms of popular music and is intended primarily for the rhythm section consisting of piano, guitar, bass and drums.

Popular Print Music

Popular music includes pop songs, R&B, dance, rock, adult contemporary, alternative, country, new age, jazz standards, gospel, contemporary Christian, and other radio hits that appear on the charts. They are printed as single *song sheets* and collections of songs in *songbooks* or *folios*.

Popular print music includes *sheet music, mixed folios*, or collections of songs by a variety of artists around a theme such as *Hits of the Sixties*, or *Country Song Hits of the Nineties, matching folios*, those that match a specific record album, movie, TV show, or Broadway musical and have the same cover art or photo, and *personality folios*, which include collections of an artist's or group's songs or greatest hits.

Major publishers of popular music will not print sheet music for a song unless it has become a *hit single* as a recording, and has more than likely been on the *Billboard Hot 100 Chart* or is a *Top 100 Album*. Print publishers will often publish various *arrangements* of popular songs, in addition to a sheet music version that matches the key and style of the original recording.

Not all hit songs are considered marketable as sheet music. Because printing costs are high, print publishers will print only those songs that have made it to the top of the popular song charts, are well suited as piano/vocal/guitar arrangements, or those that have become standards over time. For example, a popular groove-oriented dance tune with two chords may never be released as sheet music as the arrangement would be "thin" and the demand would more than likely be minimal.

Sheet music buyers are often musicians who want to learn how to play songs for performances such as weddings, casuals, or piano bars, music teachers and students, or hobbyists on their instrument. The sheet music section of a local music store will usually include racks of current hits and many standards from all eras.

Current popular print music formats include *Piano/Vocal/Guitar, Easy Piano, Five-Finger Piano (Very Easy), Guitar Tablature, E-Z Play*, and *Fake Books*. Piano/Vocal/Guitar arrangements consist of three staves, with the top line including the melody line and song lyrics. Sometimes the song lyric is written all the way through on multiple pages. In some cases, only the first verse, chorus, and bridge are written out, with any additional lyrics typed on the last page and direction signs instructing the player to repeat certain sections. Above the top line will appear guitar chord symbols either as alphabet letters or actual tablature.

The bottom two lines of a Piano/Vocal/Guitar arrangement will include a treble and bass clef with a piano accompaniment (indicated by a brace joining the two lower staves), that may or may not include the song melody. It is usually the Piano/Vocal/Guitar arrangement that most closely resembles the original recording. When these arrangements are written in the same key, as they often are, they can actually be practiced along with the original recording.

Easy piano arrangements consist of two staves, usually treble and bass clef, and include the song melody, a simple piano accompaniment, the song lyric, and chord symbols above the top staff. Because these are "easy" piano arrangements, they are sometimes not in the same key as the original recording and are often in the "easy" keys of C, F, or G major, or a related relative minor key.

Five-finger piano arrangements are written on two staves, usually treble and bass clef, and include only the song melody as single notes played between the two hands, with a few accompaniment notes, and in easy keys. Song lyrics and simple chord symbols may be included.

Guitar tablature books are written for guitarists and include the guitar chords, song lyrics, and, occasionally, guitar solo transcriptions. Fake books include only the melody line, lyrics, and chords of a song and are usually used by professional performing musicians who can improvise around the tune at a glance. E-Z Play books are similar to fake books, but the print is usually larger and the actual note names are printed on the note heads. They are frequently used for playing the organ or electronic keyboards with one-finger chord accompaniment functions.

While some popular songs work well as piano arrangements, especially those that are "piano-based," meaning the piano was used substantially in the original recording, others do not. For example, a student will have a hard time playing a heavy metal guitar song on the piano, especially if there is no clearly defined melody line, and the original recording is comprised primarily of melodic fragments and guitar riffs. Similarly, a "piano-based" song might not lend itself well to guitar chord strumming or finger-picking patterns.

The popular songs that sell the most as sheet music editions are those that cross over into a variety of instrumental markets. A recent example of a major sheet music seller is the theme from the movie *Titanic* by James Horner, *My Heart Will Go On*. Melodically, this song adapted to many different instrumental arrangements. Other examples of extremely popular sheet music sellers include *Theme from Love*

Story, Theme from Ice Castles, The Rose, Music Box Dancer, and any of the twentieth-century popular songs that have become standards.

Educational Print Music

Although many arrangements of popular songs can be found in educational print music, especially piano and guitar methods and those for school bands and orchestras, chart action is not a factor when considering original educational material.

Educational print publishers look for work that fits into their publishing program and is appropriate for those who use their music, such as private teaching studios, school and church choirs, and school bands or orchestras. Unlike popular song publishers, choral, religious, and educational print music publishers want a fully written arrangement included in a submission package. A print music publisher needs every note of the arrangement to be legible, clear, and complete. Composers and arrangers must be familiar with the capabilities of school age performers or church musicians.

Educational print music includes choral, band, orchestral and instrumental ensemble arrangements, and *instrumental method* or *how-to books.* There are companies who print both popular and educational music, those who produce just popular music, and those that fall into various areas of educational print music, such as piano methods or band and orchestra. There are religious print publishers who publish sheet music, books, and choral music, and distribute primarily to churches and religious bookstores.

Educational and religious print companies accept original songs suitable for choral arrangement, in some cases requesting 2-, 3-, or 4-part harmony. When submitting a choral piece to a print publisher, it is a good idea to also send a recording of the piece being performed by singers in the age group for which the arrangement is intended, such as elementary or high school students. This will show that the notes in the arrangement are within the singing range of the particular age group. Look for material similar to the composition and direct submissions to that publisher. Submissions should be made to someone on the choral publisher's editorial staff. It is a good idea to call before submitting to get a contact name.

Other educational print publishers look for original piano, jazz band, concert band, marching band, or instrumental ensemble pieces. Instrumental arrangements for high school marching and jazz bands and college or community orchestras make up a large market. Submissions of band and orchestra arrangements to potential print publishers are made in the same format as submissions of choral arrangements.

When submitting an arrangement for a marching band, the piece needs to be in 4/4, 2/4, or 6/8 time (march tempo) on a full score lead sheet. Do not send the individual parts that each musician reads. The publisher will want to hear a recorded performance of the arrangement by a high school band or community orchestra. The cover letter should be similar to the one used for a choral arrangement submission.

Arrangements

Many music educators have done some arranging for their students. The issue of copyright must be considered before making an arrangement. An arrangement of a copyrighted work done without permission from the copyright owner is considered an infringement of copyright.

One of the five exclusive rights granted to copyright owners is "the right to prepare derivative works based on the copyrighted work." A derivative work is defined as any adaptation of a copyrighted work. In music, derivative works include arrangements, transcriptions, simplified editions, adaptations, translations of texts, orchestrations, and instrumental accompaniments to vocal publications and parody lyrics. Permission must be granted before arranging, adapting, simplifying, editing, or translating a copyrighted work.

To obtain permission to make an arrangement, it is first necessary to identify the copyright owner. The copyright notice at the bottom of the first page of a printed sheet music edition provides this information, or the credits on a CD label or insert. This information can also be obtained from ASCAP, BMI, or SESAC, with the exact title and writer information. Always check the copyright date. If the work was published before 1923, it is in the public domain and permission is not necessary to make an arrangement.

After locating the copyright owner, it is necessary to write and request permission to make an arrangement of the work. It is important to be specific and provide as much information as possible, including the type of arrangement, the number of copies or parts, who will be performing the arrangement, who will actually be making the arrangement, and whether or not the arrangement will be sold.

It is also important to note if the arrangement is to be used for one occasion only, or if it will be performed regularly. The more information provided, the better the chance of getting a response from the publisher. This information is necessary for them to decide if permission should be granted to make the arrangement, and whether or not to charge a fee. A copyright owner is not obligated to grant permission to make arrangements. For example, if the type of arrangement suggested has already been done, the publisher may deny the request. If the request is within reason, the copyright owner will grant permission to arrange and may or may not charge a fee.

The copyright owner will always require a copyright notice to be shown on an arrangement and will specify how it should be stated. In the case of an instrumental arrangement, the copyright notice should appear on the score and all the accompanying parts.

If permission to arrange is denied, then an arrangement should not be done as the arranger could be sued for copyright infringement.

Publishers consider the sale of unauthorized arrangements a serious copyright infringement. Several popular music publishers have successfully sued jazz and marching band arrangers who have sold unauthorized arrangements, resulting in stiff fines and penalties from the courts. One more important point: arrangements themselves are copyrightable and may not be adapted or orchestrated without permission, even if the basic work is in the public domain.

Adaptations

An adaptation of a work can range anywhere from a complete orchestration to changing several notes in one part of a choral work. Permission must be obtained to adapt a musical work in any way. Any adaptation which may result in lost sales for the publisher, or which changes the character of the work, requires permission from the copyright owner. This includes instrumental accompaniments to vocal or choral works.

One Fair Use that covers adaptations is the case of printed copies that have already been purchased. They may be edited or simplified, as long as the fundamental character of the work is not distorted or the lyrics changed, or lyrics added if there were none. The general principle of Fair Use will help to determine whether or not permission should be requested to adapt a work.

Transcriptions

Prior to transcribing a copyrighted musical work or arrangement from one format to another, for example, from a chamber ensemble to a piano duet, permission must be obtained from the copyright owner of the work. Parody lyrics, altered texts, and translations also require permission from the copyright owner.

Writing, Arranging, and Copying

Writing, arranging, and copying can be a good source of income for musicians skilled in these areas. This includes writing lead sheets, full arrangements, and scores. It is a good idea to network at recording studios, jingle agencies, music schools and conservatories, music stores, music trade conventions, and songwriter groups to meet the people who need these services. Transcribers, arrangers, and specialists on their instrument can have lucrative careers.

Lyric Sheets

A lyric sheet is a sheet of paper containing the typed lyrics or words to a song. The purpose of the lyric sheet is to make the lyrics of a song accessible to the listener and to avoid the possibility of misheard lyrics. When submitting songs to song publishers, it is essential that a lyric sheet be included with the song demo.

Lyric sheets should be typed or computer generated on standard-sized paper (8.5- x 11-inch) with the title at the top. The song title should be in capital letters. The chorus should be in capital letters or indented, or both. It is also acceptable to type all the lyrics in capital letters, and type the title and chorus in boldface caps. In either case, the style should be consistent.

The lyric should be centered from top to bottom and symmetrically aligned with the margins. Set the lyrics up so that the parts of the song stand out. The way a lyric is set on the page should clearly indicate the sections of the song. Labeling the verse, chorus, and bridge is optional but not necessary. It is also not necessary to retype a chorus that has identical wording. Typing "Chorus" or "Repeat Chorus" or "Chorus Repeats" is sufficient.

A lyric sheet should be as clean and uncluttered as possible. It is not necessary to insert chord changes over the lyrics or the melody note names. Handwritten lyric sheets or a typed lyric sheet with handwritten chord notations look unprofessional. Never make ink or pencil corrections on a lyric sheet. If there are errors, retype the lyric sheet.

Besides the lyrics themselves, the only information the lyric sheet needs to contain is the copyright notice and the name, address, phone number, and e-mail address of the songwriter(s). If the lyric sheet is typed on plain paper, this information should appear at the bottom of the page, at least two spaces below the copyright notice.

Using letterhead stationery gives a more professional look to a lyric sheet, although lyrics typed neatly on plain white paper are perfectly acceptable. Most word processing programs can generate a letterhead each time a lyric sheet is printed.

It is easy enough to purchase special paper, for example, "gray marble" to add a letterhead to, with each separate printing of the lyric sheet. This can help the writer to avoid the cost of having stationery specially printed and having leftover, unused, or shelf-worn paper.

Custom printed or typed cassette, J-card or CD labels, envelopes, and address labels also look much more professional than handwritten ones. The songwriter should be prepared with multiple copies of lyric sheets for demo and recording sessions as well as song pitching opportunities.

Lead Sheets

Lead sheets communicate the melody, chords, and lyrics of a song in written format. Before the Copyright Act of 1976, songwriters were required to submit a lead sheet with any song sent in for registration with the United States Copyright Office. As of the new law effective January 1, 1978, a cassette recording and lyric sheet are considered sufficient documentation for copyright registration.

Lead sheets are no longer required as part of the copyright registration process, nor are they appropriate or necessary to send as part of a song submission package to a song publisher. They may still be used for copyright purposes, however. It is not necessary to submit a complete piano arrangement of the song. The melody line, lyrics, and chords are sufficient. There is also the argument that a paper copy of a song may have a longer shelf life than a magnetic tape. CDs are also more durable than a cassette tape for the purpose of copyright registration.

A lead sheet is musical manuscript handwritten, engraved, or computer generated on five-line staff paper. Lead sheets made on ten-stave paper are easier to read than those done on twelve-stave paper. If the melody notes and rests are written in pencil, mistakes can be easily erased and corrected. There are many computer software notation programs available that can produce lead sheets as well as complete scores in a variety of formats. A properly formatted lead sheet should include the following:

(1) The song's title and the author(s) of the words and music; (2) contact information, including name, address, telephone number, e-mail address, and/or Web site; (3) copyright notice on the first page, even if the song has not been registered with the Copyright Office; (4) the style or tempo of the music should be placed above the first measure such as "waltz" or "moderately"; (5) a treble clef sign as all lead sheets are written in the treble clef; (6) the key signature indicated by accidentals after the treble clef sign; (7) the time signature directly after the key signature; (8) vertical bar lines separating the measures; (9) notes below the third line should have stems going up and on the right side; notes on or above the third line should have stems going down and on the left side; (10) even spacing; (11) complete measures; each measure must contain the exact combination of note and/or rest values as indicated by the top number of the time signature; (12) the lyric typed below the musical staff with each word or syllable placed directly under the note it corresponds to; for a sustained note such as a tie or whole note, insert the word or syllable directly under the note and draw a straight line from the bottom of the last letter of the word or syllable to the beginning of the next note or rest; (13) chord symbols should be written in their proper places above the musical staff, above a particular note, rest, or beat; (14) measure or rehearsal numbers; (15) section breaks.

It is important to keep a master copy of a lead sheet, sending out only duplicate copies. The three basic techniques for reproducing lead sheets and other music manuscripts include the diazo process white-print reproduction, photocopying, or photo-offset reproduction.

The diazo process white-print reproduction is the most flexible method of manuscript reproduction. Copies come in many sizes, they can be printed on one or both sides, and they may be bound in many ways. Paper with a special diazo chemical coating is used for this process. The transparent master copy of a work, preferably dense, black engrossing ink printed on a special kind of onion skin paper referred to as deschon or vellum, is placed in contact with the paper and is then exposed to ultraviolet light, then developed in ammonia fumes. The copies come out as black print on white paper.

Photocopying is the reproduction of copies by photocopying machines. It is a convenient method to use because of the availability of photocopying machines and the most economical when only small quantities are needed. Two-sided prints can be punched and bound with a plastic binding. Photocopying machines can reproduce 8.5- x 11-inch and 11- x 17-inch copies as well as color copies for attractive covers.

Photo-offset reproduction or offset printing is the most economical process to use when over five hundred copies of a work are needed. In this process, the manuscript is photographed and a printing plate is made from the photographic negative. This plate is then mounted on a rotary press, inked, and the image is printed onto a rubber blanket on the press. The resulting copies are clear and professional.

For more information and prices on reproduction techniques, consult a music copyist or printer listed in the yellow pages online and offline under *Music Copyist, Music Manuscript Reproductions,* or *Music Printers and Engravers,* or in advertisements in trade magazines, or do a search online.

Those unable to write or generate a computer lead sheet can seek the help of someone who knows how to notate music. They can sing, present on cassette tape, or play the song on an instrument to a music copyist or stenographer, arranger, musician, music teacher, or friend who is able to write a lead sheet.

A fee will be charged for the transcription of the melody onto paper and the notation of the chord symbols and lyrics. Professionals can be found in the yellow pages under *Music Copyists, Music Arrangers, Music Teachers,* or in the trade magazines or online.

Many arrangers will use a lead sheet when writing out the musical parts of a song. While some parts are worked out intuitively or by ear, other songs are recorded by groups of musicians who read off charts. In writing out the charts, the arranger works from the original lead sheet of the song. It is best if the lead sheet is written as uncomplicated as possible so that a vocalist or musician can interpret the song without becoming confused.

A lead sheet can be helpful in the demo-making process of a song, especially when hiring musicians who do not know the song. However, experienced musicians will usually make a spontaneous *head arrangement*, using only a chart showing the chord changes written over the lyrics on the lyric sheet.

In Nashville, charts using the Nashville Number System are used with session players. These charts include the chords written as Arabic numerals that can easily be transposed to any key. A work-tape of a song demonstrating the suggested style and groove is helpful for a demo-recording session. A great song demo is useful for communicating the song's intended interpretation to a publisher or producer. Despite all the technological advancements in computer-generated lead sheet production, in today's market, it is still the recorded demo that sells the song.

If a song is going to be recorded by an artist for commercial release, it is a good idea to supply the producer with a full lead sheet, showing melody, chords, rhythms, and lyrics, in addition to a quality song demo. The degree to which the songwriter's ideas are adapted in the final recording can vary considerably. Having strong ideas initially, such as a strong intro lick or groove pattern, will best help to influence the final outcome of the production.

Only if a popular song is a hit will sheet music be printed. At this stage, it is very important that the music publisher be supplied with an accurate lead sheet to use as a reference. Most music publishers want the sheet music to be like the final recording, reflecting the creative changes that took place in the studio. The most important quality of a professional-looking lead sheet is legibility. The musical notation must be accurate. The notes must add up to the correct number of beats per measure, and the stems must face the right direction. The lyrics should be clearly written and accurately placed under the notes.

Many successful singer/songwriters do not play an instrument or know how to write songs down. Many of the great jazz and blues artists did not use writing to communicate their songs and arrangements to others. They learned by listening and played by ear. This method is used by many pop and rock musicians today. It is not necessary to know how to notate music in order to create it. Writing down music is simply another form of communication and documentation, another skill. A good natural ear can create great music with or without this skill.

Lead sheets may be used to teach songs to others, especially for songwriters who can't sing on key. Lead sheets are a convenient reference on the songwriter's piano or shelf. Having a lead sheet makes it possible to play a song on the spot, be it for pleasure, to share with others or to rework the song. Tunes or parts of a tune may be written out then returned to later when the writer is inspired to finish it.

A tape recorder is a powerful songwriting tool and can be used as an auditory notebook. Using a tape recorder gives the songwriter an opportunity to review his or her ideas as well as a way to communicate ideas to a collaborator or other musicians working on a song. Synthesizers, drum machines, sequencers, MIDI devices, and music software have created many new possibilities for musical experimentation and home recording for the songwriter. Chapters 3 and 4 list many of the options available.

Chord Charts

The standard lead sheet format is not always necessary. Many instrumentalists find a chord chart to be sufficient, even preferable. A chord chart must clearly show the chords and when they change. Typing out the complete lyric of the song and placing each chord symbol directly above the word or syllable where the change occurs accomplishes this.

Some chord charts are written out using rhythm-figure notation or slash marks. These marks use the same system of open and filled-in noteheads and stems, flags, and beams as standard notation, except that the quarter-note slash mark is usually drawn without a stem. When the rhythm is consistent, only quarter-note slashes are used. Important riffs or musical hooks can be indicated in standard notation. Stops, pushes, or anticipated rhythms can be written in as well as chords that change off the beat. This type of chord chart can be used by any instrumentalist and by singers when the lyric is added.

The Nashville Number System

Most Nashville musicians substitute Arabic numerals in place of chords or note symbols when making musical notations. This quick and effective system has become standard. Using this method, musicians can hear a song one time, write out the numbers, and then play it. If the key of the song is too low or too high for the singer, the musicians can easily transpose or change key while using the same number chart.

Tablature

When tablature is used, musical notes are represented on a staff in which the staff lines depict the strings of the instrument played, usually the guitar. This is in contrast to a normal staff where the lines represent musical tones. Bends, slides, pops, hammers, and strums are represented by different symbols and are displayed according to the position and sequence in which they are performed.

Reading and Writing Music

There is no mystery to reading and writing music, and it is not a difficult task to become musically literate. It is simply a matter of practice. Usually a person who plays an instrument is familiar with notes, chords, and their names. Those who play or sing entirely by ear will need some help writing down music. In either case, it is a good idea to become familiar with the accepted formats. There are many useful Web sites and music software programs available for learning basic music theory and notation skills.

Sample Scores

Sample scores in a variety of formats, including those mentioned previously, can be found on the CD-ROM that accompanies this book.

Print Music and Copyright Terms

Abridgment of Music Removing or changing parts of a song to create a new arrangement.

Administration When a songwriter retains ownership of the copyright and assigns a portion of the publisher's share of rights to a publisher in exchange for its services in administering the copyright.

American Society of Composers, Authors, and Publishers (ASCAP) Founded in 1914; the first performing rights organization in the United States.

Arrangement A new and different version or adaptation of the lyrics, melody, instrumental, or vocal parts of a song; a new orchestration of an instrumental; an orchestration to which new ideas are added; an enhancement of the performance of a song.

Arranger One who orchestrates or adapts a musical composition by scoring for voices or instruments other than those for which it was originally written.

Author One who creates or originally writes the lyrics and/or music to a musical composition; the author's name.

Blanket Performing License A license purchased from a performing rights organization; licensee obtains the performance right for all works written and/or published by all the members of the organization.

Broadcast Music, Inc. (BMI) U.S. performing rights organization; founded in 1939.

Broadcast/Public Performance License The right to broadcast a copyright on radio, television, Internet streaming, or to perform it in concert; issued to broadcasters, arenas, and clubs; issued by performing rights organizations (ASCAP, BMI, SESAC); rate varies by usage.

Catalog A collection of all the songs owned by a music publisher.

Chromolithography Lithography adapted to use multicolored inks.

Collaborator Co-writer; person(s) with whom musical works are written.

Compose To write a musical work.

Composer A person who composes.

Composition An intellectual and artistic creation of music; a musical work.

Contractor Anyone who is under contract or works for another under contract; an independent contractor; a music contractor.

Contracts Written legal agreement between two or more parties.

Co-publishing When a songwriter transfers part of the copyright and assigns all or a part of the publisher's share of the rights to a publisher for an advance.

Copy Reproduction of an original work; to reproduce an original work; work ready to be printed.

Copyist Person who copies music from a lead sheet or score in written or computer manuscript form.

Copyright Infringement A violation of any of the exclusive rights granted by law to a copyright owner.

Copyright Owner Owner(s) of any or all exclusive rights granted under copyright law.

Co-writer Collaborator.

Derivative Works Based on one or more preexisting works; arrangement, dramatization, transcription, orchestration, or simplified edition; a derivative or sample license issued by the publisher is required.

Distortion Any changing of the fundamental character or melody of a copyrighted work.

Dramatic Work Performing arts work such as a play, musical play, opera, or ballet, which is primarily dramatic in nature.

Electrical Transcription The right to use a copyright as background music on an airplane, electronic game, Karaoke system, or jukebox; an electrical transcription license issued by the publisher is required.

Engraving The production of music notes, letters, or illustrations by means of incised lines on a metal plate.

Exclusive Rights The specific rights granted under copyright law to a copyright owner or his licensee.

Exempt Performance A public performance covered by one or more of the limitations placed upon the performance right by the Copyright Act of 1976.

Fair Use A limitation placed on an exclusive right of a copyright owner.

First Sale Doctrine A portion of the U.S. Copyright Act stating that anyone who purchases a recording may then sell or otherwise dispose of that recording; the seller may not keep, sell, or give away any other copies.

First Use The right to record and commercially release a copyright for the first time; a first use license issued by the publisher to a company or individual commercially releasing the copyright is required; fee is negotiable.

Fixed The way in which music is fixed is legally separated into two classes: (1) sound recordings, including records, CDs, and tapes; (2) all others, including material copies such as printed copies, and audiovisual copies such as video, and motion picture synchronizations; a work's physical existence where it is embodied in a tangible medium of expression; the fixation must be done by, or under the authority of, the author; the embodiment must be sufficiently permanent or stable to permit it to be perceived, reproduced, or otherwise communicated for a period of more than transitory duration; a fixed work is in contrast with a "non-fixed" work as a piece that is memorized or a work that is performed or played from memory.

Folio A collection of songs of printed sheet music; the songs may be by a particular artist or group, or by a number of different artists.

Full Publishing When a writer transfers the copyright and assigns all of the publisher's share of the right to a publisher, usually in exchange for an advance.

Grand Rights Another name for performance rights in dramatic works.

Harry Fox Agency, Inc., The For the licensing of recordings of copyrighted musical works.

Head Arrangement A spontaneous arrangement of a musical work where a musician plays from memory, experience, and habit.

Independent Contractor A person or business who performs a service for another under verbal or written contract, as opposed to a person who works for wages or salary or an employee; contractor retains control of the means, method, and manner of production or execution concerning the work or service contracted; neither the contractor nor the contracted may independently terminate the contract before completion of the work by the contractor; an independent contractor is not, by tax law, considered to be an employee.

Instrumental A composition written for a musical instrument; a musical performance involving only musical instruments; a recorded performance of a musical instrument.

License A contractual permission to act; given by written agreement granted by an authority that is legally authorized to grant such permission; a grant of one or more of the exclusive rights of copyright owners by the owner of that right to another party.

Literary Work A non-dramatic work of prose or poetry.

Lithography The process of printing from a flat surface such as stone or a metal plate; the surface on which the image is printed is ink receptive and the blank area is ink repellant.

Lyric License License to print lyrics.

Lyric Sheet A page with only the lyrics or words to a song.

Lyricist A person who writes the words to a song.

Lyrics The words of a song.

Mechanical Reproduction License The right to mechanically reproduce a copyright on a CD or tape, or to digitally download it to a hard drive; a mechanical license is issued to record companies by a publisher or license clearance agency such as the Harry Fox Agency.

Mechanical Right One of the exclusive rights granted to copyright owners; the right to record the copyrighted work.

Music Manuscript A set of symbols used to fix a musical composition in written manuscript form; the music notation symbols are placed on a five-line staff and convey the meter, key, notes, rests, etc., of a musical composition.

Music Publishers Association of the U.S. An association of publishers of primarily serious and/or educational music.

Musical Play A dramatic work, such as a musical, musical comedy, or operetta, incorporating music as an integral part of the work.

Musical Work A term used in copyright law that refers to the actual notes and lyrics used in a song.

National Music Publishers Association An association of publishers of primarily popular music.

No Electronic Theft Act The No Electronic Theft Act of 1997 amends the U.S. Copyright Act to define "financial gain" to include the receipt of anything of value, including the receipt of other copyrighted works.

Nondramatic Work A work of the performing arts, such as a musical work, which is not dramatic in nature.

Nonexempt Performance A public performance that falls under the purview of the performance right.

Orchestra Large group of musicians performing on brass, woodwind, string, and percussion instruments; may include the piano or unique instruments not usually associated with the western European orchestra; genre-specific orchestras include the klezmer and tango orchestras, consisting of traditional and ethnic instruments.

Orchestral Sketch Linear form of writing music; harmonic content shown with symbols.

Orchestration Written music for orchestra separated into performance parts for specific instruments.

Orchestrator A person who transcribes a musical composition for orchestra with performance specifications.

Original Material Song, lyrics, or music written or composed by an individual or group of individuals.

Original Work Independently created work of authorship.

Out-of-Print Music A music publication which is no longer available for sale; the copyright on a musical work does not expire when the work is placed out of print.

Parody Lyrics Any lyric that replaces the original lyric of a vocal work.

Performance Right One of the exclusive rights granted to copyright owners; the right to publicly perform the work.

Performing Rights Organization An organization which administers the performance rights in musical works for its publisher and writer members; in the United States, these are ASCAP, BMI, and SESAC.

Print To make a copy by use of a machine that prints or transfers print from an inked or carbon surface, or applies ink, carbon, or other printing material to paper.

Print License Defines the agreement to assign the print rights of a copyrighted work; the assignment is made by the legal owner of the print right, or his representative (licensor), to another (licensee); usually assigned to, and administered by, the music publisher.

Print License Fee The monetary compensation paid to a print right licensor to obtain a print license; the payment is a negotiated rate.

Print Publisher One who issues a printed edition of a work; may or may not be the copyright owner of the work.

Print Right The right, authorized by copyright law, to reproduce a copyrighted work in printed form; one of the exclusive rights granted to copyright owners, that being the right to print copies of the work.

Print Royalties The standard royalty paid on all printed sheet music collected and distributed by publishers; the compensation paid to a copyright owner for the printed use of his work in, for example, song

folios and sheet music; if the work has been assigned to a music publisher by the songwriter(s) who created the work, the royalty is paid by the music publisher to the songwriter(s); the amount paid is proportionate to the license fees received by the publisher from its print publisher licensees or from the sales gross if the publisher is printing and publishing in-house; the royalty rate paid is defined by the songwriter/publisher contract.

Public Domain The absence of copyright; a work is in the public domain if no copyright is claimed on the work or if the copyright on the work has expired; arrangements of works in the public domain are copyrightable.

Public Performance To perform or display a work at a public place live or by any device or process capable of transmitting or recording an image of a performance or display.

Published Work A work that has been distributed to the public in copies or recordings by sale, rental, lease, or lending.

Publishing License Defines the agreement to assign the publishing rights of a copyrighted work; assignment is made by the legal owner or licensor of the publishing; publishing licenses include the print license, mechanical license, compulsory license, purchase license, transcription license, and synchronization license.

Publishing Rights The administration of a copyright divided into two parts: the writer's share (50%) and the publisher's share (50%); publishing rights can be assigned without transferring ownership of the copyright; ownership of a copyright can be transferred without assigning publishing rights.

Register of Copyrights The director of the United States Copyright Office.

Rental Music Music distributed through the rental of scores and/or parts rather than through the sale of copies; a rental work is considered a published work, and is granted the same copyright protection.

Reproduction Right The exclusive right, granted by copyright law, to reproduce a copyrighted work in copies of phonorecords, piano copies, CDs, cassette tapes, and all fixed material objects that can be perceived, reproduced, or otherwise communicated.

Reversion Clause A statement requiring the publisher to provide a release of a commercial recording on the national level within a specified period of time; if this requirement is not met, the contract terminates and all rights revert to the songwriter.

Right of Attribution Concerns the right of the creator to be known as the author of his/her work, the right to prevent others from being named as the author of his/her work and the right to prevent others from falsely attributing to him/her the authorship of work that the author has not written.

Right of Integrity Concerns the right to prevent others from making deforming changes in the author's work, the right to withdraw a published work from distribution if it no longer represents the views of the author, and the right to prevent others from using the work or the author's name in such a way as to damage his/her professional standing.

Role of the Publisher The primary publisher functions are authorizing the use of a copyright, collecting income generated by the copyright, protecting the copyright against illegal use, and promoting the copyright.

Royalties Payment made to a composer by an assignee or copyright holder for each unit or copy sold of the composer's work; royalty income sources, according to the contractually agreed-upon amount, include mechanical, which covers CD, tape, and album sales; sheet music sales; sync licenses for synchronization of music to film, movie videos, etc.; background music for elevators and similar uses; special licenses such as commercial, merchandising, etc.

Royalty Rates In the royalty rates section of a song contract, the percentage rate of royalty payment for various uses of the song.

Royalty Statement An accounting statement made by the user licensee to the licensor or by the copyright assignee; statement shows the dates and sources of income, itemized deductions and costs, total sales, royalty rates, and royalties owed and paid out; sent out quarterly by registered mail.

Self-Publishing The act of carrying on the duties of a music publisher by oneself.

SESAC The smallest of the three performing rights organizations in the United States.

Sheet Music Printed music that is sold to the public.

Single-Song Contract Where a publisher signs one song; term is typically for the duration of copyright; common with new writers.

Small Rights Performance rights in non-dramatic works.

Software Publishers Association Publishers of computer software.

Song Dex Index system that lists the writer, publisher, copyright proprietor, lyrics, and melody line of various songs.

Song File A publisher's checklist and data sheet for an individual song that is part of its catalog; file contains various information, including the song name, the songwriter(s) name(s), the date of the songwriter/publisher contract, royalty income distribution dates, when and to whom mechanical licenses were granted, when and to whom compulsory li-

censes were granted, when and to what performance rights society a publisher registration card was sent, the date of copyright, the copyright registration number, and the song's status as published or unpublished.

Song Registration The act of establishing a written record to substantiate the ownership and date of ownership of a song.

Song Rights All the legal rights in a musical composition that may be sold or assigned.

Song Royalties Royalties received from the sale of the rights to a song from performance, publishing, compulsory, jukebox, or derivative work licenses.

Song Shark Any person who charges a fee to publish a song; anyone who profits by exploiting the ignorance of a novice songwriter.

Songwriter's Biography Form A form kept by a music publisher with information concerning one of their contracted or affiliated songwriters; includes the songwriter's name, professional name, address, address of a close relative, birth date, birthplace, citizenship, driver's license (state and number), social security number, music organization affiliates, union membership, spouse's name, children's names, published songs, and other publishers of the songwriter's music.

Stereotype Process A solid metal duplicate of a relief printing surface that is made by pressing a molding material such as wet paper pulp against it to make a matrix; molten metal is then poured into the matrix to make a casting, which may then be faced with a harder metal to increase durability.

Subpublishing When a publisher licenses the copyright and the publishing rights associated with the copyright to a third party to administer; used most often when dealing with foreign territories; subpublisher receives a percentage of the publishing share.

Synchronization Right The right to affix, or synchronize, a musical work in an audiovisual work such as a film or video; the right to use a copyright by "syncing" it up with a visual picture, such as in film or television; a synchronization or sync license is issued to a film or TV production company by the publisher or license clearing agency.

Union Contractor Union musician that performs supervisory functions for a recording session; contractor that employs union labor.

Universal Copyright Convention An organization of nations, all of which agree to provide copyright protection in their countries to copyright works from all member nations; the United States is a member.

Unpublished Work A work which has not been distributed to the public in copies or recordings by sale, rental, lease, or lending; unpublished works may be protected by copyright.

WIPO The World Intellectual Property Organization; negotiates treaties that help make copyright laws more consistent between nations; the WIPO treaties, negotiated in 1996 by more than one hundred countries, make it possible to fight piracy worldwide, regardless of the location of the copyright holder or the infringer.

Work for Hire When a writer is hired or contracted to write for a company or other second party; often utilized in jingles, corporate themes, and some TV and film uses; the employer is the copyright owner.

Copyright, Legal, and Tax Information— Performing and Mechanical Rights— Government Grants Web Sites

AFM (American Federation of Musicians) www.afm.org Musicians union; New York headquarters; how to hire musicians; member groups; booking agents; member benefits; history of the organization founded in the 1890s.

AFTRA (American Federation of Television and Radio Artists) www.aftra.com Broadcast/News; Entertainment Programs; Commercials; Industry and New Technologies; Sound Recordings: FAQ.

AKM (Staatlich Genehmigte Gesellschaft Der Autoren Komponisten Und Musikverlager) www.akm.co.at Performing rights organization of Austria.

APRA (Australasian Performing Right Association) www.apra.com.au Australasia.

ASCAP (American Society of Composers, Authors, and Publishers) www.ascap.com Performing rights organization; collects performance royalties; active members are composers, lyricists, songwriters, and music publishers; award-winning Web site; music database; legislative; licensing; insurance; music business; catalogs; links; created in 1914 to provide the essential link between the creators of music and the users of music; only performing rights organization in the U. S. whose board of directors is made up entirely of writers and publishers elected by and from its membership.

BayTSP www.baytsp.com San Jose, CA, based corporation; developer, patent holder, and provider of effective means of branding and tracking online content over the Internet; software products and services are aimed to deter theft of online content as well as aid in the prosecution of those who engage in copyright infringement.

Better Business Bureau www.bbb.org Online site.

Blue Spike, Inc. www.bluespike.com Information on digital watermarking.

BMI (Broadcast Music Incorporated) www.bmi.com Performing rights organization; collects license fees on behalf of its songwriters, composers and music publishers and distributes them as royalties to those members whose works have been performed; writer and publisher member catalogs; licensing.

BUMA (Het Bureau voor Muziek-Auteursrecht) www.buma.nl Performing rights organization of the Netherlands.

California Lawyers for the Arts www.calawyersforthearts.org Nonprofit tax-exempt service organization founded in 1974; provides lawyer referrals, dispute resolution services, educational programs, publications and a resource library to artists of all disciplines and arts organizations.

Canada Council for the Arts www.canadacouncil.ca Art Bank; Public Lending Right Commission.

Catalog of Federal Domestic Assistance www.gsa.gov/fdac Types of assistance; FAQ.

Center for Financial & Tax Planning www.taxplanning.com Tax information.

CMRRA (Canadian Musical Reproduction Rights Agency Ltd.) www.cmrra.ca Home page; reproduction rights in Canada.

Content Delivery and Storage www.contentdeliveryandstorage.org/ Content delivery and Storage association.

Copyright Alliance www.copyrightalliance.org Grass roots non-profit based in Washington, DC working to protect the interest of all creators and publishers of intellectual property; principles; alliance members; copyright and you; documents and research; newsroom; blog.

Copyright Clearance Center www.copyright.com Copyright tools, resources, and information.

Copyright Office of the United States www.lcWeb.loc.gov/copyright Copyright information; copyright law; forms; legislation.

Digital Media Association www.digmedia.org/ Shaping the future of online media.

EAU (Eesti Autorite Uhing) www.eauthors.ee Performing rights organization of Estonia.

Electronic Frontier Foundation www.eff.org Civil-rights organization for the online community; general information on copyright; links; articles on issues of debate; freedom of speech rights.

Entertainment Publisher www.entertainmentpublisher.com Automated contracts for a fee; music industry; film; TV.

Essential Links to Taxes www.el.com/elinks/taxes Tax information.

Federal Government Information www.usa.gov/
Federal laws and more; United States government's official Web site.

FedWorld www.fedworld.gov Search for government
reports and Web sites.

Find Law www.findlaw.com Legal news; legal professionals; business resources; public and consumer resources; corporate council; student resources; services for lawyers.

Future of Music Coalition www.futureofmusic.com
Not-for-profit collaboration between members of
the music, technology, public policy, and intellectual property law communities; seeks to educate the media, policymakers, and the public
about music technology issues; aims to identify
and promote innovative business models that
will help musicians and citizens to benefit from
new technologies; attempts both to address
pressing music technology issues, and to serve as
a voice for musicians and citizens in Washington, DC, where critical decisions are being made
regarding intellectual property rights.

*GEMA (Gesellschaft Fur Musikalische Auffuhrungs
Und Mechanische)* www.gema.de Performing
rights organization of Germany.

GPO Access Services
www.gpoaccess.gov/index.html Disseminates official information from all three branches of the
federal government.

IMRO (Irish Music Rights Organization)
www.imro.ie Performing rights organization of
Ireland.

Incorporated Society of Musicians www.ism.org
UK's professional association for musicians.

International Trademark Association www.inta.org
Representing the trademark community since
1878.

IP Watchdog www.ipwatchdog.com/copyright.html
Copyright law; information; basics; links; industry associations; articles.

*KODA (Selskabet til Forvaltning af Internationale
Komponistrettighederi Danmark)* www.koda.dk/
Performing rights organization of Denmark.

Library of Congress Home Page www.loc.gov Information resources.

MCPS (Mechanical Copyright Protection Society)
www.mcps.co.uk UK collection agency.

Music Business Solutions www.mbsolutions.com
Helping musicians, songwriters and industry professionals start and grow successful music businesses through vital information and creative
management strategies.

Music Rewards Fundraising
www.raisemoremoney.com CDs and cassettes
from top artists; year-round, holiday, Christian
family, Latin, and children's programs; FAQ.

Musician's Intellectual Law and Resources Links
www.aracnet.com/~schornj/index.shtml Notes
on copyright: new legislation; copyright in compositions; copyright in sound recordings; collection of royalties; mechanical royalties; trademarks and servicemarks; miscellaneous intellectual law links; thoughts on contracts; analysis of
recording contract clauses; musician resources;
my favorite musician-related links; jazz and music magazines; record company links; booking
agents, managers, and music publishers; international venues; American venues; musicians'
Web pages.

Musician's Union UK www.musiciansunion.org.uk
Information on local offices; press releases;
FAQs; links; members; gig list; copyright.

Music-Law.com www.music-law.com Legal issues
concerning musicians.

National Endowment for the Arts (NEA)
www.arts.endow.gov Learn about work being
done by artists and arts organizations across the
country; helping nonprofit organizations link
with federal arts resources; applications.

National Foundation for Advancement in the Arts
www.ARTSawards.org Arts recognition and talent search.

PRS (Performing Right Society) www.prs.co.uk UK
association of composers, songwriters, and music publishers; administers performing rights.

Public Domain Music www.pdinfo.com Lists music
in the public domain.

Public Domain Music Works www.pubdomain.com
Monthly subscription available; approximately
10,000 hand-picked PD music titles and growing, specially selected by the editors of *Public
Domain Report;* search music by title, genre,
composer, keyword, lyric, or any word or phrase;
updated monthly with hundreds of new titles;
Rotating Editor's selection of top 100 PD songs
with Real Audio sound clips; subscribers receive
unrestricted, password protected access; sheet
music offered for thousands of titles; custom
copyright research available; copyright forums;
articles, tips, tricks, and techniques for practical
PD usage.

Quicken Financial Services www.quicken.com
Budget and tax planning.

RAO (Russian Authors Society) www.rao.ru Performing rights organization of Russia.

Recording Industry Association of America (RIAA)
www.riaa.com Official Web site; copyrights;
legislation; technology; Web licensing; censorship; parental advisory; Gold and Platinum
awards; links.

Revenue Canada www.ccra-adrc.gc.ca/menu-e.html
Tax information.

Rock Out Censorship www.theroc.org Grassroots anticensorship organization; First Amendment rights.

SABAM (Societe Belge Des Auteurs Compositeurs Et Editeurs) www.sabam.be Performing rights organization of Belgium.

SACEM (Societe Des Auteurs Compositeurs Et Editeurs De Musique) www.sacem.fr Performing rights organization of France.

SESAC www.sesac.com Performing rights organization; privately owned; licensing; repertory; writer/publisher links; news and events; SESAC Latina; search.

SGAE (Sociedad General De Autores De España) www.sgae.es Performing rights organization of Spain.

SIAE (Societa Italiana Degli Autori Ed Editori) www.siae.it Performing rights organization of Italy.

Small Business Administration www.sba.gov Government office.

Small Business Taxes and Management www.smbiz.com Tax information.

SOCAN (Society of Composers Authors & Music Publishers Of Canada) www.socan.ca Performing rights organization of Canada.

SODRAC Inc. www.sodrac.com Canadian performing rights organization (French).

SoundExchange, Inc. www.soundexchange.com The not-for-profit corporation responsible for collecting and distributing sound recording performance royalties to artists and copyright owners from digital audio transmissions over the Internet, satellite radio, cable, and other platforms.

Stanford University Libraries Comprehensive Copyright Site fairuse.stanford.edu/ Copyright history; statutes; regulations; treaties; articles; links.

STIM (Svenska Tonsattares Internationella Musikbyra) www.stim.se Performing rights organization of Sweden.

TEOSTO (Bureau International Du Droit D'Auteur Des Compositeurs Finlandais) www.teosto.fi Performing rights organization of Finland.

The British Phonographic Industry www.bpi.co.uk British music industry; statistics; links.

The Copyright Website www.benedict.com Copyright information; all forms and subjects.

The Electronic Privacy Information Center www.epic.org Furthering online privacy.

The Harry Fox Agency www.harryfox.com Mechanical royalties and licenses; database of songs and publishers; current statutory mechanical rate.

The Privacy Rights Clearinghouse www.privacyrights.org Devoted to furthering online privacy.

The United States Senate www.senate.gov Information on the Senate.

TONO (Norsk selskap for forvaltning av fremføringsrettigheter til musikkverk) www.tono.no Performing rights organization of Norway.

United States Nonprofit Gateway www.nonprofit.gov Directory of information about grants, regulations, taxes, and government services.

UBC (Uniao Brasilera de Compositores) www.ubc.org.br Performing rights organization of Brazil.

United Nations www.un.org Information about the United Nations.

What is Copyright? www.whatiscopyright.org Basic definitions regarding copyrights; written using the Berne Union for the Protection of Literary and Artistic Property (Berne Convention).

World Intellectual Property Organization www.wipo.org News and information resources.

3
Children's Music
Software, Instructional Media and Web Sites

Action Songs Children Love (www.musicmotion.com): Actions songs to enhance language development, sequencing ability, and using both sides of the brain; songs include old and new favorites pitched in keys that go no lower than middle C for children's singing voices; each CD contains over fifty minutes of music in a split-track format that works well for rehearsal or performance; twenty-eight+ songs per CD listed under teaching focus: Keep the Beat, High Low, Changing Tempo, Movers and Shakers, Brain Teasers, Finger Fun, Leave It Out, Expression; teaching suggestions; three volumes by Denise Gagne; Volume 1 PreK - Grade 2; Volume 2 K-Grade 3; Volume 3 Grades 2-5. SYSTEM SPECS: Book and Audio CD.

Adventures in Musicland CD-ROM (www.ecsmedia.com/indivprods/musaim.shtml): Animations; colorful graphics; general music program; listening skills; music notation; White Rabbit serves as a guide; Music Match tests identification of musical symbols, notes, rests, and instruments; Sound Concentration tests aural memory skills, including various sounds, single notes, intervals, triads, and scales; in Melody Mix-Up students duplicate a melody with pitches from a major triad, pentatonic scale, or the major scale; in Picture Perfect students identify instruments, musical signs, or composers; can save scores in the Hall of Records; characters from Carroll's *Alice in Wonderland*; for beginners, grades K-6. SYSTEM SPECS: Hybrid CD-ROM.

Alfred's Kid's Course (www.alfred.com): Titles include: *Alfred's Kid's Drum Course; Alfred's Kid's Drumset Course;* and *Alfred's Kid's Guitar Course*; full color books and illustrations for young beginners at the early elementary level. SYSTEM SPECS: Book and Audio CD.

American Cultures for Children DVD Set (www.libraryvideo.com): Tony Award-winning actress Phylicia Rashad introduces children to the tapestry of world cultures in America today; each culture is presented in educational segments that celebrate the community's values and traditions; programs include geography and history segments about the culture's original country of origin; tours of neighborhood restaurants, markets, and festivals; foreign language segments in which children learn to count to ten and say "hello," "goodbye," "thank you" and "friend"; arts and crafts demonstrations; a traditional animated folktale and a traditional folksong performed by a chorus of children and musicians; teacher's guides; includes African-American Heritage, Arab-American Heritage, Central American Heritage, Chinese-American Heritage, Irish-American Heritage, Japanese-American Heritage, Jewish-American Heritage, Korean-American Heritage, Mexican-American Heritage, Native American Heritage, Puerto Rican Heritage, and Vietnamese-American Heritage. SYSTEM SPECS: Instructional DVD.

American Idol Jam Trax CD-ROM (www.sonycreativesoftware.com/products/childrenssoftware.asp) Create and perform music; record live vocals and instruments; mix and match over 600 loops; add turntable scratch and other effects; e-mail songs. SYSTEM SPECS: Windows.

Animusic (www.animusic.com): Combines cutting edge computer animation with a diverse collection of modern musical grooves and soundscapes; seven unique music animations bring extraordinary musical instruments to life; virtual concerts with note for note precision; running time approximately seventy-five minutes; additional two hours of bonus material; for all ages. SYSTEM SPECS: Instructional DVD.

Ann Rachlin's Classical Music and Stories (www.funwithmusic.com): Complete set of sixteen CDs of stories to classical music told by Ann Rachlin; imaginative and entertaining; involves the listener with thoughtful questions and suggestions; history and anecdote; forty-sixty minutes each; stories of the composers, classical ballet, or adventures based on themes of a composer; beautifully and artfully done; includes Happy Birthday, Mr. Beethoven, Mr. Handel's Fireworks Party, Mozart: The Miracle Maestro, Once Upon the Thames, Papa Haydn's Surprise, Cinderella, The Firebird, Romeo & Juliet, Sleeping Beauty, Swan Lake, The King Who Broke His Promise, Love for Three Oranges, Mandy and the Magic Butterfly, The Man Who Never Was, Season's Greeting from Vivaldi. SYSTEM SPECS: Audio CD.

Baby Jamz (http://kids.babyjamz.com/?#music): Hip-Hop inspired preschool line; color and fun book; thirteen nursery songs sung in hip-hop fashion. SYSTEM SPECS: Book and Audio CD.

Baby Loves Jazz (www.babylovesjazz.info): Music played by great young jazz players; Miles the Crocodile plays the colors; scatting with Ella Elephant; counting the beat with Charlie Bird; beboppin' through the zoo with Duck Ellington; board books; CDs have the story and music, either songs or instrumentals; set of four. SYSTEM SPECS: Book and Audio CD.

Baby Loves Music Series (www.babylovesmusic.com): Disco, Jazz, Blues, Hip-Hop, Salsa, and Reggae; fun and creative CDs for babies and toddlers. SYSTEM SPECS: Audio CD.

Bach to Rock (www.friendshiphouse.com): Upbeat, light approach to music from different periods; meet composers from the Baroque, Classical, and Modern periods, including jazz, blues, ragtime and rock; offers young people an easy-to-understand anthology of composers and their music; 150-page illustrated activity book is easy to follow and fun; CD has excerpts from thirty-two of the recommended works in sequential order; thirty-minute video is live-action, fast-paced, and provides an overview of the world of music; for grades three-eight. SYSTEM SPECS: Book, Audio CD, and Instructional DVD.

Beethoven Lives Upstairs DVD (www.friendshiphouse.com): Best-loved and best-selling of all Classical Kids stories; arrival of an eccentric boarder turns a young boy's life upside down; Ludwig van Beethoven has moved in upstairs; at first Christoph resents their new tenant but slowly he comes to understand the genius of the man, the torment of his deafness, and the beauty of his music; in the end he is won over by the music and true incidents from the great composer's life. SYSTEM SPECS: Instructional DVD.

Beethoven's Wig Book and CDs (www.beethovenswig.com): Based on the award-winning Sing Along Symphonies music series; combines adventure with illustrations woven throughout Beethoven's Fifth Symphony; hardcover book with CDs; thirty pages; Beethoven's Wig Sing Along Symphonies CDs are fun lyrics set to the greatest hits of classical music; filled with information about notable composers and their masterpieces; opens the door to serious music in a fun way. SYSTEM SPECS: Book and Audio CD.

Boomwhacker Books and CDs (www.boomwhackers.com): Books and CDs used for teaching music with boomwhackers tuned percussion tubes; brightly colored plastic tubes tuned by length to musical notes; six different sets available; five of the six sets combine to create two and a half chromatic octaves; the sixth set, the C Major Pentatonic Scale, is a subset of the C Major Diatonic Scale; used to teach rhythm, melody, and harmony; get exercise. SYSTEM SPECS: Book and Audio CD.

Can You Hear It? (www.friendshiphouse.com): Examples of pictorial music matched to masterpieces from the Metropolitan Museum of Art; introduction to music and art appreciation for young listeners; CD features twelve short works and an introduction to the orchestra and instruments; hardcover; for ages four-ten. SYSTEM SPECS: Book and Audio CD.

Carnival of the Animals Set (www.musicmotion.com): Hardback book with accompanying CD; commentary helps children follow each musical section; introduces the instruments; tells why Saint-Saëns created the work and chose specific instruments to represent the different animals; DVD hosted by Gary Burghoff; verses of Ogden Nash; live animals from the San Diego Zoo; animation; outdoor concert by the Mormon Youth Symphony; live orchestra allows kids to see which instruments are playing to characterize the different animals; for all ages; running time thirty minutes. SYSTEM SPECS: Book, Audio CD, and Instructional DVD.

Children's Fiddling Method Volumes 1 and 2 (www.melbay.com): Carol Ann Wheeler, assisted by eleven-year-old fiddler Collin Bay and guitarist John Standefer, play through the seventy-three lessons from Volume 1, and sixty-three lessons from Volume 2; covers fiddling techniques in a step-by-step manner; learn thirty-two fiddling solos in tunes such as *Liberty, McNabe's Hornpipe, Boil the Cabbage, Red Fox Waltz*; numerous twin fiddling arrangements. SYSTEM SPECS: Book and Instructional DVD.

Children's Guitar Chord Book and DVD (www.melbay.com): Creative approach to playing simple guitar chords; chords taught with exercises that build upon each other; student plays logical and common chord progressions including I-iii-vi-ii-V-I and twelve bar blues in different keys; chords shown in chord diagram form with detailed illustrations showing finger positions in relationship to fretboard; open chords for folk music as well as power chords for rock music presented clearly; complete easy chord chart and capo chart provided at end of book for easy reference; examples and exercises presented in strum bar notation. SYSTEM SPECS: Book and Instructional DVD.

Children's Guitar Method Volumes 1-3 (www.melbay.com): For teaching guitar to young children; integrates chord playing with note reading; student starts with easy one finger chord forms and strums accompaniments to numerous songs; note reading is then introduced; features Ron Wheeler's cartoon artwork. SYSTEM SPECS: Book, Audio CD and/or Instructional DVD.

Children's Music Journey Volumes 1-3 (www.adventus.com): Addresses music reading and objectives identified by elementary school music curriculums; provides a background for continued development with the piano and preparation for band programs; interactive lessons taught by famous composers Beethoven, Bach, Scott Joplin, and more; practice sessions with "Miss Melody" the practice room teacher; learn to play songs and famous pieces; games to reinforce theory and make learning fun; composing and improvising with dozens of instruments, sounds, beats, and pre-loaded arrangements from classical to rock 'n roll. SYSTEM SPECS: Windows.

Children's Piano Method Level 1 (www.melbay.com): Comprehensive piano course for young beginners; colorful presentation; well organized; play-along CD is included; several songs are recorded twice, the first time as written and the second with a separate accompaniment; listening to songs and playing together with accompaniment aids the student's learning process and provides good ear training. SYSTEM SPECS: Book and Audio CD.

Children's Recorder Method Volumes 1 and 2 (www.melbay.com): Lyrics to all songs; large notes; each melody is illustrated; clear and concise instructions introduce technique and notation concepts gradually; Icelandic songs and folk songs; introduction of many unusual melodic and rhythmic elements; first book is based on the six easiest notes on the recorder; accompaniment will help student gain a firm rhythmic feeling; second book carries on where the first left off, introducing F-sharp and B-flat and includes some duets. SYSTEM SPECS: Book and Audio CD.

Children's Tinwhistle Method (www.melbay.com): Easy method for learning tinwhistle; big notes and illustrations; children's songs scored and graded for the D tinwhistle; written partially in easy-play notation, where the letter names of the notes are written inside the note heads, and partially in large standard notation; play-along CD contains every song in the book and serves as a guide; all recorded examples include solo whistle with multi-instrumental back-up. SYSTEM SPECS: Book and Audio CD.

Classical Baby Music Show (www.musicmotion.com): Baby conductor enters the stage; animal orchestra is tuned and ready; features short works of classical music and imaginative visuals of the title genre; conceptual animation set to classical and jazz standards; for baby through Pre-Kindergarten; running time thirty minutes. SYSTEM SPECS: Instructional DVD.

Classical Kids – A Symphony of Stories for All Ages Audio CDs and DVDs (www.childrensgroup.com/sections/classical/classical_index.html): Award-winning series introduces children and adults to classical music; a dramatic story, a little bit of history, and the world's best-loved classical music set the scene for fun-filled musical adventures. SYSTEM SPECS: Audio CD and Instructional DVD.

Classical Music Through Stories - Books and CDs (www.friendshiphouse.com): Set of four books; follow a modern interpretation of a classical song; music inspires imaginations as the tale progresses; story, music, and pictures creates a three-dimensional experience; each illustrated book is accompanied by a CD that features a recording of the classical piece; paperback; thirty-six pages each; for ages six-ten; Jupiter Cove (*Jupiter* from *The Planets Suite* by Holst); The Crazy Alien Ball (*A Night on a Bare Mountain* by Mussorgsky); William the Crackshot Kid (*Overture: William Tell* by Rossini); Billy Briggs Big on Skates (*The Moldau* from *Ma Vlast* by Smetana). SYSTEM SPECS: Book and Audio CD.

Classroom Music for Little Mozarts, Books 1 & 2 (www.alfred.com): Learn about music in the classroom and the Music Play Center; comprehensive approach; develops singing, movement, and listening skills; appreciation of musical styles and concepts; lesson plans for ten weeks; includes stories, visuals, and coloring pages; for ages four-six. SYSTEM SPECS: Book and Audio CD.

Clifford the Big Red Dog Musical Memory Games (www.interactiveclassics.com): Nineteen challenges; activities adapt according to user's progress; popular characters and voices from the hit TV show; automatic help; memory; problem solving; creativity. SYSTEM SPECS: Hybrid CD-ROM.

Discover Bach Three-Disc Set (www.interactiveclassics.com): Documentary; sixteen music jigsaw puzzles; nine reversed music jigsaw puzzles; sixteen melody puzzles; Bach and music trivia game; Bach, Baroque, and beyond interactive encyclopedia; early reading. SYSTEM SPECS: Audio CD, Instructional DVD, and Windows CD-ROM.

Disney's Little Einstein's (http://atv.disney.go.com/playhouse/littleeinsteins/music/index.html): Musical journeys to real-world destinations; sing, clap, pat, dance, laugh, and problem solve; learn about music, art, and teamwork; DVDs feature a revolutionary blend of animation, live-action footage, famous works of art, exciting classical music, and educational interactive games; for ages two-eight; approximately sixty minutes each. SYSTEM SPECS: Instructional DVD.

Easy Guitar Deluxe CD-ROM (www.interactiveclassics.com): Split-screen video showing both hands; lessons for acoustic and electric guitar; over sixty exercises and songs; built-in metronome and tuner; complete dictionary of over 1000 chords; print out chords and sheet music to practice. SYSTEM SPECS: Hybrid CD-ROM.

Easy Piano (www.interactiveclassics.com): Covers the basics; step-by-step video lessons; print out chords and easy tunes to practice; watch as an expert shows the right way to play; lessons and tunes at basic and advanced levels; pieces and chords to print and practice; complete guide to reading music; piano history and famous players; easy-to-follow lessons; main menu. SYSTEM SPECS: Hybrid CD-ROM.

Every Kid's Mozart Two-Disc Set (www.interactiveclassics.com): Orchestra Game; The Gazebo Game; Mozart Music Jigsaw Puzzles; The Castle Game; Truly Twisted Music Riddles; The Pond Game; Music Memory Game; The Musical Air Balloon Game; The Music Tree Game; The Finest Music Trivia; Interactive Encyclopedia of Musical Instruments; The Magic Flute Tale; Mozart's Biography for Kids; The Mozart Jukebox; Papageno's Magic Feathers; automatic help. SYSTEM SPECS: Audio CD and Windows CD-ROM.

Extreme Music Fun (www.disney.go.com): Mickey and friends warm up their voices with musical antics; "Mickey's Grand Opera," featuring Clara Cluck and Donald in a duet full of surprises; Goofy attempts to learn "How To Dance;" collection of eight Disney cartoons. SYSTEM SPECS: Instructional DVD.

Fortune Cookie Basic Skills CD-ROM (www.wrldcon.com/maestro/): Basic skill development for piano, vocal, and instrumental students; nine learning modules; tutorial explanations; drill and practice sequences; optional speech for pre-reading and special needs users; available for older and newer operating systems; for ages five to six. SYSTEM SPECS: Hybrid CD-ROM.

Fun With Composers Series (www.funwithcomposers.com): Interactive approach brings classical music to life; storytelling draws children into the world of classical music; nurtures the many ways in which children learn; fun visuals; imaginative stories; many opportunities for creative improvisation; promotes creativity by encouraging the child to create fun, imaginative characters and bring them to life through drama, song, creative movement, and instrumental play; caters to the many different needs of children; Teacher's Guides; Just for Kids Guides; for ages three-twelve. SYSTEM SPECS: Book, Audio CD, and Instructional DVD.

Hearing Music Hybrid CD-ROM (www.emediamusic.com/hmusic.html): Introduces a unique way to hear music as expressive communication; virtual playground features games; breaks musical concepts down to patterns and levels that pose a challenge to listeners; beginner to advanced; children learn to identify different parts of music; for ages eight and up. SYSTEM SPECS: Hybrid CD-ROM.

Hip Hop For Kids (www.hiphop4kids.net): Thirty-minute DVD/CD entertainment set introduces kids to Hip Hop; host Roger G has been featured with Jay Z; leads kid dancers through a fun Hip Hop workout; carefully designed warm up for kids; learn the latest Hip Hop steps from Melissa, Adia, Shani, Antoine, and Chi-Chi; stretch, dance, work out; CD has the song *The Hip Hop Bounce* to enjoy at home or at a party; for ages six-twelve; Parent's Choice Award. SYSTEM SPECS: Audio CD and Instructional DVD.

Hip Hop for Kids POP! LOCK! & BREAK! (www.hiphop4kids.net): DVD/CD entertainment set; Hip Hop Master Roger G takes students through the classic hip hop styles and the hottest new moves; kids learn to Pop, Lock, Shake and Break dance; great workout doing the Chingy, the Ponytail, The Uprock, and more; includes a soundtrack CD to play at a party or at home with friends; bonus chapters include hip hop performances by such greats as Roger G (who is featured in videos with Jay Z and has appeared with Def Comedy Jam and 106 & Park) and Ms. Twist and Poker; kid-friendly nutrition and workout segment to keep the junior rap set in top dancing form; one hour long; CD of soundtrack; for ages seven-sixteen. SYSTEM SPECS: Audio CD and Instructional DVD.

Hunk-Ta-Bunk-Ta (www.hunktabunkta.com): Music for children by platinum-selling and award-winning singer-songwriter Katherine Dines; songbooks and CDs; activity guides; performances; workshops; newsletter. SYSTEM SPECS: Book and Audio CD.

Instrumental Classmates 5-DVD Series (www.friendshiphouse.com): Entertaining, educational, musical adventure; interactive series developed to assist educators in introducing children to the major musical instrument families and the instruments that make music; host PJ has an intense love and knowledge of music; in each episode, PJ introduces a particular family of instruments in a fun and entertaining way; assisted by unique on-screen graphics called Brain Blasts that reinforce key points; for grades two-six. SYSTEM SPECS: Instructional DVD.

Interactive Classics Series CD-ROMs (www.interactiveclassics.com/educators_page1.htm): Music appreciation software for Kindergarten-Sixth Grade; Volume I Tchaikovsky's Nutcracker; Volume II Alice in Vivaldi's Four Seasons; Volume III Mozart's

Magic Flute; interactive musical CD-ROMs for elementary school students; variety of musical games, puzzles, riddles, animated encyclopedias, listening rooms, music trivia, and other educational music-related activities. SYSTEM SPECS: Windows.

Jim Gamble's Video Introduction to Classical Music (www.jimgamble.com): Award-winning puppeteer Jim Gamble presents marionette productions of five stories; set to the music of Grieg, Tchaikovsky, Humperdink, Saint-Saens, and Prokofiev; full color; each is thirty minutes long; for ages three and up. SYSTEM SPECS: Instructional DVD.

Juilliard Music Adventure CD-ROM (www.lentines.com): Interactive game for students geared towards developing music skills; elaborate animation; intriguing music problems must be solved in order to meet the game's objective: rescue the kidnapped queen by finding the keys to free her; music appreciation and elementary music theory concepts are presented; introduces rhythm, melody, and orchestration to aspiring young musicians. SYSTEM SPECS: Hybrid CD-ROM.

K. I. D. S. (www.ecsmedia.com): Keyboard Introductory Development Series: Getting Ready to Play; teaches beginning music concepts; objective is to reinforce concepts encountered by the young child in beginning music study which are adaptable to computer-based learning; select between the keys of C, G, or F; choose either letter names or solfege names to be displayed; for pre-school to grade three. SYSTEM SPECS: Hybrid CD-ROM.

Kids Can Play Guitar DVD (www.b2bmusicsales.com): Simple and effective method; guitar types; guitar parts; how to hold the guitar; fingering, chords, and chord diagrams; guitar tablature and how to read guitar music; tunes to play and songs to sing; full performances of country, rock, blues, and classical pieces; guitar trivia. SYSTEM SPECS: Instructional DVD.

Kids Can Play Keyboard DVD (www.b2bmusicsales.com): Simple and effective method for the younger keyboard player; sitting at the keyboard; naming the notes; fingering; reading rhythm; reading notes; playing tunes; scales and arpeggios; chords and songs; tunes include *Yellow Bird, Ode To Joy;* keyboard trivia; practice tips and more. SYSTEM SPECS: Instructional DVD.

Kids Can Play Recorder DVD (www.b2bmusicsales.com): Simple method for the younger recorder player; fingering; tonguing; reading music; tunes to play; tunes include *When The Saints Go Marching In, Go Tell Aunt Rhody, Jingle Bells;* clear explanations; easy to follow computer graphics. SYSTEM SPECS: Instructional DVD.

Kidsongs (www.kidsongs.com): Performances of favorite kids' songs, sung, danced, and acted by the Kidsong Kids; for ages two to ten; lyric booklet included with each half-hour DVD; twenty-four episodes include 300+ classics; includes: *A Day With The Animals, A Day At The Circus, A Day At Old MacDonald's Farm, I'd Like To Teach The World To Sing, Very Silly Songs, What I Want To Be, I Can Dance, I Can Bop With The Biggles,* and *Yankee Doodle Dandy;* also available: *The Kidsongs TV Show.* SYSTEM SPECS: Instructional DVD.

Kidtunes (www.pianopress.com): Includes thirty songs by award-winning singer-songwriters from the U.S. and Canada; fun and delightful mixture of musical styles (folk, bluegrass, country, rock); children's and adult's voices; over seventy minutes of family friendly entertainment; recorded and produced in Nashville and in other studios around North America; tunes are easy to listen to and sing along with; great for classroom use; accompanying songbook and activity guide includes lead sheets with lyrics, melody line, and chords; reproducible coloring pages and mazes; songs include *Rock 'n' Roll Teachers, School Is Cool, Addicted to the Dictionary;* for pre-school to fifth grade. SYSTEM SPECS: Book and Audio CD.

Make Mine Music (www.disney.go.com): Imaginative stories and music in Disney's eighth full-length animated classic; musically charged animated shorts featuring "Peter and the Wolf"; narrated by the voice behind Winnie the Pooh; also includes "Casey at the Bat," "The Whale Who Wanted to Sing at the Met," and "Johnnie Fedora and Alice Bluebonnet," the adventure of two hats who fall in love in a department store window. SYSTEM SPECS: Instructional DVD.

Make Music Come Alive Books and CDs (www.friendshiphouse.com): Colorful illustrations; engaging stories; accompanying CDs; introduction to classical music; includes *Carnival of the Animals, Pictures at an Exhibition, The Heroic Symphony, The Story of the Orchestra, Peter and the Wolf, Bach's Goldberg Variations, Gershwin's Rhapsody in Blue.* SYSTEM SPECS: Book and Audio CD.

Making More Music Hybrid CD-ROM (www.emediamusic.com/mmmusic.html): Kids become a composer, a musician, and the audience; learn the basics of rhythm, theme and variation; search the virtual encyclopedia; write and edit music with graphic interface; print and save compositions; play games that enhance musical understanding; choose from over two dozen instruments; conduct a virtual orchestra; draw notes on an animated screen; experiment with different instruments; assemble sections of a score; games and easy-to-use music-making tools; children are exposed to a creative learning experience that brings the musical heritage of Western culture to life; for ages eight and up. SYSTEM SPECS: Hybrid CD-ROM.

Making Music Hybrid CD-ROM (www.emediamusic.com/mmusic.html): Children learn the basics of musical composition at their own pace; after drawing notes on the screen, kids can manipulate them; learn about sixteen instruments from their sounds and shapes; melody and rhythm maker; variety of games and activities; for ages five and up. SYSTEM SPECS: Hybrid CD-ROM.

Melody Time (www.disney.go.com): Features seven classic stories, each enhanced with high-spirited music and characters; Donald Duck puts on a display of jazzy antics as the star of "Blame It On The Samba"; music becomes an adventure for a busy bumble bee in "Bumble Boogie"; meet a mischievous young tugboat in "Little Toot" and heroes of legend and myth in "Johnny Appleseed" and "Pecos Bill." SYSTEM SPECS: Instructional DVD.

Merry Christmas Happy Hanukkah – A Multilingual Songbook and CD (www.pianopress.com): Includes sixteen Christmas and sixteen Hanukkah songs arranged for elementary and intermediate-level piano students with duet accompaniments; guitar chords; lyrics in English, Hebrew, Spanish, German, French, and/or Latin. SYSTEM SPECS: Book and Audio CD.

MiDisaurus Eight-Volume CD-ROM Series (www.town4kids.com/us_ecom/products/midi_about.htm): Award-winning edutainment; musical dinosaur introduces music with animation, games, and songs to play and sing; on-screen keyboard; MIDI keyboard optional; user friendly; 510 activities; read, play, compose, and appreciate music; from simple to basic to advanced concepts; relates graphics or animated sequences with sound; instructions on screen and read aloud; grounding in music fundamentals; for private teacher and schools; accounts for up to 250 students; Volumes 1-8 include Notation, Rhythm, Instruments, and Composers; for ages four to eleven. SYSTEM SPECS: Hybrid CD-ROM.

Mr. Bach Comes to Call (www.friendshiphouse.com): Live-action, full color DVD tells the story of a young, present-day music student who gets an unexpected visit from the great composer; family entertainment; more than twenty excerpts of Bach's best-loved works; main feature is fifty-four minutes long; includes an additional fifty minutes of music from the award-winning "Classical Kids" series. SYSTEM SPECS: Instructional DVD.

Music Explosion and Music Mania (www.friendshiphouse.com): Award-winning, integrated early childhood curriculums; includes popular children's songs to help students learn across the curriculum; each set's units start off with a circle time song followed by easy-to-use ideas in reading, science, math, social studies, art, and music; accompanying CD includes all of the songs; convenient lesson plans; for ages three-seven; paperback. SYSTEM SPECS: Book and Audio CD.

Music Expressions DVDs (www.alfred.com): Literacy-focused music curriculum; includes a wide range of classroom resources for teachers of grades K-8; each lesson focuses on a particular set of music standards set forth in the National Standards for Arts Education; provides elementary school students with the curricular foundation needed for secondary-school music disciplines including band, orchestra, chorus, and jazz ensembles; spiral structure builds music skills cumulatively from class to class and year to year; embedded assessments, authentic recordings, diverse content. SYSTEM SPECS: Instructional DVD.

Music Games CD-ROM (www.alfred.com): Provides an innovative and fun way for piano students to learn important music theory concepts; includes note names, rhythm, intervals, music terms and more; entertaining, interactive software environment; seven fun, educational games that teach different aspects of music theory; for ages seven and up. SYSTEM SPECS: Hybrid CD-ROM.

Music Makers (www.friendshiphouse.com): Six episodes introduce children to the instrument families; instruments and their sounds; how they are played; character P.J. demonstrates each of these lessons through a collection of quirky scenarios and wild adventures that help foster and develop an interest in music; interactive activities and Web access to a musical terms video glossary; printable learning games and activities. SYSTEM SPECS: Hybrid DVD-ROM.

Musical Life of Gustav Mole (www.musicmotion.com): Musical mole family; includes a plush hand puppet of Gustav with his violin; two hardbacks, two CDs, and the hand puppet. SYSTEM SPECS: Book and Audio CD.

My Christmas Fun Songbook and CD (www.pianopress.com) Features eighty-eight Christmas songs by award-winning songwriters; traditional favorites, contemporary standards, and fun, new originals; spiral-bound for easy use; elementary to intermediate-level piano arrangements; includes guitar chords and lyrics; coloring pages. SYSTEM SPECS: Book and Audio CD.

My Electric Guitar Children's CD-ROM (www.emediamusic.com/myelectric.html): Animated character Rocky the Guitar leads lessons by Charles McCrone; covers the basics; tuning; learning about gear; reading music, playing songs, and more; animated fretboard shows where to put fingers as live recorded audio plays; with MIDI tracks, speed of music can be adjusted; automatic tuner, metronome, chord dictionary, and digital recorder; for ages nine and up. SYSTEM SPECS: Hybrid CD-ROM.

My Guitar Children's CD-ROM (www.emediamusic.com/myguitar.html): Animated character named Gary the Guitar leads kids through lessons; covers tuning, chords, reading music, playing songs, and more; animated fretboard shows where to put fingers as live recorded audio plays; with MIDI tracks, the speed of the music can be adjusted so student can learn at own pace; automatic tuner, metronome, chord dictionary, and digital recorder; for ages six and up. SYSTEM SPECS: Hybrid CD-ROM.

My Halloween Fun Songbook and CD (www.pianopress.com) Original Halloween songs by award-winning songwriters; spiral-bound; elementary to intermediate-level piano arrangements; includes guitar chords and lyrics; coloring pages, recipes, and more. SYSTEM SPECS: Book and Audio CD.

My Piano Children's CD-ROM (www.emediamusic.com/mypiano.html): Animated character Pam the Piano leads kids through lessons by Irma Irene Justicia, M.A.; covers the basics; learning notes, counting rhythm, playing chords, reading music, playing songs, and more; animated keyboard shows where to put fingers as live recorded audio plays; with MIDI tracks, the speed of the music can be adjusted so student can learn at own pace; metronome and digital recorder included; for ages six and up. SYSTEM SPECS: Hybrid CD-ROM.

My Violin Children's CD-ROM (www.emediamusic.com/myviolin.html): Animated character named Val the Violin leads lessons by Sabina Skalar; covers the basics; tuning; playing notes; reading music; playing songs; and more; animated fingerboard shows where to put fingers as live recorded audio plays; Finger Tracker listens to playing and shows whether fingers are on the right spot; with MIDI tracks, speed of music can be adjusted so student can learn at own pace; automatic tuner, metronome, and digital recorder; for ages six and up. SYSTEM SPECS: Hybrid CD-ROM.

Once Upon a Sound (www.clearvue.com): Meet the four families of instruments through lively stories, songs, and listening activities; illustrations; hear the tales of how each instrumental group began; meet the modern instruments with humorous songs to help remember their characteristics; for primary and intermediate ages; kit includes video, teacher's guide, and reproducible activity sheets; running time fifty-five minutes. SYSTEM SPECS: Instructional DVD.

Penn and Teller Present the Basics of Music Making (www.friendshiphouse.com): Educational and entertaining; animation, special effects and live performances used to teach melody with composer Alan Toussaint; rhythm with percussionist Max Roach; and texture with conductor Jo Ann Falleta; hosted by magic team Penn and Teller; for grades K-6; thirty minutes each. SYSTEM SPECS: Instructional DVD.

Perfect Harmony (www.disney.go.com): Boyhood friendship and the love of music overcome racial prejudice in South Carolina in the 1950s; Taylor, the star of his prep school's renowned, all-white boys' choir, and Landy, an orphaned black teenager with a gift for the blues, develop a friendship in spite of the racial barriers that divide the school and town; features uplifting music. SYSTEM SPECS: Instructional DVD.

Piano Mouse Goes to Preschool CD-ROM (www.pianomouse.com): Introduces young children to beginning music theory; covers the musical alphabet, notes, patterns, and instruments; learn about the lives and music of four great composers; easy to use; fully narrated. SYSTEM SPECS: Hybrid CD-ROM.

Playing Music Hybrid CD-ROM (www.emediamusic.com/pmusic.html): Child explores the expressive elements of the musical experience; allows children to play with expression in music and experience some of the joys and surprises these elements can bring; includes over twenty musical scores by eleven of the world's most famous composers; nine videos; interactive animation; games; glossary and more; for ages eight and up. SYSTEM SPECS: Hybrid CD-ROM.

Progressive Young Beginner Guitar Book 1 (www.learntoplaymusic.com): For young beginning guitarists; easy arrangements of over twenty favorite children's songs; introduces five notes and four easy chord shapes; illustrated in full color. SYSTEM SPECS: Book, Audio CD, and Instructional DVD.

Progressive Young Beginner Guitar 1 Giant Coloring Book (www.learntoplaymusic.com) Fun and enjoyable way to learn the guitar for the young student; illustrations to color; very easy arrangements of over twenty favorite children's songs while introducing the student to five different notes. SYSTEM SPECS: Book, Audio CD, and Instructional DVD.

Progressive Young Beginner Keyboard Book 1 (www.learntoplaymusic.com) Suitable for all types of electronic keyboard; graded lesson by lesson method for the younger student; very easy arrangements of over twenty favorite children's songs; introduces five notes with the right hand and three one finger chords with the left hand; illustrated throughout in full color. SYSTEM SPECS: Book, Audio CD, and Instructional DVD.

Progressive Young Beginner Keyboard 1 Giant Coloring Book (www.learntoplaymusic.com) Fun and enjoyable way to learn the keyboard for the younger student; each page contains beautiful illustrations for the child to color; very easy arrangements of over twenty favorite children's songs. SYSTEM SPECS: Book, Audio CD, and Instructional DVD.

Progressive Young Beginner Piano 1 Giant Coloring Book (www.learntoplaymusic.com) Beautiful illustrations for the child to color; easy arrangements of favorite children's songs; introduces five notes on each hand using the white keys only. SYSTEM SPECS: Book, Audio CD, and Instructional DVD.

Progressive Young Beginner Piano Book 1 (www.learntoplaymusic.com): Carefully graded method for the younger student; very easy arrangements of over twenty favorite children's songs; introduces five notes on each hand using the white notes only; beautifully illustrated throughout in full color. SYSTEM SPECS: Book, Audio CD, and Instructional DVD.

Progressive Young Beginner Recorder 1 Giant Coloring Book (www.learntoplaymusic.com): Fun and enjoyable way to learn the recorder for the younger student; each page contains beautiful illustrations for the child to color in as they progress through the book; very easy arrangements of favorite children's songs; introduces five notes for the left hand only. SYSTEM SPECS: Book, Audio CD, and Instructional DVD.

Progressive Young Beginner Recorder Book 1 (www.learntoplaymusic.com): Carefully graded, lesson-by-lesson learning method for the younger student; very easy arrangements of favorite children's songs; introduces five notes for the left hand only; beautifully illustrated throughout with full color; contains ten lessons. SYSTEM SPECS: Book, Audio CD, and Instructional DVD.

Rabbit Ears Storybook Collection: Stories through Song (www.clearvue.com): Includes the music of celebrated artists and stories; twenty-four DVDs; award-winning programs; covers music from jazz to rock to classical to reggae; features narration by well-known celebrities; students and teachers will realize how much music contributes to storytelling. SYSTEM SPECS: Instructional DVD.

Reading Rainbow Eight DVD Series (www.friendshiphouse.com): Music-themed videos; host LeVar Burton takes kids on a musical journey through New York City in Berlioz the Bear; Zin! Zin! Zin! A Violin features a visit with young musicians at the Juilliard School of Music; Ty's One Man Band explores the city sounds of rap, doo-wop, jazz, and salsa; Barn Dance! travels to the hills of Tennessee for a look at bluegrass music and clog dancing; Follow the Drinking Gourd explores the history, heroes, and music of the African-American culture which emerged from slavery; Borreguita and the Coyote teaches kids about Mexican-American music, art, stories, and language; in Abiyoyo, a South African folktale is retold and sung by its author, Pete Seeger, and LeVar reveals some of the ways a story can be told with music; in Hip Cat explores jazz music and examples of improvisations in music, literature, art, and dance; thirty minutes each. SYSTEM SPECS: Instructional DVD.

Sesame Street Elmo's Musical Adventure (www.musicmotion.com): Discover how music and imagination can tell a story; Baby Bear goes to hear the Boston Pops Orchestra perform Peter and the Wolf and imagines his Sesame Street friends as characters in the Prokofiev story; he and Elmo learn the secret to making beautiful music. SYSTEM SPECS: Instructional DVD.

Sesame Street Fiesta (www.musicmotion.com): Songs in English and Spanish; singing and dancing with the Sesame gang; guest performers include Linda Ronstadt and Celia Cruz; running time thirty minutes. SYSTEM SPECS: Instructional DVD.

Sesame Street Get Up and Dance (www.musicmotion.com): Join Big Bird's dance party; do The Jelly, The Airplane, Birdland Jump, The Grouch, and more; features tap-dancer Savion Glover, jazz vocalist Joe Williams, and cameos by Garth Brooks, Kevin Kline, the Neville Brothers, and others; thirty minutes. SYSTEM SPECS: Instructional DVD.

Sesame Street Let's Make Music (www.musicmotion.com): Explore the world of music and rhythm with the Sesame Street gang and the cast of STOMP, the international percussion sensation; Telly loses his tuba and thinks he will never make music again; crew shows that everyday items, like Oscar's trash can, can make music; running time forty minutes. SYSTEM SPECS: Instructional DVD.

Sesame Street Music Maker (www.interactiveclassics.com): Visit with Elmo and make songs with special musical stickers; sing-along with the Muppets; sing Karaoke; explore the World of Sound at the zoo, the city streets, the home, and the farm; join Elmo and Ernie on guitar, Grover on keyboards, and Cookie on drums for a jam session; get down and boogie at Studio 543; compose songs with Elmo's help. SYSTEM SPECS: Windows.

Singing Coach Kidz (www.carryatune.com): Offers children ages six and up an interactive way to learn to sing on pitch and in rhythm while having fun; animated vocal coaches teach kids the basics of breathing as well as how to sing their favorite songs through a complete and interactive singing course. SYSTEM SPECS: Windows.

Song Play (www.singers.com): For classroom teachers and music specialists; each songplay section includes a detailed step-by-step teaching process, opportunities for cross-curricular connections, and a listing of recommended literature readings; includes a coaching CD with musical prompts and song demonstrations in various keys by an adult solo voice for use in preparing each lesson; over forty songs. SYSTEM SPECS: Book and Audio CD.

Super Duper Music Looper for PC (www.sonycreativesoftware.com/products/childrenssoftware.asp): Fun and exciting way for kids to create music; for kids ages six to ten and beyond; can be used at home for furthering a child's musical experiences, or by schools for exploring the fundamental basics behind music creation; instruments and sound effects; kids can record vocals, e-mail songs; pick from nine instruments, mix them together, and create a complete song in minutes; animations as they dance to the music; create music with recordings of actual musicians; over 700 studio-quality sounds and instruments; drums, keyboards, guitars, horns, percussion, and more; Cool

FX effects and other sounds; plug in a mic and record vocals. SYSTEM SPECS: Windows.

Superstart! Piano for Kids (www.interactiveclassics.com): Tempo bar adjusts to match learning speed; left and right hand movements taught separately and together; ladybug follows the notes as the tune is played back; look up musical terms in the glossary; well-known tunes; sheet music with finger positions and notes to color; introduction to the basics of general music theory; puzzles; games; drag and drop exercises with fun sounds and animations to support the lessons; touch and click piano helps kids learn where the notes are on the piano keyboard and the staff. SYSTEM SPECS: Hybrid CD-ROM.

Teaching Kids to Sing, Volumes One and Two (www.singers.com): By Chris and Carole Beatty; interactive training tool for teachers, parents, choir directors, and children; clear presentation of material; entertaining format makes learning fun; includes Posture, Breathing, Tone, and Warming Up the Voice. SYSTEM SPECS: Instructional DVD.

The Biscuit Brothers: Go Make Music! (www.biscuitbrothers.com): Wonderful way to get a child interested in making music; each DVD features three full episodes from the hit PBS program; sing and dance along with the Emmy nominated show that uses music education as a gateway for children to explore interpersonal and community values, and to think critically about the world around them; for ages one to eight. SYSTEM SPECS: Instructional DVD.

The Mozart Effect - Music for Children (www.mozarteffect.com): Series of audio recordings for babies and children based on the best-selling books, "The Mozart Effect" and "The Mozart Effect for Children," by noted author, teacher and musician, Don Campbell; designed to achieve a particular effect, including enhancing intelligence, inspiring creativity, or exploring body movement and motion; combines up-to-date medical and psychological research in creativity and intelligence to provide a rich listening and learning experience for children. SYSTEM SPECS: Audio CD.

The Music Factory DVD Set (www.friendshiphouse.com): Six thirty-minute programs explain melody, harmony, rhythm, tonality and more; short segments profile famous composers; introduces families of instruments; features young musicians performing; classroom segments show teachers and students having fun with musical concepts; for Grades K-4. SYSTEM SPECS: Instructional DVD.

The Ultimate Nutcracker Three-Disc Set (www.interactiveclassics.com): Complete Nutcracker Ballet by the Mussorgsky Theater of Opera and Ballet; The Nutcracker Suite and Highlights CD by the London Symphony Orchestra; award-winning Nutcracker Music Game CD-ROM featuring: The Orchestra Game; The Nutcracker Music Jigsaw Puzzle Game; The Nut House Game; The Music Memory Game; The Flying Instruments Game; Find Me on a Tree Game; The Funky Monkey Game; The Children's Album Game; The Nutcracker Music Trivia Game; Interactive Encyclopedia of Musical Instruments; The Nutcracker Tale in a Nutshell; A History of the Nutcracker Ballet; Tchaikovsky's Biography for Kids; The Nutcracker and Children's Listening Room. SYSTEM SPECS: Audio CD, Instructional DVD, and Windows CD-ROM.

The Wheels on the Bus DVD (www.musicmotion.com): Movement, singing, and instruments for class room participation; *Dem Bones* sung by Bob Barner adds a lesson on the bones and their functions; title song by Paul O. Zelinsky; *Over in the Meadow* by John Langstaff; *I Know an Old Lady Who Swallowed a Fly* by Rose Bonne and Alan Mills; *I Want a Dog* by Dayal Kaur Khalsa; *The Chinese Violin* by Madeleine Thien; running time forty-five minutes. SYSTEM SPECS: Instructional DVD.

This Is Music! Series (www.alfred.com): For teaching music in a classroom setting with young children, ages preschool-grade three; each book and CD set has eight thematic lessons; reproducible pages. SYSTEM SPECS: Book and Audio CD.

Tubby the Tuba (www.tubbythetuba.com): Includes the classic characters in a colorful picture book; hear Paul Tripp's performance complete with full orchestration; hardcover; thirty-two pages. SYSTEM SPECS: Book and Audio CD.

Tunes Buddies Music Makers (An Introduction to the Instruments): (www.alfred.com): Special features; musical glossary of terms; beginning music theory instruction; printable coloring pages; interactivity. SYSTEM SPECS: Instructional DVD.

Wee Sing (www.weesing.com): Singing, dancing, and drama based on the popular series; platinum-selling albums and videos; *Best Christmas Ever!, The Big Rock Candy Mountain, Grandpa's Magical Toys, King Cole's Party, Marvelous Musical Mansion, Sillyville, Together, Train,* and *Under the Sea.* SYSTEM SPECS: Book, Audio CD, and Instructional DVD.

Children's Music Web Sites

A to Z Kids Stuff www.atozkidsstuff.com Name That Tune; link to the American Symphony Orchestra League; instruments; lesson plans and games.
America's Story—Children's Songs www.americaslibrary.gov/cgi-bin/page.cgi/sh/kidsongs History and stories.
Andy Z www.andyz.com/home.htm Children's artist; CDs; shows; school performances.
Babyuniversity.com www.babyuniversity.com Songs and more for the very young.

Best Children's Music.com
www.bestchildrensmusic.com Children's music for parents and teachers.

Bratz www.bratz.com Fashion dolls; CDs; movies.

Buck Howdy www.buckhowdy.com Cowboy songs for kids; activities; store.

Burl Ives www.burlives.com Classic American balladeer; songs for children; gospel; holidays.

Cathy Fink and Marcy Marxer www.cathymarcy.com Grammy winning children's artists and songwriters; CDs and instructional books.

Children's Music Network www.cmnonline.org Music for children; information; resources; links.

Children's Music Web www.childrensmusic.org Nonprofit organization; resources; information; links; guide to children's music online; children's concert calendar; database of musicians; children's radio list; music education.

Children's Music Workshop www.childrensmusicworkshop.com Instrumental music instruction to public and private schools throughout the greater Los Angeles area.

Children's Music www.childrensmusic.co.uk UK-based Web site for children's music.

Coloring.com www.coloring.com Coloring pages.

Creating Music www.creatingmusic.com By Morton Sobotnick; place for kids to compose music; musical performance; music games and puzzles.

Dan Zanes danzanes.com/pages/news.php Children's music artist; CDs; videos; tour.

Dave Kinnion www.songwizard.com CDs; concerts; information for parents and teachers.

Disney disney.go.com/index All things Disney; music; graphics.

Dr. Toy www.drtoy.com Guide to children's products; links; awards.

Free Kids Music www.freekidsmusic.com Songs by contemporary artists as well as traditional songs.

International Kids' Space www.kids-space.org To make a difference in the future educational use of the Internet and in understanding each other.

JazzKids Music Program www.jazzkids.com Useful information about jazz.

Jeanie B Music www.jeaniebmusic.com Children's songs for kids, teachers, and students; teacher's guides; concerts; news and reviews.

Kid Pan Alley www.kidpanalley.org Inspiring kids to be creators, not consumers; founded by Paul Reisler; songwriting workshops in schools.

KIDiddles Mojo's Musical Museum: Complete Song List www.kididdles.com/mouseum/allsongs.html Lyrics to hundreds of children's songs and lullabies; stories; games; contests; search by title.

Kids Camps www.kidscamps.com Directory of camps.

Kids Games www.kidsgames.org Games for first- through twelfth-graders; links.

Kids Music Planet www.kidsmusicplanet.com Pod casts; children's music radio stations.

KidsCom www.kidscom.com Creative for kids.

Kidtunes www.pianopress.com Popular children's CD with accompanying songbook and activity guide; thirty songs by award winning children's songwriters and performers.

Kidz Bop kidzbop.com/ CDs of children singing current pop hits; videos and more.

Kindermusk www.kindermusik.com Early childhood music instruction.

Kool Songs www.koolsongs.com Personalized children's songs.

Laurie Berkner www.twotomatoes.com/site/index.php Children's artist; CDs; tours.

Mama Lisa's World www.mamalisa.com/world/ Children's songs and rhymes of all nations.

Mister Rogers' Neighborhood www.pbs.org/rogers Online version of the popular TV series.

Music for Young Children www.myc.com Music education program for children.

Music Together www.musictogether.com Early childhood music workshops.

Music4KidsOnline www.music4kidsonline.com Everything musical for children.

Musik Garten www.musikgarten.org Early childhood music education workshops.

NIEHS Kids' Pages www.niehs.nih.gov/kids/musicchild.htm or www.niehs.nih.gov/kids/music.htm MIDI files and lyrics to children's songs.

Nursery Rhymes www-personal.umich.edu/~pfa/dreamhouse/nursery/rhymes/ Alphabetical listing of nursery rhymes.

Nursery Songs www.nursery-songs.com/songs_and_engravings.htm Lyrics and pictures to many nursery songs.

PBS Jazz Kids www.pbs.org/jazz/kids/ Children's jazz Web site.

PBS Kids Web Site www.pbskids.org Links to many children's television programs.

Pete Seeger www.peteseeger.net/ Legendary songwriter and activist; children's songs.

Play Music www.playmusic.org Introduces kids to the instruments of the orchestra.

Preschooleducation.com www.preschooleducation.com/song.shtml Music and songs.

Radio Disney www.radiodisney.com Children's instructional software, DVDs, videos.

Raffi www.raffinews.com Children's recording artist.

San Francisco Symphony Kids Site www.sfskids.org Instruments of the orchestra; music lab; concerts.

Sandman Records www.sandmanrecords.net/ Featuring award winning children's songwriter Lanny Sherwin; lullaby CDs and more.

Screen It! www.screenit.com Reviews for parents.

Songs for Scouts www.macscouter.com/Songs/index.html Campfire songs, silly songs, and chants for leaders.

Strike a Chord www.strikeachord.com Dynamic, interactive, character building music program for elementary students by Karl and Jeanne Anthony.

The Children's Group www.childrensgroup.com Titles include: *Classical Kids, Song of the Unicorn, The Mozart Effect.*

The New York Philharmonic Kidzone www.nyphilkids.org Musician's Lounge; Composers Gallery; Composers Workshop.

The Teacher's Guide to Children's Songs www.theteachersguide.com/ChildrensSongs.htm Lyrics and MIDI files to children's songs.

The Uncle Brothers www.unclebrothers.com/index.html Family friendly children's music; concerts and more; featuring Tommy Gardner and Danny Quinn.

The Wiggles www.thewiggles.com.au/us/home/ Popular Australian children's music artists; CDs; DVDs.

Yahooligans www.yahooligans.com Web guide for kids; music links and more.

Young Composers www.youngcomposers.com Compositions of kids, teens, and young adults.

4
Music Theory Fundamentals—Ear Training and Aural Skills Software, Instructional Media and Web Sites

Aural Skills Trainer (www.ecsmedia.com): Intervals; basic chords; seventh chords; student records; diagnostic information; progress reports; completion scores; advanced. SYSTEM SPECS: Hybrid CD-ROM.

Auralia (www.risingsoftware.com): Aural training course; includes Cadences, Chords, Chord Progression, Cluster Chords, Interval Recognition, Interval Singing, Jazz Chords, Meter, Pitch, Rhythm Dictation, Rhythm Elements, and Scales; each subject area has several levels of difficulty; lower levels for beginners; testing features; give test a name, save, and use again; for beginner to advanced, ages twelve and up. SYSTEM SPECS: Macintosh; Windows.

Berklee Music Theory: Book 1 (www.berkleepress.com): Covers pitch, rhythm, scales, intervals, chords, harmony, and notation; fundamental concepts; how to read music; how to form scales; major and minor keys; how music works. SYSTEM SPECS: Book and Audio CD.

Berklee Music Theory: Book 2 - Fundamentals of Harmony (www.berkleepress.com): Focuses on harmony; triads, seventh chords, inversions, and voice leading for jazz, blues, and popular music styles; lead sheets. SYSTEM SPECS: Book and Audio CD.

Challenge Musicus (www.ecsmedia.com): Second title in series; rests are introduced; 9/8, 12/8, 7/8, and 7/4 meters; understanding of the relative lengths of notes and rests as well as combinations of tied notes; move note blocks of rhythms to complete lines of music; hear completed lines played at end of game. SYSTEM SPECS: Hybrid CD-ROM.

Clef Notes (www.ecsmedia.com): In a drill, students use the mouse or arrow keys to move the note to match the indicated note name; student must successfully complete ten tries in a row to place a designated note on the treble, bass, tenor, or alto staff; student is prompted to try again if a mistake is made until the correct answer is given; help menu shows the name for all notes on a particular staff; timed games encourage students to improve the speed at which they accurately identify notes on the staff; students choose note names by selecting from a musical alphabet displayed at the bottom of the screen; at the end of each game a screen displays the percent of correct answers and the time in seconds; program automatically makes a record for each student tracking the time and score for the first and last game and an average for all games played; Hall of Fame displays top ten scores; student may choose one clef or all clefs; instructor may view or print the roster or individual records; program is copy protected; a backup copy cannot be made; for all music students ages six to fourteen; reading skills. SYSTEM SPECS: Hybrid CD-ROM.

Cloud 9 Music (www.ecsmedia.com): Educational music software; children explore pitch, duration, and rhythm in four different scenarios; Freeform Flyer leaves small clouds at various altitudes to assist learning about pitch through unstructured compositional techniques; Pitch Pilot concentrates on understanding relative pitch differences; Head To Tail offers introductions, verses, and endings of a variety of compositions that children can freely arrange into their own compositions; Rhythm Drops explores beats and rests. SYSTEM SPECS: Hybrid CD-ROM.

Computer Activities (www.pbjmusic.com): Note identification; half and whole steps; intervals; major/minor five-finger positions; triads; scales in C, F, G, D, and B-flat major and A minor; 2/4, 3/4, 4/4, and 6/8 meters; eighth notes; cadences; major key signatures; scales; key signatures in A, E, D, G, C, and

B-natural and harmonic minor; major and minor intervals; major and minor triads and inversions; diminished triads; primary and secondary triads; dominant seventh chords; 2/2, triplets, sixteenth notes; analysis of repetition, sequence, and imitation in music. SYSTEM SPECS: Hybrid CD-ROM.

Counterpointer (www.ars-nova.com/cp/): First software ever to offer evaluation of both species and free counterpoint; can serve as a self-contained introduction to counterpoint and as a tool to accompany counterpoint textbooks; includes notation tools for entering and saving music and more than 150 user-controllable style rules; species counterpoint exercises based on the Fux examples (2, 3, and 4 parts); species counterpoint exercises based on a cantus firmus invented by the computer; exercises in realizing Roman numerals in 4-part vocal harmony based on Bach examples; exercises in realizing figured bass in 4-part vocal harmony from Bach examples; free counterpoint in 2-8 voices using choice of style rules; onscreen manual offering a basic introduction to counterpoint and explanations of each rule; compositions can be saved, heard, printed, and exported as MIDI files; student file is the same type as those used by *Practica Musica*. SYSTEM SPECS: Macintosh; Windows.

Dolphin Don's Music School (www.dolphindon.com): Nine games, each with ten skill levels that can be set up for treble, alto, tenor, or bass clef; in Read Notes students identify notes on the staff; in Hear Notes two notes are played and student identifies the second; a one-measure rhythm is shown with one hidden note in Rhythm Read; in Hear Rhythm a short rhythm is played and student selects the correct written version from the three displayed; in Read Keys students identify the correct key for the key signature shown; Interval and Chord games are similar; games may be paused; examples may be replayed or wrong answers tried again, but timer continues to run; final score and the highest recorded score are displayed; games begin by clicking on the Start button; computer counts backward from ten; points are scored equal to the amount of time left when the player enters a correct answer; answers are selected from a multiple-choice list or group of possible notes; a large Yes appears for correct answers, along with a rippling chime sound; in hearing drills, the correct response is played again as reinforcement; for wrong answers, a visual No, Try Again appears; each game advances to the next level upon achieving a score of ninety or more points; progress tallied by giving a rank, which has both a number and an ocean-related name such as Seaweed or Octopus; highest rank is Dolphin; students can view their scores any time; teacher can view or print all students' scores by entering a password; maximum of fifteen players is recorded; a well-sequenced program; complete set of theory and ear-training skills for the

young student; for music students ages six to ten; reading skills; rhythm skills; video resolution is restricted to 640 x 480 pixels; most all multimedia computers default to higher resolutions, requiring users to reset the video and restart Windows. SYSTEM SPECS: Windows.

Ear Challenger (www.ecsmedia.com): Listening skills, hand-eye coordination; pitches are played by the computer, each represented by a different color key; student plays back pitches on the MIDI keyboard; correct answer is shown in response to right or wrong answers; helps student develop good listening habits; students visualize the notes and hear the intervallic movement among the pitches; seven levels of difficulty based on the number of pitches presented; students advance at their own pace; one or two players may play at the same time; Hall of Fame records student scores; self-explanatory; quick and easy installation; aural-visual music game designed to increase player's ability to remember a series of pitches as they are played by the computer; for beginners, all ages. SYSTEM SPECS: Windows.

Ear Training Coach (www.adventus.com): Well-rounded and entertaining combination of assessment and constructive activities, graded by year of music study; carefully selected supply of music content; ear-training and sight-reading tests; interactive activities; five disk series that will take the student through a 10-grade curriculum in ear training and sight-reading. SYSTEM SPECS: Windows.

Ear Training Expedition Parts 1, 2, and 3 (www.trailcreeksystems.com): Tutorial introductions; elementary, intermediate, and advanced; practice drills; listening skills games; high and low pitch recognition; ascending and descending note patterns; recognizing major and minor triads and scales; identifying intervals; general theory concepts. SYSTEM SPECS: Windows.

Early Music Skills (www.ecsmedia.com): Introduces four basic musical concepts: line and space recognition, numbering lines and spaces on the staff, direction of melodic patterns, and steps and skips; multiple-choice answers; if a MIDI keyboard is used, answers are played on the keyboard; for beginners, grades K-3. SYSTEM SPECS: Hybrid CD-ROM.

EarMaster Pro (www.earmaster.com): Ear-training tutor; graded exercises; design own course; covers intervals, scales, chords, rhythm, and melody. SYSTEM SPECS: Windows.

EarMaster School (www.earmaster.com): Premium edition of Earmaster Pro; extra features for classroom use; customized reports; overview results. SYSTEM SPECS: Windows.

Earope Ear Training (www.cope.dk): Ear-training software; aural training of scales, chords, intervals, melody, rhythm, inversions, progressions, and more. SYSTEM SPECS: Windows.

Ear Power Ear-Training Program (www.earpower.com/earpower.htm): To be used as a daily routine; compact and easy to use; many features; for anyone, from the hobbyist to the professional musician; downloads; used in over sixty countries. SYSTEM SPECS: Windows.

Echos (www.ecsmedia.com): Sight-reading skills, rhythm and note reading; students echo musical examples of notes from bass C to treble C on the staff, and rhythms up to eighth notes at the keyboard; dotted quarter notes in Level II; ability to identify key signatures up to five flats and sharps is assumed; six sharps and flats for Level II; sight-reading/ear-training combination; students hear each example before they play it; wrong notes are highlighted; student is given three tries to play correctly; when played correctly, the program gives a praise word; if played incorrectly three times, program states, No, but let's go on; holds up to fifty names and passwords; keeps record of last time student used program only; gives percentage of correct responses for each section; Music Reading, Sight-Reading Boxes, and Mystery Boxes; repetition of musical examples; for students ages ten to eighteen. SYSTEM SPECS: Windows.

Elements of Music (www.ecsmedia.com): Beginning music program for children or adults; random drills; includes naming major and minor key signatures and naming notes on the staff or keyboard; progress tests and reports for each drill; instructor file for access to student records; for beginners, grades K-adult. SYSTEM SPECS: Hybrid CD-ROM.

Essentials of Music Theory Volumes 1-3 (www.alfred.com): Interactive way to learn music; for classroom or individual instruction; exercises reinforce concepts; narration, musical examples, and animations; ear-training exercises with acoustic instruments and scored reviews; Glossary of Terms; spoken pronunciations; audio and visual examples of each term; scorekeeping; record keeping; custom tests; Student and Educator versions available; for ages eight to adult. SYSTEM SPECS: Hybrid CD-ROM.

Explorations in Music (www.kjos.com): By Joanne Haroutounian; comprehensive theory series which integrates ear training, listening lessons, compositions, and analysis; seven levels of work/textbooks span beginning through advanced levels of theory; carefully sequenced writing and listening assignments; series parallels the Music Teacher's National Association and affiliated state organizations' theory guidelines; can be used with all piano or instrumental methods and in all class situations; CD and cassette recordings available with each Student Book provide recorded examples for ear training and musical analysis using examples of piano and instrumental solo, chamber, and orchestral literature; Teacher's Guides give teaching tips, learning objectives, and Extend and Excel enrichment activities to fit the needs of each student. SYSTEM SPECS: Books and Audio CD.

Explorations: Music Fundamentals (www.mhhe.com/catalogs/1559346981.mhtml): Music fundamentals course with textbook and computer software; intended for students with no previous knowledge of music or computers; covers note recognition, intervals, diatonic melody, rhythm and meter, triads, voice leading, key signatures, seventh chords, scales (major, three forms of minor, and modal), and chord function; textbook provides written explanations, suggested activities for exploring musical elements on the computer, creative exercises, written exercises, and a step-by-step guide on using the software program and MIDI keyboard; software explores each musical subject; practice sessions and tests separated into written theory skills and ear-training skills; students enter musical information using the computer by writing notation with the mouse, entering answers by clicking on interval names, solfege and so on, and playing music on a MIDI instrument or the on-screen keyboard; practice session mode includes detailed feedback; in test mode, students respond to a series of questions and are told how many have been attempted and how many were correct; Music Editor for music writing assignments and compositions; can collect test scores; automatic record keeping; easy-to-use comprehensive music fundamentals program; adult beginners may use the software and textbook for self-instruction; tool bar for entering music notation; choice of solfege or musical alphabet for identifying melodies; exploration mode for learning each subject; for music students, ages ten to adult; listening skills; rhythm skills; music notation. SYSTEM SPECS: Macintosh.

Functional Harmony (www.ecsmedia.com): Drill packages; displays grand staves with four-voice chords; key signatures provided; select answers by moving cursor through boxes identifying chord types; covers borrowed and altered chords, diatonic sevenths, and secondary dominants; cannot hear sound on a single-voice Apple II computer; MIDI keyboard required to hear sound; in Section 1, the user practices analyzing basic chords in major or minor keys and in root position or inversions; Section 2 presents diatonic seventh chords; Section 3 presents secondary dominants; Section 4 covers borrowed and altered chords; instructor may select the number of problems in each quiz; when using the MIDI option, the chord displayed on the screen will play through the audio device to aid in chord identification; for high school students and above. SYSTEMS SPECS: Hybrid CD-ROM.

Gary Ewer's Easy Music Theory CD-ROM (www.musictheory.halifax.ns.ca/): Veteran teacher, composer, and arranger; twenty-five critical music theory lessons on double CD-ROM set; complete music theory course; over 600 pages of materials. SYSTEM SPECS: Book and Hybrid CD-ROM.

Groovy Music (www.sibelius.com): Music software for elementary school children ages five to eleven years; Groovy Shapes teaches basic music concepts to children ages five-seven; Groovy Jungle introduces children ages seven-nine to notes and notation, ostinato, major and minor, and simple music terms, and allows them to experiment with composition; in Groovy City, kids ages nine-eleven learn more about notation, and complete more complex listening tasks; teaches the basics of sound, rhythm, pitch, and composition using pictures and animation, progressing to the study of simple notation as well as major and minor scales; integrate technology into teaching; control children's screens and workflow in a networked environment; makes time with students more efficient; uses the latest educational standards and teaching methodologies; students learn at their own pace and own level; uses an imaginative virtual environment where students arrange shapes, characters, and images to create music; can be used on a single computer, whiteboard, or network; vocal instructions guide children, so no reading is required. SYSTEM SPECS: Macintosh; Windows.

Harmonic Progressions (www.ecsmedia.com): Designed to help the user in analysis of functional harmony; includes root position chords, inverted chords, and the V7, embellishing sixth chords and the V7, diatonic sevenths, and cadence patterns; over 200 chord sets; practice analyzing chords, harmonic dictation, and aural identification; user must detect quality of chord sounded harmonically as well as position and voicing of chord; correct answer given at end of example; for advanced students, high school to college. SYSTEM SPECS: Hybrid CD-ROM.

Inform (www.ecsmedia.com): Analysis of musical form while listening to and viewing music; understand the impact of seeing a musical score while analyzing its musical structure; user can mark-up the score as they listen, stopping and starting the playback; includes high-quality music performances from the Naxos record catalogue as MP3 files and scrolling graphical music scores. SYSTEM SPECS: Hybrid CD-ROM.

Interactive Musician (www.alfred.com): Pitch Training, Sight-Reading, and Rhythm; designed to enhance recognition of intervals, chords, and scales, and improve ability to sight-read; various types of rhythms; self-paced program identifies strengths and weaknesses; multiple levels to choose from; customize own level with control over the content and difficulty of the program. SYSTEM SPECS: Hybrid CD-ROM.

MacGAMUT (www.macgamut.com): Drill and practice in aural identification and notation skills; Intervals, Scales, Chords, Melodic and Harmonic Dictation; easy to use; interaction with computer is done with mouse; can control the number of times a student may hear a particular example; printout of student statistics; for high school to college music students. SYSTEM SPECS: Hybrid CD-ROM.

MiBAC Music Lessons I and II (www.MiBAC.com): Comprehensive music theory and ear-training program; eleven drill types: Note Names, Circle of Fifths, Key Signatures, Major/Minor Scales, Modes, Jazz Scales, Scale Degrees, Intervals, Note-Rest Durations, Intervals Ear-Training, and Scales Ear-Training; each drill has five to eight levels of difficulty; user can choose to work with treble, bass, alto, or random choice of clefs; in some drills, students enter answers by clicking on a note on the on-screen keyboard or by playing a key on a MIDI keyboard; in other drills, students enter answers by clicking an answer button with the mouse; students may select any of the eleven drills as well as the level of difficulty by clicking one of eleven buttons at the top of the screen; a black diamond shape appears above an answer box for a correct answer and the number of correct responses, the number of tries and a percentage score are shown on the screen throughout the exercise; incomplete drills show a zero percent; complete drills show a score for each level and an average score for all levels for that drill type; requires no musical background. SYSTEM SPECS: Macintosh; Windows.

Music Ace (www.harmonicvision.com): Includes Music Ace and the Music Doodle Pad; colorful graphics; animated conductor named Maestro Max teaches music fundamentals from the staff through key signatures and scales; six students may be enrolled at one time; students select their name, then one of the twenty-four lessons or twenty-four correlating games; instruments may be presented in treble and bass, treble only, or bass only; lesson control buttons include: skip forward, skip backward, volume control, pause/resume, and a game button; each lesson and game has several sections to complete to win the game; games include "The ABC's of the Piano Keyboard," "The ABC's of the Treble Staff," "Half Steps and Whole Steps," and "Introduction to Major Scales"; "Lesson Progress Tracking" shows how many times a user has completed each lesson section; "Game Progress" screen shows if a game was won as well as the total score; "High Scores" section allows users to see who has the highest score on each of the twenty-four games; with the "Music Doodle Pad" users can listen to and change sample melodies or create and hear their own; sample songs are selected and played by clicking the "Jukebox" button; new melody can be created by dragging a "face"; melodies can be heard on six different instruments: piano, guitar, oboe, trumpet, marimba, and synthesizer; each "face" sings as it is played; introduction to music fundamentals; for beginning music students ages eight to adult. SYSTEM SPECS: Hybrid CD-ROM.

Music Ace 2 (www.harmonicvision.com): Standard notation, rhythm, melody, key signatures, harmony, intervals, and more; Maestro Max; choir of Singing Notes; over 2,000 musical examples; new instruments; introduction to music fundamentals and theory; twenty-four lessons; games; composition tool; tracks progress through lessons and games; Music Doodle Pad. SYSTEM SPECS: Hybrid CD-ROM.

Music Ace Deluxe (www.harmonicvision.com): Combines thirty-six of the music lessons from *Music Ace* and *Music Ace 2* into a carefully sequenced, single product. SYSTEM SPECS: Hybrid CD-ROM.

Music Ace Maestro (www.harmonicvision.com): Combines all forty-eight lessons from *Music Ace* and *Music Ace 2* with *Maestro Manager*, a suite of student assessment and curriculum management tools. SYSTEM SPECS: Hybrid CD-ROM.

Music Flash Cards (www.ecsmedia.com): Important music material in a drill-and-practice format; nine lessons; Section 1 includes names of notes, rhythm values, and rhythm value equivalents; Section 2 includes major scales, minor scales, modal scales, and key signatures; Section 3 includes intervals and basic chords; user evaluation displayed at the end of each lesson; for beginner to early advanced, grades K-9. SYSTEM SPECS: Hybrid CD-ROM.

Music Skill Builder (www.ecsmedia.com): User decides what to include and omit from each set of questions; interactive music software program that lets the user determine the material to be presented. SYSTEM SPECS: Hybrid CD-ROM.

Music Study (www.musicstudy.com): Ear-training and music theory instruction software; downloads. SYSTEM SPECS: Windows.

Music Terminology (www.ecsmedia.com): Five programs for improving student's knowledge of music terminology; Glossary of Terms, Categories of Terms, True/False Test, Multiple-Choice Test, and Fill-In Questions; programs randomly select questions from a pool of over one hundred terms; summary of terms to be reviewed is displayed at the end of each program; for beginner to intermediate, grades 5-12. SYSTEM SPECS: Hybrid CD-ROM.

Music Theory Builder (www.ecsmedia.com): Identify visually or aurally major, minor, diminished, and augmented intervals as well as major, minor, diminished, and augmented chords; options to choose from including selection of inversion and clef for the drill; program features student evaluation and record keeping. SYSTEM SPECS: Hybrid CD-ROM.

Music Theory Drill and Practice (www.wrldcon.com/maestro/index.html): Topic specific; three traditional drill and practice programs for upgrading skills in naming notes, recognition of intervals, and identifying chromatic structures; advanced. SYSTEM SPECS: Macintosh; Windows.

Music Theory for Dummies (www.dummies.com): Covers note value and counting notes; treble and bass clefs; time signatures and measures; naturalizing the rhythm; tempo and dynamics; tone, color, and harmonics; half steps and whole steps; harmonic and melodic intervals; key signatures and circles of fifths; scales, chords, and their progressions; elements of form; music theory history; CD demonstrates ideas with musical excerpts on guitar and piano. SYSTEM SPECS: Book and Audio CD.

Music Theory Series Levels 1 and 2 (www.wrldcon.com/maestro/index.html): Two tutorial programs to teach an actual course in music fundamentals; electronic equivalent of a fundamentals or theory method which would accompany most keyboard, band, orchestra, or choral programs; for grades three-seven. SYSTEM SPECS: Macintosh; Windows.

Musical Stairs (www.ecsmedia.com): Interval reading; screen displays an interval in the treble or bass clef; student reproduces the interval at the MIDI keyboard; ten problems in each session; scoring is based on the number correct out of ten; Hall of Fame for the top ten scores; covers intervals within one octave on the white keys; for kindergarten through grade three. SYSTEM SPECS: Hybrid CD-ROM.

Musicus (www.ecsmedia.com): Students complete measures in a given meter with music blocks; five levels of difficulty; players are not required to understand the rhythmic notation, only to fit the blocks of notes into a given space; falling note blocks of rhythm must be put into measures of specific meters; student selects the space for the note block to fall by pressing a button; another note appears at the top of the screen for placement; each game is timed and the speed that notes fall can be adjusted at the beginning of each session; total points are accumulated by completing lines of rhythms with the note blocks; each note offers a different point value that is added to the total score; user has the option to hear their completed rhythmic lines at the end of the game; for elementary to middle-school students. SYSTEM SPECS: Hybrid CD-ROM.

MusIQ Challenger Game (www.adventus.com): Beginner to advanced students can analyze their musical intelligence in a strategy game; understand the relationships between musical devices; prepare for the study of composition and harmony; levels range from beginner to advanced; all genres played. SYSTEM SPECS: Windows.

Musique (www.ecsmedia.com): Self-paced exercises for theory instruction; ear-training and theory drills present immediate feedback; maintain achievement scores for student and instructor; interval and chord analysis, harmonic dictation, aural identification of chord function within a chord series, keyboard topography, note placement, scales and modes, and over one hundred basic music terms; for advanced, high school to college. SYSTEM SPECS: Hybrid CD-ROM.

Musition (www.risingsoftware.com): Educational music theory package; drill-based teaching; covers Scales, Intervals, Instrument Range, Note Reading, Advanced Clefs, Key Signatures, Scale Degrees, Symbols, Terms, Musical Concepts, Chord Recognition, Meter Recognition, Rhythm Notation, and Transposition; customize to needs; set up tests; define contents of test; extensive reporting features; twenty built-in reports. SYSTEM SPECS: Windows.

Note Speller (www.ecsmedia.com): Players identify words created by on-screen staff notation; each game has a ten-example quiz; clef options include treble, bass, grand staff, alto, and upper or lower ledger lines; game speed options are adagio, moderato, or allegro; word length can be short (three to four letters) or long (up to seven letters); user clicks the on-screen Answer button, the example disappears and the user types the correct spelling of the notational word with the computer keyboard or plays the alphabetical spelling of the word on a MIDI keyboard; Continue button is clicked when finished; if word is spelled correctly, points are awarded based on the time it takes to answer; negative points are given if an incorrect answer is given; higher points for using faster game speeds, but not for using longer words or ledger lines; if the user runs out of time on an example but gives a correct answer, no points are awarded; no second rides for incorrect answers; up to ten student names can be listed in the Hall of Fame; four Halls of Fame include Treble, Bass, Treble and Bass (grand staff), and Alto; Help menu includes the sayings Every Good Boy Does Fine, Great Big Dogs Fight Animals, and All Cows Eat Grass for identifying grand staff lines and spaces; alphabetical spelling also appears to the right side of the staves; alphabetical note identification; easy to use; on-screen graphics; for beginners, grades K-6. SYSTEM SPECS: Hybrid CD-ROM.

Perfect Pitch Ear Training Super Course (www.perfectpitch.com): Ear-training instruction series for musicians of all instruments; learn multiple aural skills. SYSTEM SPECS: Book and Audio CD.

Piano Mouse Music Theory FUNdamentals (www.pianomouse.com): Basic foundation for beginning music students; introduction to keyboard basics; sixteen lessons and games; review tests and games; four ear-training lessons; introduction to basics; keyboard, pitch, and musical alphabet; treble clef and bass clef notes; note and rest values; time signature and counting; sharps, flats, and naturals; enharmonic notes, half steps, and whole steps; five finger pattern. SYSTEM SPECS: Hybrid CD-ROM.

Pitch Challenger (www.ecsmedia.com): Program to improve pitch-matching and pitch discrimination skills; The Explorer section presents two pitches to be matched visually and aurally; The Challenger randomly plays two pitches to be judged in tune, sharp or flat; The MultiPitch Challenger requires the user to judge each of several pitches sharp, flat, or in tune; visual feedback reinforces learning to tune and match pitches; student scores and records can be saved and printed. SYSTEM SPECS: Hybrid CD-ROM.

Play It by Ear (www.alfred.com): Recognize, identify, and play single notes, melodies, scales, chords, and intervals; six levels; customize to fit specific needs; visual feedback with on-screen keyboard or guitar fret board; tracks progress; ear-training/dictation program appropriate for beginning theory classes through advanced college classes. SYSTEM SPECS: Windows.

Practica Musica (www.ars-nova.com): Comprehensive music-literacy training; includes textbook, Exploring Theory with Practica Musica, with tutorial and references to specific activities; to reinforce classroom and studio learning or to be used as an independent study package; each learning activity has four levels of difficulty; includes Pitch Matching, Reading and Dictation; Rhythm Matching, Reading and Dictation; Pitch and Rhythm Reading and Dictation; Scales and Key Signatures; Interval Playing, Spelling, and Ear Training; Chord Playing, Spelling, and Ear Training; Chord Progression Ear Training; Melody Writing and Listening; students can select the musical elements they wish to practice in one of several clefs; answers are entered with a MIDI keyboard, an on-screen keyboard, or guitar fretboard or computer keyboard; assumes a certain level of musical skill for students at Level One of each activity; difficulty of exercises presented changes with the student's success; students earn points toward a mastery goal; shows student progress toward goal during each practice session; points are displayed in a colored box that matches a chart on the title page of the program when student masters an activity; instructors can create custom exercises using the Melody Writing activity or by using Songworks; Student Files can be used if multiple students use the program on one computer; interactive; beginner to advanced, middle or high school and college theory courses. SYSTEM SPECS: Macintosh; Windows.

Rhythm Divide (www.ecsmedia.com): Compose unique electronic musical pieces by sectioning off notes in the game field; assign specific instruments sounds as well as percussion instrument sounds; as notes collide with other objects, will hear piece begin to develop. SYSTEM SPECS: Hybrid CD-ROM.

Rhythm Performance Test (www.ecsmedia.com): Test for tapping a steady beat and rhythm patterns; for children ages four to twelve; screening tool; research and assessment. SYSTEM SPECS: Windows.

Smack-A-Note (www.ecsmedia.com): CD-ROM; speed up note recognition and reflexes; note-letter critters creep out across the screen; "smack" if they match the note displayed on a music staff; includes Solfege option. SYSTEM SPECS: Hybrid CD-ROM.

Super Ear Challenger (www.ecsmedia.com): Aural-visual game designed to increase a student's memory of a series of pitches played by the computer; based on a twelve-note chromatic scale, a major scale, and a minor scale; each pitch is represented visually by a color on the on-screen keyboard; for beginner to intermediate. SYSTEM SPECS: Macintosh.

Super Musicus (www.ecsmedia.com): To help learn time values of notes; whole, half, quarter, eighth, sixteenth, and triplets; combinations of tied notes of equal values and tied notes of unequal value or dotted notes; how these note values relate to different musical meters, including 6/8 and 5/4; follow-up to Musicus. SYSTEM SPECS: Hybrid CD-ROM.

Symbol Simon (www.ecsmedia.com): Game-based drill format; nautical metaphor; two games; drills symbols, terms, rhythm values, time signatures, and note names; displays definitions and examples; Hall of Fame records highest scores; for beginners, grades three-six. SYSTEM SPECS: Windows.

Tap-It (www.ecsmedia.com): Aural and visual rhythmic examples at four levels; each level includes three levels of difficulty and seven tempo choices; students play rhythms at the computer keyboard; quiz and percentage scores are given at the end of each level; automatic scorekeeping; final quiz is the "All-Pro" level; ear training and sight-reading; for beginners, all age groups. SYSTEM SPECS: Hybrid CD-ROM.

Tap-It II (www.ecsmedia.com): Sequel to Tap-It; more difficult rhythm patterns; syncopation, eighth, and sixteenth note values; actual note heads are introduced; help menu; three levels include new rhythms; Tutorial; Listening and Tapping; Reading and Tapping; each level has a quiz of twenty measures; seven different tempo settings; full record keeping; for intermediate to early advanced. SYSTEM SPECS: Hybrid CD-ROM.

Tap-It III (www.ecsmedia.com): Most advanced in the series; 5/8, 7/8, and 10/8 meters are included with three different difficulty levels; each level includes a non-stop quiz of twenty measures; recordkeeping; different tempo setting options; for advanced level users. SYSTEM SPECS: Hybrid CD-ROM.

The Art of Listening (www.clearvue.com): Develop active listening skills; numerous types of music and sound; explanations of melody, harmony, timbre, and rhythm; many examples from numerous forms; for beginners, grades four through nine. SYSTEM SPECS: Instructional DVD.

Theory Games (www.alfred.com): Each game covers a different topic, from note names and intervals to musical terms and rhythms; to be used with Alfred's Basic Piano Library; may also be used with other methods; games include: Name That Key, Note Names Race, Chord Name Race, Cross the Road, Melodic Intervals, Counting Game, Scale Game, Carnival Fun, Invader, and Composer Game; for beginners, all ages. SYSTEM SPECS: Hybrid CD-ROM.

Music Theory Fundamentals— Ear Training and Aural Skills Web Sites

Absolute Pitch www.silvawood.co.uk/pitch-intro.htm Ear-training application for Windows to help acquire absolute or perfect pitch, the ability to name any note played, without the aid of a reference note; perfect pitch differs from relative pitch, where a musician can identify notes by knowing the intervals between them.

Big Ears www.ossmann.com/bigears/ The original online ear trainer.

Center for the History of Music Theory and Literature www.music.indiana.edu/chmtl Joint venture of Indiana University's School of Music and the Office of Research and the Univ. Graduate School.

Chord Wizard www.chordwizard.com/theory.html Music theory tutorials.

Clarion www.red-sweater.com/clarion/ Fine-tune musical ear; customizable quiz partner for interval ear training; Macintosh only.

Complete Chords www.completechords.com Roedy Black's chord posters; products; free information for songwriters; reference charts.

Ear Power www.earpower.com/index.php Ear training site offers software tools to help musicians at any level; *Ear Power, Sight-Singer, Metronome, Vocal Express,* and *EarSteady;* Windows only.

Earplane http://earplane.com/modules/earplane_main/ Ear training practice; identify intervals, melodies, rhythms, chords, and modes.

EMusic Theory www.emusictheory.com/ Designed to help students of music theory improve their proficiency; basic skills.

Gary Ewer's "Easy Music Theory" www.musictheory.halifax.ns.ca Free music theory lessons on the Internet; scales, chords, triads, etc.

GNU Solfege www.solfege.org Free ear training program; recognize melodic and harmonic intervals; compare interval sizes; sing the intervals the computer asks for; identify chords; sing chords; scales; dictation; remembering rhythmic patterns; Windows only.

Good-Ear.com www.good-ear.com Offers ear-training and theory skills.

Guitar and Bass Ear Training www.byear.com Ear training software course for guitar and bass players; Windows only.

Hearing and Writing Music www.rongorow.com
  Professional training; self-study.
I Breathe Music www.ibreathemusic.com Music
  theory; tips; tutorials; reviews.
Journal of Music Theory Home Page www.yale.edu/jmt
  Published twice a year by Yale University.
KBA Software www.musicstudy.com Ear training and
  music theory software; includes *Pitch ID, Rhythm
  ID, Chord ID, Spell ID*, and *Melodic ID;* demo
  downloads; Windows only.
Listen www.imaja.com/listen/index.html Ear-training
  software program; matching and multiple-choice
  exercises; Macintosh only.
Metronimo-Educational Musical Games
  www.metronimo.com Music theory; classic
  composers; musical culture; instruments of the
  symphony orchestra; in English and French.
MIBAC Music Lessons
  www.mibac.com/Pages/Theory/Main_Theory.htm
  Music theory reference.
Music Arrangers www.musicarrangers.com/star-theory
  Music theory explanations.
Music Theory
  library.thinkquest.org/15413/theory/theory.htm?tqs
  kip1=1&tqtime=0907 Basics of music theory.
Music Theory Online
  www.societymusictheory.org/mto/ Online resource
  for music theory.

Musical Flash Cards
  http://courses.wcupa.edu/frichmon/usetech/musical
  flashcards/aaaindex.html Practice identifying notes
  in all clefs.
MusicTheory.net www.musictheory.net Free online
  music theory lessons; drills; trainers;
  comprehensive coverage of all music theory topics.
Practical Music Theory
  www.teoria.com/exercises/index.htm Identify and
  write scales, chords, and intervals.
Rhythm Is Easy www.rhythmiseasy.com Flash cards for
  learning rhythm sequentially.
Sibelius Academy
  www2.siba.fi/Kulttuuripalvelut/theory.html Music
  research and music theory.
THEMA www.uga.edu/~thema Music Theory of the
  Middle Ages; transcriptions of Latin theoretical
  treatises on music theory.
Theory Time www.theorytime.com Comprehensive
  music theory course; believes a music theory
  course is essential for any music student.
Treblis Software www.treblis.com/ear_training.htm
  Seven ear training lessons; Windows only.
Yahoo! Entertainment:Music:Theory
  www.yahoo.com/Entertainment/Music/Theory
  Music theory site.

Music Appreciation—Music History and Composers— Music Education Software, Instructional Media and Web Sites

Accent on Composers (www.alfred.com): Reproducible music appreciation course; twenty-two featured composers including bios, portraits, and musical style; time line; listening examples. SYSTEM SPECS: Book and Audio CD.

Amazing Music (www.friendshiphouse.com): Entertaining and educational DVDs feature the Dallas Symphony Orchestra in special young people's concerts; Emotions in Music shows how music can evoke specific feeling; Pictures in Music examines the pictorial and descriptive abilities of music; Families of the Orchestra is a tour of the orchestra, with members demonstrating how each instrument works; Jazz features jazz greats Billy Taylor and Roy Hargrove exploring the history of jazz; selections range from "Star Wars" to Beethoven and Tchaikovsky; kids participate in the programs; full color and stereo; for the whole family. SYSTEM SPECS: Instructional DVD.

Ars Antiqua: Sounds of a Distant Tyme (www.musicmotion.com): For students grades three-eight; Medieval and Renaissance periods; filmed live before a student audience; costumed musicians perform vocal and instrumental music of the era on period instruments; informative narration; audience participation in the singing and accompaniment; hear madrigals, canons, and more from the 13th century through Henry VIII's own compositions sung and played on the krummhorns, a consort of recorders, rauschpfeifes, and more; two thirty-minute videos; manual; activities and quizzes. SYSTEM SPECS: Instructional DVD.

Art and Music DVD Series (www.clearvue.com): Interactive series; exploration through history from the medieval era through surrealism; shows parallels between art and architecture and music; humanities in a new light; series of eight includes the following titles: MEDIEVAL ART AND MUSIC: The art, architecture, and music of the era were created for and governed by the Church; evolution of art and music during Medieval times; RENAISSANCE ART AND MUSIC: Renaissance artists and composers, influenced and inspired by the new humanistic philosophy, developed new forms and techniques from painting with oils to four-part polyphony; BAROQUE ART AND MUSIC: Examples of the dramatic effect of art from Caravaggio to Rembrandt; the energetic, expressive style of music from Frescobaldi to Handel; the drama of opera; EIGHTEENTH CENTURY ART AND MUSIC: Developments in painting and sculpture parallel music's changing styles; comic opera, Viennese classical style, emerging Romanticism; art and music of the French Revolution; comparison between the works of David and Beethoven; ROMANTICISM IN ART AND MUSIC: Berlioz's Requiem and Delacroix's Liberty Leading the People; numerous works of music and art that are related; IMPRESSIONISM IN ART AND MUSIC: Impressionist art and music; parallels between the artist's use of color and light and the composer's use of instrumentation; TWENTIETH CENTURY ARTISTIC REVOLUTIONS: Significant artistic developments; abstraction in art and atonality in music emerge, followed by Fauvism and Cubism; SURREALISM IN ART AND MUSIC: Parallels between the artistic methods of Ernst, Magritte, and Dali and the musical works of Satie, Bartok, and Cage; all titles are in hybrid format; for intermediate to advanced, grades seven-college. SYSTEM SPECS: Instructional DVD.

Beethoven Sound and Fury (www.musicmotion.com): Explores his life, work, and legacy through extensive interviews with Issac Stern, Kurt Masur, and others; hear extended performances of his greatest works; running time fifty minutes. SYSTEM SPECS: Instructional DVD.

Broadway: The American Musical 3-DVD Set (www.pbs.org/wnet/broadway/): Hosted by Julie Andrews and seen on PBS; six-part series tells two stories including the 100-year history of the American musical theater and its relationship to 20th-century American life; includes facts, stars, still photos, archival footage, first-person accounts, on-camera interviews, and songs; scenes from *Show Boat, Porgy and Bess, My Fair Lady, Chicago, West Side Story, Rent* and many more; over three hours of bonus material not seen on television; total running time approximately ten hours. SYSTEM SPECS: Instructional DVD.

CD Time Sketch (www.ecsmedia.com): To facilitate listening and analyzing music; create listening lessons with any audio CD; for fundamentals and appreciation courses, or music history courses at any level; annotated listening format can be applied to classes and activities and the music performance curriculum; glossary of terms includes dynamics, tempo markings, stylistic expression markings, music symbols, and standard musical terms. SYSTEM SPECS: Windows.

Classical Destinations Mixed Media Kits (www.classicaldestinations.com): Go to Europe without leaving the classroom; unique set of six mixed-media DVDs; introduces the world of classical music to young people in grades five-twelve; covers the music and cultures of six European countries; each destination kit includes a DVD and CD-ROM with footage of each country's landscape; audio and MIDI files featuring interactive quizzes and specially-designed orchestral scores to introduce key concepts of classical music; includes Austria, the Czech Republic, Germany, Italy, Russia, and Scandinavia. SYSTEM SPECS: Instructional DVD and Hybrid CD-ROM.

Classical Music for Dummies (www.dummies.com): Covers the various forms of classical music, from symphonies to string quartets; what goes on behind the scenes and on stage; how to recognize, by sight and by sound, the instruments that make up an orchestra; components of classical music, from rhythm to harmonic progression; CD containing over sixty minutes of masterpieces compiled especially for the book; CD also includes a demo version of the Angel/EMI Classics For Dummies multimedia interface to use on a Windows-based PC or Macintosh computer. SYSTEM SPECS: Book and Enhanced CD.

Classical Orchestra Notes for Windows (www.hoptechno.com/classic.htm): Almost 2,000 program notes, many with complete vocal text in their original language with English translations; 500 text-audio links; read about a piece and hear music examples of timeless masterpieces; CD-ROM; full-text search; portraits of over 500 composers; picture library and text covering scores of instruments; hypertext classical glossary with hundreds of music terms; information on the world's greatest conductors and music directors. SYSTEM SPECS: Windows.

Decades of Dance (www.halleonard.com): Journey through decades of dance with John Jacobson; step-by-step visual instructions for over seventy-five different dances in a number of styles from the 1920s through today; booklet included with a complete list of steps and historic background of the styles presented; for all ages. SYSTEM SPECS: Instructional DVD.

Every Note Counts – Instruments of the Orchestra (www.musicmotion.com): Meet the families of instruments with a live orchestra of both students and professionals; student audience interacts; conductor John Sinclair, with the help of the performers, demonstrates and explains how the orchestra interacts as a team and the role of the conductor; each interactive kit has two live-action thirty-minute videos; teacher's manual; activities and quizzes; for grades three-twelve. SYSTEM SPECS: Instructional DVD.

Famous Music Stories (www.musicmotion.com): Hear the tales and the beautiful music these stories have inspired; each kit features two works with the narrated story, colorful illustrations, and musical excerpts; online resources, including a complete teacher's guide, reproducible worksheets, and an answer key; for elementary through middle school; includes *Hansel and Gretel* (Humperdinck) and *The Firebird* (Stravinsky), twenty-two minutes; *Swan Lake* (Tchaikovsky) and *Midsummer Night's Dream* (Mendelssohn), twenty minutes; *William Tell Overture* (Rossini) and *Sleeping Beauty* (Tchaikovsky), thirty minutes; *Aida* (Verdi) and *The Barber of Seville* (Rossini), twenty-six minutes; *Scheherazade* (Rimsky-Korsakov) and *The Magic Flute* (Mozart), twenty-four minutes; *The Nutcracker Suite* (Tchaikovsky) and *Peer Gynt Suite* (Grieg), twenty minutes. SYSTEM SPECS: Instructional DVD.

Gramophone Classical Good CD Guide DVD (www.musicsales.com): Edited by Emma Lilley; over 3,500 reviews of classical CDs and DVDs written by the critics of Gramophone; each review is rated so that readers can see at a glance the best disks in each repertoire area; includes suggested basic library, composer biographies, and critics' appraisals of the world's finest musicians; includes CD sampler of music by favorite composers. SYSTEM SPECS: Instructional DVD.

Great Composers and Their Music DVDs (www.clearvue.com): Six-volume series covers the most influential men in classical music history; teaches students about their childhood, musical experiences, and evolution into great composers; narrator relates interesting stories about each musical master; viewers listen to famous works throughout; student host prefaces each program with general information about the featured composer, as well as some of his more recognizable pieces; by learning about the lives of these great composers, students will better understand the influence of their works and will better appreciate the enduring qualities of their music; Further Learning Web site supplements each program, providing learning objectives, Internet resources approved for content, an online teacher's guide, and more; Johann Sebastian Bach; George Frideric Handel; Wolfgang Amadeus Mozart; Ludwig van Beethoven; Franz Joseph Haydn; Franz Schubert; for all music students, ages six-eighteen. SYSTEM SPECS: Instructional DVD.

Hansel and Gretel (www.halleonard.com): 1954 feature set to Englebert Humperdinck's classic 1893 opera; stop-action animation and hand-sculpted dolls and sets create fantasy legend; Grammy nominated; over thirty scene selections; composer biography; story synopsis; seventy-two minutes. SYSTEM SPECS: Instructional DVD.

History of Music Volumes 1 and 2 (www.musicmotion.com): Survey of the Western classical tradition; presented in historical context; graphics and illustrations; survey of non-Western music and the role of music in early and modern civilizations; covers musical concepts such as polyphony, homophony, tonality, and form; teacher's guide includes a booklet of program notes, full text of the narration, a glossary, and complete identification of all works performed; divided into four sections for classroom convenience; for grades seven-twelve; running time ninety minutes each. SYSTEM SPECS: Instructional DVD.

Instruments of the Orchestra (www.clearvue.com): Hosted by musician and educator Stephen Titra; videos introduce orchestral instruments; combines interviews with school-age musicians with a dramatic formal concert; each segment highlights a different family of instruments: woodwinds, brass, or percussion; each family is demonstrated by a group of young performers from the Green Bay Youth Symphony Orchestra, who share details of their lives and their love of music; students will meet the players, not just as musicians, but as real kids; for both general music teachers and for classroom teachers without a music background. SYSTEM SPECS: Instructional DVD.

Instruments of the Symphony Orchestra CD-ROM (www.clearvue.com): Select instrument and view summary of its history and development; identify instruments by appearance, sound, and musical capability; how to hold and play each instrument; music; colorful photography; detailed narration; for beginners, grades 7-12. SYSTEM SPECS: Macintosh; Windows.

Introduction to Music: Let's Go to a Concert! (www.clearvue.com): Visit a variety of concerts and concert settings; learn how to dress for the occasion, rules of behavior, and how they can participate in the event; covers indoor and outdoor venues; children's concerts; parades; classical, jazz, and folk performances; and more; introduction to live music. SYSTEM SPECS: Instructional DVD.

Introduction to Music: Let's Go to a Concert! (www.clearvue.com): Features informative narrative segments and classroom activities; learn music basics such as rhythm, melody, and tempo; the four families of musical instruments; how music functions in human culture; the wide variety of musical styles that exist across time and place; see students exploring, creating, and responding to music. SYSTEM SPECS: Instructional DVD.

Is It Music? (www.clearvue.com): Nurtures valuable skills in music analysis and discrimination; includes informative historical segments and two in-depth musical field trips; master class with saxophonist Odeon Pope; explores the traditions of American folk music with a street musician; topics covered include harmony and fugue, jazz improvisation as a musical form, and the social and individual meanings of music; outlines a range of musical forms, functions, and traditions. SYSTEM SPECS: Instructional DVD.

Leonard Bernstein's Young Peoples Concerts on DVD (www.leonardbernstein.com): From 1958 through 1973, Leonard Bernstein and the New York Philharmonic gave audiences these many wonderful concert experiences; telecast around the world, the Young People's Concerts created a generation of music lovers; winner of multiple Emmy, Peabody, and Edison awards; set of twenty-five hour-long concerts on nine DVDs; programs include *What Does Music Mean?*, *What is Melody?*, *What is American Music?*, and more. SYSTEM SPECS: Instructional DVD.

Marsalis on Music Four DVD Set (www.friendshiphouse.com): Young peoples concert series; Wynton Marsalis presents a lively and informative four-part program: "Why Toes Tap" on rhythm; "Listening for Clues" on form; "Sousa to Satchmo" on jazz; and "Tackling the Monster" on practice; filled with wit and music by the Wynton Marsalis Jazz Orchestra and the Tanglewood Music Center Orchestra; features Seiji Ozawa and Yo-Yo Ma; for all ages; four DVD set. SYSTEM SPECS: Instructional DVD.

Meet the Music Makers (www.clearvue.com): Spotlights each instrument family and its key instruments; in each program, a member of the instrument group explains the history of its family and illuminates the modern instrument members and their sounds; student host introduces each program, while a young audience listens; to teach instruments and music concepts; Further Learning Web site supplements each program, providing learning objectives, Internet resources approved for content, an online teacher's guide, and more. SYSTEM SPECS: Instructional DVD.

Meet the Musicians Five DVD Set (www.meetthemusicians.us): Actor/pianist Dennis Kobray portrays Bach, Mozart, Beethoven, Gershwin, and Scott Joplin; drama and powerful piano performances; viewer is drawn into the composer's world of hardship, sacrifice, and ultimate triumph; each video is approximately fifty minutes long; for all ages. SYSTEM SPECS: Instructional DVD.

Mozart's The Magic Flute Story (www.halleonard.com): English narration; sung in the original German; story of Prince Tamino and Princess Pamina, young lovers who use the powers of a magic flute to battle the forces of evil that threaten to keep them apart; lavish opera; forty-two minutes. SYSTEM SPECS: Instructional DVD.

Intermediate Music Appreciation Series (www.clearvue.com): Cultivates in students a greater understanding of and appreciation for classical masterpieces; series of five DVDs presents famous compositions set to classic footage, from the Southwest to space to history; host discusses information about the composer and guides students through the sections of the featured composition; learn more about well-known pieces and the visual sides of music; Further Learning Web site supplements each program, providing learning objectives, Internet resources approved for content, an online teacher's guide, and more. SYSTEM SPECS: Instructional DVD.

Music Appreciation Course: Intermediate Level (www.clearvue.com): Interactive, two-part program; each part briefly explains the scientific principles of sound; historical tour of the musical changes and achievements of the Baroque, Classical, Romantic, And Modern Eras; part one focuses on rhythm and melody and part two concentrates on dynamics and tone; students will hear the music of Bach, Beethoven, Handel, Vivaldi, Haydn, and Copland; uses a variety of musical instruments to demonstrate essential musical concepts; menu allows users to watch the disc glossary of key terms; teacher's guides for each of the two sections enhance the ideas found in the program and aid in content integration. SYSTEM SPECS: Instructional DVD.

Music Appreciation Course: Primary Level (www.clearvue.com): Designed by music educators especially for primary-grade students; Stephen Titra uses a collection of instruments to explore melody, rhythm, and dynamics; relates concepts to selections from the classical repertoire and to his own music and art; students are invited to participate in singing, hand clapping, and other activities; easy-to-use kits improve students' knowledge of music, enhance their listening skills, build their self-confidence in creative expression, and encourage music appreciation; reproducible worksheets reinforce the skills conveyed in the program and are included in the teacher's guides; activity suggestions, project ideas, and discussion topics. SYSTEM SPECS: Instructional DVD.

Music Composer Quiz CD-ROM (www.ecsmedia.com): Twenty questions randomly selected from a pool; users have three chances to answer a question correctly before the answer is displayed; instructor may edit or print any of the one hundred quiz questions; feedback is given at the end of each quiz session; student records are retained; for grades 6-college. SYSTEM SPECS: Hybrid CD-ROM.

Music Curriculum Connections (www.clearvue.com): Each program provides teachers with fresh ideas to increase music appreciation, literacy, vocabulary, sequencing, and other essential early learning skills; narration and demonstrations; fun and multidimensional activities; Further Learning Web site supplements each program, providing learning objectives, an online teacher's guide, and more. SYSTEM SPECS: Instructional DVD.

Music Factory (www.musicmotion.com): Six part elementary and middle school program sequentially lays a foundation of music knowledge and appreciation; hosts, children, and guest performers; each DVD introduces musical concepts with activities, dramatic skits, demonstrations, and experiments; fifty-five page Teacher's Guide includes outlines, activities, references, resources, glossary, and illustrated index of instruments arranged by families; thirty minutes each; set includes: *Vol. 1: What is Music?; Vol. 2: Rhythm Basics; Vol. 3: Tone, Dynamics, Pitch, Duration, Timbre; Vol. 4: Scales; Vol. 5: Melody; Vol. 6: Harmony.* SYSTEM SPECS: Instructional DVD.

Music from the Inside Out DVD (www.musicfromtheinsideout.com): Cinematic exploration of the magic and mystery of music told through the stories, passion, and artistry of the 105 musicians of the Philadelphia Orchestra; jazz, bluegrass, salsa, classical, and world music interwoven with the musicians' personal stories; for all ages; running time ninety minutes. SYSTEM SPECS: Book, Audio CD, and/or Instructional DVD.

Music History Review: Composers CD-ROM (www.ecsmedia.com): Test knowledge of composers; Renaissance to twentieth century; select quiz from ten categories; multiple-choice format; feedback; coordinated with A History of Western Music, 4th ed., by Grout and Palisca (published by W. W. Norton); student records; for beginners, grades 6-college. SYSTEM SPECS: Hybrid CD-ROM.

Music in Time Series (www.musicmotion.com): Authoritative and comprehensive history of Western music; running time sixty minutes each; VIBRATIONS AND PAGAN RITES - Chronologically backward from Ligeti to Gregorian chant; demonstrates how ageless and universal music-making is; depth of understanding of music history determines appreciation for the art; excerpts from many works; THE FIRST SECULAR MUSIC – Covers the early music of the Eastern churches to the Christian liturgy to the birth of secular song; excerpts from Gregorian, Hebrew, and Greek chants through Landini, Dunstable and Dufay; THE RENAISSANCE - Follows the patronage of the

Dukes of Burgundy and the Kings of France and the continued influence of the church; music, like philosophy, moved away from elaborate formality to purer forms; includes Binchois, Ockeghem, Josquin des Pres, Palestrina, de Lassus, Gabrieli, Taverner, and more; THE GOLDEN AGE - Covers the wealth of music during the age of Elizabeth I in England; the emergence of opera in Italy and France; madrigals; includes the music of Byrd, Purcell, Monteverdi, Lully, Morley, and more; LUTHER AND THE REFORMATION - Covers the impact of the reformation on the history of music; the work of J.S. Bach, church organs, chorale singing; includes choral, organ, string, flute, chamber ensemble, and more; THE ADVENT OF FASHION - Covers music written for public performance in concert halls and theaters; required composers to keep abreast of popular styles; includes Handel's Music for the Royal Fireworks and Zadok the Priest, Messiah plus Rameau, Telemann, Scarlatti, John Gay's The Beggar's Opera, and more; THE SEASONS AND THE SYMPHONY – Covers Vivaldi's musical celebration of the seasons; Gluck's transformation of an opera into a dramatic as well as musical experience; new ideas in symphonic composition and Haydn; VIENNA – Covers Mozart and Schubert and the musical scene in Vienna; parts of the Mozart Requiem, his piano concertos, symphonies, operas; Schubert's songs, chamber, and piano music; THE REVOLUTIONARY – Covers Beethoven, who changed the course of music; THE ROMANTICS - Covers the composers who strove for self-expression and reacted against the orderliness and 18th century classicism and 19th century industrialization; includes Chopin, Mendelssohn, Brahms, Schumann, Bruckner; NATIONALISM AND REVOLUTION - Beginning with the French Revolution, composers began to identify with causes and expressed them in music; includes Berlioz' and Verdi's Requiems, Wagner, Liszt, and more; LAND OF OUR FATHERS – Covers Smetana, Dvarak, Janacek, Grieg, de Fallas, Vaughan Williams, Kodaly, and Sibelius who all used folk songs in their music to express the culture and landscape of their individual countries; THE MIGHTY FISTFUL - From folk traditions to the founding of the Russian style by Glinka; Balakirev, Mussorgsky, Rimsky-Korsakov, Borodin, Scriabin, and Tchaikovsky; THE TURN OF THE CENTURY - Hear the transition from Romanticism to Modernism, from self-expression to Realism, and the attempts to escape to bygone eras; includes Puccini, Debussy, Mahler, Schoenberg, Wagner, Berg, and Richard Strauss; WAR AND PEACE - Composers sought to express the jarring and discordant sense of civilization gone awry, but during the same time, jazz burst upon the international scene; includes Shostakovich, Britten's War Requiem, Gershwin, Elgar, Joplin, Hindemith, Milhaud, Weill, Bartok, and others; TODAY AND TOMORROW - Presents a broad cross-section of modern music and musical trends; includes Lennon and McCartney, Varese, Stravinsky, Copland, Tippett, Messiaen, Stockhausen, Berio, Ligeti, Henze, and Cage. SYSTEM SPECS: Instructional DVD.

Notion Conducting (www.notionmusic.com): Teaching/learning tool that combines the playback and tempo control of Notion with a selection of score excerpts of varying difficulty especially suited to training effective conductors; to augment existing curriculums; provides full class involvement, immediate feedback, useful homework, and independent study assignments; allows the instructor to concentrate on each individual student's continued improvement; can be installed in the music computer lab to permit class instruction; on students' personal computers it facilitates self-learning with the benefit of a responsive full-sound orchestra; under the baton of a classmate, each student actively participates in the ensemble; responsive feedback not possible using a recording; enables the teacher to focus on the students' development. SYSTEM SPECS: Macintosh; Windows.

P.D.Q. Bach DVDs (www.acornmedia.com): Highbrow slapstick comedy for the musically minded; Professor Peter Schickele is a musical satirist who juxtaposes serious classical music with folk tunes, comedic visual cues, farce, and instrumentation; *P.D.Q Bach in Houston: We Have a Problem* is a special live concert performance of P.D.Q. Bach's greatest hits, celebrating forty years of this act featuring Professor Schickele with Orchestra X; *The Abduction Of Figaro* is a grand opera in three acts and the largest work by P.D.Q. Bach performed by the Minnesota Opera; for middle school and up. SYSTEM SPECS: Instructional DVD.

Peter and the Wolf DVD (www.friendshiphouse.com): Prokofiev's musical score; Emmy award-winning DVD starring Kirstie Alley, Lloyd Bridges, and a new cast of animated characters from Chuck Jones; animated Peter and friends try to outwit the mighty wolf; intertwined with the animation is a live-action story of another boy named Peter who discovers the magic of imagination and the spirit of adventure; fifty minutes; for all ages. SYSTEM SPECS: Instructional DVD.

Piano Mouse Meets Great Composers (www.pianomouse.com): CD-ROM; introduction to the lives and music of eight great composers from the Baroque, Classical, and Romantic periods; biographies; games. SYSTEM SPECS: Hybrid CD-ROM.

Primary Music Appreciation Series (www.clearvue.com): Five DVDs feature five classic compositions by celebrated composers; uses visuals to enhance students' understanding of musical themes, patterns, instruments, and important works; live host introduces the composer, composition, story, and key musical elements to a classroom of young students; students will expand their knowledge of music and will understand the importance of music throughout the world; Further Learning Web site supplements each program, providing learning objectives, Internet resources approved for content, an online teacher's guide, and more. SYSTEM SPECS: Instructional DVD.

Protégé (www.notionmusic.com): Interactive software that allows anyone to create, perform with, and explore music; develop musical skills with the intuitive environment where music can be seen, heard, and changed with immediate, realistic feedback; accompaniment tool; play instrument with world-class musicians in your own home or anywhere; accompany children as they practice; NTempo feature of PROTÉGÉ allows user to direct the London Symphony Orchestra as child plays along; used by private music teachers; can accompany student with a full orchestra and control the tempo; use to help build music theory skills; turn computer into a live accompaniment tool or backup band by composing own piece or downloading favorite titles from the Performance Repertoire; can transpose the playback; sounds of the London Symphony Orchestra, recorded at Abbey Road Studios; click and drag notes; note audition; expandable and customizable sound library; no external hardware or software needed; NTempo: real-time conducting of the score; global key changes and tuning adjustments; instrument audio mixer: mute, solo, decay, pan, and balance; export to WAV file; open and play full Notion files; write for up to eight instruments in a single score; automatic score layout and alignment; shortcuts for every element; enter and edit up to ninety-nine verses of lyrics; *Performance Repertoire* downloadable library of performance ready music for use within Notion or Protégé; collection includes many styles ranging from full orchestral symphonies to solo pieces to popular titles; features the music of well-known composers including Bach, Beethoven, Fauré, Mozart, Puccini, and others. SYSTEM SPECS: Macintosh; Windows.

Spirits of Music (www.spirits-of-music.com): World-famous musicians celebrate the masters of classical music in a series of concerts live from Leipzig, Germany; *Swinging Bach* features both jazz and classical musicians including Bobby McFerrin, the Jacques Loussier Trio, the King's Singers, Gil Shaham and Adele Anthony, the Turtle Island String Quartet, and more as they perform some of Johann Sebastian Bach's most well known compositions; in *Spirits of Music Parts I and II* musicians from Britain, Bulgaria, Cuba, Germany, Norway, Poland, Syria, and the U.S.A. take an enthusiastic audience on an unusual musical journey through the centuries and over continents, from spirituals to Ravel, from Bach to Klezmer, from African folk music to Mozart. SYSTEM SPECS: Instructional DVD.

Tap Dogs (www.tapdogs.com.au/): Award-winning; six young dancers from Australia take tap dancing out of the ballroom and into the new millennium; approximately seventy-five minutes; for grades seven and up. SYSTEM SPECS: Instructional DVD.

The Complete Encyclopedia of Musical Instruments (www.musicmotion.com): Set includes The Complete Encyclopedia of Music Instruments, Instruments of the Orchestra CD Set, and World Instruments CD. SYSTEM SPECS: Book and Audio CD.

The Composers' Specials Six-DVD Set (www.friendshiphouse.com): Family entertainment; dramatic stories of what it might have been like to cross paths with the great composers; brings the composer and his world vividly to life; stresses the importance of self-esteem, hard work, and following one's dreams; great musical scores; includes *Bach's Fight for Freedom, Bizet's Dream, Handel's Last Chance, Liszts' Rhapsody, Rossini's Ghost,* and *Strauss: The King of Three Quarter Time*; for all ages; fifty-three minutes each. SYSTEM SPECS: Instructional DVD.

The Famous Composers Series DVD Set (www.friendshiphouse.com): Covers their professional and personal lives; for high school and college students; composers were not always rich and famous people, and students identify with their struggles and victories; each DVD is thirty-five minutes long; full-color, live action programs, filmed on location. SYSTEM SPECS: Instructional DVD.

The Great Composers DVD Series (www.friendshiphouse.com): Landmark BBC TV series presents the lives and works of Bach, Beethoven, Mozart, Tchaikovsky, Mahler, and Puccini; examines the backgrounds, influences, and relationships that make these six composers part of the fabric of the history of western music; each composer's life and work is presented through extensive performance sequences, interviews, and comments from some of today's greatest artists and most respected authorities; each DVD is approximately sixty minutes; for middle school and up. SYSTEM SPECS: Instructional DVD.

The History of Music (www.clearvue.com): Eight DVD series; explores the history of music from ancient civilizations to the present day; host opens each program by prefacing the important musical developments, key composers and works, and enduring themes of the presentation; students use their eyes and ears; musical examples and samples of period artwork; affect of historical events on music, the grandeur of music eras, and the majesty of significant composers' works; complement to any music or history course; Further Learning Web site supplements each program, providing learning objectives, Internet resources approved for content, an online teacher's guide, and more. SYSTEM SPECS: Instructional DVD.

The Unanswered Question: Six Talks at Harvard by Leonard Bernstein DVDs (www.friendshiphouse.com): Course in music appreciation; taken from lectures Bernstein gave while a professor at Harvard; examines music from every age and place; talks are illustrated with performances by the Boston Symphony Orchestra, the Vienna Philharmonic, and by Bernstein himself; over thirteen hours on three DVDs; boxed collector's set. SYSTEM SPECS: Instructional DVD.

The Young Persons Guide to the Orchestra (www.clearvue.com): Updated version of the classic program; footage of musicians in performance, with close-ups of individual instruments; complement to Benjamin Britten's composition of the same name; highlights the four instrument families in the orchestra - woodwinds, brass, percussion, and strings; emphasizes the unique characteristics of instruments within each group; orchestra members demonstrate how to handle and play each instrument and show where in the orchestra they belong; for students who are interested in joining the orchestra but are uncertain about which instrument to play; shows the distinct sounds of several instruments and the specific roles they play in an orchestra. SYSTEM SPECS: Instructional DVD.

TimeSketch Editor (www.ecsmedia.com): Designed to facilitate listening and aurally analyzing CD music under CD-ROM and computer control; can be used to create teacher-developed listening lessons with any audio CD, MP3 file, MIDI file, WAV file, or AIFF file; for fundamentals courses, appreciation courses, and music history courses at any level; annotated listening format can be applied to a number of classes and activities and the music performance curriculum. SYSTEM SPECS: Hybrid CD-ROM.

TimeSketch Editor PRO (www.ecsmedia.com): Designed to facilitate listening and analyzing music with an easy-to-use interface to create guided listening lessons from any audio CD, MP3, MIDI, Wave or AIFF file; choose which area of a musical piece or performance to analyze and begin adding chart marks for a bubble chart sketch to be displayed; add synchronized text which displays at specific offsets as the audio track is played; when user has finished creating the analysis, it may be published as a file which can be sent over the Internet with the TimeSketch Player for other users to experience. SYSTEM SPECS: Hybrid CD-ROM.

TimeSketch Series (www.ecsmedia.com): Each sketch includes a recording and a form analysis of the piece; for use in music fundamentals, music appreciation, and music history courses; listening lab or private studio; for all grade levels; includes Portrait of Bach, Toccata and Fugue in D Minor; Portrait of Beethoven, Symphony No. 5; Portrait of Brahms, Symphony No. 3; Portrait of Mozart, Symphony 40; Portrait of Schubert, Unfinished Symphony; Portrait of Dvorak, New World Symphony; Pathetique Sonata, Beethoven; Piano Concerto, Beethoven; Brubeck Sketches No. 1, Jazz Series; Miles Davis Sketches No. 1, Jazz Series; Grainger

Sketches No. 1, Lincolnshire Posey. SYSTEM SPECS: Hybrid CD-ROM.

Vivaldi: The Four Seasons DVD (www.friendshiphouse.com): Listen to Vivaldi's concerto as the season's change in the beautiful city of Venice; for home or classroom viewing; running time forty-two minutes. SYSTEM SPECS: Instructional DVD.

What Is Music? (www.musicmotion.com): Explore the phenomena of sound and why some sounds are musical and others are noise; a look at the cultural context of musical perception; for middle school and up; running time sixty minutes. SYSTEM SPECS: Instructional DVD.

Music Appreciation Web Sites

Artist Web Sites

To find any artist's Web site, simply type his or her name into a search engine and click on the link(s). Look for the "Official Web Site" among the fan sites. Signed artist Web pages can also be found at their record label's Web site.

Ballet—Ballroom and Modern Dance Web Sites

American Ballet Theater www.abt.org/default.asp Performances; dancers; education and training.
Ballet www.Ballet.co.uk/ UK dance Web site and discussion group.
Ballet and Dance Art www.danceart.com E-zine for dancers; articles; chat and message boards; interviews with famous dancers; advice from teachers.
Ballet on the Net www.cyberdance.org Companies; colleges; schools; news; education; programs.
Ballroom Dance Music Resource-Dance Plus www.danceplus.com Ballroom dance supply company; ballroom dance CDs from all over the world.
Centuries Dance www.centuriesdance.org Professional performance troupe dedicated to recreating and presenting period social dances in a historically accurate manner; founded in January 2000 by Renée Camus; captures the look and feel of many eras through its costumes, music, and dances.
Critical Dance www.ballet-dance.com Moderated bulletin board; news articles; interviews with dance celebrities; performance reviews; extensive links.
Dance Books Online www.dancebooks.co.uk/ Books, CDs, videos, and DVDs on dance and human movement.

Dance Magazine www.dancemagazine.com Magazine on dance music.

Dance USA www.danceusa.org Programs and publications; meetings; facts and figures; members.

Dancer Universe danceruniverse.com Dance information; teachers; studios; retailers; links.

DanceWeb www.danceWeb.co.uk/ Interactive directory; searchable database for all sorts of dance-related information.

English National Ballet www.ballet.org.uk/ UK's premier touring ballet company; news; performances; resources.

New York City Ballet www.nycballet.com/nycballet/homepage.asp Repertoire; dancers; educational resources; schedule; tickets.

Nutcracker Ballet www.nutcrackerballet.net/ History of the Nutcracker Ballet; music; links; movies; information on performances.

Russian Classical Ballet www.aha.ru/~vladmo History; outstanding choreographers; ballet teachers; ballet dancers; musicians; education; photo gallery.

The Art of Ballet www.artofballet.com/classics.html Dance information; photos; clip art; ballet class; performing arts; adult beginners; instructional; classics; MIDI; famous ballets; steps; exercises; stretching tips; recommended books and videos.

The International Guild of Musicians in Dance www.dancemusician.org Membership; publications; conferences.

The National Ballet of Canada www.national.ballet.ca/home.php Repertoire; tickets; subscriptions; artists; performances.

The National Ballet School www.nationalballetschool.org School of ballet.

USA International Ballet Competition www.usaibc.com Official International Ballet Competition site in the United States.

Voice of Dance www.voiceofdance.com Online resource for dance; insights; calendar.

Classical Music and Composers Web Sites

All Classical Guide www.allclassical.com Explore classical music; search by composer/performer, work title/keyword, or album title; top composers listed by period and genre.

American Classical Music Hall of Fame www.americanclassicalmusic.org Dedicated to honoring and celebrating the many facets of classical music in the United States; seeks to recognize those who have made significant contributions to classical music.

American Composers Forum www.composersforum.org Arts service organiza-

tion which provides grants, fellowships, recordings, and other services for composers of contemporary music; national programs; regional chapters.

Arsis Press: Music by Women Composers www.instantWeb.com~arsis Publisher of concert and sacred music by women composers; music for chorus, solo voice, keyboards, and chamber ensembles.

Artek Recordings—Classical www.artekrecordings.com Range of classical music that spans traditional and well-known repertoire and rarely heard masterpieces from little-known composers.

BBC Music Magazine www.bbcmusicmagazine.com Classical music reviews; reviews by subject; search by composer; search by type of music: orchestral, opera, choral and song, chamber instrumental.

Cadenza www.cadenza.org Resources and information for classical and contemporary music and musicians; program note library; musicians; concerts; glossary; MIDI diary.

Classical Archives www.classicalarchives.com Thousands of classical music files to listen to or download; over 1,500 works arranged alphabetically by composer; public domain files.

Classical Composers Database www.classical-composers.org Ever-growing list of composers; over 3,500 entries and 8000 individual compositions; links and contributions accepted.

Classical Music Broadcast www.classicalmusicbroadcast.com/ Classical music Internet radio; 24/7.

Classical Music History Timelines on the Web . . . The History Beat www.search-beat.com/composer.htm Classical music history time lines; composer history resources.

Classical Music Pages w3.rz-berlin.mpg.de/cmp/classmus.html Variety of information on music in the Western culture.

Classical Music UK www.classicalmusic.co.uk Links, videos, CDs, concerts, and jobs; guide to classical music Web sites in the UK.

Classical Net www.classical.net/music Features more than 2,500 CD reviews; 5,800 files; over 4,000 links to other classical music Web sites.

Classical NPR Music www.npr.org/templates/story/story.php?storyId=10 003 Concerts; interviews; profiles.

Classical Piano MIDI Page www.piano-midi.de/ Composers of classical piano music; MP3s.

Classical.com www.classical.com Unlimited listening to entire catalog; subscriptions; downloads.

ClassicalUSA.com classicalusa.com Resources; links.

ClassicWeb www.classicWeb.com Classical links.

Early Music FAQ www.medieval.org/emfaq/misc/ Early music links and resources; recordings; concerts; performers.

Early Music News www.earlymusic.org.uk Event listings, concerts, and festivals for Baroque, choral, Renaissance, and early music; promotes the understanding and enjoyment of early music and historically informed performance.

Early Music on the Web . . . The Classical Music Beat www.search-beat.com/earlymusic.htm Classical music history Internet links; time lines; composer history resources on the Web.

Essentials of Music www.essentialsofmusic.com Music facts and information; from Sony Classical and W. W. Norton; basic information eras; terms; composers; audio examples.

Gramophone www.gramophone.co.uk UK classical music Web site and magazine.

Hopkins Technology www.hoptechno.com/classic.htm *Classical Notes* CD-ROM.

Impulse Classical Music Website www.impulse-music.co.uk Pages on contemporary classical composers and performers; photographs; biographies; reviews; downloadable musical tracks.

Meet the Composer www.meetthecomposer.org Information on composers.

MIDIWorld.com Classical midiworld.com/classic.htm Classical music MIDI files listed by composer.

MIDIWorld.com Composers midiworld.com/composers.htm Alphabetical listing of links to composer information and MIDI files.

Music Resources on the Internet www.skdesigns.com/internet/music Free music graphics; links to regional symphony orchestras and music organizations.

Musical Online-Classical Music Directory www.musicalonline.com Classical music directory; music education; music instruction; virtual concert hall; online music directory listing service and Web page design source for artists, musicians, and performers; resource for locating professional musicians and companies; listings of opera singers and instrumentalists as well as composers and conductors; opera companies and orchestras are indexed.

Naxos: Composers Biographies and Their Works www.naxos.com/qcomp.htm Links to information on composers and their works in alphabetical order; classical music record label.

Performance Today performancetoday.publicradio.org/ Features; stations.

REC Music Foundation www.recmusic.org Promotes new classical music composers, primarily through the development of new computer tools.

Society of Composers, Inc. www.societyofcomposers.org Home page; members; performers; recordings.

Sony Classical www.sonyclassical.com Artists and new releases; sound clips; tour schedules; releases.

Symphony Orchestra Schedules www.hoptechno.com/symphony.htm Links to major symphony orchestra home pages.

The Classical Music Navigator www.wku.edu/~smithch/music/index2.htm Basic library of notable works; geographical roster; index of forms and styles of music.

The J. S. Bach Home Page www.jsbach.org Extensive biography; tour of Bach's life in Germany; catalog of complete works; bibliography; recommended recordings; other Bach resources on the Web.

Vox Music Group www.voxcd.com Catalog of classical compact disks and recordings.

Worldwide Internet Music Resources www.music.indiana.edu/music_resources/outline.html William and Gayle Cook Music Library Indiana University School of Music; links to information on many music topics.

Yahoo Classical Music Artists dir.yahoo.com/Entertainment/music/artists/by_genre/classical/ By instrument; composers; conductors; ensembles; opera; orchestras; vocal.

Yahoo Classical Music Index dir.yahoo.com/Entertainment/music/genres/classical/ Links to a variety of classical music sites.

Young Concert Artists, Inc. www.yca.org Home page; roster of artists; concerts.

Holiday Music Web Sites

Black History Month, Kwanzaa, and Martin Luther King Day Resources www.creativefolk.com/blackhistory/blackhistory.html Provides the origins of Black History Month, Kwanzaa, and Martin Luther King Day; links to recipes, songs, games, and speeches.

Christmas and Holiday Music www.christmassongs.com Christmas and holiday song publisher; owned by Justin Wilde; audio samples; catalog; track record; how to submit.

Halloween—History and Traditions of the Holiday wilstar.com/holidays/hallown.htm History and customs of Halloween.

Hanukkahh Celebrations at the Holiday Spot www.theholidayspot.com/hanukkah/ Free Chanukkah wallpaper, recipes, letterhead, music, history.

Happy Thanksgiving www.theholidayspot.com/thanksgiving Greetings; clip art; recipes.

Hatikvah Music hatikvahmusic.com Jewish Music; Klezmer, Yiddish, Ladino, Sephardic, Cantorial, Israeli, and children's holiday CDs, DVDs.

Haunted Halloween www.animatedfun.com/halloween.htm Interactive haunted house file with spooky 2D and 3D animations, pictures, music, and sounds.

Have Yourself a Merry Little Christmas Page
www.kate.net/holidays/christmas Large categorized list of Christmas links; holiday music.

Holiday Stuff for Children
home.amaonline.com/teacherstuff/holiday.htm Thanksgiving and Christmas sites; arts and crafts, coloring pages; holiday stories.

Merry-Christmas.com www.merry-christmas.com/music/index.htm MIDI files; holiday jukebox.

Merry Christmas Happy Hanukkah—A Multilingual Songbook & CD www.pianopress.com Thirty-two traditional favorites arranged for five-finger and easy piano with duet accompaniments; sing-along/play-along CD; lyrics in English, Hebrew, Spanish, German, French, and Latin.

New Year's Day
www.wilstar.com/holidays/newyear.htm History, traditions, and customs of New Year's Day and how it is celebrated.

Piano Press Holiday Fun Series www.pianopress.com Elementary to intermediate level piano sheet music for the holidays; *My Christmas Fun Books; My Halloween Fun Books; Merry Christmas Happy Hanukkah – A Multilingual Songbook and CD;* sheet music solos and more.

Santa Claus Online www.santaclausonline.com E-mail a letter to Santa Claus and he will respond personally; fun and games; holiday music; free clip art; free Christmas cards; toys and much more; listen to Santa read *'Twas the Night before Christmas.*

Santa Land www.santaland.com/songs.html Christmas carols and lyrics.

Sheryl's Holidays Site
www.sherylfranklin.com/holidays Collection of pages and links related to all holidays.

The Holiday Page-History and Customs
wilstar.com/holidays Customs and history of most holidays; games, graphics, music, and poetry.

Music Education— Instructional Media Web Sites

Adventus www.adventus.com Music instruction software for Windows; *Piano Suite; Ear Training Coach; Musiq; Internet Music Studio.*

All Things Musical www.allthingsmusical.com National music education resource guide.

American Music Conference www.amc-music.com National nonprofit educational association founded in 1947; dedicated to promoting the importance of music, music-making, and music education to the general public; goal is to build credibility for music and music education, especially at an early age, and to expand that portion of the population that enjoys and makes its own music.

American Orff-Schulwerk Association www.aosa.org Professional organization of music and movement educators dedicated to the creative teaching approach developed by Carl Orff and Gunild Keetman; believe that learning about music—learning to sing and play, to hear and understand, to move and create—should be an active and joyful experience.

Ars Nova Music Software www.ars-nova.com Educational music software; *Practica Musica; Songworks; Kidmusic.*

Association for Technology in Music Instruction www.music.org/atmi Serves as a forum for the scholarly presentation of technical information by and for specialists in the field of computer-assisted instruction (CAI) in music; delivers such information to an audience of nonspecialists who are users of music CAI.

Berklee College of Music Home Page www.berklee.edu Pragmatic educational approach to jazz, pop, rock, world music, and classical music; Boston, MA.

Casa de la Musica www.casamusica.com *Time Signature 2000* Studio Management Software.

Cassette & Video Learning Systems www.cvls.com Music instruction videos, books with CDs, DVDs, tabs, tablature, and lessons for learning on acoustic guitar, electric guitar, bass guitar, rock guitar, blues guitar, keyboards, harmonica, drums, snare drum, banjo, mandolin, violin, and fiddle; free guitar lessons online on video; free banjo lessons online.

Children's Music Workshop
www.childrensmusicworkshop.com Music education online; links.

Clarus Music, Ltd. www.clarusmusic.com Worldwide K-12 catalog mail order dealer; sell to music and non-music educators.

Coalition for Music Education in B.C.
www.bcmusiccoalition.org Music education advocacy information for parents, educational decision makers, and teachers.

Crown Trophy www.crowntrophy.com Medals and awards for music students.

Dolphin Don's Music School www.dolphindon.com Music education software.

Educational Activities www.edact.com Educational software, children's music, educational videos; early childhood recordings.

Educational Cyber Playground www.edu-cyberpg.com Award winning Web site; links to arts and music Web sites; vendor directory.

Educational Programs Network
www.educationalprograms.com Adjudication festivals and resources for music educators.

Educator's Music Annex www.educatorsmusic.com Educational supplier.

Edumart www.edumart.com Collection of educational stores and/or school supply distributors in the educational industry.

Electronic Courseware Systems (ECS) www.ecsmedia.com Educational music software company based in Champaign, IL; downloadable demos; developers of music instructional, multimedia, and MIDI software.

eMedia Music www.emediamusic.com Series of instructional software for guitar, piano, bass, and voice; chord dictionary with audio playback; Macintosh; Windows.

Enrichment Works www.enrichmentworks.com Los Angeles schools assembly programs, classroom events, and workshops in the arts.

Experience Music Project www.emplive.com Seattle-based; interactive exhibits, unique artifacts, and space for live performances; created to celebrate the past, present, and future of music; explore; archives; summer camps; museum; tours; contests.

Exploding Art Music Productions www.explodingart.com Committed to research, promotion, and development of music education; specializing in contemporary music practices, including music technology and rock music.

Expression Center for New Media www.xnewmedia.com Digital visual media and sound arts education.

Festivals of Music educationalprograms.com/festivalsofmusic/index.asp Adjudication festivals for vocal and instrumental ensembles.

Happy Note! www.happynote.com/music/learn.html Computer game; learn how to read music.

Harmonic Vision www.harmonicvision.com Educational music software; *Music Ace.*

Heritage Festivals/Bowl Games of America www.heritagefestivals.com Band, choir, and orchestra festivals.

Homespun Tapes Online www.homespuntapes.com Wide selection of music instruction on videos, CDs, and DVDs for all instruments and styles.

Homework Spot www.homeworkspot.com/theme/classicalmusic.htm Links to classical music sites.

International Schools Service www.iss.edu Providing services to overseas schools and meeting the educational needs of companies abroad.

International Society for Music Education www.isme.org Serving music educators and promoting music education worldwide.

Introduction to Music omnidisc.com/MUSIC/index.html Web-based course.

Lessons4you.com www.lessons4you.com Online music lessons; instructors.

Maestro Music Software www.wrldcon.com/maestro/ Educational music software.

MiBAC Music Software www.mibac.com Products; theory reference; music instructional software; *MiBAC Jazz* and *Music Lessons.*

MidiSoft www.midisoft.com/idd/DesktopDefault.aspx?tabindex=0&tabid=1 Music creational and educational software.

Mike Mangini's Rhythm Knowledge Online www.rhythmknowledge.com Rhythm instruction materials for all instruments.

Mollard Conducting Batons Inc. www.mollard.com Mollard & Brite Stixs.

Mr. Holland's Opus Foundation www.mhopus.org Supports music education and its many benefits through the donation and repair of musical instruments to underserved schools, community music programs, and individual students nationwide.

Murphy Cap and Gown www.murphyrobes.com Choir robes.

Music Data Management Software www.winband.com WinBand; WinChoir; WinEnsemble.

Music Education at Datadragon datadragon.com/education/ Music education links.

Music Education Council www.mec.org.uk/ Umbrella body for all organizations connected with music education in the UK.

Music Education Madness www.musiceducationmadness.com Gathering place for music educators.

Music Education Online www.musiceducationonline.org Member-driven Web site for music teachers, music directors, performers and parents interested in music programs.

Music Education Software www.musicmall.com/cmp/educatin.htm A variety of music software for learning piano, guitar, ear training, and music theory.

Music Educators Market Place www.musicedmarket.com Online retailer of music educational products.

Music Educators National Conference (MENC) www.menc.org Mission is to advance music education by encouraging the study and making of music by all.

Music in the Parks www.musicintheparks.com Adjudication festivals for ensembles.

Music Minus One www.musicminusone.com or www.pocketsongs.com *Music Minus One; Pocket Songs;* accompaniment music; play-along and sing-along for all musicians and vocalists; popular, classical, jazz, rock, and country.

Music Notes www.musicnotes.net Publishes *Music You Can Read*; music curriculum for elementary music teachers, home schoolers, or persons interested in learning to read music.

Music Reading www.musicreading.com Teaching and learning tool; sample lessons and tests; CD-ROM.

Music Simply Music www.musicsimplymusic.com Helping teachers, parents, and students share the gift of music.

Music Staff www.musicstaff.com Find a music teacher; add a listing.

Music Teacher's Helper www.musicteachershelper.com Online software for music teachers; bookkeeping; student information database; online billing; monthly fee; e-newsletter.

Music Teachers National Association (MTNA) www.mtna.org Member and program benefits; convention information; publications; resources; online ordering; links.

Music Technology Learning Center www.mtlc.net Music technology in the schools and at home; retailer.

Musica www.musica.uci.edu Music and science information; computer archive; research notes and abstracts on the effects of music on the brain.

Musical Online www.musicalonline.com/pedagogy.htm Links to information on how to practice.

Musician's Workshop www.musicians-workshop.com Video and audio music instruction since 1973.

Musicianship Basics www.dragnet.com.au/~donovan/mb Music education software for schools and piano teachers; graded ear training and theory activities for all music students; demos for Macintosh and Windows.

MusickEd.com musicked.com Study guides and learning tools for all instruments; membership includes free access to chat rooms and other musical services; online lessons for beginners to professionals.

Musicline Publications www.musicline-ltd.com Stage musicals and shows for schools and youth theaters.

National Federation of Music Clubs www.nfmc-music.org/ Membership of 155,000+ musicians and non-musicians who support the performing arts; non-profit; the largest philanthropic musical organization in the world; founded in 1898; chartered by the Congress of the United States; available at the Local, State, and National Federation levels.

North American Music Festivals www.greatfestivals.com Festivals for students.

Organization of American Kodály Educators oake.org Mission is to enrich the quality of life of the people of the United States through music education by promoting the philosophy of Zoltán Kodály.

Pedagonet www.pedagonet.com Learning material and resource center.

Peery www.PeeryProducts.com Risers and skirting for performances.

PlayPro Software, Inc. www.PlayPro.com Guitar and keyboard instructional software.

Private Lessons www.privatelessons.com Locate a private local music teacher.

PureGold Teaching Tools www.puregoldteachingtools.com Teaching aids for classroom teachers, private teachers, parents, students, homeschoolers, and music therapists.

Quia www.quia.com/dir/music/ Students can test their music knowledge with quizzes, matches, concentration card games, and other activities.

ScholarStuff www.scholarstuff.com Directory of education sites; colleges and universities; educational software; financial aid.

Silver Burdette www.sbgmusic.com Music educational materials for the classroom; articles; samples.

Singlish www.singlish.com Develop language skills in children through the singing of classic and contemporary folk songs; Volumes 1 and 2 for Pre-K through 2nd grade classroom.

Smart Music www.smartmusic.com Access online accompaniments that function as virtual accompanists; *Smart Music* CD-ROM; practice program for woodwinds, brass players, and vocalists.

SmarterKids.com www.smarterkids.com Educational books, audio materials, and software for music.

Songs for Teaching www.SongsForTeaching.com Links to songs used for teaching a variety of subjects; articles; educational lyrics and recordings; tips; store.

Sound Tree www.soundtree.com Music technology services for education; resource guide.

Suzuki Association of the Americas, Inc. www.suzukiassociation.org Coalition of teachers, parents, educators, and others who are interested in making music education available to all children.

Suzuki Music Academy www.suzukimusicacademy.com Suzuki Method classical music study; two and up.

Suzuki Musical Instruments www.suzukimusic.com Educational musical instruments.

The Copernicus Education Gateway www.edgate.com/musichall/educator/ For educators, students, and parents.

The Grove School Without Walls www.dickgrove.com College-level music courses.

The Land of Music www.landofmusic.com Tapes and materials for teaching music to young children.

The Practice Spot www.practicespot.com Information about how to practice.

The Technology Institute for Music Educators www.time.org Assists educators in applying technology to improve teaching and learning in music.

Thinkquest Internet Challenge Library www.thinkquest.org/library/cat_show.html?cat_id=17&cid=1 Online guide to music education.

Tritone Music www.tritonemusic.com Multimedia online music education systems for schools and internet distant learning environments; specialize in incorporating professionally developed content for K-12 with the latest in technology.

Watch and Learn www.cvls.com Books with CDs, DVDs, tabs, tablature, and lessons for learning on acoustic guitar, electric guitar, bass guitar, rock guitar, blues guitar, keyboards, harmonica, drums, snare drum, banjo, mandolin, violin, and fiddle.

Wenger www.wengercorp.com Instrument storage.

Worldwide Internet Music Resources www.music.indiana.edu/music_resources/mused.html Music education links and online music resources for music educators.

Music History Web Sites

Academic Info – Music History www.academicinfo.net/music.html Music history and studies; digital library; musical databases and archives; classical music composers; folk music; jazz resources; music libraries; music centers.

Basic Music: Your Guide to Music of the Western World www.basicmusic.net Biographies, compositions, and recommended recordings of composers of all genres and styles of music; This Day in Music; musical glossary; musical forms.

Early Music FAQ www.medieval.org/emfaq Comprehensive information on Medieval and Renaissance; repertory overview; CDs; links.

Encyclopedia Smithsonian www.si.edu/resource/faq/nmah/music.htm Musical history; artists and exhibitions.

Essentials of Music www.essentialsofmusic.com From Sony Classical and W. W. Norton; basic information about classical music; eras; terms; composers.

Gregorian Chant Home Page www.music.princeton.edu/chant_html The Nassau Edition of Gregorian Chant.

History Happens www.ushistory.com Stories from American history on music video.

History Net www.TheHistoryNet.com History on the Internet.

Library of Congress American Memory Site memory.loc.gov/ammem/amhome.html Thousands of historical public domain MP3 files; photos.

Music History Articles www.essortment.com/in/Music.History/ Links to many music history sites.

Music History for Music Education musicandyou.com/musichistory.htm Links; MP3s; sheet music.

Music History Resources members.tripod.com~papandr/musicology.html Collection of outlines on music history topics.

Music History Resources www.nerdworld.com/nw1240.html Information on music history; links.

MUSIClassical.com musiclassical.com/ Today in classical music history.

Open Directory dmoz.org/Arts/Music/History/ Music history links.

Orpheon www.orpheon.org Museum of historical musical instruments.

Stylistic Timeline of Music History www.stevenestrella.com/composers/index.html?styletimeline.html Time line by date or name.

The Galpin Society www.music.ed.ac.uk/euchmi/galpin/ For the study of musical instruments.

The 100 Most Important American Musical Works of the Twentieth Century www.npr.org/programs/specials/vote/list100.html NPR special features cover music from a wide variety of genres; classical, jazz, rock, country, R&B, musical theater and film scores; aired on *All Things Considered, Morning Edition*, and NPR's weekend news magazine programs.

The History of Today www.on-this-day.com Daily historical facts and events; music history.

The Internet Public Library www.ipl.org/div/mushist/ Music History 102; guide to western composers and their music; middle ages to the present.

The Music Room www.empire.k12.ca.us/capistrano/Mike/capmusic/music_room/themusic.htm Music history sites.

The Use of Music and Dance in Teaching United States History pw2.netcom.com~wandaron/history.html Teaching history with the use of music and dance.

This Day in Music History datadragon.com/day/ Birthdays; releases; charts; shows and plays.

Those Were the Days, Today in History www.440.com/twtd/today.html Daily summary of news events, famous birthdays, and hit music that happened on this day in history.

Worldwide Internet Music Resources www.music.indiana.edu/music_resources/mcology.html Musicology and music history links.

Yahoo! Entertainment:Music:History www.yahoo.com/Entertainment/Music/History Music history.

6
Country—Folk—Traditional and World Music
Software, Instructional Media and Web Sites

A Vision Shared – A Tribute to Woody Guthrie and Leadbelly (www.musicmotion.com): The lives of two influential folk singers, each singing about life as he found it; these men made the country aware of the plight of people as in *Deportee, I Aint Got No Home,* and *Do Re Mi,* and new developments and their impact as in *Grand Coulee Dam;* they spoke against injustice in *I've Got to Know* and *Union Made;* they also wrote fun songs for children and proud songs like *This Land Is Your Land;* songs are sung by well-known singers in tribute; footage of Woody and Leadbelly; interviews and comments from those who knew them; running time seventy-two minutes. SYSTEM SPECS: Instructional DVD.

African Dance and Drumming DVD Kit (www.musicmotion.com): Interactive introduction to the rich heritage of African culture through dance, music, song, language, and clothing; two live-action thirty-minute films with interactive performances before student audiences; teacher's manual; activities and quizzes; for grades three-twelve. SYSTEM SPECS: Instructional DVD.

American Roots Music Series (www.musicmotion.com): PBS series featuring historic footage and musical performances by the pioneers of American music; traces the cultural evolution that shaped and influenced the music; hear masters of folk, country, blues, gospel, western swing, bluegrass, Cajun, zydeco, Tejano, and Native American music; rare footage; includes music of the Carter Family, B. B. King, Muddy Waters, Woody Guthrie, Leadbelly, Elvis Presley, Weavers, and many more; color and black and white; two DVD set. SYSTEM SPECS: Instructional DVD.

Anyone Can Play Bluegrass Banjo (www.melbay.com): Teaches the basics of bluegrass

banjo playing to the beginning student with no previous music experience; discussion of Scruggs style banjo playing; brief introduction to melodic-style playing; Bluegrass standards such as Cripple Creek, Lonesome Road Blues, Little Maggie, Bury Me Beneath the Willow, and many others; free instructional booklet. SYSTEM SPECS: Instructional DVD.

Anyone Can Play Country Fiddle (www.melbay.com): Designed to teach beginners of any age how to play country fiddle; no previous musical experience needed; learn basics of bowing, fingering, chord playing, shuffle bowing, and several famous fiddle tunes; free instructional booklet; forty-five minutes. SYSTEM SPECS: Instructional DVD.

Anyone Can Play Harmonica DVD (www.melbay.com): By Phil Duncan; different techniques and styles taught including folk, gospel, country, and blues; requires ten-hole diatonic harmonica pitched in key of C; free instructional booklet; thirty minutes. SYSTEM SPECS: Instructional DVD.

Anyone Can Play Mandolin DVD (www.melbay.com): By Paul Hayman; designed for beginning mandolin students; teaches fundamentals of mandolin chord strumming, single-note melody picking, and explains tablature; does not require any previous musical experience or note-reading ability; learn several well-known bluegrass songs in both strumming and picking styles; free instructional booklet. SYSTEM SPECS: Instructional DVD.

Banjo for Beginners (www.alfred.com): Get started playing the banjo; reading tab; basic technique; bluegrass classics. SYSTEM SPECS: Book, Audio CD, and/or Instructional DVD.

Barrage: The World on Stage DVD (www.barrage.ca): Combining Celtic, East Indian, big band swing, and American folk music; concert presentation fuses song, dance, and theater; highlights resourceful stringed instruments; upbeat blend of different cultures and musical styles. SYSTEM SPECS: Instructional DVD.

Barrage: Vagabond Tales DVD (www.barrage.ca): Features the international, multi-talented Barrage group as it performs a new, eclectic mix of music, dance, theater and song; story is told through the recollections of an old man, as he remembers his time in a roving group of Gypsy musicians, the adventures he undertook and the romance that shaped his life; running time one hour. SYSTEM SPECS: Instructional DVD.

Basic Blues Harmonica Method DVD (www.melbay.com): By David Barrett; accompanies the book and CD Basic Blues Harmonica Method; large charts, diagrams, and many playing examples. SYSTEM SPECS: Instructional DVD.

Basix Harmonica Method (www.alfred.com): Special note-reading system for chromatic or diatonic harmonica; listening suggestions; musical examples. SYSTEM SPECS: Book and Enhanced CD.

Beginning Mandolin (www.alfred.com): Learn the basics; easy chord forms; basic strumming; covers fiddle tunes, bluegrass, and blues styles; alternate picking, tremolo, and slides. SYSTEM SPECS: Book, Audio CD, and/or Instructional DVD.

Blues Harmonica 1 & 2 (www.alfred.com): Choosing a harmonica; blowing and drawing; first position and cross harp; playing notes; bending; blues phrasing; vibrato and trills; playing octaves and chords. SYSTEM SPECS: Instructional DVD.

Blues Harmonica for Beginners (www.alfred.com): Tablature; photos and diagrams. SYSTEM SPECS: Book and Enhanced CD.

Caribbean Carnival (www.musicmotion.com): Introduces a live student audience to rhythms and musical styles of Soca, Calypso, Reggae, and more; see how steel drums are made; two thirty-minute, live-action videos; teacher's guide. SYSTEM SPECS: Instructional DVD.

Celebrations Around the World! and Celebrations Around the World Again! (www.alfred.com): Celebrate holidays in countries around the world; covers customs, cultures, and languages; cross-cultural study of music; teacher's handbook. SYSTEM SPECS: Book and Audio CD.

Chinese Opera (www.musicmotion.com): Colorful mixture of music, mime, acting, dance, acrobatics, and martial arts; evolved from ancient traditions; was banned during Mao's Cultural Revolution; indoor and outdoor theaters, an opera school, a percussion factory showing the making of a gong, a silk fan factory, and a dance class practicing with fans and parasols; see musicians rehearsing on traditional instruments, acrobatic training, singers applying elaborate makeup, Ming Dynasty costumes, live opera scenes, and more; running time twenty-eight minutes. SYSTEM SPECS: Instructional DVD.

Clawhammer from Scratch Volumes 1 and 2 (www.melbay.com): By Dan Levenson; history of the five-string banjo; covers the parts of the banjo, holding the banjo, right- and left- hand styles and basic clawhammer strum; strum is broken down into the steps of the finger and thumb; based on Dan's Meet the Banjo program; no prior experience; using one tune, Spotted Pony, student is guided through chords, scale, and individual notes of tune; tips and frequently asked questions; two-page pamphlet included. SYSTEM SPECS: Instructional DVD.

Come West along the Road (www.musicmotion.com): Traditional Irish music from the archives of RTE TV from 1960s through 1980s; songs in Irish and English; jigs, reels, hornpipes, and aires; step dances, set dances, and ceili dances; running time 145 minutes. SYSTEM SPECS: Instructional DVD.

Conjunto Button Accordion DVD (www.melbay.com): By Joe Torres; the three-row button accordion gives Tex-Mex music its unique sound; learn to play in the authentic Norteno style; basic scales and chords; step by step; overview of Spanish music terminology used by conjunto musicians. SYSTEM SPECS: Instructional DVD.

Dance in Bali: Upon the Sacred Stage (www.musicmotion.com): From simple village settings to royal courts; explores the rich musical heritage of Bali where culture, religion, and life are woven together; ten of Bali's most dramatic dances, including a trance dance performed barefoot on hot ashes; gamelan orchestras; elegant headdresses; masks and traditional costumes; running time twenty-eight minutes. SYSTEM SPECS: Instructional DVD.

Discovering American Indian Music (www.musicmotion.com): Documentary illustrates the wide diversity of American Indian music; includes themes of Indian music and dance and the importance of keeping these traditions alive; shot on location with native instruments and beautiful costumes; running time twenty-four minutes. SYSTEM SPECS: Instructional DVD.

Folk Rhythms (www.halleonard.com): Learn to play spoons, bones, washboard, hambone, and the paper bag; David Holt teaches musicianship, feeling, and enthusiasm; well-paced, step-by-step demos of rhythm making using simple materials and body and voice percussion; for all ages; running time forty-seven minutes. SYSTEM SPECS: Instructional DVD.

Fun with the Banjo (www.melbay.com): By Joe Carr; chords, strums, and songs; beginner's course for five-string banjo; concert C tuning. SYSTEM SPECS: Instructional DVD.

Fun with the Mandolin DVD (www.melbay.com): By Joe Carr; teaches material in book of same title; twenty-two songs; tuning and hand positions briefly discussed; 4/4, 3/4, and 2/4 rhythm chord accompaniments in C, G, and D Major; chords are shown in picture diagram form. SYSTEM SPECS: Instructional DVD.

Fun with the Ukulele (www.melbay.com): By Mel Bay; taught by Joe Carr; simple chords, strums, and songs; beginner's course for ukulele in C tuning. SYSTEM SPECS: Instructional DVD.

Games Children Sing Series (www.alfred.com): Favorite children's songs from each country; authentic; English adaptations; supplementary notes; titles include: *Games Children Sing – China, Games Children Sing – India, Games Children Sing – Japan, Games Children Sing – Malaysia, Games Children Sing Around the World.* SYSTEM SPECS: Book and Audio CD.

Harmonica Basics, Blues (www.alfred.com): How to hold; blow and draw; beginning notes and melodies; playing a major scale; articulation; chords and arpeggios; bugle calls; train sounds; hand vibrato; shakes and more. SYSTEM SPECS: Instructional DVD.

Homespun Tapes Instructional DVDs (www.halleonard.com): Titles include *Bluegrass Fiddle Boot Camp; The Sam Bush Mandolin Method; Classic Bluegrass Banjo Solos; Essential Techniques for Dobro; Essential Techniques for Mandolin; Tony Trischka's Essential Practice Techniques for Bluegrass Banjo; Lead Singing and Rhythm Guitar—Finding Your Bluegrass Voice,* and more. SYSTEM SPECS: Instructional DVD.

Into the Circle (www.musicmotion.com): Authentic presentation of the powwow, or gathering of the tribe; introduction to Native American music; native people danced in a circle around the drum for celebration, fellowship, renewal, and healing; traditions continue still; set in the original Indian Territory of Oklahoma; live powwows from different tribes show fully costumed dancers from national champions to toddlers and singers; interviews with tribal elders, dancers, drummers, and singers; different dance steps and drum patterns; how the powwow evolved; written outline guide; running time fifty-eight minutes. SYSTEM SPECS: Instructional DVD.

It's a Wonderful World! (www.alfred.com): Twenty-five songs from countries A-Z; learn multicultural musical styles; information about the countries. SYSTEM SPECS: Book and Audio CD.

Latin Legends (www.musicmotion.com): Live performances introduce Afro/Cuban music in a historical and geographical context from its beginnings to its current trends; five musicians demonstrate techniques and styles including Son, Rumba, Mambo, Cha-Cha, Merengue, Songo and Cha-Cha, Merengue, Songo and Afro/Cuban Jazz using claves, congas, bongos, timbales, cowbells, guiro, drumset, piano and bass; teacher's guide; running time two thirty-minute videos. SYSTEM SPECS: Instructional DVD.

Music and Culture (www.clearvue.com): Covers the music and traditions of Polynesian, African, and North American Indian peoples; instruments, vocal music, and dance; authentic recordings and graphics; audiovisual presentation with text linked to an encyclopedia and glossary; multiple-choice questions for quizzes; identifies the four major instrument groups classified by ethnomusicologists; for beginners to intermediate, grades 7-college. SYSTEM SPECS: Hybrid CD-ROM.

Music of Our World (www.halleonard.com): Books and CDs from Music Express for grades four to eight; learn a song in the language and discover the cultural festivals around the world; accompaniment CDs use the world instruments mentioned in the text. SYSTEM SPECS: Book and Audio CD.

Myth, Music, and Dance of the American Indian (www.alfred.com): Multicultural activity-oriented source; activities; historical and cultural information; musical analysis; English texts. SYSTEM SPECS: Book and Audio CD.

No Excuses Guide: Celtic (www.musicsales.com): Comprehensive guide for players of all abilities; practice in a variety of styles as part of a real band. SYSTEM SPECS: Instructional DVD and Hybrid CD-ROM.

No Excuses Guide: Didgeridoo (www.musicsales.com): Comprehensive guide for players of all abilities; practice in a variety of styles as part of a real band. SYSTEM SPECS: Instructional DVD and Hybrid CD-ROM.

No Excuses Harmonica Guide (www.musicsales.com): Comprehensive guide for players of all abilities; practice in a variety of styles as part of a real band. SYSTEM SPECS: Instructional DVD and Hybrid CD-ROM.

Power Pickin' Volume I—Up the Neck Backup for Bluegrass Banjo DVD (www.melbay.com): By Bill Evans; visual method for learning the basic techniques used to play bluegrass banjo accompaniment in up the neck positions; step-by-step approach appropriate for all levels of pickers; tab booklet included; techniques covered include vamping with variations, 3/4 time backup, roll patterns based on chord forms, classic backup licks, two finger backup for slower songs, and bluesy backup styles. SYSTEM SPECS: Instructional DVD.

Putumayo World Music CDs (www.putumayo.com): Established in 1993 to introduce people to the music of other cultures; label grew out of the Putumayo clothing company founded by

Dan Storper in 1975 and sold in 1997; CD covers feature the art of Nicola Heindl, whose colorful, folkloric style represents one of Putumayo's goals: to connect the traditional to the contemporary and to create products that people love; combines appealing music and visuals while supporting its releases with creative retail promotions and marketing; one of the industry's most innovative companies. SYSTEM SPECS: Book and Audio CD.

Ready to Sing Series (www.alfred.com): Songs arranged for voice and piano; for young singing groups; melody line song sheets; titles include: *Ready to Sing – Christmas, Ready to Sing – Folk Songs*, and *Ready to Sing – Spirituals*. SYSTEM SPECS: Book and Audio CD.

Roots of Rhythm (www.musicmotion.com): Covers the melding of history, cultures, and peoples that became Latin music; Harry Belafonte narrates; begins in Africa with tribal celebrations; Moorish Spain with the flamenco; Cuba, where the African slaves and Spaniards combined these sounds in celebrations; United Sates introduction through musicals and bands led by Xavier Cugat and Desi Arnaz; continuing into jazz with Dizzy Gillespie; tour of the history and development of rhythm; running time three hours. SYSTEM SPECS: Instructional DVD.

Songs of Hispanic Americans (www.alfred.com): Multicultural activity-oriented source; historical and cultural information; musical analysis; English texts. SYSTEM SPECS: Book and Audio CD.

Songs of Latin America (www.alfred.com): Twelve songs featuring native singers on the CD; maps; cultural information; lesson plans integrate music and social studies; arrangements for Orff instruments. SYSTEM SPECS: Book and Audio CD.

Step One: Play Harmonica DVD (www.musicsales.com): All-in-one package for learning to play the harmonica; guidebook; practice with accompanying audio tracks; DVD features demonstration with an expert; chapter menus and more for easy navigation through the lessons. SYSTEM SPECS: Book, Audio CD, and Instructional DVD.

Step One: Teach Yourself Harmonica DVD (www.musicsales.com): Guidebook; practice along with accompanying audio tracks; DVD features demonstration with an expert; chapter menus and more for easy navigation through the lessons. SYSTEM SPECS: Book, Audio CD, and Instructional DVD.

Teach Yourself to Play Harmonica (www.alfred.com): Interactive; for beginners with no musical experience; free Hohner Harmonica; licks in the style of the Beatles, Bob Dylan, and Stevie Wonder; demonstrates chording, single-note playing, advanced techniques, and more. SYSTEM SPECS: Book and Enhanced CD or Hybrid CD-ROM.

The History of Folk Music CD-ROM (www.clearvue.com): Information about the European and African influences on the development of American folk music; five sections: Roots of American Folk Music, Country Music, Black Folk Music, Folk Music in History, and Folk Music in History, Part II; tracks the roots of American folk music from early Native American music, to the music of new settlers, to country music, and to African American music; in-depth surveys; includes aural examples of folk instruments, singing, and chanting; spoken text between the examples; color pictures showing costumed groups singing, playing different instruments, and dancing; main program runs through the musical examples and spoken text; click on different icons to access extra information and references, question and answer sections, and quizzes; Intro to Power CD answers questions about how to access other areas of the program such as references, printing, and quizzes; Question and Answer icon takes user through several multiple-choice questions; when an incorrect choice is made, the correct answer is shown, and the reasons why; preparation for the seven timed quizzes; score and the correct answers are given at the end of each timed quiz; quiz topics include Ethnic and Cultural Aspects, Important People, and Styles of Music; quiz scores are automatically recorded; information can be printed; references given for more in-depth research; clicking the Magnifying Glass icon enlarges the picture on the screen; helps users see instrument and costume details; addition to any American music history curriculum; technical support; for ages ten to adult. SYSTEM SPECS: Hybrid CD-ROM.

The Interactive Blues Harp Workshop (www.melbay.com): By Steve Baker; CD-ROM; starting from beginners level; multimedia tutorial features play-along tracks and more than 100 exercises with loop function; covers the basics to advanced playing techniques; background information on the history of the harp; important players; how to tune and repair harp; recommended recordings, mics and amps; graphics, audio files, pictures, text files. SYSTEM SPECS: Windows.

The Instruments and Music of China (www.musicmotion.com): Visit the Great Wall and instrument and silk factories; hear outstanding performances on traditional instruments like the guqin and more; introduction to the music of China; running time twenty-seven minutes. SYSTEM SPECS: Instructional DVD.

The Sounds of Mexico (www.inside-mexico.com): Rich and diverse musical heritage; each region has its own styles of singing, playing, and dancing, as well as folk dress and handicrafts; Oaxacan marimbas, sacred instrument of the Mayans, revived later by the African slaves; Mariachis of Jalisco; songs of Michoacan that echo pre-Hispanic roots, and more; narrated musical tour of Mexico; beautiful colonial settings; sights and colors of Mexico blend with the music; running time forty-five minutes. SYSTEM SPECS: Instructional DVD.

Traditional Songs of Singing Cultures (www.alfred.com): Explores the musical heritage of cultures around the world; features maps, cultural information, and activities to enhance the listening experience; gives students a greater understanding of the music that has developed in different cultures. SYSTEM SPECS: Book and Audio CD.

Ultimate Beginner Series: Bluegrass Banjo Basics and Beyond and Bluegrass Mandolin Basics and Beyond (www.alfred.com): By Dennis Caplinger, bluegrass multi-instrumentalist; learn classic bluegrass techniques using bluegrass standards; back-up parts; playing solos; working with a bluegrass band. SYSTEM SPECS: Instructional DVD.

West African Drum and Dance (www.alfred.com): Rhythms and dances of Guinea, West Africa; multimedia collection; traditional West African music, dance, and culture. SYSTEM SPECS: Book, Audio CD, and Instructional DVD.

Woody Guthrie – Ain't Got No Home (www.woodyguthrie.org): From the Dust Bowl and the Depression, he permeated America's music and social conscience, inspiring the folk revival of the 1950s and 1960s; he wrote, sang, and painted about everything from labor to laundry to love; his legacy endures today; documentary of the real-life American legend includes PDFs of a biographical essay and Director Peter Frumkin's Q & A; running time ninety minutes. SYSTEM SPECS: Instructional DVD.

World Beat Fun: Multicultural and Contemporary Rhythms (www.alfred.com): Interactive set; world music styles and contemporary themes; allows students to hear and see notes and rhythms; encourages the use of different instruments; reinforces learning through rote and reproducible handouts; helpful notations for students; easy-to-follow teaching suggestions; play along with the seven tracks; students learn to maintain a steady beat; discover cultural music awareness; reinforce note values and rhythm reading; perform call-and-response rhythms as ostinatos, and more; for grades K-8. SYSTEM SPECS: Book and Audio CD.

World Dance Series (www.alfred.com): Easy to follow dance graphics with accompaniment, background notes, and Orff or percussion arrangements; titles include *Canadian Folk Dances; Folk Dances from Around the World; Folk Dances from France; Folk Dances from Latin America,* and *Mexican Folk Dances.* SYSTEM SPECS: Book and Audio CD.

You Can Teach Yourself Banjo DVD (www.melbay.com): For five-string bluegrass banjo; teaches tuning, how to read tablature, roll patterns, chords, licks, and other basic information needed to play bluegrass and melodic-style banjo; explains first twenty-two lessons from book of same title; demonstrates examples slowly and at regular speed; can be used by itself to learn by ear, or with tablature found in companion book; companion book sold separately; sixty minutes. SYSTEM SPECS: Instructional DVD.

You Can Teach Yourself Blues Harp (www.melbay.com): Taught by Phil Duncan; play rhythm chords; designed to be used with book of same title; demonstrates selected examples from book; student is guided in developing ability to hear blues progressions and styles; helps student develop ability to handle demands of most blues music. SYSTEM SPECS: Instructional DVD.

You Can Teach Yourself Dobro DVD (www.melbay.com): By Janet Davis; presents several popular styles used in playing the Dobro, including bluegrass, old time, blues, country, and Hawaiian; no previous musical knowledge needed; tunes included are Good Night Ladies, Dark Hallow, Jon Henry, Dixie, and many more; presented in G tuning with tablature only; companion book recommended. SYSTEM SPECS: Instructional DVD.

You Can Teach Yourself Dulcimer DVD (www.melbay.com): By Madeline Macneil; companion to book of same title; covers tuning, scales, strumming, fingering, chord studies, alternate tunings, use of capo, and notes; demonstrates dulcimer arrangements. SYSTEM SPECS: Instructional DVD.

You Can Teach Yourself Fiddling DVD (www.melbay.com): By Craig Duncan; complements first seventeen lessons of companion text; covers tuning, holding fiddle and bow, left-hand position, basic A, D, and G scales, shuffle bowing, slurs, double stops, and tunes, including Liza Jane, Shortening Bread, Going to Boston, and Bile Them Cabbage Down. SYSTEM SPECS: Instructional DVD.

You Can Teach Yourself Hammered Dulcimer (www.melbay.com): By Madeline Macneil; information on playing hammered dulcimer; tuning, major and minor keys, duplicated notes, repeated notes, modulations, walking bass lines, chromatic notes, drone harmony, back-up chords, interval harmony, and more; arrangements of twenty-five tunes. SYSTEM SPECS: Book and Instructional DVD.

You Can Teach Yourself Harmonica (www.melbay.com): Guides viewer through solos and techniques in companion book; fifty minutes playing time. SYSTEM SPECS: Instructional DVD.

You Can Teach Yourself Mandolin (www.melbay.com): By Dix Bruce; play-along examples and tunes; basics of mandolin and mandolin playing; accompanying self and others; common chords and useful strums; reading simple melodies;

playing mandolin folk songs; musical examples and tunes written in standard notation and tablature; diagrams principal chords used on mandolin; Chord Appendix; drawings and photographs of vintage instruments. SYSTEM SPECS: Instructional DVD.

You Can Teach Yourself Uke DVD (www.melbay.com): By William Bay; teaches basics of uke playing; how to hold the uke; strum in different time signatures; fifty-eight ukulele songs in keys of C, G, D, F, and Bb; step-by-step instruction; C tuning. SYSTEM SPECS: Instructional DVD.

Country Music—Cowboy Songs—Line Dancing—Western Swing Web Sites

Academy of Country Music www.acmcountry.com
Awards; news; events; membership; history.
Bill Bader's Line Dance Links
www.billbader.com/line-links.htm Line dance.
Birthplace of Country Music
www.birthplaceofcountrymusic.org Concerts and events; musical heritage; museum; education.
Canadian Country Music
www.canehdian.com/genre/country.html Information on country music in Canada.
CMT Canada www.cmtcanada.com/index.asp Canadian country music.
Country Music Association (CMA)
www.cmaworld.com Founded in 1958; first trade organization formed to promote a type of music; now has more than 6,000 members in 43 countries; to guide and enhance the development of country music throughout the world; to demonstrate it as a viable medium to advertisers, consumers, and media; and to provide a unity of purpose for the country music industry; awards.
Country Music Association of Australia
www.countrymusic.asn.au Information on country music in Australia.
Country Music Classics
www.countrymusicclassics.com Free weekly newsletter; classic country music.
Country Music Hall of Fame
www.countrymusichalloffame.com Information on Hall of Fame members; museum; programs; music history; *Journal of Country Music*; Hatch Show Print.
Country Music History
thanksforthemusic.com/history Information on favorite country stars; news; articles
Country Music People
www.countrymusicpeople.com Country music magazine; new country, roots, honky-tonk, Americana, traditional, acoustic, country-rock, old time, bluegrass, Nashpop, cowboy,

rockabilly, western swing, singer-songwriter, alternative.
Country Music Store www.cmstore.co.uk Over 4,000 CDs available from stock.
Country Music Television (CMT) www.cmt.com Music videos; news; artists; tours; radio; hall of fame; top twenty countdown.
Country Standard Time
www.countrystandardtime.com Country music features, articles, and reviews.
Country Weekly www.countryweekly.com Online magazine; artist tour dates by state; country notes; star stats; history.
Country-Time www.country-time.com Line dances online; country dance music CDs for sale; homepages for well-known choreographers.
Cowboy Songs
www.lonehand.com/cowboy_songs.htm Western music; history; Pickin' Parlor; old West events.
Cowboy Songs www.mcneilmusic.com/cowboy.html CDs; songbooks; historical collections; music samples; links; Civil War songs; Revolutionary War songs.
Cowboy Songs and Range Ballads
www.bbhc.org/events/cowboySongs.cfm Exhibitions; events; museums; library; store; programs and education.
Gene Autry Oklahoma Film & Music Festival
www.geneautryokmuseum.com/ Annual event in September; Gene Autry Oklahoma Museum.
Goodwin Music www.goodwinmusic.com Country music artists; music; lyrics; sheet music; guitar reference; videos; country links.
Greatest Films-Nashville (1975)
www.filmsite.org/nash.html Detailed review, synopsis, and discussion of the film.
Hillbilly Music www.hillbilly-music.com Artists; groups; news; press; jukebox; library; reviews; publications; music sources; organizations.
Honky Tonkin' honkytonkinmusic.bizland.com Wide variety of Independent music CDs including country, Texas, western swing, cowboy, bluegrass, alternative country, traditional country and honky-tonk along with various other genres.
Las Vegas Country Music and Cowboys
www.2steppin.com/vegas.htm Country music Las Vegas style.
Line Dance Fun www.linedancefun.com San Francisco area; streaming MP3s.
Nashville City Search nashville.citysearch.com City guide, clubs, music, etc.
PBS Songs of the West
www.pbs.org/weta/thewest/resources/archives/five/songs.htm Songs of the plains; cowboy songs.
Roughstock's History of Country Music
www.roughstock.com/history Country music

history; artists from Gene Autry, Roy Acuff, Bob Wills, Hank Williams to Patsy Cline, Lefty Frizzell, Willie Nelson, Garth Brooks, and many others; cowboy music; western swing.

The Canadian Country Music Association www.ccma.org/ccmatoday/index.htm Canadian country music industry; events; CCMA Awards archives; Hall of Fame; links to artists; radio stations; magazines; record labels; organizations.

The Roughstock Network www.roughstock.com Contemporary country music; COWPIE archives; chords; sheet music; Country Countdown; charts.

The Western Music Association www.westernmusic.org Nonprofit whose purpose is the preservation and promotion of the traditional and contemporary music of the Great American West and the American Cowboy.

The Wild West www.thewildwest.org/cowboys/songs.html Songs and poetry.

Voices West www.cowboysong.com/index.html Cowboy poetry and songs.

Western Swing www.westernswing.com Music news and information; links.

Western Swing Monthly wswing.home.texas.net/ Complete and up to the minute listing of dances, shows, festivals and events.

Western Swing Music Society of the Southwest www.wsmss.com Hall of Fame; history.

Women of Country www.womenofcountry.com Featured artists; album reviews; news; interviews; concert reviews; music store; wallpaper.

Folk and Traditional Music and Instruments—Folk Dancing—Bluegrass Web Sites

---

Acoustics Records (UK) www.acousticsrecords.co.uk Virtuoso recordings of Celtic and classical mandolin, Irish accordion, folk and children's songs.

AcuTab Publications www.acutab.com Authorized tab transcriptions from top bluegrass pickers; banjo accessories and software; DVDs.

American Melody www.americanmelody.com Award-winning recordings of folk, bluegrass, and children's music and stories; audio samples.

ARC Music www.arcmusic.co.uk/ Folk and world music.

Bluegrass Now www.bluegrassnow.com Magazine; festival calendar in each issue; features; reviews; tour schedules; group news.

Bluegrass Unlimited www.bluegrassmusic.com Magazine; annual festival directory; features; interviews; band news; tour schedules.

Breezy Ridge Instruments Ltd. www.jpstrings.com Strings; hammered dulcimers; guitar products; capos; finger picks; vintage thumb picks; videos; Nuage Gypsy Strings.

Cajun/Zydeco Music and Dance snipurl.com/zydemagic Cajun/Zydeco music and dance Web site; national and international festivals and special events information; regional reporters; bands and artists.

CajunZydeco.net cajunzydeco.net Links to other associated Web pages; schedules and newsletters; bands; festivals and dance camps; dance instructors; online dance instruction; online audio and video; Louisiana culture.

Country Dance and Song Society www.cdss.org Celebrating a living tradition of English and Anglo-American dance and music since 1915.

Crafters of Tennessee www.crafterstn.com Products; news; history; banjos; mandolins; guitars.

Creativefolk.com creativefolk.com Resources; links; calendar of events nationwide and more.

Cybergrass www.cybergrass.com For bluegrass music enthusiasts; over 175 pages of information; artists; concerts; events; associations; bluegrass magazines; downloadable sound files; links; articles on bluegrass musicians; history of bluegrass.

Deering Banjo Co. www.deeringbanjos.com Banjo manufacturer.

Dirty Linen www.dirtylinen.com Online folk music magazine; tour schedules in each issue; venues and contact information; folk, world music, roots music, Celtic; features; interviews; new releases.

Dr. HorsehairMusic Co. www.drhorsehair.com Banjo recordings and instruction books; modern-day clawhammer banjo or frailing style; old-time minstrel banjo stroke style.

efolk Music efolkmusic.org/ Folk, bluegrass, Celtic, and children's music; downloads; CDs.

Encyclopedia of Cajun Culture www.cajunculture.com Cajun music and culture.

Fiddler Magazine www.fiddle.com Informative, educational, and entertaining resource for fiddlers, accompanists, and appreciative listeners.

Flea Market Music, Inc. www.fleamarketmusic.com Jumpin' Jim's ukulele products.

Folk Corporation www.folkcorp.co.uk UK folk music Web site; links.

Folk Dance Association www.folkdancing.org Calendar; directory; library; camps; cruises.

Folk Den www.folkden.com Roger McGuinn; continues the tradition of the folk process of telling stories and singing songs, passed on from one generation to another by word of mouth.

Folk Image www.folkimage.com Internet DJ's folk music audio Web site; archives.

Folk Music Home Page
www.jg.org/folk/folkhome.html Informative links to folk music sites.

Folk Music Index www.ibiblio.org/folkindex/ Index to recorded sources.

Folk Music Links
Web.ukonline.co.uk/Members/martin.nail/commerc.htm Links to record companies, publishers, retailers, and artist agents in England.

Folk of the Wood www.folkofthewood.com Acoustic instruments; information; lessons; accessories.

Folk Roots Home Page www.frootsmag.com England's leading roots, folk, and world music magazine; charts; reviews.

Folkcraft Instruments www.folkcraft.com Hammered dulcimers; folk harps.

FolkLib www.folklib.net/ Library of folk music links.

Folklinks.com www.folklinks.com Informative folk and acoustic music Web site.

Folkmusic.org www.folkmusic.org Comprehensive source for folk and acoustic music resources.

Harmonica Lessons www.harmonicalessons.com Complete harmonica source on the Internet.

International Bluegrass Music Association (IBMA)
www.ibma.org Venue, presenter, media, and membership mailing lists available; membership required; events and programs.

International Folk Culture Center www.ifccsa.org U.S., Canadian, and international folk dance and music groups, camps, festivals, institutes, parties, symposia, tours, weekend centers, college and university folk dance and folklore programs, directories, libraries, museum, organizations.

John C. Campbell Folk School www.folkschool.com Held in Brasstown, NC.

Kerrville Music Foundation Inc. Kerrville Directory www.kerrville-music.com Folk festival information; listings of folk venues, press, radio stations, newsletters, publications, record companies, agents, managers, performers, and publicists.

Mandolin Bros. Ltd. www.mandoweb.com Mandolins and guitars.

Musicmaker's Kits, Inc. www.musikit.com Acoustic instrument do-it-yourself kit company; catalog of early music and folk instruments.

National Storytelling Association (NSA)
www.storynet.org Directory of organizations; storytellers; workshops; festivals; production companies; publishers; bimonthly magazine; National Storytelling Conference.

Old Town School of Folk Music
www.oldtownschool.org Held in Chicago, IL.

PrinceGeorge.Com
www.princegeorge.com/georgemusic/ Bagpipes, tin whistles, and mandolins.

Ridge Runner www.ridgerunner.com Music instruction mail-order company; videos for guitar, fiddle, mandolin, dobro, banjo, and more.

Sheet Music for Harmonica
www.harmonicaspot.com/cat67.htm List of items available.

SingOut! Magazine www.singout.org Annual directory of folk festivals; features; reviews; regular columns; to preserve and support the cultural diversity and heritage of all traditional and contemporary folk music; to encourage making folk music a part of our everyday lives; nonprofit.

Sound to Earth, Inc. www.soundtoearth.com Instruments; players; dealers; products.

Southeast Celtic Music Association www.scmatx.org Promoting Celtic music in the southwest.

The Folk Alliance—North American Folk Music and Dance Alliance www.folkalliance.org/ Folk and traditional music; annual conferences held in different locations; membership required.

The Gumbo Pages www.gumbopages.com New Orleans music and culture.

Traditional Dance in Toronto www.dancing.org Information on traditional dancing.

Weber Mandolins www.Webermandolin.com Mandolin manufacturer.

World Folk Music Association wfma.net/ Events; folk music links; store.

Latin and Caribbean Music Web Sites

ART-COM International Latin Music Megastore
www.artcomintl.com/music.htm Latin pop, Latin rap, danza, flamenco, mariachi, merengue, salsa, tango, and tejano.

Batanga www.batanga.com/sp/default.asp Latin music Internet radio.

Bembe Records www.bembe.com/cgi-bin/SoftCart.exe/store/index.html?E+scstore Cuban music record label.

Billboard Latin Music Conference and Awards
www.billboardevents.com/billboardevents/latin/index.jsp Schedule; finalists and winners; show.

Caribbean Beat www.caribbeat.com.jm Caribbean artists; online promotion and distribution of music products and services from the Caribbean.

Descarga.com
www.descarga.com/db/pages/catalog.html Artists; journal archives; glossary of terms;

Glossary of Latin Music Terms
www.salsaholic.de/glossary.htm Definitions.

Heartbeat Records www.rounder.com/heartbeat Jamaican ska, rocksteady, early reggae, and dub; modern roots and cultural dancehall.

Hispanic Online www.hispaniconline.com Arts and entertainment.

Hispano Music and Culture of the Northern Rio Grande memory.loc.gov/ammem/rghtml/rghome.html Juan B. Rael Collection of religious and secular music of Spanish-speaking residents of northern New Mexico; essays in English and Spanish.

Hot Salsa www.chez.com/abri/e/index.htm Archives, forum, and more.

Jammin Reggae Archives niceup.com Gateway to reggae music on the Internet; search; sounds.

Just Salsa www.justsalsa.com Web magazine dedicated to Latin music, dance, and culture.

LaMusica.com stories.lamusica.com Bilingual Latin music and entertainment site, featuring original content, music reviews, Web casts, celebrity chats, concert info, contests, artist interviews, videos, and online shopping.

LARitmo www.laritmo.com *Latin American Rhythm Magazine*; interviews; articles; charts.

Latin American Folk Institute www.lafi.org Nonprofit organization dedicated to building community through art education and affordable cultural programs; promotes the art, music, and folklore of the Caribbean.

Latin American Music Center www.music.indiana.edu/som/lamc Research and performance of Latin American art music.

Latin Jazz Club www.LatinJazzClub.com Online magazine dedicated to the advancement, education, and historical preservation of Latin Jazz.

Latin Music Specialists www.latinmusicspecialists.com Latin music library for TV, film, and commercials.

Latin Real Book, Latin-Jazz www.shermusic.com/latrealb.htm Contemporary and classic salsa, Latin jazz, and Brazilian music arrangements; exactly as recorded, to help bands play in authentic Latin styles.

Latin Sequences of Miami www.latinosequences.com Cumbia, merengue, salsa, and all Latin rhythms; free catalog; over 4,000 Latin rhythm sequences.

Latin/Jazz Reviews www.warr.org/latinjazz.html Reviews of recordings by Latin and Jazz artists.

Latin-Beat.net latin-beat.net/ Latin music, culture, recordings, and shopping; Latin dances; music samples and steps; stars, posters, magazines, leathers, instruments.

Latino Web www.latinoweb.com Latino culture.

LatinWorld www.latinworld.com Articles; travel; adventure; music.

Library of Congress/HLAS lcWeb2.loc.gov/hlas *Handbook of Latin American Studies.*

Music in Latin America-LANIC lanic.utexas.edu/la/region/music Latin American resources; links.

MusicaPeruana.com www.musicaperuana.com Music of Peru.

Puro Mariachi www.mariachi.org The Mexican musical genre; conferences; musicians and bands.

Ratango www.ratango.com New Latin dance combining authentic Argentine tangos with hip-hop beats and rap; English lyric adaptations; featuring Marina Dorell.

Reggae Lyrics Archive hem.passagen.se/selahis Reggae lyrics.

Reggae Train www.reggaetrain.com Largest and most comprehensive reggae music portal on the web; free e-mail, festival guide, concert calendar, reggae forum, and more; detailed information on record labels, record distributors, radio stations, music charts, clubs and venues, and publications.

Salsa Dance Site www.salsadancesite.com Mission is to connect salsa dance lovers and their friends around the world, providing reliable information, services and products.

Salsa Web www.salsaweb.com/home.htm Online magazine; music; artists; videos and more.

Samurai Latino Web www.s-latino.com Informative site devoted to the Latin music of the Caribbean.

Sounds of Brazil www.sobs.com New York City club; World and Latin music; news; calendar.

Tango Reporter www.tangoreporter.com Monthly magazine published in Spanish in Los Angeles with interviews, biographies, CD and book reviews, tango lyrics, milongas, and tango news.

Todotango.com www.todotango.com Original tango master recordings; online tango music club featuring unique tango classics.

Trinidad & Tobago Instruments Ltd. www.steelpansttil.com Steel drums; Panland.

Tropical Music www.tropical-music.com Newsboard; world music; Cuban music; MP3.

Tropical Music & Pro Audio www.tropicalmusic.com Wholesale distribution.

World Music—International— Ethnomusicology Web Sites

200 International Music Links http://ingeb.org/midimidi.html Links and MIDI files to countries and ethnic music.

4Arabs Music www.4arabs.com/music/ Arabic music to download; Arabic CDs; online forum.

Africa Sounds www.africasounds.com Music concerts and cultural events.

Africa1.com www.africa1.com World music radio.

African-American Mosaic
lcWeb.loc.gov/exhibits/african/intro.html African American history and culture.

Afrojazz www.afrojazz.com Promotes talent, originality, social and cultural respect; alternative and new music from around the world.

Ancient-Future.Com: World Music Online www.ancient-future.com World music movement; traditional world music education; global music and dance forums.

Arab Music
trumpet.sdsu.edu/M151/Arab_Music1.html Major influences; assimilated cultures; Medieval Europe; structure of modern-day Arabic music including maqam and iqa.

Arabic Music Info Source
members.aol.com/amisource Resource for Arabic music.

Archive of World Music
http://hcl.harvard.edu/libraries/loebmusic/collections/archive.html Collection of the Loeb Music Library, Harvard University.

Archives of African American Music and Culture www.indiana.edu/~aaamc African American music; links.

Archives of Traditional Music
www.indiana.edu/~libarchm/ At Indiana University; largest university-based ethnographic sound archives in the United States.

Arts, Culture, and Music in India
www.Webindia.com/india/music.htm Art forms and entertainment in India; classical music and dance, movies, theater, photography; links.

Belly Dance Home Page www.bdancer.com Local features; schedule of dancers; FAQ; educational.

Bhargava & Co. www.indianmusicals.com Indian musical instruments.

Blissco www.blisscorporation.com Italian electronic and dance music; for DJs and musicians.

Books on Music of India
www.vedamsbooks.com/music.htm Annotated catalog of books on various aspects of music of India; detailed descriptions.

California Newsreel-African American Music and Cultural History
http://newsreel.org/nav/topics.asp?cat=2&sub=1 2 Videos on African American music.

California Worldfest www.worldmusicfestival.com Mission is to present incredible music and dance along with fine food and quality crafts for the whole family; children's program and music and dance workshops are included.

Center for World Music
www.centerforworldmusic.org World music center based in San Diego, CA; concert series; world music in the schools; cultural tours; workshops; image galleries.

Ceolas Celtic Music Archive
www.ceolas.org/ceolas.html Celtic music Web site; tunes; tunebooks.

Classical Music of St.Petersburg, Russia
www.classicalmusic.spb.ru All about classical music in St. Petersburg; concert halls; musical theaters; musicians; Russian composers; classical MP3; Russian musical links.

Condor Records www.condorrecords.com World music with free audio samples; Andean and Native American music.

Culturekiosque www.culturekiosque.com Cultural topics; articles in different languages.

Djembe Online www.djembe.dk Scandinavian forum for cross-culture and world music; African and Latin American culture debate; world music record reviews; film and book reviews.

Ethnomusicology, Folk Music, and World Music Links www.lib.washington.edu/music/world.html Extensive and comprehensive list of links to all world music cultures; organizations; institutions; archives; research centers; bibliography; periodicals; online publications; record labels and distributors; videos.

Ethnomusicology Online
research.umbc.edu/eol/eol.html Peer-reviewed multimedia e-journal.

Finnish Music Information Centre www.fimic.fi Finnish music; composers, artists, and groups of contemporary music; folk and world.

Folk Music of England, Scotland, Ireland, Wales, and America www.contemplator.com/folk.html Traditional music; lyrics; tune information; historical background; MIDIs; related links.

France MP3 www.francemp3.com Download site.

Global Fusion Catalog
www.global.fusion.ndirect.co.uk Traditional world music, classical world music, and world fusion music ranging from acoustic English folk, to Latin jazz, to cutting edge dance remixes.

Hardanger Fiddle Association of America
www.hfaa.org Dedicated to preserving and promoting the Norwegian Hardanger fiddle and related traditions of Norwegian music and dance.

House of Musical Traditions www.hmtrad.com Carry acoustic instruments, accessories, and books from around the world, including rare and exotic instruments.

IMMEDIA! www.immedia.com.au AustralAsian music industry directory.

Indian Music Glossary
www.chandrakantha.com/tablasite/glossary.htm Glossary of terms used in Indian music.

Irish Music Box www.dojo.ie/musicbox Online resource for Irish music.

Irish World Music Centre www.ul.ie/~iwmc University of Limerick; set up by Dr. Súilleabháin.

Italia Mia-Italian Music www.italiamia.com/music.html Italian music.

JewishMusic.com www.jewishmusic.com Jewish music books; software; videos.

Lo'Jo www.lojo.org World music, concerts, and press kit; French and English.

Lotus www.lotusarts.com Music and dance multicultural studio.

M.E.L.T. 2000 www.melt2000.com World music.

Mathers Museum of World Cultures www.indiana.edu/~mathers/home.html Exhibits, events, and educational programs.

Mondomix—Musiques du Monde www.mondomix.org World Music; traditional music; downloads.

Moroccan Music www.moroccanmusic.com Music of Morocco.

Music India OnLine www.musicindiaonline.com Updates; mailing list; audio samples.

Music of the World www.musicoftheworld.com Independent label that produces quality recordings of traditional and contemporary world music.

Musica Russica www.musicarussica.com Russian choral music.

Musicanews www.musicanews.com Italian music.

NativeWeb www.nativeWeb.org Information of interest to indigenous peoples; seeks to represent all indigenous peoples of the planet.

Oud Home Page www.kairarecords.com/oudpage/Oud.htm Information about the Middle-Eastern lute, or oud.

Rampant Scotland Directory—Music and Dance www.rampantscotland.com/music.htm Scottish music and dance.

RootsWorld www.rootsworld.com Magazine of world music; culture, art, and music.

Scandinavian Indie www.lysator.liu.se/~chief/scan.html Internet guide to Scandinavian independent music.

Swedish Music Festivals www.musikfestivaler.se From spring to autumn there are festivals throughout Sweden; folk music, chamber music, opera, jazz, or choral music; program folder available in Swedish, English, and German.

The Society for Ethnomusicology www.ethnomusicology.org Founded in 1955 to promote the research, study, and performance of music in all historical periods and cultural contexts; over 2,000 members from six continents.

Traditional World Music Influences in Contemporary Solo Piano Literature http://www.scarecrowpress.com/Catalog/SingleBook.shtml?command=Search&db=^DB/CATALOG.db&eqSKUdata=0810833808 "Everything But Bach, Beethoven and Brahms," comprises this *multicultural* repertoire guide for pianists, composers, music teachers and students, world music enthusiasts, and scholars; identifies pieces in the contemporary solo piano literature which show world music influences not traditionally associated with the standard repertoire of Western European art music; includes pieces which use or attempt to emulate non-Western scales, modes, folk tunes, rhythmic, percussive or harmonic devices and timbres.

Traditional World Music Recordings www.medieval.org/music/world.html Quick menu; how to buy.

World Beat Planet www.worldbeatplanet.com World music portal.

World Fusion Music Links www.ancient-future.com/links/index.html Links page for the world music and dance movements; traditional and world fusion music.

World Music www.worldmusic.org Nonprofit organization; presenter of global culture, featuring music and dance from around the world.

World Music Central www.worldmusiccentral.org/ World music resource; links.

World Music Charts Europe www.wmce.de/ Current charts.

World Music Institute www.heartheworld.org Encourages cultural exchange between nations and ethnic groups; supports traditional music by providing opportunities for visiting and local artists; presents the finest in traditional and contemporary music and dance from around the world; works towards a greater understanding of the world's music and dance traditions.

World Music Network www.worldmusic.net/ In-depth information and sound samples of all releases including Rough Guide introductions to music from around the world, fund-raising CDs for Amnesty, Oxfam and New Internationalist, and single artist releases on the Riverboat label.

World Music Press www.worldmusicpress.com Multicultural music books; recordings.

World Music Store www.worldmusicstore.com Multicultural media.

Worldwide Internet Music Resources www.music.indiana.edu/music_resources/ethnic.html National, international, and world music links.

Jazz—Blues—Ragtime—
New Age—Rock and Popular Music
Software, Instructional Media and Web Sites

A Great Day In Harlem (www.a-great-day-in-harlem.com): In 1958 photographer Art Kane assembled fifty-seven of the greatest jazz stars of all time and took a picture that would live forever; narrated by Quincy Jones, the film tells the story behind the legendary photograph; rare, archival footage of live performances and interviews with thirty jazz greats; navigate to any image in the photo to see the musician's name; click on the name to bring up a selection of related scenes in the documentary including outtakes; 1995 Academy Award nominee for Best Documentary; running time sixty minutes. SYSTEM SPECS: Instructional DVD.

Berklee Press (www.berkleepress.com): Titles include: *A Guide to Jazz Improvisation; A Guide to Jazz Improvisation (Bass Clef Instruments); A Guide to Jazz Improvisation (Bb Instruments); A Guide to Jazz Improvisation (Eb Instruments); Arranging for Large Jazz Ensemble; Blues Improvisation Complete (Bb Instruments); Blues Improvisation Complete (C Bass Instruments); Blues Improvisation Complete (C Instruments); Blues Improvisation Complete (Eb Instruments); Jazz Composition—Theory and Practice; Modern Jazz Voicings—Arranging for Small and Medium Ensembles; Jazz Improvisation: A Personal Approach with Joe Lovano; Jazz Expression: A Toolbox for Improvisation; Jazz Improvisation: Starting Out with Motivic Development; Latin Jazz Grooves;* and more. SYSTEM SPECS: Book, Audio CD, and/or Instructional DVD.

Blue Man Group DVD (www.blueman.com): Three bald, blue characters take the viewer through a multi-sensory experience that combines theatre, percussive music, art, science, and vaudeville; live rock concert footage; three full-length music videos; bonus material including tracks with surround sound; ninety minutes. SYSTEM SPECS: Instructional DVD.

Blues for Dummies (www.dummies.com): Covers blues from the Mississippi Delta to Chicago's gritty South Side and points beyond; blues guitarist Lonnie Brooks guides through the life and times of the blues, from Robert Johnson and Son House to the urban blues men and women of today: John Lee Hooker, Robert Cray, B.B. King, Etta James, Koko Taylor, and Stevie Ray Vaughan; styles and eras of the blues; four generations of blues musicians; the best blues clubs; some of the greatest blues recordings of all time are on the CD. SYSTEM SPECS: Book and Audio CD.

Blues Journey and Jazz Set (www.musicmotion.com): The blues and jazz verbally, visually, and musically explored; inspired verse backed by memorable collages in blue ink and brown paper; guitar and singing with the narration on the CD; for grades four and up; forty pages each. SYSTEM SPECS: Book and Audio CD.

Bluesland (www.musicmotion.com): Traces the roots of blues from the beginning of the century through the Mississippi Delta to Louisiana, Texas, Kansas City and Chicago; footage of the era; narration; performances by Big Bill Broonzy, Sonny Boy Williamson, Joe Turner, Muddy Waters, Bessie Smith and more. SYSTEM SPECS: Instructional DVD.

Elements of the Jazz Language for the Developing Improvisor (www.alfred.com): Comprehensive book on jazz analysis and improvisation; elements used in jazz improvisation examined in recorded solos; suggestions are made for using each element in the jazz language; specific exercises provided for practicing the element; ideal environment for developing fluency with the jazz language; for intermediate to advanced, ninth grade and up. SYSTEM SPECS: Book and Audio CD.

Ella Fitzgerald – Something to Live For DVD (www.musicmotion.com): Documentary of the jazz singer; her stylings; she recorded more that 2000 songs and won fourteen Grammys over her sixty-year career; features rare footage of performances and exclusive interviews; running time eighty-six minutes. SYSTEM SPECS: Instructional DVD.

Jamey Aebersold Jazz Books with Play-Along Audio CDs and Instructional DVDs (www.aebersold.com/Merchant2/merchant.mvc): Since 1967 the name Jamey Aebersold has been synonymous with the very best in jazz education materials; world-class performer; charismatic teacher/lecturer; mission is to teach people how to play jazz and improvise; over one-hundred titles. SYSTEM SPECS: Book, Audio CD, and Instructional DVD.

Jazz for Young People (www.musicmotion.com): Produced by Jazz at Lincoln Center; written and narrated by Wynton Marsalis, Artistic Director; complete curriculum; history, style, form, improvisation, arranging, composing, personalities, and more; Marsalis is a fantastic teacher, using metaphor, example, interaction, straight talk, and great music; short talks, asking for participation, and example after example in a step-by-step approach keeps students listening and involved; Teaching Guide presents each lesson, suggests participatory activities and additional resources as well as integrates National Standards; whole narrative is on CD-ROM available to be printed; nine CDs present seventeen units in thirty sessions; thirty student guides feature focused listening charts, activities, historical summaries, bios, and photos; video shows the Lincoln Center Jazz Band recording in their studio; use all or part of the interactive curriculum. SYSTEM SPECS: Book, Audio CD, and Hybrid CD-ROM.

Jazz Theory and Practice (www.alfred.com): Introduction to jazz theory; examples from the jazz repertoire; for performers, arrangers, and composers; theoretical foundations of jazz; supplemental exercises for ear-training and sight-reading practice; tutorials. SYSTEM SPECS: Book and/or Macintosh CD-ROM.

Journey Through Jazz (www.musicmotion.com): Traces the history and development of jazz with musical selections from blues, ragtime, swing, be-bop, cool jazz, fusion, and avant-garde; includes the Dan Jordan Trio performing Armstrong, Waller, Ellington, Basie, Goodman, Parker, Coltrane, and more; DVD kit has two live-action thirty-minute films with interactive performances before student audiences; teacher's manual; activities and quizzes; for grades three-twelve. SYSTEM SPECS: Book and Instructional DVD.

Joy of Improv Books 1 and 2 (www.halleonard.com): Twelve to twenty-four-month foundation course for music improvisation on all in-struments; total of fifty-two lessons; emphasizes practice rather than theory; strengthens all aspects of playing, including technique, theory, and ear training; organized for beginning and intermediate players having some basic music reading skills and at least a year of experience playing any musical style; experience real-time synthesis of feeling, hearing, and playing. SYSTEM SPECS: Book and Audio CD.

Hal Leonard DVDs (www.halleonard.com): Titles include: *Breakthrough to Improv: The Secrets of Improvisation—Freedom for All Musicians; Dizzy Gillespie—A Night in Chicago; Gordon Goodwin's Big Phat Band—Swingin' for the Fences; Joe Lovano—Improvisation—Developing a Personal Approach; The Ladies Sing the Blues,* and more. SYSTEM SPECS: Instructional DVD.

Jazz – A Film by Ken Burns (www.pbs.org/jazz/): Epic celebration of the music that defines America from its humble origins in blues and ragtime through its evolution into swing, bebop, and fusion; contains 75 interviews, over 500 pieces of recorded music, 2400 still photographs, and over 2000 historic film clips, many rare or never before seen; highly recommended for all ages; explores the heritage of this uniquely American music; nineteen hours on ten volumes. SYSTEM SPECS: Instructional DVD.

MiBAC Jazz (www.MiBAC.com): MiBAC (Music Instruction By A Computer) breaks jazz into four main styles; each of these main styles has three different tempo subgroups that can be mixed and matched with any of the other styles or groups; many playing options; manual includes a tutorial that covers all twelve styles; how to type in chord progressions; printing charts; tempos and transposition; based on the basic blues progressions; user can experiment with the rhythm section, intros, voicings, and chord alternations; section on printing and setup; last section is a complete reference for all of the commands used; detailed discussions on the twenty-eight possible chord combinations; tool for developing jazz improvisational skills; practice examples; play with a jazz combo on any tune; play in any key, at any tempo; twenty-three jazz styles, including 4/4 and Ballad, Swing, Bebop, Rock Shuffle, Bossa Nova, Samba, Slow 12/8, and Two Beat; for all music students, intermediate to advanced, ages fifteen to adult. SYSTEM SPECS: Macintosh; Windows.

MIDI Jazz Improvisation Volumes I and II (www.ecsmedia.com): Instruction and practice in jazz improvisation for all instruments; jazz ensemble is played through MIDI synthesizer and records student's solo keyboard improvisation; each exercise is organized into eight separate tracks: Bass Line, Chords, Melody, Riff or Counter Melody, Scale Study, Sample Improvised Line, Drums (Vol. II only), and User Solo; Volume I covers ii-V-I progressions and twelve-bar blues; Volume II covers advanced materials and assumes student knowledge of scales and basic improvisation techniques such as harmonic substitution and complex ii-V-I progressions; knowledge of MIDI operation is essential; detailed learning sequence provided to give students guidance and goal-oriented practice; for middle-school through adult keyboard students. SYSTEM SPECS: Hybrid CD-ROM.

Musicians Institute Press (www.halleonard.com): Titles include: *A Modern Approach to Jazz, Rock and Fusion Guitar; An Approach to Jazz Improvisation—A Step-by-Step Guide for All Musicians; Basic Blues Guitar—Essential Progressions, Patterns and Styles; Blues—Workshop Series; Blues Hanon—50 Exercises for the Beginning to Professional Blues Pianist; Blues/Rock Soloing for Guitar—A Guide to the Essential Scales, Licks and Soloing Techniques; Classic Rock—Workshop Series; Jazz Guitar Chord System; Jazz Guitar Improvisation; Jazz Hanon; Jazz-Rock Triad Improvising for Guitar; Modern Rock Rhythm Guitar—A Guide to the Essential Chords, Riffs, Rhythms and Grooves; Rock Lead Basics—Techniques, Scales and Fundamentals for Guitar; Rock Lead Guitar—Techniques, Scales, Licks, and Soloing Concepts for Guitar; Rock Lead Performance—Techniques, Scales and Soloing Concepts for Guitar; Rock Lead Techniques—Techniques, Scales and Fundamentals for Guitar; Slap and Pop Technique for Guitar; Texas Blues Guitar—Private Lessons*, and more. SYSTEM SPECS: Book and Audio CD.

Oscar Peterson Multimedia CD-ROM (www.pgmusic.com): Fourteen complete audio/video performances by Oscar Peterson; ten MIDI transcriptions of his famous blues performances; signature CD-ROM; integrates interactive audiovisual performances with on-screen piano display and notation; see and study exactly what the master is playing; musical journey through his life and career; comprehensive multimedia autobiography with audio and video clips; exclusive photographs from Oscar Peterson's private collection. SYSTEM SPECS: Windows.

Oscar Peterson Note for Note Transcriptions Book (www.pgmusic.com): Transcriptions of Oscar Peterson's jazz piano performances; authorized volume of eighteen full-length transcriptions all taken directly from original recordings; selected and approved by Oscar Peterson. SYSTEM SPECS: Book and Audio CD.

Pop Music in the Twentieth Century (www.clearvue.com): Two DVDs; covers pop music from turn-of-the-century sounds that marked technical advances to new wave, heavy metal, and the introduction of music videos; documentary film footage of historical events; film clips and stills of music performances; the social background and events against which each style of music developed; includes ragtime, jazz, swing, the song era, and 1950s and 1960s rock and roll; the rise of folk music, hard rock, country, punk rock, disco, soul, funk, and reggae. SYSTEM SPECS: Instructional DVD.

Robben Ford—Playin' the Blues (www.alfred.com): Famed blues and jazz guitarist teaches blues scales and phrases along with his unique fingerings. SYSTEM SPECS: Instructional DVD.

Robben Ford—The Blues and Beyond (www.alfred.com): Innovator in contemporary jazz fusion reveals his advanced concepts for improvising and comping; learn from one of the modern master of blues. SYSTEM SPECS: Instructional DVD.

Rock Roots (www.musicmotion.com): Featured on PBS; evolution of American popular music and rock 'n roll; narrated live performances of ethnic dance, folk, blues, swing, R & B, country, rockabilly, Motown, British Invasion, rap, and more; historical, political, and geographical references combined with audience participation; entertaining and educational; includes two thirty-minute videos; teacher's manual; activities and quiz. SYSTEM SPECS: Instructional DVD.

Saxophone Lessons with Alan Neveu (Parakeet): Twenty multimedia saxophone lessons; finger technique, embouchure, articulation, reeds, vibrato, intonation, time, repertoire, and more; lessons on soprano, alto, tenor, and baritone sax playing specifics; multimedia experience; movie clips; CD-quality sounds; color photos; music notation; rich text. SYSTEM SPECS: Macintosh; Windows.

Say Amen Somebody (www.musicmotion.com): Inspirational documentary about gospel music and its development; Willie Mae Ford Smith, Thomas A. Dorsey, and other pioneers of the genre; bonus fifteen-song CD; running time 120 minutes. SYSTEM SPECS: Audio CD and Instructional DVD.

Stephen Foster (www.musicmotion.com): Follow the American songwriter's meteoric rise and lonely decline; discover the tremendous impact his music had on American popular culture; running time sixty minutes. SYSTEM SPECS: Instructional DVD.

The Best of Jazz and Blues – Hollywood Rhythm (www.kino.com): Eleven early black and white mini-musicals or shorts feature Louis Armstrong, Duke Ellington, Billie Holiday, Cab Calloway, Bessie Smith, Fats Waller, and more; despite segregation, jazz slipped in the backdoor of Hollywood; film-making and music making history; running time 123 minutes. SYSTEM SPECS: Instructional DVD.

The Complete Monterey Pop Festival DVD (www.clearvue.com): Revisit the spirit and music of the 1960s; documents the 1967 Monterey International Pop Festival; three-DVD set features classic and rare footage taken by D. A. Pennebaker; first disk contains the legendary 1968 concert film of the festival, highlighting the performances of such greats as the Who, Jimi Hendrix, and Ravi Shankar; second disk includes "Jimi Plays Monterey" and "Shake! Otis at Monterey"; both provide detailed looks at the sets of Jimi Hendrix and Otis Redding; third disk offers two hours of amazing outtake performances and showcases the Byrds, Buffalo Springfield, Quicksilver Messenger Service, Simon and Garfunkel, the Mamas and the Papas, and others; DVD features include crisp digital picture and sound, audio commentaries, photographs, and trailers. SYSTEM SPECS: Instructional DVD.

The Great American Songbook (www.musicmotion.com): Documents popular music from its roots in English folk songs, African slave rhythms and spirituals, European operettas, Irish and Jewish immigrant influences, through Tin Pan Alley, Vaudeville, Ragtime, Jazz, Broadway, and Hollywood; narrated by Michael Feinstein; rare footage of the songs, musicians, and composers; historical events that shaped the national character; introduction to American music for all ages; running time 174 minutes. SYSTEM SPECS: Instructional DVD.

The History of Jazz (www.clearvue.com): History of jazz; performers; jazz from different cities; 1900s to present; interactive; shows how jazz was created by the descendants of the slaves brought from Africa; preserves the spirit and beat of African drum music; includes jazz music legends Louis Armstrong, Dizzy Gillespie, Scott Joplin, Duke Ellington, Benny Goodman, and others; for beginner to intermediate, grades 4-college. SYSTEM SPECS: Hybrid CD-ROM.

The History of Rock 'n' Roll (www.musicmotion.com): Five-DVD set; collection of concert and archival footage; extensive interviews; the most complete history available; from the beginning in blues, gospel, and jazz through today; the movers and shakers; for the fan, library, and for classes on the history of American music; some lyrics inappropriate for children; running time fifty-six minutes. SYSTEM SPECS: Instructional DVD.

The Instrumental History of Jazz CD-ROM Set (www.clearvue.com): History of jazz; audio CD and CD-ROM; ragtime; Dixieland; swing through twentieth century; roots of instrumental jazz; twenty-two audio tracks; archival photos; video clips; different types of jazz; virtual time line; fifty-six-page book with text and photos. SYSTEM SPECS: Macintosh; Windows.

The Jazz Channel Presents DVDs (www.clearvue.com): Familiarize students with some of the greatest names in contemporary jazz; highlighting famed performances at Black Entertainment Television Studio II; each program includes a candid interview and features the artist performing some of his or her most memorable songs; thirteen DVDs; includes B. B. King, Ben E. King, Bobby Womack, Brenda Russell, Chaka Khan, Earl Klugh, Freddie Jackson, Herbie Hancock, Jeffrey Osborne, Keiko Matsui, Kenny Rankin, Lou Rawls, Soul Conversation: Mark Whitfield and JK. SYSTEM SPECS: Instructional DVD.

The Jazz Play-Along Series (www.halleonard.com): Learning tool for all jazz musicians; includes lead sheets, melody cues, and other split-track choices on the audio CD; each tune includes a split track with melody cue with proper style and inflection; professional rhythm tracks; choruses for soloing; removable bass part; removable piano part; additional full stereo accompaniment track without the melody; additional choruses for soloing. SYSTEM SPECS: Book and Audio CD.

The Jazz Saxophonist (www.pgmusic.com): Music program with studio recordings of great jazz saxophone music; learn riffs and tricks; each instrument (sax, piano, bass, and drums) recorded on a separate track; listen to each part independently; multimedia features; study arrangements; hear music; play along with top studio musicians; tips and techniques; integrates multitrack audio, MIDI, chord symbols, and music notation. SYSTEM SPECS: Windows.

The Jazz Soloist (www.pgmusic.com): Jazz quartet arrangements of fifty songs per volume; each song features a jazz solo played by jazz musicians, piano comping, bass, and drums; over three hours of jazz soloing on each volume; MIDI files; for intermediate to advanced, high school and up. SYSTEM SPECS: Macintosh; Windows.

The Rock Saxophonist (www.pgmusic.com): Music program with studio recordings of great rock and roll saxophone music; learn riffs and tricks; each instrument recorded on a separate track; listen to each part independently; multimedia features; study arrangements; hear music; play along with top studio musicians; tips and techniques; integrates multitrack audio, MIDI, chord symbols, music notation, and chord progressions. SYSTEM SPECS: Windows.

The Story of the Blues (www.musicmotion.com): Archival imagery and performance footage capture the essence of the music, the people, and the places that shaped the blues; from slavery and rural uprooting to urban dislocation, discrimination, and poverty; black musicians found in blues an outlet for their pain and frustrated dreams; homemade instruments like the jug for the double bass, the kazoo, and washboard played with thimbles for the drum; used for real instruments which were beyond the means of early blues musicians; traces the traditions and contribution of blues to the development of jazz, rock, and country western music; hear Blind Lemon Jefferson, B.B. King, Robert Johnson, Jelly Roll Morton, King Oliver, Louis Armstrong, Ma Rainey, Bessie Smith, Duke Ellington, and more; running time 120 minutes. SYSTEM SPECS: Instructional DVD.

The Story of Jazz (www.musicmotion.com): Performances, narration, and history; personal profiles and first-hand observations of dozens of artists; begins with the slave dances in Congo Square in New Orleans in

1830 through the cross-cultural influences of the twentieth century; witness the growth of jazz-America's major musical contribution to the world; an introduction to jazz for all ages; running time ninety-seven minutes; color and black and white. SYSTEM SPECS: Instructional DVD.

The Wonderful World of Louis Armstrong (www.musicmotion.com): An intimate portrait of the man and his music; from his humble beginnings in New Orleans, Louisiana, Louis Armstrong rose from singing on street corners to becoming the legendary father of jazz; the DVD is filled with rare archival footage, clips, interviews, and great music; running time sixty-five minutes. SYSTEM SPECS: Instructional DVD.

Jazz—Blues—Swing Web Sites

A Passion 4 Jazz www.apassion4jazz.net Information; resources; links.

Acoustic Records home.c2i.net/acousticrecords Independent Norwegian jazz record label; artist information; reviews; MP3 samples and more.

Aebersold Jazz Online www.jajazz.com Producer of play-along disks and educational materials.

All About Jazz www.allaboutjazz.com Reviews and more; guide to jazz.

Alligator Records www.alligator.com Foremost authority on blues music and blues artists; view artist bios and liner notes; online catalog.

Bird Lives! www.birdlives.com Weekly jazz-zine.

Blue Note Records www.bluenote.com Jazz label; reviews; news; online catalog, artist and tour information; RealAudio clips.

Blues Express www.bluesexpress.com TV; records; CDs; DVDs.

Blues for Peace Cafe www.bluesforpeace.com Web radio, blues books, art, CDs, gifts, and more.

Blues Lab www.blueslab.com Youth enrichment programs; after school programs.

Blues News www.bluesnews.com Blues information.

Blues on Stage www.mnblues.com Comprehensive blues guide; reviews.

Blues Paradise-Classic Blues Musicians www.bluesparadise.com Links to national and regional blues acts; schedule for regional blues venues; festival information and more.

Blues Revue www.bluesrevue.com Magazine site with blues MP3s.

BluesNet www.hub.org/bluesnet Articles, photographs, and more; traditional and historical blues artists.

Contemporary Jazz www.contemporaryjazz.com News; releases; reviews; interviews; forums.

Contemporary List of Jazz Links riad.usk.pk.edu.pl/~pmj/jazzlinks/ Artists; education; radio; links.

Cyberjaz.com www.cyberjaz.com Jazz Web site; hard-to-find and rare recordings.

Dr. Jazz Operations www.drjazz.com Independent radio and print media record promotion firm in the United States; jazz, blues, and world music.

East Coast International Blues and Roots Music Festival www.bluesfest.com.au Australian festival.

Electric Blues www.electricblues.com Hundreds of blues CD ratings; biweekly CD reviews with RealAudio, RealAudio Blues Jukebox, and Real Audio Blues links; all artists linked to discographies/soundclips.

Europe Jazz Network www.ejn.it/ Concerts; bulletin board.

Fivenote Music Publishing www.fivenotemusic.com Publishes music books containing jazz improvisation method, theory, and resources for learning and improving skills for beginning through advanced players of treble clef instruments.

Glenn Miller Orchestra www.glennmillerorchestra.com History; personnel; tour schedule; reviews; links.

House of Blues www.hob.com Live concert cybercasts; music news; on demand concert archives; interviews; music reviews; Internet radio; editorial.

JAZCLASS www.jazclass.aust.com Music lessons on music theory, blues, jazz, improvisation, chords, and scales on all instruments; saxophone technique.

Jazz and Blues www.jazzandblues.org KJAZ radio and Internet radio; program grid; host bios.

Jazz and Blues Report www.jazz-blues.com Reviews of jazz, blues, fusion, and swing music from record labels like Alligator, Rounder, Blind Pig, and more.

Jazz Clubs Worldwide www.jazz-clubs-worldwide.com Organized by continents and countries; links.

Jazz Corner www.jazzcorner.com Great jazz site with MIDI files, jazz artists Web pages, and other jazz related material.

Jazz Is www.jazzis.com Online retailer of jazz music recordings.

Jazz IZ www.jazziz.com Features; reviews; news; subscriptions.

Jazz Master www.jazzmaster.com Information; resources; links.

Jazz Net www.culturekiosque.com/jazz Jazz Web site; news; reviews.

Jazz Online www.jazzonline.com Monthly Webzine; news; features; links; artist reviews; Jazz 101; introduction to the world of jazz.

Jazz Radio www.jazzradio.org From Lincoln Center in New York City; concert series.

Jazz Review www.jazzreview.com Submit music.

Jazz Roots www.jass.com Early jazz history.

Jazz Scale Suggester System www.w-link.net/~jsss/jsss.htm Enter jazz chord chart; suggests and explains solo scale possibilities.

Jazz Times Magazine, Inc. www.jazztimes.com Club Guide in September issue; night clubs; managers; booking agents; features; reviews; news; photography; subscriptions.

Jazz West.com www.jazzwest.com The Bay Area's online jazz network.

Jazz World www.jazzworld.com Information; resources; links; new faces in jazz; artist network.

Jazz, Blues, Flamenco, and World Music Posters www.arrakis.es/~artstudiohita Limited-edition prints.

Jazzbreak www.jazzbreak.com Jazz guide; history; musicians; fanzine; news.

JazzFM www.jazzfm.com The home of jazz on the Internet.

Jazzharmony.com www.jazzharmony.com Contemporary methods for piano, ear training, chords, and jazz voicings; jazz standard fake books; free monthly chord post; includes teaching and learning tips about chords.

JazzInternet.com jazzinternet.com Jazz resources worldwide; jazz radio; RealAudio sites; "Jazz Club" with message board and chat; resource.

JazzUtopia www.jazzutopia.com Jazz music books, videos, and CDs for listening, practicing, and learning.

Jazzworx! www.jazzworx.com.au Set of learning tools; lesson by lesson on a double CD and book; three-volume series; beginning, intermediate, and advanced.

Montreal Jazz Festival www.montrealjazzfest.com/Fijm2008/splash.aspx In French and English.

New Mexico Jazz Workshop www.nmjazz.org/ Dedicated to American jazz; premier jazz presenting and education organization.

New Orleans Jazz and Heritage Festival www.nojazzfest.com Schedules; tickets.

New Orleans Music Radio: WWOZ www.wwoz.org Listener supported jazz and heritage station for New Orleans and the surrounding region; from blues to jazz, cajun, zydeco, gospel, Brazilian, and Caribbean.

Newworldnjazz.com www.newworldnjazz.com Full-service marketing, promotion, and consulting company for the Jazz, Smooth Jazz, and World Music formats; work with over 1,000 radio stations in the United States and Canada.

PBS www.pbs.org/jazz/ *Jazz;* film by Ken Burns.

Photographs from the Golden Age of Jazz memory.loc.gov/ammem/wghtml/wghome.html William P. Gottlieb Collection; over 1,600 photographs of celebrated jazz artists; documents the jazz scene from 1938 to 1948 in New York City and Washington, DC.

Pittsburgh Blues Women www.pghblueswomen.com Chicago and New Orleans are known for blues music; many female blues performers are from these cities.

Play Jazz www.playjazz.com Jazz web site.

Posi-Tone Jazz World posi-tone.com For jazz enthusiasts; links to tribute sites, legends, and more.

Real Blues Magazine www.realbluesmagazine.com Guide for blues music.

SaxTrax.com www.saxtrax.com/cgi-bin/cp-app.cgi Smooth jazz, traditional jazz, and new age CDs.

Sher Music www.shermusic.com Publisher of jazz educational materials; *The New Real Book;* Brazilian and Latin songbooks.

SkyJazz Internet Radio www.skyjazz.com Jazz in four categories: Big Band, Light & Easy, Straight Ahead, and All Requests.

Smooth Jazz www.smoothjazz.com/ The world's smooth jazz radio station.

Smooth Jazz Vibes www.smoothvibes.com/ For fans of contemporary jazz or smooth jazz.

Sonny Boy Lee's "Ain't nothin' but the blues!" www.sonnyboylee.com Blues artists pages and links to blues music sites worldwide.

Southwest Blues www.southwestblues.com Festival.

Stanford Jazz Workshop www.stanfordjazz.org Jazz education.

Swedejazz.se www.swedejazz.se Web site about Swedish jazz.

The Blue Zone bluezone.org Blues bands.

The Blues Fake Book www.netstoreusa.com/music/002/HL00240082.shtml Fake book of over 400 songs for all "C" instruments; sheet music.

The Blues Foundation www.blues.org Organized and founded in 1980 to promote and preserve blues.

The Jazz Pages: Jazz in Deutschland www.jazzpages.com Jazz in Germany.

The Jazz School www.jazzschool.com Specializes in jazz education.

The Jazzserver www.jazzserver.org Interactive jazz database; jazz groups; samples; venues and festivals from all over the world.

The JazzSource www.jazzsource.com Comprehensive international resource to the world of jazz.

The Red Hot Jazz Archive www.redhotjazz.com History of jazz before1930.

Village Vanguard www.villagevanguard.net Famous jazz club; recording venue; schedules.

What is Jazz? town.hall.orgArchives/radio/Kennedy/Taylor/ Four lectures.

Yahoo! Entertainment: Music: Genres: Blues www.yahoo.com/Entertainment/Music/Genres/Blues Blues music.

Music and Health—Healing Music— Recovery Music Web Sites

12 Step Radio www.12stepradio.com Recovery music streamed 24/7; links to CDs; submit music.

Advanced Brain Technologies www.advancedbrain.com Combines extensive clinical experience with neuroscience and music research to create products, programs, and services that enhance health, learning, and productivity.

Alexander Center www.alexandercenter.com/pa/index.html Alexander Technique for musicians; articles; links.

Alexander Technique www.alexandertechnique.com Systematic guide to information and resources on and off the Internet.

American Music Therapy Association www.musictherapy.org Find a music therapist; career options.

Center for Voice Disorders www.wfubmc.edu/voice Information about the causes and treatments of voice disorders; singer's problems.

Crystal Singing Bowls Relaxation Massage Music www.crystalmusic.com Massage relaxation music played on thirty-five pure quartz crystal bowls; for deep relaxation, insomnia, and stress reduction.

Dalcroze Society of America www.msu.edu/user/thomasna Training programs; biography; articles about Dalcroze Eurhythmics.

Donna Michael www.donnamichael.com Healing music; performances; CDs; workshops; artistic collection of piano and hammered dulcimer recordings.

Ear, Nose, and Throat Information Center www.sinuscarecenter.com Public information brochures; symptoms; self-help; hearing loss.

H. E. A. R. www.hearnet.com Hearing protection; earplugs; referral for hearing help; artist of the month.

Hand Health www.handhealth.com *Finger Fitness* program; help for hands.

Hands On! www.lunnflutes.comho.htm Online newsletter about performance health for flutists; list of performance health clinics; links.

HealingMusic.Net www.healingmusic.net *Love Is a Sound* CDs and books; MidiVox Voice to MIDI products; singing courses; composing and songwriting services; sound healing and music healing techniques and resources.

Healthwindows.com www.healthwindows.com Articles on music and wellness.

House Ear Institute-Hearing Conservation www.hei.org Sound Partner Program; HIP-Hearing is Priceless; research.

Internet Resources on the Alexander Technique www.life.uiuc.edu/jeff/alextech.html Collection of links; articles.

Jana Stanfield www.janastanfield.com Motivational performer; combines music with a message that entertains, inspires, and encourages; mission is to give organizations a "faith-lift."

Karen Taylor-Good www.karentaylorgood.com Healing music; performances; CDs; keynote speaker; workshops; hit songwriter.

Mental Health Net www.mentalhelp.net Directory of online mental health resources.

Music and Health www.musicandhealth.co.uk/ Links to articles and organizations.

Music Maker Relief Foundation www.musicmaker.org Charity honors and aids traditional Southern musicians over the age of fifty-five who earn less than $18,000 a year.

Musician's Health www.musicianshealth.com Health information for musicians.

Musicians On Call www.musiciansoncall.org Mission is to use music to complement the healing process for patients in healthcare facilities; Bedside Performance Program; CD Pharmacies.

Performing Arts Medicine www.ithaca.edu/hshp/pt/pt1/index.html Newsletter; information for the performer and health practitioner; links to resources.

Share Songs www.sharesongs.com Songs of hope, awareness, and recovery for everyone; mission is to use the power of Nashville music to bring attention to the pervasive problem of alcohol and drug abuse; to raise awareness and funds through an album project using songs from recording artists and featuring a song to be recorded by a group of Nashville artists; funds from album sales benefit prevention and treatment programs.

Sober Café Podcast www.sobercafepodcast.com Sponsored by Sunlight of the Spirit Music; using the power of music to support recovery from alcoholism and addiction in all its forms.

Special Music by Special People www.specialmusic.org Compact disks; MP3 and Quicktime music projects; music composed by people with developmental disabilities.

Sunlight of the Spirit www.sunlightofthespirit.com Web site featuring music exclusively by artists in recovery; created by Gracie Vandiver; carries over 100 CDs; order online.

Twelve Songs www.twelvesongs.com Songs for each of the Twelve Steps of the A. A. Program.

New Age and Ambient Music Web Sites

Amazing Sounds www.amazings.com/ingles.html New age and ambient music Webzine.

Ambience for the Masses www.sleepbot.com/ambience Search by label, artist, or type of music.

Ars Electronica www.aec.at/en/index.asp Center; Future Lab; Festival; Prix; Archives.

AstroStar Astrology and New Age Resources www.astrostar.com Eclectic array of astrology and New Age resources; conferences; chat room; astrology; books; Atlantean crystals; romance.

Backroads Music www.backroadsmusic.com *Heartbeats Catalog*; source for over 6,000 titles of ambient, new age, space, tribal and global sounds, and other music and videos since1981.

Bliss Relaxation CDs www.relaxationcds.co.uk/ New age/spiritual music.

East West Spiritual and New Age Books and Tapes www.eastwest.com Spiritual and new age books and tapes on the Internet; alternative health and healing; personal growth; self-help; world religions and teachers; mythology; psychology.

Epsilon www.hyperreal.org/music/epsilon Ambient music information Web site; links.

Higher Octave Music www.higheroctave.com Record label; contemporary instrumental music; smooth jazz, new age, ambient, world, and flamenco.

Invincible Music www.invinciblemusic.com Features yoga music, new age music, therapy music, guitar music, healing music, massage music, and Reiki music.

iVibes www.ivibes.nu/ Guide to electronic dance music; trance, techno, house, progressive, and more; news; reviews; interviews; artists; labels.

Makoche-Native American and New Age Music www.makoche.com Makoche Native American Indian music; label and sound studio; online catalog; ordering; concert information.

Music A La Carte www.musicalacarte.net/ New age and world music custom CDs; wide variety of categories, instruments and artists.

Music for a New Age www.mfna.org/index2.html New age music; links.

Music Mosaic www.new-age-music-shop.com New age music compilations by theme; meditation music; healing music; relaxation music.

Narada www.narada.com Record label; new instrumental, jazz and world music; influenced by jazz, world, folk, rock, pop, and classical music.

New Age Information www.newageinfo.com/ New age resource for body, mind, and spirit; articles; music and more.

New Earth Records www.newearthrecords.com New Age artists, world music, trance, meditation relaxation music, and Reiki.

New World Music www.newworldmusic.com Relaxation, world, Celtic, Native American music.

North Star Music www.northstarmusic.com Music for living.

Obsolete www.obsolete.com Ambient and techno.

Only New Age Music www.newagemusic.com Founded by Suzanne Doucet and James Bell to serve the New Age Music industry in all aspects; online retail store, record label, and publishing company.

Peaceful Paths www.peacefulpaths.com Enlightening products: books, music, artwork, aromatherapy products, authentic Native American products, candles, Feng Shui items; all in themes of Spirit and Wholeness.

Quarterlight Productions www.donnamichael.com New Thought keyboard/vocal artist Donna Michael; CDs; bookings; workshops; ministry.

Serenity www.serenitymusic.com New age record label; music for massage, Reiki, relaxation, and guided imagery.

Sheet Music Plus—New Age Music www.sheetmusicplus.com/enter.html?s=googleds& t=new+age&e=a Over 100 titles.

Shining Star www.shiningstar.com Music featuring the acoustic guitar music of Bruce BecVar and Brian BecVar, vocals from Aurora Juliana Ariel, Indian and Sanskrit chants from Nada Shakti and chants of the Drepung Loseling Monks and their Tibetan Sacred Temple Music.

Spotted Peccary Music www.spottedpeccary.com/artists.php News; releases; listen; artists; order.

Yahoo Directory—New Age Music dir.yahoo.com/Entertainment/Music/Genres/New_ Age/ Links to Electronica, artists, CDs, labels.

Yahoo Directory—New Age Music Artists dir.yahoo.com/Entertainment/Music/Artists/By_Ge nre/New_Age/ Links to New Age artists in alphabetical order.

Popular Music and Culture—Fashion— Dance Music—Techno—Electronica— Rock 'n' Roll—Oldies—Punk— Heavy Metal Web Sites

---

A Biased History of Glam Rock www.doremi.co.uk/glam Chronological history; links and more.

A Brief History of Banned Music in the United States www.ericnuzum.com/banned Selected online chronicle of music that has been banned or censored in the United States.

Access Place Music www.accessplace.com/music.htm News; reviews; online audio; MP3 files; genres; artists; songs; lyrics; concerts; tickets; CD stores; instruments; references; acoustics; electronics.

All Time Favorites www.alltimefavorites.com/Entertainment.htm Complete entertainment resources.

Armani Exchange www.armaniexchange.com Fashion industry.

Art Rock www.artrock.com Dealer in rock and roll collectibles.

Bazaar www.bazaar411.com Fashion industry.

Blue Eyes.com www.blue-eyes.com Frank Sinatra fan site.

Canadian Musician www.canadianmusician.com Pop music magazine.

Celebrity Corner www.premrad.com Audio interview clips.

Celebrity Site of the Day www.net-v.com/csotd Links to celebrity sites.

Chronology of San Francisco Rock Music 1965-1969 www.sfmuseum.org/hist1/rock.html Museum of City of San Francisco.

Classic Rock Daily www.classicrockdaily.com Hard rock and heavy metal Web site.

CNN Style www.cnn.com/STYLE Fashion journalism.

Comics.com www.comics.com United Media.

Cover Heaven freespace.virgin.net/love.day/coverheaven Record cover artwork.

Disco Music www.discomusic.com Disco music Web site.

DJ Union www.djunion.com DJ music and equipment.

DJ.net www.dj.net Amplify your attitude.

Donna Karan www.donnakaran.com Fashion industry.

Drum and Bass Arena www.breakbeat.co.uk News; reviews; interviews; dance e-zine.

ERock www.erock.net Rock music Web site.

Eurodance Hits www.eurodancehits.com Information on artists; releases in European dance music; Annual Cyberspace Euro-Energy Awards.

Fashion Angel www.fashionangel.com Fashion industry.

Fashion.net www.fashion.net Guide to Internet fashion sites.

FirstView www.firstview.com The latest fashions displayed online.

Flash Rock www.flashrock.com Rock music site.

George Starostin's Classic Rock Album Reviews starling.rinet.ru/music/index.htm Detailed reviews of 1960s and 70s rock and pop music; ratings; best of lists; etc.

Gianni Versace www.versace.com Tribute to Versace's life and work.

Guess www.guess.com Fashion Web site.

Hard Rock Cafe hardrock.com Hotels, casinos, restaurants.

Hard Rock Hotel www.hardrockhotel.com Las Vegas hotel and casino.

Hard Rock Live www.hardrocklive.com Live music venues.

Heavy Harmonies www.heavyharmonies.com Metal and hard rock bands; discography.

Levi's www.levi.com Fashion Web site.

Lilith Fair www.lilithfair.com Official Web site of the 1999 concert tour.

Look Online www.lookonline.com Fashion industry.

Losing Today www.losingtoday.com Pop music.

Metal Hammer www.metalhammer.co.uk Hard rock and heavy metal Web site; magazine.

Metal Maniacs www.metalmaniacs.com Metal magazine.

Mishatzar www.mishatzar.com Fashion industry.

Modern Rock www.modernrock.com Rock music Web site.

Music Fan Clubs www.musicfanclubs.org Links to fan club Web sites.

Music.com www.music.com Affiliate partner of DreamWorks label; free downloads.

Mutha Funkas www.muthafunkas.com Funk music Web site.

Oldies Music www.oldiesmusic.com History, trivia and charts of the 50s, 60s, and 70s.

Online Rock www.onlinerock.com Rock music site.

Peace Rock www.peacerock.com Collectibles.

Peaceville www.peaceville.com Hard rock and heavy metal Web site.

Pop Culture Madness Music Charts www.popculturemadness.com/Music/index.html List top hits by decade and category.

Pop History www.mrpophistory.com Features a random year in pop history every weekday; covers music, television, movies, news, and politics.

Pop.com www.pop.com Pop music Web site.

Raga Rock www.ragarock.com Rock music Web site.

Rave-Club Info and Electronic Music Links around the World spraci.cia.com.au/ravew.htm Easy-to-use links page.

Rhythm Net www.rhythmnet.com New music.

Rock 108 from Key J www.keyj.com Hard rock and heavy metal Web site; information; news; radio service.

Rock Around the World www.ratw.com Photo library; radio show archive; 1970s.

Rock Daily www.rockdaily.com Rock music Web site.

Rock Music Music Network www.rock.com Guide; streaming audio; online store.

Rock News www.rocknews.com Rock music.

Rockabilly www.rockabilly.nl Rockabilly, Surf, 1950s and 1960s music.

Rockabillyhall.com www.rockabillyhall.com Rockabilly Hall of Fame Web site.

Rockfest www.rockfest.org Rock festivals.

Rockhall.com www.rockhall.com Official Web site of the Rock and Roll Hall of Fame Museum located in Cleveland, OH; popular music used in interdisciplinary teaching.

Rockhouse www.rockhouse.de Rock music Web site.

Rusmetal.ru www.rusmetal.ru Russian metal music.

Style 365 www.style365.com Directory of fashion Web sites.

The Beatles www.thebeatles.com/core/home/ Official web site; links to related sites; albums.

The Beatles www.getback.org/beatles.html The Internet Beatles album.

The Beatles Sheet Music www.rarebeatles.com/sheetmu/sheetmu.htm Collecting Beatles sheet music.

The Center for Popular Music popmusic.mtsu.edu/ Popular music information and resources.

The Dance Music Resource Pages www.juno.co.uk Complete weekly listing of new UK dance releases; catalog numbers and distributor information; future releases; UK dance radio listings; over 500 dance-related links.

The Dark Site of Metal metal.de/ Hard rock and heavy metal Web site.

The Fillmore www.thefillmore.com In San Francisco; famous for booking big names in the 60s; Joplin; Hendrix; Grateful Dead; Jefferson Airplane.

The Gap www.gap.com Fashion site.

The Musical World of Rocky Horror www.rockymusic.org Audio and more; largest Rocky Horror sounds collection on the Internet; images; lyrics; reviews.

The Wanderer www.wanderers.com/wanderer First oldies Web site on the Internet.

Tommy Hilfiger www.tommy.com Designer site.

Trouser Press www.trouserpress.com Rock magazine; archives online.

UK-Dance www.uk-dance.org Mailing list for people to discuss everything to do with dance music culture in the UK.

Videogame Music Archive www.vgmusic.com 11,000+ game music MIDI files.

R&B—Rap—Hip-Hop and Soul Web Sites

88HipHop.com www.88hiphop.com Current events; reviews; music; videos; links; indie artists.

Altrap.com www.altrap.com Hip-hop culture and perspective.

Davey D's Hip-Hop Corner www.daveyd.com Radio shows; visitor polls; boards; newsletters; news.

DJ Rap www.dj-rap.com DJ rap music Web site.

E-Jams www.ejams.com R&B music site; interactive music survey; contests; chat rooms; trivia; music charts; bulletin boards; links and information.

Hip-Hop Directory www.hiphopdirectory.com Hip-hop music; links; global hip-hop community.

Hip-Hop Elements www.hiphop-elements.com Free subscription to the Elements Newsletter; news; charts; playlists; album reviews; free CD drawings.

Hip-Hop Spot www.hiphophotspot.com Interactive Web site; dedicated to helping indie artists achieve their goals; free resources.

HipHopCity.com www.hiphopcity.com Hip-hop directory; top100; add a site; search.

HipHopSite.com www.hiphopsite.com New releases; reviews.

Original Hip-Hop Lyrics Archive www.ohhla.com Large database.

Rap Sheet www.rapsheet.com Channels; community.

Rap Station www.rapstation.com Today in hip-hop.

Rhythm & Blues Foundation www.rhythm-n-blues.org Preserving America's soul.

Rock Rap www.rockrap.com Rap music Web site.

Support Online Hip-Hop www.sohh.com News section; bulletin boards; music and culture.

The Source www.thesource.com Hip-hop; rap; features; reviews.

Underground Hip-Hop www.undergroundhiphop.com Streaming audio of singles; emerging artists.

Vibe www.vibe.com Hip-hop urban music and culture.

Ragtime Web Sites

Colin D. MacDonald's Ragtime-March-Waltz Website Welcome Page www.ragtimemusic.com Ragtime, march, and waltz MIDI files.

John Roache's Ragtime members.aol.com/ragtimers Ragtime, jazz, and stride piano MIDI sequences; online catalog for ragtime, stride, and novelty piano music.

Music Links www.rtpress.com/links.htm Links to music sites; ragtime, oldtime, and stride; American variety stage; vaudeville; entertainment 1870-1920.

Northern Virginia Ragtime Society (NVRS) www.nvrs.org Mailing list; events; links.

Paragon Ragtime Orchestra www.paragonragtime.com Professional organization performing ragtime-era music; vaudeville hits; silent movie accompaniments; dance-hall favorites.

'Perfessor' Bill Edwards Ragtime Sheet Music Covers and MIDI Files www.perfessorbill.com Restored sheet music covers and MIDI files.

Player Piano www.ragtimewest.com Close to one hundred pages; WAV files; MIDI files.

Ragtime Alphabetic Index www.rtpress.com/titles.htm Alphabetic listing of song titles and authors; live MIDI performances.

Ragtime Jazz Vaudeville 1920s Vintage Recordings on Cassette and CD www.vintage-recordings.com Large selection; online catalog.

Ragtime MIDI by Walt E. Smith members.aol.com/waltesmith/ragtime.htm For noncommercial use only.

Ragtime MIDI Files by Warren Trachtman www.trachtman.org/ragtime Ragtime MIDI files of pieces by Scott Joplin, James Scott, Joseph Lamb, Jelly Roll Morton, Eubie Blake, Piano Soundfonts.

Ragtime Sheet Music Collection library.msstate.edu/ragtime/ Digital library collection; search.

Ragtime the Musical www.imagination.com/moonstruck/albm53.html Information; cast albums; sheet music.

Ragtime Tunes www.discoverynet.com~ajsnead/ MIDI files.

Ragtime-Blues-Hot Piano www.doctorjazz.co.uk/index.html Ragtime piano music; MIDI files of some of the great ragtime artists; photographs; document archives.

Scott Joplin International Ragtime Foundation www.scottjoplin.org Located in Sedalia, Missouri, the Cradle of Ragtime.

Swedish Ragtime Home Page www.ragtime.nu Ragtime MIDI files; rags written by Swedish, international, classic, and contemporary ragtime composers.

The Ragtime Centennial Show www.rrragtimer.com Online show takes audience back one hundred years to the beginnings of ragtime.

The Ragtime Ephermeralist home.earthlink.net/~ephemeralist/ Devoted to the preservation and dissemination of articles and items relating to nineteenth- and early twentieth-century popular music.

The Ragtime Story www.wnur.org/jazz/styles/ragtime/ragtime-story.html History of ragtime.

Vaudeville and Ragtime Show www.bestwebs.com/vaudeville Early ragtime and vaudeville performers; songs and routines.

Vintage Music-Ragtime Jazz Vaudeville www.vintage-music.com/ragtime Antique ragtime; jazz; vaudeville; links.

West Coast Ragtime Society www.westcoastragtime.com Official Web site.

Western Social Dance memory.loc.gov/ammem/dihtml/diessay7.html Ragtime dance.

21st Century Americana Intermediate Piano Solos with General MIDI Accompaniment (www.melbay.com): By Elisabeth Lomax; includes folk songs collected by John and Alan Lomax; variety of styles for solo piano, including soft rock ballad, fandango, lullaby, new age, blues, and more; complete lyrics; melodies in lead sheet format; historical notes; suggestions for related study topics; for historians and pianists; solos may be performed independently, with the enclosed CD, or with included part for second piano; companion CD features MIDI-generated accompaniments for pieces with piano included and without. SYSTEM SPECS: Book and Audio CD.

Absolute Beginners: Keyboard DVD (www.musicsales.com): Step-by-step exercises; play along with professional backing track; learn how to maintain posture and playing position, read basic music notation, play with hands separately and then together, and perform songs; includes a thirty-two page booklet matching the exercises on the DVD. SYSTEM SPECS: Book, Audio CD, and Instructional DVD.

Alfred's Anthology Series (www.alfred.com): Titles include *Anthology of 20th Century Piano Music with Performance Practices in Early 20th Century Piano Music DVD; Anthology of Baroque Keyboard Music with Performance Practices in Baroque Keyboard Music DVD; Anthology of Classical Piano Music with Performance Practices in Classical Piano Music DVD; Anthology of Impressionistic Piano Music with Performance Practices in Impressionistic Piano Music DVD; Anthology of Romantic Piano Music with Performance Practices in Romantic Piano Music DVD;* SYSTEM SPECS: Book and Instructional DVD.

Alfred's MAX Series (www.alfred.com): Hear and see performance; beginning keyboard method; read music and play chords in different styles; *Alfred's MAX Blues Keyboard, Alfred's MAX Keyboard 1, Alfred's MAX Keyboard 2, Alfred's MAX Keyboard Complete.* SYSTEM SPECS: Book and Instructional DVD.

Alfred's Piano Library (www.alfred.com): Library of piano methods assists teachers in introducing the piano through a sequenced presentation of technical concepts and a variety of musical compositions; piano methods for children under age seven: Music for Little Mozarts, Alfred's Basic Prep Course; piano methods for children ages seven to nine: Alfred's Basic Piano Course, Premier Piano Course, Later Beginner, All-in-One Course, Sacred All-in-One Course, Group Piano Course; piano methods for children ages ten to fifteen: Chord Approach, Jazz/Rock Course, Electronic Keyboard Course, Group Piano Course; piano methods for ages sixteen and up: Adult Piano Course, Adult All-in-One Course, Adult Jazz/Rock Course, Chord Approach, Chord Approach Electronic Keyboards, Electronic Keyboard Course. SYSTEM SPECS: Book, Audio CD, and/or MIDI Accompaniment Disk.

Anyone Can Play Piano (www.melbay.com): For beginners and amateur players; chord formulas, chord progressions, left-hand accompaniment techniques, and right-hand melody work; no previous knowledge of music necessary; free instructional booklet; forty-five minutes. SYSTEM SPECS: Instructional DVD.

Artists DVDs (www.alfred.com): Titles include: *Chick Corea: Electric Workshop, Keyboard Workshop; George Duke, Volumes I and II.* SYSTEM SPECS: Instructional DVD.

Bastien Piano Library and Bastien Piano Basics (www.kjos.com): Elementary piano method includes Piano, Theory, Performance, and Technic books as well as many supplementary books including solos, duets, sight reading, and more SYSTEM SPECS: Book, Audio CD, and/or MIDI Accompaniment Disk.

Berklee Press (www.berkleepress.com): Titles include: *Berklee Instant Keyboard; Berklee Practice Method: Keyboard; Hammond Organ Complete— Tunes, Tones and Techniques for Drawbar Keyboards; Piano Essentials – Scales, Chords, Arpeggios, and The Contemporary Pianist; Solo Jazz Piano—The Linear Approach.* SYSTEM SPECS: Book and Audio CD.

Century of Jazz Piano CD-ROM (www.halleonard.com): Dick Hyman; history of jazz piano; re-creates styles of sixty-three pianists; 103 tunes; over five hours of music; twenty-one rare historical videos; over one hundred historical photographs; more than 500 pages of documentation by Joel Simpson, Dick Hyman, and others; biographies; stylistic analyses; discographies; complete bibliography. SYSTEM SPECS: Hybrid CD-ROM.

Clavisoft Book and Disk Accompaniments (www.yamahamusicsoft.com): Book and disk collections; "You are the Artist" series; educator collections; disk orchestra collection; complete instrumental accompaniments. SYSTEM SPECS: MIDI compatible keyboard or computer.

Complete Blues Keyboard Method, Complete Jazz Keyboard Method, and Complete Rock Keyboard Method (www.alfred.com): Each style has beginning, intermediate, and advanced level books each with an accompanying listening and play-along audio CD; from the National Keyboard Workshop. SYSTEM SPECS: Book, Audio CD, and/or Instructional DVD.

Cuetime Smartkey for Disklavier Pianos (www.yamahamusicsoft.com): Control tempo of prerecorded instrumental background by how fast or slow user plays at the keyboard; mixed genre song selections. SYSTEM SPECS: Yamaha Clavinova digital pianos; Smartkey equipped Disklavier pianos.

Discover Blues (www.fjhmusic.com): Comprehensive approach for the beginning blues player; instruction in improvisation and theory; pieces with improvisation options, blues technique, and blues ear training. SYSTEM SPECS: Book, Audio CD and/or MIDI Accompaniment Disk.

Dozen a Day (www.halleonard.com): Classic Edna Mae Burnham finger exercise series; graded levels. SYSTEM SPECS: Book and Audio CD.

Early Keyboard Skills (www.ecsmedia.com): Helps teach keyboard positions; five different sections drill the student; show the note letter for a pressed key; show the staff position for a pressed key; drill on which key matches a given note letter; drill on which key matches a given staff position; drill on which note letter

corresponds to the presented key. SYSTEM SPECS: Hybrid CD-ROM.

Easy Piano MIDI Play Along (www.halleonard.com): Includes a 3.5 disk of professional performances and arrangements in Easy Piano format; disk works with any general MIDI keyboard; listen to performances; play or sing along; remove the melody and play the lead; alter tempo; play arrangements alone without the disk. SYSTEM SPECS: Book and Disk.

Electronic Keyboards (www.voyetra.com): Software companion for MIDI musical keyboard; dynamic, well-rounded multimedia environment for learning basic piano keyboard skills; comprehensive overview of MIDI technology and the history of keyboard instruments; perform with the interactive MIDI Songbook; bonus tutorial "Understanding MIDI and Synthesis" offers information on how PCs and keyboards generate sound and make music; record performances and compositions in the "Recording Station." SYSTEM SPECS: Windows.

Fast Track Keyboard (www.halleonard.com): A quick way for beginners to learn to play; play-along CD to help hear how the music should sound; last section of the FastTrack method books for different instruments is the same so that players can form a band and jam together. SYSTEM SPECS: Book and Audio CD.

Finger Power (www.alfred.com): Classic Schaum finger exercise series; graded levels. SYSTEM SPECS: Book and Audio CD.

FJH Piano Library (www.fjhmusic.com): Orchestrations for Piano Adventures and PreTime to BigTime Piano Supplementary Library; feature instrumentation of marching band, Baroque chamber group, jazz ensemble, chamber orchestra, rock group, etc.; exposure to the sounds of ensembles; can play along; General MIDI format offers teachers and students option of modifying tempos without changing pitch; isolate parts, solo, or mute selected instruments to match individual practice needs. SYSTEM SPECS: Book, Audio CD, and/or MIDI Accompaniment Disk.

Frances Clark (www.alfred.com): "Music Tree" elementary piano method. SYSTEM SPECS: Book, Audio CD, and/or MIDI Accompaniment Disk.

Frederick Harris Music Series for Piano (www.frederickharrismusic.com): Celebration Series; The Piano Odyssey; Celebrate Piano!; Composer Library; Souvenirs for Piano; introductory piano repertoire and method books. SYSTEM SPECS: Book, Audio CD, and/or MIDI Accompaniment Disk.

Hal Leonard Piano and Keyboard DVDs (www.halleonard.com): Titles include *Play Piano Today!; Beginning Keyboard Volume One*, and more. SYSTEM SPECS: Instructional DVD.

Hal Leonard Piano Method (www.halleonard.com): Elementary piano method.

SYSTEM SPECS: Book, Audio CD, and/or MIDI Accompaniment Disk.

Harmony Road Music Course (www.harmonyroadmusic.com): Program designed to help children discover the world of music through motivating materials and activities that develop the whole child. SYSTEM SPECS: Book and Audio CD.

Heritage Music Press Accompaniments (www.lorenz.com/heritage.html): Accompaniments for Piano Discoveries and works by Carol and Walter Noona. SYSTEM SPECS: Book, Audio CD, and/or MIDI Accompaniment Disk.

Homespun Tapes Instructional DVD (www.halleonard.com): Titles include *Learn to Play Gospel Piano; A Pianist's Guide to Free Improvisation,* and more. SYSTEM SPECS: Instructional DVD.

iSong (www.halleonard.com): Teaching tool; animated score and tab; interactive sheet music; synced instructor video; arrangements in varying levels of difficulty; virtual keyboard; tempo control; looping with exact cueing; classical piano; artists. SYSTEM SPECS: Hybrid CD-ROM.

Intermediate Piano and Keyboard Method (www.emediamusic.com): Improve playing, gain control of the keyboard, and develop musicianship; play pieces by famous composers in a broad range of musical styles, from Baroque to the present; develop musical creativity by learning how to improvise; guides the student with video demonstrations of techniques and practical advice that will elevate playing to a new standard; covers conventional scales, chord progressions, finger techniques, blues form, scales, and patterns needed to create improvisations and songs. SYSTEM SPECS: Hybrid CD-ROM.

Kalmus CD-ROM Editions (www.alfred.com): Each contains hundreds of pages of music from the most prolific composers for piano, including Bach, Beethoven, Chopin, Mozart, Debussy, and Ravel; print libraries of the Kalmus piano editions with minimal or no editing. SYSTEM SPECS: Hybrid CD-ROM.

Keyboard Arpeggios (www.ecsmedia.com): Covers key signatures, notes, and fingerings in major and minor two-octave arpeggios; designed to review arpeggio performance and fingerings; students enter correct fingering, then play the requested arpeggio on the MIDI keyboard; program is presented in five parts: Instructions, Hand-over-Hand Triads (major and minor), Major Triads (two octaves), Minor Triads (two octaves), and a Final Quiz; two-octave triads are presented to the user for both right-hand and left-hand fingerings; final exams record percentage scores; top ten scores are listed; evaluation is stored in student records for the instructor; for beginners to intermediate, grades 3-7. SYSTEM SPECS: Hybrid CD-ROM.

Keyboard Blues (www.ecsmedia.com): Blues chords; twelve-bar blues; practice playing and hearing chord changes, first with the music, then without; drill-and-practice section scores student's knowledge of simple blues chords; student creates an original solo with a computer accompaniment; student evaluation and record keeping; requires MIDI; beginners, grades 4-8. SYSTEM SPECS: Hybrid CD-ROM.

Keyboard Chords (www.ecsmedia.com): Tests students' knowledge of major and minor triads in all positions; one note of a triad is provided and student answers by spelling the triad or playing the triad on the keyboard; percentage scores are recorded; presents qualities of simple chords; composed of a tutorial on major, minor, diminished, and augmented chords; chord spelling drill; keyboard drill; test; drill-and-practice programs allow user to select the inversion (root, first, or second) and the clef (treble or bass) for the drill; score is displayed after student correctly answers ten consecutive items; test randomly selects the inversion and clef for each item, and the student's score is displayed; student evaluation and record keeping; for intermediate to advanced pianists, all age groups. SYSTEM SPECS: Hybrid CD-ROM.

Keyboard Coach (www.keyboardcoach.com): Keyboard Roll shows how to play; Music Coach checks and corrects playing; Video Coach includes over fifty video sequences; Real-time Cues; Track Mixing and Accompaniments; Practice Loops; CD-ROM. SYSTEM SPECS: Windows.

Keyboard Extended Jazz Harmonies (www.ecsmedia.com): Sequel to Keyboard Jazz Harmonies; designed to teach students to identify and build ninth, eleventh, and thirteenth chords; tutorial presents option to hear each chord played through MIDI synthesizer keyboard; four sections are included in the lesson: Visual Chord Recognition, Aural Chord Recognition, Chord Symbol Drill, and Chord Spelling Drill; final quiz included; student record keeping allows instructor to monitor progress; for advanced, all age groups. SYSTEM SPECS: Hybrid CD-ROM.

Keyboard Fingerings (www.ecsmedia.com): Combines scale construction with fingering practice; major, natural, and harmonic minor scales presented in standard and special fingerings for student review and practice; for both the right and left hands; single staves are used, with treble for the right-hand exercises and bass for the left hand; students enter scale fingerings, then play the same scales correctly at the MIDI keyboard; automatic scorekeeping; student roster and scores are available for printout; Hall of Fame provides top scores; computer judges the accuracy of the scale performance in each section and on the final test; for beginners to intermediate. SYSTEM SPECS: Windows.

Keyboard for the Absolute Beginner (www.alfred.com): Learn notes, rhythms, time and key signatures, fingerings, and more. SYSTEM SPECS: Book and Instructional DVD.

Keyboard Intervals (www.ecsmedia.com): Designed to help music students learn to play major, minor, diminished, and augmented intervals; must be able to read music and play notes on a keyboard; student evaluation and record keeping; for intermediate students, all ages. SYSTEM SPECS: Hybrid CD-ROM.

Keyboard Introductory Development Series (KIDS) (www.ecsmedia.com): Four disk series for very young beginners; Zoo Puppet Theater introduces learning correct finger numbers for playing the piano; Race Car Keys teaches the layout of the keyboard by recognizing solfege syllables or note names; Dinosaurs Lunch teaches notes on the treble staff; Follow Me asks the student to play notes after hearing them; computer graphics; designed to correlate with Yamaha Music Education System Primary One Course; for grades K-3. SYSTEM SPECS: Hybrid CD-ROM.

Keyboard Jazz Harmonies CD-ROM (www.ecsmedia.com): Teaches chord symbols, seventh chord recognition, and chord spelling; basic knowledge of traditional harmonies and musical intervals required; tutorial; four drills and quizzes; final quiz uses MIDI to provide aural chord examples; advanced, all ages. SYSTEM SPECS: Hybrid CD-ROM.

Keyboard Kapers (www.ecsmedia.com): Staff-to-keyboard drills for pitch identification, melodic dictation, and sight-reading; scores are kept for correct answers per clef; no automatic record keeping; three challenging piano keyboard games: Keyboard Clues plots a note on the grand staff and requires that the note be played on the keyboard; ?Mystery? Notes presents one note visually and aurally, then asks the student to identify other notes(s) played by the computer; Kwik Keys is a timed game requiring the student to play back notes presented on the screen as quickly as possible; two levels of difficulty and Halls of Fame; scores are displayed; for beginner to intermediate, all age groups. SYSTEM SPECS: Hybrid CD-ROM.

Keyboard Note Drill (www.ecsmedia.com): Designed to increase speed in identifying notes randomly placed on the bass and treble staves; musical keyboard used to allow for selection of correct answers; twenty notes must be identified to complete each session; summary score presented at the end of each session; response time can be adjusted to the level of difficulty; for beginners, all age groups. SYSTEM SPECS: Hybrid CD-ROM.

Keyboard Speed Reading (www.ecsmedia.com): Sight-reading program flashes groups of notes on a monitor; students then play notes on a MIDI keyboard and are graded for speed and accuracy; completion time can be set by the user; Hall of Fame records top ten scores; for beginner to intermediate, all ages. SYSTEM SPECS: Hybrid CD-ROM.

Keyboard Tutor (www.ecsmedia.com): Provides tutorial and drill for students beginning to learn note location on the grand staff; presents exercises for learning elementary keyboard skills, including knowledge of names of the keys, piano keys matched to notes, notes matched to piano keys, and whole steps and half steps; each lesson allows unlimited practice of the skills; for beginning keyboard students, all age groups. SYSTEM SPECS: Hybrid CD-ROM.

Learn2 Play Piano (www.adventus.com): For beginner players; contains limited editions of two popular series - Piano Suite Premier and Ear Training Coach; the two combined programs are used for learning to read music and play the piano by ear; future upgrades available; eighty piano pieces at three skill levels; multi-track recording; fourteen musical games; five ear training activities each with hundreds of exercises at each level. SYSTEM SPECS: Windows.

Learn to Play Keyboard (www.alfred.com): Step-by-step interactive lessons; adjust tempo; mix accompaniment parts; record performance. SYSTEM SPECS: Hybrid CD-ROM.

Master Blues Piano Solos (www.pgmusic.com): Includes thirty full tunes with Pop/Rock/Jazz Blues piano solos in the style of the great Blues pianists Jelly Roll, DrJ, MontyA and more; gives a foundation for many styles of music; includes comping examples along with easy, medium and difficult soloing styles; all solos are integrated with an on-screen piano display and notation; can see and hear note-for-note exactly what is being played; can loop any portion of a solo, slow a solo down, or step through a solo one note at a time; can print solos out for further study; all tunes are done in standard MIDI and Band-in-a-Box MGU formats with either solo piano or a complete band arrangement (drums, bass, guitar and piano soloing; stand-alone product; includes files in Band-in-a-Box format for Band-in-a-Box users. SYSTEM SPECS: Windows.

Master Composer Library (www.kjos.com): New editions by Keith Snell of classical repertoire by J. S. Bach, Bartók, Beethoven, Burgmüller, Chopin, Clementi, Debussy, Diabelli, Grieg, Gurlitt, Haydn, Kabalevsky, Kuhlau, Lynes, Mendelssohn, Mozart, Scarlatti, Streabbog, and Tchaikovsky; Sonatina Collections; First Sonata Album; Quiet Classics. SYSTEM SPECS: Book and Audio CD.

Masterworks Library (www.alfred.com): Standard piano repertoire edited with high musicological standards; artistic covers with reproductions of classic paintings to reflect the spirit of each composer and musical period; publications are prepared from original sources, first printings, or the most reliable sources from the composer; musically accurate editions; prefaces give historical and stylistic context for the pieces; high-quality engraving and printing. SYSTEM SPECS: Book and Audio CD.

Mel Bay Piano and Keyboard (www.melbay.com): Titles include: *121 Fills for*

Gospel and Country Piano; Children's Piano Method, Level 1; First Lessons Piano; Improvisation Step By Step: Improvising Classical Music on Piano; Jazz Piano for the Young Beginner; Joy of Six for Solo Piano or Keyboard; Play Jazz, Blues, & Rock Piano by Ear, Books One, Two, and Three; You Can Teach Yourself Blues Piano; You Can Teach Yourself Gospel Piano; You Can Teach Yourself Jazz Piano; You Can Teach Yourself Piano by Ear; You Can Teach Yourself Piano Chords, and more. SYSTEM SPECS: Book, Audio CD, and/or Instructional DVD.

Memorization in Piano Music (www.alfred.com): Lecture for those who fear memory loss in performance; five memorization processes are outlined; techniques to aid in memorization problems; suggestions for teaching memorization. SYSTEM SPECS: Instructional DVD.

Music Sales Piano and Keyboard (www.musicsales.com): Titles include: *Improvising Blues Piano; Fast Forward: 12-Bar Blues Piano; Fast Forward: Cool Blues Keyboard; Fast Forward: Real Blues for Keyboard; In a Box: Starter Pack Piano DVD Edition; 100 Tips for Keyboards You Should Have Been Told, Parts 1 & 2; The Complete Keyboard Player, Books 1-3; You Can Play Piano!; Let's Play Keyboard Interactive Master Pack,* and more. SYSTEM SPECS: Book and Audio CD and/or Instructional DVD.

Musicians Institute Press (www.halleonard.com): Titles include: *Dictionary of Keyboard Grooves: The Complete Source for Loops, Patterns, and Sequences in All Popular Styles; Funk Keyboards: A Contemporary Guide to Chords, Rhythms, and Licks; Keyboard Technique; Keyboard Voicings: The Complete Guide; Music Reading For Keyboard: The Complete Method; R&B Soul Keyboards: The Complete Guide; Salsa Hanon: 50 Essential Exercises for Latin Piano,* and more. SYSTEM SPECS: Book and Audio CD.

No Excuses Keyboard Guide (www.musicsales.com): Comprehensive guide for players of all abilities; practice in a variety of styles as part of a real band. SYSTEM SPECS: Instructional DVD and Hybrid CD-ROM.

Note Detective (www.ecsmedia.com): Helps beginning students locate notes on grand staff and keyboard; graphic tutorial and game series designed to help students develop keyboard skills; Section 1 introduces beginners to basic concepts such as high and low sounds, the musical alphabet, and staff note reading; Section 2 helps students develop fluent music reading skills; practice in note reading on the grand staff, ledger line recognition, interval recognition, and reading sharps and flats; letter name answers are entered at the computer keyboard and notes at the computer MIDI keyboard; Sherlock provides guidance and instructions throughout the program; automatic scorekeeping for up to fifty student records; records

provide information only on levels completed; for beginning keyboard students of reading age and above, grades K-5. SYSTEM SPECS: Hybrid CD-ROM.

Performance Practices in Baroque Keyboard Music DVD (www.alfred.com): Composers in the Baroque period (1600-1750) produced some of the greatest and most exciting keyboard music; looks at conventions and knowledge that help the performer create a more historically informed performance; practical aid to today's performers and teachers; basic touches, articulations, dynamics and ornamentation are discussed in detail; includes a lecture on the history of Baroque dance and the relationship between dance movements and the performance of keyboard music; dances broken down into component steps for learning by the viewer; nine of the most popular court dances (minuet, sarabande, gigue, allemande, bourrée, polonaise, courante, gavotte and rigaudon) performed to Dr. Hinson's keyboard accompaniment by dancers in Baroque costume; approx. 107 minutes. SYSTEM SPECS: Instructional DVD.

Performance Practices in Classical Piano Music DVD (www.alfred.com): Dr. Maurice Hinson; piano music by composers in the Classical Period including Beethoven and Mozart; historical context. SYSTEM SPECS: Instructional DVD.

Performance Practices in Early 20th Century Piano Music DVD (www.alfred.com): Covering music from approximately 1890 to 1914; music by Bartók, Debussy, Joplin, Grainger, Hindemith, MacDowell, Coleridge-Taylor, Satie, Schoenberg, and more; performed in context of the performance challenges and stylistic explorations of the period; approx. one hour. SYSTEM SPECS: Instructional DVD.

Performance Practices in Impressionistic Piano Music DVD (www.alfred.com): Impressionist painters, symbolist writers, imagery, and other influences on impressionist composers are methodically presented; performance techniques; plainsong; the whole tone scale; folk music and more are discussed and demonstrated. SYSTEM SPECS: Instructional DVD.

Performance Practices in Late 20th Century Piano Music DVD (www.alfred.com): Dr. Stewart Gordon offers insights into how to interpret, perform, and teach the piano music of the late twentieth century. SYSTEM SPECS: Instructional DVD.

Performance Practices in Romantic Piano Music DVD (www.alfred.com): Piano repertoire of the Romantic era is explored; Dr. Maurice Hinson examines the performance practices of the era and discusses the influence that literature and art had on the composers of the period; dance forms, nationalistic influences, pedaling, dynamics, ornamentation, Italian terms, and tempo markings are covered in depth; interesting historical anecdotes about the composers; one hour. SYSTEM SPECS: Instructional DVD.

Piano and Keyboard Method CD-ROM (www.emediamusic.com) On-screen instructor is Irma Irene Justicia, MA, of the Juilliard School of Music; learn the skills needed for sight-reading and playing music; method is song based; MIDI accompaniments; quizzes reinforce skills learned; feedback to help students correct any mistakes made while playing; 250 lessons. SYSTEM SPECS: Hybrid CD-ROM.

Piano for Dummies (www.dummies.com): Covers buying a piano - acoustic versus electronic; how a piano works and how to care for one; left- and right-hand piano technique; examining keys, scales, melodies, harmonies, and chords; musical examples to play; history of piano musical styles; advice for piano teachers; Top Ten list of pianists. SYSTEM SPECS: Book and Audio CD.

Piano Literature Series (www.kjos.com): Edited by the Bastiens; introduction to the master composers of the Baroque, Classical, Romantic, and Contemporary eras; VOLUME 1: Bach, Kabalevsky, Schumann, Beethoven, Bartók, Spindler, Mozart, and Shostakovich, Levels 2–4; VOLUME 2: Bach, Bartók, Schumann, Kabalevsky, Clementi, Beethoven, and Rebikoff, Levels 4–5; VOLUME 3: For the intermediate grades; Grieg, Bach, Burgmüller, Beethoven, Kirnberger, Tchaikovsky, Kuhlau, Kabalevsky, eleven others, Level 5–6; VOLUME 4: For the early advanced grades; Chopin, Schubert, Schumann, Kabalevsky, seventeen others, Level 6; VOLUME 5: Advanced Level pieces; all the music from Piano Literature, Volumes 1–5 is available on CD; listening to a musical performance enhances and reinforces the emphasis on phrasing, touch, dynamics, and balance provided during lessons; performed by Diane Hidy. SYSTEM SPECS: Book and Audio CD.

Piano Press (www.pianopress.com): Holiday Fun Series; Kidtunes; Merry Christmas Happy Hanukkah— A Multilingual Songbook and CD; Pieces for Piano Series; Contemporary American Composers Series; World Music Through the Piano Series; audio samples on Web site. SYSTEM SPECS: Book and Audio CD.

Piano Repertoire Series (www.kjos.com): Edited by Keith Snell; Prep-Level 10; CD recordings available for each level; each CD includes the music of all three books at each level; Preparatory Level and Level One are included on one CD; piano interpretations by Diane Hidy closely follow the editions as a practical example for students. SYSTEM SPECS: Book and Audio CD.

Piano Suite Basic (www.adventus.com): Customizable and expandable tools; interactive voice tutor; continuous feedback; in-depth interactive theory lessons; large musical repertoire; personal and musical biographies of over 150 composers and performers; compositions can be exported to MIDI format and made available on the Internet; contains one hundred musical pieces covering Classical, Jazz/Blues, Country,

Pop/Rock, Children's, Folk/Traditional, and more. SYSTEM SPECS: Windows.

Piano Suite Premier (www.adventus.com): Customizable and expandable tools; record music; display and print musical notation; add own composition with a photo to Learning Library repertoire; includes Piano Player: supervised piano practice with audiovisual feedback; Library: over 400 pieces from Pop/Rock, Classical, Folk, and Jazz/Blues; sixty-five licensed songs; animation, lyrics, and voice recordings; Theory Thinker: hundreds of narrated, step-by-step theory lessons with practice exercises to teach notation, sight-reading, and playing skills; Composers Corner: compose, edit, and print music; pieces can be saved to a custom library and learned by others; Personal Profile: individual performance records to review progress; tracks results of every piece practiced or game played for any number of users; History Happens: biographies of famous composers and performers; free add-on Adventus Internet Music Studio. SYSTEM SPECS: Windows.

Pianosoft Solo and Pianosoft Plus Collections (www.yamahamusicsoft.com): Artists; Broadway; children's; Christmas; classical; contemporary; country; international; jazz; movie and TV themes; pop; sacred; standards; accompanist; educational. SYSTEM SPECS: Yamaha or compatible keyboard with disk player.

Play Today Piano (www.halleonard.com): Complete guide to the basics; listen and learn at own pace; can be used by students who want to teach themselves or by teachers for private or group instruction; full-demo tracks and audio instruction; students can learn at their own pace; each book includes over seventy songs and examples. SYSTEM SPECS: Book and Audio CD.

Play With The CD Series (www.halleonard.com): Titles include: *Christmas Hits; Christmas Favorites; The 1950s; The 1960s; The 1970s.* SYSTEM SPECS: Book and Audio CD.

Progressive Beginner Keyboard Audio CD and DVD (www.learntoplaymusic.com): By Gary Turner; for all types of electronic keyboards; for the complete beginner; covers note reading, finger technique, using the automatic accompaniment function, and playing chords with the left hand. SYSTEM SPECS: Book, Audio CD, and Instructional DVD.

Progressive Beginner Piano Audio CD and DVD (www.learntoplaymusic.com): By Gary Turner; for the complete beginner; covers note reading, music fundamentals, finger technique, and playing chords with the left hand; includes many well-known songs in a variety of styles. SYSTEM SPECS: Book, Audio CD, and Instructional DVD.

Ricochet (www.ecsmedia.com): Innovative music game; in Ricochet Random, play highlighted keys after random balls ricochet off piano keys on computer screen; number of balls and movement speed will increase at higher level of difficulty; in Ricochet Melody, choose a melody from a play list and try to play the notes before the ball leaves the screen; tempo can be changed. SYSTEM SPECS: Windows.

Schirmer Performance Editions (www.halleonard.com): Titles include: *Bach: First Lessons in Bach, Selections from the Notebook for Anna Magdalena Bach, Two-Part Inventions; Beethoven: Für Elise and Other Bagatelles, Selected Piano Works, Six Selected Sonatas, Sonata in C Minor, Opus 13 ("Pathétique"), Sonata in C-Sharp Minor, Opus 27, No.2 ("Moonlight"), Two Short Sonatas, Opus 49; Burgmüller: 25 Progressive Pieces, Opus 100; Chopin: Preludes, Selected Preludes; Clementi: Sonatinas, Opus 36; Gurlitt: Albumleaves for the Young, Opus 101; Heller: Selected Piano Studies, Opus 45 & Opus 46; Kabalevsky: 24 Pieces for Children, Opus 39; Kuhlau: Selected Sonatinas; Mozart: 15 Easy Piano Pieces, 15 Intermediate Piano Pieces, Sonata in C Major, K.545; Schumann: Scenes from Childhood (Kinderscenen, Opus 15, Selections from Album for the Young, Opus 68; Sonatina Album: Clementi, Kuhlau, Dussek, and Beethoven - 9 Sonatinas*; historical and stylistic commentary. SYSTEM SPECS: Book and Audio CD.

SongXpress (www.alfred.com): Titles include: *SongXpress Keyboard: Yuletide Tunes, Vol. 1* and *SongXpress Singles for Keyboard: The Star Spangled Banner*; learn songs step by step. SYSTEM SPECS: Instructional DVD.

Sparky's Magic Piano (www.musicmotion.com): Eight-year-old Sparky hates to practice; one day his piano speaks and makes a secret pact with him; a big concert tour follows, ending with the lesson there is no shortcut to success; classical music; clever animation; the voices of Mel Blanc, Tony Curtis, Cloris Leachman, and Vincent Price; running time forty-eight minutes. SYSTEM SPECS: Instructional DVD

Sports Scores (www.alfred.com): Ballpark music; sporting themes; titles include: *Sports Scores: Baseball for Keyboards* and *Sports Scores: Rock the Arena for Keyboards*. SYSTEM SPECS: Instructional DVD.

Step One: Play Piano (www.musicsales.com): Designed for the learner to understand the keys and play scales and chords for any keyboard; audio tracks allow listener to hear correct sounds while DVD presentation demonstrates proper hand and finger positioning. SYSTEM SPECS: Book, Audio CD, and Instructional DVD.

Step One: Teach Yourself Keyboard DVD (www.musicsales.com): Learn the keys and play scales and chords for any keyboard; audio tracks allow listener to hear correct sounds while the DVD presentation demonstrates proper hand and finger positioning; chapter menus and more for easy navigation through

the lessons. SYSTEM SPECS: Book, Audio CD, and Instructional DVD.

Suzuki Piano Method (www.alfred.com): The Suzuki Piano Method, created at Shinichi Suzuki's Talent Education Institute, is a natural extension of the Suzuki Method, first applied to violin study. SYSTEM SPECS: Book and Audio CD.

Teach Me Piano (www.voyetra.com): Over 150 lessons; over 100 exercises; beginners learn basic techniques; advanced players reinforce musical skills; Keyboard Lessons include note reading in treble and bass clefs, rhythm and timing, finger numbering and finger positions, key signatures, time signatures, scales, and chords; keeps records; Songbook organizes songs; Trainer Screen for practice; Performance Screen to play with full accompaniment; Musician's Reference for commonly used musical terms; includes MediaCheck; for beginner to intermediate, ages ten to adult. SYSTEM SPECS: Windows.

Teach Yourself Keyboard Audio CD and DVD (www.learntoplaymusic.com): By Gary Turner; for all types of electronic keyboards; covers basics of reading music and playing melodies; contains diagrams showing fingerings for automatic chordal accompaniment and a lesson on left-hand fingering as it applies to the keyboard. SYSTEM SPECS: Book, Audio CD, and Instructional DVD.

Teach Yourself Piano Audio CD and DVD (www.learntoplaymusic.com): By Gary Turner; for beginning pianists; learn to read and play piano music; learn chords, chord progressions, and over twenty-five songs using a range of two octaves; classical, folk, pop, rock, and blues. SYSTEM SPECS: Book, Audio CD, and Instructional DVD.

Teach Yourself to Play Piano CD-ROM (www.alfred.com): Uses same teaching approach as the best-selling book; interactive, audiovisual format; for beginners of all ages; learn the notes of the entire keyboard, how to form the most important scales and chords, basic rhythms, and how to play expressively and with feeling; exercises reinforce technique as follow along with music on screen; with interactive song player can change tempos, adjust audio levels, and record performance; video of an instructor teaching and demonstrating lessons; customizable ear-training program. SYSTEM SPECS: Hybrid CD-ROM.

The Art of Piano - Great Pianists of the 20th Century (www.musicmotion.com): As seen on PBS; from Paderewski in 1936 to Claudio Arrau in 1970; illustrates a broad range of pianistic styles as displayed by Horowitz, Rubinstein, Cortot, Richter, Gould, Hofmann, Rachmaninoff, and others; fascinating selections, historically and musically, from film and television archives; includes commentaries on all eighteen artists given by Daniel Barenboim, Sir Collin Davis, Evgeny Kissin, Gary Graffman, and other artists of today; in color and black and white; running time 108 minutes. SYSTEM SPECS: Instructional DVD.

The Beginner Piano Master Class CD-ROM (www.pgmusic.com): Pianist Miles Black illustrates basic keyboard skills and theory; designed for the beginner piano or keyboard student; helps develop skills on its own or as a valuable addition to any existing course of study. SYSTEM SPECS: Windows.

The Blues Pianist (www.pgmusic.com): Large library of original blues tunes performed by top studio musicians; wide variety of styles: Boogie Woogie, Slow/Fast Boogies, Jazz Blues, New Orleans Style, Chicago Blues, and more; styles made famous by Pete Johnson, Albert Ammons, Jelly Roll Morton, Jerry Lee Lewis, etc.; Trivia and Guess the Song games; notes; biographies; all levels can use the games and biographies; advanced, all ages. SYSTEM SPECS: Macintosh; Windows.

The Blues Piano Master Class (www.pgmusic.com): Master Pianist Miles Black; multimedia software program designed to illustrate basic skills to the beginner; start to learn how to play the Blues; first twenty lessons will deal with Blues history, basic Blues form, simple chord construction, and learning to improvise a simple Blues melody over a few basic Blues styles; Blues Piano styles included are Boogie, Barrelhouse, Rag Blues, Jazz Blues, Rock Blues, and more. SYSTEM SPECS: Windows.

The Concert Performer Collection (www.musicsales.com): Twenty classical, ragtime, and folk songs for piano; includes three CDs with audio and MIDI format tracks, a concert performance track, and a special study track for each piece; MIDI CD has two channels for each song: one for the left hand, and one for the right hand; changeable tempo. SYSTEM SPECS: Book and Audio CD.

The Concert Performer Series (www.musicsales.com): Piano pieces presented on a strong, high-sheen card; CD-ROM has both audio and MIDI to help with practicing; titles include works by Bach, Beethoven, Brahms, Chopin, De Falla, Debussy, Elgar, Mozart, Pachelbel, Schubert, and Joplin. SYSTEM SPECS: Book and Hybrid CD-ROM.

The Jazz Piano Master Class, Volumes 1 and 2 (www.pgmusic.com): Interactive piano lessons; illustrates basic skills to the beginning pianist; enhances skills of more advanced pianists; includes over sixty topics such as Roots and Shells, Block Chords, Stride Piano, Playing the Blues, Scales, Common Progressions, Improvisation, and more; practice exercises; backing tracks; eleven tunes included in the program; over five hours of verbal instruction; nearly one hundred exercises; practice tip for each exercise; multimedia features. SYSTEM SPECS: Windows.

The Latin Pianist (www.pgmusic.com): Over fifty tunes played on MIDI keyboard by Rebecca Mauleon-Santana; authentic Latin and Salsa piano songs and styles: Conga, Cumbia, Merengue, Son, Mambo, Cha-Cha-Cha, Guaracha, Samba, Partido Alto, and more; on-screen piano keyboard shows what pianist is playing; slow down piece or step through chord by chord; learn music note for note watching notes on screen; load MIDI files for further study; advanced. SYSTEM SPECS: Macintosh; Windows.

The Modern Jazz Pianist (www.pgmusic.com): Top jazz/studio pianists play over fifty jazz standards in a wide variety of styles; on-screen piano keyboard shows exactly what is being played; slow down piece or step through chord by chord; learn the music note for note by watching the piano notes on the screen; load MIDI files into programs for further study; Music Trivia and Guess the Song games; program notes; biographies; music dictionary and more; all levels can use the games and biographies; advanced. SYSTEM SPECS: Macintosh; Windows.

The New Age Pianist (www.pgmusic.com): Collection of solo piano compositions inspired by the natural world; covers New Age piano music; full range of piano techniques presented; over four hours of music; song memory, biographies, and information on important New Age musicians; advanced, all ages; all levels can use the games and biographies. SYSTEM SPECS: Macintosh; Windows.

The Piano Master Class (www.pgmusic.com): Master Pianist Miles Black; software program that illustrates basic keyboard skills and theory; designed for the beginner piano or keyboard student; helps develop skills on its own or as a valuable addition to any existing course of study; fifty included topics from the rudiments of playing keyboard to reading music from the staff; includes The Major Scale, Triads, Comping, Improvisation, and the Minor Scale; integrates audio lessons with on-screen piano display and notation; advanced multimedia features link each lesson to a suitable exercise; the loop, pause, advance and backup controls make learning fun and practicing easy; almost three hours of digitally recorded verbal instruction, plus exercises, study tunes, and lead sheets linked to multimedia features that allow student to see and hear exactly what Miles Black is teaching. SYSTEM SPECS: Windows.

Tune 1000 (www.halleonard.com): General MIDI files with arrangements to songs of top artists; lyrics can be displayed on keyboards, computers, and software sequencers with lyric read-out capabilities; back-up vocal parts for use with compatible harmonizer voice processors. SYSTEM SPECS: General MIDI File.

UBSJr.: Learn Basic Keyboards (www.alfred.com): Start playing the keyboard; learn the notes, how to play basic melodies, and about the keyboard. SYSTEM SPECS: Instructional DVD.

Ultimate Beginner Series: Blues Keyboards (www.alfred.com): Learn how to play twelve bar progressions, triplets, shuffle beats, inversions, turnarounds, blues scales, and blues licks; includes examples using a band that will help demonstrate the lessons. SYSTEM SPECS: Instructional DVD.

Ultimate Beginner Series: Keyboard Basics (WEA): Covers the basics of keyboard playing, finding notes, body position; using both hands simultaneously; major and minor chords and scales; basic improvisation. SYSTEM SPECS: Instructional DVD.

Ultimate Beginner Series: Rock Keyboard (www.alfred.com): Instructor David Garfield; compiles Volumes 1 and 2 of previously released programs; study minor seventh chords, the dorian mode, improvisation, and playing in a band; introduces the blues form, dominant seventh chords, rock and roll style, and how to select sounds and create a part. SYSTEM SPECS: Instructional DVD.

Ultimate Beginner Xpress: An Introduction to Musical Styles for Keyboard (www.alfred.com): Learn the essentials of keyboard playing in many different popular styles, including blues to rock to Latin to funk; covers posture, technique, chords structure, inversions, arpeggios, basic theory, and more. SYSTEM SPECS: Instructional DVD.

Virtuoso Piano Performance Software (www.yamahamusicsoft.com): Artist recordings for reproducing pianos, digital keyboards, and multimedia computers. SYSTEM SPECS: Yamaha Disklavier, Yamaha Clavinova, PianoDisc, Roland KR and HP Series, Baldwin Concert Master, and Kurzwel Mark Series.

Yamaha General MIDI Compatible Style Disks (www.halleonard.com): Titles include: *60s Pop; Amy Grant—Heart In Motion; Big Band—Volume I; Christmas Hits; Classical and Folk; Contemporary Pop; Country and Western; Country Sound; Dancefloor; Eric Clapton; Jazz; Latin—Volume I; Latin Ballroom; Latin Pop; Pops of The 60s and 70s; Rock N' Roll; Songs of The 60s; Soul; Sting; The Beatles—Greatest Hits I; The Beatles—Greatest Hits II; The Beatles—Greatest Hits III; The Best of Elvis Presley; The Best of Marvin Hamlisch; Traditional Dance.* SYSTEM SPECS: General MIDI Compatible.

Yamaha Musicsoft for Disklavier and Clavinova (www.yamahamusicsoft.com): Music software, accessories, and digital downloads. SYSTEM SPECS: Disklavier; Clavinova.

You Can Teach Yourself Piano (www.melbay.com): By Matt Dennis; taught by L. Dean Bye; teaches basic music reading skills; essential technique and theory for playing in all contemporary keyboard styles; technical and theoretical concepts; graded material; ear training and modern harmony.

SYSTEM SPECS: Book, Audio CD, and/or Instructional DVD.

You're the Star! by Turbo Music (www.halleonard.com): Series of popular songbooks with MIDI accompaniments; change tempo and keys; create own orchestration and mix; improvise solos; for computers and instruments with disk drives and a digital keyboard; some with E-Z play notation. SYSTEM SPECS: Hybrid CD-ROM.

Piano—Keyboard—Organ Web Sites

American Guild of Organists www.agohq.org Magazines; competitions; convention; membership; regions and chapters.

American College of Musicians / National Guild of Piano Teachers http://pianoguild.com/ Membership; auditions and programs; awards and benefits.

American School of Piano Tuning www.piano-tuning.com Has been training piano technicians since1958, offering a complete home study course in piano tuning and repair in just ten comprehensive lessons.

Anybody Can Play the Piano www.anybodycanplay.com Books and videos for beginners as young as three years; information for parents, piano teachers, and caregivers about different piano methods.

Associated Board of the Royal Schools of Music www.abrsm.org/?page=home World's leading music examining board; over 600,000 candidates take the music exams each year in more than ninety countries around the world; professional development courses for teachers; ABRSM Publishing publishes a wide range of repertoire, music books, and CDs.

Baldwin Pianos and Organs www.gibson.com/en-us/Divisions/Baldwin/ Baldwin products and accessories; Chickering; Wurlitzer; Pianovelle.

Casio, Inc. www.casio.com Maker of electronic keyboards and digital pianos.

Chopin Foundation of the United States www.chopin.org Chopin competitions; publications and concerts.

Classical Piano MIDI Page www.piano-midi.de/midicoll.htm MIDI and MP3 sequences for all friends of classical music.

Clavier www.instrumentalistmagazine.com Magazine for pianists and piano teachers; reviews; articles; events; subscribe online.

Clavier's Piano Explorer www.instrumentalistmagazine.com For piano teachers and students; students can send in compositions, questions, comments, music-related stories, poetry about music, artwork, and photos.

Estonia Piano Factory www.estoniapiano.com Estonia Pianos.

European Piano Teachers Association www.epta-europe.org/ News; membership; subscriptions.

Fun Brain www.funbrain.com/notes/ Game involving reading music; Pianomus Platypus.

German Piano Imports, LLC www.bluthnerpiano.com Bluthner; Haessler.

Harpsichord Clearing House www.harpsichord.com Comprehensive resource for early keyboard instruments, including the harpsichord, virginal, spinet, clavichord, fortepiano, or continuo organ in North America.

History of the Piano www.uk-piano.org/history/ Piano history; UK piano page.

International Piano Festival www.festival-piano.com Program; press; archives.

International Piano www.pianomagazine.com Magazine for pianists and piano enthusiasts; interviews with top pianists from around the world; comprehensive reviews of the latest piano CDs, DVDs, concerts, and sheet music; insights into piano repertoire and technique; profiles of great historic pianists as well as their recordings; up-to-date news and piano events.

International Piano Supply www.pianosupply.com/ips/ Pianos for sale.

Kawai America www.kawaius.com Descriptions of products; technical information; download page has free patch libraries, operating system updates and sound demos; lists company's pianos, digital keyboards, home keyboards, and synths; links to sites containing patches, librarians, and more.

Kawai Japan www.kawai.co.jp/english/index.html Japanese headquarters; home page is in English.

Keyboard Companion www.keyboardcompanion.com Current issue; multimedia articles; past website issues; index of past print issues; links; gallery.

Keyboard Education www.piano-masterclass.net/ Music site for keyboard players; jazz piano instruction material; teaching professional melody and harmonic ideas; fills, run, licks.

Keyboard Magazine www.keyboardmag.com Latest news on keyboards, digital pianos, and new products; features, interviews, and more.

Keyboard Magazine TV www.keyboardmag.tv Online streaming videos for keyboard players; lessons; interviews; performances; products.

Keyboard Player www.keyboardplayer.com Longest running keyboard magazine in the UK.

Kurzweil www.kurzweilmusicsystems.com Company has been acquired by Young Chang; can access FTP site to download files for Kurzweil

instruments; online catalog; discussion forums; technical support; links.

L. Bosendorfer Klavierfabrik GMBH www.bosendorfer.com L. Bosendorfer pianos.

Louis Renner GMBH & Co. www.rennerusa.com Renner Upright; Grand Piano Actions; Hammerheads; and Piano Tools.

Lowrey Organ Co. www.lowrey.com Lowrey home organs.

Luciano's Piano Bar www.piano-bar.com Popular music in MIDI format played at the piano.

Mason & Hamlin www.masonhamlin.com Mason & Hamlin pianos.

Music and You www.musicandyou.com Online piano lessons; beginners to advanced players; jazz, blues, classical, theory, arranging, and more.

National Conference on Keyboard Pedagogy www.francesclarkcenter.org Annual conference; keynote speakers; teaching demonstrations; workshops; group forums; technology hubs.

Organ Historical Society Catalog www.ohscatalog.org Catalog sales division of the organ historical society; sells pipe organ related books, CDs, videos, and sheet music.

Organ Stop www.organstop.com Keyboards for the home and church organist; customer support materials and activities; large sheet music department.

Organ1st www.organ.co.uk Worldwide mail-order shop; organs; sheet music.

OrganTutor Organ 101 www.organtutor.byu.edu CD-ROM and workbook with sixty-two lessons teaching organ registration, technique, and hymn playing; classical and traditional sacred style.

Orgel www.orgel.com Pipe organs; extensive information on pipe organs and organ music; listen to classical as well as modern organ music; RealAudio; virtual photo gallery.

Patti Music www.primamusic.com/pattimusic/ Piano sheet music, methods, and classical repetoire; for teachers, classical pianists, and organ players.

Perfectly Grand Piano Accessories, Inc. www.perfectlygrand.com For pianists.

Pianist Magazine www.pianistmagazine.com Interviews, features, and reviews; specially selected sheet music for players at beginner, intermediate, and advanced levels; each issue contains a forty-page pullout section of sheet music from all genres with expert notes; includes a four-page Method section called Keyboard Class, where the focus is on gaining freedom at the keyboard and learning how to improvise; UK-based; recorded tutorial CD comes free with every issue.

Piano - The Movie www.fys.uio.no/~magnushj/Piano/ Information on the movie; links.

Piano 300 piano300.si.edu/ Celebrating three centuries of people and pianos.

Piano Home Page www.serve.com/marbeth/piano.html Information for piano teachers.

Piano Lane www.pianolane.com The world of piano at your fingertips.

Piano Nanny on the Net www.pianonanny.com Online courses using QuickTime movies to teach piano lessons and pop music theory, including some jazz and blues; beginning to advanced levels; free public educational service.

Piano Net www.pianonet.com Official Web site of the National Piano Foundation; comprehensive guide to everything about pianos.

Piano Pal www.piano-pal.com Store and reference for piano books and sheet music scores; popular, classical, sacred, and educational material.

Piano Passion www.pianopassion.com Guide to search free classical piano sheet music.

Piano Pedagogy Plus www.pedaplus.com Music and resources for piano teachers and students.

Piano Power www.pianopower.com Endorsed by musicians and medical professionals; book series takes student to new levels of technical and musical proficiency while optimizing time and avoiding injury.

Piano Press Studio www.pianopress.com Piano, keyboard, theory, and voice lessons; recitals; festivals; MTNA and MTAC member; original music; publications; online newsletter.

Piano Productions Press www.pianoproductions.com Piano-related materials; publications.

Piano Spot www.pianospot.com Piano sheet music and accessories.

Piano Supplies www.pianosupplies.com Supplies for the pianist.

Piano Teaching www.pianoteaching.com Nancy and Randall Faber; Piano Adventures; PreTime to BigTime; Developing Artist; supplementary books; forum; bio; news and events; teaching materials.

Piano Teams www.pianoteams.com Ensemble project.

Piano Technicians Guild, Inc. www.ptg.org Find a technician; daily tips; events; merchandise.

Piano Today www.pianotoday.com Magazine for pianists with an interest in classical music and jazz; filled with great pieces from all eras and styles; jazz arrangements by today's top artists; inside stories; lessons and playing tips; whole section for the beginning level.

Piano Tuning www.pianotuning.com Courses, reference books, and materials for learning how to tune pianos professionally.

Piano Vision www.pianovision.com Community of teachers, students, performers, and music aficionados; World Piano Pedagogy Conference.

Piano Women www.pianowomen.com Women concert pianists.

Piano World www.pianoworld.com Pianos; keyboards; digital pianos; resource for information about the piano; free sheet music; locate a piano tuner, teacher, dealer; e-newsletter; interesting facts about the piano; list of piano movers and pianos for sale; trivia quiz; competitions; links.

PianoDisc www.pianodisc.com Leading manufacturer of player piano systems.

Pianomate Co. www.pianomate.com Pianomate.

Pianosoft Express www.pianosoftexpress.com Yamaha Disklavier and Clavinova software products.

Pipedreams pipedreams.mpr.org/index.html Minnesota Public Radio presents live broadcasts of organ music; recordings of show segments online; links to background information; listening tips; organ-related articles.

Piporg-l www.albany.edu/piporg-l Electronic mailing list devoted to pipe and electronic organs, organists, and organ music.

Play Piano Now pianomusic.hypermart.net/index.html Learn to play the piano and keyboard by ear, without relying on sheet music.

Play Piano Today www.playpianotoday.com Piano lessons unlimited.

Premiere Piano www.premierepiano.com Skills Mastery System; series of workbooks designed to coordinate with the MTAC Certificate of Merit Program; books for all levels.

Pro Piano www.propiano.com/index.html Instrument rentals; recital series.

Rhodes Pianos www.rhodespiano.com/ Information; FAQ; downloadable manual.

Roland Contemporary Keyboards www.rolandus.com Roland Corporation; musical instrument manufacturer; product and upgrade information; downloads; history of General MIDI.

Schimmel Piano Corp. www.schimmel-piano.de Schimmel pianos.

School of Music, University of Canterbury www.music.canterbury.ac.nz Christ Church Town Hall pipe organ; follow progress on video clips as the 3,372 pipes were gradually pieced together; learn about how the instrument works.

Sheet Music for Electronic Keyboard www.pianospot.com/cat20.htm List of items.

Smithsonian's National Museum of American History "PIANO 300: Celebrating Three Centuries of People and Pianos" piano300.si.edu/ Exhibition celebrating the 300th anniversary of the invention of the piano; composers' manuscripts, photographs, and other memorabilia; 250 pianos and keyboards.

Steinway and Sons www.steinway.com Factory tour; learn about Steinway and Boston Piano products.

Suzuki Corporation www.suzukipianos.com Digital
pianos; portable keyboards; QChord; harmonicas.

The Canadian Piano Page
www.canadianpianopage.com Information; links.

The CM Keyboard Technique DVD
www.jwpepper.com Instructional DVD by Linda
Rohmund; supplement for teaching or learning the
Certificate of Merit Keyboard Technique; in
compliance with the Music Teachers' Association
of California (MTAC) 2007 Keyboard Syllabus;
clear view of both hands and fingering; all
elements are identified.

The Herschell Carousel Factory Museum
www.carousels.com/ The carousel and band organ
manufacturing business in America.

The Pianist www.thepianistmovie.com About the
movie; trailer; flash site.

The Pianist's Guide to the Internet
www.rainmusic.com/pianomusic/piano.htm Piano
links; resources for students and teachers.

The Piano Education Page pianoeducation.org
Resource for piano teachers and students.

The Piano Place www.pianoplace.com Online catalog;
piano books; CDs; videos; software.

The Player Piano Page www.pianola.demon.co.uk/
Information on player pianos or the pianola.

*Van Cliburn International Piano Competition-Van
Cliburn Foundation* www.cliburn.org Information
on the competition and foundation.

Weber Piano Co. www.weberpiano.com Weber;
Rieger-Kloss; Ridgewood; Sagenhaft.

Yamaha Corporation of America www.yamaha.com
Yamaha pianos, digital pianos, and more.

Yellow Cat Publishing www.yellowcatpublishing.com
Music teaching materials for piano students; color
coded system for note recognition.

Young Chang Worldwide www.youngchang.com
Information about products and services; piano
models; history; dealer locater; room designer;
quality; links.

9
Guitar and Bass
Software, Instructional Media and Web Sites

101 Essential Riffs for Bluegrass Guitar (www.pgmusic.com): Learn Bluegrass riffs; each of the 101 phrases displays correctly on the Guitar Fretboard window; toggle through the notes manually, or slow down the tempo and loop the lick. SYSTEM SPECS: Macintosh; Windows.

101 Essential Riffs for Country Guitar (www.pgmusic.com): Licks essential for every player to know; each phrase is a short Band-in-a-Box file with a descriptive memo; phrases range in difficulty from easy to advanced including lots of bends and quasi-steel guitar licks; each lick was played on guitar and displays correctly on the Guitar Fretboard Window. SYSTEM SPECS: Macintosh; Windows.

101 Jazz Guitar Phrases (www.pgmusic.com): Includes 101 jazz guitar riffs, each with a Band-in-a-Box file and Audio Memo; four-bar Jazz guitar phrases help learn exactly how the pros play; hear the music, see the notation and guitar tablature, and watch the on-screen guitar fretboard to see exactly how the phrases are played; recorded with a MIDI Guitar Controller so the displayed fingerings on the Guitar Fretboard Window will be exactly how they were originally played; change the key and tempo to learn the phrases in all twelve keys; includes Audio Memos for each file with an on-call, personal instructor who plays and describes each phrase in detail. SYSTEM SPECS: Macintosh; Windows.

200 Guitar Licks (www.halleonard.com): Comprehensive source for the essential licks in all rock styles; interactive CD-ROM; multimedia synchronization of tab notation, video, audio, jam tracks, lessons and fretboard animation; learn 200 licks in a variety of styles, from blues rock to rockabilly, surf to Latin rock, grunge/alternative to heavy metal and fusion, and many more; background information on

each style; theory behind the licks; adjust the tempo of the notation and audio without changing the pitch. SYSTEM SPECS: Windows.

50 Licks Series (www.halleonard.com): Guitar technique DVDs; *50 Licks Blues Style; 50 Licks Country Style; 50 Licks Jazz; Style; 50 Licks Rock Style.* SYSTEM SPECS: Instructional DVDs.

Absolute Beginners: Bass Guitar DVD (www.musicsales.com): Step by step tutor; exercises; play along with professional backing track; learn how to tune bass, pluck the strings using fingers or a pick, and read basic notation and bass tab; practice scales and arpeggios; play first complete bass lines along with a band; includes thirty-two page booklet containing all the music examples shown on the DVD. SYSTEM SPECS: Book, Audio CD, and Instructional DVD.

Absolute Beginners: Guitar DVD (www.musicsales.com): Step by step tutor; play along with professional backing track; learn how to tune guitar; develop techniques using fingers or a pick; practice sense of rhythm; play essential chord shapes; perform first complete solo; includes thirty-two page booklet matching the exercises on the DVD. SYSTEM SPECS: Book, Audio CD, and Instructional DVD.

Acoustic Master Class Series (www.alfred.com): Titles include: *Acoustic Blues Solos; Acoustic Guitar Solos; David Cullen: Jazz, Classical, and Beyond; DADGAD Guitar Solos; Mike Dowling: Uptown Blues (American Roots Guitar); Laurence Juber: Acoustic Guitar Essentials, Vol. 1; Laurence Juber: The Guitarist; Laurence Juber: The Guitarist Anthology, Volumes 1 and 2; Doug MacLeod: 101 Blues Guitar Essentials; Al Petteway: Celtic, Blues, and Beyond; Doug Smith: Contemporary Instrumental Guitar; Kenny Sultan: Guitar Blues.* SYSTEM SPECS: Book and Audio CD and/or Instructional DVD.

Acoustic Methods and Technique (www.alfred.com): Titles include: *Basic Classical Guitar Method, Book 1; Complete Acoustic Blues Method: Beginning Acoustic Blues Guitar; Complete Acoustic Guitar Method: Beginning Acoustic Guitar; Complete Fingerstyle Guitar Method: Beginning Fingerstyle Guitar; A Fingerstyle Summit with Adrian Legg, Martin Simpson & Ed Gerhard; Martin Simpson Teaches Alternate Tunings; Pumping Nylon.* SYSTEM SPECS: Book and Audio CD and/or Instructional DVD.

Alfred's Books and Enhanced CDs for Guitar (www.alfred.com): Titles include: *Alfred's Basic Guitar Method, Book 1; Alfred's Teach Yourself to Play Guitar; Basic Blues Guitar Method, Books 1 & 2; Basix Guitar Method; Basix TAB Guitar Method; Bass for Beginners; Blues Guitar for Beginners; Classical Guitar for Beginners; Complete Blues Guitar Method: Beginning Blues Guitar; Folk Guitar for Beginners; Girl's Guitar Method; Guitar for the Absolute Beginner, Books 1 & 2; Kid's Guitar Course; Rock Guitar for Beginners; Teaching Guitar; Ultimate Play-Along Bass: Green Day; Ultimate Play-Along Guitar: Green Day,* and more. SYSTEM SPECS: Book and Enhanced CD.

Anyone Can Play Blues Guitar DVD (www.melbay.com): By Vern Juran; for the beginning to intermediate guitarist; learn blues chord progressions; variety of blues strumming and picking patterns; basic blues scales; lead guitar techniques; combination rhythm and lead playing; basics of slide guitar and open tuning; no music reading required but student should understand basic chords and strumming. SYSTEM SPECS: Instructional DVD.

Anyone Can Play Bottleneck Blues Guitar (www.melbay.com): Designed for the beginning slide guitar player; will also help intermediate player develop bottleneck technique; learn standard and alternate tunings, reading slide tablature, basic left- and right-hand technique, and classic bottleneck blues riffs; free tablature booklet of examples from the video included. SYSTEM SPECS: Instructional DVD.

Anyone Can Play Electric Bass DVD (www.melbay.com): By Scott Miller; designed for people who want to play bass in a small group or ensemble; presents all the most common musical forms; learn bass techniques for rock, country, pop, and other popular music styles; no music-reading ability required; free instructional booklet included. SYSTEM SPECS: Instructional DVD.

Anyone Can Play Fingerstyle Guitar DVD (www.melbay.com): By Paul Hayman; lessons derived from easy-to-learn method which doesn't require student to read music; learn basic accompaniment patterns; alternating bass styles; fingerstyle classics; free instructional booklet. SYSTEM SPECS: Instructional DVD.

Anyone Can Play Guitar Chords (www.melbay.com): By Vern Juran; learn the most commonly used chords; split-screen viewing; learn how the chords are fingered and how they should sound; learn major, minor and seventh chord forms and diminished and augmented chord shapes on first four frets of fingerboard; thirty minutes. SYSTEM SPECS: Instructional DVD.

Anyone Can Play Guitar Volume I (www.melbay.com): By Vern Juran; for beginning acoustic and electric guitar students; practical, easy-to-learn approach; no previous knowledge of music necessary; teaches tuning, the parts of the guitar, how to hold the guitar and pick, and proper right and left hand positioning; numerous close-ups and diagrams both on-screen and in accompanying booklet; learn to strum basic chords for four folk songs and two blues progressions; free instructional booklet. SYSTEM SPECS: Instructional DVD.

Anyone Can Play Popular Chord Progressions (www.melbay.com): By Vern Juran; for the beginning guitarist who already understands and uses chords in first position; learn standard chord changes used in thousands of folk, country, blues, and rock songs, and in the development of faster chord changing; helps songwriters to write better songs; learn to play all the friendly guitar keys; booklet included. SYSTEM SPECS: Instructional DVD.

Bass Artists (www.alfred.com): Titles include: *Steve Bailey and Victor Wooten: Bass Extremes, Bass Extremes Live; Bill "The Buddha" Dickens: The Collection, Funk Bass and Beyond; Jaco Pastorius: Modern Electric Bass; Jaco Pastorius and Jerry Jemmott: Modern Electric Bass (Revised); John Patitucci: Electric Bass, Electric Bass Complete; Rufus Reid: The Evolving Bassist, The Evolving Bassist Mega Pak; Billy Sheehan: Advanced Bass and Basic Bass; Victor Wooten: Bass Day 97 Highlights.* SYSTEM SPECS: Book and Audio CD and/or Instructional DVD.

Bass Guitar for Dummies (www.dummies.com): Includes exploring the anatomy of a bass guitar; getting started, holding the bass, positioning hands, and striking notes; reading bass notation and understanding chords, scales, and octaves; creating a groove and playing solos and fills; examining different bass-playing styles, from rock and funk to blues and reggae; care, cleaning, changing strings; buying a bass and accessories; Top Ten lists on bassists one should know about. SYSTEM SPECS: Book and Audio CD.

Bass Guitar Method (www.emediamusic.com): Beginning level; 114 step-by-step lessons by John Arbo; full-motion video with multiple angles and close-ups; over 200 songs and exercises; triads; fills; syncopation; creating a bass line; multitrack recorded audio; variable-speed MIDI; bass-only and no-bass options; songs by the Grateful Dead, Bob Dylan, and others; animated fretboard; automatic tuner; recorder and metronome. SYSTEM SPECS: Hybrid CD-ROM.

Bass Methods and Technique (www.alfred.com): Titles include: *Bass for Beginners / Rock Bass for Beginners; Bass for the Absolute Beginner; Rock Bass for Beginners; 30-Day Bass Workout; Alfred's MAX Bass; Complete Electric Bass Method – Beginning Blues Bass; Complete Electric Bass Method: Beginning Electric Bass; No Reading Required: Easy Rock Bass Lines; UBSJr.: Learn Basic Bass; Ultimate Beginner Series: Bass Basics; Ultimate Beginner Series: Blues Bass; Ultimate Beginner Series: Rock Bass; Ultimate Beginner Series Bass Jam With Songbook: Classic Blues; Ultimate Beginner Xpress: An Introduction to Musical Styles for Bass.* SYSTEM SPECS: Book and Audio CD and/or Instructional DVD.

Beginner Guitar Lessons for Macintosh (www.iplaymusic.com): Learn to play hit songs from artists like the Beatles, Eric Clapton, Johnny Cash, and Bob Marley; lessons are optimized for the Macintosh and iLife Suite; export and view lessons on the video iPod; create and record own version of a song in GarageBand and podcast performances using iWeb. SYSTEM SPECS: Macintosh.

Beginner Guitar Lessons for Windows (www.iplaymusic.com): Learn to play hit songs from artists like the Beatles, Eric Clapton, Johnny Cash, and Bob Marley; export and view lessons on the video iPod; create and record own version of a song using Sony's ACID XMC Music creation software (CD included). SYSTEM SPECS: Windows.

Beginner Guitar Lessons Levels 1 & 2 (www.iplaymusic.com) Learn the essentials to start playing songs without learning complex theory or reading music; play songs by Eric Clapton, the Beach Boys, Willie Nelson, Creedence Clearwater Revival and more; full video lessons teach guitar basics, chords and strumming; song lessons have scrolling chords and lyrics for easy play-along; background music provided. SYSTEM SPECS: Instructional DVD.

Berklee Press (www.berkleepress.com): Titles include: *A Modern Method for Guitar—Volume 1; A Modern Method for Guitar—Volume 2; Afro-Cuban Slap Bass Lines; Berklee Instant Bass; Berklee Instant Guitar; Berklee Jazz Guitar Chord Dictionary; Berklee Practice Method: Bass; Berklee Practice Method: Guitar; Chop Builder for Rock Guitar; Essential Rock Grooves for Bass; Instant Bass—Play Right Now!; Jazz Guitar Techniques: Modal Voicings; Jazz Improvisation for Guitar: A Melodic Approach; Jim Kelly's Guitar Workshop; Modern Method for Guitar (French Edition); Modern Method for Guitar (Spanish Edition); More Guitar Workshop; Playing the Changes – Bass: A Linear Approach to Improvising; Playing the Changes – Guitar: A Linear Approach to Improvising; Rock Bass Lines; Slap Bass Lines; The Chord Factory;*

The Guitarist's Guide to Composing and Improvising; Voice Leading for Guitar—Moving through the Changes, and more. SYSTEM SPECS: Book, Audio CD, and/or Instructional DVD.

Beyond Basics Series (www.alfred.com): Titles include: *Acoustic Blues Guitar; Acoustic Slide Guitar; The Fingerstyle Christmas Guitar Collection, Volumes 1 and 2; Fingerstyle Christmas Guitar: 12 Beautiful Songs & Carols for Solo Guitar; Fingerstyle Guitar; Fingerstyle Solo Guitar; Introducing Alternate Tunings for Fingerstyle Guitar; Solo Acoustic Blues Guitar.* SYSTEM SPECS: Book and Audio CD and/or Instructional DVD.

Beyond Power Chords (www.halleonard.com): Covers intermediate and professional guitar techniques; number of chords used will increase dramatically; gives means to play all types of chords including major, minor, seventh, and more in all keys; includes 85-track audio CD with almost 300 examples performed by the author. SYSTEM SPECS: Book and Audio CD.

Blues Artists (www.alfred.com): Titles include: *Albert Collins; Robben Ford: Back to the Blues, The Blues and Beyond, Highlights, Playin' the Blues; Johnny A.: Taste-Tone-Space; B.B. King: Blues Master, Blues Master Highlights.* SYSTEM SPECS: Book and Audio CD and/or Instructional DVD.

Blues Guitar for Dummies (www.dummies.com): Covers all aspects of blues guitar; play scales, chords, progressions, riffs, solos, and more; musical examples, chords charts, and photos help to explore the genre and play the songs of the great blues musicians; choose the right guitar, equipment, and strings; hold, tune, and get situated with the guitar; play barre chords and strum to the rhythm; recognize the structure of a blues song; musical riffs; master melodies and solos; make guitar sing, cry, and wail; jam to any type of blues. SYSTEM SPECS: Book and Audio CD.

Blues Guitar Legends (www.emediamusic.com): Learn to play classic blues songs from the masters; music notation is highlighted as songs play; animated fretboard displays fingerings in real time; learn to play ten blues classics from the original master recordings; variable-speed MIDI tracks; simplified chord versions for beginners; note-for-note transcriptions; biographical material. SYSTEM SPECS: Hybrid CD-ROM.

Blues Methods and Technique (www.alfred.com): Titles include: *Basic Blues Guitar Method 1; Beginning Delta Blues Guitar; Beyond Basics: Blues Guitar Rhythm Chops; Beyond Basics: Electric Slide Guitar; Complete Blues Guitar Method: Beginning Blues Guitar; Complete Blues Guitar Method: Intermediate Blues Guitar; Complete Blues Guitar Method: Mastering Blues Guitar; Getting the Sounds: Classic Blues Guitar; Getting the Sounds: Jump, Jive 'n' Swing Guitar; No Reading Required: Easy Blues Guitar Licks; Ultimate Beginner Series:*

Blues Guitar; Ultimate Beginner Series Guitar Jam w/Songbook: Classic Blues. SYSTEM SPECS: Book and Audio CD and/or Instructional DVD.

Chords, Scales, and Reference (www.alfred.com): Titles include: *Alfred's Teach Yourself Guitar Repair & Maintenance; The Seymour Duncan Guide to Pickups; Theory for the Contemporary Guitarist; Ultimate Beginner Series: Guitar Theory Basics.* SYSTEM SPECS: Book and Audio CD and/or Instructional DVD.

ChordWizard (www.chordwizard.com): Software for players of guitar, banjo, mandolin, bass guitar, ukulele, bouzouki, and other stringed instruments; free music theory tutorial; practical applications such as accompaniment, improvisation, and songwriting; *Songtrix Gold, Songtrix Silver, Music Theory, ChordWizard Gold, ChordWizard Silver.* SYSTEM SPECS: Windows.

Complete Blues Guitar Instructional DVD (www.melbay.com): Covers basic concepts in blues guitar; performance level blues solos and techniques. SYSTEM SPECS: Instructional DVD.

Complete Jazz Guitar Method Volume 1 and 2 (www.melbay.com): By Mike Christiansen; combines all material previously presented in two-volume video set; parallels book of same title; guides guitarist through barre chords, dead-string chords, bass-string chords, comping, chord inversions, altered seventh chords, major scales, concept of tonal centers, chord construction, ways of connecting chord forms, chord embellishment, transposition, chord substitution, blues progressions, pentatonic and blues scales, sequencing, diminished chords and the diminished scale, augmented chords, and the whole-tone scale; also presents Latin rhythms, the Dorian and Mixolydian modes applied separately and in combination, improvising over the ii-V-I progression in various keys, the Lydian, Aeolian, Phrygian, Locrian, and Super Locrian modes, "targeting" of chord tones, guide tones, phrasing, constructing a solo, secondary arpeggios, the Parker Cycle, improvising around a melody, quartal harmony as applied to the blues, chord substitution using quartal harmony, single-note soloing using fourths, and concept of moving geometrical chord shapes from one fret to another, or from one set of strings to another; hands-on demonstrations. SYSTEM SPECS: Instructional DVD.

Country Artists (www.alfred.com): Titles include: *Albert Lee: Country Boy, Country Legend, Highlights; Arlen Roth: Masters of the Telecaster.* SYSTEM SPECS: Book and Audio CD and/or Instructional DVD.

Country Methods and Technique (www.alfred.com): Titles include: *Getting the Sounds: Classic Country Guitar; Getting the Sounds: Hot Nashville Guitar; Ultimate Beginner Series: Bluegrass Guitar Basics & Beyond.* SYSTEM SPECS: Book and Audio CD and/or Instructional DVD.

Electric Guitar Coach (www.guitarcoach.com): Practice partner with full band backing tracks and multimedia instruction; refine Technique, Lead, and Rhythm playing; songs to work on; step by step guide to getting started in the right way; immediate chance to start playing easy lead guitar solos and famous tracks; each lesson starts off by introducing something new such as a fret hand technique, a new scale, or new chord ideas; learn a Cool Track or Study to help perfect it; practice what you learn with video and backing tracks at different speeds; extensive video uses the most advanced technology to bring clear views of exactly what to play; full range of angles, shots, and speeds to choose from; CD-ROM. SYSTEM SPECS: Windows.

Essential Elements for Guitar (www.halleonard.com): Popular songs in a variety of styles; quality demonstration and backing tracks on the accompanying CD; designed to meet the National Standards for Music Education, with features such as cross-curricular activities, quizzes, multicultural songs, basic improvisation and more; concepts covered include: getting started; basic music theory; guitar chords; notes on each string; music history; ensemble playing; performance spotlights, and more. SYSTEM SPECS: Book and Audio CD.

Everybody's Guitar Method, Books 1 & 2 (www.fjhmusic.com): Step-by-step approach for contemporary guitar students of all ages; single-note playing is well-paced; solo playing; basic notation is reinforced throughout the book; chords are introduced with examples; includes new music and arrangements; music encompasses a wide variety of musical styles: rock, blues, folk, jazz, country, and classical; orchestrated play-along CD completes the method. SYSTEM SPECS: Book and Audio CD.

Fast Track Guitar (www.halleonard.com): A quick way for beginners to learn to play; play-along CD to help hear how the music should sound; last section of the FastTrack method books for different instruments is the same so that players can form a band and jam together. SYSTEM SPECS: Book and Audio CD.

Flamenco Guitar Volumes 1, 2, and 3 (www.melbay.com) Flamenco guitar video instruction series produced entirely in Spain; for those who already have a command of basic classic guitar technique; insights on sitting and hand positions; thumb/index technique; the "picado," the "picado falseta," and the "golpe"; demonstrates various "rasgueos" executed with and without the thumb and presents the "tango" and "soleas" rhythms; booklet included with English and Spanish text and music in notation and tablature; tracks in four languages: Spanish, English, French, and Japanese. SYSTEM SPECS: Instructional DVDs.

Fretwriter Lite (www.alfred.com): Create and print original songs with guitar tablature; lead sheets and custom chord grids; listen to work on choice of instruments; select time and key signatures; add lyrics, text, and titles; music is automatically formatted and ready to print. SYSTEM SPECS: Hybrid CD-ROM.

Fun with the Guitar (www.melbay.com): By Mel Bay and Joe Carr; beginner's video teaching simple chords, strums, and songs; for guitarists of any age. SYSTEM SPECS: Instructional DVD.

G7 (www.sibelius.com): Support for all guitars: acoustic, classical, and electric; compose, arrange, or write out an existing song and then print it, publish it on the Internet, and burn it to CD using the Kontakt sample library from Native Instruments; songwriters can create additional parts such as keyboards, drums, and other instruments; import any MIDI or ASCII tab file into G7 and learn the fingerings from the on-screen fretboard. SYSTEM SPECS: Macintosh; Windows.

Guitar Chord Finder (www.musicsales.com): See and hear every chord played on the virtual guitar neck; standard music notation and chord boxes; 350 most-used chords fully illustrated; how to tune guitar. SYSTEM SPECS: Hybrid CD-ROM.

Guitar Coach (www.guitarcoach.com): Innovative method focused on developing good hand skills, musical awareness, and a thorough understanding of the guitar; over fifty hours of video and audio instruction teach the solo, picking, and strumming techniques essential for good all-round playing; key skills presented form the foundation for a lifetime of playing the guitar; CD-ROM. SYSTEM SPECS: Windows.

Guitar Expressions: Teacher Edition (www.alfred.com): Uses multiple learning styles combining note reading with learning by ear and rote; solos, duets, ensembles. SYSTEM SPECS: Book, Audio CD, and Hybrid CD-ROM.

Guitar for Dummies (www.dummies.com): Presents an easy method for learning to play guitar; step-by-step method does not require viewer to read music; shows how to play in tune and in rhythm, how to form chords, fingerpick, and strum in different patterns; demonstrates how to apply these techniques in actual songs; leads the viewer through a number of popular favorites. SYSTEM SPECS: Book and Audio CD.

Guitar Magic (www.sdgsoft.com): Guitar software for both electric and acoustic guitar players; video; virtual fretboard; audio; text and graphics; notation and tab; products include *Guitar Magic* and *Bass Magic*. SYSTEM SPECS: Windows.

Guitar Method (www.emediamusic.com): Beginning guitar; 155 comprehensive lessons cover basics; chord strumming, playing melodies and fingerpicking; over seventy songs, including hits from artists such as Bob Dylan, Grateful Dead, and Steve Miller; over thirty videos; over three hours of audio from guitar instructor/national performer Kevin Garry, PhD; animated fretboard; multitrack audio for hit songs; variable-speed MIDI tracks to slow down any song or exercise; learn songs in either guitar tablature or standard music notation as the notes on the screen highlight and fingering is displayed on the animated fretboard; built-in automatic tuner to interactively tune guitar; digital metronome; recorder with playback; Internet song guide; 250-chord dictionary. SYSTEM SPECS: Hybrid CD-ROM.

Guitar Methods and Technique (www.alfred.com): Titles include: *Guitar Method 1; Guitar Method 1 Mega Pak w/DVD; 30-Day Guitar Workout; Adam Levy: Play the Right Stuff; Alfred's MAX Guitar 1, 2, and Complete; Alfred's MAX TAB Guitar 1, 2, and Complete; Barre Chord Basics Mega Pak; Beginning Electric Slide Guitar; Beginning Guitar for Adults; Chord Basics Mega Pak; Girl's Guitar Method Complete; Guitar Expressions; Guitar for the Absolute Beginner, Book 1; UBSJr.: Learn Basic Guitar; Ultimate Beginner Series: Acoustic Guitar Basics; Ultimate Beginner Series: Electric Guitar Basics; Ultimate Beginner Series: Guitar Basics; Ultimate Beginner Xpress: An Introduction to Musical Styles for Acoustic Guitar; Ultimate Beginner Xpress: An Introduction to Musical Styles for Electric Guitar.* SYSTEM SPECS: Book and Audio CD and/or Instructional DVD.

Guitar Playing for Songwriters (www.garytalley.com): Learn from Nashville-based instructor Gary Talley of the sixties group the Box Tops; workbook included; guitar lessons; workshops. SYSTEM SPECS: Instructional DVD.

Guitar Pro (www.guitar-pro.com/en/index.php): Multitrack tab editor for guitar, banjo, and bass; writes scores; useful resource for guitarists from beginner to experienced levels to progress, compose, or accompany themselves. SYSTEM SPECS: Macintosh; Windows.

Guitar Songs (www.emediamusic.com): Learn to play hit songs in all styles, including rock, blues, country, classical, and folk genres; variable-speed MIDI track for slowing down music; separate audio tracks, including no guitar, guitar only and bass only; over twenty songs made famous by artists such as Eric Clapton, Melissa Etheridge, Heart, Willie Nelson, Bonnie Raitt, Santana, Talking Heads, Stevie Ray Vaughan, the Who; song playing tips are included for both bass and guitar players; animated fretboard shows bends and vibrato in addition to fingering positions in real time; automatic tuner and metronome; options for guitar tablature or standard notation available on each song. SYSTEM SPECS: Hybrid CD-ROM.

Guitar Star Volumes 1 and 2 (www.pgmusic.com): Press different keys on the computer keyboard to play a guitar solo complete with a back up rhythm section; learn to play guitar riffs; each note is displayed in notation as the music plays; guitar tablature and on-screen guitar fretboard; video tutorials with pro tips. SYSTEM SPECS: Windows.

Guitar Toolbox (www.emediamusic.com): Guitar accessory tool; integrates a built-in automatic tuner, metronome, recorder, and chord dictionaries onto one CD-ROM; automatic tuner analyzes sound for each guitar string, then visually displays if sharp or flat until exactly in tune; prerecorded reference notes; 900-chord dictionary displays variations of each chord for three positions on the guitar neck; simplified 250-chord dictionary displays fingering charts and features audio playback for chords played in the first position; digital metronome helps work on picking speed and develops rhythm and timing; built-in recorder to record playing; save and retrieve recordings for future playback. SYSTEM SPECS: Hybrid CD-ROM.

Guitropolis (www.alfred.com): Based on *Alfred's Basic Guitar Method;* interactive; play-along tunes; on-screen graphics; musical game play; award-winning game design; live video; solid guitar techniques for the beginning guitarist; licks; chords; popular melodies. SYSTEM SPECS: Hybrid CD-ROM.

Hal Leonard Guitar and Bass (www.halleonard.com): Titles include: *Basic Guitar and String Set Up; Bass Day 1998; Beginning Bass Volume One; Beginning Guitar Volume One; Fender Presents Getting Started on Acoustic Guitar; Fender Presents Getting Started on Electric Guitar; Flea—Instructional DVD for Bass; Fretboard Roadmaps; Hal Leonard Guitar Method; Jim Kelly's Guitar Workshop; Jimi Hendrix—Learn to Play the Songs from Are You Experienced; Play Bass Today!; Play Guitar Today!; Playing in the Style of the Fender Stratocaster Greats; Slap Bass—The Ultimate Guide; Victor Wooten and Carter Beauford—Making Music; Victor Wooten: Live at Bass Day 1998,* and more. SYSTEM SPECS: Instructional DVD.

Hal Leonard Guitar Method Books 1, 2, & 3 (www.halleonard.com): Second edition; new engravings and popular songs; riffs and licks; recordings with demonstration and play-along tracks; co-written by original method author Will Schmid and Greg Koch. SYSTEM SPECS: Book and Audio CD.

Homespun Guitar (www.halleonard.com): Titles include: *Muriel Anderson's All-Star Guitar Night; Norman Blake's Guitar Techniques; An Introduction to Open Tunings and Slide Guitar; Learn to Play the Songs of John Denver; Easy Steps to Guitar Fingerpicking; The Guitar Style of Richie Havens; The Blues Guitar of Keb' Mo'; Learn to Play Bottleneck Blues Guitar; Learning to Flatpick; Roger McGuinn's Basic Folk Guitar; The Tony Rice Guitar Method; You Can Play Guitar,* and more. SYSTEM SPECS: Instructional DVD.

Intermediate Guitar Coach CD-ROM (www.guitarcoach.com): Many songs and solos to help build a repertoire; increase skill level and understanding in many areas; array of multimedia features, including over 100 video clips, real audio 'minus 1' backing tracks, variable speed practice tracks, and Guitar Karaoke tracks. SYSTEM SPECS: Windows.

Intermediate Guitar Method CD-ROM (www.emediamusic.com): Learn to play lead guitar and more; goes beyond basic chords and melodies; new techniques demonstrated in over 175 lessons; full-motion video; variable-speed MIDI; recorded audio; animated fretboard; lead guitar skills; rhythm and fingerstyle chapters; lessons on improvisation; scale directory provides fingerings, recordings, and variable-speed MIDI for over 200 scales; automatic tuner; digital metronome; recorder and 1000-chord dictionary with audio playback. SYSTEM SPECS: Hybrid CD-ROM.

iSong Series (www.halleonard.com): Teaching tool; animated score and tab; synced instructor video; varying levels of difficulty; virtual fretboard; tempo control; looping with exact cueing; titles include popular guitar artists and classical guitar standards. SYSTEM SPECS: Hybrid CD-ROM.

Jazz, Fusion, Funk, and Latin Artists (www.alfred.com): Titles include: *An Evening with John Abercrombie; Al Di Meola; Herb Ellis: Swing Jazz Soloing & Comping; An Evening with Tal Farlow: Jazz Guitar; Frank Gambale: Chopbuilder – The Ultimate Guitar Workout, Concert with Class, Modes – No More Mystery, Monster Licks & Speed Picking; Scott Henderson: Jazz-Rock Mastery; Pat Martino: Quantum Force; Don Mock: The Blues from Rock to Jazz; Joe Pass: An Evening with Joe Pass, Jazz Lines, On Guitar; John Scofield: Jazz-Funk Guitar.* SYSTEM SPECS: Book and Audio CD and/or Instructional DVD.

Jazz, Fusion, Funk, and Latin Methods and Technique (www.alfred.com): Titles include: *Beyond Basics: Funk Guitar Rhythm Chops; Beyond Basics: Jazz Guitar Rhythm Chops; Complete Jazz Guitar Method: Beginning Jazz Guitar.* SYSTEM SPECS: Book and Audio CD and/or Instructional DVD.

Just Enough/Learn to Play Bass Instructional DVD Kit (www.melbay.com): Instructional package for beginning electric bass guitar; includes DVD, interactive CD-ROM, and portable book/CD set; DVD Video introduces the instructors, shows how they got started, what it is like to perform, what music means to them, and how to buy first gear; learn basic techniques; play with band in interactive Virtual Jam Session; CD-ROM contains over fifty bass lessons; learn the twelve-bar structure, how to play with a steady beat, and bass lines for country, soft rock, heavy metal, jazz, pop, rap, and funk; AudioBook pocket reference manual works with CD; match tracks in book to tracks on CD and follow along. SYSTEM SPECS: Macintosh; Windows.

Just Enough/Learn to Play Guitar Instructional DVD Kit (www.melbay.com): Instructional package for beginning guitar; includes DVD, interactive CD-ROM, and portable book/CD set; DVD Video introduces the instructors, shows how they got started, what it is like to perform, what music means to them, and how to buy first gear; learn basic techniques; play with band in interactive Virtual Jam Session; CD-ROM contains over fifty guitar lessons; animated content includes chord charts, twelve-bar blues structure, lead boxes, and video tips taught by fifteen-year-old guitarist Andrew; AudioBook pocket reference manual works with CD; match tracks in book to tracks on CD and follow along. SYSTEM SPECS: Macintosh; Windows.

Learn to Play Bass (www.alfred.com): Step-by-step interactive lessons; adjust tempo; mix accompaniment parts; record performance. SYSTEM SPECS: Hybrid CD-ROM.

Learn to Play Guitar (www.alfred.com): Step-by-step interactive lessons; adjust tempo; mix accompaniment parts; record performance. SYSTEM SPECS: Hybrid CD-ROM.

Mastering the Guitar Class Method Level 1 (www.melbay.com): Tool for teacher who is teaching a guitar class; pedagogical information regarding techniques such as holding position, strumming, playing single-note melodies, and improvisation are demonstrated; how to set up and rehearse a guitar ensemble. SYSTEM SPECS: Instructional DVD.

Mel Bay Guitar and Bass DVDs (www.melbay.com): Titles include: *Acoustic Guitar Anthology; Advance Touch Technique for Solo Guitar; Advanced Fingerpicking Guitar Techniques: Ragtime Blues Guitar; Advanced Fingerpicking Guitar Techniques/Blues Guitar; African Fingerstyle Guitar; African Guitar - The Mighty Popo; African Guitar: Solo Fingerstyle Guitar Music; Anyone Can Play C6 Lap Steel Guitar; Anyone Can Play Classic Guitar; Anyone Can Play Country Guitar; Anyone Can Play Electric Blues Guitar; Anyone Can Play Jazz Guitar; Anyone Can Play Nashville Lead Guitar; Anyone Can Play Praise Guitar; Anyone Can Play Rock Guitar; Back Porch Picking; Bag of Tricks Pocketful of Licks; Basic Country Flatpicking Guitar; Basic Swing Guitar; Bass Chords Made Easy; Beginner Touch Technique for Solo Guitar; Beginner's Blues Guitar; Beginner's Country Guitar; Beginner's Fingerpicking Guitar; Beginner's Rock Guitar; Beginning Bass with Missy Raines; Beginning Bass: Learn Bluegrass by Ear; Better Lead Guitar Through Chords; Blues, Rags and Slide Guitar; Bottleneck Blues Guitar; Bottleneck Slide Guitar: Acoustic and Electric Guitar Techniques; British Fingerstyle Guitar; Celtic Fingerstyle Guitar According to Tony McManus, Volumes 1 & 2; Celtic Melodies & Open Tunings; Celtic Melodies For Flatpicking Guitar; Children's Guitar Method Volume 1; Christmas Carols and Songs for Fingerstyle Guitar; Classic Guitar Anthology; Classic Guitar Artistry; Classic Ragtime Guitar; Complete Country Guitar; Contemporary Guitar Greats; Country Blues Guitar 3-Volume Set; Country Blues Guitar Duets; Country Blues Guitar in Open Tunings; Dadgad Guitar With Simon Fox; Delta Blues Guitar Duets; Developing Classical Guitar Technique; Doc's Guitar Jam; Downhome Flatpicking Guitar; Electric Blues Guitar; Essentials of Jazz Guitar; Fingerpicking Blues Guitar Solos; Fingerpicking Country Blues Guitar: A Repertoire Lesson; Fingerpicking Guitar Solos; Fingerpicking Guitar Techniques: A Two Volume Set; Fingerstyle Blues Guitar; Fingerstyle Guitar from the Ground Up Volumes One and Two; Fingerstyle Guitar: New Dimensions & Explorations Volumes 1-3; Fingerstyle Jazz Guitar: Bop to Modern; Fingerstyle Jazz Guitar: Improvisation; Fingerstyle Jazz Guitar: Swing to Bop; Flatpicking Country Classics; Flatpicking Guitar Country Style: The Roots of Bluegrass Guitar; Fun with the Guitar; Gene Bertoncini - Art of Solo Jazz Guitar; Great Guitars of Jazz; Guide to the Capo; Guitar Aerobics: Exercises for the Advanced Contemporary & Traditional Fingerpicking Guitarist; Guitar Chords Encyclopedia; Guitar Chords Made Easy; Guitar Portraits; Hawaiian Lap Style Slide Guitar; Hindustani Slide Indian Classical Guitar; How to Play Blues Guitar, Lessons 1-3; Intermediate Bass: Learn Bluegrass by Ear; Intro to Lead Guitar; Introduction to Alternate Tunings; Introduction to Celtic Fingerstyle Guitar; Introduction to Fingerstyle Swing Guitar; Introduction to Gospel Fingerstyle Guitar; Introduction to Thumbstyle Guitar; Irish Guitar Encores; Irish Traditional Guitar Accompaniment; Jazz Classics for Fingerstyle Guitar, Volumes 1 & 2; Jazz for the Electric Blues Guitarist; Jazz Guitar Real Book; Jeff Berlin - Bass Logic from the Players School of Music; Joe Beck: Solo Jazz Guitar; Joe Diorio: Solo Guitar Concepts; Larry Coryell's Blues Guitar; Larry Coryell's Jazz Guitar, Volumes 1, 2, & 3; Legacy of Country Fingerstyle Guitar Vol. 1 & 2; Legends of Bottleneck Blues Guitar; Legends of Country Blues Guitar Volume One, Two and Three; Legends of Country Guitar; Legends of Flatpicking Guitar; Legends of Jazz Guitar Volumes One, Two, and Three; Legends of Old Time Music; Legends of the Delta Blues; Legends of Traditional Fingerstyle Guitar; Legends of Western Swing Guitar; Masters of Fingerstyle Guitar, Volume 1; Mastery of the Flamenco Guitar Series Volumes 1-3; Medieval and Renaissance Music for Fingerstyle Guitar; Modern Classical Guitar Method, Grade 1; Nashville Picking 1 & 2: Guitar Solos of Merle Travis, Jerry Reed, and Chet Atkins; Open Tunings for Beginners; Peppino D'Agostino: Contemporary Fingerstyle Guitar; Playing & Understanding Jazz Guitar; Rags to Rock: Advanced Fingerstyle Guitar Solos; Richard Smith: Fingerstyle Artistry; Robin Bullock - Acoustic Guitar Artistry; Rockabilly Guitar; Rockabilly Slap Bass; Romane: The Gypsy Sound; Sacred Music for Fingerstyle Guitar;*

Slap Bass - The Ungentle Art; Slide Guitar In Standard Tuning; Stan Lassiter Electric Guitar Insights; Stephen Bennett: Harp Guitar Artistry; Steve Baughman - Celtic Fingerstyle Guitar; Strings and Frets; Super Electric Blues Guitar Picking Techniques; Super Fingerpicking Guitar Techniques; Super Jazz Guitar Picking; Super Jazz, Rock & Blues Techniques: (For Electric Bass); Take Me Back to Tulsa - An Anthology of Western Swing; Texas Blues Guitar; The Art of Fingerstyle Guitar; The Art of Solo Fingerpicking Guitar: Advanced Techniques; Touch Technique for Solo Guitar; Understanding Slide Guitar with Doug Cox; Up the Neck; World of Fingerstyle Jazz Guitar; World of Slide Guitar, and more. SYSTEM SPECS: Instructional DVD.

Modern Guitar Method Grade 1 (www.melbay.com): Guitarist learns basic notes on the guitar, single note playing, thirds, triads, chords, and chord progressions; solos, duets, scales, and chords in the keys of C, A minor, G, and E minor while learning to read musical notation; offers added instruction and tips along with split-screen right- and left-hand views of exercises, solos, and duets; music is shown on screen (in notation only); can use video without book, but book is recommended; 105 minute video. SYSTEM SPECS: Book and Instructional DVD.

Music Made Easy: Guitar (www.alfred.com): Fun, step-by-step lessons; interactive; for kids ages five and up; learn the notes on the guitar; how to read music; technique. SYSTEM SPECS: Hybrid CD-ROM.

Music Sales Guitar and Bass DVDs (www.musicsales.com): Titles include: *Advanced Metal: Riffs, Arpeggios, and Speed Run; Bass Slappin' and Poppin'; Guitar for Girls; House of Blues: Learn to Play Beginner Acoustic Guitar; House of Blues: Learn to Play Blues Guitar Levels 1 & 2; Learn Rock Acoustic: Beginner Program; Learn Rock Acoustic: Intermediate; Learn Rock Bass: Beginner Program; Learn Rock Bass: Intermediate; Learn Rock Guitar: Beginner and Intermediate Programs; Lick Library: Electric Blues Volumes 1 & 2; London Licks; Play It All Acoustic Guitar; Play It All Bass Guitar; Play it All Electric Guitar; Rock House: Learn Rock Guitar; Blues Riffs, Rhythms and Secrets; Rock House: New Dimensions for Bass; The Secrets of Funk: Using It and Fusing It.* SYSTEM SPECS: Instructional DVD.

Musicians Institute Press Publications (www.halleonard.com): Titles include: *Advanced Guitar Soloing—The Professional Guide to Improvisation; Advanced Scale Concepts and Licks for Guitar—Private Lessons; Arpeggios for Bass—The Ultimate Reference Guide; Bass Fretboard Basics—Essential Scales, Theory, Bass Lines and Fingerings; Bass Playing Techniques—The Complete Guide; Chord Progressions for Guitar—101 Patterns for All Styles from Folk to Funk!; Classical and Fingerstyle Guitar Techniques; Contemporary Acoustic Guitar; Creative Chord Shapes—Guitarist's Guide to Open-String Chord Forms; Essential Rhythm Guitar—Patterns, Progressions and Techniques for All Styles; French Diminished Scale for Guitar; Funk Guitar—The Essential Guide; Grooves for Electric Bass—Essential Patterns and Bass Lines for All Styles; Guitar Basics—Essential Chords, Scales, Rhythms and Theory; Guitar Fretboard Workbook—A Complete System for Understanding the Fretboard for Acoustic or Electric Guitar; Guitar Hanon—Private Lessons; Guitar Soloing—The Contemporary Guide to Improvisation; Harmonics—Guitar in the Style of Lenny Breau, Ted Greene, and Ralph Towner; Latin Bass—The Essential Guide to Afro-Cuban and Brazilian Styles; Latin Guitar—The Essential Guide to Brazilian and Afro-Cuban Rhythms; Modes for Guitar; Music Reading for Bass—The Complete Guide; Music Reading for Guitar; Odd Meter Bassics—A Comprehensive Source for Playing Bass in Odd Time Signatures; Outside Guitar Licks—Lessons and Lines for Taking Your Playing Over the Top; Practice Trax for Guitar—Musicians Institute Press; The Art of Walking Bass—A Method for Acoustic or Electric Bass; The Diminished Scale for Guitar; The Guitar Lick-tionary; The Musician's Guide to Recording Acoustic Guitar; Rhythm Guitar—The Complete Guide,* and more. SYSTEM SPECS: Book and Audio CD.

No Excuses Guitar Guide and No Excuses Bass Guide (www.musicsales.com): Comprehensive guide for players of all abilities; practice in a variety of styles as part of a real band. SYSTEM SPECS: Instructional DVD and Hybrid CD-ROM.

Play Guitar With Ross Bolton (www.halleonard.com): Learn basic guitar playing skills; play with the band or take a lesson; learn music theory; develop chops using the animated fingerboard. SYSTEM SPECS: Hybrid CD-ROM.

Play Music Together (www.iplaymusic.com): Video lessons teach guitar chords and strumming; song lessons have scrolling chords and lyrics for easy play-along; background music provided; over thirty-five videos and six full song lessons; for all ages. SYSTEM SPECS: Instructional DVD; Macintosh; Windows.

Play Today Guitar (www.halleonard.com): Complete guide to the basics; listen and learn at own pace; can be used by students who want to teach themselves or by teachers for private or group instruction; full-demo tracks and audio instruction; students can learn at their own pace; each book includes over seventy songs and examples. SYSTEM SPECS: Book and Audio CD.

Play with the CD Series (www.halleonard.com): Titles include: *Christmas Hits; Christmas Favorites; The 1950s; The 1960s; The 1970s.* SYSTEM SPECS: Book and Audio CD.

Progression (www.notionmusic.com): Write in tab or notation; automatic updating between tab and notation; record and enter from a MIDI guitar or keyboard; supports custom tab and alternate tunings; interactive fretboard and chord library; dozens of drum patterns; audio file export; integrated audio mixer; 1.5 GB sample library; MIDI file import, export, and output; real-time tempo control with NTEMPO feature; built-in amp simulator and VST effects support; velocity overdub. SYSTEM SPECS: Macintosh; Windows.

Progressive Beginner Bass Instructional DVD (www.learntoplaymusic.com): By Gary Turner; for beginning bassists; introduction to playing electric bass; essential techniques and music fundamentals as applied to bass playing. SYSTEM SPECS: Book, Audio CD, and Instructional DVD.

Progressive Beginner Classical Guitar (www.learntoplaymusic.com): By Brett Duncan; for beginning guitarists; introduction to classical guitar playing; introduces chords, scales, arpeggios, and essential techniques for both hands; includes pieces by Tarrega, Giuliani, Sor, Carcassi, etc. SYSTEM SPECS: Book, Audio CD, and Instructional DVD.

Progressive Beginner Guitar Instructional DVD (www.learntoplaymusic.com): By Gary Turner; for beginners; covers melody and chord playing using standard notation and tablature; introduces essential techniques and music fundamentals; includes chords and melodies of many well-known songs in a variety of musical styles. SYSTEM SPECS: Book, Audio CD, and Instructional DVD.

Progressive Guitar Method Book One (www.learntoplaymusic.com): For beginning guitarists; basics of guitar; how to read music; covers notes on each of the six strings and basic elements of music theory; how to play melodies and chord arrangements of many well-known traditional, rock, blues, ragtime, and folk songs. SYSTEM SPECS: Book, Audio CD, and Instructional DVD.

Progressive Guitar Method Book One — Supplement (www.learntoplaymusic.com): Over seventy well-known songs with chord symbols; can be used alone or with Progressive Guitar Method Book 1; contains eight more lessons, including information on major scales, keys, triplets, 6/8 time, sixteenth notes, syncopation, etc. SYSTEM SPECS: Book, Audio CD, and Instructional DVD.

Progressive Guitar Method Book One—Tab (www.learntoplaymusic.com): Comprehensive, lesson by lesson introduction to the guitar; covers notes on all strings, reading music and tablature, picking technique, and basic music theory; well known traditional, pop/rock, folk, and blues songs. SYSTEM SPECS: Book, Audio CD, and Instructional DVD.

Progressive Guitar Method—Bar Chords (www.learntoplaymusic.com): By Gary Turner; beginner to advanced; introduces useful bar, rock, and jazz chord shapes used by rock/pop/country and blues guitarists; includes major, minor, seventh, sixth, major seventh, minor seventh, suspended, etc.; bar chords discussed in detail; suggested bar chord rhythm patterns including percussive strums, dampening, and sixteenth note rhythms. SYSTEM SPECS: Book, Audio CD, and Instructional DVD.

Progressive Guitar Method—Chords (www.learntoplaymusic.com): By Gary Turner; beginner to advanced; open, bar, and jazz chord shapes of frequently used chord types; chord progressions to practice and play along; tuning; how to read sheet music; transposing; the capo; easy chord table, chord formula, and chord symbol chart. SYSTEM SPECS: Book, Audio CD, and Instructional DVD.

Progressive Guitar Method—Fingerpicking (www.learntoplaymusic.com): By Gary Turner; beginner to advanced; introduces right-hand fingerpicking patterns that can be used as an accompaniment to any chord, chord progression, or song; covers alternate thumb, arpeggio, and constant bass style used in rock, pop, folk, country, blues, ragtime and classical music. SYSTEM SPECS: Book, Audio CD, and Instructional DVD.

Progressive Guitar Method—Lead DVD (www.learntoplaymusic.com): By Gary Turner; beginner to advanced; covers scales and patterns over the entire fretboard so can improvise against major, minor, and blues progressions in any key; learn licks and techniques used by lead guitarists, such as hammer-ons, slides, bending, vibrato, pick tremolo, double notes, slurring, and right hand tapping. SYSTEM SPECS: Book, Audio CD, and Instructional DVD.

Progressive Guitar Method—Rhythm DVD (www.learntoplaymusic.com): For beginning guitarists; introduces open chord shapes for major, minor, seventh, sixth, major seventh, minor seventh, suspended, diminished, and augmented chords; learn to play over fifty chord progressions, including twelve-bar blues and turnaround progressions. SYSTEM SPECS: Book, Audio CD, and Instructional DVD.

Ramble to Cashel—Celtic Fingerstyle Guitar Volume 1 (www.melbay.com): Irish and Scottish music adapted to fingerstyle by Martin Simpson, Steve Baughman, Pierre Bensusan, Duck Baker, Tom Long, Pat Kirtley, and El McMeen; follow in the footsteps of Scottish guitarist Davey Graham, who developed the D-A-D-G-A-D tuning, now the predominant tuning for Irish guitarists; features performances of Believe Me If All These Endearing Young Charms; Waters of Tyne; Shepherd's Delight; Lowlands of Holland; Bony Crossing the Alps; Ramble to Cashel; Cullen Bay;

Murtagh McKann; Flamorgan Air; and many more. SYSTEM SPECS: Instructional DVD.

Richie Sambora (www.enteractive.com): CD-ROM features Richie Sambora, lead guitarist of Bon Jovi; teaches different riffs and techniques; play lead with the band; rock star shares his photo collection, popular music videos, personal interviews, and more; includes tuner, scale charts, chord dictionary, and over forty rock guitar techniques; interactive multimedia; user-friendly. SYSTEM SPECS: Windows.

Rock Artists (www.alfred.com): *Pete Anderson: Roots Rock Workshop; Paul Gilbert: Intense Rock – Complete, Terrifying Guitar Trip; Yngwie Malmsteen; Steve Morse: The Definitive Steve Morse, Highlights; John Petrucci: Rock Discipline; Carlos Santana: Influences; Carl Verheyen: Intervallic Rock.* SYSTEM SPECS: Book and Audio CD and/or Instructional DVD.

Rock Guitar for Dummies (www.dummies.com): Learn how electric guitars and amplifiers work; how to chose the right guitar and amp and how to care for them; left-hand and right-hand guitar techniques; styles of rock guitar playing; creating great riffs; the history of rock guitar; buying accessories; Top Ten lists of the guitarists one should listen to, the rock albums one must have, and the classic guitars one should know about. SYSTEM SPECS: Book and Audio CD.

Rock Guitar Method (www.emediamusic.com): Over 100 audio- and video-enhanced guitar lessons; learning to play rock hits including songs from Black Sabbath, Blue Oyster Cult, Silverchair, and more; presents rock songs, chords, riffs, and gear tips; requires no previous music experience; play favorite hit songs; instructor is Charles McCrone, a graduate of the Guitar Institute of Technology, with over twenty-five years of playing and teaching experience; variety of techniques needed to play rock, punk and metal; movable power chords, barre chords, effects pedals, yanks, hammer-ons, pull-offs, palm muting, distorted riffs, the blues scale, using feedback, the whammy bar, and more. SYSTEM SPECS: Hybrid CD-ROM.

Rock Methods and Technique (www.alfred.com): Titles include: *Beyond Basics: Rock Guitar Rhythm Chops; Complete Rock Guitar Method: Beginning Rock Guitar; Complete Rock Guitar Method: Beginning Rock Guitar, Lead & Rhythm; Getting the Sounds: Classic Guitar Effects; Getting the Sounds: Classic Rock Guitar; No Reading Required: Metal Guitar Licks; Shred Is Not Dead; Ultimate Beginner Series: Rock Guitar; Ultimate Beginner Series: Rock Guitar Basics; Ultimate Beginner Series Guitar Jam with Songbook: Classic Rock.* SYSTEM SPECS: Book and Audio CD and/or Instructional DVD.

Signature Licks Series (www.halleonard.com): Learn trademark riffs and solos from guitar legends; the Allman Brothers Band; Black Sabbath; Freddie King; Lennon and McCartney; Stevie Ray Vaughn; T-Bone Walker; Muddy Waters, and more. SYSTEM SPECS: Book, Audio CD, and Instructional DVD.

SongXpress (www.alfred.com): Titles include: *SongXpress: Acoustic Guitar; SongXpress: Blues Guitar; SongXpress: Rock Guitar;* includes GuitarView Virtual Song Player with high-quality, customizable, digital audio playback, ChordXpress LE with ninety-six of the most common and useful chords, and a fully interactive tuner. SYSTEM SPECS: Hybrid CD-ROM.

SongXpress Series (www.alfred.com): Learn favorite songs on guitar; learn all the chords, riffs, and guitar patterns for each song from a computer; on-screen diagrams and tablature; titles include: *Austin Blues, Barre Chord Basics, The California Sound, Classic Acoustic, Classic Bad Boys of Rock and Roll, Classic Blues, Classic Folk Songs, Classic Rock, Classic Surf, Country Ballads, Country Rock, Early Rock & Roll, Going Solo, Guitar Chord Basics, Heavy Metal, Inspirational Songs, Modern Rock, Party Tunes, Women of Modern Rock, Yuletide Tunes;* also, Personality Folios and Singles. SYSTEM SPECS: Instructional DVD.

Stefan Grossman's Guitar Workshop (www.guitarvideos.com): Comprehensive series of video and audio guitar lessons in a wide variety of styles, featuring world-renowned instructors; huge selection available online; DVD guitar lessons; audio book/CD lessons; Vestapol DVDs; Guitar Artistry DVDs; The Reverend Gary Davis; books; CDs; catalog; e-mail list; specials; archival photos; radio broadcasts; tabs; interviews; reviews; YouTube; The Woodshed discussion area and forum. SYSTEM SPECS: Book and Audio CD and/or Instructional DVD.

Step One: Play Guitar (www.musicsales.com): Learn how to play notes, chords, and chord progressions; learn proper playing techniques on the CD and DVD; chapter menus and more for easy navigation through the lessons. SYSTEM SPECS: Book, Audio CD, and Instructional DVD.

Step One: Teach Yourself Guitar (www.musicsales.com): Learn how to play notes, chords, and chord progressions while using the book and accompanying audio tracks; teacher demonstrates proper playing techniques on DVD; chapter menus and more for easy navigation through the lessons. SYSTEM SPECS: Book, Audio CD, and Instructional DVD.

Super Guitar Chord Finder (www.ready4music.com): Learn, search for, analyze, and play guitar chords; SYSTEM SPECS: Windows.

Teach Me Blues Guitar (www.voyetra.com): Video clips; animation; voice-overs; classic blues riffs, solos, and songs; comes with picks, chord dictionary, and software-based tuning system; for beginners and advanced players. SYSTEM SPECS: Windows.

Teach Me Guitar (www.voyetra.com): Play chords and songs with videos, intuitive charts, and diagrams; online instructor demonstrates techniques; talks user through lesson; animated fretboard shows neck fingerings in real time; control tempos or loop sections to learn songs at own pace; play with virtual backup band; comes with picks, a chord dictionary, and software-based tuning system; for beginners and advanced players. SYSTEM SPECS: Windows.

Teach Me Rock Guitar (www.voyetra.com): Vidoes, charts, and diagrams; animated fretboard shows fingerings on guitar neck in real time; control tempos or loop sections; learn songs at own pace; jam and play along with band; comes with picks, chord dictionary, and software-based tuning system; for beginners and advanced players. SYSTEM SPECS: Windows.

Teach Yourself Bar Chords Instructional DVD (www.learntoplaymusic.com): For beginners; contains the most useful bar chord shapes for every type of chord; includes major, minor, seventh, sixth, major seventh, minor seventh, suspended, ninth, etc.; section on reading sheet music, chord symbols, and jam along progressions. SYSTEM SPECS: Book, Audio CD, and Instructional DVD.

Teach Yourself Bass Instructional DVD (www.learntoplaymusic.com): By Gary Turner; for beginning bassists; introduces fundamentals of both left- and right- hand technique; covers music reading using standard notation and tablature; scales, arpeggios, riffs, and how to create bass lines. SYSTEM SPECS: Book, Audio CD, and Instructional DVD.

Teach Yourself Blues Guitar Instructional DVD (www.learntoplaymusic.com): By Brett Duncan; for beginning blues guitarists; covers blues rhythm guitar playing, involving open chords, and movable chord patterns, together with classic blues triplets and shuffle rhythms; teaches lead guitar playing. SYSTEM SPECS: Book, Audio CD, and Instructional DVD.

Teach Yourself Classical Guitar Instructional DVD (www.learntoplaymusic.com): By Brett Duncan; for beginning guitarists; introduces basics of reading music; variety of left- and right- hand techniques introduced; learn pieces through study of chords and arpeggios as well as notes. SYSTEM SPECS: Book, Audio CD, and Instructional DVD.

Teach Yourself Fingerpicking Guitar DVD (www.learntoplaymusic.com): For beginning fingerpicking guitarists; right-hand fingerpicking techniques and patterns which can be applied to any chord or chord progression; covers basics of fingerpicking accompaniment styles. SYSTEM SPECS: Book, Audio CD, and Instructional DVD.

Teach Yourself Guitar Chords Instructional DVD (www.learntoplaymusic.com): For beginning guitarists; easy to use chord dictionary containing the most useful open, jazz, and bar chord shapes of all the most commonly used chord types; includes special sections on tuning, reading sheet music, transposing,

and using a capo. SYSTEM SPECS: Book, Audio CD, and Instructional DVD.

Teach Yourself Guitar Instructional DVD (www.learntoplaymusic.com): By Gary Turner; for beginning guitarists; introduction to playing the guitar; types of guitars available; basic chord shapes and chord progressions; covers standard music notation, guitar tablature, and basic music theory. SYSTEM SPECS: Book, Audio CD, and Instructional DVD.

Teach Yourself Lead Guitar Instructional DVD (www.learntoplaymusic.com): For beginning guitarists; comprehensive introduction to lead guitar playing; demonstrates essential techniques and scales; learn important rhythms, note bending, slides, hammer-ons, pull-offs, and right-hand tapping. SYSTEM SPECS: Book, Audio CD, and Instructional DVD.

Teach Yourself Rhythm Guitar Instructional DVD (www.learntoplaymusic.com): For beginning guitarists; introduction to chords and rhythm guitar; learn to play over fifty chord progressions, including twelve-bar blues and turnaround progressions; learn a variety of rhythm patterns. SYSTEM SPECS: Book, Audio CD, and Instructional DVD.

Teach Yourself Rock Guitar Instructional DVD (www.learntoplaymusic.com): For beginning guitarists; introduces popular rock guitar techniques; covers important bar chords along with two string rock chords and other movable chord shapes; teaches techniques such as slides, hammer-ons, pull-offs, and string bending. SYSTEM SPECS: Book, Audio CD, and Instructional DVD.

Teach Yourself Slap Bass Instructional DVD (www.learntoplaymusic.com): For beginning slap bassists; slapping, popping, left-hand hammers, slides, bends, ghost notes, and double-stops; scales, arpeggios, and fingering. SYSTEM SPECS: Book, Audio CD, and Instructional DVD.

Teach Yourself to Play Bass (www.alfred.com): Tips on buying and maintaining instrument; how to read Tab and standard music notation; covers a wide range of popular styles including rock, metal, blues, country, jazz, and more; accompaniments for songs and exercises. SYSTEM SPECS: Hybrid CD-ROM.

Teach Yourself to Play Guitar (www.alfred.com): Interactive audiovisual format; for beginners of all ages; learn to read standard music notation and TAB; perform songs in a variety of styles; play chords, scales, and cool licks on either acoustic or electric guitar; exercises reinforce technique as follow along with music right on screen; interactive song player to change tempos, adjust audio levels, and record performance; videos of an instructor teaching and demonstrating lessons; bonus games reinforce concepts; customizable ear-training program; interactive guitar tuner; Deluxe Edition also available. SYSTEM SPECS: Hybrid CD-ROM.

The Art of Acoustic Blues Guitar: Ragtime and Gospel (www.musicsales.com): By Woody Mann; book and DVD package; showcases the songs and techniques of two of the most fundamental and exciting styles of traditional fingerstyle guitar playing as exemplified by the legendary virtuoso Reverend Gary Davis; illustrates how the music of one of America's greatest guitarists offers a complete lesson in the beauty and subtleties of ragtime and gospel guitar playing; includes music and instruction for six full blues tunes. SYSTEM SPECS: Book and Instructional DVD.

The Art of Acoustic Blues Guitar: The Basics (www.musicsales.com): By Woody Mann; covers basic techniques; capture the essence of traditional blues styles; exercises, tunes, and clear explanation in print and on video; practical ways to develop fundamental technique offers insights into the musical logic of blues guitar; includes music and instruction for six full blues tunes. SYSTEM SPECS: Book and Instructional DVD.

The Blues Guitarist (www.pgmusic.com): Music programs containing studio recordings of performances; listen to session players perform blues music; learn riffs, licks, and tricks; each instrument (guitar, piano, bass, and drums) recorded on a separate track; listen to each part independently; multimedia features; study arrangements; hear music; play along with top studio musicians. SYSTEM SPECS: Windows.

The Complete Idiot's Guide to Playing Bass Guitar (www.idiotsguides.com): Provides a strong foundation in reading music, purchasing the right equipment, and care and maintenance of the bass guitar; CD of original music helps bass players practice their skills; features examples and practice music for a wide range of styles including blues, rhythm and blues, country, hip-hop, rock, swing, jazz, Latin, reggae, and more. SYSTEM SPECS: Book and Audio CD.

The Complete Idiot's Guide to Playing the Guitar (www.idiotsguides.com): Covers the anatomy of a guitar, identifying all components, and how to string and tune it properly; practice techniques from scales to full pieces; expanded coverage on musical styles from folk to flamenco to blues; audio CD with eighty-three tracks and 125 practice pieces including verbal instructions, page reference, and identifying title for each piece. SYSTEM SPECS: Book and Audio CD.

The FJH Beginner Guitar Method, Books 1-3 (www.fjhmusic.com): Graded guitar method designed especially for the younger beginner; engages students with lively songs instead of exercises; addresses the National Standards for Arts Education. SYSTEM SPECS: Book and Audio CD.

The Gospel Guitar of Rev. Gary Davis (www.melbay.com): Century of different techniques, styles and ideas; many musical formats such as blues, ragtime, folk, gospel, marching songs and Tin Pan Alley hits; four full-length video lessons; Ernie Hawkins teaches fourteen of Rev. Davis's most requested and famous gospel guitar arrangements; rare footage of Rev. Davis playing; detailed rundown of each arrangement, analyzing the structure and timing of each phrase, verse and chorus and replaying everything slower on a split screen with close-ups of both hands; comprehensive eighty-page tab/music booklet included; almost six hours of instruction. SYSTEM SPECS: Instructional DVD.

The Guitar Master Class (www.pgmusic.com): Master Guitarist Oliver Gannon; illustrates basic guitar skills and theory; specifically designed for the beginner guitar student; helps develop skills on its own or as a valuable addition to any existing course of study. SYSTEM SPECS: Windows.

The Guitar of Chet Atkins (www.melbay.com): Taught by Certified Guitar Player Chet Atkins; for intermediate and advanced fingerstyle guitarists; performs and describes in detail, phrase by phrase, the playing of nine of his classic arrangements; split-screen techniques; study left- and right-hand movements; eighty-four-minute DVD; booklet is not included, but may be downloaded from guitarvideos.com. SYSTEM SPECS: Instructional DVD.

The Guitar of Elizabeth Cotton (www.melbay.com): Elizabeth Cotten (1893-1987) occupies a unique niche in American finger-picked guitar; composer of the perennial favorite Freight Train; taught herself to play left-handed on her older brother's guitar, which was strung right-handed, leaving her playing left-handed, and upside down as well, picking alternating bass with her index finger and melody with her thumb; lived with and worked for the Seeger family; exceptional attention to details of phrasing and voice leading; strong improvisatory element; includes rare film footage of Elizabeth Cotten performing the songs that are taught; accompanying booklet includes TAB/standard notation transcriptions and song lyrics; 102 minutes. SYSTEM SPECS: Instructional DVD.

The Guitar of Mississippi John Hurt Volumes One and Two (www.melbay.com): Musician of his time and place; played within a tradition but with own subtleties of touch, phrasing, and use of the guitar; famous for fingerpicking in alternating bass style; employed omitted beats or syncopated runs rather than sticking to an unvaried alternation; was comfortable playing in a variety of keys; instruction in John Hurt's repertoire; songs chosen to showcase his playing in different keys; rare documentary silent film footage; accompanying booklet includes TAB/standard notation transcriptions and song lyrics. SYSTEM SPECS: Instructional DVD.

The Jazz Guitar Master Class (www.pgmusic.com): Illustrates basic skills to the beginning guitarist; enhances skills of more advanced guitarists; sixty lessons, including Chord Voicings,

Inversions, Right-Hand Techniques, Comping, Scales, Modes, Arpeggios, Common Progressions, Improvisation, Chord Melodies, and more; each lesson has an accompanying exercise and a practice tip; ten program tunes feature common chord progressions in a variety of styles and tempos; reference sheets and practice backing tracks; integrates interactive audio lessons with on-screen guitar display and notation. SYSTEM SPECS: Windows.

The Master Flatpick Guitar Solos (www.pgmusic.com): Fully-featured interactive music program with professional flatpick arrangements of fifty-one songs; each song features a flatpick guitar solo as well as accompanying piano (comping), bass, drums, and strings. SYSTEM SPECS: Windows.

The Master Jazz Guitar Solos (www.pgmusic.com): Interactive music program with professional jazz quartet/quintet arrangements of fifty songs; each song features a jazz guitar solo played by a top studio musician; accompanying piano, bass, drums, and strings; almost five hours of jazz guitar soloing; on-screen fretboard shows which notes and chords are being played; guide notes for typical positions for the key; note names to help learn the fret/string positions; large library of jazz solos; all solos are mainstream playing based on typical chord progressions; most use eighth notes or triplets; each song contains six full choruses; hear solos, slow them down, or step through one note at a time; solos may be printed out; notation also contains TAB; advanced looping features; loop a number of bars, what is on screen, or entire song; adjust tempo or key. SYSTEM SPECS: Macintosh; Windows.

The Rock Guitarist (www.pgmusic.com): Programs containing studio recordings of performances; listen to session players perform rock music; learn riffs, licks, and tricks; each instrument recorded on a separate track; listen to each part independently; multimedia features; study arrangements; hear music; play along with top studio musicians. SYSTEM SPECS: Windows.

The Sor Studies (www.pgmusic.com): Classical guitar performances of 121 of Sor's studies for guitar; music notation and chord symbols on-screen; audio performance; on-screen guitar, fretboard, and fingering; print a high-resolution copy; three CD-ROMs; biography of Sor; historical time line; multimedia features. SYSTEM SPECS: Windows.

Video Guitar Lessons Series (www.pgmusic.com): Play like the pros; video guitar lessons; each volume features hours of video instruction by master guitarists; each program includes on-screen video guitar fretboard, transcribed notation, tab, and complete printout; lessons include riffs, songs, tips, techniques, and guitar settings; *Essential Blues Guitar, Volumes 1 and 2; Essential Rock Guitar, Volumes 1 and 2; Essential Jazz Guitar, Volumes 1, 2, and 3*. SYSTEM SPECS: Macintosh; Windows.

You Can Teach Yourself Blues Guitar (www.melbay.com): Companion video to book of same title; in-depth look at basics of acoustic blues guitar; blues progression, blues chords, strum patterns, how to accompany a blues song, 6/8 blues, minor blues, power chords, movable chords, barre chords, the blues scale, turnarounds, fill-ins, the capo, double stops, blues licks, bass line accompaniments, 12/8 blues, blues techniques, how to build and play an improvised solo, and fingerpicking blues; dozens of blues solos and nine new blues songs. SYSTEM SPECS: Instructional DVD.

You Can Teach Yourself Classic Guitar (www.melbay.com): Learn to play classic guitar in all basic keys; Renaissance to 20th Century masterpieces by Sor, Carcassi, Carulli, Diabelli, Giuliani, Bach, Handel, and Dowland; studies for playing in the second, third, fourth, and fifth positions; hands on method. SYSTEM SPECS: Instructional DVD.

You Can Teach Yourself Country Guitar (www.melbay.com): Beginners/intermediate players; how to tune guitar; basic major, minor, and seventh guitar chords; guitar accompaniment strums from current country hits; examples from the book; basic flatpick technique; how to use a capo; easy play-along country songs. SYSTEM SPECS: Instructional DVD.

You Can Teach Yourself Electric Bass (www.melbay.com): For the working bass player; thorough and easy to understand instruction; covers popular bass techniques like slap and pop and hammering. SYSTEM SPECS: Instructional DVD.

You Can Teach Yourself Guitar DVD (www.melbay.com): Popular guitar method; moves at a slow, steady pace; play chord accompaniments in seven primary guitar keys; learn to strum blues chords and begin to play fingerstyle backgrounds; ninety-minute video. SYSTEM SPECS: Instructional DVD.

You Can Teach Yourself Rock Guitar (www.melbay.com): William Bay teaches essential elements of contemporary rock and blues guitar; rock rhythm and rock solo techniques are shown; solo, power chords, barre chords, licks, improvising, scales and rhythm chord progressions shown in keys of E, G, D, A, C, F, and B flat; for each key, solos and studies are contained in various positions on the guitar fingerboard. SYSTEM SPECS: Instructional DVD.

Guitar and Bass Web Sites

12 Tone Music Publishing www.12tonemusic.com Guitar and bass instructional materials; DVDs; *Fretboard Flashcards; Guitar EncycloMedia.*
Acoustic Guitar Magazine www.acguitar.com or www.acousticguitar.com Features; interviews.

Active Bass www.activebass.com Online community.

All Parts www.allparts.com Strings, pedals, cases, etc.

Analog Man www.analogman.com Strings, pedals, parts, cases, etc.

Azola Basses www.azola.com Bug Bass; Mini Bass; Baby Bass; Deco Bass; Jazzman.

Bass Guitar Magazine www.bassguitarmagazine.com Subscribe; gear tests.

Bass Player www.bassplayer.com Bass guitar magazine; technology; news; reviews.

Bass Tab Archive www.basstabarchive.com Tab index.

Basslines www.basslines.com Bass accessories.

Blue Book, Inc. www.bluebookinc.com Prices and values of guitars.

Books for Guitar www.booksforguitar.co.uk/ Handbooks for electric guitar, classical guitar and bass guitar; books and audiocassettes covering all aspects of guitar from beginners to advanced; performance and improvisation.

Chord Find www.chordfind.com Guitar fingerings for chords in various positions.

Chord Melody Guitar Music www.chordmelody.com Chord harmonization; guitar sheet music and tab books; videos and instructional guitar music in all styles: jazz, classical, rock, country, blues, flamenco, acoustic, religious, and Christmas.

Crate Amps www.crateamps.com Amplifiers.

Crossroads Guitar www.crossroads-guitar.com Interactive online guitar courses; over 110 one-hour lessons with streaming video, soundfiles, notation, tab, and text; practice tracks, playing tips, introductory lessons, and contact with instructors.

Cyberfretbass www.cyberfretbass.com Online lessons.

Daddario www.daddario.com Strings, pedals, parts, cases, etc.

D'Andrea, Inc. www.dandreausa.com D'Andrea Picks & Music Gear, Ice Pix, Tribal Planet, Snarling Dogs, Wallacher, Stagerig, Rocky Mountain Slides, Planetone Harmonicas, Rebel Straps, Brooklyn Gear, Pick Boy, KSD Basses, Cadence Harbour.

Danelectro www.danelectro.com Guitar manufacturer; guitar accessories; amplifiers; effects; strings.

Dream Guitars & Apparel www.dreamguitars.com Custom instruments; accessories.

Electro-Harmonix www.ehx.com Analog effects for guitar and bass.

Elixir Guitar Strings www.elixirstrings.com Guitar strings; polyWeb coating.

Epiphone www.epiphone.com Division of Gibson Guitar Corp.; acoustic and electric guitars; amplifiers; accessories.

Ernie Ball www.ernieball.com Guitars, basses, strings.

EVD String Instruments www.evd303.com Variations on traditional acoustic guitars, banjos, and lyres; view custom designs and testimonials.

Experience Hendrix www.jimi-hendrix.com Information on Jimi Hendrix.

Fastfingers www.fastfingers.co.uk Guitar tuition courses covering all styles.

Fender Guitars www.fender.com Product catalog; technical support; find date guitar was made with serial number; contests; e-zine.

Fernandes Guitars www.fernandesguitars.com Guitar manufacturer.

Finger Style Guitar www.fingerstyleguitar.com Features; reviews; news.

Flamenco Guitar Transcriptions www.ctv.es/guitar The flamenco guitar throughout the twentieth century in standard notation and tablature.

Flamenco World www.flamenco-world.com Music and dance videos; CDs; interviews and biographies of the world's greatest guitarists and singers.

Flamenco.org www.flamenco.org Flamenco events.

Flat Pick www.flatpick.com Guitar magazine.

Fodera Guitars www.fodera.com Bass guitars; accessories; electric bass strings.

FretsOnly www.fretsonly.com Educational products for guitar, banjo, mandolin, and violin.

Genz Benz Enclosures www.genzbenz.com Products.

George Furlanetto's Bass www.fbass.com Models; specs; price list; dealers.

GHS Strings www.ghsstrings.com Guitar strings.

Gibson Guitar www.gibson.com Home page; guitar manufacturer based in Nashville; acoustic and electric; strings and accessories; merchandise; music news; references; free online appraisal; dealer directory; auction.

Gig Mate www.gigmate.com Strings, pedals, parts, cases, etc.

GMW Guitarworks www.gmwguitars.com Empire Guitars.

Gretsch www.gretsch.com Guitar and drum manufacturer.

Gruhn Guitars www.gruhn.com Nashville-based vintage guitar dealer; catalog; photo gallery.

Guild Guitars www.guildguitars.com What's new; resources; online store.

Guitar and Bass Guitar Lessons on the Web www.visionmusic.com Free online music lessons for the evolving guitarist or bassist.

Guitar Auction www.guitarauction.com/guitarauctionfrontpage.html Auction source for used, new, and vintage guitars by Martin, Gibson, Fender, Takoma, etc.

Guitar Center www.guitarcenter.com Guitars; amps; drums; keyboards; software; recording and P.A. gear; DJ and lighting; fifty-seven locations.

Guitar College, Inc. www.guitarcollege.com Home study courses for guitar.

Guitar Concept guitarconcept.home.att.net Guitar lessons online or by United States mail.

Guitar Connection www.guitarconnection.com Sheet music, videos, software, and DVDs.

Guitar Gallery Sheet www.guitargallerymusic.com Catalog of guitar music and instructional videos; also banjo, mandolin, fiddle, bass, dulcimer, harmonica, penny whistle, autoharp, songbooks.

Guitar Geek www.guitargeek.com Guitar rig database.

Guitar Lessons at Home www.guitar-lessons-at-home.com In-home lessons; transcriptions.

Guitar Lessons at Musiclearning.Com www.musiclearning.com Lessons with play-along MIDI files and RealAudio examples.

Guitar Net www.guitar.net Chord Archive features a different chord every week; Tab Planet; G.E.A.R.

Guitar Nine Records www.guitar9.com Guitar recordings; books; news.

Guitar Noise www.guitarnoise.com Free online lessons.

Guitar Notes www.guitarnotes.com Guitar links; lessons; MP3s; tabs; shopping; reviews; listings of over 600 guitar dealers.

Guitar One Magazine www.guitaronemag.com Guitar Webzine; tab and notation; MP3s.

Guitar Online www.guitar-online.com Guitar courses online, via e-mail or CD-ROM; videos, scores, and tablatures; MIDI files; online tuner and metronome; English; French; Spanish.

Guitar Player Magazine www.guitarplayer.com Buyer's guide; features; lessons; reviews.

Guitar Simplified www.guitarsimplified.com The "Guitar Barre" method; online sales of a lesson book and a play-along video; for beginners.

Guitar Sounds www.guitarsounds.com The Peter Pupping Quartet.

Guitar World www.guitarworld.com Features; reviews.

Guitar.com www.guitar.com Guitar guide; chord generator; instructors; artists; MP3; tablature; chat.

GuitarLessons.net www.guitarlessons.net Free 24/7 guitar lessons taught by a professional guitarist.

Guitarras Manuel Rodriguez & Sons; S.L. www.guitars-m-r-sons.com Classical and Flamenco; Cutaway Models; Cadete and Señorita.

GuitarSite.com www.guitarsite.com For guitarists by guitarists; updated daily.

Harmony Central: Bass Resources www.harmony-central.com/Bass/ Links to bass Web sites.

Harmony Central: Guitar Tab www.harmony-central.comGuitar/tab.html Tablature.

Highly Strung www.highlystrung.co.uk Strings, pedals, parts, cases, etc.

Hot Licks Productions www.hotlicks.com Instructional media.

International Guitar Seminar www.guitarseminars.com Classes; seminars; FAQ; links.

J. Jennings Publishing Company www.jenningspublishing.com Instructional DVDs for guitar and other instruments.

Jackson Guitars www.jacksonguitars.com Guitar manufacturer; resources.

Jazz Guitar Online www.jazzguitar.com For jazz guitarists; lessons; forum; features; news.

Jean Larrivee Guitars, Ltd. www.larrivee.com Guitar manufacturer.

Johnson Amp www.johnson-amp.com Amplifiers.

Just Strings www.juststrings.com Large selection of strings for all string instruments.

Kaman Music Corp. www.kamanmusic.com Ovation; Takamine; Hamer; Toca; Gibraltar; CB.

Ken Smith Basses, Ltd. www.kensmithbasses.com Bass guitars.

La Bella Strings www.labella.com La Bella; Criterion; Electrics; Super Steps; Deep Talkin' Bass; Slappers; Pacesetter; Folksinger; Elite Series; Series 2001; Silk & Steel; Kapalua; New Yorkers.

Lakland Basses www.lakland.com Standard; Deluxe; Classic; Joe Osborn Signature; Bob Glaub Signature; Jerry Scheff Signature.

Levy's Leathers, Ltd. www.levysleathers.com Guitar straps, gig bags.

Martin Guitar Company www.martinguitar.com Guitars; strings; pedals; parts; cases; etc.

Mesa Boogie www.mesaboogie.com Guitar amplifiers; photos; product information; English and German.

Metal Method www.metalmethod.com Weekly free lessons include tablature, WAV, and MP3 files.

MetalTabs.com www.metaltabs.com Heavy metal guitar tabs.

Music Theory Course for Guitar www.guitar-jimsuttoninst.comMT.html International correspondence guitar school.

Musical Instrument Makers Forum www.mimf.com Acoustic guitar making; electric guitar building; guitar repair; violin making; online interactive course in instrument making; forum; community for musicians and instrument makers.

National Guitar Summer Workshop www.guitarworkshop.com Held June through August in various locations.

PDS Music www.pdsmusic.com Guitar lessons offered by international mail-order correspondence.

Pedal Boards www.pedalboards.com Pedal racks.

Phantom Guitar Works, Inc. www.phantomguitars.com Phantom Guitars; Teardrop Guitars; Mando Guitars.

Picks by the Pound www.picksbythepound.com Guitar picks.

Pignose Amps www.pignoseamps.com Amplifiers.

Play Guitar www.nl-guitar.com Download program to learn how to play guitar; music educational programs for schools.

RainSong Graphite Guitars www.rainsong.com WS 1000; WS 2000; WS 1100; JZ 1000.

Renaissance Guitars www.renaissanceguitars.com
    Renaissance Guitars and Basses; Rick Turner
    Guitars; Electroline Basses; Model T Guitars.
Rio Grande Pickups www.riograndepickups.com
    Pickups.
Sabine www.sabineusa.com Chromatic tuners.
Samson Technologies Corp. www.samsontech.com
    Strings, pedals, parts, cases, amplifiers.
Santa Cruz Guitar Co. www.santacruzguitar.com
    Maker of fine guitars.
Schecter Guitar Research www.schecterguitars.com
    Custom Guitars and Basses; Diamond Series
    Guitars; Basses and Seven-String Electrics.
Seymour Duncan www.seymourduncan.com Pickups.
Spector Design, Ltd. www.spectorbass.com Bass
    guitars and strings.
Steinberger www.gibson.com/products/steinberger
    Headless guitars and basses; company information.
String Letter Publishing www.stringletter.com Guitar
    magazines, books, songbooks, and CDs.
Tacoma Guitars USA www.tacomaguitars.com Tacoma
    USA; Olympia.

Taylor Guitars www.taylorguitars.com Guitar
    manufacturer based in El Cajon, CA; newsletter.
TCguitar.com www.tcguitar.com Magazine.
Teaching the Folk Guitar
    www.radioyur.com/yufpub.html Basic skills.
The Classical Guitar Home Page
    www.guitarist.com/cg/cg.htm Created in 1994;
    resources; sheet music; MIDI files; lessons.
The Natural Approach to Guitar
    www.thenaturalapproach.com Teaches students to
    see and hear the neck as one unit; no memorizing
    scales; improvise in any style.
TrueFire.com www.truefire.com Digital self-publishing
    and distribution system for guitar instruction;
    original music, literature, art, and reference
    materials; available in multiple formats.
VintageGuitar.com www.vguitar.com Guitar magazine.
W. Paul Guitars Inc. www.wpaulguitars.com Timeless
    Timber guitars and bass guitars.
Washburn International www.washburn.com Acoustic
    and electric guitars and basses; artists; resources;
    dealer locater.

10
Drums and Percussion
Software, Instructional Media and Web Sites

Absolute Beginners: Drums (www.musicsales.com): Step-by-step exercises; play along with professional backing track; set up drum kit; tune drums; read drum music; understand rhythm; coordinate bass drum, snare, hi-hat, rash, and ride cymbals; perform first drum part; includes a thirty-two page booklet with exercises matching the DVD. SYSTEM SPECS: Book, Audio CD, and Instructional DVD.

Alfred's Drum Method (www.alfred.com): Alfred's Drum Method, Books 1 and 2 prepare beginning players for all styles of snare drum and percussion performance; Book 1 contains eighty pages of sequential instruction covering rudimental studies, roll studies, contest solos, and bass drum and cymbal technique; also includes twenty-three solos suitable for recitals and contests; Book 2 covers additional rudimental studies, tonal properties of the snare drum, theme and variations, musical forms, solos and duets; also covers traditional rudimental style, corps style (by Jay Wanamaker), orchestral style, accessory instruments, and multiple percussion techniques; videotapes include demonstrations of all the rudiments and accessory instruments, plus solo performances by the authors. SYSTEM SPECS: Book and/or Instructional DVD.

Alfred Methods and Technique (www.alfred.com): Titles include: *30-Day Workout (An Exercise Plan for Drummers); Alfred's Drumset Method; Alfred's MAX Drumset; The Drum Along Drum Circle Video; Drum Solos Revisited; Drum Tips: Double Bass Drumming; Drum Tips, Part I: Developing a Groove/Power Solos; Drum Tips, Part II: Double Bass Drumming/Funky Drummers; The Drummer's Toolkit; Drums for the Absolute Beginner; International Drum Rudiments; New Orleans Drumming; New Orleans Jazz and Second Line Drumming; No Reading Required: Easy Rock Drum Beats; World Rhythms! Arts Program Presents West African Drum & Dance: A Yankadi-Macrou Celebration; Together in Rhythm,* and more. SYSTEM SPECS: Book, Audio CD, and/or Instructional DVD.

All About Bongos, All About Congas, and All About Jembe by Kalani (www.alfred.com): In-depth coverage of popular percussion instruments, including history, tuning, maintenance, techniques, exercises, ensembles, and more; world renowned educator and performer; multimedia content; demonstrations of rhythms, techniques, and tunings. SYSTEM SPECS: Book and Enhanced CD.

Anyone Can Play Drum Set (www.melbay.com): By Gene Holter; designed for anyone who wants to learn to play the drum set; learn popular techniques used in modern music; step-by-step process; no previous musical experience necessary; learn rock, swing, jazz, and country styles; drum music reading, counting, and proper drum setup; free booklet. SYSTEM SPECS: Instructional DVD.

Artist Drum DVDs (www.alfred.com) Large catalog of instructional materials for drummers by artists including Henry Adler, Carmine Appice, Kenny Aronoff, Billy Ashbaugh, Carter Beauford, Terry Bozzio, Brian "Brain" Mantia, Dennis Chambers, Tony Royster, Jr., Billy Cobham, Changuito, Luis Conté, Wilson "Chembo" Corniel, Virgil Donati, Cassio Duarte, Peter Erskine, Joe Franco, Steve Gadd, Richie Gajate-Garcia, David Garibaldi, Michael Spiro, Jesus Diaz, David Garibaldi, Bob Gatzen, Robby Ameen, Jim Greiner, Gavin Harrison, Horacio "El Negro" Hernandez, Giovanni Hidalgo, Steve Houghton, Bobby Jarzombek, Bashiri Johnson, Kalani, Will Kennedy, Bob Gatzen, Gene Krupa, Rick Latham, Russ Miller, Marco Minnemann,

Pablo "Chino" Nuñez, Babatunde Olatunji, Neil Peart, Simon Phillips, Raul Rekow, Karl Perazzo, Buddy Rich, Bobby Rock, Chad Smith, Steve Smith, Ed Soph, Horacee Arnold, Jerry Steinholtz, Ed Thigpen, Steve Thornton, Dave Weckl, Zoro, and more. SYSTEM SPECS: Book, Audio CD, and/or Instructional DVD.

Berklee Press (www.berkleepress.com): Titles include *Berklee Instant Drum Set; Berklee Practice Method: Drum Set; Beyond the Backbeat; Brazilian Rhythms for Drum Set and Percussion; Mastering the Art of Brushes; Rudiment Grooves for Drum Set*, and more. SYSTEM SPECS: Book and Audio CD.

Buddy Rich: The Lost West Side Story Tapes (www.voyetra.com): State-of-the-art audio mix; solos of selected performers; track selection menu; additional commentary by Dave Weckl and Gary Reber; includes interviews, behind-the-scenes footage of Buddy, and more. SYSTEM SPECS: Instructional DVD.

Complete Modern Drum Set DVD (www.melbay.com): Companion to Complete Modern Drum Set Book; challenging material for the intermediate to advanced drummer; special effects have been removed and sound track has been encoded in Dolby Digital stereo; twenty-one play-along tracks; CueLink; metronome; jazz, Latin, rock, R&B, African, and more; Frank Briggs presents masterful performances and cutting edge concepts such as metric modulation, displaced beats, polyrhythms, etc.; complete performances of Red Moon, Home, Along the Mohawk, Sketch/Electric, and more; over 115 minutes of drumming; hear what patterns sound like in context. SYSTEM SPECS: Instructional DVD.

Drum Circle: A Guide to World Percussion (www.alfred.com): Covers twenty-eight different instruments; descriptions and performance techniques; exercises; traditional music notation and time box notation. SYSTEM SPECS: Book and Enhanced CD; Macintosh; Windows.

Drums for Dummies (www.dummies.com): Discover how to bang out basic rhythms with or without sticks; understand fundamental drumming techniques; explore other percussion instruments; find the perfect drum set; purchase, tune, and maintain drums; CD-ROM has MP3 files of each rhythm and beat to play along with; rhythms for hand drums from the bongos and congas to the surdo, tar, and udu; drum solos. SYSTEM SPECS: Book and CD-ROM.

Drums on Demand (www.drumsondemand.com): Live drum loops for drum tracks; from rock to country, jazz to blues; Acid loops, Apple Loops, or Rex files; drum loops organized in easy-to-use Song Sets featuring as many as seventy-two verse, chorus, fill, bridge, break, intro, ending, and other loops; find the Master Loop that fits the drum beat of the original song and use the matching drum loops and segments to build a drum track that feels like a session drummer; drum loops for

Pro Tools, Cakewalk, Cubase, Logic, DP, Garageband, Acid, Live and more; My Co-Writer. SYSTEM SPECS: Macintosh; Windows.

Eight-Note Bell Songbook and CD (www.musicmotion.com): Forty-six songs and an accompaniment CD to be used with bells, boomwhackers, step bells, resonator bells, any eight-note instrument. SYSTEM SPECS: Book and Audio CD.

Fast Forward: Hip Hop Drum Patterns (www.musicsales.com): Play along with the tracks on the CD; learn about hip-hop, funk, and soul beats; Guide to Drums pull-out chart. SYSTEM SPECS: Book and Audio CD.

Fast Forward: Rock Solid Drum Patterns (www.musicsales.com): Learn the essentials of rock rhythms, including bass and snare drum variations, drum fills, syncopated rhythms, and more. SYSTEM SPECS: Book and Audio CD.

Hal Leonard Drum and Percussion DVDs (www.halleonard.com): Titles include *Beginning Drums Volume One; Buddy Rich—At the Top; Classic Drum Solos and Drum Battles; Classic Drum Solos and Drum Battles—Vol. 2; Classic Jazz Drummers; Drummers Collective 25th Anniversary Celebration and Bass Day 2002; Getting Started on Drums; John Blackwell—Technique, Grooving and Showmanship; Learn to Play the Drumset; Modern Drummer Festival 2000; Play Drums Today!; Snare Drum Basics; Steve Jordan—The Groove Is Here; Steve Smith—Drum Set Technique/History of the U.S. Beat*, and more. SYSTEM SPECS: Instructional DVD.

How to Play Drums from Day One (www.melbay.com): By Jim Payne; basics of rock and blues drumming; assigns singing drum sounds or solfege syllables to five basic components of drumset; addresses holding the sticks, playing the bass drum, and traditional notation and singing syllables of the hi-hat, bass drum, cymbals, and toms; rock and blues tunes with various grooves and tempos; awareness of song form; on-screen samples in both standard notation and drum sounds. SYSTEM SPECS: Instructional DVD.

Hudson Music (www.hudsonmusic.com): Large catalog of instructional materials for drummers by artists including Mike Portnoy, Thomas Lang, Steve Smith, Steve Gadd, John Blackwell, Gregg Bissonette, Jeff Queen, Antonio Sanchez, Buddy Rich, Tito Puente, Hank Marvin, Marco Minnemann, and more. SYSTEM SPECS: Book, Audio CD, and/or Instructional DVD.

Just Enough Drums (www.melbay.com): Instructional package for beginning drum set; introduces instructors, shows how they got started, what it is like to perform, what music means to them, and how to buy first gear; learn basic techniques; play with band in inter Virtual Jam Session; contains over fifty drums lessons; Gavin, Ben, and Nikki teach how to get set up and start jamming; learn twelve-bar structure, rolls, fills, and how to play beats for funk, jazz, rock, rap, pop, and more; AudioBook pocket reference manual works with Audio CD; contains over fifty lessons; match tracks in Book to tracks on CD player and follow along. SYSTEM SPECS: Book, Audio CD, Instructional DVD, and Hybrid CD-ROM.

Learn to Play Drums (www.alfred.com): Step-by-step interactive lessons; adjust tempo; mix accompaniment parts; record performance. SYSTEM SPECS: Hybrid CD-ROM.

Mel Bay Drum and Percussion Methods (www.melbay.com): Titles include: *100 Famous Funk Beats; A Rhythmic Vocabulary; Absolute Beginners Bodhran Tutor; Advanced Jazz Drumset; Advanced Rock Drumset; Afro-Latin Polyrhythms; Anthology of Rock Drumming; Anyone Can Play Djembe; Anyone Can Play Drum Rudiments; Arabic Percussion; Art of Arabic Drumming; Art of Bongo Drumming; Banda - Percussion, Volumes 1 & 2, Spanish Only; Bateria Volumes 1, 2, & 3 (Spanish): You Can Play Drums Now; Blues Drums Method: An Essential Study of Blues Drums for the Beginning-Advanced Player; Blues Drums Play-Along Trax; Bodhran Tutor: Absolute Beginner's; Bodhran, Bones & Spoons; Bongo Drumming: Beyond the Basics; Bongos World Percussion; Complete Music for the Fife and Drum; Conga Drumming: A Beginner's Guide to Playing with Time; Crosstraining: A Method for Applying Rhythms and Techniques to Drum Set, Hand Percussion, and Mallet Instruments; Darbuka Method; Darbuka World Percussion; Djembe World Percussion; Drum Basics; Drum Circle Spirit - Facilitating Human Potential Through Rhythm; Drum Lessons for Kids of All Ages; Drum Set Dailies: Rudimental Applications for Drum Set; Drum Set SMART Book: Style, Mechanics, Applications, Routines, Tips; Drum Set Styles Encyclopedia; Drum Set Tunes Book; Drumming Facts, Tips and Warm-Ups; Drumset 101; Drumset for the 21st Century; Drumstick Finger Systems and Techniques; Drum-Talk, Volumes 1 & 2: Fundamental Rhythm Studies for Drums; Earth Rhythms Catalog; Ethnic Asian Rhythms for the Modern Drummer; Fill Workbook; First Lessons Djembe; First Lessons Drumset; Fun with Bongos; Fundamentals of Mallet Playing; Fundamentals of Rhythm for the Drummer; Funk Drumming; Fusion Drum Styles; Hands on Drumming Sessions 1-4; Hip Grooves for Hand Drums: How to Play Funk, Rock & World Beat Patterns on Any Drum; How to Play Djembe; How to Play Drums from Day One; How To Play The Bodhran; Inside The Big Band; Intermediate Jazz Drumset; Intermediate Rock Drumset; Introduction to Rock Style Drumming; Introduction to Swing-Style Drumming; Jazz & Blues Drumming; Jazz Combo Drumming: A Drummer's Workshop DVD Guide to Playing with a Modern Rhythm Section; Jazz Drumset Basics; Jazz Time Part One - The Basics; Just Enough/Learn to Play Drums; Killer-Fillers: Drum Set Exercises for Today's Drummer; Latin Concepts for the Creative Drummer; Latin Elements for the Drum Set; Learn How to Play the Flamenco Cajon; Learning the Tabla; Musical Drumset Solos for Recitals, Contests and Fun; Natural Development in Drumming Technique; Natural Drumming: Lessons 1-6; Percussion Volumes 1-3, Spanish Only: You Can Play Percussion Now!; Play the World: The 101 World Instrument Primer; Pocket Rhythms For Drums; Practice the Flamenco Cajon; Rhythm is the Cure, Southern Italian Tambourine; Rock Drumming & Soloing Methods; Rock Drumset Basics; Rock Studies for Drumset; Rock: Take Off 1; Rock: Take Off 2; Rudimental Drum Method for the Intermediate Drummer: Follow-up to Fundamentals of Rhythm for the Drummer; Rudiments on the Drumset; Rumba Soloing Technique, Volumes 1 & 2: Afro-Cuban Conga Drum Improvisation; Secrets of the Greats: Drumset Exercises for a Professional Sound; Set Up and Play!; Skin It, Tune It, Play It; Slap Happy; Stick Tricks; Studies in Drumset Independence; The Art of Transcribing: Drum Set; The Beatlife Book: Playing & Teaching Samba Beyond Stick Control: For the Snare and Drum Set Player; The Bongo Book; The Drummer's Cookbook; The Drummer's Guide to the Funk Shuffle and Other Sextuplet Based Grooves Best Seller; The Irish Drum: A Bodhran; The Magnificient Darbuka Rhythms; The Soul of Hand Drumming; The Tomás Cruz Conga Method, Volumes I, II, & III: Beginning: Conga Technique as Taught in Cuba; Traditional Afro-Cuban Concepts in Contemporary Music; Understanding Groove for Drum Set the Easy Way*, and more. SYSTEM SPECS: Book, Audio CD, and/or Instructional DVD.

Mike Portnoy Liquid Drum Theater DVD (www.voyetra.com): Two-disk set featuring live performances by Dream Theater and Liquid Tension Experiment; over twenty minutes of new footage; full-length commentary; camera switching option allows the viewer to "direct" four studio performances; photo gallery, and more. SYSTEM SPECS: Instructional DVD.

Modern Drummer Festival 2000 Highlights (www.voyetra.com): Don Brewer, Vinnie Colaiuta, Horacio "El Negro" Hernandez with Marc Quinones, Akira Jimbo, Hilary Jones, Paul Leim, Dave Lombardo, and Billy Ward; first-ever DVD for musician's market; 170 minutes of performances, clinics, and interviews. SYSTEM SPECS: Instructional DVD.

Musicians Institute Press (www.halleonard.com): Titles include: *Afro-Cuban Coordination for Drumset—The Essential Method and Workbook; Blues Drumming—The Drummer's Guide to Blues Drumming Styles and Grooves; Brazilian Coordination for Drumset—The Essential Method and Workbook; Chart Reading Workbook for Drummers; Drummer's Guide to Odd Meters—A Comprehensive Source for Playing Drums in Odd Time Signatures; Encyclopedia of Reading*

Rhythms—Text and Workbook for All Instruments; Funk and Hip-Hop Drumming—Essential Grooves, Fills and Styles; Latin Soloing for Drumset; Working the Inner Clock for Drumset, and more. SYSTEM SPECS: Book and Audio CD.

No Excuses Drum Guide (www.musicsales.com): Comprehensive guide for players of all abilities; practice in a variety of styles as part of a band. SYSTEM SPECS: Instructional DVD and Hybrid CD-ROM.

Progressive Beginner Drums DVD (www.learntoplaymusic.com): For beginning drummers; explains and demonstrates essential sounds and techniques used in modern drumming styles; music fundamentals; coordination and rhythm studies, and making effective use of the whole drum kit. SYSTEM SPECS: Book, Audio CD, and Instructional DVD.

Pulse: A Stomp Odyssey DVD (www.friendshiphouse.com): World percussion; hear the primal rhythms and polyrhythms of Africa, Asia, Europe, and the Americas; spectacular visuals and celebratory rhythms of the world; forty minutes. SYSTEM SPECS: Instructional DVD.

Realistic Rock 35th Anniversary Special Edition (www.alfred.com): One of the top twenty-five drum books of all time; includes material from the first edition printing in 1972; video rockumentary; instruction by Carmine Appice of the band Cactus. SYSTEM SPECS: Book and Enhanced CD.

Rock Drums for Beginners (www.alfred.com): Correlates to the method book Rock Drums for Beginners; author shows the concepts and techniques discussed in the book; step-by-step, easy-to-understand approach; teaches how to set up and tune drums; covers two methods of holding sticks and basic stroke technique; close-ups of the hands and feet, split screens, and other video techniques. SYSTEM SPECS: Book and/or Instructional DVD.

Sound Shape Playbook: Drumming Games and Other Music Activities for Percussion (www.musicmotion.com): Twenty-two activities and games to show groups ages three to adult the power of rhythmic expression and communication; mix of chants and songs using Sound Shapes and other percussion; games and activities involving listening, call and response, improvisation, creative movement, reading readiness and more; CD of demos and accompaniment. SYSTEM SPECS: Book and Audio CD.

Stomp Out Loud (www.stomponline.com): Filmed live in New York, NY; features the cast of the off-Broadway hit show; uses ordinary objects like mop handles and trashcan lids to make music; for all ages; running time fifty minutes. SYSTEM SPECS: DVD.

Teach Yourself Drums Instructional DVD (www.learntoplaymusic.com): By Peter Gelling; for beginning drummers; introduces basics of playing rock, funk, blues, jazz, and other popular styles; exercises for developing independence between all four limbs; lesson on how to play in a band. SYSTEM SPECS: Book, Audio CD, and Instructional DVD.

The Complete Idiot's Guide to Playing Drums (www.idiotsguides.com): Second edition; by Michael Miller; learn drum basics and more. SYSTEM SPECS: Book and Audio CD.

UBSJr. Learn Basic Drums (www.alfred.com): Learn how to play the drums; how to hold the drumsticks; what each drums is; basic patterns; how to get in the groove. SYSTEM SPECS: Instructional DVD.

Ultimate Beginner Series (www.alfred.com) Titles include: *Ultimate Beginner Series: Blues Drums; Ultimate Beginner Series: Rock Drums; Ultimate Beginner Series: Drum Jam With Songbook, Classic Blues; Ultimate Beginner Series: Have Fun Playing Hand Drums, Bongos; Ultimate Beginner Series: Have Fun Playing Hand Drums, Congas; Ultimate Beginner Series: Have Fun Playing Hand Drums, Djembe; Ultimate Beginner Series: Have Fun Playing Hand Drums (For Bongo, Conga, and Djembe Drums).* SYSTEM SPECS: Book, Audio CD, and/or Instructional DVD.

Ultimate Beginner Series: Drum Basics (www.alfred.com): Provides all the basics; how to hold a drumstick; drummer's function within the framework of a band; how to play a simple drum fill and basic rock and blues beats. SYSTEM SPECS: Book, Audio CD, and/or Instructional DVD.

Ultimate Beginner Xpress: An Introduction to Musical Styles for Drums (www.alfred.com): Covers posture, proper stick technique, basic grooves, fills, and rhythms. SYSTEM SPECS: Instructional DVD.

World Drum DVD (www.musicmotion.com): Experience 250 of the world's greatest percussionists at Vancouver's Expo 1986; hear African drummers, rock drummers, Indonesian gamelan orchestras, military drum corps, Inuit elders, Caribbean steel drum orchestra, and more; John Wyre narrates; running time forty-five minutes. SYSTEM SPECS: DVD.

World Music Drumming - A Cross-Cultural Curriculum (www.musicmotion.com): Learn drumming techniques; sing songs using drumming techniques and movement; create connections to African and Latin cultures; teach team building, listening, respect, and other life skills; step-by-step approach. SYSTEM SPECS: Instructional DVD.

You Can Teach Yourself Drums DVD (www.melbay.com): Useful information for the beginning drummer of any age; introduces drumset basics from setup and basic sticking patterns to rock and funk grooves and fills involving syncopation; sixty-seven minutes. SYSTEM SPECS: Instructional DVD.

Drums and Percussion Web Sites

2box AB www.2box.se Drumit Electronic Percussion.

A. M. Percussion Publications www.ampercussion.com Repertoire for percussion recitals and ensembles.

Ahead Drumsticks www.aheaddrumsticks.com Drumsticks; snares; accessories.

American Drum School www.americandrumschool.com Drums; instructional drum videos; accessories.

American Drum www.americandrum.com Online retail store for percussion.

Aquarian www.aquariandrumheads.com Brands include Studio-X, Super-2, Super-Kick and Hi-Energy Drumheads, Cymbal Springs, Studio Rings, Kick Pads, and Power-Sleeve Drumsticks.

Audix www.audixusa.com Drum microphones.

Ballistic Drums www.ballisticdrums.com Play feet like hands; free pounding audiotape and report.

Basix Percussion www.basixpercussion.com Brands include Basix, Royce, and Drumcraft.

Battlefield Drums www.battlefielddrums.com Drum company.

Bazhou Basix Musical Instrument Co., Ltd. www.basixdrums.com Drums unlimited.

Beatboy www.beatboy.com Drum pattern programmers; product info; demos.

Beato, Inc. www.beatobags.com Carries drum bags, orchestra covers, drum kit dust covers, and percussion covers.

Big Bang Distribution www.bigbangdist.com Ahead Drumsticks, Protection Racket, Bass Drum O's, Big Dog, Flix Fibre Brushes, Metrophones, and RTOM.

Bosphorus Cymbals www.bosphoruscymbals.com Brands include Bosphorus Cymbals, Bopworks Drum Sticks, and Cymbal Swipes.

Canopus Co., Ltd. www.canopusdrums.com Brands include Zelkova Snare Drum, Club-Kit, Be-Bop Kit, Vintage Snare Wire, Back Beat Snare Wire, Hybrid Hardware, Ligh Weight Hardware, Neo-Vintage Series, Bolt Tight, and R.F.M. Series.

Clearsonic www.clearsonic.com ClearSonic Panel drum shield and SORBER free-standing sound absorption.

Discrete Drums, Inc. www.discretedrums.com Discrete Drums: Series One Two, Earthbeat, Heavy Mental, Discrete Percussion, Turbulent Filth Monsters, Apple Loop Editions, Ruff Drumz, Bitch, I-Studio Live Recording Sessions.

Drum Bum www.drumbum.com Gifts and accessories for drummers.

Drum Connection www.drumconnection.com Drum tip of the day; videos; events; classes; store.

Drum Corps World www.drumcorpsworld.com Drum Corps world history; scholarships; schedules; photos; auctions.

Drum Grooves Publications www.drumgrooves.com Seventy-two page book with CD; fifty play-along songs in many styles with accompanying scores; for beginning through intermediate drummers.

Drum Machine Museum www.drummachine.com Drum machines; links.

Drum Network DrumNetwork.com Developed to help drummers find out about drums, drum tuning, drum sets reviews, and more; on-line drum shop; "today's lick" drum lesson.

Drum Tech www.drumtech.com Drum technology; electronic drums.

Drum Trax www.drumtrax.com MIDI file drum pattern library.

Drum Workshop, Inc. www.dwdrums.com Products; artists; information.

Drum! Magazine www.drummagazine.com/html/ Publication for drummers.

Drum-A-Long www.drumalong.com Practice pads; educational kits.

Drummers Web www.drummersweb.com Links; ads.

Drums and Percussion Music Software www.hitsquad.com/smm/cat/DRUMS_PERCUSSION/ Links organized by platform.

Drums on the Web www.drumsontheweb.com Artists; forum; behind the music.

Drums.com www.drums.com Links; lessons; interviews; articles; forums.

Drums.org www.drums.org Information resources and links; global hand drum and dance community.

Drumtech Drum and Percussion School www.drumtech.co.uk Drum school in Europe; beginner to advanced; private lessons; three-month full-time course; one-year diploma; three-year music degree.

Empire Music www.empire-music.com Bongos; congas; Latin percussion; recorders; kazoos; tambourines; rhythm.

Everyone's Drumming Co. www.everyonesdrumming.com Hand drums.

Fat Congas www.fatcongas.com Cajón drums.

GrooveMaker www.groovemaker.com IK Multimedia; combination of remixing software and sounds for creating hypnotic dance tracks in real time; groove combinations in every dance style; ready-to-use loops; professional drum grooves; synth pads; sound effects; ambient loops; add-on loop libraries.

Harmony Central—Drums and Percussion www.harmony-central.com/Drums/ Resources.

Kaman Music Corporation www.kamanmusic.com Percussion instruments and more.

LP Music Group www.lpmusic.com Manufacturer of Latin percussion instruments; congas; bongos; udu drums; cowbells; tambourines; maracas.

Ludwig Drums www.ludwig-drums.com Brands include Classic Birch Series Drums, Rocker and Accent Series Drums, Educational Percussion Kits, Musser Mallet Percussion Instruments, and Timpani and Concert Drums.

Mountain Rythym www.mountainrythym.com Handcrafted percussion instruments; Drums; Ashiko; Djembe; Conga; Simple Twist Tuning System.

Music Room www.musicroom.com/drums.html Drums and percussion songbooks.

Neztech Software www.neztech.com *SequBeat PRO* drum sample sequencing packaging for PC.

Not So Modern Drummer www.notsomoderndrummer.com Drum magazine.

Pearl www.pearldrum.com Departments; forum; artist roster; news.

Percussive Arts Society www.pas.org Music service organization promoting percussion education, research, performance, and appreciation.

Platinum Samples www.platinumsamples.com Master Engineer Series drum samples.

Pork's Pie Percussion www.porkpiedrums.com Products; artists; swag; news; support.

Premier Percussion www.premier-percussion.com Percussion products; artists.

Pro Percussion www.propercussion.co.uk/ Percussion; drums; drum kits; cymbals.

Pure Sound Percussion www.puresoundpercussion.com Blasters, Speedball, and Puresound.

R.E.T. Percussion www.retpercussion.com First software-based drum company.

Remo www.remo.com Drum heads.

Rhythm Band Instruments, Inc. www.rhythmband.com Aulos Recorders, Kidsplay, Charlie Horse Music Pizza Rhythm Band Set, Sweet Pipes Recorder Music, Belleplates, and Chromaharp.

Rhythm Fusion, Inc. www.rhythmfusion.com Wide variety of percussion instruments.

Rhythm Tech www.rhythmtech.com Percussion instruments and accessories.

Rhythm Traders www.rhythmtraders.com Drums and percussion; four sites to all genres.

Rhythms Exotic Afro Percussions, LLC www.afrorhythms.com Specializes in the manufacture of Afro Percussion instruments traditionally found in areas of the Caribbean and West Africa.

Roots Jam: Collected Hand Drum Rhythms www.alternativeculture.com/music/drumming.htm Music instruction book for African drumming; drum rhythms and drumming tips; easy notation for beginners or advanced drum groups.

Sabian www.sabian.com Cymbals; accessories; artists.

Submersible Music www.submersiblemusic.com DrumCore, DrummerPacks, KitCore.

The Overseas Connection www.overseasconnection.com Brands include Rhythmkids, Agogo Gongs, Realafrica, Shekeres, Djembes, Djun Djuns, and Udu Drums.

Toontrack Music AB www.toontrack.com Superior Drummer, EZ Drummer, EZX, EZPlayer, DFH, Drumkit From Hell, DrumTracker, ToonTrack.

Trueline Drumsticks www.trueline.com T6 Trueline Grip, Natural Diamond Grip, Classic Drumsticks.

WaveMachine Labs www.drumagog.com Drumagog.

Zildjian www.zildjian.com Cymbals; percussion accessories; instructional tips; QuickTime video clips.

11
Vocal—Choral—Opera and Musical Theater Software, Instructional Media and Web Sites

10 Great Hollywood Film Duets (www.musicsales.com): Sing ten great film hits with a duet partner to the backing tracks or with the pre-recorded professional singers; includes male and female voices; full demonstration tracks; full piano accompaniment and vocal arrangements for all ten songs; complete lyrics and guitar chords. SYSTEM SPECS: Book and Audio CD.

Alfred Vocal and Choral Methods and Technique (www.alfred.com): Titles include: *Follow Me to the Top! A Choral Movement Video; On the Stage! A Choral Movement Video; That's Entertainment: A Choral Movement Video; Creative Rehearsal Techniques for Today's Choral Classroom; Jazz Style and Improvisation for Choirs; Performance Vocals; Rock Your Vox Vocal Performance Instruction; Ultimate Beginner Series: Blues Vocals; Ultimate Beginner Series: Rock Vocals; Zen of Screaming; Basix Rock Singing Techniques*, and more. SYSTEM SPECS: Book, Audio CD, Enhanced CD, or Instructional DVD.

American Idol Singer's Advantage (www.idoladvantage.com): Voice training program based on Seth Rigg's speech level singing; free karaoke; voice evaluation system helps identify vocal problems; learn the five secrets to mastering any song; sing along to all styles of music including pop, hip-hop, rock, country, gospel, jazz, and opera. SYSTEM SPECS: Book, Audio CD, and Instructional DVD.

Audio Mirror (www.ecsmedia.com): Practice singing and matching pitches; listens to notes in real time and determines the note being sung and how sharp or flat the note is in cents; set the sensitivity of the program to compensate for various mic level inputs and impedances; record keeping is included so progress can be tracked and performance evaluated; for all ages. SYSTEM SPECS: Windows CD-ROM.

Audrey Hunt (www.singtome.com/cd.htm): Includes *Anyone Can Sing, Complete Ear Training, Breath Control, Starting a Singing Career, Develop Vibrato, Practice Guidance and Singing Tips,* and *Total Vocal Warm-Up.* SYSTEM SPECS: Audio CD.

Born to Sing (www.vocalpowerinc.com): By Elisabeth Howard and Howard Austin; step-by-step demonstrations; orchestrated tracks; over 300 song phrases and exercises; Technique section covers breath support, vibrato, range, resonance, falsetto, head voice, chest voice, smoothing out the break between registers, volume control, projection, holding notes and long phrases, and more; Style section covers pop, rock, country, blues, R&B, Broadway, phrasing, improvisation, personal style; Super Vocals gives licks and tricks for every style; Sing-Aerobics is a thirty-minute daily workout. SYSTEM SPECS: Book, Audio CD, and Instructional DVD.

Breck Alan: Lead Singer – Vocal Techniques (www.rockhousemethod.com): Includes *From Pop to Rock, Levels One and Two* and *From Heavy Rock to Metal, Levels One and Two;* comprehensive learning system integrates multimedia and online lesson support; start with basics including proper posture, relaxing, breath control, and how male or female vocalists can find and develop their full singing range; warm-up routines and exercises that bring voice to its highest performance level while maintaining vocal health; techniques for singing in all styles. SYSTEM SPECS: Book, Audio CD, and Instructional DVD.

Carry-a-Tune: Singing Coach Limited (www.carryatune.com): Pitch-tracking system; microphone/headset; tracks progress for three songs; vocal range analyzer; twenty singing lessons; twelve practice songs; four free downloads from the online music store. SYSTEM SPECS: Windows CD-ROM.

Daily Workout for a Beautiful Voice (www.musicmotion.com): By Charlotte Adams and the Cherry Creek High School Girls' 21 from Denver; choir known for their free, clear, warm, and open sound; uses techniques of visualization, movement, and reinforcement; group goes through a daily workout encompassing two-three exercises each in the areas of resonance, breath support, lifted soft palate, range, and agility; guide notates the exercises and gives more hints for using them; running time thirty-four minutes. SYSTEM SPECS: Instructional DVD.

Discover Your Voice (www.singers.com): By Tona de Brett; includes Learning to Sing: Must I learn to Read Music?; Practice makes Perfect; Breathing Exercises; Your Body Your Dreams; Aural Awareness; Vocal Register Imitation; Strain; The Microphone; Preparing to Perform; Choosing a Teacher; Basic Exercises: Exercises 1-14; Vocal Flexibility: Exercises 1-9; Word Exercises; Studio Work: Sound Engineers; Studio Microphones; Effects; Performing in the Studio. SYSTEM SPECS: Book and Audio CD.

Global Voices in Song CD-ROM (www.globalvoicesinsong.com): Aural and visual model of vocal music from different cultures; interactive CD-ROM with music and cultural information; resource guide; supplementary audio CD and videotape; for multicultural and choral studies; all ages. SYSTEM SPECS: Hybrid CD-ROM.

Hal Leonard Vocal Publications with Companion CDs (www.halleonard.com): Titles include: *3 Arias for Baritone/Bass; 3 Famous Tenor Arias; 3 Puccini Arias for Soprano; 3 Seductive Arias for Mezzo-Soprano; 10 Contemporary Hymn Arrangements - High Voice; 10 Contemporary Hymn Arrangements - Low Voice; 10 Popular Wedding Duets; 10 Wedding Solos - HIGH VOICE; 10 Wedding Solos - LOW VOICE; 12 Christmas Favorites - High Voice; 12 Christmas Favorites - Low Voice; 12 Sacred Songs - High Voice; 12 Sacred Songs - Low Voice; 14 Sacred Solos - High Voice; 14 Sacred Solos - Low Voice; 15 American Art Songs - HIGH VOICE; 15 American Art Songs - LOW VOICE; 15 Easy Folksong Arrangements - High Voice; 15 Easy Folksong Arrangements - Low Voice; 15 Easy Spiritual Arrangements for the Progressing Singer - HIGH VOICE; 15 Easy Spiritual Arrangements for the Progressing Singer; 21 Bebop Exercises; 24 Italian Songs & Arias - Medium High Voice; 24 Italian Songs & Arias - Medium Low Voice; 36 Solos for Young Singers; '80s Gold for Female Singers; '80s Gold for Male Singers; American Arias – SOPRANO; American Arias - MEZZO-SOP.; American Arias – TENOR; American Arias – BARITONE; Arnold Book of Old Songs - HIGH VOICE; Arnold Book of Old Songs - LOW VOICE; Broadway for Teens - Young Women's Edition; Broadway for Teens - Young Men's Edition;* *Broadway - Full Dress Performance; The Broadway Junior Songbook - Young Women's Edition; The Broadway Junior Songbook - Young Men's Edition; Broadway Songs - For Female Singers; Broadway Songs - For Male Singers; Cantolopera: Arias for Soprano - Volumes 1-4;; Cantolopera: Puccini Arias for Soprano Volume 1; Cantolopera: Verdi Arias for Soprano Volume 1; Cantolopera: Arias for Mezzo-Soprano - Volumes 1-3; Cantolopera: Arias for Tenor - Volumes 1-4; Cantolopera: Puccini Arias for Tenor Volume 1; Cantolopera: Verdi Arias for Tenor Volume 1; Cantolopera: Arias for Baritone - Volumes 1-4; Cantolopera: Arias for Bass - Volumes 1-3; Cantolopera: Duets for Soprano/Tenor - Volume 1; Cantolopera: Tosti - Favorite Songs, Volumes 1 & 2; Children's Sacred Solos; Christmas Solos for Kids; Christmas Standards for Female Singers; Christmas Standards for Male Singers; Church Solos for Kids; Classical Carols - High Voice; Classical Carols - Low Voice; Classical Contest Solos - Soprano; Classical Contest Solos - Mezzo-Soprano; Classical Contest Solos - Tenor; Classical Contest Solos - Baritone/Bass; The Classical Singer's Christmas Album - High Voice; The Classical Singer's Christmas Album - Low Voice; Contemporary Hits - For Female Singers; Contemporary Hits - For Male Singers; Contemporary Theatre Songs – SOPRANO; Contemporary Theatre Songs; Contemporary Theatre Songs - MEN'S EDTN.; Daffodils, Violets and Snowflakes - High Voice; Daffodils, Violets and Snowflakes - Low Voice; Disney Solos for Kids; Easy Songs for the Beginning Soprano; Easy Songs for the Beginning Mezzo-Soprano/Alto; Easy Songs for the Beginning Tenor; Easy Songs for the Beginning Baritone/Bass; English Songs: Renaissance to Baroque - High Voice ; English Songs: Renaissance to Baroque - Low Voice ; Favorite French Art Songs - Volume 1, High Voice; Favorite French Art Songs - Volume 1, Low Voice; Favorite German Art Songs - Volume 1, High Voice; Favorite German Art Songs - Volume 1, Low Voice; Favorite Spanish Art Songs - High Voice; Favorite Spanish Art Songs - Low Voice; The First Book of Broadway Solos - Soprano; The First Book of Broadway Solos - Mezzo-Soprano; The First Book of Broadway Solos - Tenor; The First Book of Broadway Solos - Baritone/Bass; The First Book of Soprano Solos; The First Book of Mezzo-Soprano/Alto Solos; The First Book of Tenor Solos; The First Book of Baritone/Bass Solos; The First Book of Soprano Solos - Part II; The First Book of Mezzo-Soprano/Alto Solos Part II; The First Book of Tenor Solos - Part II; The First Book of Baritone/Bass Solos - Part II; The First Book of Soprano Solos - Part III; The First Book of Mezzo-Soprano/Alto Solos Part III; The First Book of Tenor Solos - Part III; The First Book of Baritone/Bass Solos - Part III; Gilbert & Sullivan for Singers – Soprano; Gilbert & Sullivan for Singers -*

Mezzo-Soprano; Gilbert & Sullivan for Singers – Tenor; Gilbert & Sullivan for Singers - Baritone/Bass; Singer's Gilbert & Sullivan - Women's Edition; Singer's Gilbert & Sullivan - Men's Edition; Great Songs from Musicals for Teens - Young Women's Edition; Great Songs from Musicals for Teens - Young Men's Edition; Hymn Classics - High Voice; Hymn Classics - Low Voice; Italian Tenor Arias; Jazz Ballads for Singers - Women's Edition; Jazz Ballads for Singers - Men's Edition; Jazz Standards - For Female Singers; Jazz Standards - For Male Singers; Jazz Tracks for Singers - Women's Edition; Jazz Tracks for Singers - Men's Edition; Kids' Broadway Songbook ; Kids' Stage & Screen Songs; Learn to Sing Harmony; Lovers, Lasses & Spring – SOPRANO; Lyric Soprano Arias: A Master Class with Evelyn Lear; More Disney Solos for Kids; Mozart Arias for Soprano; Mozart Arias for Mezzo-Soprano; Mozart Arias for Tenor; Mozart Arias for Baritone/Bass; Musical Theatre Anthology for Teens - Young Women's; Musical Theatre Anthology for Teens - Young Men's; Musical Theatre Anthology for Teens - Duets; Musical Theatre Classics – SOPRANO; Musical Theatre Classics - Soprano Volume 2; Musical Theatre Classics - Mezzo-Soprano/Belter Volume 1; Musical Theatre Classics - Mezzo-Soprano/Belter Volume 2; Musical Theatre Classics – Tenor; Musical Theatre Classics - Baritone/Bass; Musicianship for Singers; My Heart Will Go On - Vocal Solo; Popular Solos for Young Singers; Practical Vocal Method (Vaccai) - High Voice; Practical Vocal Method (Vaccai) - Low Voice; Sacred Classics - High Voice; Sacred Classics - Low Voice; The Sanctuary Soloist - Volume III – HIGH VOICE; The Sanctuary Soloist - Volume III - LOW VOICE; The Second Book of Soprano Solos; The Second Book of Mezzo-Soprano/Alto Solos; The Second Book of Tenor Solos; The Second Book of Baritone/Bass Solos; The Second Book of Soprano Solos - Part II; The Second Book of Mezzo-Soprano/Alto Solos Part II; The Second Book of Tenor Solos - Part II; The Second Book of Baritone/Bass Solos - Part II; Sight Singing Made Simple; Sing a Song of Christmas - 12 Christmas Favorites - HIGH VOICE; Sing a Song of Christmas - 12 Christmas Favorites - LOW VOICE; Sing The Lord's Prayer with Orchestra - High Voice; Sing The Lord's Prayer with Orchestra - Medium High Voice; Sing The Lord's Prayer with Orchestra - Medium Voice; Sing The Lord's Prayer with Orchestra - Medium Low Voice; Sing the Songs of Frank Loesser (Vocal) - HIGH VOICE; Sing the Songs of Frank Loesser (Vocal) - LOW VOICE; Sing the Songs of Rodgers & Hammerstein - HIGH VOICE; Sing the Songs of Rodgers & Hammerstein - LOW VOICE; The Singer's Musical Theatre Anthology - Volume 1 – SOPRANO; The Singer's Musical Theatre Anthology - Volume 2, Revised – SOPRANO; The Singer's Musical Theatre Anthology - Volume 3 – SOPRANO; Singer's Musical Theatre Anthology - Volume 4 – SOPRANO; The Singer's Musical Theatre Anthology - Volume 1, Revised; The Singer's Musical Theatre Anthology - Volume 2, Revised; The Singer's Musical Theatre Anthology - Volume 3; Singer's Musical Theatre Anthology - Volume 4; The Singer's Musical Theatre Anthology - Volume 1, Revised – TENOR; The Singer's Musical Theatre Anthology - Volume 2, Revised; The Singer's Musical Theatre Anthology - Volume 3 – TENOR; Singer's Musical Theatre Anthology - Volume 4; The Singer's Musical Theatre Anthology - Volume 1, Revised; The Singer's Musical Theatre Anthology - Volume 2, Revised – BARITONE; The Singer's Musical Theatre Anthology - Volume 3 – BARITONE; Singer's Musical Theatre Anthology - Volume 4; The Singer's Musical Theatre Anthology - Volume 1; The Singer's Musical Theatre Anthology - Volume 2; Singing in the African American Tradition; Solos for Kids; Solos from Musicals for Kids; Standard Ballads - Women's Edition; Standard Ballads - Men's Edition; Standard Vocal Literature - An Introduction to Repertoire; Standard Vocal Literature - An Introduction to Repertoire; Standard Vocal Literature - An Introduction to Repertoire – TENOR; Standard Vocal Literature - An Introduction to Repertoire; Standard Vocal Literature - An Introduction to Repertoire – BASS; Teach Yourself to Read Music; Teen's Musical Theatre Collection - Young Women's; Teen's Musical Theatre Collection - Young Men's; Torch Songs - Women's Edition; Torch Songs - Men's Edition; Tunes for Teens from Musicals - Young Women's Edition; Tunes for Teens from Musicals - Young Men's Edition; Wedding Classics - High Voice; Wedding Classics - Low Voice. SYSTEM SPECS: Book and Audio CD.

Harmony Singing and Vocal Arranging (www.pennynichols.com): Learn to sing in Harmony with Penny Nichols; double CD set features six songs with six artists including: Tom Prasada-Rao, Small Potatoes, Michael Monagan, Deborah McColl, Severin Browne, Penny Nichols, and others; seven complete lessons and over forty-six tracks of exercises and examples to choose and sing along. SYSTEM SPECS: Audio CD.

Harmony Vocals—The Essential Guide (www.halleonard.com); by Mike Campbell and Tracee Lewis; learn to sing harmony; instructors at Hollywood's Musicians Institute; building harmonies; reading music; scales, chords and intervals; stage and studio techniques; drills for the advanced singer; includes eighteen songs in pop, rock, blues, funk, soul, and country styles; CD with ninety-nine full-demo tracks. SYSTEM SPECS: Book and Audio CD.

Heavenly Voices (www.musicmotion.com): Covers 1000 years of the choral tradition from 10th-century Gregorian chant to the Christian rock band;

inspiring musical journey to cathedrals, churches, and abbeys throughout Britain; divided into eight fifteen-minute segments ideal for educational use; running time 120 minutes. SYSTEM SPECS: Instructional DVD.

I'm Not Crazy, I'm Vocalizing! Audio CD (www.vocalizing.com): By Karen Oleson, founder of VoiceTech; warm-up exercises; helpful adjunct to teaching; mini vocal lesson before each exercise; twenty-minute warm-up exercise recording with vocal guide; twenty-minute warm-up on own with horn guide; instruction booklet includes musical notation and guidance for each exercise, along with tips on vocal health care; car bumper sticker. SYSTEM SPECS: Book and Audio CD.

I'm Vocalizing 2! (www.vocalizing.com): Variety of instrumental ensembles in styles ranging from urban funk, jazz scat, or operatic, to selections with southeast Asian and middle eastern influences; recorded examples come both with and without the guide vocals; suitable for all voices from bass to high soprano; vocalises challenge ear, versatility, and develop voice; package includes a CD and a piano/vocal score with helpful hints for improving singing. SYSTEM SPECS: Book and Audio CD.

Jazz Style and Improvisation for Choirs (www.musicmotion.com): Interactive journey into scat and improvisation; demonstration choir; begins with simple blues chords, adds scat syllables; uses three notes to improvise; call-and-response; trade fours; ten segments with an intro and conclusion; for upper elementary. SYSTEM SPECS: Instructional DVD.

Jeffrey Allen's "Secrets of Singing" (www.vocalsuccess.com): Includes the basic principles of singing, mastery of the upper voice, achieving the power of an open throat, and phrasing and diction on a professional level; designed to bring out the unique qualities in any singer's voice; learn to practice, audition, perform, and record professionally. SYSTEM SPECS: Book and Audio CD.

Just Enough Vocals Instructional DVD Kit (www.melbay.com): Instructional package for beginning vocals; includes DVD, interactive CD-ROM, and portable book/CD set; DVD Video introduces instructors, shows how they got started, what it is like to perform, what music means to them, and how to buy first gear; learn basic techniques; sing with band in interactive Virtual Jam Session; CD-ROM contains over fifty vocal lessons; Allen, Anna, Aron, Daniel, Lillian and SaBella, teach how to use voice, find range, and learn to sing different styles of music; includes karaoke-style practice tracks; AudioBook pocket reference manual works with Audio CD; contains over fifty lessons; match tracks in Book to the tracks on CD player. SYSTEM SPECS: Macintosh; Windows.

Karaoke Maker (www.replayinc.com) Remove or reduce vocals in real time from any wav file; change pitch in real time without changing the tempo; automatically convert MP3 files to wav format; copy tracks from any audio CD to wav files; display and scroll lyrics as the song is playing; remove or reduce vocals in any wav file and save the results; change the pitch of any wav file and save the results; load a wav file of any size, regardless of available computer memory; loop an entire song or just sections; supports customized play lists. SYSTEM SPECS: Windows.

Kool Karaoke (www.koolkaraokestudio.com): Adjust tempo, pitch, melody, and volume; lyrics display; over fifty popular songs; download songs; for all ages. SYSTEM SPECS: Windows CD-ROM.

L'Or des Anges (www.musicmotion.com): Three documentaries highlight the singing, challenges, and choices of the boy choir experience; guided on the journey by a young chorister with the assistance of five choirs; hear from directors and students; running time 150 min. SYSTEM SPECS: Instructional DVD.

Learn to Sing like a Star! (www.learntosing.biz): Vocal instructional method created by Berklee College of music graduate and professional singer Ava Tracht Landman; for all singers; includes Breathing Technique/Exercises; Vocal Register (Range); Vocal Placement and Style; Various Scale Exercises. SYSTEM SPECS: Audio CD.

Musicians Institute Press (www.halleonard.com): Titles include *Sight Singing—The Complete Method for Singers; The Musician's Guide to Recording Vocals; Vocal Technique*, and more. SYSTEM SPECS: Book and Audio CD.

My Voice (www.emediamusic.com): Software designed to remove the vocals from a CD in real time; replace the singer; hide the main vocals; change the key; change the tempo; adapt the songs to any singing style; add lyrics; use studio quality effects; record and mix own voice over the original song; create and burn songs to CD; studio effects, recorder, burner, ripper, and more; no need to buy special equipment; includes microphone. SYSTEM SPECS: Windows.

No Excuses Singers Guide (www.musicsales.com): Comprehensive guide for players of all abilities; practice in a variety of styles as part of a real band. SYSTEM SPECS: Instructional DVD and Hybrid CD-ROM.

Opera for Dummies (www.dummies.com): Covers opera from the Baroque and Roman periods through today; interpret characters, orchestra, chorus, and other players; understand what's happening, both on stage and off; choose the best seats; identify famous operas; build a great collection of opera recordings; locate opera sites and chat groups online; the words, the music, and the people who sing it; the history of opera and the lives of the great composers; tips for getting tickets, preparing for the opera, dressing for the opera; musical and theatrical conventions used in opera; in-depth synopses of the world's most beloved operas; more than sixty minutes of music compiled especially for the book. SYSTEM SPECS: Book and Audio CD.

Pitch Exercises Volumes One and Two (www.judyclark.net): Complete training guide for improving pitch; includes printed music and a practice log; all of the exercises were a part of Maestro David Kyle's training program during his over fifty years of teaching. SYSTEM SPECS: Book and Audio CD.

Pro Vocal Series (www.halleonard.com): Collections of popular songs by contemporary artists. SYSTEM SPECS: Book and Enhanced CD.

Progressive Beginner Singing DVD (www.learntoplaymusic.com): For beginner to intermediate; for anyone who wants to learn to sing or sing better; essential information on breathing, posture, and tone production; introduction to the basics of reading and understanding music and copying melodies by ear; performing in public, overcoming nerves, and microphone technique; perform many well-known songs in a variety of styles. SYSTEM SPECS: Book, Audio CD, and Instructional DVD.

Reach for the Stars Complete Vocal Training Kit (www.judyclark.net): 128 page book; sheet music; one demo CD; one pitch exercise CD in five different vocal ranges; five vocal exercise compact discs; an instructional DVD featuring a private lesson from Judy Clark; instruction in diction and enunciation; breathing exercises; stage presence and attitude; diet program for optimum vocal clarity; setting goals; determining your vocal range; music business tips. SYSTEM SPECS: Book, Audio CD, and Instructional DVD.

Roger Burnley's EZ Vocal Method (www.rogerburnley.com): Hollywood vocal coach; for singers of all levels and styles; how to exercise voice to obtain maximum potential; create new sense memories; increase range, power, and control. SYSTEM SPECS: Audio CD and Instructional DVD.

SHOWTRAX Background Tracks (www.halleonard.com): Background tracks to popular songs; choral CDs of popular music, holiday music, show tunes, traditional music, and more; arranged for SATB, etc. SYSTEM SPECS: Audio CD.

Sight Singing Made Simple Book and Audio CD (www.halleonard.com): Solfege; hear sounds music symbols represent; for home or school; over sixty exercises; for vocal and choral studies; audio CD. SYSTEM SPECS: Book and Audio CD.

Sing Like the Stars! (www.singers.com): By Roger Love; master the art of breathing; conquer stage fright; sing hit songs with the unique program; work on sound, look, moves; bonus warm-up CD with over twenty exercises; includes personal performance tips. SYSTEM SPECS: Book and Audio CD.

Sing! (www.alfred.com): Featuring the original Elisabeth Howard Vocal Power Method of Singing; includes four CDs that focus on singing techniques such as power, range expansion, vibrato control, volume, dynamics, pitch; singing styles such as pop, rock, country, blues, R&B, Broadway; phrasing; improvisation; personal style; "Licks and Tricks" for every style; Sing-Aerobics includes a thirty minute workout for male and female voices. SYSTEM SPECS: Book, Audio CD, and Instructional DVD.

Sing at First Sight (www.alfred.com): Sight-singing curriculum; sequential text; reading concepts; rhythm and pitch exercises; excerpts from actual choral music; review for each unit. SYSTEM SPECS: Book and Audio CD.

Singing for Dummies (www.singers.com): Step-by-step instructions; helpful tips, hints, vocal exercises, reminders, and warnings for both men and women; includes advice on the mechanics of singing, discovering your singing voice, developing technique, singing in performance, maintaining vocal health, performing like a pro, proper posture and breathing, perfecting articulation, finding the right voice teach, how to train for singing, selecting music materials, acting the song, overcoming stage fright, auditioning for musical theater; comes with a CD full of useful instruction and songs, including: demonstrations of proper technique, exercises to develop technique and strength, scales and pitch drills, practice songs for beginning, intermediate, and advanced singers. SYSTEM SPECS: Book and Audio CD.

Singing for the Stars (www.alfred.com): By Los Angeles-based vocal and opera coach Seth Riggs; speech level singing and master classes; complete index and table of contents; vocal therapy and technique for singing; lecturer and teacher; consultant; performer; includes: How Your Voice Works; How Your Voice Works Best; How to Get Your Voice to Work for You; Practical Exercises; Building Confidence; Toward Speech-Level Singing; Technique Maintenance; The Author Speaks Out; Health and Care of the Singer's Voice. SYSTEM SPECS: Book and Audio CD.

Singing Fundamentals (www.musicmotion.com): Video and kit of tools that help teach singing to all children; begins with a vocal checkup to identify the type of child's voice; vocal pyramid of posture, breath, sound, embouchure, and diction is demonstrated by a choir and using the materials in the kit; running time forty-five minutes; bonus footage of a dynamic choir warm-up. SYSTEM SPECS: Instructional DVD.

Singing! Basic Vocal Technique (www.pennynichols.com): Six one-hour CD's, equal to a month of private lessons; for all levels and styles; rock and roll, bluegrass, folk songs, pop, or show tunes; helps to increase vocal range, tone, power, and stamina. SYSTEM SPECS: Book and Audio CD.

Teach Yourself to Sing (www.alfred.com): Covers the basics of singing; breathing, posture, warming up, and more; discusses the mind/body connection to singing; easy and comprehensive approach to reading music; covers rock, jazz, blues, and other popular styles; can transpose accompaniment to any key. SYSTEM SPECS: Book with Enhanced CD or Hybrid CD-ROM.

Teach Yourself to Sing—10 Easy Lessons (www.learntoplaymusic.com): For beginning vocalists; learn the basic principles of singing; covers vocal tone, vocal control, breathing, posture, microphone technique, performance ideas, etc. SYSTEM SPECS: Book, Audio CD, and Instructional DVD.

The Bach Chorales (www.pgmusic.com): Performance of Bach's four-part Chorales; professional choral ensemble; detailed multimedia history; each voice (soprano, alto, tenor, and bass) recorded on a separate track; listen to independently; interactive program; vocal music; history of Bach; time line. SYSTEM SPECS: Windows.

The Barbershop Quartet (www.pgmusic.com): Interactive multimedia history of barbershop singing in America; each voice (tenor, lead, baritone, and bass) recorded on a separate track; listen to each part independently; study arrangements; hear music; sing along; made with the assistance of the Society for the Preservation and Encouragement of Barbershop Quartet Singing in America. SYSTEM SPECS: Windows.

The Chorus - A Union of Voices (www.clearvue.com): Traces the history of choral music from its beginnings to the present; includes many musical examples from all periods; beautiful illuminated manuscripts, paintings, and photographs; running time forty-minutes; divided into two parts for classroom flexibility; includes a teacher's guide, text of narration, and identification of music examples; for grades seven-twelve; Part 1: Gregorian Chant through Renaissance polyphony, Baroque opera and oratorio, Classical and Romantic works; Part 2: Late Romantic through the 20th century; introduces the professional chorus, school and church choirs, the folk chorus; choral technique and commentary by leading figures in choral music. SYSTEM SPECS: Instructional DVD.

The Complete Idiot's Guide to Singing (www.idiotsguides.com): Topics include finding an ideal singing range, tips on how to stand and breathe properly, techniques for singing in various styles, advice on overcoming stage fright, and more; audio CD includes examples of different techniques and accompaniments for the singing exercises in the book. SYSTEM SPECS: Book and Audio CD.

The Contemporary Singer Book and Audio CD (www.berkleepress.com): Berklee Guide by Anne Peckham; elements of contemporary vocal technique; learn how to use and protect voice properly; develop stage presence, microphone technique, stamina, range, and sound. SYSTEM SPECS: Book and Audio CD.

The Instant Singer (www.popeil.com): DVD Series by Lisa Popeil; begin with the Basic Edition, a twenty-five-minute show of her eight best vocal tips; next comes the Advanced Edition, with seven great tips including Larynx Positions and Throat Shapes for Vocal Colors, Gesture, Reducing Performance Anxiety, Enhancing Charisma, Mic Technique and Maintaining Vocal Health; The Kid's Edition will show children six to twelve the basics of healthy vocal technique including: posture, support, singing with a 'facey' sound, how not to 'strain' on high notes, vibrato, safe and beautiful belting, gesture, confidence, and creating a solid foundation of excellence for a life-time of singing. SYSTEM SPECS: Instructional DVD.

The Perfect Blend (www.shawneepress.com): Using material from his book, Seelig gives two hours of warm-ups demonstrated by adult singers; calls it a five-course meal; Appetizer is Posture; Soup is Breathing; Salad is Phonation; Entre is Resonance; Dessert is Blend; visit a vocologist at Baylor Medical Center; see vocal folds in action and hear tips to keep them healthy; running time two hours. SYSTEM SPECS: Instructional DVD.

The Perfect Rehearsal (www.shawneepress.com): Resource that will help maximize rehearsal time to the fullest and lead to more efficient, effective, productive rehearsals and to a better choir; sequel to Dr. Seelig's *The Perfect Blend;* entertaining journey through the ins and outs of choir rehearsal. SYSTEM SPECS: Instructional DVD.

The Pop Singers Warm-Up Kit Book and Audio CD (www.thesingersworkshop.com): By Lis Lewis; vocal instruction for pop singers; a dozen warm-up exercises specific to men and women; each exercise begins with a sung example, then piano plays exercise; includes warming up lower and upper voices, connecting the two voices, loosening the throat, placing the sound forward, relaxing the tongue, breath and volume control, increasing vocal range, pitch accuracy, stabilizing tone, and more; book shows practical objectives of each exercise and gives helpful pointers for success. SYSTEM SPECS: Book and Audio CD.

The Sam West Vocal Workout DVD for Singers (www.samwest.co.uk/index.htm): First of its kind to have been produced in the UK; still a best seller in music stores and mail order companies in the UK and Europe; begins by explaining the principles of voice production; graphics are used to illustrate certain points; Sam West, with the aid of two singers, Candi McKenzie and Bridget Lynch-Blosse, explains and demonstrates various singing techniques; includes Breath Control, Range, Resonance, Vibrato, Aural (ear) training, and more; in the workout section, ten different exercises are presented, each going through various keys accommodating both low and high voiced singers; each of the ten exercises are intended for specific areas of vocal technique; viewers can select different parts of the program quickly, varying their practice routines; the written musical accompaniment to the exercises can be viewed on-screen via the DVD menu; for singers of various styles, from Classical to Contemporary; running time is fifty-nine minutes. SYSTEM SPECS: Instructional DVD.

The Singer's First Aid Kit Book and Audio CD (www.thesingersworkshop.com): By Lis Lewis; book and vocal warm-up CD; twenty-minute Singer's Warm-Up; use on the way to rehearsals or gigs, at the recording studio, or at home; warm up before voice lesson; protect vocal instrument and keep it stronger and healthier; book includes chapters on recording, rehearsing, performing, auditions, vocal health, and more; The Singer's Troubleshooting Guide gives insider tips needed to be successful. SYSTEM SPECS: Book and Audio CD.

The Total Singer (www.popeil.com): By Lisa Popeil; voice-training program; includes a ninety-minute DVD, a forty-eight-page booklet and a sixty-minute audio CD with warm-up and training exercises for both classical and popular singers; available in downloadable format; outlines the Voiceworks Method; vocal instruction program developed over a forty-year period; systematic approach used by thousands of singers from beginners to professionals; covers Posture, Breathing, Support, Ring, Registers and Break Elimination, Larynx Positions, Vibrato, Control of Nasality and Breathiness, Range, Power Techniques; covers all vocal styles including Pop, Rock, Jazz, Country, R&B, Belt, Legit, and Classical. SYSTEM SPECS: Book, Audio CD, and Instructional DVD.

The Ultimate Practice Guide for Vocalists (www.berkleepress.com): By Donna McElroy; shows how to use the whole body to become the best singer; works with a vocal student one on one, demonstrating how to use different muscle groups to increase vocal strength and endurance; provides lifestyle tips and simple everyday exercises to help cultivate and protect the voice and sing better; running time fifty-one minutes. SYSTEM SPECS: Instructional DVD.

The Vienna Boys Choir (www.clearvue.com): Institution was founded before Shakespeare was born; visit them at school, watch them rehearse, record, sing in chapel, perform an opera, play sports, travel; discipline and skill development is obvious, as is the joy in singing; teacher's guide offers questions and suggestions, lists vocabulary and songs performed, and provides the scripted narrative; running time twenty-eight minutes. SYSTEM SPECS: Instructional DVD.

The Vocal Visions Warm-Up CD (www.vocalvisions.net): By Ellen Johnson; for soloists, choirs, bands, studio musicians, and anyone who sings; seventeen exercises designed for all levels; instruction booklet included; CDs made for male high or low

voice, female high or low voice; helps get voice ready to perform; increases musicianship skills. SYSTEM SPECS: Book and Audio CD.

Tune Your Voice - Tune Your Life (www.tuneyourvoice.com/cd.htm): By Christine Grimm; each track has one tone and its related vowel in four octaves; twelve tracks, five minutes each; the twelve chromatic tones of the scale are sung by human voices; sing the notes in the most comfortable octave; sing C low and B high, if possible; singers can use the CD as vocal attunement by singing along with the tracks in various octaves, as well as practicing fifths and other intervals; tracks can also be used as drone tones for improvisation. SYSTEM SPECS: Audio CD.

Tune Your Voice (www.singers.com): By Darlene Koldenhoven; comprehensive resource for vocalists of all levels; learn correct vocal techniques; course includes five teaching CDs, one listening CD, and one singing CD; for private study, classroom, or home-school use; sing in tune, sing in harmony; compose and sight-read music; learn any instrument faster or by ear; interactive series for exploring the space-time code of music to develop the musical ear. SYSTEM SPECS: Book and Audio CD.

Ultimate Sing-Along Series (www.alfred.com): *Volume 1: Broadway Divas (Female Voice): Volume 2: Broadway (Male Voice); Volume 3: Country Divas (Female Voice): Volume 4: Lounge (Male Voice); Volume 5: Disco Divas (Female Voice); Volume 6: 1960s (Male Voice); Volume 7: Movies (Female Voice); Volume 8: 1970s (Male Voice); Volume 9: Pop Divas (Female Voice); Volume 10: Rock (Male Voice).* SYSTEM SPECS: Book and Enhanced CD.

Vocal Coach Singer (www.vocalcoach.com): By Chris Beatty; produce better sound by understanding how vocal cords work in conjunction with head, chest, and entire body; increase stamina and ability to control voice; develop systematic warm up habits that avoid straining the voice; understand how to match songs to the tone and personality of your voice; expand range; regular vocal exercises that will strengthen your voice. SYSTEM SPECS: Book and Audio CD.

Vocal Gymnastics (www.judyclark.net): Consists of the majority of voice exercises that were taught by the late Maestro David Kyle of Seattle, WA; five CD's that contain the same exercises, each recorded in a different key to accommodate various voice ranges; thirty-page booklet includes the exercises in musical format, printed in the key of C, as a reference; tips on how to practice the exercises; information on how to properly care for the voice and much more; booklet includes a training log to track daily practice. SYSTEM SPECS: Book and Audio CD.

Vocal Technique DVD (www.berkleepress.com): By Anne Peckham; learn proper vocal techniques to help prevent injuries and maximize potential; featured exercises help singer gain technical and expressive command of voice; lessons include how to warm up your voice, proper posture, breathing and tone, maintaining vocal health, improving stamina, range, and sound. SYSTEM SPECS: Instructional DVD.

Vocal Techniques for the Young Singer (www.musicmotion.com): By Henry Leck and the Indianapolis Children's Choir with Steven Rickards; covers stylistic technique, vocal modeling, exercises to demonstrate vocal concepts, and warm-ups to improve intonation and tone quality; provides a fine choir sound and visual model; running time sixty-three minutes. SYSTEM SPECS: Instructional DVD.

Vocal Workouts for the Contemporary Singer (www.berkleepress.com): Companion book to Anne Peckham's first book, *The Contemporary Singer;* includes a vocal workout CD which features exercises in many styles including jazz, pop, rock, and R&B with rhythm section accompaniments; CD is divided into several complete vocal workout routines including the Warm-Up for All voices, Basic Workout, Advanced Workout, and Singing Harmony: Two- and Three- Part Exercises. SYSTEM SPECS: Book and Audio CD.

Voice Lessons to Go, Volumes One - Four (www.singers.com): By Ariella Vaccarino; includes Vocalize and Breath; Do, Re Mi Ear and Pitch Training; Pure Vowels; Stamina; well organized, comprehensive, vocal instructional program; vocal exercises designed to challenge and strengthen any singer's abilities. SYSTEM SPECS: Audio CD.

Working With Male Voices DVD (www.musicmotion.com): Presented by Jerry Blackstone; demonstration topics include tone and the singing male, consistency throughout the range, communicative choral singing, intonation issues, effective rehearsal procedures, voice classification, and live performances; running time fifty-four minutes. SYSTEM SPECS: Instructional DVD.

You Can Sing! (www.pennynichols.com): By vocal coach Penny Nichols; for beginners; one-hour DVD is an encouraging and enjoyable lesson that will turn listeners into singers; helps break down inhibitions; covers pitch perception and basic music theory. SYSTEM SPECS: Instructional DVD.

Musical Theater Web Sites

Academy for New Musical Theatre (ANMT)
www.anmt.org Educational programs; workshops.
American Association of Community Theater
www.aact.org Events and festivals; books; CDs.
American Musical Theater
www.theatrehistory.com/american/musical030.html History of the musical theater in the United States.

American Theatre Wing
www.americantheatrewing.org/ Founder of the Tony Awards; audio/video; programs; support; e-mail list; career guides; podcasts.
Applause Tickets www.applause-tickets.com Theater and entertainment service; Broadway, Off Broadway, concert and ballet tickets; sightseeing and more in New York City.
Arts and Entertainment at Musical Theater West www.musical.org Southern California's oldest professional musical theater companies; current and past productions; tickets; auditions.
Artslynx www.artslynx.org Links to theatre, dance, music, and more.
Broadway Theater www.broadwaytheater.com Theater industry; tickets; reviews; multimedia.
Circle in the Square Theater School www.circlesquare.org Professional acting and musical theater training at the heart of Broadway.
Concert Tickets www.musicalchairstickets.com Ticket agency specializing in all types of tickets including concert tickets, theater tickets.
Eldridge Plays and Musicals www.histage.com Theater plays and musicals for all occasions; full-length plays; one-act plays; melodramas; holiday themes; children's and full-length musicals; skits and theater collections.
Invisible Sound Design http://invisibleobjects.net/ Custom software solutions for the entertainment industry; sound design services for musical theater.
London Theater Guide www.londontheatre.co.uk What's playing in London.
Music Theater International www.mtishows.com Major Broadway and Off-Broadway shows; youth shows, revues; musicals which began in regional theater.
Musical Stages Online www.musicalstages.co.uk Guide to musical theater.
Musical Youth Artists Repertory Theater www.myart.org Musical theater for young performers; performances using kids and young people in legitimate Broadway plays.
Musicals 101 www.musicals101.com The Cyber Encyclopedia of Musical Theater, TV and Film.
Musicals.Net www.musicals.net Index to many Broadway musicals; song lists; synopses; lyrics; discussion forums.
National Alliance for Musical Theatre www.namt.org Service organization dedicated exclusively to musical theatre; members include theatres, presenting organizations, universities, and individual producers.
Playbill Online www.playbill.com Source of theater information; published by the same company that has printed *Playbill Magazine* on Broadway for over 100 years; international theater news.

Stage Directions www.stage-directions.com Theater industry.

The American Musical Theater Reference Library www.americanmusicals.com Internet directory.

The Guide to Musical Theater www.nodanw.com World of musical theater.

The Really Useful Company Presents Andrew Lloyd Webber www.reallyuseful.com Musicals and other productions by Sir Andrew Lloyd Webber.

The Tony Awards www.tonyawards.com/en_US/index.html Honoring the best of Broadway annually; nominees; winners.

Theater Development Fund www.tdf.org Nonprofit theater organization for the performing arts.

Theater Net www.theatrenet.co.uk Theater industry; news archives; links.

Theatricopia www.saintmarys.edu/~jhobgood/Jill/theatre.html Links and more for musical theater fans.

Whatsonstage.com www.whatsonstage.com UK guide to theater, classical music, opera, and dance productions; news; seating plans; online shop.

Writing Musical Theatre www.writingmusicaltheatre.com Online course.

Religious and Gospel Music—Inspirational Web Sites

1Christian.net www.1christian.net Christian music network.

A Little Religion and Romance Music www.greaterthings.com/Music Online MIDI albums and singles; originals and arrangements of spiritual, romantic, and patriotic songs, hymns, anthems, medleys; CD available.

Bible Gateway www.bible.gospelcom.net Bible-search resource.

Black Gospel Music Clef www.blackgospel.com/tools/ Provides resources and information for participants and supporters of black gospel music.

CCM Online www.ccmcom.com Christian Music magazine; radio charts; countdown; Christian stations reporting.

Christian Answers.Net www.christiananswers.net/midimenu Christian background music; TM page; 100+ MIDI files.

Christian History Institute www.gospelcom.net/chi/GLIMPSEF/Glimpses/glmps089.shtml Slave songs.

Christian Music Place www.placetobe.org/cmp/central.htm Resources for writers of Christian music.

Christian Songwriters Group www.christiansongwriters.com Christian music songwriters.

Church Assist www.churchassist.com *Worship Assistant* software.

Church Music Master www.churchmusicmaster.com Christian music software.

Coalition of Internet Church Music Publishers www.redshift.com~bowms1/cicmp Dedicated Christians who compose and publish music for Christian worship; independent publishers.

Contemporary Christian Music www.ccmusic.org Directories of Christian music and artists sites; concert dates.

Get Christian Music www.getchristianmusic.com Online Christian music store.

Gospel Flava www.gospelflava.com Gospel site.

Gospel Music Association (GMA) www.gospelmusic.org Membership; links; resources for writers of Christian music.

Harlem Spirituals www.harlemspirituals.com Gospel and jazz tours.

Heart Songs www.heartsongs.org Christian music; MIDIs; songs; chat.

Hymns and Spirituals www.iath.virginia.edu/utc/christn/chsohp.html Songs; information.

K-LOVE Radio KLOVE.com Contemporary Christian music heard around the world; listener-supported; noncommercial.

Lammas Records www.lammas.co.uk Solo, choral, and organ music from Britain's cathedrals.

Negro Spirituals www.negrospirituals.com History; singers; songs; composers.

Negro Spirituals xroads.virginia.edu/~HYPER/TWH/Higg.html Article from the *Atlantic Monthly*, June 1867.

Negro Spirituals xroads.virginia.edu/~HYPER/TWH/twh_front.html Hypertext edition; links.

Praise Charts www.praisecharts.com Worship resource center; sheet music to popular worship songs; supplied by a growing network of arrangers.

Reflection Christian Music Resources www.users.zetnet.co.uk/mlehr/reflec/reflec.htm Original Christian worship music; MIDIs and sheet music available for downloading and use.

Religious Information Source—BELIEVE www.mb-soft.com/believe/index.html Hundreds of informative articles on important words, subjects, and terms in Christianity and other major world religions; source of information for deeper understanding of religious subjects.

Religious Resources on the Net www.religiousresources.org/ Comprehensive, searchable database of religious and Christian Web sites; over one hundred topics or use our search engine to generate a listing of religious resources containing selected words or phrases.

Religious Society of Friends www.quaker.org The official Quaker home page; large listing of Quaker links; hosting for a number of Quaker groups.

Sacred Harp and Shape-Note Music Resources www.mcsr.olemiss.edu/~mudws/harp.html Describes printed music, literature, recordings, and other related resources.

Sacred Heart www.sacredheart.com/music.htm Religious music.

Shape Note Singing www.fasola.org Shape notes; information and links; print and audio examples.

Stravinsky's Religious Works www.cco.caltech.edu/~tan/Stravinsky Includes *Symphony of Psalms, Mass,* and *Requiem Canticles*; illustrated biography of Stravinsky's life; listening guide and commentary.

The Almost Definitive Contemporary Christian Music Hot-Page www.afn.org~mrblue/ccm/ccm.html Artist and band links; brief history.

The California Mission Site www.californiamissions.com Histories for each of the twenty-one California Missions; music; color and black-and-white photographs.

The Singing News www.singingnews.com Southern gospel music; features; charts.

The Spirituals Project www.spiritualsproject.org Information on Spirituals, our Mission Statement, Educational Programs, Sponsorship, Projects, Resources, and more.

The World of Christian Music www.worldofcm.com Online magazine of Contemporary Christian music charts; top artists, albums, reviews, etc.

Today's Christian Music www.todayschristianmusic.com Contemporary Christian; live RealAudio feed.

Top Christian Music Titles www.emmanuel.kiev.ua/music_groupE.html Music hit parade of Christian musicians; MP3s.

WeddingMusic2Dance.com www.weddingmusic2dance.com Home page.

Worldwide Internet Music Resources www.music.indiana.edu/music_resources/gospel.html Religious music links.

Worship Music www.worshipmusic.com Christian worship music; praise music media.

Vocal Music—Choral and Opera— Singing Web Sites

Academic Choir Apparel www.academicapparel.com Choir robes.

America Sings www.americasings.org Non-competitive choral music festivals.

American Choral Directors Association (ACDA) www.ACDAonline.org News; about ACDA;
officers; staff; chapters: divisions, states, students; *Choral Journal;* national convention; division conventions; repertoire and standards; membership.

Anyone Can Sing www.singtome.com Audrey Hunt, vocal coach; articles and tips; links; advice column; monthly newsletter; CDs; downloads.

Aria Database www.aria-database.com Quick search; arias; operas; composers; roles; diverse collection of information on over 1,000 operatic arias; for singers and nonsingers; includes translations and aria texts of most arias; collection of MIDI files of operatic arias and ensembles.

Audio-Technica www.audio-technica.com Microphones.

Barbershop Harmony www.spebsqsa.org Locate a barbershop quartet or chorus; find arrangements and songbooks; purchase CDs and videos.

Choral Clewes Vocal Music Instruction Series www.choralclewes.com For teachers, choral directors, home schoolers, and professional singers.

Choral Music home.att.net/~langburn Information on over one hundred published compositions and arrangements; accompanied and a cappella; mixed and treble; sacred and secular; reviews; performances; repertoire suggestions; ordering.

ChoralNet www.choralnet.org Internet launching point for all choral music; collection of links including reference and research resources; database for choral repertoire, events, and performances; news; Web message boards; worldwide directory of choirs on the Web; archives; e-mail lists; support.

Choristers Guild www.choristersguild.org Home page.

Classical Singer www.classicalsinger.com For singers of classical music; directories; forums; events; magazine; site tools; store.

Classical Vocal Repertoire www.classicalvocalrep.com The Web site of classical vocal reprints.

International Vocalist www.vocalist.org Resource and database for singers.

ISong.com www.isong.com Accompaniment tracks.

Jeannie Deva www.jeanniedeva.com/ Los Angeles based vocal coach; free online lessons.

Karaoke Scene www.KaraokeScene.com Club directory; articles; forum; magazine.

KJPro Karaoke Software www.kjpro.com *KJ Pro* Windows program for creating karaoke songbooks.

La Scala lascala.milano.it/ World famous opera house.

Lisa Popeil—The Total Singer www.popeil.com Video course for all styles and levels.

Metropolitan Opera www.metopera.org/home.html Schedules; performer bios; opera quiz.

Metropolitan Opera Broadcasts www.metopera.org/broadcast International radio broadcasts; telecast series.

Music Contact International www.Music-Contact.com Choir tours.

National Association of Teachers of Singing www.nats.org Home page; membership; resources.

Neumann www.neumann.com Microphones.

New York City Opera www.nycopera.com Opera company.

Opera News www.operanews.com News on opera-related features and events.

Operabase www.operabase.com Schedules; venues; festivals; reviews; links.

Optimal Breathing for Singing www.breathing.com Manual with exercises for the singing voice.

Pocket Songs www.pocketsongs.com Instrumental track sing-along CDs and cassettes of popular music and standards; large catalog.

Primarily A Cappella Catalog www.singers.com A cappella recordings, videos, and vocal arrangements; vocal jazz, gospel, choral, doo-wop, folk, barbershop, and contemporary.

ProSing www.prosing.com Pocket Songs, Forever Hits, Sound, Star Disk, Zoom, Legends, Chartbusters, Vocopro, V2GO, IXT, Emerson, North Star, Stage Stars, Monster Hits, Music Minus One, RSQ, Tropical Zone, CAVS.

Showoffs Studio www.nefsky.com For performers; singing classes; workshops; talent showcase.

Shure www.shure.com Manufacturer of microphones.

Sing Your Life www.singyourlife.com Self-teaching manual emphasizing vocal strength and endurance.

Singing for the Soul www.singingforthesoul.com Singing lessons on tape.

Singing Store www.singingstore.com Everything for the singer; tracks.

Sound Choice www.soundchoice.com Accompaniment tracks for singers.

The Academy of Vocal Arts www.avaopera.com Academic program; theater.

The Choral Public Domain Library www.cpdl.org Devoted exclusively to free choral sheet music; over 230 contributors and 5,000 scores.

The Gregorian Chant Home Page silvertone.princeton.edu/chant_html Links to chant sites; Medieval music theory sites; resources for chant performance; ecclesiastical, historical, humanistic, and information sciences.

The Metropolitan Chorus www.metchorus.org The 100-voice Metropolitan Chorus presents concerts featuring music of great variety, spanning time from the Renaissance to the twentieth century; strong emphasis on American composers.

The Singer's Workshop www.thesingersworkshop.com Insider information for pop singers: preparing for the stage; breath control; finding the right voice teacher; session singing; music industry insights; rehearsing a band; creating charisma; created by professional singing coach Lis Lewis; Los Angeles-based.

Vocal Power Academy www.vocalpowerinc.com Elisabeth Howard's Vocal Power Method; vocal training; proper breathing techniques; singing lessons; performance workshops; seminars; private lessons; books; CDs; videos.

Vocal Visions www.vocalvisions.net Jazz vocalist and coach Ellen Johnson; workshops; warm-up book and CD; performances.

Vocalist.org www.vocalist.org.uk/index.html Articles; careers; resources for singers and teachers.

Voice Lesson www.voicelesson.com Mark Baxter's in-depth knowledge and unique approach to vocal improvement; *The Rock and Roll Singers Survivor Manual.*

Voice Teachers www.voiceteachers.com Find a teacher; add a new teacher; listed by state.

Voice-Craft Electronics Co., Ltd. www.voice-craft.com.tw Voice-Craft; Dynasonic.

Yodeling Instructional Video www.yodelers.com Intended to help find natural yodel voice break.

You Can Sing with Impact! www.singwithimpact.com Daily warm-up workout; singing exercises.

12
Band and Orchestra—Patriotic Music—Classroom and Studio Management Software, Instructional Media and Web Sites

101 Ways to Harmonize the Madness (www.friendshiphouse.com): How-to survival kit for music educators, created for teachers, by teachers; manage music classroom or musical group; sample letters to parents; recruitment data and tools; handbook and policy guidelines; concert programs; budget and financial forms; schedule models; ready-to-use letterheads and more; ready-to-use PDF, Word, and Excel files. SYSTEM SPECS: Hybrid CD-ROM.

3D (www.pyware.com): Premier drill design product on the market; most widely used drill design software; used by high school, college, university, and corps around the world; uses a patented count to count technology; view, edit or print any count of the drill at any time; with Morph feature can create transitions by morphing existing formation instead of tediously recreating formations from scratch; Time Track process removes the limitation that requires all transitions to begin and end at the same time; employs True Automatic animation handled by computer behind the scenes; records every move and then uses that information to automatically create animation in the background; Rewrite technology allows user to rewrite drill in seconds. SYSTEM SPECS: Macintosh; Windows.

3D Director's Viewer (www.pyware.com): Designed specifically for directors and drill designers; provides a restricted version of the actual 3D Interactive program that animates, prints coordinates and thumbnail charts. SYSTEM SPECS: Macintosh; Windows.

3D Performer's Practice Tools (www.pyware.com): Downloadable Performer's Practice Tools for performers or students; suite of tools used at home by a performer for viewing, practicing, and printing their drills; no personal email account, no downloading of email attachments, no handling of data files; everything is done automatically; most current copy of a drill is loaded directly into the program on the performer's computer, ready to use; suite of tools includes: The Drill Explorer, The 3D Performance Simulator, The Drill Book printout, The Coordinate List printout, and The Thumbnail Charts print out. SYSTEM SPECS: Macintosh; Windows.

Anyone Can Play Violin DVD (www.melbay.com): Self-guided beginner's violin course; designed for anyone of any age; no previous musical experience necessary; teaches basics for all types of performance, from classical to country; step-by-step process compatible with Suzuki pedagogy; instrument care, tuning, positioning, note reading, playing pizzicato on open strings, fingering, and use of the bow; instructional booklet included; sixty-five minutes. SYSTEM SPECS: Instructional DVD.

Artistry in Strings (www.kjos.com): Fifty-six page beginning string method for the classroom or private studio; comprehensive approach includes music theory, composition, listening exercises, ensemble performances, and interdisciplinary studies; many music styles are featured, including classical, jazz, country, rock, and folk music from a variety of cultures around the world; note reading; artistry with the bow; rhythm charts feature creative rhythmic word associations; note values and rhythm patterns; "Swingercises" emphasize left- and right-hand technical development; solos, duets, rounds and orchestrated arrangements; bow strokes such as martelé are introduced and reinforced; scales, thirds, and arpeggios in the keys of D, G, and C Major are included in the back of each part book; multiple image photographs, graphics, and artwork; complete Teacher's Score and Manual with Enrichment CD containing excerpts of symphonic classical music and world folk music; full-length recordings of the four ensembles featured in the book; articles; worksheets;

separate books available for all string instruments. SYSTEM SPECS: Book and Audio CD.

Band Music Direct (www.bandmusicdirect.com): Downloadable print music; digital titles for bands; browse by ensemble type, grade level, and/or composer/arranger; official, authorized and licensed service; generates royalties for the relevant publishers and composers. SYSTEM SPECS: Macintosh; Windows.

BandQuest Series (www.halleonard.com): Titles include: *A+: A Precise Prelude and an Excellent March; American Composers Forum; Alegre; City Rain; Grandmother Song; Hambone; New Wade 'n Water; Old Churches; Ridgeview Centrum; Spring Festival,* and more. SYSTEM SPECS: Hybrid CD-ROM.

Berklee Press (www.berkleepress.com): Titles include *Berklee Practice Method: Teacher's Guide; Berklee Practice Method: Alto and Baritone Sax; Berklee Practice Method: Tenor and Soprano Sax; Berklee Practice Method: Trombone; Berklee Practice Method: Trumpet; Berklee Practice Method: Violin; Berklee Practice Method: Vibraphone,* and more. SYSTEM SPECS: Book and Audio CD.

Blast (www.blasttheshow.com): Brings together sixty-eight brass, percussion, and visual performers; vaudeville, ballet, and circus-type performances with music from classical to techno-pop; running time 115 minutes. SYSTEM SPECS: Instructional DVD.

Buy a Band Series (www.boosey.com): Works like karaoke; play solo with audio CD backings; use the CD-ROM to print out other parts; word sheets; find out about the composer; mix and arrange own backings with MIDI software; suitable for all treble clef instruments; high quality specially recorded backing tracks; optional bass parts; MIDI Player is included (PC only) that enables player to add or subtract parts on the recording to create a unique arrangement; alter playback speed to help with rehearsals; for all C, B-flat, and E-flat instruments. SYSTEM SPECS: Enhanced CD and CD-ROM.

Canadian Brass (www.halleonard.com): Titles include: *Beginning Trumpet Solos (Piano/Trumpet); Easy Trumpet Solos (Piano/Trumpet); Intermediate Trumpet Solos (Piano/Trumpet).* SYSTEM SPECS: Book and Audio CD.

Canadian Brass: Inside Brass DVD (www.friendshiphouse.com): Three educational programs; "Strings, Winds and All That Brass" features school-age musicians telling why they chose to participate in their schools' music programs; "Master Class" is a hands-on guide to performance improvement which teaches lessons on posture, breathing, tonguing, embouchure, musical performance, and playing with an ensemble; "Brass Spectacular" is an on camera meeting of the Canadian Brass, the New York Philharmonic, and the Boston Symphony Orchestra. SYSTEM SPECS: Instructional DVD.

Church Music Master for Windows (www.churchmusicmaster.com) Visual interface for organizing church music program; customizable; free demo download. SYSTEM SPECS: Windows.

Concert Time Beginning Band Book 1 (www.fjhmusic.com): Collection of pieces dedicated to strengthen, reward, and challenge students; fifteen pieces, all of which differ in style, compositional technique, and theme; for use with first-year band students and to start off the year with second-year students. SYSTEM SPECS: Book and Audio CD.

Concert Time Developing Band Book 1 (www.fjhmusic.com): Second book of band pieces; to challenge and reward young students; fifteen progressive pieces; different in style, compositional technique, and theme. SYSTEM SPECS: Book and Audio CD.

De Haske Play-Along Book/CD Packages (www.halleonard.com): Alto Saxophone and Romance; Clarinet and Romance; Euphonium and Romance; Flute and Romance; Oboe and Romance; Pini Di Roma; Ponte Romano; Tenor Saxophone and Romance; Trombone and Romance; Trumpet and Romance. SYSTEM SPECS: Book and Audio CD.

Digital Metro-Tuner (www.ecsmedia.com): Includes a metronome and a tuner; metronome turns computer into a device to assist with playing more accurately in tempo; tempos can be set from 40 to 220 beats per minute (bpm); tuner is designed to help play or sing in tune; sing or play any note and program shows if singing or playing is sharp, flat or in tune; for musicians of any skill and age. SYSTEM SPECS: Hybrid CD-ROM.

Digital Music Mentor CD-ROM (www.ecsmedia.com): For classroom or private instruction; teacher records exercises or tunes for study; student can study on their own by hearing how the piece is supposed to sound and then record their version of the piece; teacher can review and discuss with the student; all ages. SYSTEM SPECS: Hybrid CD-ROM.

Dynamic Marching and Movement, Volumes 1 & 2 (www.halleonard.com): By experienced teacher, judge, and clinician Jeff Young and his staff; system of teaching visual fundamentals; covers the basics of posture, marching, and body movement; system is built upon warm-up, stretch, and dance basics that teach the performer proper techniques in all aspects of body movement; Vol. 1 - Posture, Instrument Carriage, Body and Dance Basics, Marching Fundamentals, and Strength & Fitness; Vol. 2 - Full Stretch and Body Warm-up Routine, Block Drills, Across-the-Floor Drills, and Advanced Specialty Drills. SYSTEM SPECS: Instructional DVD.

Dynamic Music (www.halleonard.com): By composer, arranger, teacher, judge, and clinician Richard Saucedo; system of teaching music fundamentals; method for teaching the basics of posture, breathing, sound production, and ensemble listening skills; not limited to the marching band genre; includes: Philosophy of Teaching, Breathing, Sound Production, and Listening in the Ensemble. SYSTEM SPECS: Instructional DVD.

Essential Elements 2000 for Band, Essential Elements 2000 for Strings, and Essential Elements 2000 for Jazz (www.halleonard.com): Uses popular songs in a variety of styles; quality demonstration and backing tracks on the accompanying CD; designed to meet the National Standards for Music Education, with features such as cross-curricular activities, quizzes, multicultural songs, basic improvisation, and more. SYSTEM SPECS: Book and Audio CD.

Essential Elements 2000 Band Director's Communications Kit and Essential Elements for String Orchestra Director's Communication Kit (www.halleonard.com): Letters focusing on music advocacy, the importance of the arts in the schools, and the benefits of musical study in the development of the child; additional letters written specifically for band; time savers for the busy band director. SYSTEM SPECS: Hybrid CD-ROM.

Expressive Conducting DVD-ROM (www.expressiveconducting.com): Interactive, multimedia presentation of the conductor's skills and gesture grammar; moving animations; begins with the most basic gestures; progresses to complications faced by professionals; program coordinated with textbook; for the classroom or independent study; 756 video clips; 200 animations; 137 scores; 1150 instrumental parts; fourteen chapters of text with graphics; author is an experienced teacher of conducting and a choral/orchestral conductor; program will run from CD or may be installed to hard drive; installer checks for adequate space and provides required version of QuickTime. SYSTEM SPECS: Hybrid DVD-ROM.

Fast Forward Series (www.musicsales.com): Instructional series; chamber instruments. SYSTEM SPECS: Book and Audio CD.

FastTrack Series (www.halleonard.com): Instructional series; standard and pocket size; all instruments and vocal; Spanish editions. SYSTEM SPECS: Book and Audio CD.

Hal Leonard DVDs (www.halleonard.com): Titles include: *Play Alto Sax Today!; Play Clarinet Today!; Play Flute Today!; Play Trumpet Today!*, and more. SYSTEM SPECS: Instructional DVD.

iPAS - Interactive Pyware Assessment System (www.pyware.com): Assessment software that automatically guides students through an assigned exercise or musical passage allowing unsupervised practice and accountability; each exercise is presented to the student in the form of a lesson which steps the student through a prearranged course of practicing and learning; first listening, then practicing, and then recording for a grade

is sent back to a school account; an assignment sheet is generated and the results of the student's practice session can be uploaded to the instructor; the instructor can then see the graded results or click a button and hear the actual performance; many new features including: fingering and alternate fingerings, tempo adjustments with score based on tempo chosen, hands free automatic reference pitch, tuner note name is in the key of the instrument played and CD quality playback. SYSTEM SPECS: Macintosh; Windows.

Jazz Pedagogy: The Jazz Educator's Handbook and Resource Guide (www.alfred.com): Comprehensive guide; jazz concept; rhythm section; jazz improvisation and styles; Latin jazz; audio/video demonstrations. SYSTEM SPECS: Book and Instructional DVD.

Lessons in Performance Book 1: Around the World (www.fjhmusic.com): For beginning and developing bands; fifteen pieces with full score analyses, techniques for conducting and teaching, background information, and supplemental exercises; for cross-curricular teaching; all supplemental material incorporates the National Standards. SYSTEM SPECS: Book and Audio CD.

Marching Bands and Me DVD (www.musicmotion.com): Watch and enjoy marching bands, bagpipe bands, brass bands, drill bands, military bands, show bands, and bands on horseback; learn about the different instruments; for Pre-K-Elementary; running time thirty minutes. SYSTEM SPECS: Instructional DVD.

Master Music Manager Software (www.musicmanager.com): Music library; membership files; personnel directory; inventory/uniform manager; recordings library; for all choral and instrumental educators; access commands by pulling down menu bar or clicking on buttons; datafile capacity limited only by the amount of hard disk space. SYSTEM SPECS: Macintosh; Windows.

Music Administrator (www.pyware.com): Easy to use and fully modifiable data base; contains templates for Student Files, Music Library, Equipment and Uniform Inventory and General Ledger; most of the same functions and features contained in the Music Office System are also contained in the Music Administrator; provides pre-designed file templates; no set up involved. SYSTEM SPECS: Macintosh.

Music Clip Art (www.friendshiphouse.com): Use to find a list of musical terms and their definitions; put together a quiz identifying different instruments; create a bulletin board with a musical theme; find images of famous composers; over 2,300 images carefully organized. SYSTEM SPECS: Hybrid CD-ROM.

Music of the Heart (www.musicmotion.com): For all teachers who have fought for funding for quality music education programs; true story; Roberta Guaspari, played by Meryl Streep, begins a violin program in a tough inner-city neighborhood in East Harlem; when her program is cut, she fights back; Isaac Stern, Itzhak Perlman, and Joshua Bell join her students in the performance of a lifetime; rated PG; running time 124 minutes. SYSTEM SPECS: Instructional DVD.

Music Office (www.pyware.com): For record keeping, including student grades, student addresses, music in music library, fund-raising, or uniform and equipment inventories; maintenance and accounting; export data function in file menu; copy to/from floppy feature so files can be easily transferred between computers; added font options allowing better control of fonts during printing; added restore function to revert a data file easily to a backup; additional backup security to protect work. SYSTEM SPECS: Windows.

Music Terminology for Bands, Orchestra, and Choirs (www.ecsmedia.com): Covers fundamental music terminology; includes dynamics, tempo markings, stylistic expression markings, music symbols, key signatures, scales, and string terminology; final test of fifty questions and record keeping included; for beginner to intermediate, grades 5-12. SYSTEM SPECS: Hybrid CD-ROM.

Music Word Wall (www.musicmotion.com): Print out a music word wall; select from over 150 terms, symbols, composers, instruments, and more; colorfully illustrated and defined; also effective when printed in black and white on colored stock; includes bonus graphics. SYSTEM SPECS: Hybrid CD-ROM.

New Directions for Strings (www.fjhmusic.com): Written by a team of pedagogues representing each of the four stringed instruments; equal integration of all instruments; tetrachord-based approach to support proper development of the left hand; assessment opportunities; attention to bow control. SYSTEM SPECS: Book and Audio CD.

No Excuses Band Jam Guide (www.musicsales.com): Comprehensive guide for players of all abilities; practice in a variety of styles as part of a real band. SYSTEM SPECS: Instructional DVD and Hybrid CD-ROM.

Orchestra Music Direct (www.orchestramusicdirect.com): Downloadable print music; digital titles for orchestras; browse by ensemble type, grade level, and/or composer/arranger; official, authorized and licensed service; generates royalties for the relevant publishers and composers. SYSTEM SPECS: Macintosh; Windows.

Play Sax from Day One (www.alfred.com): Complete introduction to the saxophone for the beginner; putting the instrument together; fingerings; tone production; tonguing; scales; daily practice routines; play along section. SYSTEM SPECS: Instructional DVD.

RCI Music Library CD-ROM (http://riden.com/index.shtml): Organize and track performances; create program notes; catalog composers; keep track of music and instrument loans; access music library by title, composer, arranger, or accompaniment; keep track of concert and recital dates; order music from publishers; keep track of robes and uniforms; print customized reports. SYSTEM SPECS: Macintosh; Windows.

Rhythm Section Workshop for Jazz Directors (www.alfred.com): For instrumental jazz ensembles, small group combos, vocal jazz ensembles, and praise and worship bands. SYSTEM SPECS: Book, Audio CD, and/or Instructional DVD.

Sibelius Instruments (www.sibelius.com): Guide to orchestral and band instruments; interactive encyclopedia of instruments, bands, orchestras, and ensembles; complete information on every orchestral and band instrument, with full details of their characteristics, how to write for them, and hundreds of high-quality recordings; explains about different orchestras, bands, and ensembles, including their historical development and repertoire; extensive quiz; for schools, colleges, universities, teachers, students, composers, and arrangers; over fifty instruments, from alto clarinet to xylophone; over twenty types of band, orchestra, and ensemble, from string quartet to marching band; instrumental writing and playing techniques such as range, bowing, mutes, glissandi, harmonics, mallets, and multiphonics; lesson plans, student assignments, and recommended listening; quiz with 500 listening and general questions. SYSTEM SPECS: Macintosh; Windows.

Sibelius Starclass (www.sibelius.com): Lesson plans and resources for the elementary and primary school; 180 ready-to-use lesson plans which support MENC and QCA standards; includes full explanations of musical concepts for nonspecialist teachers; hundreds of music clips and printable pictures; ninety-nine-track audio CD to play in class; classroom resource; well-presented and impressively structured lesson plans; saves hours of preparation. SYSTEM SPECS: Macintosh; Windows.

SlowBlast! and SlowGold for Windows (www.slowgold.com): Help practicing difficult musical passages; slows music down; play along or transcribe riffs and tunes at own speed instead of at full pace; master difficult phrases. SYSTEM SPECS: Windows.

SmartMusic Studio (www.smartmusic.com): CD-ROM; practice program for woodwinds, brass players, and vocalists; improvement in the ability to perform solo repertoire comes from working with accompaniment; provides accompaniment and follows player; metronome; practice loops; vocal warm-ups; vocal and instrument microphones included; foot pedal; practice with 20,000 professional accompaniments featuring authentic basso continuo, full orchestra, jazz piano combos, and rock/pop bands; accompaniments to over 50,000 skill-building exercises; subscribe online. SYSTEM SPECS: Hybrid CD-ROM.

Spell & Define (www.ecsmedia.com): Create up to sixteen different vocabulary lists, each containing up to fifty different words and definitions with a voice speaking the words; tool for teachers and parents to customize a learning environment. SYSTEM SPECS: Hybrid CD-ROM.

Standard of Excellence Enhanced Comprehensive Band Method (www.kjos.com): Each book comes with two CDs containing all the full band accompaniments for all the exercises and the iPAS Interactive Pyware Practice and Assessment Software; provides numeric performance scores; Tuner and Metronome included with iPAS; iPAS Teacher's Edition gives directors objective assessment and record-keeping tools. SYSTEM SPECS: Book and Audio CD; Macintosh; Windows.

Step One Series (www.musicsales.com): Instructional series; all instruments. SYSTEM SPECS: Book and Audio CD.

Sousa and His Band (www.musicmotion.com): John Philip Sousa Marches to greatness; he set the tempo for American life in the early 1900s; we are still marching to his beat; documentary narrated by E.G. Marshall includes historical performances; running time twenty-four minutes. SYSTEM SPECS: DVD.

Tap It Rhythm Creator (www.ecsmedia.com): Designed as a development tool to create new rhythms for use with the Tap It Rhythm Player; using the two programs in combination allows teachers to develop exercises and drills for students; use the Tap It Rhythm Player to open and perform the rhythm studies; drag-and-drop interface allows quick creation of rhythm patterns; standard 2/4, 3/4 and 4/4 time signatures can be selected before placing pre-determined rhythm beat patterns into each measure; number of measures in each exercise can be unlimited; create an entire lesson series of rhythm patterns; lessons can be saved and exported. SYSTEM SPECS: Hybrid CD-ROM.

Tap It Rhythm Player (www.ecsmedia.com): Free program to be used in conjunction with Tap It Rhythm Creator; use Tap It Rhythm Creator to create custom rhythm lessons and distribute the lessons to students for use in Tap It Rhythm Player; when students have imported the rhythms, they can use the lesson an unlimited number of times; when the lesson is completed the student can export their scores and send them to the teacher for easy record keeping; available for free download. SYSTEM SPECS: Macintosh; Windows.

The Orchestra Musician's Library (www.orchmusiclibrary.com): Orchestral repertoire; compilation of printed parts; view or print letter-sized copies. SYSTEM SPECS: Hybrid CD-ROM.

Timesketch Editor (www.ecsmedia.com): For listening to and analyzing music with computer; create teacher-developed listening lessons with any audio CD; for fundamentals courses, appreciation courses, or mu-

sic history courses at any level; annotated listening format can be applied to classes, activities, and music performance. SYSTEM SPECS: Hybrid CD-ROM.

Ultimate Beginner Series—Alto Sax (www.alfred.com): Covers assembling the instrument, proper breathing, forming the embouchure, producing a sound, holding the instrument, correct posture, basic theory, learning notes, playing a song, and basic maintenance; demonstrations of good tone and proper technique; contains everything needed to get one started on the alto sax. SYSTEM SPECS: Instructional DVD.

Ultimate Beginner Series—Cello (www.alfred.com): Learn to play simple tunes; learn the history of the instrument, instrument maintenance, the proper way to hold the instrument, simple finger patterns, bowing, plucking methods, and how to develop a rich full tone; for the new student or as a refresher course at the intermediate level. SYSTEM SPECS: Instructional DVD.

Ultimate Beginner Series—Clarinet (www.alfred.com): Covers assembling the instrument, proper breathing, forming the embouchure, producing a sound, holding the instrument, correct posture, basic theory, learning notes, playing a song, and basic maintenance; demonstrations of good tone and proper technique; contains everything needed to get one started on the clarinet. SYSTEM SPECS: Instructional DVD.

Ultimate Beginner Series—Flute (www.alfred.com): Covers assembling the instrument, proper breathing, forming the embouchure, producing a sound, holding the instrument, correct posture, basic theory, learning notes, playing a song, and basic maintenance; demonstrations of good tone and proper technique; contains everything needed to get one started on the flute. SYSTEM SPECS: Instructional DVD.

Ultimate Beginner Series—Trombone (www.alfred.com): Covers assembling the instrument, proper breathing, forming the embouchure, producing a sound, holding the instrument, correct posture, basic theory, learning notes, playing a song, and basic maintenance; demonstrations of good tone and proper technique; contains everything needed to get one started on the trombone. SYSTEM SPECS: Instructional DVD.

Ultimate Beginner Series—Trumpet (www.alfred.com): Covers assembling the instrument, proper breathing, forming the embouchure, producing a sound, holding the instrument, correct posture, basic theory, learning notes, playing a song, and basic maintenance; demonstrations of good tone and proper technique; contains everything needed to get one started on the trumpet. SYSTEM SPECS: Instructional DVD.

Ultimate Beginner Series—Viola (www.alfred.com): Learn to play a simple tune; learn the history of the instrument, instrument maintenance, the proper way to hold the instrument, simple finger patterns, bowing, plucking methods, and how to develop a rich, full tone; for the new student or as a refresher course at the intermediate level. SYSTEM SPECS: Instructional DVD.

Ultimate Beginner Series—Violin (www.alfred.com): Introduction to playing the violin; covers instrument care to playing techniques; also covers the history of the instrument, the proper way to hold the instrument, simple finger patterns, bowing and plucking methods, and various techniques that allow the player to develop own distinctive tone; for beginners and novices. SYSTEM SPECS: Instructional DVD.

WinBand and WinChoir (www.winband.com): Music data management software; complete student, parent, and booster records; individual fund-raising accounts with automatic tab and project totals; grade tabulations; complete music library information; equipment and uniform inventory; shortcut keys. SYSTEM SPECS: Windows.

WinEnsemble (www.winband.com): For scheduling solo and ensemble festivals; make complete schedules and reports; automatic scheduling of events; flexible start, break, and event interval times; random or specific time scheduling; automatic matching of event type to judge; labels for comment sheets; mailing labels for participating schools and judges; imports data from WinBand, WinChoir, or WinEnsemble. SYSTEM SPECS: Windows.

Worship Assistant and Ministry Assistant (www.churchassist.com): For anyone who plans, organizes, and manages worship services, concerts, holiday productions, etc.; keep track of worship songs; plan worship services and musical productions; present song lyrics using a video projector; manage worship teams, choir members, and more. SYSTEM SPECS: Windows.

Brass and Woodwind Instruments Web Sites

A Physical Approach to Playing the Trumpet www.trumpetbook.com Method book.

A Tutorial on the Fife beafifer.com Tutorial book and CD with seventy-five lessons keyed to tracks; forty-nine tunes of varying difficulty; tips on how to buy a new fife or recondition an old one.

AAIIRR Power AcoustiCoils for Brass and Woodwinds www.dmamusic.org/acousticoils Produces enhanced response for all brass and woodwind musical instruments.

Bam Cases www.bamcases.com Wide range of cases for wind instruments.

Bassoon Spot www.bassoonspot.com/cat28.htm Sheet music for bassoon.

Brass Band World www.brassbandworld.com Webzine for the brass world.

Buffet Crampon www.buffet-crampon.com/en/ French maker of clarinets, oboes, bassoons, and saxophones.

Calicchio Brass Musical Instruments www.calicchio.com Hand-crafted horns.

Canadian Brass canbrass.com/frontpage.html Brass quintet; over 60 recordings of classical repertoire.

Cannonball www.cannonballmusic.com Manufacturer of saxophones, trumpets, and clarinets; accessories.

Charles Double Reed Company www.charlesmusic.com Reeds.

Chartier www.chartierreeds.com Reeds.

Conn-Selmer, Inc. www.conn-selmer.com Leading manufacturer and distributor of band and orchestral instruments.

Custom Music Co. www.custommusiccorp.com Tubas; euphoniums; trumpets; trombones; bassoons; oboes; brass winds.

E. M. Winston Band Instruments www.emwinston.com Band instruments; orchestra instruments; stands; sax straps; recorders; percussion; educational toys; mouthpieces.

Emerson Musical Instruments www.emersonflutes.com Emerson flutes.

Empire Brass Sheet Music www.empirebrass.com/sheet.html Brass arrangements.

F. Lorée www.loree-paris.com/engl/accueil.html French oboe manufacturer; English horns; bass oboes; piccolo oboes.

Flute Talk www.instrumentalistmagazine.com Magazine for flute players, teachers, and students.

Flute World www.fluteworld.com Flutes; piccolos; sheet music; accessories.

Flute.net Publications www.flute.net/publications Works for flute choir.

Fox Products www.foxproducts.com Oboes; bassoons; contrabassoons; English horns; accessories.

Gemeinhardt www.gemeinhardt.com Flutes and piccolos.

Giardinelli www.giardinelli.com Band and orchestral instruments and accessories.

Haynes Flutes www.wmshaynes.com One of the world's finest flutes; since 1888.

Horn Place www.hornplace.com Music instruction books, CDs, videos, and software for tenor saxophone, alto saxophone, baritone saxophone, soprano saxophone, flute, trombone, and trumpet.

J. L. Smith and Co. www.flutesmith.com Flute specialists; teacher locator; buyers guide; road shows.

John Myatt www.myatt.co.uk/ UK woodwind and brass instrument specialists.

Julius Keilwerth www.schreiber-keilwerth.com/englisch/general/home_keilwerth.htm Saxophones since 1925.

Jupiter Band Instruments, Inc. www.jupitermusic.com Jupiter Brass & Woodwinds; Ross Mallet Instruments.

Leblanc www.gleblanc.com Wind instrument manufacturer and distributor.

Lighthouse Media Group www.lighthousemediagroup.com Tips and Techniques videos for repairing band instruments, string, and percussion.

Mouthpiece Express.com www.mouthpieceexpress.com Mouthpieces and accessories for brass and woodwind instruments.

Muramatsu Flutes www.muramatsu-america.com American distributor; fine handmade flutes.

Music by Arrangement www.musicbyarrangement.co.uk/index.html Music for orchestras, bands, and ensembles; specially arranged for the instruments available; catalog; based in the UK.

National Association of School Music Dealers www.nasmd.com Trade association dedicated to sales, rental, and service of band and orchestra instruments, accessories, and published music.

Pearl Flutes www.pearlflutes.com Flutes; handmade craftsmanship; Pinless Mechanism; One-Piece Core-Bar construction.

Rayburn Musical Instrument Company www.rayburn.com Brass, woodwind, and string instruments; new and used; accessories.

Rico International www.ricoreeds.com Reeds; mouthpieces.

Sax on the Web www.saxontheweb.net Online forum for saxophone players.

Sax Puppy www.saxpuppy.com/index.html Sheet music for saxophone.

Saxophone U.S. www.saxophone.us Web resource for saxophone players.

Softwind Instruments www.softwind.ch/Synthophone.asp Synthophone MIDI Sax.

SR Mouthpieces www.srtechnologies.com SR Technologies; SR Mouthpieces.

Stephanhöuser www.gemstonemusical.com/stephanhouser/history.htm Revolutionary new saxophone.

Suzuki Band Instruments www.suzukibandinstruments.com For intermediate, advanced, and professional players.

Tap Music Sales www.tapmusic.com Woodwind and brass instrument recordings on compact disks, tapes, records, and videocassettes; imported and artist produced; publishes sheet music.

The Bandstand, Ltd. www.bandstand.ab.ca Wind instrument specialists; source for school band.

The Clarinet Pages www.woodwind.org/clarinet/ Clarinet pedagogy; equipment; hints; techniques.

The Instrumentalist www.instrumentalistmagazine.com Magazine for band and orchestra teachers and students; subscribe online.

The International Saxophone Home Page www.saxophone.org Information; resources; links.

The Woodwind and the Brasswind www.wwbw.com Music store; large selection of musical instruments and accessories.

Trombone Puppy www.trombonepuppy.com/index.html Sheet music for trombone.

Trombone USA www.trombone-usa.com Over 4,000 trombonists listed; links.

Trumpet Studio www.trumpetstudio.com/home.html Resource for trumpet players; practice suggestions.

Vandoren Reeds www.vandoren.fr/en/home.html Reeds and mouthpieces for saxophone and clarinet.

Vandoren Scores www.vandorenscores.com Collection of sheet music and CDs for saxophone and clarinet.

Verne Q. Powell Flutes Inc. www.powellflutes.com Handmade metal flutes, wooden flutes, and piccolos; clarinet, alto sax, and tenor saxophone reeds.

Westwind Brass www.westwindbrass.org San Diego-based brass quintet; performances; recordings; concert calendar; education.

Wind Player www.windplayer.com Webzine.

Windband www.windband.co.uk Specialists in woodwind, brass, folk, and early musical instruments; bagpipes, banjos, bassoons, clarinets, concertinas, flutes, folk instruments, mandolins, saxophones.

Windcraft Limited & Dawkes Music Limited www.windcraft.co.uk or www.dawkes.co.uk Woodwind and brass instruments; accessories; mouthpieces; spares; repair materials and tools.

Yamaha Band and Orchestral Instruments www.yamaha.com/bandhome/0%2C%2CCTID%2525253D231200%2C00.html Brass; woodwinds.

Yanagisawa Saxophones www.yanagisawasax.co.jp/en/ Japanese manufacturer of saxophones; soprano, alto, tenor, baritone.

Zachary Music www.zacharymusic.com Clarinet, trumpet, trombone, flute, and saxophone.

Patriotic Music—Marches and Marching Bands Web Sites

American and Patriotic Music my.homewithgod.com/heavenlymidis/USA/ MIDI files of songs.

Flags of the Native Peoples of the United States users.aol.com/Donh523/navapage/index.html Photos and histories of Native American flags.

Independence Day wilstar.com/holidays/july4.htm Links to America's historic documents.

Military Women on Sheet Music userpages.aug.com/captbarb/sheetmusic.html History of women in the military from the revolutionary war to the present day.

Music for the Nation: American Sheet Music, 1870-1885
memory.loc.gov/ammem/smhtml/smhome.html Tens of thousands of songs and instrumental pieces registered for copyright in the post-Civil War era.

NIEHS Kid's Pages
www.niehs.nih.gov/kids/musicpatriot.htm Patriotic songs with lyrics; print an American flag.

Operation Just Cause Jukebox www.ojc.org/sounds/ Audio files.

Patriotic Greeting Cards
www.prairiefrontier.com/pfcards1/patriotic.html Patriotic multimedia greeting cards by Prairie Frontier.

Patriotic Melodies
http://lcweb2.loc.gov/diglib/ihas/html/patriotic/patriotic-home.html Tells the stories behind the songs.

Patriotic MIDIs and Marches
www.laurasmidiheaven.com/Patriotc.shtml Audio files.

Patriotic Songs
www.angelfire.com/tx/scout21/patriotic.html Audio files and song lyrics.

Patriotic Songs
www.digitaltimes.com/karaoke/singers/patriotic/ Song lyrics.

Patriotic Songs and Hymns www.usflag.org/songs.html Song lyrics.

Prairie Frontier Patriotic Music MIDI Files
www.prairiefrontier.com/pfcards/Xtrapgs/patriotic.html MIDI file collection.

Scout Songs
www.scoutsongs.com/categories/patriotic.html Index of patriotic songs.

Sheet Music about Lincoln, Emancipation, and the Civil War memory.loc.gov/ammem/scsmhtml/scsmhome.html From the Alfred Whital Stern Collection at the Library of Congress.

Student Travel and Tours for Marching Bands and Choirs www.travelgroups.com Student travel and tour packages for marching bands, choirs, sport teams, and class trips; festivals and competitions.

The 4th of July Page-Patriotic Fantasy
www.wilstar.com/holidays/july4.htm Uncle Sam's dream; contains many historic American documents; listen to patriotic MIDI music.

The Fifties Web www.fiftiesweb.com/usa/ustunes.htm Patriotic songs.

Stringed Instruments—Violin—Viola—Cello—Bass—Harp Web Sites

About the Violin
www.nelson.planet.org.nz/~matthew/cbt.html The violin and its history.

Amateur Chamber Music Players www.acmp.net/ Nonprofit; facilitates informal playing and singing by people of all ages and nationalities, beginners to professionals; 5,400 members.

American Federation of Violin and Bow Makers www.afvbm.com Members; tips; programs.

American Harp Society www.harpsociety.org Local chapters; awards and competitions.

American School of Double Bass www.asodb.com Clinics; retreat; books; recordings; facilities.

American String Teachers Association
www.astaweb.com Member benefits; resources; events; jobs.

American Viola Society www.americanviolasociety.org Membership; local chapters; join.

Berg Bows www.bergbows.com Bows.

Bernard Ellis www.ellisium.cwc.net Handmade early string instruments; supply worldwide to professional and amateur musicians, museums, cultural foundations, and university departments.

Cello Classics www.celloclassics.com CDs; news; reviews; distribution.

Cellos2go.com www.cellos2go.com Buying and renting; accessories.

Chamber Music America www.chamber-music.org Membership; programs; events; publications.

Double Bass Links Page
www.gollihurmusic.com/links.cfm Tons of links.

Double Bassist www.doublebassist.com Magazine for double bass teachers, students, players, makers.

International Society of Bassists
www.ISBworldoffice.com./ Events; publications.

International Violin Company
www.internationalviolin.com Since 1933; customers include violin and guitar makers, repair people, music stores, schools and universities.

Internet Cello Society www.cello.org FAQ; What's New; links; newsletter; forums; tips; festivals.

Ithaca Stringed Instruments www.ithacastring.com Custom guitars, violins, violas, and cellos; catalog.

Johnson String Instruments www.johnson-inst.com Violins, violas, cellos, and their bows; new and antique violins, violas, bows, and cellos; online catalog; repairs and rentals.

Jordan Electric Violins www.jordanmusic.com Electric violins; electric violas; electric cellos; electric basses; links.

Lashof Violins.com www.lashofviolins.com Care and maintenance of string instruments.

Meisel Stringed Instruments www.meiselmusic.com Meisel; Mittenwald; Mozart; Spitfire; Skyinbow; GIG Stands; Innovation Strings.

Orchestras www.music.indiana.edu/music_resources/orchestr. html Extensive list of inks to orchestra sites.

Otto Musica U.S.A., Inc. www.ottomusica.com Violin bows; violin cases; cello cases; violin strings; violin shoulder rests; violin rosin; violins; cellos.

PBS Great Performances www.pbs.org/wnet/gperf/shows/artofviolin/artofvio lin.html The Art of Violin; flash video; links.

Shar Music www.sharmusic.com Online violin shop; sheet music for stringed instruments.

Southwest Strings www.swstrings.com Music products; strings; sheet music.

String Works www.stringworks.com Sales and rentals.

Stringnet www.stringnet.com String instruments; violin; viola; cello; bass; bows and accessories.

Strings Magazine www.stringsmagazine.com All things strings.

Super-Sensitive Musical String Company www.supersensitive.com Strings and accessories for bowed instruments.

Suzuki Violin Teachers Central www.suzuki-violin.com Teachers directory; forum; teaching points.

Tempest Music www.violin-world.com/sheetmusic Classical specialist; music and accessories for stringed instruments.

The Cello Handbook www.cellohandbook.com Instruction book.

The Cello Page home.thirdage.com/Music/cellomar/ All about the cello.

The Double Bass and Violone Internet Archive www.earlybass.com Articles; links; resources.

The Harp Mall www.harpmall.com The harp world.

The Joy of Cello Playing www.wimmercello.com Harry Wimmer; studio tour; books; links.

The String Pedagogy Notebook www.uvm.edu/~mhopkins/string/ Resource for teachers and performers.

The Viola Web Site www.viola.com Portal for violists on the Web.

The Violin Society of America www.vsa.to/ Membership; conventions; competitions; journal.

The Violin Tutor www.theviolintutor.com Practice software for Windows.

Thomastik-Infeld Vienna www.thomastik-infeld.com Dominant perlon violin strings.

Viola da Gamba Society of America vdgsa.org Not-for-profit dedicated to the support of activities in the U.S. and abroad; society of players, builders, publishers, distributors, restorers and others sharing a serious interest in music for viols, and other early bowed string instruments.

Violin Acoustics www.phys.unsw.edu.au/~jw/violindex.html Basics; publications.

Violin Making www.centrum.is/hansi/ Sound; construction; care and maintenance; pictures.

Violin Online www.violinonline.com Music and instruction for all ages.

Violin Scale Charts option-wizard.com/vsc/violin_scale_charts.shtml Finger positions for major and minor scales and arpeggios.

Violin-World www.violin-world.com Stringed instruments; violin; viola; cello; double bass; strings; bows; cases; sheet music; online store and catalog; announcements; classifieds; teachers directory; sound advice; articles; music jokes.

Virtuoso www.webcom.com/virtvirt/ Practice tools for string players; Practice Assistant; Performance Assistant; Duets; Scale Master; Support; Order Form; based on MIDI files; for Windows.

Yahoo Directory: Classical Violinists dir.yahoo.com/Entertainment/Music/Artists/By_Ge nre/Classical/By_Instrument/Violin/ Links to Web sites; listed by popularity and alphabetically.

Zeta Music Systems www.zetamusic.com Violins; basses; cellos; violas; amps.

13
Songwriting—Accompanying—Music Industry
Software, Instructional Media and Web Sites

A Zillion Kajillion Rhymes and Cliches (www.eccentricsoftware.com): Thesaurus for rhymes; for songwriting, poetry, parodies, plays on words, jingles, product names, and more; enter word and will produce a list of rhyming words. SYSTEM SPECS: Macintosh; Windows.

Alfred Methods and Techniques for DJs (www.alfred.com): Titles include: *Latin DJ Techniques: Miami Style; Run DMC's Master Jay – Be a DJ; DJ Styles Series: DJ Mixing and Remixing; DJ Styles Series: DJing in a Band; DJ Styles Series: DJing with CDs; Ultimate Beginner Series: Digital DJ; Ultimate Beginner Series: The DJ's Guide to Scratching; Ultimate Beginner Series: The Turntable DJ.* SYSTEM SPECS: Book and Audio CD and/or Instructional DVD.

Band-In-A-Box (www.pgmusic.com): Intelligent automatic accompaniment program; enter chords to a song, choose a style of music, and Band-in-a-Box does the rest, generating a full band arrangement complete with Bass, Piano, Drums, Guitar, Strings, and more; arrange, listen to, or play along with songs in hundreds of musical styles. The MIDI and audio tracks that Band-in-a-Box creates are automatically played out through computer's built-in sound card or synthesizer; music notation is displayed in a lead sheet window; broad range of uses; music composition tool for exploring and developing musical ideas with instant feedback; educational tool, used both by professional musicians to sharpen their skills, and as a learning aid by people with little or no musical background; essential program for practicing instrument in a full band setting; play instrument while Band-in-a-Box takes the place of the other band members; The Soloist, Melodist, and Audio Chord Wizard are examples of intelligent features; the Soloist generates professional quality solos over any chord progression; the Melodist can create entire songs from scratch with Chords, Melodies, Intros, and Solos; the Medley Maker can combine songs to create interesting medleys; the Audio Chord Wizard can figure out the chords in any audio file; encompasses a diverse range of musical genres including Pop, Rock, Latin, Country, Classical, World, Blues, Bluegrass, New Age, Techno, and much more; over 1500 styles are currently available from PG Music and more are always being developed, many based directly on customer requests; each style is a large database of musical patterns and ideas so the song arrangements will always be fresh, never sounding exactly the same each time. Basic Steps: Input chords for song; choose a key/tempo and set the number of bars/choruses/loops, etc.; type in the chord symbols using the computer keyboard, play the chords from a connected MIDI keyboard and use MIDI Chord Detection, use the built-in Chord Builder, or have Band-in-a-Box figure out the chords in any MIDI or audio file; chords can include common chord symbols such as C7, Cm, and Cmaj7, or more complex chords; over 100 chords are supported; can enter an alternate root for any chord (slash chord); choose a style of music using the StylePicker Window; preview song in many different styles, or listen to original demo songs for any of the PG Music styles available; Styles use up to five tracks for the accompaniment, depending on what is suitable for that specific style; arrange song using automatic intros, two-bar endings, sub style variations, drum fills, intelligent chord substitutions, pushes, shots, rests, and more; Press Play to have Band-in-a-Box instantly develop an original arrangement for song, which is played back through the sound card or

MIDI synthesizer; for playback, can use a software synth such as the VSC-DXi included with Band-in-a-Box, or a hardware synth, e.g., a sound card synth/MIDI keyboard/sound module; generates original audio tracks called RealDrums and RealTracks; input own instrumental melody/solo track using an external MIDI keyboard, or by using the computer mouse and keyboard in the Editable Notation window; or have Band-in-a-Box create the solo and melody using the Melodist and Soloist; Record an audio track; use a microphone to record singing; harmonize vocal track using the built-in audio harmonizer; make an audio CD of music. SYSTEM SPECS: Macintosh; Windows.

CD Looper (www.replayinc.com): Learn to play any song directly from computer's CD player; can slow down two, three, or four times without changing pitch; learn songs note for note; set loop points anywhere within a track; can set a loop point for every two-bar phrase; loop options can play each loop once, twice, or continuously, pausing between each loop or user-settable amount of time; highlight multiple loops and loop an entire section. SYSTEM SPECS: Windows.

Copyright and Publishing Law: For Musicians and Songwriters DVD (www.mixbooks.com): Understanding Legal Ownership; Intro to Intellectual Property; Learning Legal Lingo; Copyright With or Without Registration; How to Legally Protect Your Music/Songs; ABC's of Typical Contracts; Major and Independent Music Labels; Granting Terms; Terms and Termination; Compensation. SYSTEM SPECS: Instructional DVD.

Decomposer (www.replayinc.com): Advanced filtering program; filter out a single instrument or sections of instruments from any digital audio file. SYSTEM SPECS: Windows.

DJ Styles (www.alfred.com): *Mixing and Remixing*: mixing and remixing as a DJ; by acclaimed DJ KNS; includes tips on beat matching, blending vocals, working with beats, bars and breaks, and more; *DJing in a Band*: DJs KNS and Ucada give the lowdown on being the turntable guru in a band; included are tips on scratching, creating beats, understanding bars and breaks and more; *DJing with CDs*: learn all the techniques of DJ-ing with CDs from DJ Gerald "World Wide" Webb; master such areas as scratchable and non-scratchable CDs, beat matching techniques, creating loops, and matching beats and breaks. SYSTEM SPECS: Instructional DVD.

Finale Songwriter (www.finalemusic.com): Print professional-quality sheet music; create MP3 files; e-mail songs; experiment with melodies; click notes onto the staff and hear pitches; drag notes up and down to find the right pitches; play a MIDI keyboard and see the music appear instantly; import and export MIDI files; add lyrics with multiple verses; explore different arrangements; try any tempo; transpose to any key; type

a chord name to hear how it sounds and see its guitar fretboard; select automatic drum grooves for different styles; add automatic harmonies; experiment with more than 128 professional instruments; print sheet music; save MP3 files to create audio CDs or to play on an iPod; hear songs with a professional software synthesizer; use Human Playback to make songs sound like they're performed live; entry-level version of the Finale music software; create melodies and songs; for creating all types of lead sheets, including Christian music lead sheets, guitar lead sheets, piano lead sheets, and more. SYSTEM SPECS: Macintosh; Windows.

Guitar Playing for Songwriters (www.garytalley.com): By Gary Talley, guitar player for the Box Tops; unique, effective, and streamlined approach to teaching guitar especially designed for songwriters; fun and innovative; three-lessons; fifty-five-minutes. SYSTEM SPECS: Instructional DVD.

Home Concert (www.timewarptech.com): Play a piece of music on a MIDI instrument, reading the music off the computer screen, while music's accompaniment is synchronized to playing; play solo part on keyboard; plays the accompaniment, following the player's timing, tempo, and dynamic changes. SYSTEM SPECS: Macintosh; Windows.

How to Find Gigs That Pay Big Bucks (www.halleonard.com): Advice from music industry heavy-hitters; Kevin Eubanks, musical director for Tonight Show band, shares thoughts on getting major work as a musician in today's market; guitarist Richie Sambora talks about critical elements to launching a music career; Kevin Cronin (REO Speedwagon), Eric Schenkman (Spin Doctors), and Joe Satriani give inside scoop about finding good-paying gigs, agents, and learning from mistakes; Carnival Cruise Lines supervisor J. B. Buccafusco gives ideas on how to get booked on cruise ships; Steve Schirripa, former entertainment director for Las Vegas Riviera, gives insight into casino bookings nationwide; tips from concert and festival promoters, studio musicians, and talent buyers; thirty-eight minutes. SYSTEM SPECS: Instructional DVD.

How to Mic a Band for Ultimate Live Sound (www.musicsales.com): Professional mic techniques and placement for vocals, guitars, bass, horns, and percussion; learn about room acoustic variations, setting up a final mix, effects usage, compressors, gates, types of PAs, and microphones; full mixer explanation included. SYSTEM SPECS: Instructional DVD.

Jammer Live (www.soundtrek.com): Interactive virtual professional backup band that jams to chord changes in real time and interacts with melodies upon command; captured the feel of top pros; photographic user interface; professionally recorded style riffs in a wide variety of styles; "state of the art" graphic style editor for styles. SYSTEM SPECS: Windows.

Jammer Professional (www.soundtrek.com): Virtual studio musicians ready to improvise, harmonize, exchange ideas, and lay down original tracks; control the style of each musician on each track; over 200 band styles; complete control over player styles, note ranges, velocities, and transitions; blend multiple styles together; 25-track MIDI studio located in the PC; six-part harmony; load and save individual drum styles; automatic fades and crescendos; "Real Feel" composition engine; 32-bit graphic user interface. SYSTEM SPECS: Windows.

Jammer Pro Band and Drum Styles Volumes 1-4 (www.soundtrek.com): Vol. 1: over seventy assorted professional band-style grooves, intros, breaks, stops, holds and endings for ballads, fast jazz swing, moderate swing rock, slow guitar blues, slow R&B, upbeat country, reggae, swing, and hip hop; plus 100 assorted professional drum styles including jazz, rock, blues, and country beats with dynamic drum fills; Vol. 2: over seventy assorted professional band-style grooves, intros, breaks, stops, holds and endings for pop-rock, bossanova, boogie woogie, jazz fusion, new age, upbeat soul, slow country swing, funk-rock swing, and easy listening; plus 100 assorted professional drum styles, including Latin, jazz, and rock beats with dynamic drum fills; Vol. 3 over seventy professional band-style grooves, intros, breaks, stops, holds, and endings for contemporary jazz, slow rock, moderate rock, upbeat rock swing, upbeat Latin rock, mambo, salsa, merengue, techno dance, and gospel waltz; plus 100 drum styles including Latin, jazz, rock, funk, and country beats with dynamic drum fills; Vol. 4 over seventy assorted professional band-style grooves, intros, breaks, stops, holds, and endings for medium alternative rock, upbeat alternative rock, pop funk, inspirational, 50s R&B swing, country rock, Irish jig, Irish reel, big band swing, and big band ballads; plus 100 assorted drum styles, including rock, ballad, fusion, hip-hop, and dance beats with dynamic drum fills. SYSTEM SPECS: Windows.

Jammer Songmaker (www.soundtrek.com): 256-track single-port MIDI sequencer with built-in studio musicians; 200 assorted band style grooves, intros, breaks, stops, holds, and endings in a wide variety of styles; 50 drum styles, harmony composers, and more; upgradeable to Jammer Pro SYSTEM SPECS: Windows.

Lyricist (www.virtualstudiosystems.com): Word processor for lyricists, musicians, songwriters, and poets; rhyming dictionary, spell checker, thesaurus, chord charting and editing, chord wizard, online file copyright, programmable text styles, Web link button, database-oriented storage, album categorization, and more. SYSTEM SPECS: Windows CD-ROM.

MasterWriter (www.masterwriter.com) Collection of tools for songwriters; rhyming dictionary

with over 100,000 entries; pop-culture dictionary with over 11,000 icons of American and World Culture; dictionary of over 35,000 phrases, idioms, clichés, sayings, and word combinations; *Rhymed-Phrases Dictionary* with over 36,000 entries; *Alliterations Dictionary* in existence; *American Heritage Dictionary* and *Roget's II Thesaurus*; state-of-the-art database to keep track of all lyrics, melodies and information related to the songs written; stereo Hard Disk Recorder for recording melodic ideas; Songuard online date-of-creation Song Registration Service; over 250 tempo adjustable MIDI Drum Loops; Word Processing. SYSTEM SPECS: Hybrid CD-ROM.

Music for New Media (www.berkleepress.com): Learn to write for videogames, websites, and other new media; devices, sounds, and techniques for supporting stories and responding to user actions; technical and dramatic requirements necessary for each type of new media. SYSTEM SPECS: Book and Audio CD.

Music Publisher (www.yeahsolutions.com/): Features for publishing administration, A&R, copyright, licensing, royalties, product royalties, sub-publishing, and other business; additional support packages and demo version available. SYSTEM SPECS: Windows.

MusicMaker (www.halleonard.com): Play fifteen pop hits with five options: One Key Play: tap out timing to play melody along with backing track; Jamtrax: play any key; Drum Along: choose between four kits to drum along with tracks; Quiz: take a musical quiz; Melody Play: play melody on keyboard. SYSTEM SPECS: Windows.

MusicWrite Songwriter (www.turtlebeach.com): Select a staff; select the instruments; musical creations can be viewed, printed, and played back; notate a wide variety of musical styles, from single staff guitar tablature with lyrics to an eight-piece band; create music in a variety of ways including mouse click entry and MIDI recording; use symbols and markings for more complicated passages; organize compositions with the Track Sheet, a summary of track information used for naming, moving, deleting, and editing tracks and track parameters; keep complex compositions organized. SYSTEM SPECS: Windows.

Number Chart Pro Software (http://www.robhainesstudio.com/numchart/index.htm): Custom font enables users to create any sized professional Nashville Number System song charts; computer-generated charts can be archived, updated, e-mailed. SYSTEM SPECS: Macintosh; Windows.

Secrets of Songwriting Success CD-ROMs (www.jaijomusic.com): Jai Josef's live seminar on two-CD-ROM set; author of *Writing Music for Hit Songs*; live clips of actual workshops; text; graphics; interactivity; links to useful resources. SYSTEM SPECS: Macintosh; Windows.

SetMaker Freeware Application Download (www.sweetwater.com/download) Make set lists; key field; filter songs by key; new key column in every set list; open multiple set lists simultaneously; drag and drop between set lists; print all songs in the songs window; songs in the songs window are saved with every modification; print preview print jobs; more control over final printed output; backwards compatibility with SetMaker 1.0/1.1 set lists; "song manager" allows songwriter to keep "database" or "list" of song information; data are automatically saved with program and can be categorized, filtered, and manipulated in useful ways; set list creator allows songwriter to quickly select songs from database, put them in a set list, and print out a list of songs to use for live performance, general reference, etc.; create and save unlimited number of sets. SYSTEM SPECS: Macintosh; Windows.

Song Sheet (www.dsbsoft.com/): Designed to help organize lyric sheets and save time; toggle between formatted text (standard text) and unformatted text (chordpro text) with the ability to edit in both modes; use tags and comments to make lyrics sheets easy to understand; create word sheets, fake books, lead sheets, and more; open and edit ChordPro files and save back as Song Sheet files; place lyrics, chords, and chord diagrams on a single page; type in the words and place the chord names within the lyrics using the insert chord name method or type them in; transpose function allows user to go up or down by 1/2 steps; create chords using up to and including the 16th fret; over 500 chord diagrams; create a chord in the Chord Editor and hear it using the Play Chord function; use the Word Sheets function to produce a two-column printed page of selected songs or save as an .rtf file or text for editing; create Fake Books or Song Books; save the lyric sheets to the .rtf format, compatible with Word or WordPad; can be used by the worship leader for home groups or in the church; free unlimited technical support via e-mail. SYSTEM SPECS: Macintosh; Windows.

SongTracker and SongTracker Pro (www.bizbasics.net/songtrkr.html): Manage the business side of songwriting or a music-industry company; office database system designed in FileMaker Pro; comprehensive contact manager; automates and prepares: Copyrights, ASCAP/BMI registration forms, DAT/CD/cassette inserts, contracts, songplugging correspondence, and more; digital sounds can be stored or played; optional PRO version offers network of coworkers a set of management/tracking modules for the contract, licensing, administration, and royalty aspects of publishing/record company needs; over 130 reports provide music industry information.; demo version available; keep music business organized; manage and administrate entire song catalog; Song Shopping module tracks results and gets music out faster; prints effective reports. SYSTEM SPECS: Macintosh; Windows.

Songworks (www.ars-nova.com): Compose music, notate music, hear music, and print music on Computer; use for leadsheets (melody and chord symbols) or choral music or instrumental scores; tools include transposition, idea generators, and harmony suggestions; provides accompaniment for practice, to learn a part in a chorale, or to improvise on the letter keys; notate compositions on multiple staves with up to eight voices per staff; invents tune ideas and suggests chord progressions; with Active Listening, can perform one part of a composition while computer plays the others; explore polyphony; experience being part of a music ensemble; can export music to an AIFF, MIDI, or PICT file for use on multimedia projects; MIDI compatible. SYSTEM SPECS: Macintosh; Windows.

Tab, Lyrics, and Chords (www.tabslyricschords.com/): For guitarists and users of tablature and lyric sheets; take a plain text lyric sheet and transpose to any key; insert finger positions for all chords in a song; generate almost any scale in any key and insert it directly into the text; create tab frames for tabbing own songs; edit with tab editor; store 1000s of songs in database format; create and manage printed booklets of songs with table of contents; create downloadable ZIP files and/or matching HTML for songs; share tab and lyrics; record songs directly to hard drive. SYSTEM SPECS: Windows.

The Complete Music Business Office (www.halleonard.com): Includes over 125 essential contracts and forms for conducting music and entertainment industry business; includes United States Government documents for filing copyrights; CD-ROM containing contract library for use with Windows and Macintosh computers. SYSTEM SPECS: Book and Hybrid CD-ROM.

The Indie Bible (www.indiebible.com): The Indie Bible is over 330 pages and contains: 4000 publications from around the world that will review CDs; 3200 radio stations from around the world that will play songs; 500 vendors and services that will help sell music; 200 sites where one can upload music files; 500 useful resources to help promote. SYSTEM SPECS: Macintosh; Windows; download.

The Lead Sheet Bible Book and Audio CD (www.halleonard.com): Guide to writing lead sheets and chord charts; by Robin Randall and Janice Peterson; book/CD package for singer, songwriter, or musician who wants to create a lead sheet or chord chart that is easy-to-follow; CD includes over seventy demo tracks; covers: song form, transposition, considering the instrumentation, scales, keys, rhythm, chords, slash notation, and other basics, beaming, stemming, syncopation, intervals, and chord symbols; includes sample songs, common terms, and important tips for putting music on paper. SYSTEM SPECS: Book and Audio CD.

The MIDI Fakebook (www.pgmusic.com): Hundreds of favorite tunes; load songs into Band-in-a-Box and play or sing along; create own arrangements on computer; learn traditional jazz and improvisational skills with Soloist feature; 300 songs in a variety of styles; Traditional/Original Jazz and Pop, fifty songs; Classical, 200 songs; Bluegrass, fifty songs. SYSTEM SPECS: Macintosh; Windows.

The Music Registry recordXpress (www.recordXpress.net): Download music industry contact information to computer; updated daily; real-time contact management system. SYSTEM SPECS: Macintosh; Windows; download.

The Music Review Database Downloads (www.musreview.com/musicdata.html): Promote CD; databases available for download; Radio Station Data Base includes call letters, address, state, zip and telephone numbers, web site, email address, program director, format to all known U.S. stations on a national level; information available for immediate download; current and is updated on a daily basis; subscribers receive a free one year update anytime the data bases change; follow the emailed URL to the download site. SYSTEM SPECS: Macintosh; Windows.

The Professional Musician's Internet Guide (www.halleonard.com): Learn about opportunities for musicians to market and sell music on the Internet; addresses various technical issues musicians face preparing and uploading music to a Web site; details on how to get online companies to sell music; how to upload music using Mac and Windows computers; accompanying CD-ROM provides simple HTML templates and audio test files in various Web-ready formats to test Web audio files. SYSTEM SPECS: Book and Hybrid CD-ROM.

The Songwriter's Survival Kit (http://www.nancymoran.com/songwriters_survival_kit.htm): By Danny Arena, Sara Light, Fett, and Nancy Moran; over two hours of tips, ideas, and practical "prescriptions" to heal songwriting ailments, strengthen creative muscles, and lead to success. SYSTEM SPECS: Audio CD.

The Songwriter's Workshop: Harmony (www.berkleemusic.com): By Jimmy Kachulis; covers fundamental techniques behind current hit songs; exercises; colors of chords and keys; adapt and embellish chords and progressions; learn the most common chord progressions used in hit songs; practice songs with accompaniment on play-along CD. SYSTEM SPECS: Book and Audio CD.

The Songwriter's Workshop: Melody (www.berkleemusic.com): By Jimmy Kachulis; teaches fundamental techniques behind today's hit songs; easy-to-follow exercises; develop melodies that express

unique spirit of lyrics; choose notes, rhythm, and section structures to effectively express lyric meaning; write memorable choruses and verses that work together as a complete song; follow examples and tips from professional songwriters; practice songs with accompaniment on play-along CD. SYSTEM SPECS: Book and Audio CD.

The Successful Songwriter's Motivation and Meditation CD (www.songwritermotivation.com): By Nashville-based Penny Dionne and Troy McConnell; twelve tracks include: Intro; Create the Vision; Power of Thought; Power of Emotions; Faith; Persistence; Habits; Imagine and Visualize; The Law of Attraction; Affirmations; Meditation Intro; Meditation; over seventy-three minutes. SYSTEM SPECS: Audio CD.

You Can Write Hits, Volumes 1 and 2 (www.jasonblume.com): By hit songwriter Jason Blume, author of "Six Steps to Songwriting Success" and "This Business of Songwriting" and songs recorded by the Backstreet Boys, Britney Spears, Jesse McCartney, Collin Raye, and more; Writing Hit Melodies with Jason Blume, Volume 1: Topics: The Power of Repetition; Using Short Phrases; Repeating Rhythms; Magic Moments; Writing A Cappella; Prosody; Appropriate Range, Signature Licks; Varying Your Rhythms and Keeping Them Fresh; Rewriting; seven new exercises and more. Writing Hit Lyrics with Jason Blume, Volume 2: Topics: Writing for Yourself vs. Other Artists; Developing Great Titles and Concepts; Focusing Your Lyrics; Writing "Melody-Friendly" Lyrics; Finding a Market for Your Talent; Evoking Emotion with Action, Detail and Imagery; Writing Strong Opening Lines; Bridges; five new exercises and more. SYSTEM SPECS: Audio CD.

Booking—Touring—Gigging— Clubs and Venues Web Sites

American Bed & Breakfast Association www.abba.com Directory of B and Bs.

Amtrak www.amtrak.com Train schedules and reservations.

Atlanta Entertainment www.atlantaentertainment.com/ATLANTA/ By date, type, and venue; attractions; tickets; events.

Barnes & Noble www.barnesandnoble.com Chain store venue; list of stores nationwide; contact the community relations coordinator; book signings.

Billboard International Talent & Touring Guide www.billboarddirectories.com/bb/biz/directories/index.jsp Thousands of listings; artists; managers; venues; instrument rentals; booking agents; security services; staging and special effects; hotels; reference source; digital guides available online for download.

Borders Books and Music
www.borders.com/stores/index.html Chain store venue; list of stores by state; events.

ClubPlanet.com
www.clubplanet.com/default.asp?site=14 New York music clubs.

CNN Airport cnn.com/airport Flight information; travel news; weather.

CNN Weather cnn.com/WEATHER Four-day forecasts for towns in the United States and many cities around the world.

CNN: Travel Guide www.cnn.com/TRAVEL Travel journalism and multimedia.

Coffee House Tour www.coffeehousetour.com Comprehensive resource and tour guide.

Cowriter Connection www.cowriterconnection.com Sponsored by Barbara Cloyd; tool designed to help songwriters find collaborators; member fee.

Demo Singer www.demosinger.com Find a demo singer; hear audio samples; contact info.

EF Performing Arts Tours www.efperform.com Educational tours for teachers and students.

Expedia www.expedia.com Booking and issuing of airline tickets.

Foreign Languages for Travelers
www.travlang.com/languages Multilingual phrases.

Gig Masters www.gigmasters.com Nationwide database of talent; all genres and types of events; secure online bookings.

Gig Page www.gigpage.com Interactive; add, edit, or delete a gig; page is immediately updated online; choose colors; annual fee.

GigMaster www.shubb.com/gigm.html Mac software; lists, organizes; for every aspect of gigging.

Google Maps maps.google.com/ Find any location.

HouseConcerts.com www.houseconcerts.com Venues; singer-songwriters; hosting concerts; photos; press; links; featured artists.

LA Music Scene www.lamusicscene.com Bands; forum; articles; clubs; calendar; links.

Las Vegas Leisure Guide www.mesquite-nv.com/lvnight.htm Las Vegas nightlife.

Live Nation www.livenation.com/ Concerts and tickets.

London Clubs
www.londonnet.co.uk/ln/out/ent/clubs.html Regularly updated guide to London's best clubs from dance music to retro; club listings; venues; reviews; previews; free tickets.

Los Angeles Bars and Dance Clubs
weekendevents.com/LOSANGEL/lamusic.html Club guide.

Map Quest www.mapquest.com Road maps online; directions to and from anywhere.

Maps On Us www.mapsonus.com Interactive maps.

Musi-Cal www.musi-cal.com Concert calendar listing dates for musicians and venues; all genres.

National Weather Service www.nws.noaa.gov Weather disaster warnings.

On Stage Magazine onstagemag.com Live performance magazine for bands and musicians; interviews popular artists on the realities of touring and the business; new performance product information.

Peak Performance Tours
www.peakperformancetours.com Customized tour packages for touring student groups.

Pollstar www.pollstar.com Subscription includes weekly magazine plus five biannual directories; tour itineraries, music industry news, box office summaries, *Concert Pulse Charts* for album sales and radio airplay in nine formats; directories include *Talent Buyers & Clubs, Concert Venues, Concert Support Services, Agency Rosters, Record Company Rosters;* directories available separately.

Power Gig www.powergig.com Book gigs online.

Rand McNally www.randmcnally.com Maps; driving directions.

Roadie.net www.roadie.net True stories from roadies.

Roadsideamerica.com www.roadsideamerica.com Unusual tourist attractions.

Russ and Julie's House Concerts www.jrp-graphics.com/houseconcerts.html Chance to experience music in a warm and intimate environment; meet performers; social evening of friends and neighbors; upcoming and past concerts.

Sdam.com www.sdam.com San Diego music scene.

SetMaker
www.sweetwater.com/download/?download=setmaker Free software for gigging musicians.

South Florida NightLife
www.floridagoldcoast.com/nightlife/index.htm Nightclubs; bars; dancing; clubs; pubs; listings of nightclubs organized by region and format.

Southwest Airlines Internet Specials
www.southwest.com Weekly e-mail listings of special fares; online reservations.

The John F. Kennedy Center for the Performing Arts www.kennedy-center.org Information on the performing arts center.

The Musician's Guide to Touring and Promotion www.musicianmag.com or www.musiciansguide.com Lists agents, bands, clubs, labels, lawyers, press, fan magazines, radio stations, music stores, and more.

The Nashville Music Business Directory and Entertainment Guide
www.nashvilleconnection.com Complete directory of the Nashville music business; contacts.

The Rough Guide www.travel.roughguides.com Budget travel advice.

The Universal Currency Converter
www.xe.net/currency Count in foreign denominations.

The Weather Underground www.wunderground.com Weather updates.

This Is London www.thisislondon.co.uk Guide to the city; nightclubs.

Time Out www.timeout.com Travel guide.

TravelASSIST Magazine travelassist.com Online magazine; bed and breakfast directory.

Travelocity www.travelocity.com Full-service online travel agent.

United States Chamber of Commerce www.uschamber.com/default Information on United States cities and locals.

United States Gazetteer www.census.gov/cgi-bin/gazetteer Maps of the United States.

World Clubs Net www.worldclubs.net Guide to clubs around the world.

Worldwide Guide to Hostelling www.hostels.com Hostel database on the web.

Conferences and Showcases— Festivals and Fairs Web Sites

All American Music Festival www.bandfest.com Provides a great experience for students around the world; concert bands, marching bands, jazz bands, orchestras, choral groups, color guard, drill teams, dance groups, and other performance groups.

Appel Farm Festival www.appelfarm.org Held the first Saturday in June in Elmer, NJ.

Arts Midwest www.artsmidwest.org Individuals and families from America's heartland share in the art and culture of the region and the world.

Association for the Promotion of Campus Activities (APCA) www.apca.com Annual conference in early March; trade show; showcases performance types interested in the college market.

Association of Performing Arts Presenters (APAP) www.artspresenters.org Annual conference in mid-January in NYC; regional conferences include early Sept. Western Arts Alliance Association; mid-Sept. Midwest Arts Conference; late Sept. Southern Arts Exchange.

Atlantis Music Conference www.atlantismusic.com Held in Atlanta, GA.

Audio Engineering Society (AES) Conventions www.aes.org Held in various cities around the world; devoted to audio technology.

Augusta Heritage Center Music Camp www.augustaheritage.com Held in August in Elkins, WV; vocal week; festival.

Calgary Folk Music Festival www.calgaryfolkfest.com Held in July in Calgary, Alberta, Canada.

Canadian Music Week www.cmw.net Annual music conference in early March; trade show; all genres.

Chamber Music Northwest www.cmnw.org One of the leading festivals of chamber music in North America; festival musicians have international solo and ensemble careers.

City Stages www.citystages.org Held in Birmingham, AL in June.

CMA Music Festival (formerly Fan Fair) www.fanfair.com Held in Nashville in June.

CMJ Music Marathon & Music Fest www.cmj.com Fall conference and showcase in NYC clubs and at the Lincoln Center; all genres of music; college radio chart reports.

Colgate Country Showdown www.countryshowdown.com Judged country music artist showcases; annual local, state, regional, and national winners compete for cash and a recording contract.

Common Ground on the Hill www.commongroundonthehill.com Held in July at Western Maryland College, Westminster, MD; workshop; festival.

Consumer Electronics Show www.cesWeb.org January in Las Vegas.

Country Music Showcase International, Inc. www.cmshowcase.org Directory; event calendar.

Country Stampede Music Festival www.countrystampede.com Four days of country music in June in Kansas and Kentucky.

Dawson City Music Festival www.dcmf.com Held in July in Dawson City, Yukon, Canada.

Durango Songwriters Expo durangosong.com Annual event held in Colorado, Santa Barbara, and various other locations; blend of music business seminars and workshops, song listening/critique sessions, live songwriter showcases, and a live hit-writer concert to close the event.

Edmonton Folk Music Festival www.efmf.ab.ca Held in August in Edmonton, Alberta, Canada.

Falcon Ridge Folk Festival www.falconridgefolk.com Held in July in New York.

Festival Finder www.festivalfinder.com Comprehensive guide to music festivals in North America; search by genre, date, location, performer, or festival name.

Festivals.com www.festivals.com Information on music festivals.

GrassRoots Festival www.grassrootsfest.org Held in July; Cajun, Zydeco, stringband, African music; over forty bands on four stages over four days.

High Sierra Music Festival www.hsmusic.net Held in July in California.

Independent Music Conference www.indiemusicon.com Conference; trade show; showcases; all styles of commercial music; in Philadelphia in the fall.

International Association of African American Music
(IAAAM) www.IAAAM.com Presents series of
educational seminars; conference tour sponsorship;
concert production.

International Bluegrass Music Association (IBMA)
www.ibma.org Annual week-long trade show,
showcase, and festival in early October; showcase
new and established bluegrass acts; membership.

Kerrville Folk Festival www.kerrville-music.com
Annual folk event held in late May to early June
(through Memorial Day weekend) in Kerrville, TX;
songwriting; networking; performances.

Lamb's Retreat for Songwriters
www.springfed.org/Songwriters.html Held in
November and April in Michigan.

Lotus World Music and Arts Festival www.lotusfest.org
Series of events that offer opportunities to
experience, celebrate, and learn about the diversity
of the world's cultures; named after Lotus Dickey.

MerleFest www.merlefest.org Held in Wilkesboro, NC
in the spring.

MIAC (Music Industries Association of Canada)
www.miac.net Trade Show held in August.

NAMM (International Music Products Association)
www.namm.com Annual conferences; trade shows;
concerts; winter, Anaheim; summer, Nashville;
thousands of exhibitors and registrants;
international products and services displayed.

National Academy of Recording Arts & Sciences
(NARAS) www.grammy.com Check for future
showcase opportunities; sponsor showcases for
unsigned and independent label rock bands.

National Association for Campus Activities (NACA)
www.naca.org Annual conference, showcase, and
exhibit hall in mid-February; regional conferences
include the Southeast, South Central, Upper
Midwest, East Coast, Great Lakes, Pacific
Northwest, Heart of America, New England, Far
West, Illiana, Wisconsin; showcase music of all
genres, comedy, theater, and performance art.

National Association of Record Merchandisers (NARM)
www.narm.com Annual conference, trade show,
and showcase; presented by member labels.

New Orleans Jazz & Heritage Festival
www.nojazzfest.com Annual event held in late
April and early May in New Orleans.

Newport Folk Festival www.newportfolk.com Held in
August in Newport, RI.

North By North East (NXNE) www.nxne.com Annual
music conference held in June in Toronto.

Northeast Regional Folk Alliance Conference
www.nefolk.org Held in November in
Philadelphia, PA.

Ottawa Folk Festival www.ottawafolk.org Held in
August in Ottawa, Ontario, Canada.

Philadelphia Folk Festival www.folkfest.org or
www.pfs.org Held in August in Philadelphia, PA;
always before Labor Day.

Rocky Mountain Folks Festival www.bluegrass.com
Held in August in Lyons, CO; Planet Bluegrass.

Sierra Nevada World Music Festival www.snwmf.com
Three-day Reggae and World Music festival held
in Marysville, CA, in June.

Sisters Folk Festival www.sistersfolkfestival.com Held
in Sisters, Oregon.

South By Southwest Music and Media Conference
(SXSW) www.sxsw.com Annual conference and
showcase held in mid-March in Austin, TX;
international talent; all genres.

Strawberry Music Festival www.strawberrymusic.com
Held in May on Memorial Day weekend and in
September on Labor Day weekend in Sonora, CA.

Taxi Road Ralley www.taxi.com Free annual
convention held in Los Angeles; music industry
panels; song and demo critiques; networking.

Telluride Bluegrass Festival www.bluegrass.com Held
in June in Telluride, CO.

The Association for Recorded Sound Collections
(ARSC) www.arsc-audio.org Annual conferences
in different parts of the United States.

The Folk Alliance www.folkalliance.org Annual
international folk music and dance conference held
in mid-February; rotate regional locations;
Northwest and Midwest annual conferences;
showcase folk, acoustic, world, ethnic music, and
dance; membership required.

The International Association of Fairs and Expositions
www.fairsandexpos.com Directory listing county,
state, and international fairs and events in the
United States, Canada, and the world; associate
memberships for performers and agents.

The Rhythms of the World www.harbourfront.on.ca
Includes the JVC Jazz Festival; mid-June through
September in Toronto, Ontario, Canada.

The South Florida Folk Festival
www.southfloridafolkfest.com Annual event held
in January; folk festivities; songwriting.

The Swannanoa Gathering www.swangathering.org
Held in late July and early August in Ashville, NC;
Guitar and Folkweek.

Tin Pan South www.tinpansouth.com NSAI annual
week-long event held in April in Nashville; club
showcases of songwriters from everywhere.

Vancouver Folk Festival www.thefestival.bc.ca Annual
event held in July in Vancouver, BC, Canada.

Walnut Valley Festival www.wvfest.com Held in
September in Winfield, KS.

West Coast Songwriters
www.westcoastsongwriters.org/ Annual
Songwriters Conference held in September;

networking; seminars; workshops; song critiques; panel discussions; annual song contest.

Wildflower Arts & Music www.wildflowerfestival.com Held in May in Richardson, TX.

Winter Music Conference www.wintermusicconference.com Miami Beach, FL; network with industry professionals; DJs; radio forums; exhibition area; technology.

Addicted to Songwriting www.addicted-to-songwriting.com/ Resource for songwriting information, articles, news, tips, and more.

American Songwriter Magazine's Lyric Writing Competition www.americansongwriter.com Song lyric writing contest.

American Songwriter www.americansongwriter.com Magazine for songwriters; features; interviews; reviews; events listings; lyric writing competition.

Austin Songwriters Group Annual Song Contest www.austinsongwritersgroup.com Songwriting contest.

Baltimore Songwriters Association baltimoresongwriters.org/ Regional songwriters organization.

Barbara Cloyd www.barbaracloyd.com Hit songwriter, performer, and open mic host at Nashville's Bluebird Café; songwriting teacher, consultant, and workshop host; Ready for the Row and Play for Publishers Workshops; song critiques.

Beaird Music Group www.beairdmusicgroup.com Nashville-based demo studio; Larry Beaird, owner, guitarist; testimonials; online order form.

Belfast Nashville Songwriter's Contest www.belfastnashville.com Songwriting contest.

Beth Nielsen Chapman www.bethnielsenchapman.net Prolific Nashville-based songwriter; career; upcoming performances.

Billboard Song Contest http://billboardsongcontest.com/ Annual song contest; deadlines, rules; entry form; winners.

California Coast Music Camp musiccamp.org Held in July.

Camp Summer Songs www.summersongs.com Weeklong summer camps for songwriters in New York and California started by Penny Nichols; workshops; seminars; critiques; performances.

Central Oregon Songwriters Association cosa4u.tripod.com Regional organization.

Chord Coach www.chordcoach.com/songwriting/ Songwriting and chord tips; screen shots.

Chris Austin Songwriting Contest www.merlefest.org/songwritingcontest.htm Annual songwriting contest.

Christian Songwriting Competition www.christiansongwritingcompetition.com Songwriting contest.

Woody Guthrie Free Folk Festival www.woodyguthrie.com Annual event held in July in Midwest City, OK.

Songwriting—Songwriting Contests and Camps—Tip Sheets Web Sites

Chuck Cannon www.chuckcannon.com Nashville-based hit singer-songwriter; Nashville Underground; former president of NSAI.

Circle of Songs www.circleofsongs.com Songwriters; live music; workshops; radio.

CMT/NSAI Song Contest www.nashvillesongwriters.com Songwriting contest.

Colorado Music Association www.coloradomusic.org Home page.

Connecticut Songwriters Association www.ctsongs.com Home page.

Contemporary Christian Songwriting Contest www.christiansongwriting.com Songwriting contest.

Cooch Music's Amateur Songwriting Contest www.coochmusic.com Amateur songwriting contest; music publisher.

Dallas Songwriters Association www.dallassongwriters.org Regional songwriters organization; contest.

Denny Martin Music www.dennymartinmusic.com Nashville-based recording and production studio; song demos; recording projects.

Diane Warren www.realsongs.com Prolific songwriter of popular music.

District of Columbia Songwriters Association of Washington www.saw.org Home page.

Eccentric Software www.eccentricsoftware.com A Zillion Kajillion Rhymes and Cliches.

ElectricEarl.com www.electricearl.com/mlinks09.html Songwriting and publishing music links.

Exit In www.exit-in.com Nashville club; Billy Block's Western Beat; Roots Revival; writer's night.

FlightSafe Music QuickLaunch Song Contest www.flightsafemusic.com Songwriting contest.

Fort Worth Songwriter's Association www.fwsa.com Regional songwriters organization.

Frank Brown International Songwriters Festival www.fbisf.com Annual event in Perdido Key, Florida, in November; songwriters; schedule.

Georgia Music Industry Association, Inc. www.gmia.org Home page.

Guild of International Songwriters and Composers www.songwriters-guild.com Member services; copyright assistance; song critiques; demos.

Harlan Howard www.harlanhoward.com Legendary country music songwriter; hundreds of hits.

Harriet Schock www.harrietschock.com Hit singer-songwriter based in Los Angeles; correspondence courses; author of *Becoming Remarkable*.

Hitquarters www.hitquarters.com Source of information for songwriters, artists, musicians, and producers; online directory of record company A & Rs, managers, publishers, and producers.

How to License Your Music www.howtolicenseyourmusic.com Online newsletter with licensing advice.

I Write the Songs Love Song Competition www.iwritethesongs.com Songwriting contest.

Independent Songwriter www.independentsongwriter.com Online magazine for songwriters.

Inspirations for Songwriters groups.yahoo.com/group/DIFS/ E-newsletter dedicated to songwriters; helpful hints; links; written by Ande Rasmussen.

International Narrative Song Competition www.narrativemusic.ca/insc.html Songwriting contest.

International Songwriters Association (ISA) www.songwriter.co.uk Songs and songwriting; *The Songwriter* founded in 1967.

International Songwriting Competition www.songwritingcompetition.com Entry form; rules; judges.

Irene Jackson's Songwriting Workshop www.irenejackson.com Tips; links to relevant sites; post lyrics or discuss songwriting on the songwriting board; tools.

Jai Josefs www.jaijomusic.com Author of *Writing Music for Hit Songs; Secrets of Songwriting Success* CD-ROM; workshops; classes; song critiques.

Jason Blume www.jasonblume.com Tips for songwriters; workshops and seminars; critique service; author of *Six Steps to Songwriting Success, Inside Songwriting*, and *This Business of Songwriting;* instructional CDs.

Jeff Mallet's Songwriter Site www.lyricist.com Large collection of useful links and resources for songwriters; FAQ; updates.

John Braheny www.johnbraheny.com Los Angeles-based songwriting coach; author of *The Craft and Business of Songwriting;* musician; songwriter; performer; recording artist.

Just Plain Folks www.jpfolks.com or www.justplainfolks.org Created by Brian Austin Whitney; online group of over 51,000 songwriters, recording artists, music publishers, record labels, performing arts societies, educational institutions, recording studios and engineers, producers, legal professionals, publicists and journalists, publications, music manufacturers and retailers;

helpful resources including mentor program, chat, bulletin board, e-newsletter; tours.

Kim Copeland Productions www.kimcopelandproductions.com Nashville-based independent record and demo producer.

Kiss This Guy www.kissthisguy.com Archive of misheard lyrics.

LadySixString Annual Lyric Contest www.ladysixstring.com/lyricwritingcontest Songwriting contest; for females only.

Let's Sing It www.letssingit.com Thousands of lyrics to all styles of music.

Li'l Hanks Guide for Songwriters www.halsguide.com Resources for songwriters; newsgroups; links.

Licensemusic.com www.licensemusic.com Artist and band pages; upload songs, photos, and bio; pitch and licensing opportunities.

Live on the Net www.liveonthenet.com Venue in Nashville broadcasts nightly show called *Live from the Spoke in Nashville;* over the Internet nightly from 8-9 PM CST.

Lyric Crawler www.lyriccrawler.com Lyrics search engine; more than 130,000 songs.

Lyric Find www.lyricfind.com Over 11,000 lyrics.

Lyricalline Songwriting Resource Forum www.lyricalline.com/theforum/index Resources for songwriters; free e-newsletter; forum; radio show; Q&A; interviews; articles; services.

LyricPro www.lyricpro.com Software for songwriters; archive song titles and ideas; edit lyrics with a rhyming dictionary; track publishers and submissions; create charts; Windows.

Lyrics Review www.lyricsreview.com Submit lyrics to be reviewed.

Lyrics World www.lyricsworld.com Index; links; songs found in *Top 40 Hits of 1930-1999, #1 Songs of 1930-1999, Top Singles by Decade*, and *Artist Collections*.

Lyrics www.lyrics.com Words to songs.

Marc-Alan Barnette www.marcalanbarnette.com Nashville-based singer-songwriter; Nashville Tours; workshops and seminars; book *Freshman Year in Nashville*; CDs.

MasterWriter www.masterwriter.com Software program for songwriters; suite of songwriting tools; product info; reviews; free trial.

Memphis Songwriters' Association www.memphissongwriters.org Regional songwriters organization.

Merriam-Webster Dictionary www.m-w.com/home.htm Online dictionary.

Metro Detroit Songwriting Contest www.detroitsongs.com Songwriting contest.

Mid-Atlantic Song Contest www.sonicbids.com/midatlanticsong Songwriting contest.

Minnesota Association of Songwriters www.mnsongwriters.org Regional songwriters organization.

Muse's Muse www.musesmuse.com Founded by Jodi Krangle; large archive of songwriting resources, services, tips, and tools; chat; articles; free monthly e-newsletter; reviews; links.

Music Row www.musicrow.com Information for songwriters; industry news and articles; *Row Fax* tip sheet subscriptions; current listings.

Music Theory for Songwriters members.aol.com/chordmaps Questions about chords; music theory.

My Hit Online www.myhitonline.com Pitch opportunities for songwriters; upload songs, tracks, and bio; membership fee.

Nancy Moran www.nancymoran.com Coaching and consulting; workshops; song critiques; co-author of *The Songwriter's Survival Kit.*

NashCamp Songwriting School www.nashcamp.com Songwriter summer camp in Nashville with pro-writers and music industry professionals; week long session of songwriting workshops.

Nashville Convention and Visitors Bureau www.nashvillecvb.com Meeting professionals.

Nashville Muse www.nashvillemuse.com Weekly Nashville songwriting and music industry events listings; e-newsletter by Doak Turner.

Nashville Publishers Network www.songpublishers.com Dedicated to networking in the Nashville songwriting community.

Nashville Scene www.nashvillescene.com Entertainment newspaper; back issues; classifieds.

Nashville Songwriters Association International (NSAI) www.nashvillesongwriters.com Nonprofit service organization for songwriters of all levels and genres; annual Spring Symposium; Fall Songposium; Song Camps; weekly and regional workshops; free song critique service for members; insurance plans; Songwriter Achievement Awards.

Nashville Songwriters Foundation www.nashvillesongwritersfoundation.com Non-profit dedicated to honoring and preserving the songwriting legacy of the Nashville Songwriters Hall of Fame; principal purposes are to educate, archive, and celebrate songwriting that is uniquely associated with the Nashville Music Community.

NashvilleSongService.com www.nashvillesongservice.com Work with lyric writers to help them accomplish their goals.

New Music Nashville www.newmusicnashville.com Radio show; audience and affiliate resources.

New on the Charts www.notc.com By subscription; Publisher Leads and Soundtrack Leads tip sheets; latest signings; charts in all genres; cross-referenced contact info on artists, producers,

managers, record labels, and booking agents of hits; Video Spotlight; International Deals.

North Carolina Songwriters Co-Op Song Contest www.ncsongwriters.org Songwriting contest.

OneLook Dictionaries www.onelook.com Definitions searched by keyword.

Open Directory dmoz.org/Arts/Music/Songwriting/ Songwriting links.

Pacific Songwriting Competition www.pacificsongwritingcompetition.com Songwriting contest.

Pamela Phillips-Oland www.pamoland.com Hit songwriter; lyricist; lyric samples; listen to songs; collaboration discussion group; author of *The Art of Writing Great Lyrics* and *The Art of Writing Love Songs;* articles.

Parade of Stars www.paradeofstars.com Songwriter's tip sheet since 1972; by subscription; authentic listings.

Pat and Pete Luboff www.writesongs.com Songwriting coaches; authors of *101 Songwriting Wrongs and How to Right Them* and *12 Steps to Building Better Songs;* song consultations; coached songwriting; instruction; workshops.

Pat Pattison www.patpattison.com Lyric writing instructor; author of *Songwriting: Essential Guide to Rhyming, Songwriting: Essential Guide to Lyric Form and Structure,* and *Writing Better Lyrics;* lyric tips and links.

Performing Songwriter www.performingsongwriter.com Magazine; current issue; resource center; festivals; competitions; contact information; DIY reviews.

Pitch This Music www.pitchthismusic.com Nashville-based country music tip sheet; subscriptions.

Positive Pop Song Contest www.positivepopsongcontest.com Songwriting contest.

PublishSongs.com www.publishsongs.com Pitch songs; create an account; add songs; songwriter profile; FAQ; traffic stats.

Pump Audio www.pumpaudio.com Independent labels and artists can submit music to license for film, TV, and advertising.

Rhymer www.rhymer.com WriteExpress Online Rhyming Dictionary; word rhyme; end rhymes; last syllable rhymes; double rhymes; and more.

Rhymezone.com www.rhymezone.com Online rhyming dictionary; find phrases.

Roget's Thesaurus thesaurus.reference.com Online version of the thesaurus.

RowFax (www.rowfax.com): Country music industry tip sheet based in Nashville; online subscription.

Ryman Auditorium www.ryman.com Nashville venue; original home of *The Grand Ol' Opry.*

San Diego NSAI Regional Workshop
www.pianopress.com/sandiegonsaiworkshop.html
Regional workshop focusing on the craft and
business of songwriting; monthly meetings; special
events with pro-writers and industry guests; group
song critiques; quarterly showcase; networking.

Select Tracks www.selecttracks.com Music licensing
site; composers; clients; projects; Bug Music.

Seth Jackson's Songwriting and Music Business Info
www.sethjackson.net/ Web site for songwriters;
Los Angeles NSAI regional workshop; links.

Software for Songwriters www.musicbusinessstore.com
Music contracts; tour management.

Song of the Year www.songoftheyear.com/ Song
contest; supporter of VH-1 Save the Music;
monthly and annual winners; all genres.

Song Planet www.songplanet.com Creation;
collaboration; community.

Song Rights www.songrights.com Song rights; legal
aspects of songwriting; topics; summary; reviews;
primer on legal issues facing songwriters.

Songbook.net www.songbook.net Information and
resources for songwriters; links.

SongCatalog.com www.songcatalog.com Designed to
connect publishers, labels, independent artists,
songwriters, and producers with companies looking
to license music for commercial use; on and offline
services; innovative services designed to offer a
convenient way to access music; clients include ad
agencies, film and TV music supervisors, record
labels, music publishers, indie artists, and
producers; songwriter/composer/publisher receives
100% of licensing fee from client; membership fee.

SongCritic.com www.songcritic.com Register; listen
and review song lyrics; shop; chat; advertise; FAQ.

SongDoor www.songdoor.com/ International
songwriting competition; prizes; sponsors; judges.

Songfile.com www.songfile.com Harry Fox Agency
song licensing; online form.

SongLink International www.songlink.com Tip sheet
publication; international listings for all types of
music and artists; listings include the artist, label,
style of music needed, and contact information.

Songprize.com International Songwriting Competition
www.songprize.com Songwriting contest.

SongQuarters (www.songquarters.com): Tip sheet for
music industry song pitches; subscriptions.

SongRamp.com www.songramp.com New music
community focused on the creative aspects of
songwriting; artist pages; open mic; Artist of the
Month; songs and CDs for sale.

SongRepair.com www.songrepair.com Songwriter and
song development service; song demos; song
reviews; Nashville happenings.

Songs Alive www.songsalive.org How to get started in
the music business; nonprofit dedicated to the

nurturing, support, and promotion of songwriters
and composers worldwide; founded by Gilli Moon.

Songs for Sale www.songsforsale.co.uk Online music
publisher.

Songs Inspired by Literature Contest
www.artistsforliteracy.org Songwriting contest.

Songs Wanted www.songswanted.com Germany's
leading song casting publication for professional
songwriters and music publishers.

Songscope.com www.songscope.com Online song
shopping catalog; artist development.

SongU.com www.songu.com Songwriting courses
online; created by Danny Arena and Sara Light;
provides online coaching, co-writing, and pitching
opportunities; over fifty multi-level courses
developed by award-winning songwriters; ten-day
free trial; song evaluations; Yearbook Page.

Songwriter Universe www.songwriteruniverse.com
Founded by Dale Kawashima; information;
resources; links; services for songwriters; contests.

Songwriters Directory www.songwritersdirectory.com
Comprehensive reference tool and songwriter
database; opportunities for recording artists to find
songs, producers to find new music for movies and
television, and record labels to find new artists.

Songwriters Resource at Writers Write
www.writerswrite.com/songwriting Information
for songwriters.

Songwriting Consultants, Ltd. www.songmd.com
Molly-Ann Leikin; songwriting consultant.

Songwriting Software www.songwriting-software.com
Songwriting items, programs, and services
designed to enhance songwriting development.

Steve Seskin www.steveseskin.com Hit songwriter;
seven #1 hit songs; performer; songwriting teacher;
CDs; gigs; online press kit.

TAXI www.taxi.com Independent A&R Vehicle;
connects artists, bands, and songwriters with major
record labels, publishers, and film and TV music
supervisors; biweekly listings in all genres; song
critiques; related links; free TAXI Road Rally in
LA in November; Michael Laskow, founder.

Texas Songwriters' Cruise Contest
www.texassongwriterscruise.com Songwriting
contest; workshops; annual event.

The Bluebird Café www.bluebirdcafe.com Famous
Nashville venue for songwriters; writer's nights;
open mic; guest performers.

The Boston Songwriters Workshop
www.bostonsongwriters.org Regional organization.

The Chicago Songwriters Collective
www.chicagosongwriters.com Regional
songwriters organization.

The Essential Secrets of Songwriting
www.secretsofsongwriting.com/ Advice for
songwriters by Gary Ewer.

The Great American Song Contest
www.GreatAmericanSong.com Entry form; rules.

The Guild of International Songwriters & Composers
www.songwriters-guild.co.uk/ International songwriting organization based in England.

The John Lennon Songwriting Contest www.jlsc.com
Check for updates on the current year's contest; winners; prizes; print contest application.

The L.A. Songwriters Network www.SongNet.org
Network; showcase; links; e-mail group.

The Lyrics Library tinpan.fortunecity.com/blondie/313
Links to many different lyric Web sites.

The Music Row Show
www.themusicrowshow.com/TheMusicRowShow.
com/index.html Weekly radio show from Nashville for songwriters; guests; podcasts.

The Original Songwriters Showcase
www.showcaselondon.co.uk London showcase.

The Songwriters Association of Washington
www.saw.org Regional songwriters organization.

The Songwriters Connection
www.songwritersconnection.com Inspirational and useful resource for songwriters; free online newsletter and weekly e-tips.

The Songwriters Guild of America (SGA)
www.songwritersguild.com Membership; SGA songwriter's contract; educational workshops; regional offices and events; contests.

The Songwriter's Tip Jar www.songwriterstipjar.com
Free e-newsletter; resources; links; forum.

The USA Songwriting Competition
www.songwriting.net Annual competition; fifteen categories, including lyrics only; see Web site for updates, contest rules, prizes, contest winners.

Tunesmith.net www.tunesmith.net Song critique forum; seminar info; latest news; Radio Tunesmith.

UK Songwriting Contest
www.songwritingcontest.co.uk/ Entry form; prizes.

Ultimate Songwriting
www.ultimatesongwriting.com/index.html Resources for songwriters; software; books; tips.

Unisong International Songwriting Contest
www.unisong.com Created by songwriters, for songwriters; to unite a world community bonded by the creation of music; links; annual and monthly songwriting contests; winners; prizes.

Virginia Organization of Composers and Lyricists
www.vocalsongwriter.org/index.php Songwriter organization.

Washington Area Music Association
www.wamadc.com Regional organization.

Webster's Dictionary www.m-w.com/dictionary.htm
Look up words online.

West Coast Songwriters Association
www.westcoastsongwriters.org/ Annual conference; networking and performance opportunities; workshops; songwriting contest.

Yahoo Directory: Songwriting
dir.yahoo.com/Entertainment/Music/Composition/
Songwriting/ Links to songwriting Web sites.

Yahoo Groups: Songwriting
dir.groups.yahoo.com/dir/Music/Songwriting?show
_groups=1 Join a songwriting group.

Your First Cut www.yourfirstcut.com Questionnaire; sample book chapters from *Your First Cut—A Step-by-Step Guide to Getting There* by Jerry Vandiver and Gracie Hollombe; forum; workshops; links; newsletter.

14
Composition—Scoring—Notation—Film, TV and Video Game Music Software, Instructional Media and Web Sites

"abc" Musical Notation Language (www.walshaw.plus.com/abc/software.html): Language designed to notate tunes in plain text format; designed primarily for folk and traditional tunes of Western European origin such as English, Irish, and Scottish which can be written on one stave in standard classical notation; introduced at the end of 1991; many software tools can read "abc" notation and either process it into staff notation or play it through the speakers of a computer; freeware and shareware programs available to read and edit. SYSTEM SPECS: Macintosh; Windows.

AudioScore Pro (www.neuratron.com): Create scores using only a musical performance via a microphone or MIDI keyboard; manually create scores by manipulating a simple, automatically generated performance without the need for any musical knowledge; for musicians of all levels; performance training; allows user to build up a full score using MIDI instruments; can determine intended rhythm and create accurate and musical score notation; play directly into a notation editor or sequencer without the need for a MIDI keyboard; choose the Neuratron AudioScore MIDI recording device and hit Record; MIDI file to score converter. SYSTEM SPECS: Windows.

Capella Software (www.capella-software.com): Capella music notation program; Capella Reader can display, playback, and print Capella files; Capella-Scan can scan sheet music with text and then edit with Capella; Capella-PlayAlong can create sing-along and play-along CDs from over 7500 free scores; digital score library has 7500 Capella scores for free usage; Tonica creates automatic four-part compositions in the styles of J.S.Bach and others and does automatic harmonizing; Tonica Plus creates automatic four-part composition in the styles of J.S.Bach and others plus

can create own styles and do automatic harmonizing and automatic canon composition. SYSTEM SPECS: Windows.

CD Sheet Music (www.cdsheetmusic.com): Printable scans of sheet music on CD-ROM for piano, vocal, opera, choral, organ, strings, woodwinds, guitar, full scores.; all have a Table of Contents; cannot be used with other notation software; from standard available public domain editions. SYSTEM SPECS: Hybrid CD-ROM.

CD Sheet Music—Pop and Classical (www.halleonard.com): Each popular song is in piano/vocal/guitar arrangements; view and print music; hear a MIDI playback; transpose to different keys; masterworks series by composers of classical music are from out-of-copyright standard editions; disks include biographical and analytical information; economical. SYSTEM SPECS: Hybrid CD-ROM.

CD Sheet Music—Manuscript Paper (www.halleonard.com): Variety of staff paper for composing and arranging; print staff paper right from Mac or PC; single-line paper; guitar and bass tablature paper; grand staff paper; guitar or keyboard with vocal paper; viewable with Adobe Acrobat Reader on screen and printable; includes music basics; music notation guide; guitar, bass, and drum notation legends; instrument ranges, standard articulations, and transpositions for jazz bands and orchestras and more; installation instructions. SYSTEM SPECS: Hybrid CD-ROM.

Composer Notes (www.ecsmedia.com): Includes Teacher's Guide; explains instrumentation and composition to student composers using both traditional and electronic instruments; allows users to play over 500 recordings from orchestral, jazz, and contemporary musicians in a variety of formats: from their own computer, with included MIDI files using a sequencer, or from a CD player with the included audio CD; topics covered include arranging, texture, tempo and meter, musical form and structure, melody, motifs, phrases, MIDI, ensemble writing, and writing for strings, woodwinds, brass, and rhythm instruments; teachers also can use the program to generate related worksheets for distribution in the classroom. SYSTEM SPECS: Hybrid CD-ROM.

Composing Digital Music for Dummies (www.dummies.com): Digital music basics; how to work with the necessary hardware and software; templates on CD-ROM; save in different formats; add instruments to score; set tempos and keys; create chord symbols and show fretboards; add lyrics to tune; write and arrange digital music; determine what equipment is needed; create ringtones and MP3s; compose with a MIDI controller or a mouse; work with notation software; use keyboard shortcuts; publish creations on the Internet; build tune from scratch; extract parts from score for each instrument; CD-ROM includes a demo of Sibelius 5 and audio files for all music examples in the book. SYSTEM SPECS: Book and Hybrid CD-ROM.

Copyist (www.sionsoft.com): Music notation software; treats notes, staves, clefs and other musical characters as graphical elements; can put musical objects on page regardless of musical rules; can create small excerpts to be included in work that is predominantly text, as well as very complex scores which are difficult to create using software which must follow musical rules; works with existing QuickScore files; fine-tune any score created in QuickScore Elite or QuickScore Elite Level II by saving your work as a Copyist file and loading it into Copyist; can save scores as .BMP, TIFF, .EMF or .EPS files so can incorporate them into Microsoft Word, Corel WordPerfect, Corel Draw, Adobe Illustrator, Adobe PageMaker and many other types of documents. SYSTEM SPECS: Windows.

Django Early Music Software (http://josquin.musickshandmade.com/pub/pages/django): Tab editor and composer for lutes, guitar, cittern, bandora, mandolin, gamba, and other plucked instruments, such as banjo, ukulele, theorbo, mandora, dulcimer, etc. SYSTEM SPECS: Windows.

eGigVision (www.egigvision.com): Sheet music management software; store sheet music to a database; view scores on LCD, laptop, or tablet PC; import music from notation software programs; create playlists; organize songs. SYSTEM SPECS: Windows.

Encore (www.gvox.com): Complete scoring features, part extraction, and MIDI playback; play directly into Encore or transcribe MIDI files; accurate notation and printouts; extract parts, transpose for different instruments, and play music as originally conceived; graphically displays and plays back dynamic marks, repeats, multiple endings, pedal marks, or any MIDI

controller; flexible page layout; guitar tablature; fine-tune with a move of the mouse; on-screen palettes to enter dozens of marks and symbols; add lyrics and text; page layout control; TrueType® and PostScript® support; polyphonic part voicing; editable expressions palettes; transcribe music into guitar tablature with correct fingering and guitar fret diagrams; create and publish everything from simple lead sheets to symphonies. SYSTEM SPECS: Macintosh; Windows.

Finale (www.finalemusic.com): Compose, arrange, notate, and print engraver-quality sheet music; note entry options include from MIDI to mouse, from scanning to Finale's MicNotator; create SmartMusic accompaniments; support for linked parts, repeats, and more; Exercise Wizard, Studio View to teach composition, educator templates, and more; includes more than 300 world-class instrument sounds from the makers of Garritan Personal Orchestra, ranging from orchestral instruments to choirs, jazz brass to marching percussion, handbells, world instruments, and more; Record/Import Audio with a real vocal or instrumental track; record or import a mono or stereo audio file to enhance playback; time-saving tools include linked parts, multiple page editing, ScoreMerger, and more; creation, entry, moving, and editing of dynamics, tempo indications, and other text and markings has been streamlined; multiple page editing; can simultaneously view and edit as many pages as user chooses to view on monitor; includes more than 100 instrument sounds from Tapspace Virtual Drumline marching and concert percussion software instrument; Garritan Aria Player is included; compatible with all VST/AU instruments; specify which VST/AU plug-ins load, eliminating conflicts and assisting troubleshooting; checks plug-ins for compatibility before loading; tracks which plug-ins were previously checked; triplet recognition in SmartScore Lite Scanning; improvements to engraver slurs; Human Playback enhancements; FinaleScript and updates to MusicXML; ASIO support for Windows users provides more accurate playback, reduced latency, and increased compatibility with a wider variety of sound cards. SYSTEM SPECS: Macintosh; Windows.

Finale Allegro (www.finalemusic.com): For educators, performing musicians, composers, arrangers, worship directors, and students; Launch Window; Setup Wizard and pre-designed templates; QuickStart Videos; enter notes with mouse, computer keyboard, and/or MIDI keyboard (including sustain pedal) in step- or real-time; enter notes by playing brass or woodwind instrument into a mic with MicNotator; scan sheet music with SmartScore Lite (included) and import or export MIDI files; runs natively on both Intel- and PowerPC-based Macs as well as Windows computers; add two- and three-voice auto-harmonization from Band-in-a-Box Auto Harmonizing; add Drum Grooves;

Exercise Wizard creates warm-ups for the band, orchestra, or choir; Setup Wizard includes diverse options, including Orff instruments and marching percussion; create quizzes and tests that students can open, edit, print, and play with the free, downloadable Finale NotePad; play back with integrated software sounds (including Row-Loff marching percussion) or via external MIDI devices; Human Playback adds expression, phrasing, swing, and dynamics automatically; mixer offers control of volume, panning, patch, and reverb as well as the choice of mute, solo, or record; MIDI tool allows user to edit MIDI data; transpose, edit page layout, and add chord symbols, guitar fretboards, guitar tablature, lyrics, slash, or rhythmic notation; print score or parts; Allegro files can be opened, edited, printed, and played by others using Finale NotePad, a free download, Finale SongWriter, Finale PrintMusic, and Finale; save as audio file, including MP3, to create CDs; export TIF graphics files to add music to word processing documents. SYSTEM SPECS: Macintosh; Windows.

Finale Notepad (www.finalemusic.com): Compatible with Windows XP and Vista and runs natively on both Intel and PowerPC based Macintosh computers; import and export MIDI Files; open and save Format 1 MIDI files; MIDI Input and Output; notes can be entered in step time using MIDI keyboard or other MIDI controller; compositions can be played back through external MIDI devices; Selection Tool offers regional selection, stack selection, and partial measure selection; measures can be selected using the computer keyboard; Streamlined User Interface simplifies how user will cut/copy/paste/insert/delete music; redesigned menus, a consolidated interface with fewer tools, and the ability to change pages using the computer keyboard's Page Up/Page Down button; Setup Wizard allows users to initially specify the number of measures in their piece and provides improved page layout automatically; Documentation System provides information quickly and easily; free download. SYSTEM SPECS: Macintosh; Windows.

Finale PrintMusic! (www.finalemusic.com): For songwriters, students, teachers, church musicians, and band leaders; Setup Wizard configures key and time signatures, transpositions, pickup measures, and more; engraved or handwritten look; select a document style to personalize appearance of music; easy entry; play MIDI keyboard with a metronome and watch music appear on screen in real time; play a brass or woodwind instrument into a microphone using MicNotator; click notes into place with a mouse; enter notes in step-time from computer or MIDI keyboard; scan music with SmartScore Lite 3.3 (included); advanced playback features; free Software Synthesizer with 128 instrument sounds and marching percussion sounds from Row-Loff; Human Playback gives music nuance, as if performed by live musicians; Band-in-a-Box Auto-Harmonizing adds harmonies to melodies; save music as an audio file to burn CDs or save on an iPod; new mixer fine-tunes playback; geared towards educators, musicians, composers, and others who don't need the advanced engraving capabilities of Finale 2008 or the other advanced features in Allegro. SYSTEM SPECS: Macintosh; Windows.

FreeHand Systems MusicPad Pro (www.freehandsystems.com): Digital music notebook; music management system; store entire music library; download over 98,000 digital music scores already formatted from www.freehandmusic.com; scan music library into a computer and convert; zoom in and zoom out while writing; add or erase rehearsal marks and notations; easy-to-read personal on screen color notes; extensive library of notation symbols; text annotation via a virtual keyboard; half-page turn option for look-ahead viewing in portrait mode; two-page display in landscape mode; remote easy page turning; audio player for MIDI; Solero viewer; file browser and search. SYSTEM SPECS: Macintosh; Windows.

Goodfeel Braille Music Translator (www.dancingdots.com): Quickly transcribe to braille from Finale, Sibelius, and other popular music notation software used by band, orchestra, and choir directors; synchronized scrolling of print and braille notation for current musical measure; ships with Lime 8 which simplifies entering of text annotations and has a new MusicXML import/export feature; blind musicians can now scan, read, and write musical scores with the Lime notation editor that ships with Goodfeel via the Lime Aloud JAWS-based access features; Lime Aloud is a new way for the blind to read and write music; JAWS 5.1 through 7.x required; blind musicians can easily create print and equivalent braille transcriptions for collaboration with sighted or blind teachers, colleagues, or students; optional integration with the Duxbury (literary) Braille Translator to facilitate transcription of theory or method books that have large blocks of expository text. SYSTEM SPECS: Windows.

GuitarMaster (www.guitarmaster.co.uk/): Transcription and notation aid for the electric guitarist; produces guitar tablature and MIDI files directly from the audio signal generated by the instrument; plug in and play; enter notes and chords into Cubase or Sibelius without using a keyboard - this software lets the user do so by playing the electric guitar; export the MIDI file it produces to any standard notation package. SYSTEM SPECS: Windows.

IntelliScore (www.intelliscore.net): Convert WAV to MIDI, MP3 to MIDI, CD to MIDI; compose MIDI music by singing or playing any instrument; helps remove vocals for karaoke singing; record MIDI directly into sequencer software using voice or any acoustic instrument; generate cell phone ringtones in conjunction with Mobile Music or other ringtone conversion program; view notation from music; see chord names and key; change individual notes, swap instruments, transpose, etc.; polyphonic: WAVE, MP3, CD, and live music can contain several notes at a time. SYSTEM SPECS: Windows.

Lime (www.cerlsoundgroup.org): Instructions for familiarizing user with Lime from the web site: "Run Lime and open pieces in Examples folder; print out User's Manual; step-by-step example; use Record option with MIDI keyboard; experiment with Parts and Voices option; create and delete parts, reorder them, notate two voices together on one staff, stop and start printing voices at various points in piece, and make a percussion staff; Group Select notes and change their articulation or accidentals; add key or clef changes in several places at once with Group Select; use This Staff Only in the Key and Clef dialogs; add text and line annotations; Leave Space annotation control; type a MIDI control change, and try it out using the Hear option; copy a text annotation, then Group Select notes and Paste to all the notes at once; see how Horizontal Lock and Vertical Lock affect Multiple Paste; use Duplicate at Each System to label staves; open two Lime pieces at once; copy and paste between them; start building up a single page Lime piece with useful stuff to copy to other pieces; enter all the notes for a score, then use the Notation Contexts option to create parts; change a note in a part notation context, then look at the updated score; see how Only in Score and All Notation Contexts affect the appearance of annotations in a score and its parts; experiment with Duplicate Part Label; experiment with piano tablature; enter a piano score in standard notation, then use the Parts and Voices option to convert it to piano tablature notation; create a guitar piece that has notes in standard notation on one staff, and guitar tablature on another; copy and paste between the staves; make any necessary corrections to Lime's automatic fingering; experiment with Parameters; try the microtonal accidentals in the Special Accidentals option; define some new accidentals using Parameters; copy music excerpts from Lime to Microsoft Word; use Copy Rectangle in Lime, then Paste Special in Word; music can be resized in Word, but not edited; scan sheet music using SharpEye Music Reader or Musitek SmartScore, then use Lime's Import NIFF to import the scanned music." SYSTEM SPECS: Macintosh; Windows.

MagicScore Maestro Music Editor (www.dgalaxy.net/products.php#MagicScore): Musical editor; music notation software allows creating compositions of any complexity, including polyphonic; virtual piano, guitar tones, partita entry from a MIDI-device, ability to work with chords, extensive opportunities for editing and fine adjustment of sound of composition; program will compute the playback of effects; partita

editing; adjust the sound of each note and of the entire composition; prepare for concerts and performances. SYSTEM SPECS: Windows.

MagicScore Music Editor (www.dgalaxy.net/products.php#MagicScore): Interface for a set of musical score; data input by means of the virtual keyboard, external MIDI devices and set of musical symbols; automatic and manual formatting of the musical score; reproduction and printing of the musical score; saving in MIDI format; reading from format MIDI; support of editing operations, copying, and removal of a set of the allocated elements of the musical score; wide choice of elements of registration; adjustment of force of impact of each note at sound reproduction; extended opportunities of navigation. SYSTEM SPECS: Windows.

Manuscript Maker (www.notationware.com): Create manuscript paper to own specifications; setup wizard; select time and key signatures; number of staves and measures, and more; enter titles, text, staff names, copyright dates; chose measure numbering, measures per system, and systems per page. SYSTEM SPECS: Hybrid CD-ROM.

Music Notation: Preparing Scores and Parts (www.berkleepress.com): Notation textbook; learn the skills necessary for improving music's legibility and representation; score and part preparation based on contemporary publishing industry practice; resource for both written and software notation. SYSTEM SPECS: Book and Audio CD.

MusicTime Deluxe (www.gvox.com): Produce musical scores; intuitive user interface; notate up to sixteen staves with up to eight instruments per staff; prints sheet music; enter music with mouse or from computer keyboard; record performance live using a MIDI keyboard for instant display of notation; add guitar chord diagrams and chord names to scores and lead sheets; transpose and hear music in any key; lyric entry formats words with music for up to eight lines; cross-staff beaming extends beams across staves; automatic import/export of any standard MIDI file or Master Tracks Pro; displays and prints any item in score; place notes and rests anywhere on scores by clicking mouse; enter text anywhere on a page in any font, size, and style; enter song lyrics that line up with the notes; change the key, clef, and time signature anywhere in score; chord symbols transpose automatically when transpose music; place notation symbols by selecting from symbol palettes; change any element: notes, accidentals, markings, lyrics, text, etc.; scores live playing with beaming; audition and select different MIDI instruments for each staff; set the playback levels of each staff with on-screen volume controls; view the music as it plays to both see and hear composition; piano keyboard window keys light up in color as music plays; prints standard MIDI files as finished sheet music; print the entire score or individual pages. SYSTEM SPECS: Macintosh; Windows.

Musicator (www.musicator.net/): Program to be used as both a notation tool and a sequencer tool; for creating a printed arrangement for a musical ensemble; music production tool; high quality internal sampler; complete musical workstation for notation, sequencing, and audio recording. SYSTEM SPECS: Windows.

MusicEase (www.musicease.com): Music notation software; full-featured, intelligent music notation editor; produces publication quality, printed music; automatically generates accompaniments consisting of any number of general MIDI instruments including drums; play, print, or save as a MIDI file; includes support for scanned music; works much like a word processing program; any scalable Windows fonts/sizes can be used for titles, lyrics, dynamics, chords, etc.; all Windows printers are supported; reformat pieces; experiment with different looks; import scanned music and then transpose and edit it; automatically convert from standard notation to tablature and vice/versa; add figured bass; play using any General MIDI instruments; create Southern shape note songs, guitar tablature pieces, hymns, orchestral pieces, pop, rock, and folk songs; import any of thousands of SongWright, abc, and MIDI files from the Internet and print the corresponding sheet music. SYSTEM SPECS: Windows.

MusicWrite Series (www.turtlebeach.com): Starter Kit; Songwriter; Maestro; compose, play, edit, and print music on PC; create and print sheet music; connect MIDI keyboard to PC, play the keys, and see the music transcribed on the screen; use mouse to edit compositions with drag-and-drop ease; copy, paste, insert notes, chords and ties, add lyrics and copyright info to sheet music; see the notes on PC screen; hear it played on MIDI synthesizer or PC soundcard; print sheet music for others to play; listen to compositions played by a MIDI Orchestra; compose with an orchestra of different instrument sounds; edit every nuance; print a score that represents exactly how song will sound when played by other musicians; printed music makes it easier to compose and rehearse with sheet music with each part written out; printout options include the whole score or just the drum notation and the second harmony. SYSTEM SPECS: Windows.

Myriad Software (www.myriad-online.com): Programs include: *Harmony Assistant, Melody Assistant, Melody Player, Myriad Music Plug-In;* music software for computer-assisted tune writing and composition; multilingual programs: English, French, German, Dutch, Spanish, Italian, Portuguese, and Japanese. SYSTEM SPECS: Macintosh; Windows.

Nightingale (www.ngale.com/index_02a.html): Produces professional quality output; can play and record with accurate timing using MIDI instruments; creates scores quickly; cut and paste, transpose, drag any-

thing in score; add and delete parts and extract them with one click. SYSTEM SPECS: Macintosh.

Notation Composer Software (www.notation.com/midinotate.htm): Arrange and compose music; provides all of the features of Musician; arrange and prepare music for practice, or choir or instrumental group; compose music from scratch; enter notes using mouse, computer keyboard, or by recording live from a MIDI instrument; places the music symbols in the score automatically; edit both the notation and MIDI playback sound of music scores. SYSTEM SPECS: Windows.

Notation Musician Software (www.notation.com/midinotate.htm): See, hear and print music; find and download music MIDI files from the Internet; automatically convert MIDI files to high quality sheet music; watch the notes on the screen as they play; sing or play instrument along with the band; listen to and watch songs one after another in a playlist; add lyrics and annotate the score with accent marks, dynamic marks, slurs, etc.; print the music; print parts for members of vocal or instrumental group. SYSTEM SPECS: Windows.

Notationware (www.notationware.com): Products include Play Music: compose, play, and print own sheet music; Fretwriter Lite: for guitarists to compose, playback, and print original songs; Manuscript Maker: create custom manuscript paper from computer; KeyboardStudio.net: new way to use MIDI keyboard; free demos. SYSTEM SPECS: Windows.

Noteheads Igor Engraver (www.noteheads.com): Offers the professional engraver control over all aspects of the notation of music; easy to use for beginners; cross-platform scores; can install for use on two computers; movies show how basic procedures in Igor Engraver work; advanced movie shows more advanced features such as lyrics input, coloring, tablature, and Internet publishing; playback capabilities include interpretation of trills, arpeggios, and more. SYSTEM SPECS: Macintosh; Windows.

NoteWorthy Composer Software (www.noteworthysoftware.com): Music composition and notation processor; create, record, edit, print, and play back musical scores; built-in transpose feature; print feature makes it possible to publish sheet music; save notation as a MIDI performance for use in other MIDI applications, including software karaoke players; evaluation edition available as a free download. SYSTEM SPECS: Windows.

Notion (www.notionmusic.com): Solution for notation and playback; music production tool to get user from score to final product; realistic playback of a score and live performance capability; compose, conduct, perform, teach, and learn; brings music notation to life; uses the sounds of the London Symphony Orchestra recorded at Abbey Road Studios; responds to standard musical notation with intelligence, playing compositions in realistic sound; NTempo feature allows user to conduct the music to add a realistic feel, accompany live musicians, or perform as a member of an ensemble; tool for practice or live performance; performance engine features; ease of use; advanced score features; supported formats; completely integrated full orchestral library of the London Symphony Orchestra, recorded at Abbey Road Studios; full set of multi-timbre samples, articulations, performance techniques, and instructions; integrated sample management engine automatically maps every score element to the exact sound; actual Abbey Road captured reverberation decay, fully adjustable per instrument and for the entire orchestra; NTempo real-time live performance control, with virtually no latency; save and replay NTempo performances; integrated Audio Mixer; expandable sound library through a large collection of NOTION add-on kits; 15-minute learning curve; intuitive mnemonic keyboard shortcut system; two levels deep navigation sidebar without excessive toolbars or clustered menus; automatic score layout with alignment and positioning of all score elements; intelligent Copy-Paste, Transpose, and View/Hide functionality; enter notes by point and click, MIDI play-in or keyboard entry; mass edit of articulations and other score elements; no MIDI setup required; no external hardware or software required; quarter-tone support and playback; custom key signatures; custom time signatures; multiple simultaneous time signatures on separate staffs; chord symbol playback; lyrics with up to ninety-nine verses; performance instructions specific to each orchestral group; MIDI Import; MusicXML Import and Export; save as .WAV. SYSTEM SPECS: Macintosh; Windows.

Notion Music Sound Expansion Kits (www.notionmusic.com): Users can customize the sound library of Notion software; some kits provide additional playing techniques for existing instruments; other kits add completely new instruments into the mix; kits are manufactured separately; new kits are released at intervals of every one-two months. SYSTEM SPECS: Macintosh; Windows.

Overture (www.geniesoft.com): Notation software; user interface designed specifically to be easy to learn and fast to use; most entry work can be done directly on the page with a minimum of menu selection and no complex dialog boxes; create piano, band, orchestral, choral, and lead sheet notation; print arrangements of up to sixty-four instruments; comes with music and templates to get started; easy-to-use notation software; enter notes on-screen with mouse or computer keyboard, or record a MIDI performance for instant viewing; intuitive interface has editing tools and symbol palettes; for complete orchestral arrangements, lead sheets, individual cues, or simple notation examples; professional page layout; text handling functions to add or edit lyrics, page text, floating text, measure text and rehearsal marks. SYSTEM SPECS: Macintosh; Windows.

Personal Composer (www.pccomposer.com): Music notation, MIDI, sequencing, and publishing program; notate as you play a MIDI instrument, with a program-supplied metronome; record one staff while playing back others; type lyrics directly onto the score; align lyric lines globally or syllable-by-syllable; create and position titles, copyright notices, and other text; select and place chord symbols and/or fretboards easily; transpose, rebeam, and apply other changes to music with a single command, and more. SYSTEM SPECS: Windows.

PhotoScore Ultimate Music Scanning Software (www.neuratron.com/photoscore.htm): Opens PDF files, plays back, saves MIDI files, sends scores directly to Sibelius and G7, saves MusicXML, NIFF and PhotoScore files for opening in Finale and other notation programs, saves WAV/AIFF audio files (also for burning to CD); handwritten music recognition for note entry away from computer; reads slurs and ties; reads hairpins and dynamics; reads text (lyrics, title, etc.) in 120 different languages (including bold, italic, etc.), reads articulation marks, reads triplets and other tuplets, reads grace notes and cue notes, reads cross-staff notes and beams; reads guitar chord diagrams, reads 4- and 6-string guitar tab, reads 1-, 2- and 3- line percussion staves, reads double and repeat barlines, reads repeat endings, Coda, and Segno, reads ornaments and pedal markings, reads seven accidental types, reads eight clef types, shortest note value is 128th, maximum voices per staff is four, maximum staves per page is sixty-four, maximum pages per score is 400, maximum dots per note/rest is three, reads the length of irregular bars, transposes, prints scores, automatic scanning and reading after scanning, playback with realism using Espressivo licensed from Sibelius; PhotoScore MIDI Lite also available with fewer features. SYSTEM SPECS: Macintosh; Windows.

Play Music (www.notationware.com): Music composition software available; no music theory knowledge needed; user-friendly interface guides through the composition process; click on instrument sound (up to twenty-four at one time) and will play back song with those sounds; add lyrics and text; select a note, click on the desired area of score and the notes will appear; can use any MIDI keyboard or MIDI instrument to insert notes and play back song; play keyboard and Play Music will write the notes; play composition back as a violin, guitar, bass, flute, tuba, steel drum, or any sound; record live or by using step entry to create songs; can use a computer soundcard to choose from over 128 sounds to play back song; save song as a MIDI file to use with other music software programs; import MIDI files; edit MIDI files; includes over thirty templates to create new scores. SYSTEM SPECS: Windows.

QuickScore Elite (www.sionsoft.com): Mix inputs; record whole tracks or fragments of tracks in real time, step time, or while tapping own beat; mix volume, pan, and other controllers in real time; use .WAV digital audio files; look at music from all angles; score, piano roll, controller, event list, and song views; edit using comprehensive set of tools, including intelligent filters; create notation with text, lyrics, grace notes, drum notation, guitar chords, engraver spacing, multiple voices, hundreds of symbols, flexible note and staff spacing, adjustable braces and brackets, and more; cross-staff beaming with adjustable split point, six-string guitar tablature notation and multiple undo; share MIDI; play using any Windows-compatible sound card or MIDI interface; score templates; fast and easy note entry and integrated, intuitive environment. SYSTEM SPECS: Windows.

QuickScore Elite Level II Notation Software (www.sionsoft.com): Up to forty-eight tracks; editing windows include Score, Piano Roll, Controller, Event List, Song, Track Sheet, Mixer, and Comments; comprehensive set of standard editing commands in all editors including Cut, Copy, Paste, and Undo; complete control over all MIDI events; rich set of notation editing commands, including transpose chromatically or in the key, adjust enharmonic note spellings, assign notes to different voices or staves, automatically set the duration of notes to fit musical passages, and more; global graphic arranging options to cut and paste sections of songs; intelligent edit filters; loop editing; Real-time and step-time recording or record while tapping tempo from MIDI keyboard; Real-time sixteen-channel MIDI mixer controls which respond to all MIDI controllers, including volume and velocity; Punch In/Out; SMPTE/MTC and Midi Clock synchronization; optional automatic quantization of real-time recording; input and controller filters for real-time recording; playback through MIDI and all popular sound cards included; scrolling playback with synchronized window display; repeats and first and second endings automatically play; interactively edit in full-score, single-track, piano-roll, song-overview, event-list, or graphic controller formats as the music plays; play standard WAVE digital audio files; Track Sheet to mute or solo tracks and change sounds; up to ninety-six staves; independently adjust the characteristics of song title, track name, headers, footers, copyright information, four sets of lyrics, six sets of text, bar and page numbers; complete set of symbols, including groupings, fingerings, articulations, slurs, repeats, crescendos, decrescendos, dynamics, line and box drawing; all standard clefs including five-line and single-line percussion clefs; import and export standard MIDI files; export Copyist files; export Tiff, BMP, EMF, and EPS files; record and play

back multiple tracks of digital audio; synchronize with digitized movie clips. SYSTEM SPECS: Windows.

Recordare PDFtoMusic Pro (http://store.recordare.com/index.html): Create a PDF file from an old music notation program and move it into a new music program; works with PDFs created by other music programs; extracts the music-related elements from a PDF file; plays the score; Virtual Singer embedded module sings the vocal parts; export to a score format like MusicXML, MIDI, or Myr Harmony Assistant files; export to a digital audio format like WAV or AIFF; most music programs that run on Windows, Mac OS X, or Mac OS 9 can print PDF files. SYSTEM SPECS: Macintosh; Windows.

Roni Music Downloadable Software Programs (www.ronimusic.com): AMAZING SLOW DOWNER: Learn new songs and techniques while listening to repeated parts of songs; provides means to slow down music so it can be learned in real-time by playing it from a CD, MP3, WAV, AIFF (Mac only), or WMA (Windows only) file; increase music speed to up to twice normal rate; make pitch adjustments in semitones at full or lower speed; set loop points using keyboard shortcuts. MIDI SOFTWARE: Sweet MIDI Player and Sweet Sixteen MIDI Sequencer; software implementation of an arpeggiator often found on older synthesizers called Sweet MIDI Arpeggiator: computer version of an intelligent harmonizer called Sweet MIDI Harmony Maker; Sweet Little Piano lets user play sound card from the computer keyboard. AUDIO COMPANION: Three different programs in one: one to grab audio from CD (CD Ripper), one for processing MP3, WMA and WAV files (Batch Processor), and an audio recorder (Audio Splitter) for recording audio from line-in input of soundcard (with auto-split function for easy recording of vinyl records, etc). MUSICIAN'S CD PLAYER: Works like Amazing Slow Downer but does recording of desired section first; intended for slower/older Windows computers; available for download. SYSTEM SPECS: Macintosh; Windows.

Scorch (www.sibelius.com): Software for viewing, playing, customizing, printing, and saving scores from the Internet; free download; makes scores interactive; high quality print; scores download quickly; turn pages; changes which device used for playback; playback controls and tempo slider; click play button to play from the start, or click on the score to play from that point or stop; change top instrument or key; save; page setup; print; information and updates; use Page Up/Page Down and the up/down arrow keys to scroll up and down the score; play music in the background while working; set Scorch playing, then minimize the window; some scores may only play an excerpt. SYSTEM SPECS: Macintosh; Windows.

Score Writer (www.geniesoft.com): Same notation engine and user interface as Overture, but has a slimmed down feature set and eliminates some tools used for large ensembles or specific modern types of music. SYSTEM SPECS: Macintosh; Windows.

SharpEye Music Scanning (www.visiv.co.uk/): Scan music and convert printed sheet music into a notation file or a MIDI file; can be imported into a music notation program or MIDI sequencer; process is called music OCR by analogy with the more common text OCR. SYSTEM SPECS: Windows.

Sibelius (www.sibelius.com): Write scores; print sheet music; program is simple and intuitive; click the play button to hear music performed with realism; built-in Sibelius Sounds Essentials library; reads, understands, and plays back all standard markings; can buy extra sound libraries for choral music, world music, and more; produce instrumental parts; parts are already in score; flick between parts using a simple drop-down; when a change is made to the full score, the relevant parts are automatically updated, and vice versa; Ideas Hub is used to capture, tag, find, and bring together musical ideas; comes preloaded with over 2000 ready-made ideas covering all styles of music and providing useful inspiration for compositions; publish or sell music online; create web versions of scores which can be viewed by anyone using the free Scorch web browser plug-in; sell scores online via SibeliusMusic.com. SYSTEM SPECS: Macintosh; Windows.

Sibelius Compass (www.sibelius.com): Helps students learn how to compose; includes lessons, worksheets, and self-tests covering a wide range of topics; complete composition projects; for each lesson, students study relevant interactive topics, test themselves with the built-in quiz, and try out what they've learned in the Tracker; melody, harmony, scales, rhythm, dynamics, transformations, timbre, texture, and form. SYSTEM SPECS: Macintosh; Windows.

Sibelius First (www.sibelius.com): Create scores to print, share, post online, or sell; templates and plug-ins to help create lead sheets, guitar tab, and complete scores; play MIDI keyboard or MIDI guitar or use computer mouse and keyboard; turns music into notes and chord symbols; add lyrics and name; includes composing and arranging tools for up to twelve staves of music; scan in sheet music or open PDF files; instrumental parts automatically sync up with score; switch from guitar tab to notation; change key of score; playback using 128 sampled instruments; print professional-quality full scores or individual parts; export an audio file of score to burn a CD; Sibelius Scorch technology lets user post and share scores on the web for others to see and hear. SYSTEM SPECS: Macintosh; Windows.

Sibelius G7 (www.sibelius.com): Software for writing songs and playing better guitar; write tab, chords, lyrics, and notation; learn songs and riffs with the on-screen fretboard; publish music on the Internet. SYSTEM SPECS: Macintosh; Windows.

Sibelius Internet Edition (www.sibelius.com): Complete solution for publishing sheet music on the Internet; many major publishers used to publish music securely on-line; includes extra features such as secure encryption and control over the functionality available for each score on web site - play, print, and transpose; enables publishers and music websites to sell sheet music worldwide instantly; reduce printing, storage, and shipping costs; deliver scores securely straight to the customer's printer; can change key and instruments within a normal web page; provides high-quality printing, playback, and customization such as transposing; handles composing, arranging, engraving, and traditional publishing as well as Internet publishing, it provides a complete end-to-end solution; create scores with computer keyboard, mouse, or MIDI keyboard; convert existing music files, including Finale, SCORE, MusicXML, and MIDI formats; scan printed scores; once any score is in Sibelius Internet Edition, click "Save as Scorch web page" and it's turned into a file ready to go on a web site. SYSTEM SPECS: Macintosh; Windows.

Sibelius Music (www.sibeliusmusic.com/): Large collection of new scores on the web; download with Scorch; many genres, arrangers, and composers. SYSTEM SPECS: Macintosh; Windows.

Sibelius SequenceXtra (www.sibelius.com): Allows designers, developers, and authors to add MIDI sound capabilities to web pages and multimedia applications; power of a fully-featured MIDI sequencer; an Xtra for the Macromedia Director development platform; develop musical software ranging from simple games and demos up to sequencers and editors; flexible notation viewer; MIDI songs loaded into application can be displayed in standard musical notation; viewer is fully integrated with SequenceXtra; changes made to the MIDI data in the Xtra are immediately visible in the score view, and the view scrolls during playback; used by publishers, multimedia developers, universities, and research groups to deliver multimedia music applications for teaching, learning, and recreation; interactive web applications; innovative research projects. SYSTEM SPECS: Macintosh; Windows.

Sibelius Sounds (www.sibelius.com): Range of high-quality collections of sound samples for Sibelius and G7; provide realistic playback of music in a wide variety of musical styles; libraries integrate seamlessly with the software using the Kontakt sample player from Native Instruments, which provides many adjustable settings, including reverb, brightness, tuning, and other audio characteristics; export an audio file to create a CD or an MP3 file; Sibelius Sounds Essentials is a new collection of over 150 pitched and hundreds of unpitched sounds specially selected from top-name libraries. SYSTEM SPECS: Macintosh; Windows.

Sibelius Student (www.sibelius.com): Input notes via mouse, MIDI or computer keyboard; notate, play back, transpose, and print music; panorama view; hundreds of built-in ideas to help student get started; attach video files to score; up to twelve staves per system; input dynamic markings, lyrics, and other text; insert clef changes in score; publish music on the Internet; opens Sibelius, MusicXML and MIDI files; automatic backups and auto-save; exports MIDI files, web pages, and Sibelius scores. SYSTEM SPECS: Macintosh; Windows.

SmartScore (www.musitek.com): Integrated music scanning, scoring, and MIDI sequencing; advanced recognition intelligence; plays back repeats, dynamics, and articulation; displays contrapuntal voices with direct voice-to-MIDI channel linking; automatic instrument assignments according to number of staves; playback continuity; intelligent control of instrumental parts; creates scores using mouse, keyboard, MIDI instrument, MIDI file, or scanner input; control over page layout, spacing, and irregular systems; part and voice separation; notation-to-MIDI-to-notation implementation; import standard MIDI files to display, transpose, or print out scores; Pro, SongBook, Piano, MIDI, Guitar Editions. SYSTEM SPECS: Macintosh; Windows.

TablEdit Tab Editor (www.tabledit.com/): Program for creating, editing, printing, and listening to tablature and sheet music (standard notation) for guitar and other fretted, stringed instruments, including mandolin and bass; not limited to guitar; has developed support for harmonica, mountain dulcimer, diatonic accordion, drums, violin, tin whistle, recorder, Xaphoon, autoharp, pedal steel guitar, and banjo; can open/import ASCII, MIDI, ABC, MusicXML, Bucket O' Tab, TabRite, and Wayne Cripps files; files can be saved in TablEdit format or exported to ASCII, HTML, ABC, RTF, MIDI, or WAV formats; can convert MIDI instrument direct to tablature. SYSTEM SPECS: Macintosh; Windows.

TabTrax (http://2112design.com/): Tab converter/player, drum music editor, drum notation software; convert any drum tab to standard sheet music notation and playable MIDI music; learn from any tab; create drum tracks. SYSTEM SPECS: Windows.

The Vivaldi Studio (www.vivaldistudio.com): Suite of products working together; combination of music notation software, thousands of interactive digital sheet music, interactive digital teaching, and music notation scanning software from the leading music company in Italy, Allegroassai.com; ten years of development; successful test markets in Italy and Europe. VIVALDI PLAYALONG: music play-along and notation software designed by musicians for musicians; makes practicing easier by slowing down or speeding up playback to learn to play a piece more easily; designed by musicians who know how to take advantage of all the benefits of using digital sheet music. VIVALDI PLUS: notation software for teachers and everyone else; includes software, Viva score digital sheet music, learning and teaching templates; designed by music teachers who are practicing musicians for the average user of music notation; enables basic music editing software; can open, view, edit, play, and print Viva Digital Scores of any type and complexity. VIVALDI GOLD: designed by composers for composers to be easy to use, intuitive, and powerful; quickly, accurately, and intuitively write music. VIVALDI SCAN: Optical Music Recognition engine; rhythm checking and note validation tools; correct errors; add text and fingering. SYSTEM SPECS: Macintosh; Windows.

Transcribe (www.seventhstring.demon.co.uk/): Transcribe recorded music; use to work out a piece of music from a recording in order to write it out or play it, or both; copy recording to computer's hard disk as a sound file then use Transcribe instead of a cassette machine and a piano; offers many features aimed at making the transcription job smoother and easier, including the ability to slow the music down without changing its pitch and to analyze chords and show what notes are present; does not attempt to do the whole job of processing an audio file and putting out musical notation; spectrum analysis feature is very useful for working out hard-to-hear chords; must still use ear to decide which of the peaks in the spectrum are notes being played, which are harmonics, and which are the result of noise and broad-spectrum instruments such as drums; no interest in MIDI files; deals with audio sample data files; not an editor; reads, plays, and records audio files but does not modify them; downloadable shareware. SYSTEM SPECS: Macintosh; Windows.

Transkriber (www.reedkotler.com): Play music to learn on computer CD player or on an external CD or tape player hooked up to the sound card; record music using the recording panel; play music back at 3/4, 2/3, 1/2, 1/3, 1/4, or 1/26 of the original speed without changing the pitch; phrase selection to focus on one part of the music at a time; slow down algorithms, tuning, and smoothing filters; reinforce or remove certain frequency bands from the music to better focus on the part being transcribed; adjust the pitch to match the recording exactly; transpose the sound up or down as much as an octave; pitch generator identifies which note is being played on the recording; for beginning to advanced transcribers. SYSTEM SPECS: Macintosh; Windows.

Film and Television Music—Tip Sheets Web Sites

A Luna Blue www.alunablue.com Royalty-free stock footage and imagery.

Academy of Motion Picture Arts and Sciences www.oscars.org Academy Awards; events and screenings; awards database.

All Movie Guide www.allmovie.com Guide to films; new in theaters; factoid.

American Film Institute www.AFI.com News and events; catalog; membership; education.

American Movie Classics www.amctv.com Cable channel; guide; the stars; the movies; programming; forum.

Association of Independent Video and Filmmakers www.aivf.org Resources; media advocacy; regional salons; discussion; workshops.

Baseline Studio Systems www.blssi.com/ The Studio System: comprehensive and accurate film and television database; accessed daily by every studio, network, and talent firm, the system provides extensive development grids, representation rosters, and company contacts; Syndication: leading data licensor; film and TV data powers many of the world's leading online destinations, offering more than 1.5 million profiles of celebrities and other entertainment professionals; InBaseline: credits are seen daily on millions of pages on some of the biggest websites including The Studio System, Yahoo! Movies & TV, NYTimes.com, Variety.com, E!Online, Hollywood.com, and more; free to broadcast film and TV profile across the entertainment world.

Blockbuster www.blockbuster.com Rent movies and music videos offline and online.

BollywoodMusic.com www.bollywoodmusic.com Hindi, Punjabi, Pakistani, Ghazals, Pop, Filmi, and Bhangra songs in RealAudio and MP3 format; over 1,000 songs; Indian music site.

Box Office Guru www.boxofficeguru.com Comprehensive box office information.

Box Office Report www.boxofficereport.com Predicted number one film; anticipated rankings.

Bright Lights Film Journal www.brightlightsfilm.com/index.html Actor profiles; reviews; festivals.

Cannes Film Festival www.festival-cannes.com French film event; films; juries; events; awards; archives.

Cinema Confidential www.cinecon.com Current films; news and gossip; trailers; reviews; interviews; forums; gallery.

Cinema Web www.cinemaWeb.com Web site for independent films.

Cinema-sites.com www.cinema-sites.com Links to film industry-related sites.

CineMedia afi.cinemedia.org Film and media directory; over 25,000 links.

Cinemusic Online www.cinemusic.net Film music; reviews; wide variety of scores; audio clip library.

Cinemusic www.cinemusic.de German language score site; reviews.

Classical Music Used in Film www.naxos.com/musicinmovies.asp?letter=A Pieces heard in films listed in alphabetical order.

Clipland www.clipland.com/index.shtml Online music video database.

CSS Music www.cssmusic.com Royalty-free libraries on CD; themes for film and TV.

Cue Sheet www.cuesheet.net/ Confidential bulletin listing film, TV, and other media projects requiring soundtrack music, composers, songs, library music, or cues; dispatched twice a month by e-mail only to selective subscriber base consisting of music publishers, record labels, music supervisors, composers, songwriters or their managers/agents; researchers based in London and Los Angeles.

Cyber Film School www.cyberfilmschool.com Web site with instruction, tips, advice, techniques on how to make, produce, direct, shoot, light, and edit TV, films, movies, and videos.

DemoCheck www.democheck.com An online service where one can have their music or performance of music reviewed by some of the top musicians, composers, and songwriters in the industry; send them an MP3 file and receive back a review.

Disney Pictures disney.go.com/DisneyPictures/index.html Film industry; studio.

Documentary Educational Resources www.der.org Produce, distribute, and promote ethnographic and documentary films from around the world.

Documentary Educational Resources www.der.org Produce, distribute and promote ethnographic and documentary films from around the world.

Eonline Movies movies.eonline.com Movie info.

Film Connection www.film-connection.com On-the-job training in major film/video studios and television stations; video clips; news; articles; film and television resources; tips from hit directors, editors, and producers; view other helpful film-related sites.

Film Festival www.filmfestival.be Film Festival Ghent.

Film Music Institute www.filmmusicinstitute.com Offers professional courses and workshops in Los Angeles and New York designed for working professionals in the film and television music industry.

Film Music Magazine www.filmmusicmag.com Trade publication for the film and television music industry; comprehensive coverage of industry news; feature articles; investigative reporting; calendar.

Film Music Network www.filmmusic.net World's largest professional trade association for those working in the film, television, and video game music industries; chapters in leading cities including Los Angeles and New York; provides members with

job leads, industry resources, and networking meetings featuring VIP panels and industry speakers.
Film Score Monthly www.filmscoremonthly.com Online magazine of motion picture and television music appreciation.
Film Scouts www.filmscouts.com Independent site featuring original multimedia programming; movie
trailers and stills; festival coverage; celebrity interviews; information; humor; reviews; commentary.
Film Site www.filmsite.org/genres.html Lists and descriptions of film genres.
Film Sound Design-Film Sound Theory
www.filmsound.org Theoretical and practical aspects on narrative sound effects in film and TV.
FilmBaby www.filmbaby.com/ Site for independent
filmmakers; multiple genres.
FilmFestivals.com www.filmfestivals.com Portal into
the universe of cinema via its actors, directors, and
films being shown at film festivals all over the
world; over 6,000 pages and links.
Film-Makers.com www.film-makers.com Over 2,363
links to film-related Web sites.
Filmtracks Modern Soundtrack Reviews
www.filmtracks.com Reviews of recent motion
picture soundtracks; tributes to modern composers;
information about film music CD collectibles; recent releases; customer favorites; links to Ama-
zon.com and e-Bay.com; "Best of Series" organized by recent years and by decade.
Global Graffiti Music www.globalgraffiti.com Real
music for the reel world.
Greatest Films: The Sound of Music (1965)
www.filmsite.org/soun.html Detailed review, synopsis, and discussion of the film.
Guild of Canadian Film Composers www.gcfc.ca Association of professional composers and music
producers for film, TV, and new media.
Hindi Movie Songs
www.cs.wisc.edu/~navin/india/songs Hindi movie
songs.
Hollywood Creative Directory www.hcdonline.com
Online data; specials; e-mail names; mailing labels;
lists on disc; site licenses; industry links; resources;
festivals; awards; guilds; organizations; unions;
studios; business; actors; casting; celebrities; assis-
tants; media; press; services; music; education.
Hollywood Online www.hollywood.com Movie information; soundtracks.
Hollywood Reporter www.hollywoodreporter.com Inside information on film and TV upcoming projects; online subscriptions.
Hollywood Stock Exchange www.hsx.com Virtual trading in the movie industry.
Independent Feature Project www.ifp.org Source for
independent filmmakers.

Independent Film Channel www.ifctv.com First channel dedicated to independent film presented
twenty-four hours a day, uncut, commercial-free.
Inside Film www.insidefilm.com Film festivals directory; links; articles.
Internet Movie Database Pro
https://secure.imdb.com/signup/v4/?d=IMDbTab
Information resource designed exclusively for people who work in the entertainment industry; new
content; customizable searches; easy-to-use design;
in production; contact listings.
Internet Movie Database www.imdb.com Favorite stars
and movies, theater and TV show times, online
trailers, movie and trivia games.
Jeff Rona www.jeffrona.com Info on film music.
Kilima www.kilima.com/welcome.html Intriguing films
from a diverse selection of nations; films are listed
by country and subject matter; comprehensive information on the films and filmmakers; includes
art, music, and literature.
Lee Holdridge www.leeholdridge.com Official site;
audio clips.
License Music www.licensemusic.com Original, pre-
cleared songs from over seventy record labels and
music publishers; search; listen; download.
Los Angeles Film & Music Magazine www.lafm.com
Hollywood resource.
*Mandy's International Film and Television Production
Directory* www.mandy.com Database of television
film producers, facilities, and technicians world-
wide; current film/TV jobs.
Media Rights www.MediaRights.org Nonprofit; helps
media makers, educators, librarians, and activists
use documentaries to encourage action and inspire
dialogue on contemporary issues.
Megatrax www.megatrax.com Production music for
film, TV, ads, multimedia.
MGM www.mgm.com Studio site.
Michael Kamen www.michaelkamen.com A tribute to
his music.
Microcinema International www.microcinema.com
Short films distribution.
Miramax Cafe www.miramax.com Graphics; celebrity
information.
Movie Clichés List www.moviecliches.com Hollywood
clichés.
Movie Flix www.movieflix.com Large collection of
older movies available for viewing online, some
free; MovieFlix Plus monthly subscriptions.
Movie Link www.movielink.com Internet movie rentals; Windows only.
MovieFone www.moviefone.com Movie listing guide
and ticketing service; local movie show times;
tickets; trailers; film reviews; photos; celebrity and
more.

MovieSounds www.moviesounds.com Movie listing; sound tools; event sounds; trivia blitz; FAQ.

MovieWeb www.movieWeb.com Internet movie network.

Muse 411 www.muse411.com World wide online music industry directory designed to make it quick and easy to locate people and companies in the music industry; free to add a listing; search the database for networking possibilities.

Music Box Theatre's Home Page www.musicboxtheatre.com Chicago's year-round film festival.

Music from the Movies www.musicfromthemovies.com News and updates; reviews; CDs; links.

Music Library Association http://www.cftech.com/BrainBank/COMMUNICATIONS/MusLibSrc.html Music libraries for music, sound effects, and sound media sources.

National Film Board of Canada www.nfb.ca Canadian films; produces and distributes films, audiovisual and multimedia works which reflect Canada to Canadians and the rest of the world.

National Film Preservation Foundation www.filmpreservation.org/sm_index.html Nonprofit organization created by the United States Congress to help save America's film heritage; support activities nationwide that preserve American films and improve film access for study, education, and exhibition.

Netflix www.netflix.com Rent movies and music videos through the mail.

New Day Films www.newday.com/about/index.html Offers independently produced films and videos that educate and inspire.

Paramount Pictures www.paramount.com Movies and television.

Production Hub www.productionhub.com/directory/ Production directory and guide for broadcast TV, film, and video.

Production Weekly www.productionweekly.com Hollywood and international; provides the entertainment industry with a comprehensive breakdown of projects in pre-production, preparation, and active development for film and television.

RapidCue www.rapidcue.com State-of-the-art cue sheet technology for the use of music in the film, TV, and cable industries.

Screen Actors Guild www.sag.com Represents performers; member services; industry services; contracts; credit union.

Screen Archives Entertainment www.screenarchives.com Catalog of regular and rare scores; occasional auctions of collectibles.

Sonic Images Records www.sonicimages.com Soundtrack releases.

Sony Pictures Online www.sonypictures.com/index.html Studio site.

Soundtrack Express www.soundtrack-express.com One of the original score review sites.

SoundtrackNet www.soundtrack.net Art and business of film and television music; film scores to pop music that show up on soundtracks; information on composers.

Studio Systems, Inc. www.studiosystemsinc.com Projects, personnel, and production for film; The Studio System; In Hollywood; Scriptlog; information and research.

SundanceChannel www.sundancechannel.com Promotes indie films; schedule; search; store.

Tamil Film Music Page tfmpage.com Comprehensive resource for Tamil Film Music; discussion forum; song lyrics; streamed live songs; master index of artists.

Television/Film Production Information and Jobs www.crimsonuk.com Listings for the UK.

Tennessee Film, Entertainment & Music Commission www.state.tn.us/film Movie locations; music producers; cable channels; video and CD-ROM production, etc.

The Film Music Society www.filmmusicsociety.org Nonprofit dedicated to the preservation of film music; news and events; membership; merchandise; resources and links; to increase awareness of the artistic, historical, and commercial value of film and television music; to preserve and restore film and television music scores, manuscripts, orchestrations, recordings, and all related materials; to research, document, and disseminate the histories of film and television music, whether by oral means or by aural, written and/or digital media; to publish scholarly and foster, encourage, and cultivate new musical and journalistic works; to present and promote the film and television music contributions of past, present, and future composers, arrangers, and musicians.

The Henry Mancini Institute www.manciniinstitute.org/ Educational organization for composers.

The Journal of Film Music www.ifms-jfm.org/ Previous issues; submissions; subscriptions.

The Royalty Report www.royaltyreport.com Monthly publication dealing with music rights and royalties; free subscription; add email address.

The Society of Composers and Lyricists www.filmscore.org Industry forums; technology; performing rights; intellectual rights; seminars.

The Yorkton Short Film and Video Festival www.yorktonshortfilm.org Dramas; shorts; documentaries; videos; children's films; made-for-TV movies; workshops; food; music; awards; directors; producers; celebrities.

TrackSounds www.tracksounds.com Soundtrack and game soundtrack reviews; interviews.

TV Guides Movies www.tvguide.com/movies Film information; reviews; search database.

Twentieth Century Fox www.foxhome.com Information; film clips.

UCLA Film Scoring Program www.unex.ucla.edu Creative and technical challenges of film scoring; instructors are award-winning composers.

Universal Pictures www.universalstudios.com Production notes; film clips; photographs.

Varèse Sarabande www.varesesarabande.com Historical leader in score releases.

Variety www.variety.com Film; TV; music; news; world; business; legal; features.

Walt Disney Records disney.go.com/DisneyRecords Promotional site for CDs; includes audio clips.

Warner Brothers www2.warnerbros.com/web/movies/index.jsp Information; movie previews.

Women in Film www.wif.org Purpose is to empower, promote, nurture, and mentor women in the industry through a network of valuable contacts, events, and programs.

Writer's Guild of America www.wga.org Represents writers in the motion picture, broadcast, cable, and new media industries.

Music Video Games and Video Game Music Web Sites

Amiga www.amiga.com Amiga video games.

Atari www.atari.com/us/ Game information and registration; search by product, genre, price, or platform; PC downloads.

AudioGames.net www.audiogames.net Audio games based on sound and blind-accessible games.

Bemani Style www.bemanistyle.com/ Rhythm game coverage; forum; interactive; simulation; archives.

Blue's News www.bluesnews.com Game industry news.

Commodore Gaming www.commodoregaming.com Re-launched in 2007; maker of high-end purpose-built gaming computers; C-Kin allows users to customize the outer case with unique artwork.

Dance Dance Revolution www.ddrgame.com/ DDR game for Nintendo Wii, PS2, PS3, Xbox 360, and PC; platforms; dance pads; convertors.

Gamasutra www.gamasutra.com/ The art and business of making games.

Game Audio Network Guild www.audiogang.com Game industry news.

Game Boy www.gameboy.com/ Portable fun; classic system by Nintendo; hundreds of games.

Game Environment from an Auditive Perspective www.audiogames.net/pics/upload/gameenvironme nt.htm Article by Axel Stockburger.

Game Music Radio www.gamemusicradio.com Listen!

GameDev.net www.gamedev.net/ Game development needs.

GameFaqs www.gamefaqs.com/ What's new; contribute; features; boards; my games.

GameSound www.gamessound.com Theory and practice of video game music, sound effects, dialogue.

GameSound www.gamesound.org A portal to articles written about interactive sound in computer games; books; links.

GameSpot www.gamespot.com/ Previews; new releases; top games; all games; features; downloads.

GameSpy www.gamespy.com Video game news.

GameStudies.org www.gamestudies.org International journal of computer game research.

Guitar Hero www.guitarhero.com All Guitar Hero games; World Tour; community; store.

Harmonix Music Systems, Inc. www.harmonixmusic.com/ RockBand; RockBand 2; Phase; games; employment opportunites.

Interactive Audio Specialist Group www.iasig.org/ Allows developers of audio software, hardware, and content to freely exchange ideas about improving the performance of interactive applications by influencing hardware, software, and tool design.

Konami America www.konami.com/ Karaoke Revolution; Dance Dance Revolution; signature brands; find products by platform; insider news; forums.

Levels of Sound: On the Principles of Interactivity in Music Video Games www.digra.org/dl/db/07311.14286.pdf Paper by Martin Pichlmair and Fares Kayali.

Music4Games.net www.music4games.net Award-winning resource for the game music industry.

Nintendo www.nintendo.com Video game platforms; Wii; Nintendo DS; games; support.

PlayStation www.us.playstation.com/ Video game platforms by Sony; PS2; PS3; PSP; games; media and downloads; news; forums; support.

Rock Band www.rockband.com Rock Band; Rock Band 2; game info; videos; news; downloads; store.

Sound Design www.sounddesign.org.uk/ Sound design for the moving image and interactive media.

The Game Creators www.thegamecreators.com/ Game development; newsletter.

The Video Games Live Concert Series www.videogameslive.com/index.php?s=home Concerts featuring classic video game music.

Video Game Music Archive www.vgmusic.com/ Industry news; links to platform manufacturers; MIDI files of music from video games.

Video Game Music: Not Just Kid Stuff
www.vgmusic.com/vgpaper.shtml Article by Matthew Belinkie.

Xbox www.xbox.com Xbox 360 video game platform; games; accessories; Xbox LIVE; support.
Xbox365 www.xbox365.com/ Forum; cheats; games; support.

15
Digital Audio Recording and Editing—MIDI Sequencing—
Plug-Ins—Sampled Sounds and Loops—Virtual Instruments—
Software Synthesizers—CD Burning
Software, Instructional Media and Web Sites

Ableton Live (www.ableton.com): For every stage of the musical process, from creation to production to performance; offers two main views, the Session View and the Arrangement View; create, produce and perform music in a single application; Session View: acts as a musical sketch and launch pad to try out new ideas; each cell in the Session View grid can hold a recording, MIDI file, or any other musical idea; ideas can be recorded on the fly or dragged in from the Browser and played in any order and at any time; Arrangement View offers a timeline-based approach for traditional multitrack recording, MIDI sequencing, and other music production tasks; improvise in the Session View, and all actions will be recorded into the Arrangement View, where they can be edited; with Elastic Audio can manipulate the tempo and feel of the music as it plays; with Uninterrupted Creative Flow can record, mix, match, and add effects without ever stopping the music; with Defy the Timeline Freely can improvise musical structure instead of constructing it; can bring Live studio environment; Beat Creators can streamline beat production and have endless creative possibilities; Sound Designers can create radical variations of samples in real time; DJs can elevate DJ sets; remix, mash up, and produce music; no idea lost; build and browse library of musical ideas; hands on control; multitrack recording up to 32-bit/192kHz; complete nondestructive editing with unlimited undo; MIDI sequencing of software and hardware instruments; real-time time-stretching and warping of AIFF, WAV, Ogg Vorbis, FLAC, and MP3 files, for improvisation and instant remixing; comprehensive selection of built-in audio effects, including creative delays, filters, distortions, studio compressors, and EQs; built-in software instruments: Simpler for creative sample-based synthesis, Impulse for sampled drums; Instrument and Drum Effect Racks for creating and managing complex performance setups, drum kits and multi-effects; VST and AU effects and instruments support; automatic plug-in delay compensation; REX file support and native sliced audio file creation; video import and export for scoring to picture or warping picture to music; real-time control of parameters with any MIDI controller; MIDI-map it or choose from a list of popular supported controllers for instant mapping; full ReWire support; single-screen user interface for simple, creativity-focused operation; multicore and multiprocessor support; boxed version of Ableton Live includes the Essential Instrument Collection 2, a multi-gigabyte library of sampled instruments providing a selection of acoustic and electric pianos, guitars, bass, drums, orchestral strings, brass, woodwinds and more; also includes loops and construction kits; printed reference manual in English, Spanish, French, German, or Japanese (boxed version only); extensive built-in step-by-step tutorials; localized software menus, tutorials, and PDF reference manuals available in English, Spanish, French, German and Japanese. SYSTEM SPECS: Macintosh; Windows.

Ableton Live LE (www.ableton.com): Intuitive interface and pro features for recording, songwriting, remixing, and DJing; offers two main views, the Session View and the Arrangement View; create, produce, and perform your music in a single application; studio-quality recording up to 32-bit/192 kHz; sixty-four audio tracks and unlimited MIDI tracks per project; MIDI sequencing for software instruments; more than twenty built-in audio effects, including delays, filters, distortions, studio compressors, and EQs; includes two software instruments: Simpler for creative sample-based synthesis and Impulse for dynamic, sampled drums; VST and AU effects and instruments support; automatic plug-in delay compensation; real-time time-stretching and warping of AIFF, WAV, Ogg Vorbis, FLAC, and MP3 files for DJing and instant remixing; tweak Live's controls in real time with any MIDI controller; MIDI-map it or choose from a list of popular supported controllers for instant mapping; single-screen user interface for simple, creativity-focused operation; multicore and multiprocessor support; limited to two simultaneous stereo audio inputs and outputs, twelve built-in audio effects, eight built-in instruments, two AU/VST effects, and two AU/VST instruments per project; wide selection of presets for instruments and effects; extensive built-in step-by-step tutorials; printed reference manual in English, Spanish, French, German, or Japanese (boxed version only); localized software menus, tutorials, and PDF reference manuals available in English, Spanish, French, German and Japanese; Exclusive Sound Content, boxed version only; boxed version includes the Essential Instrument Collection 2 LE Edition, a comprehensive library of sampled instruments providing a choice selection of acoustic and electric pianos, guitars, drums, orchestral strings, brass, woodwinds and more. SYSTEM SPECS: Macintosh; Windows.

Ableton Sampled Instruments (www.ableton.com): *Essential Instrument Collection 2* with a selection of acoustic and electric pianos, guitars, bass, drums, orchestral instruments, and more; *Session Drums* multisampled library of acoustic drums; *Drum Machines* selection of classic drum machines; *Orchestral Instrument Collection* includes Orchestral Strings, Brass, Woodwinds, and Percussion in a comprehensive bundle; *Orchestral Strings* comprehensive selection of stringed instruments including solo and ensemble violin, viola, cello, and double bass, all recorded in their natural positions within the orchestra and with a number of articulations; *Orchestral Brass* includes solo and ensemble French horn, trombone, trumpet, and tuba, with articulations in multiple section sizes; *Orchestral Woodwinds* includes solo and ensemble flute, clarinet, bassoon, oboe, and English horn with a broad selection of articulations; *Orchestral Percussion* includes vibraphone, marimba, xylophone, crotales, glockenspiel, tubular bells, cymbals, and timpani with a variety of articulations. SYSTEM SPECS: Macintosh; Windows.

Ableton Software Instruments (www.ableton.com): Products include: *Sampler* sampling instrument with multisample playback and import and sound design capabilities; *Operator* frequency modulation synthesizer; *Electric* sounds of classic electric pianos through physical modeling synthesis; *Tension* string synthesizer with reproductions of real stringed instruments or hybrids; *Analog* emulates vintage analog synthesizers. SYSTEM SPECS: Macintosh; Windows.

Ableton Suite (www.ableton.com): Combines Ableton Live with a collection of Ableton instruments; available as a download or boxed versions; download version of Ableton Suite includes Ableton Live, Sampler, Operator, Electric, Analog, Tension, and Drum Machines; boxed version of Ableton Suite additionally includes the Essential Instrument Collection 2 and Session Drums. SYSTEM SPECS: Macintosh; Windows.

ACID Music Studio Software (www.sonycreativesoftware.com): Music creation and mixing software; tool for original song creation, multitrack audio and MIDI recording; studio-quality mixing and effects processing; burn CDs, upload to the web, prepare audio for podcasts, or export to MP3 player; built-in tutorial; composing, mixing, and mastering; mixing software with multitrack recorders; capture audio and MIDI; beat matching and music mixing; share music creations; record vocals, guitars, keyboards, and other instruments; plug microphone or instrument into PC sound card and click Record to capture audio and MIDI; 3,000 ACIDized music loops, 1,000 MIDI files, built-in effects, and other tools; import songs and MP3 files for beat-matching and mixing; burn music CDs; save the songs to popular formats for uploading to websites such as ACIDplanet.com; prepare audio for podcasts, or convert songs to MP3 format for playback on portable music player; create original music, produce DJ-style remixes, add soundtracks to videos, and burn professional-quality CDs; mixing and effects processing; mixing tools give precise control over volume and panning, effects processing, audio routing, and final output; customize songs using professional-quality audio effects including EQ, reverb, delay, chorus, flange, phase, distortion, echo, and more; use VST and DirectX audio effects, and VST instruments; add pan and volume envelopes, reverse audio, and change the pitch and tempo of mix in real time; record and edit MIDI; MIDI editing and sequencing; record and edit MIDI note and controller data on the timeline, and assign to any MIDI instrument; supports VSTi and includes over 1,000 MIDI files and ninety instruments for song creation; Show Me How tutorials include text dialogue boxes, pointers, and guides; create own CDs; disc-at-once CD layout and burning fully integrated into the software; create music and produce CDs all within one application; encoding functionality lets user save songs to popular streaming formats for uploading to the web or exporting to portable music devices. SYSTEM SPECS: Windows.

ACID Pro (www.sonycreativesoftware.com): Digital music creation; automatic loop time-stretching and tempo-matching technology; pick, paint, and play functionality; loop-based music creation tool; reformulated to add multitrack recording and full MIDI sequencing to looping functionality; loops plus multitrack plus MIDI; full-featured professional music workstation; dj mixing software, music mixing software, midi software, multitrack recorders; automatic pitch and tempo matching, real-time loop previewing, unlimited tracks; support for multiple media events per track, and automatic crossfades; includes over 1,000 Sony Sound Series loops; multitrack audio and MIDI recording; 24-bit, 192kHz sound quality production live or in-studio; on-the-fly punch in/out, unlimited tracks for audio and MIDI, control surface support, plug-in processing, and 5.1 surround mixing; comprehensive MIDI support for MIDI sequencing; real-time MIDI processing and precise control over MIDI events; note and controller data can be recorded and edited on the timeline as easily as audio tracks; new track envelopes to automate and modify modulation, expression, or other types of MIDI controller data over time; record multiple tracks of MIDI, apply real-time MIDI quantization, perform filtering and processing, create and edit drum patterns; mixing and editing; nondestructive editing, unlimited tracks, and real-time pitch and tempo matching; Groove Mapping and Groove Cloning quantization tools, real-time event reverse, freehand envelope drawing, and support for alternate time signatures; Beatmapper tool for remixing; Chopper tool helps create drum fills, stutters, and DJ-style effects; mixing and editing; professional effects and soft synth support; native support for VST instruments, as well as VST and DirectX audio plug-ins; includes the Native Instruments KOMPAKT Sony ACID Pro edition and over 20 DirectX effects; create resonant sweeps, dramatic fades, EQ changes and add effects with parameter automation; integrate with existing studio; full ReWire host and device support, ASIO, and control surface automation for devices such as the Mackie Control and Frontier Design TranzPort. Audio Control; exclusive quantization tools; transform loops and MIDI tracks into fresh, new sounds with Groove Mapping and Groove Cloning quantization tools; change the groove of a track, apply different grooves to the same track, extract a groove from one file and apply it to another, or create custom grooves; quantization tools; professional workflow features; Media Manager is a powerful way to tag, organize, and search collection of content; use new project sections to audition different arrangements of a project; folder tracks and cluster editing; use Clip

Pool to choose and arrange the events to use in compositions; place multiple media clips on one track; automatic crossfades tie everything together; deliver projects in nearly any format without leaving the ACID Pro environment; integrated DAO CD burning, AC3, AIF, ATRAC, AVI, MOV, MP3, MPEG-1 & MPEG-2, OGG, PCA, RM, W64, WAV, WMA, WMV; import and export support; includes a custom edition of Native Instruments KOMPAKT; full-featured VSTi sample playback engine comes bundled with over 120 instruments; KOMPAKT Sony ACID Pro Edition. SYSTEM SPECS: Windows.

American Idol Extreme Music Creator (www.sonycreativesoftware.com): Turn PC into a recording and mixing studio; record, mix, edit, burn, and share music; included loops create fresh tracks to support vocals; import songs from CDs and MP3s and make a custom remix; burn own demo CDs; sing along with background music; record vocals or instruments into mix; change key and tempo on the fly; import own music from CDs or MP3s; record self singing a cappella; layer an unlimited number of music tracks; remix songs and MP3s with Beatmapper tool; create special effects with reverse audio; Show Me How tutorials; click Play to preview song; export songs to personal audio players; burn demo CDs; convert songs to MP3 format; save to popular formats for uploading to the web; a loop is an audio file that repeats itself in a composition; a music loop can be a drum beat, guitar riff, keyboard part, or a vocal sample; by selecting and arranging loops in different ways, can create complete songs or background tracks; includes hundreds of professionally recorded loops in multiple genres; includes Randy Jackson's Producer's Pack Volume 1, a special CD with over 250 music loops; samples on this CD represent popular genres such as hard rock, soft rock, electro-pop, R&B, hip-hop, and dance; six prearranged projects; add own music to mix by plugging an instrument or microphone into PC to capture live vocals, guitars, keyboards, and more; play along with song; rip and burn CDs; extract audio from own CDs for immediate mixing; burn own disc-at-once CDs; convert songs to MP3 format for export to portable music player; Show Me How tutorials cover the basics of loop-based composition, recording, and mixing; text dialog boxes and guides explain steps and show where to click so can learn and do at the same time. SYSTEM SPECS: Windows.

Antares Products (www.antarestech.com): AUTO-TUNE EVO: Next generation of the worldwide standard in professional pitch correction; Evo Voice Processing Technology; sleek interface; more power; for TDM (Mac and PC), RTAS (Mac and PC), VST (Mac and PC) and Audio Units; AUTO-TUNE VOCAL STUDIO NATIVE AND TDM: Bundles Auto-Tune Evo Native or TDM with the AVOX 2 Vocal Toolkit;

AVOX 2 ANTARES VOCAL TOOLKIT: Builds on the original AVOX plug-in bundle; adds an additional five state-of-the-art vocal processing modules, including Harmony Engine Vocal Modeling Harmony Generator, to give musicians, producers, and engineers the ability to design unique vocal effects for audio post-production applications; HARMONY ENGINE VOCAL MODELING HARMONY GENERATOR: Real-time harmony generating plug-in for professional-quality harmony arrangements; tool for creating realistic harmonies; MUTATOR EXTREME VOICE DESIGNER: Provides a combination of tools for creating unusual voices; high-quality pitch shifting, throat modeling, pitch-tracking ring modulator-based "mutation," and an Alienization function; tool for unique special vocal effects and post-production sound design; ARTICULATOR VOCAL FORMANT AND AMPLITUDE MODELER: Modern-day version of the talk box; lets user extract the formant and amplitude information from a vocal or other dynamic source and apply it to any other audio track; for talking guitars, singing synths, and many special effects; WARM TUBE SATURATION GENERATOR: Based on Antares' Tube plug-in; warms up vocals with Antares' tube modeling technology; can be used on every track in a project with negligible impact on CPU usage; ASPIRE ASPIRATION NOISE PROCESSOR: Tool for modifying a voice's breathiness independently of its harmonic content; allows modification of the amount and quality of a voice's aspiration noise without affecting the vocal's harmonic characteristics; THROAT PHYSICAL MODELING VOCAL DESIGNER: Process vocals through a physical model of the human vocal tract, offering the possibility of vocal characteristics that are unattainable by any other means; DUO VOCAL MODELING AUTO-DOUBLER: Provides programmable variation in pitch, timing, vibrato depth, and timbral variation using a simplified version of THROAT's vocal modeling technology; CHOIR VOCAL MULTIPLIER: Unique processor that turns a single voice into four, eight, sixteen, or thirty-two distinct individual unison voices, each with its own pitch, timing, and vibrato variations; PUNCH VOCAL IMPACT ENHANCER: Gives vocals more dynamic impact, allowing them to cut through a dense mix with clarity and power; SYBIL VARIABLE FREQUENCY DE-ESSER: Tames vocal sibilance with a flexible compressor with threshold, ratio, attack, and decay controls as well as a variable highpass frequency to match any vocal performance. SYSTEM SPECS: Macintosh; Windows.

Apple GarageBand (www.apple.com): Personal recording studio; create own virtual onstage band and play along on favorite instrument; record, edit, and mix a song in CD quality; play with a hand-picked band on a virtual stage; generates a new project based on genre and performance styles; do arrangements; define sections of song — intro, verse, chorus — and copy, move, or delete; multi-take recording; mark a region to repeat, record a part multiple times, and pick the best performance; Visual EQ; graphically adjust frequencies for each track by clicking and dragging individual EQ bands; automation of tempo effects and instruments; set multiple edit points in a track to automate EQ and effect changes; use with GarageBand Jam Packs; TrackPaks DVD-ROMs are Apple Loops for GarageBand and Logic and are available from Hal Leonard; titles include *Classic Rock, Hip-Hop, Modern Rock,* and *R&B.* SYSTEM SPECS: Macintosh.

Apple GarageBand Jam Packs (www.apple.com): Each Jam Pack offers thousands of Apple Loops and dozens of playable software instruments; Jam Packs can also be used in Logic Express, Logic Pro, and Soundtrack Pro, offering novice and professional musicians alike a wide assortment of new sounds to stretch their musical creativity; *Voices Jam Pack:* whether song needs a soloist, backup singers, or an entire choir; over 1,500 Apple Loops featuring professional soloists and choirs in multiple genres and styles; also includes over twenty software instruments, including voices, choral ensembles, and drum kits built upon the human voice and body; *Rhythmn Jam Pack:* Rhythm Section provides a veritable drum construction kit; assemble a solid foundation of drums with varied sets of fills, grooves, and groove variations; wide variety of drum sounds available; create human-sounding performances; also provides dozens of playable instruments including ten strings, ten basses, and ten drum kits; *World Jam Pack:* go to more exotic places with World Music; recorded over the course of a worldwide expedition and featuring an unprecedented collection of world loops, ethnic percussion, exotic strings, and regional wood instruments; captures the most authentic performances in dozens of countries, genres, and playing styles; *Remix Jam Pack:* designed for electronic dance music enthusiasts who like to move to Hip-Hop, Techno, Trance, and R&B; offers beat kits, sound effects, synth sounds, and the rhythms of classic Roland drum machines; *Symphony Jam Pack:* Symphony Orchestra lets user conduct a full orchestra, from brass and percussion to strings and woodwinds; ceate classical compositions or soundtracks; add the power of a symphony to GarageBand pop, rock, and hip-hop. SYSTEM SPECS: Macintosh.

Apple Logic Express (www.apple.com): Delivers the power and streamlined interface of Logic Pro; innovative production tools and over 100 instruments and effects from Logic Studio; record, edit, and mix with quality, speed, and ease; redesigned interface and a range of powerful, easy-to-use features; offers the same powerful production tools as Logic Pro, including full notation, 24-bit/192kHz resolution, and Quick Swipe comping; Next-generation interface; redesigned interface consolidates all windows into a single, efficient workspace made for musicians; world-class instruments; thirty-six instrument plug-ins from Logic Studio, including Ultrabeat drum machine and ES2 synth; professional effects; seventy effect plug-ins from Logic Studio, including Guitar Amp Pro and full-featured Pitch Correction; redesigned, single-window interface eliminates clutter and lets user focus on music; Multitake management and Quick Swipe comping streamline the overdub process; powerful audio editing features such as snap-to-transient, graphical time stretching, and sample-accurate editing in the Arrange window let user work faster and with greater precision; comes with Ultrabeat, the premier drum machine from Logic Studio featuring twenty-five programmable voices, a built-in step sequencer, and advanced synthesis controls; with ES2 synthesizer, user can draw from a broad range of sounds, a comprehensive selection of synthesis techniques, and powerful modulation options to create radical leads or nuanced pads; EXS24 sampler provides creative flexibility, allowing user to load and play sampled instruments of near-limitless size; integrated, redesigned EXS editor lets user quickly build own sampled instruments and drum kits; new effects; comes with Guitar Amp Pro, the acclaimed guitar amp plug-in from Logic Studio featuring eleven amp models, fifteen speaker cabinets, microphone controls, and a dedicated effects section; newly bundled production effects including full-featured Pitch Correction, Ensemble, and Fat EQ help shape sound; newly bundled creative effects such as Echo, Spectral Gate, and Ringshifter provide options for transforming sound. SYSTEM SPECS: Macintosh.

Apple Logic Pro (www.apple.com): Streamlined interface; unified window design consolidates multiple edit and browser areas; library browser makes it easy to find audio files, channel strip settings, and plug-in settings; inspector provides convenient access to region and track parameters as well as primary mix functions via the Dual Channel Strip; assign tools to mouse and view current assignments directly in the Arrange window; simple multiple track creation and setup; customizable tool and transport bars; context-sensitive shortcut menus; definable startup behavior; enhanced plug-in headers for all instruments and effects; Global Tracks for graphical editing of key and time signatures, markers, tempo, and transposition; selectable time-and/or beat-based bar ruler for time-linear and/or beat-linear display in the Arrange window; Waveform zoom slider for improved visibility of low-level signals; extensive zoom tools and functions; Ultimate Writing Studio; extensive MIDI composition; region-based quantize, transpose, gate, swing, and velocity control; MIDI Groove templates; creative MIDI processing and

routing in the Environment; Caps Lock Keyboard for note entry using computer keyboard; Custom and Hermode tuning; MIDI step entry; full support for Apple Loops; Apple Loops browser for finding and previewing loops based on tempo, key, style, and mood; export of MIDI and audio regions as Apple Loops; edit plug-ins and MIDI performances for Software Instrument loops; independent loop transposition; comprehensive loop tagging and editing with Apple Loops Utility; complete music notation includes real-time transcription, instrument transposition, guitar tablature, drum notation, chord symbols, adaptive lyric input, automatic multibar rests, comprehensive palette of slurs, crescendis, and other ornaments. Staff Styles for easy recall of multiple stave attributes, Score Sets allow instruments to be combined for editing and print, layout and printing of complete professional scores; video playback features; embedded or floating video window display; Digital Cinema Desktop for display of full-screen video on second monitor; external video output via FireWire or DVCPRO HD; Global video thumbnail track; scene detect option to mark video transitions automatically; fast and intuitive region looping; global chord track with automatic chord recognition; over 980 definable key and MIDI commands; 90 recallable screen configurations; audio file and I/O resolution up to 24-bit/192kHz; internal audio resolution: 32-bit floating point; 64-bit precision where required; comprehensive surround support up to 7.1, with flexible surround mixing facilities; extended project length: 6 hours at 96kHz; 13 hours at 44.1kHz; Mac backup and sharing of preferences and settings; use of an Apple Remote to control Logic Pro from a distance, with the ability to play, stop, record, rewind, fast-forward, and move to the next or previous track; High-end POW-r dithering algorithm; seamless punch-on-the-fly recording; low latency mode to remove plug-in induced latency during recording; graphic beat mapping for creating tempo maps from existing audio; collection of production-ready templates; multiple documents open at once; bounce to AIFF, WAV (Broadcast Wave), CAF, SDII, MP3, M4A (Apple Lossless, AAC); fast, offline bouncing of single or multiple tracks; burn any bounced audio directly to CD or DVD-A (PCM only); master and author professional, Red Book-standard CDs with WaveBurner, included in Logic Studio; asset management simplifies consolidation and transport of projects and their dependent assets; MIDI note extraction from audio for drum replacement and melodic transcription; Freeze Tracks feature releases CPU resources by invisibly rendering tracks; Distributed audio processing (DAP) aggregates processing power of multiple computers on a network; serial-based copy protection; powerful folders to facilitate organization and streamline various arranging tasks; extreme compatibility; open GarageBand songs directly in Logic Pro; support for Apple Core Audio and Digidesign DAE/TDM hardware; support for TDM and AudioSuite plug-ins with DAE/TDM hardware; support for Audio Units plug-ins; support for AAF, OMF, Open TL, and XML (Final Cut Pro); streamlined ReWire support for optimized integration with Reason, Ableton Live, and other ReWire-compatible applications; intuitive region-based MIDI and audio editing; comprehensive set of editing tools assignable to left, right, and key-modified mouse buttons; effortless take management; region-based take recording and management in automatically generated take folders; pack existing tracks into take folders; single-click take selection; colorize takes on the fly; intelligent unpacking of take folders onto separate tracks; move and edit entire take folders like any other region; Quick Swipe Comping; build a comp track from multiple takes; create comps on the fly; audition comps in real time; automatic, customizable crossfades between phrases; flatten function replaces take folder with regions that represent the current comp; Flatten and Merge function replaces take folder with newly created audio file; Multiple MIDI editors include Piano Roll, Score, Hyper, Event List, and Transform; graphical time stretching and compression in the Arrange window; sample-accurate editing in the Arrange window; definable relative or absolute snap grid; nondestructive graphical fades and crossfades; snap-to-transient selection; Shuffle and Auto-Crossfade Arrange Edit modes; destructive sample editing using built-in or external sample editor like Soundtrack Pro 2; 10,000-step undo history; time-linear and/or beat-linear display in the Arrange window; professional mixing and automation; Track Mixer views simplify mixer channel navigation; dynamic channel strip creation accelerates mixer setup and configuration; easy setup of multi-output software instruments; Signal Flow view option shows all channel strips (e.g., Aux, Output, Master) within the audio signal path of the selected channel strip; Save/Load complete plug-in configurations using channel strip settings; sample-accurate, track-based 32-bit automation; track- or region-based solo and mute; track mute/solo in either Fast or CPU-Saving mode; solo safe mode for any channel strip; direct insert patching of external hardware instruments and effects; exponential or dB-linear level meter scaling; busses as sources for recording; inline input monitoring; up to 255 independent mono, stereo, or surround audio channels; up to 255 independent software instrument channels; up to 255 auxiliary channel strips; 64 busses; 15 inserts, 8 sends per channel; 32 multi-assignable channel groups for mix and edit; extensive control surface support with autolearn; EuCon protocol support for Euphonix MC and System-5-MC control surface systems; support for Smart AV Smart Console; support for active control surfaces via CS plug-ins; Curve tool for refining automation; automation features include group automation recording, inked editing of grouped automation, Automation Quick Access for easy hardware control of currently selected parameter, automate any channel strip parameter or plug-in parameter on the fly or manually input parameter values using a breakpoint interface, view multiple automation parameters for a single track at once, simultaneously view and edit automation for single or multiple tracks, read, write, touch, and latch automation modes; Comprehensive Surround; support for all standard surround configurations, including LCRS, Quad, 5.1, 6.1, and 7.1; support for multichannel interleaved and split surround audio files; play back, record, or process multichannel interleaved audio files; surround level metering; multichannel signal routing via sends, busses, and auxiliaries; Graphic Surround Panner to manipulate mono or stereo streams within a surround field; Graphic Surround Balancer to simultaneously balance all channels of surround input; support for Logic Studio True Surround plug-ins; built in multi-mono support lets user use any mono or stereo Logic Studio or Audio Units plug-in in a surround project; surround bounce and burn to DVD-A (PCM only) disc; Dolby Digital AC-3 encoding and preview with Compressor; easy mixdown to stereo and surround formats using Down Mixer plug-in. SYSTEM SPECS: Macintosh.

Apple Logic Pro Studio (www.apple.com): Contents include a DVD containing Logic Pro 8, MainStage, Soundtrack Pro 2, Studio Instruments, Studio Effects, WaveBurner 1.5, Compressor 3, Impulse Response Utility, Apple Loops Utility, QuickTime 7 Pro, and required content; six DVDs containing Jam Pack collections, sound effects, surround music beds, EXS24 samples, and impulse response files; demo DVD; printed and electronic documentation. SYSTEM SPECS: Macintosh.

Apple Main Stage (www.apple.com): Built for live performance; lets keyboardists, guitarists, and other musicians perform with software instruments and effects through a full-screen interface designed specifically for the stage; includes New View for the Stage: 3D interface created for the stage, providing the information needed for a live show; Hardware Control: from keyboards and drum pads to pedal boards and control surfaces, can use any MIDI or USB controller with MainStage; Keyboard Racks: keyboard templates featuring Studio Instruments and Studio Effects, or build own custom rack with personalized sounds, layers, and splits; Guitar Rigs: guitar templates featuring Guitar Amp Pro, or build own custom rig that user can control with hardware pedal boards; Templates for Everyone: customize live rig with a wide selection of templates designed for different instruments and performance styles; Made for Performance: provides stability under demanding conditions. SYSTEM SPECS: Macintosh.

Apple Soundtrack Pro (www.apple.com): Audio post; powerful editing tools, surround mixing, and a streamlined interface simplify audio post production for film and video; single-window design simplifies the process of creating great sound for picture; professional tools designed for audio post-production help edit and mix; restoration features let user analyze and repair field-recorded dialogue and damaged recordings; integration with Final Cut Studio makes it easy to work with Final Cut editors. SYSTEM SPECS: Macintosh.

Apple Studio Effects (www.apple.com): Shape sound; from vintage and modern compressors to distortion effects and amp models; eighty effect plug-ins; multitap Delay Designer plug-in lets user explore creative delay effects in stereo or full surround; Surround Space Designer helps user re-create the full reverberant qualities of some of the world's most compelling spaces; Guitar Amp Pro lets user play guitar through faithful re-creations of classic amplifiers and speaker cabinets; wide variety of production effects; full range of creative effects such as reverb, modulation, and delay. SYSTEM SPECS: Macintosh.

Apple Studio Instruments (www.apple.com): Produce and play nearly any sound with the largest set of instrument plug-ins available in a single box; Ultrabeat is a 25-voice drum machine with a built-in step sequencer; EXS24 Sampler lets user play and design sampled instruments; Sculpture is an advanced component modeling instrument; Vintage Keyboards are fully modeled simulations of classic keyboards; Synths include an array of FM, subtractive, and analog-modeled synthesizers. SYSTEM SPECS: Macintosh.

Apple Studio Sound Library (www.apple.com): The complete content of five Jam Pack collections: Jam Pack 1, Remix Tools, Rhythm Section, Symphony Orchestra, and World Music; provides infinite possibilities for writing, producing, and performing music; 18,000 royalty-free Apple Loops to help user establish a groove and embellish music; 2400 professionally designed channel strip settings let user create finely tuned sounds; 1300 pristine-sounding EXS sampled instruments. SYSTEM SPECS: Macintosh.

Applied Acoustics Systems (www.applied-acoustics.com): Professional Series: first-class physical modeling instruments include Tassman 4 Sound Synthesis Studio, Lounge Lizard EP-3 Electric Piano, Ultra Analog VA-1 Analog Synthesizer, String Studio VS-1 String Modeling Synthesizer, Strum Acoustic GS-1 Acoustic Guitar Synthesizer, Modeling Collection Professional Series bundle; Session Series: smart and easy to use instruments at entry level prices include Lounge Lizard Session Electric Piano, Ultra Analog Session Virtual Analog Synthesizer; Sound Bank Series: professionally crafted preset collections include Ultra Analog Sound Banks Add-on preset collections for Ultra Analog VA-1, String Studio Sound Banks Add-on preset collections for String Studio VS-1. SYSTEM SPECS: Macintosh; Windows.

Arturia Software Instruments (www.arturia.com): ANALOG CLASSICS are software recreations of the synthesizers that have been at the center of music production for the last forty years; true to the original while bringing additional features; titles include: V Collection; Analog Factory; Jupiter-8V; Prophet V; ARP2600 V; Minimoog V; CS-80V; Moog Modular V; BRASS is an instrument allowing to play the trumpet, the saxophone, and the trombone with realism; advanced physical modeling. SYSTEM SPECS: Macintosh; Windows.

Arturia Storm (www.arturia.com): Complete music creation software; emulates the environment of a production studio: synthesizers, drum machines, sample players, sequencer, effects, mixing desk; made for beginners and amateurs who do not necessarily have knowledge of studio technology; Composition Wizard provides help for learning how to compose in several musical genres. But besides this simplicity, Storm surely fulfils some of the needs of professional musicians and producers; Virtual Studio including fourteen instruments and ten effects; compose and produce with MIDI patterns, MIDI Sequencer, Piano Roll; import MIDI files; use external MIDI control; record audio and use audio samples; import Wave, Aiff, MP3 at 44.1 kHz; export songs as Wave or Aiff; automatic Tempo Synchronisation for audio samples (real time time-stretching and pitch-shifting); professional studio environment with Mixer, Mix Automation, unlimited undos, keyboard shortcuts. SYSTEM SPECS: Macintosh; Windows.

AudioEase Plug-ins (www.audioease.com): Products include: Altiverb; Impulse Responses; Speakerphone; Barbabatch; Snapper; VST Wrapper; Rocket Science; The Nautilus Bundle; Make-A-Testtone. SYSTEM SPECS: Macintosh; Windows.

AudioSurgeon (www.turtlebeach.com): Record, edit, transform, convert, manipulate, and burn music to CD; get inside digital music files for customization and control; optimize loudness, remove unwanted sections, fade out songs, remove hiss, use sound effects, and more; convert music files to and from multiple file formats, including MP3, WMA, and WAVE; audio recording, editing, and CD burning tool; digitally record songs to PC hard drive; view music as a graphical waveform showing every peak and valley in the sound; zoom in and change every nuance then burn it back to CD; companion to any music jukebox program and digital music on a PC, portable or network audio player; restore and preserve cassette and vinyl record collection; remove pops, clicks, and hiss from original recordings then convert into digital audio files on PC; create voice and music backgrounds for multimedia presentations; mix music and voice-overs together to create professional-sounding audio clips to complement PowerPoint and other visual applications; include transforms like echo, volume scaling, fades, reverse, and more; paste in sound effects and use processing to shape finished presentation; highly customizable mixer; customize faders, hide unnecessary options, control multiple sound card mixers, create own mixer applications for different functions, like recording vinyl, MP3 playback, Internet chat, and more; record and edit music and sound samples; create sample loops for drums, rhythm parts, voices, and more; loop control feature to edit nuances of audio file; import finished sample into sequencer program or other audio sampler; customize desktop with WAV sound effects, or create greeting messages for PC answering machine. SYSTEM SPECS: Windows.

BBE High Definition Sound Technology (www.bbesound.com): Sound improvement technology since 1985; BBE Sonic Maximizer signal processors; Stomp Boxes; DI boxes; B-MAX and BMAX-t bass preamps; MAXCOM Dual Compressor; MAX-X2 and MAX-X3 Electronic Crossovers; Loudspeaker Management Systems; Equalizers; VG-360 SONIC MAXIMIZER; ARS High Definition Sound processor; products used in small nightclubs to huge international tours; for both the professional audio and consumer electronic markets; next-generation audio improvement technologies; BBE ViVA, BBE Mach3Bass, and BBE MP are in consumer electronics products from major manufacturers. SYSTEM SPECS: Macintosh; Windows.

Berklee Press (www.berkleepress.com): Titles include: *Electronic and Digital Instruments; Producing and Mixing Jazz; Producing in the Home Studio with Pro Tools; Producing Music with Digital Performer; The Complete Guide to Remixing: Produce Professional Dance-Floor Hits on Your Home Computer; Turntable Technique—The Art of the DJ,* and more. SYSTEM SPECS: Book and Audio CD, or Book and Hybrid CD-ROM, or Instructional DVD.

BIAS Products (www.bias-inc.com/products/): Award-winning audio editing, processing, and mastering tools; PEAK PRO: for sound design for film, video, or multimedia, rapid-fire broadcast editing, and music production and mastering; PEAK LE: includes many of Peak Pro's core features at a lower price; PEAK PRO XT: Xtended Technology bundle includes Peak Pro, SoundSoap, SoundSoap Pro, and the Master Perfection Suite; plug-ins for mastering, audio restoration, and sound design; SOUNDSOAP: for digitizing vinyl LPs and cassettes for iPod, cleaning up recordings, improving poor quality podcasts, or

reducing background noise from home movies or DV soundtracks; SOUNDSOAP PRO: noise reduction and audio restoration with a minimum of tweaking and reduced chances of undesirable sonic artifacts; MASTER PERFECTION SUITE: for mastering and sound design professionals; state-of-the-art plug-ins were originally available as part of Peak Pro XT; full-featured multitrack audio editing and mixing at an affordable price; DECK: combination of features, speed, compatibility, and value; easy and intuitive user interface, scores of available plug-ins, and more; record, edit, process, and mix; DECK LE: more affordable version. SYSTEM SPECS: Macintosh.

Big Fish Audio Sample CDs and CD-ROMs (www.bigfishaudio.com): Quality sample libraries since 1986; extensive selection of sample library and sound effects products from around the world; all products are license free; no clearance forms or additional licenses are required; featured in hundreds of charting songs and top film scores; contain Loops/Performances and/or Sounds; extensive selection of disks; audition before buying. SYSTEM SPECS: Macintosh; Windows.

Cakewalk Alien Connections ReValver (www.cakewalk.com): Build own virtual guitar rack; arsenal of modules, including preamps, filters, effects modules, power amps, speaker simulators, and room simulators; many guitar tones; effect for wringing unique sonic characteristics out of vocals, organs, drums, and other instruments; can be used in any program that supports DirectX plug-ins. SYSTEM SPECS: Windows.

Cakewalk Audio Effects (www.cakewalk.com): Products include: Alien Connections ReValver; Audio Damage; BBE Sonic Maximizer; Bias SoundSoap 2; Boost 11 Peak Limiter; Cakewalk Audio FX 1; Cakewalk Audio FX 2; Cakewalk Audio FX 3; Cakewalk VST Adapter; Camel Audio Camelphat; Camel Audio Camelspace; Peterson Tuner; PSP Audioware Vintage Warmer; Sonitus:fx Plug-ins; Studio Devil Virtual Guitar Amp; UAD-1 Express PAK; UAD-1 Project PAK. SYSTEM SPECS: Windows.

Cakewalk Audio FX 1, FX 2, and FX 3 (www.cakewalk.com): DirectX audio plug-ins for digital audio; add real-time, 32-bit, audio processing to Windows music applications; AudioFX1 includes a compressor/gate, limiter, expander/gate, and dynamics processor; with AudioFX2, can simulate amplifiers and tape simulation to add to tone; with AudioFX3, can create custom reverb in any environment. SYSTEM SPECS: Windows.

Cakewalk Audio Loops and MIDI Groove Clips (www.cakewalk.com): Products include: Cakewalk Loops Series; Beat Fetish; Keyfax Future Beats; Keyfax Real Guitar Collection; Loopmasters Libraries;

PowerFX Loop Libraries; Smart Loops Libraries. SYSTEM SPECS: Windows.

Cakewalk Consumer Products (www.cakewalk.com): See web site for complete details of all features for the products listed; products include: PYRO AUDIO CREATOR: Virtual toolbox; recording and editing audio; burning and ripping CDs; cleaning and converting albums to CD or MP3; encoding, tagging, and organizing sound library; backing up files to data CD, DVD, or Blu-Ray; publishing music to the Internet; KINETIC 2; MUSIC CREATOR 4: Make music from home computer; plug in and record guitars, keyboards, vocals, CD samples, or any other sound source; STUDIO INSTRUMENTS; USB MUSIC PACK. SYSTEM SPECS: Windows.

Cakewalk Digital Audio Workstations and Sequencers (www.cakewalk.com): See web site for complete details of all features for the products listed; products include: PRO SUITE: includes Sonar 7, Project 5, Dimension Pro, and Rapture; create music from scratch; high audio quality; access to vintage and modern instrument sounds; studio-quality FX; timing and pitch correction; advanced mixing and bussing system; high-end mastering plug-ins, and more; SONAR 7 PRODUCER EDITION: No limits on track count, bus routing, effect or instrument inserts; ample array of audio effects, virtual instruments, and innovative technologies; feature-packed and complete music making package; impressive collection of synthesizers and effects plug-ins; used on multi-core PCs, Windows Vista, and Intel-based Macs using Bootcamp; x64 processing, multi-core and multi-processor support, and 64-bit double precision audio quality; configure studio to meet unique needs; compatible with choice of WDM or ASIO hardware from the stock sound card that ships with a PC to an SSL AWS 900+ console; load presets of keystrokes from favorite applications or make own; support for control surfaces and MIDI controllers; expand creative abilities with DSP cards and third party VST, DirectX, and ReWire effects and instruments; customize menus, toolbars, layouts, channel presets, track icons, color schemes, and more; developed by musicians who listen, understand, and respond to the discerning needs of customers, including Grammy and Emmy winning producers, engineers, and composers; complete package includes regular updates, affordably priced upgrades, user forum; technical support over both email and telephone; SONAR 7 STUDIO EDITION: Built upon the same core feature set as SONAR 7 Producer Edition; recording audio and MIDI; composing with virtual instruments; remixing with loops; mixing with professional effects; delivery of a polished final track; SONAR HOME STUDIO VERSION 6 XL: Selection of over one gigabyte of instrument sounds, Boost 11 Peak Limiter, Dimension LE, Session Drummer 2 drum

instrument, and more; SONAR HOME STUDIO VERSION 6: turn PC into a complete music production studio; record live instruments and vocals and mix them with studio-quality audio effects; edit audio, MIDI, and music notation; build backing tracks or entire songs with hundreds of included instrument sounds and tempo-syncing loops; solution for creating and sharing music; SONAR LE: included with purchased hardware from one of many partners, including Roland, Edirol, EMU, Samson, Allen & Heath, Audio Technica, and Open Labs; PROJECT5 VERSION 2: Create, record, arrange, sequence, perform, edit, mix, and promote; GUITAR TRACKS PRO VERSION 3: PC recording software; create music anywhere, anytime; no expensive hardware is required; 32-track digital recorder and virtual mixing console; IK Multimedia's Amplitube LE, a special edition of the leading guitar amp plug-in; high-quality effects; powerful looping tools with full ACID-loop support; chromatic-tuner; metronome; complete library of backing tracks; pro quality production tools; speed and ease of an old portable multi-track; KINETIC 2: Start making beats; create electronic music. SYSTEM SPECS: Windows.

Cakewalk Education Materials (www.cakewalk.com): Titles include: *Cakewalk Synthesizers: From Presets to Power User; Complete SONAR 7 Video Tutorial; Dimension Pro In-Depth; Rapture In-Depth Video Tutorial; SONAR 7 Power!; Tour:Smart by Martin Atkins*. SYSTEM SPECS: Book and Audio CD or CD-ROM and/or Instructional DVD.

Cakewalk Instrument Expansion Packs (www.cakewalk.com): Architecture Waveforms; Beat Fetish; Biolabs Vol. 1; Craig Anderton's Minimoog Tribute Pack; Digital Sound Factory Vol. 1; Dimension Pro Expansion Packs (FREE); E-MU Proteus Pack; Piscis Expansion Pack for Rapture; Rapture Expansion Packs (FREE); Session Drummer 2 Hip Hop Kit Vol. 1. SYSTEM SPECS: Windows.

Cakewalk Integrated Hardware and Software (www.cakewalk.com): Products include: SONAR REAC Recording System; SONAR Power Studio 250; SONAR Power Studio 660; Cakewalk USB Music Pack. SYSTEM SPECS: Windows.

Cakewalk MIDI FX (www.cakewalk.com): Products include: JMT Orchestrator 2.1; MusicLab Rhythm'n'Chords Pro 2.2; MusicLab VeloMaster 1.2; NTONYX Style Enhancer. SYSTEM SPECS: Windows.

Cakewalk Virtual Instruments (www.cakewalk.com): Products include: Dimension Pro; Rapture; Z3TA+; Dimension LE & Garritan Pocket Orchestra; Session Drummer 2; Studio Instruments; Pentagon I; Square I; SFZ+; Triangle DXi (FREE); Cakewalk VST Adapter. SYSTEM SPECS: Macintosh; Windows.

CD Architect (www.sonycreativesoftware.com): CD text support; support for up to 32-bit, 192kHz source audio; high-quality resampling and dithering with noiseshaping; single or multi-file playlisting; volume and ASR envelopes for any event; multiple levels of undo/redo; override validation errors option; mono-to-stereo conversion on the fly; CD transport controls; direct file open into Sound Forge® software; track creation from Sound Forge regions; trimmer window; Media Explorer; ripple editing; CD image file rendering; automatic crossfades; greater than 1:1 time zoom; reading and extraction of PQ data along with audio tracks; complete control over tracks, marker placements, and indices; preview multiple tracks or ranges of audio before extraction from a supported CD device; stereo master volume fader and adjustable envelope controls for any region; Media Pool; multiple file format support without conversion; autosave crash recovery; undo/redo history list; supports MP3, AIFF, Ogg Vorbis, Windows Media Audio, and more; mastering; over twenty real-time DirectX® plug-ins; event and master bus effects model; audio layering to create complex crossfades; event normalization; real time pitch shift/time stretch; slip trimming; audio phase invert; audio scrubbing; unlimited volume envelope points; CD design; full PQ code editing support, including track and index positions and pause times; absolute times for replication; print cue sheets and format CD liner notes; up to 99 tracks; up to 99 subindices per track; smart track reordering; automatic pause time indication; relative times for liner notes; timeline event locking; adjustable pause times; audio CD player un-mute fade emulation; CD writing; burns disc-at-once premaster CDs for professional replication; USB, FireWire, SCSI, and IDE/ATAPI CD-R and CD-RW drive support; overburn support of eighty minute and other size CD-Rs; buffer underrun protection; test burn mode; PQ list verification for Red Book compatibility prior to burn; burn speed selection; copy-inhibit flags; pre-emphasis flags; audio clipping detection; International Standard Recording Codes (ISRC); Universal Product Codes (UPC); Media Catalog Numbers (MCN). SYSTEM SPECS: Windows.

Cinescore (www.sonycreativesoftware.com): Professional soundtrack creation; precise control; customization, performance, and accuracy; automatically generate an unlimited number of musical compositions using royalty-free Theme Packs in a variety of popular styles; generates an unlimited number of fully orchestrated compositions that custom fit to video by precisely matching the time duration specified; adjust parameters such as mood, tempo, and intensity to create complex songs to short and sweet stinger tracks; create customizable songs; royalty-free themes; no loops to stack up and no complicated licensing fees; multigenre, royalty-free production music; includes one DVD featuring twenty complete themes for action sequences, weddings, corporate presentations, family vacations, and more; additional Theme Packs in a variety of genres; each Theme automatically generates an unlimited number of different arrangements and variations; 15, 30, 45, or 60 second samples of each theme; multiple editing capabilities; create a custom fit for soundtrack with precise adjustments to volume, panning, pitch, and tempo; mixing and editing; multiple media options; imports a wide range of file formats including AVI, AIF, BMP, JPG, MP3, MPEG 1 & MPEG 2 video, PCA, PSD, QT, SWF, WAV, and WMV; arrange media on the timeline, then create musical tracks for movies, slideshows, commercials, and radio productions; export to popular formats such as MPEG-2 for DVD and MPEG-4 for portable media players. SYSTEM SPECS: Windows.

Cinescore   Theme   Packs (www.sonycreativesoftware.com): Titles include: ¡con ritmo! The Latin Music Experience; Adrenaline Surge: High Energy Lifestyle; High Tech World: Kinetic Tracks; Home Studio Soundtrack Pack Volume 1; Home Studio Soundtrack Pack Volume 2; Hyperculture: New Media Soundtracks; Incredible Vistas: Visual and Emotional Panoramas; Pass the Ring: The Wedding Soundtrack Library; Take Five: Leisure Soundtracks; The Big Picture: Atmospheric Music for Film; The Ideal Vacation: Music for Life; Urban 24/7: City Soundmaps. SYSTEM SPECS: Windows.

Composing Digital Music for Dummies (www.dummies.com): Write and arrange digital music; determine what equipment is needed; create ringtones and MP3s; compose with a MIDI controller or a mouse; work with notation software; use keyboard shortcuts; publish creations on the Internet; build a tune from scratch; extract parts from score for each instrument. SYSTEM SPECS: Book and Hybrid CD-ROM.

Course Technology/CENGAGE Learning Book/CD-ROM Kits and Instructional DVDs (www.course.com/catalog/subcategory.cfm?category= Music%20Technology): Titles include: *Abelton Live 6 CSi Master; Ableton Live 4 CSi Master, Starter; Ableton Live 5 CSi Master; Ableton Live 5 Power! The Comprehensive Guide; Ableton Live 6 Power! The Comprehensive Guide; Acid 5 CSi Starter; Audio Made Easy – 4th Edition (Or How to Be a Sound Engineer Without Really Trying); Audio Plug-ins CSi Master; Audio Plug-ins, Volume 2 CSi Master; Critical Listening Skills for Audio Professionals; Cubase 4 CSi Master-Advanced Digital Audio Training; Cubase SX 2 CSi Starter; Cubase SX 3 CSi Master; Cubase SX 3 CSi Starter; Cubase Sx 4.0 Advanced Level; Cubase Sx 4.0 Beginner Level; Digital Performer 4 CSi Master; Digital Performer 4 CSi Starter; Editing Audio in Pro*

Tools – Skill Pack; GarageBand CSi Starter; Get Creative with Cubase SX/SL; Home Recording Basics; Home Recording Magazine's 100 Recording Tips and Tricks; Home Recording Presents: Miking Guitars in the Studio; Kontakt 2 Power! The Comprehensive Guide; Logic 7 – Beginner Level, Pro & Express; Logic CSi Starter; Logic Pro 7 – Advanced Level; Logic Pro 7 – Instruments & Plug-ins; Logic Pro CSi Master; Mastering Cubase 4 Presented by Electronic Musician; Mastering Music at Home; MIDI Sequencing in Reason: Skill Pack; Mixing in Pro Tools – Skillpack; Musicianship in the Digital Age; Nuendo CSi Master; Power Tools for Reason 2.5-Master the World's Most Popular Virtual Studio Software; Power Tools for Reason 3.0-Master the World's Most Popular Virtual Studio Software; Pro Tools 101 Official Courseware; Pro Tools 6 CSi Master, Second Edition; Pro Tools 6 CSi Starter, Second Edition; Pro Tools 6 Power!; Pro Tools 7 CSI Master; Pro Tools 7 CSi Starter; Pro Tools 7 Power! – Second Edition; Pro Tools 7 Power! The Comprehensive Guide; Pro Tools Surround Sound Mixing; Producing in the Home Studio with Pro Tools – Third Edition; Producing Music with Digital Performer; Project 5 InstantPro Series; Pro-Tools LE-7; Reason CSi Starter; Reason 3 CSi Master; Reason 3 CSi Starter; Reason 3.0 Advanced Level; Reason 3.0; Reason CSi Master; Reason InstantPro Series; Roger McGuinn's Guide to Home Recording on a Computer-Basic Set-Up and Advice; S.M.A.R.T. Guide to Producing Music with Samples, Loops and MIDI; Setting Up Your Surround Studio-Everything You Need to Know to Start Mixing in Surround Now; Shaping Your Sound with Microphones, Mixers & Multitrack Recording; Shaping Your Sound with Signal Processors-Professional Techniques for Creative Recording; Software Synthesizers-The Definitive Guide to Virtual Musical Instruments; Sonar 3 InstantPro Series; Sonar 5 Power! The Comprehensive Guide; Sonar 6 Advanced Level-MusicPro Guides; Sonar 6 Beginner MusicPro Guides; Sound Advice on MIDI Production; The Finale NotePad Primer-Learning the Art of Music Notation with Notepad; The S.M.A.R.T. Guide to Digital Recording Software and Plug-ins; Using Reason's Virtual Instruments: Skill Pack; Using Rewire: Skill Pack; Working with Beats in Pro Tools: Skill Pack, and more. SYSTEM SPECS: Book and Hybrid CD-ROM and/or Instructional DVD.

Critical Listening and Auditory Perception (www.halleonard.com): Sharpen skills of evaluating sound quality; hundreds of illustrations elaborate on text. SYSTEM SPECS: Book and Audio CD.

Dart (www.dartpro.com): Award-winning digital audio recording and noise reduction software products for users of all levels; for audio restoration, CD ripping and burning, or making a karaoke CD; audio control software; use DART Pro 24 for 24-bit audio cleanup to improve audio quality of older recordings like LPs with hiss, clicks, hum, and more; use DART Pro 24 as professional audio editing software or audio capture software for new recordings, and as audio mastering software to finalize a recording project; with CD Recorder 4.1 audio burning software, rip it, sweeten it, and burn audio CD disks; with Karaoke Studio make and play karaoke; remove the main vocal; synchronize lyrics; sing along; record performance; full screen playback display. SYSTEM SPECS: Windows.

DSP•FX Plug-ins (www.dspfx.com): StudioVerb; AcousticVerb; Optimizer; Aural Activator; Stereo Pitch Shifter; Multi-Tap Delay; Analog Tape Flanger; Multi-Element Chorus; Parametric EQ; Auto-Panner; Tremolo; Stereo Widener; gives PC-digital audio workstation users access to real-time effects processing with pro studio quality; works in real time with Cakewalk, Cubase, Sound Forge, and other high-end programs. SYSTEM SPECS: Windows.

Echoview Pro for Windows (http://www.mirage1.u-net.com): Integrated suite of interactive music calculating tools for musicians, sound engineers, and producers; 32-bit package; freeware; delay time calculator; delay time grid; metronome; tap tempo utility; chord cue; song length calculator; stopwatch; sample calculator; synthesisers; printing features. SYSTEM SPECS: Windows.

Essentials of Music for Audio Professionals (www.halleonard.com): For engineers, producers, directors, editors, managers, and audio/video recording professionals; music theory, musical notation, arrangements, and scores; rhythmic and pitch notation, musical expression, sound production, melody and musical form, harmony and harmonics, sound in space, modes, scales, chords, intervals. SYSTEM SPECS: Book and Audio CD.

ExpressFX 1 (www.sonycreativesoftware.com): Collection of four streamlined effects; designed for use with Sound Forge and ACID; each effect provides parameter adjustments to give control over sound processing; works with any DirectX-compatible host program; available for purchase as a downloadable product; features four discrete plug-ins: Distortion, Flange/Wah-Wah, Reverb, and Stutter; installs into and operates in any program that fully supports DirectX Plug-ins. SYSTEM SPECS: Windows.

ExpressFX 2 (www.sonycreativesoftware.com): Collection of four streamlined effects designed especially for use with Sound Forge and ACID; each effect provides parameter adjustments to give control over sound processing; works with any DirectX-compatible host program; available for purchase as a downloadable product; features four discrete plug-ins: Amplitude Modulation, Chorus, Delay, and EQ; installs into and operates in any program that fully supports DirectX Plug-ins. SYSTEM SPECS: Windows.

Hal Leonard DVDs (www.halleonard.com): Titles include: *DJ's Complete Guide; Home Recording Magazine's 100 Recording Tips and Tricks; Hudson DVD Sampler—The Finest Multimedia for Musicians; Setting Up Your Surround Studio; Shaping Your Sound with Microphones, Mixers and Multitrack Recording; Shaping Your Sound with Signal Processors; Turntable Technique—The Art of the DJ*, and more. SYSTEM SPECS: Instructional DVD.

Hal Leonard Recording Method – Six Pack (www.halleonard.com): Microphones and Mixers (One), Instrument and Vocal Recordings (Two), Recording Software and Plug Ins (Three), Sequencing Samples and Loops (Four), Engineering and Producing (Five), and Mixing and Mastering (Six). SYSTEM SPECS: Book and Instructional DVD.

iZotope (www.izotope.com): Audio signal processing products; iZotope RX: complete audio restoration application; Ozone 3: complete mastering effects system using 64-bit analog modeled processing; Trash: 64-bit modeling of classic amps, distortions, delays, and filters; Spectron: manipulate audio in the frequency domain with spectral delay, pan and morph; iZotope Radius: natural time and pitch control for Logic Pro; iDrum: drum machine for Mac OSX; pHATmatik PRO: play loops; OzoneMP: analog modeled audio enhancement. SYSTEM SPECS: Macintosh; Windows.

KVR Audio Plug-In News (www.kvraudio.com/allplug-insononepage.php): The Internet's number one news and information resource for open standard audio plug-ins; new releases, product announcements, and product updates for all VST Plug-ins, DirectX Plug-ins, and Audio Units Plug-ins; fully searchable audio plug-in database updated daily; many free member services including user reviews, product update notifications, and an active discussion forum; official support forums for many plug-in developers plus the official Receptor support forum; extensive alphabetical listing of audio plug-ins; links to manufacturers; also listed by developer; banks and patches to download and upload; ratings; forum; Wiki tutorials. SYSTEM SPECS: Macintosh; Windows.

Kyma X (www.symbolicsound.com): Sound design environment used in music and post-production studios, research labs, art installations, game developers' studios, educational institutions, home studios, and live performances; sound library of 1000+ examples; documentation; online knowledge bases; support. SYSTEM SPECS: Macintosh; Windows.

Master Tracks Pro (www.gvox.com): MIDI sequencing software; sixty-four tracks with track looping; step entry and real-time entry; automated punch-in; graphic user interface offers several views of a musical piece; any section can be deleted, moved, or copied with cut and paste edits; supports SMPTE; synchronize music to film, video, multimedia presentations, or multitrack audiotape; automatically adjust tempo to fit a specific length of time or precisely match a visual event; graphic note editor; event list editor; support for Quicktime internal synthesizer; looped overdub and record for drum machine-style recording. SYSTEM SPECS: Macintosh; Windows.

Mastering Music (www.datasonics.com.au/): Structured set of over 400 music lessons providing musical outcomes in performing, composing, digital audio, notation, aural training, music theory, and film scoring; video clips. SYSTEM SPECS: Windows.

MIDI Quest (www.squest.com): Editor/librarian; easy to use; supports over 600 instruments and sixty manufacturers; fast tips online help; comprehensive sound auditioning tools; all functions are active while playing; extensive sound sorting capabilities; sophisticated patch organization and editing for banks; store sound and banks from different MIDI devices together; Sound Checker graphic MIDI systems analysis; advanced graphic editing; more products: *MIDI Quest XL, Uniquest, Infinity, MIDI Tools,* and *Studio Suite.* SYSTEM SPECS: Macintosh; Windows.

MOTU AudioDesk (www.motu.com): Audio workstation software; 24-bit/192 KHz recording and real time, 32-bit effects processing; includes multitrack audio editing, sample-accurate placement of audio, complete virtual mixing environment with up to sixty-four stereo busses, automated mixing, graphic editing of mix and effects automation, scrubbing, trimming, spotting, crossfades, support for third-party MAS effects plug-ins, unlimited digital track bouncing including effects and automation, and much more; does not place artificial restrictions on the number of tracks user can work with; unlimited audio tracks; view audio tracks in a single, unified mixer; configure up to twenty effects inserts per audio channel, and thirty-two stereo busses; automatable, effects parameters with five advanced automation modes, beat-synchronized effects and sample accurate editing of automation data; automation system features rich set of user interface technologies such as event flags for discrete events and spline tools for manipulating control points; automation parameters displayed in real world values such as decibels and milliseconds; dozens of real-time DSP effects with easy to use graphical controls and complete automation; two-, four-, and eight-band EQ, tube-simulation and distortion effects with flexible PreAmp-1 plug-in, reverbs, compressor, synthesizer-style multimode filter, echo and delay effects, chorus, phaser, flanger, and more. SYSTEM SPECS: Macintosh.

MOTU Digital Performer (www.motu.com): Integrated digital audio and MIDI sequencing production system; provides a comprehensive environment for editing, arranging, mixing, processing, and mastering multitrack audio projects for a wide variety of applications; Digital Performer 6 includes: new user interface, streamlined operation, track comping, MasterWorks Leveler plug-in, ProVerb convolution plug-in, Final Cut Pro integration, film scoring enhancements, expanded audio file support, enhanced Pro Tools | HD support, enhanced plug-in operation, enhanced softsynth operation, direct audio CD burning, and DP6 Productivity enhancements; simultaneously record and playback multiple tracks of digital audio and MIDI data in a totally integrated, creative environment; does not place artificial restrictions on the number of tracks user can work with; unlimited audio and MIDI tracks; supports a wide range of audio hardware, including TDM (Pro Tools), Direct I/O, ASIO, Sound Manager, and MOTU audio interfaces; supports high-resolution 24-bit/192 KHz audio; view MIDI and audio tracks in a single, unified mixer; configure up to twenty effects inserts per audio channel, and thirty-two stereo busses; automatable, effects parameters with five advanced automation modes, beat-synchronized effects, and sample accurate editing of automation data; automation system features a rich set of user interface technologies such as event flags for discrete events and spline tools for manipulating control points; automation parameters are displayed in meaningful real world values such as decibels and milliseconds; includes dozens of real-time DSP effects with easy-to-use graphic controls and complete automation; two-, four-, and eight-band EQ, tube simulation and distortion effects with the flexible PreAmp-1 plug-in, three reverbs, two noise gates, including the MasterWorks Gate with real-time lookahead gating, two compressors, a synthesizer-style multimode filter, echo and delay effects including a surround delay, chorus, phaser, flanger, Sonic Modulator, and more; supports multiple processors; fully compatible with all MOTU Audio System plug-ins, including those from third-party vendors; includes a built-in waveform editor that provides a pencil tool for removing clicks and a loop tool for defining loops for sampler; auto edit cross-fades; sampler integration allows user to transfer audio from project to sampler with a drag and drop operation; sampler appears as a device inside Digital Performer; can seamlessly share data; PureDSP functions provide independent control over the duration and pitch of audio files with exceptional sound quality; tempo-conform drum loops, add vocal harmony or even gender-bend vocal tracks; audio editing is accurate to a single sample; edit MIDI with a resolution of 1/10,000.000 PPQ (pulses per quarter); when used with a USB MOTU MIDI interface, provides MIDI timing resolution to within a single MIDI byte, under one third of a millisecond; with Multirecord MIDI recording, can record on an unlimited number of MIDI tracks simultaneously; three continuous controller editing modes, creating continuous controller streams for the automation of MIDI instruments is flexible and intuitive; movie track and Quicktime support integrates Digital Performer with the video world, enabling user to see instantly how edits relate to picture; individually zoomable tracks, flexible window arrangement, and navigation tools allow for trouble-free manipulation within projects; provides many flexible editors, including Sequence Editor, Graphic Editor, Event List, Drum Editor, and QuickScribe notation; list-editing or graphical style display; score layout, or extensive drum-programming; fine-tuning of single MIDI events, or massive changes of entire sections; QuickScribe notation window lets user print out whole score or individual parts; continuous scrolling moves the music under the wiper, which stays fixed to the center of the window; provides a choice of four panner plug-ins, including a localizing room simulator; each audio track can be assigned to any surround sound format, from LCRS up to 10.2; panning movements can be automated using automation system; include complete surround submixes or record the output of a surround reverb with surround tracks; master multichannel mix with a broad assortment of variable channel effects processors, including the MasterWorks Limiter. SYSTEM SPECS: Macintosh.

MOTU Electric Keys (www.motu.com): Complete collection of classic and vintage electric pianos, clavs, organs, strings machines, tape sampler, and other electric keyboard instruments; cross-platform virtual instrument that delivers authentic sounds of fifty classic, vintage electric keyboard instruments from the last forty years; 40GB sound library includes over 20,000 meticulously crafted 24-bit 96 kHz multi-samples of legendary electric pianos, electric organs, clavinets, Wurlitzers, tape samplers, string machines, keyboard basses, and other rare and exotic electric keyboard instruments; easy to use on screen; load, save, and combine factory or custom presets; use the virtual effects rack to combine, apply, and save chained multi-effects, including chorus, reverb, delay, and more; software features include MIDI control of nearly all parameters, 256-note polyphony per instrument, ultra-low latency, efficient disk streaming for fast preset loading, UVI Engine for superb sound quality, universal plug-in compatibility, and stand-alone operation; load and play Electric Keys sounds using MachFive for convenient, consolidated operation with your other sound libraries; supports all major plug-in formats on Mac OS X and Windows (XP and Vista), including VST, DXi, MAS, Audio Units, and RTAS; also runs as a stand-alone application, turning any laptop or desktop computer into an electric keyboard instrument. SYSTEM SPECS: Macintosh; Windows.

MOTU Ethno Instrument (www.motu.com): World/ethnic instruments, loops, and phrases in a unified window; expressive ethnic instrument sounds combined with authentic world music loops and phrases in one easy-to-use window; from solo instruments to full ensembles; exotic textures; 4GB library of instrument samples from all over the world; 4GB of authentic loops and phrases, instantly tempo-locked to host software time line; slice loops with one click to trigger each beat from keyboard, or drag and drop them into host software tracks; adjust sounds quickly with the intuitive controls; place recordings in real acoustic spaces, from primordial caves to towering forests to remote canyons, reproduced with realism by the built-in convolution reverb processor; supplied both as a stand-alone application and as a universally compatible plug-in (available in all major plug-in formats for Mac OS X and Windows XP); can operate by itself to turn computer into a world instrument powerhouse with disk streaming and multiple outputs; or load it as a plug-in that saves all settings with host software documents for instant recall. SYSTEM SPECS: Macintosh; Windows.

MOTU MachFive (www.motu.com): Cutting-edge sampling technology merges four worlds of advanced sound design: samples, loops, synthesis, and effects; import, edit, synthesize, process, and play multi-sample instruments, loops, and phrases in a unified, intuitive environment; compatibility and interoperability with all major plug-in hosts, sound libraries, and sample formats on both Mac and Windows. Even if you use multiple platforms, hosts and library formats; includes four dual-layer, 8GB soundbank DVDs that contain approximately 32GB of world-class sounds; DVDs include an array of multi-sample instruments, loops and phrases, including premium material recorded at 192kHz; DVD 2 provides a 24-bit 96kHz 8GB sampled grand piano; DVD 3 supplies surround instruments and loops; DVD 4 provides the VSL Orchestra MachFive Edition, an exclusive collection of expressive orchestra sounds; Loop Lab combines the worlds of loops and multi-sample instruments; trigger both together within MachFive's intuitive environment; with Loop Lab can freely and easily edit REX, ACID, and Apple GarageBand Loops, or create own; drag audio files into the Loop Lab or audio that has not yet been sliced; instantly map slices; find or set a tempo; apply destructive or non-destructive sample level editing; assemble multiple tempo-synced loops side by side; time-stretch with no artifacts; set AutoPlay to trigger the audio when press play in sequencer application, or trigger each slice from MIDI controller; drag both MIDI and audio files from Loop Lab to desktop or tracks in sequencer; collaborate across platforms; across-the-board compatibility and interoperability; supports every major software instrument plug-in format platform (MAS, VST, AU, RTAS, and DXi), as well as stand-alone application operation on both Mac OS X (with full Universal Binary support for G5 and

Intel CPUs) and Windows (XP and Vista, 32 and 64 bit); move from one platform to another and collaborate with colleagues who use different audio software or even different computer operating systems; for example, write and track in Digital Performer or Logic on the Mac, and then move to Pro Tools running under Windows for mixing; save a MachFive 2 performance in DP or Logic, and load it into Pro Tools, along with MIDI tracks; universal software sampler; compatibility with all major sample libraries; opens and reads all major sampler library and audio file formats directly - even legacy sampler discs like Kurzweil K2xxx and the Roland S-700 series; no need for time consuming file format conversion; load presets directly from the disc; create and save disc images to any hard drive; compatibility with GigaSampler libraries, especially keyswitching and dimensions; open GigaSampler, EXS24, or Kontakt instruments in MachFive 2 directly and preset characteristics such as key switch, release, and trigger-speed sample switching are preserved and ready to go; plug-in or stand-alone operation; supports all current instrument plug-in standards on both Mac and Windows platforms; runs in any Mac or Windows sequencer that supports virtual instruments; directly compatible with notation software titles such as Finale and Sibelius; works in stand-alone mode for live performance; provides disk streaming on a per instrument basis for efficient memory usage; enable disk streaming for the included 8GB Grand Piano, so only 40MB of RAM is used to load the instrument; disable disk streaming for shorter samples, such as percussion instruments, to maximize hard drive efficiency; effects and synthesizer parameters (LFOs, envelopes, etc.) are modular, allowing for maximum CPU efficiency; for sound design, live performance, music production, or broadcast; balance of audio quality, ease of operation, and across-the-board compatibility. SYSTEM SPECS: Macintosh; Windows.

MOTU MX4 (www.motu.com): Instrument plug-in; inspired by legendary subtractive synthesizers; combines several core synthesis techniques in a unified, hybrid synthesis engine; fresh and vintage sounds; many banks and hundreds of preset; fat basses, nasty leads, analog pads, vintage electronica; save with host application projects for instant recall; tweak sounds with clearly presented controls in one window; 32-bit sound quality, unlimited voices and unlimited polyphony - as much as host computer allows; flexible programming and advanced modulation architecture provide the intimacy of a vintage synth, the flexibility of a modular synth, and the innovation of a virtual synth. SYSTEM SPECS: Macintosh; Windows.

MOTU Symphonic Instrument (www.motu.com): Create complete orchestral recordings; from solo instruments and small ensembles to full orchestral masterpieces; 8GB library of brand new sounds from world class orchestras and musicians; single-window interface; includes a built-in convolution reverb processor to produce the realistic room ambiences; authentic acoustic spaces, from orchestra sound stages to renowned concert halls to majestic cathedrals; CPU-efficient plug-in that saves with host application document for instant recall; compatible with all major plug-in formats for Macintosh OS X and Windows (VST, Audio Units, DXi, MAS, and RTAS). SYSTEM SPECS: Macintosh; Windows.

MOTU Unisyn (www.motu.com): MIDI device editor/librarian; modify a sound in Unisyn using graphic envelope controls and faders, while getting instant feedback within the context of music as Performer plays the sequence; generate entire banks of new sounds with a click of the mouse using Blend, Randomize, and Copy/Paste Parameter features; share bank names with Performer and other FreeMIDI-compatible software for accurate pop-up sound lists; can store thousands of sounds and recall them instantly using database-style search criteria. SYSTEM SPECS: Macintosh; Windows.

Muon TachyonP Sample Player (www.muon-software.com): Straightforward no-frills player with a simple, generic interface; no deep patch editing capabilities; sample library designer can take advantage of the Quick Edit features in the Tachyon Engine to present the user with the eight-most relevant parameters for each patch in the library; main screen contains a full mixer with volume, pan, mute, solo, FX sends, etc., for the user to set up their own custom layered patches and splits from the library material; compatible with the latest VST2.4, Audio Unit, and RTAS host programs for Windows and OSX computers; standalone version also available. SYSTEM SPECS: Macintosh; Windows.

Muon TachyonS Sample Editor (www.muon-software.com): Solution for creating sample libraries for Tachyon Engine products; contains a full sample keymapping editor and patch parameter editor in addition to the multi and FX editing screens in TachyonP; sample libraries created in TachyonS can be tagged with descriptive information to allow users to easily find and organize library material within the built-in browser; sample libraries can be supplied as small files alongside unencrypted source material for easy addition to existing CD-ROM products, or as fully encrypted compressed files for secure distribution; TachyonS is only available as part of a Tachyon Engine licensing deal; compatible with the latest VST2.4, Audio Unit, and RTAS host programs for Windows and OSX computers; standalone version also available. SYSTEM SPECS: Macintosh; Windows.

Muon Tau Bassline MkII (www.muon-software.com): Monophonic bass line synthesizer with a single digitally modeled analogue oscillator, filter and decay envelope; wide range of synthetic bass tones can be created and tweaked in real-time; 64-bit waveform oscillator with 2x oversampling for authentic warm analogue style sawtooth and square waveforms, without noise or digital artifacts; 18db Lowpass resonant filter modelled to have a classic, squelchy tone; Full MIDI control; fully assignable MIDI CCs; click on the user interface and link up to hardware controller; compatible with the latest VST2.4 and Audio Unit host programs for Windows and OSX computers. SYSTEM SPECS: Macintosh; Windows.

Muon Tau Pro (www.muon-software.com): Create lead riffs and basslines; took classic monosynth design of the Tau, added a second oscillator, PWM, sync, ring modulation, and an effects engine; two 64-bit waveform oscillators with eleven waveforms each; pulse-width modulation; sync and ring modulation; no noise or digital artifacts; lowpass resonant filter, with 18dB Classic, 2dB Hi-Q and 36 dB Phat modes; built-in FX unit for warm overdrive, chorus, flange and vintage-style delay effects; full MIDI control, SYSTEM SPECS: Macintosh; Windows.

Music Master (www.datasonics.com.au/) Sequencing, notation, and audio software; provides unlimited MIDI and audio tracks and can quickly turn MIDI into audio for final mix and exporting a stereo wave file; tight linking of MIDI and notation for fast and accurate songwriting to quickly move from a blank sheet to a finished song ready for playing, printing or both. SYSTEM SPECS: Windows.

Music Sales (www.musicsales.com): Titles include: *Logic: Audio Workshop; Roberts: Rhythm Programming; Electronic Projects for Musicians; Practical Recording 3: Cubase SX/SL; Macworld Music Handbook; Practical Recording 6: Music on Mac OSX; How to Remix,* and more. SYSTEM SPECS: Book and Audio CD or Book and Hybrid CD-ROM.

Musicianship in the Digital Age (www.mixbooks.com): For professional musicians, students, music enthusiasts, and multimedia specialists alike; features an integrated and practical approach to the use of music technology to compose and orchestrate original music, providing both technical instruction and theoretical discussion; concepts taught are not software or hardware specific and can be applied to products from many different manufacturers; chapters on theory, forms, arranging, and orchestration provide a cross-curricular approach to computer-based music production; companion CD provides helpful demonstrations of the composition process. SYSTEM SPECS: Book and Audio CD.

MusicLab Music Software (www.musiclab.com): Products include: RealStrat; RealGuitar; MIDIoverLAN CP; DrumTools Performance Designer; SmartFlute. SYSTEM SPECS: Macintosh; Windows.

Native Instruments Music Software Programs (www.native-instruments.com): KORE is the center-point of sound technologies from Native Instruments; the best NI instruments and effects incorporating various synthesis, sampling, and effect techniques fuse into a uniform sound-workstation; KORE SOUNDPACKS complement the KORE LINE with new premium sounds for immediate KORE expansion via instant download; finding, playing and tweaking of NI sounds is easy and intuitive; KORE 2 is the Super Instrument, a software-hardware workstation with six integrated audio engines offering complete analog-style control over the included sounds via the KORE hardware controller; KORE PLAYER is a free software instrument designed for use with KORE SOUNDPACKS; KORE SOUNDPACKS expand the sonic scope of KORE 2 or KORE PLAYER; KOMPLETE 5 is a collection of eleven first-class NI products, including samplers, synthesizers, classic emulations and a virtual guitar studio; includes MASSIVE, GUITAR RIG 3 Software Edition and KONTAKT 3; KOMPLETE SYNTHS includes the whole world of Native Instruments synthesizers: ABSYNTH 4, MASSIVE, FM8, and PRO-53 providing more than 3000 first-class synthesizer sounds of every category; KOMPLETE CLASSICS includes the sounds of legendary vintage instruments and pianos; AKOUSTIK PIANO, ELEKTRIK PIANO, B4 II, and PRO-53; REAKTOR 5 is a fully modular sound studio; provides a production environment for unique instruments and sound ideas; library contains everything from small components to complete synthesizers, samplers, effects, sequencers, and drum machines; MASSIVE creates cutting edge, contemporary sounds; interface is clearly laid out and easy to use; rugged and deep bass rumblings; smooth, gliding, and gently fluctuating pads; generates distinctive, intense, and vivid sounds; ABSYNTH 4 award-winning synthesizer; futuristic synths to rhythmic mayhem, vintage sounds to ambient layers and completely unique, alien soundscapes; semi-modular architecture; diverse spectrum of sounds; ABSYNTH 3 Tutorial DVD interactive workshop explaining how to use; FM8 is a successor to the FM7 and the popular FM synths of yesteryear; can import and faithfully reproduce any sound program in the standard FM sound formats; goes beyond emulating the classics; extended synthesis architecture includes a revolutionary sound morphing feature, programmable arppegiator, and integrated KoreSound Browser; high-class effects section, audio input, digital waveforms, and powerful modulation capabilities; B4 Organ II is an accurate software version of the legendary B3; offers many extra components and refinements, resulting in a wider sonic range and more detailed sound; tube amplifier and selection of speaker cabinets, all engineered with the acclaimed Dynamic Tube Response technology; more authentic and versatile than before;

PRO-53 carries on the tradition of the legendary days of vintage cult synthesizers; fashioned after the unique original, the PRO-53 adds brilliance, power, warmth, and beauty; KONTAKT 3 flagship sampler; expanded function range and vast 33 GB sample library; KONTAKT 2 Tutorial DVD covers all the features; KONTAKT PLAYER enhanced sample player for professional sample libraries is based on the powerful KONTAKT engine, offering a vast range of professional features and high precision sample playback; available in combination with first-class sample libraries from various library producers; BATTERY 3 is a high-end drum sample player; separate sound parameters for up to 128 sample cells, powerful modulation capabilities; sample-accurate timing, internal 32-bit resolution, and up to 128 velocity layers per cell; access to all popular sound libraries; more than 12 GB high quality samples divided into over 100 kits are already included; BANDSTAND plays MIDI music; sample-quality and ease of use establishes a benchmark far beyond conventional GM modules; 2 GB library is packed with high-end sounds; intuitive sound mixing tools and effects; AKOUSTIK PIANO combines three famed grand pianos and one upright piano into a single, versatile instrument; Steinway D, Boesendorfer Imperial, Bechstein D, and the Steingraeber 130 have been sampled; integrated convolution and script modules deliver additional room acoustics and pedal effects; ELEKTRIK PIANO unites four E-pianos into one software instrument; reproduces the sounds of the Fender Rhodes MK I and MK II, Hohner Clavinet E7, and the Wurlitzer A 200; vintage classics playable from any laptop or desktop computer; GUITAR RIG 3 professional sound equipment for guitar and bass; GUITAR RIG 3 Software Edition software-only studio package; GUITAR RIG SESSION compact recording suite for guitar, bass, and vocals; GUITAR RIG 3 XE software essentials for guitar and bass; TRAKTOR 3 professional four-deck DJ software for club and studio; TRAKTOR SCRATCH hands-on DJ system; play digital tracks using vinyl/ CD decks; AUDIO 8 DJ High-end 8 in/8 out audio interface, specially designed for DJs; AUDIO KONTROL 1 High-end 2 in/4 out audio interface and controller; TRAKTOR Tutorial DVD has practical tips and demonstrations by top DJs; BEATPORT SYNC free audio player with DJ functionality; KONTAKT Experience complement to KONTAKT 2; essential expansion pack; sampler with new features; SYNTHETIC DRUMS 2 is an award-winning collection of thirty-six top drum kits to BATTERY 2 or KONTAKT; approximately 2,400 samples produced by renowned artists; REAKTOR Electronic Instruments 2 is a collection of eight ground-breaking instruments for REAKTOR 4 und REAKTOR SESSION, comprising a state-of-the-art synthesizer and a soundscaper, one chord generator, two cutting-edge drum machines and three effect tools; REAKTOR Electronic Instruments - Vol. 1 contains seven versatile, professional-quality instruments for REAKTOR: three powerful synthesizers, three unique effects and a drum machine; BATTERY STUDIO DRUMS is a comprehensive, meticulously recorded collection of over 1.1 GB of acoustic drum samples designed for the BATTERY drum sampler; SYNTHETIC DRUMS Sample CD-ROM for BATTERY and KONTAKT includes thirty-two modern electronic drum kits for various musical styles. SYSTEM SPECS: Macintosh; Windows.

Neato CD/DVD Labels (www.neato.com): Design on any computer; print on any laser or ink-jet; apply with precision; includes assortment of CD/DVD labels, jewel case inserts, media labels, and inserts; Neato applicator; MediaFace media labeling design software; templates for most major design software; digital background art for labels; jewel cases and other media labeling needs in black and white or color; all copyright free. SYSTEM SPECS: Hybrid CD-ROM.

Noise Reduction for Windows (www.sonycreativesoftware.com): Analyzes and removes background noise such as tape hiss, electrical hum, and machinery rumble from recordings; separate click removal and vinyl restoration tools for specific conditions included. SYSTEM SPECS: Windows.

NTONYX (www.ntonyx.com): Products include: JMT Orchestrator 2.1; Onyx Arranger 2.1 LE; Onyx Arranger 2.1; Onyx Orchestrator Styles; Style Enhancer 4.0; Style Enhancer Micro 2.0; NTONYX Stylizer 1.0; NTONYX StyleMorpher 2.4; NTONYX MFX Kit 1; NTONYX MFX Kit 2; NTONYX MIDI Matrix; Asian Ethnic Sounds; Russian Native Sounds; Essential Vibraphone; SoundFonts; GigaSounds; Virtual Audio Cable 4; Virtual Audio Cable 3; Wave Clone. SYSTEM SPECS: Windows.

Open Directory Links to Samples and Loops (http://www.dmoz.org/Arts/Music/Sound_Files/Sample s_and_Loops/): Extensive, alphabetical listing of over 225 links to samples and loops. SYSTEM SPECS: Macintosh; Windows.

PowerTracks Pro Audio (www.pgmusic.com): Professional, fully featured digital audio and MIDI workstation; for musicians, students, and songwriters; integrated digital audio/MIDI recording; 32-bit version; supports Real Time DirectX Effects for live playback and monitoring; includes effects; up to four chained plug-ins can be used at once; Chord Wizard; load in any MIDI file, PowerTracks MIDI sequence file, or a work-in-progress, and the Chord Wizard will intelligently figure out the chords and display them in the Notation Window and the new Chords Window; PG Dynamics; PG Echo-Chorus; PG Flanger; PG Five Band EQ; PG Ten Band EQ; PG Reverb; PG Peak Limit; Mixer Window; Track Effects Inserts allow up to four effects

to be inserted directly into a track's signal path, so each individual track can have its own effects; LED VU meters with clipping indicator and peak-hold with gradual peak fallback; 24-bit/96 KHz audio file format is supported; Recordable audio track mixer moves for Volume, Pan, Aux1, and Aux2; automated mixes for audio tracks using MIDI controller events in the event list; user determined order for the Audio Output ports in the Audio Drivers dialog; 1-Track Stereo Audio; each audio track can play either stereo or mono; Audio I/O Latency Delay keeps audio playback/recording in sync with software MIDI synthesizers; Audio I/O Thread gives three different choices for audio playback and recording priority; paste audio tracks into the current song from the scrap buffer with the Load Scrap command; 32-bit Floating Point Processing in the audio signal path; Track data is automatically re-channeled to the MIDI channels in the Tracks view with the new "Automatically Re-channel track data when saving to a .MID" option; user-determined order for MIDI Output Ports in MIDI Driver Setup dialog; "Use Existing Channel" check-box in the Other Staff Options dialog will intelligently determine the channel number of inserted notes; clicking on a lyric or a chord in the Big Lyrics window plays the song from that location; Jazz notation font gives a "handwritten" look to notes, symbols, chords, and titles; multiple track Leadsheet window notation display; can print multiple tracks of notation; Scrub Mode in the Notation window will play the notes in the notation as drag mouse horizontally over window; slanted beams in notation window, which indicates whether the general direction of a phrase is upward or downward in pitch; New Section Text events let user place a text event at any location on the staff window; Beat Resolution settings in Notation Window; multiple levels of Edit|Undo, user-selectable from 1 to 100; Copy/Cut/Paste commands have an option to work on Chord Symbols; Lyrics window automatically switches to Chord mode when lyrics are not present; [Find] button in the Custom File Selection dialog to search for a file within the current folder; Favorite Folders button in the Custom File Selection dialog to quickly change the current folder by selecting from a list of "favorite" folders; Preferences dialog with "tabbed pages" gives access to user preferences; "Big Piano" piano settings option for sizable on-screen piano keyboard display; main toolbar displays the number of megabytes and the percentage of disk space free on the hard drive. SYSTEM SPECS: Windows.

Pro Tools (www.digidesign.com): Digital Audio Workstation platform for Mac OS and Microsoft Windows operating systems; developed and manufactured by Digidesign, a division of Avid Technology; widely used by professionals throughout the audio industries for recording and editing in music production, film scoring, television, and post production; the three types of Pro Tools systems include HD, LE, and M-POWERED; PRO TOOLS HD is the high-end package and is an integration of hardware and software; the hardware includes an external A/D converter and internal PCI or PCIe audio cards with onboard DSP; Pro Tools is similar to a multitrack tape recorder and mixer, with additional features that can only be performed in the digital medium; most highly specified version supports sample rates of up to 192 kHz and bit depths of 16 and 24 bit, opens WAV, AIFF, mp3 and SDII audio files and QuickTime video files, and features time code, tempo maps, automation and surround sound capabilities; most of Pro Tools' basic functions can be controlled within Edit or Mix windows; Edit window displays audio and MIDI tracks, and provides graphical representation of the information recorded or imported; audio can be edited in a non-linear, non-destructive fashion to the level of individual samples; MIDI information can also be manipulated; Mix window displays each track's fader channel and allows for the adjustment of a channel's volume and pan, as well as being the usual place to insert plug-in effects and route audio to and from different outputs and inputs; effects processing and virtual instruments in Pro Tools are achieved through the use of plug-ins, which are either processed by the DSP chips as TDM plug-ins, or the host computer as RTAS (Real Time AudioSuite) plug-ins; Pro Tools HD is Digidesign's high-end Pro Tools product which comes in three versions: HD 1, HD 2 and HD 3 run from a host Apple Mac or Windows PC; HD systems perform most audio processing on DSP cards, and use external, rack mountable interfaces to handle incoming and outgoing audio; TDM, a proprietary interconnect based on time-division multiplexing, is used for communication between the devices, reducing burden on the computer's PCI bus; Pro Tools systems rely on dedicated DSP cards to handle most audio processing, due to the fact that at the time Pro Tools was first developed, consumer-level computers were not powerful enough to process high-end digital audio; A HD Core PCI card or an Accel Core PCIe card is required in any HD system; the inclusion of one or two additional Accel cards upgrades the system to HD 2 or 3 respectively, and increases the system's overall processing power, allowing for higher track counts and more plug-ins; an Expansion HD product increases capability up to a total of seven cards using Digidesign's PCI-X expansion chassis product, which is available with both PCI-X and PCIe host cards for the computer; when Pro Tools HD was launched, HD Process cards were available, but due to supply problems from DSP manufacturer Motorola the line was redesigned and rebranded HD Accel, offering faster DSP chips and additional RAM; all cards contain nine DSP chips; when Apple changed the expansion

slot architecture of the G5 to PCI Express, Digidesign launched a line of PCIe HD Accel cards; the PCIe HD Core is now an Accel Core, whereas the original PCI-X Core remains non-Accel; some TDM plug-ins require the presence of Accel chips to run and therefore cannot run on the earlier non-Accel HD systems; interfaces for Pro Tools HD generally offer 16 inputs and outputs of analogue and/or digital audio; the 192 and 96 interfaces represent the highest sample rate, in kHz, that they can offer; the PRE is an HD interface with only eight inputs, but each has a built in mic pre amp; consumer-level PRO TOOLS LE systems perform all processing on the host CPU, and audio I/O is handled through a Digidesign USB or FireWire audio interface, also used as a copy protection dongle for the software; two families of external interfaces for Pro Tools LE systems; MBox 2 family connects to, and is powered by, a host computer through USB, except the FireWire connected MBox 2 Pro; all have a stereo audio output, and all but the MBox 2 Micro have two line inputs and at least one microphone pre amp; the 003 family is a series of FireWire connected interfaces, with larger I/O capabilities, additional methods of inputting audio and four microphone pre amps; Pro Tools LE software is essentially a limited version of the HD counterpart, with a smaller track count, no automatic Plugin Delay Compensation (PDC), lower maximum sampling rate and no surround sound capabilities; no additional DSP cards are required or supported, and only RTAS plug-ins can be used; VST to RTAS converter software utility made by FXpansion that will convert VST plug-ins to RTAS format; time code based grid and import of OMF and AAF files is not available in Pro Tools LE without purchase of the Digitranslator software addon; M-Audio, formerly Midiman, was acquired by Avid Technology in 2004-2005, and in April 2005, Digidesign released PRO TOOLS M-POWERED which brought almost all Pro Tools LE functionality to a subset of M-Audio USB, Firewire, and PCI interfaces; M Powered requires a separate dongle for copy protection; Digidesign control surfaces attempt to bridge the gap between old style analogue desks and modern DAWs by providing physical controls for the Pro Tools software; latest control surface is the C|24, successor to the Control|24, a 24 fader control surface with 16 built in Focusrite "A" Class Mic Preamps; new addition is the ICON: Integrated Console Environment, combining a tactile control surface and a Pro Tools|HD Accel system in one unit; VENUE, a similar system, was released for live sound applications; these large control surfaces use an Ethernet connection to the host computer, but for Pro Tools users with smaller needs, the Command|8 is a small eight fader control surface which connects via USB; an official Pro Tools training curriculum and certification program, which includes a full range of Pro Tools–related courses in music and post production, was introduced by Digidesign in 2002; curriculum is delivered by a number of schools and universities around the world; Music Production and DV Toolkits increase the capabilities of non HD Pro Tools systems; both increase the maximum number of tracks and highest possible sample rate to 96kHz and include numerous additional plug-ins; LE only DV Toolkit adds timecode; Digidesign also develops plug-ins exclusively for Pro Tools that must be bought separately from the main system, such as Eleven, a guitar amplifier emulator; Virtual instruments including Structure, Strike, Velvet, Hybrid, and Xpand! can be bought separately, with the exception of Xpand!, which is included with all ProTools systems; PRO TOOLS TIMELINE OF RELEASES: 1989 - Sound Tools stereo recording and editing system; 1991 - Original Pro Tools system is released featuring 4 voices, ProDECK and ProEDIT software, MIDI, and automation; 1994 - Pro Tools III system, provides 16-48 voices; 1997 - Pro Tools | 24 (24-bit audio); 1998 - Pro Tools | MIX with expanded DSP capabilities for mixing audio; 1999 - Digi 001 with Pro Tools LE light edition of Pro Tools; 2002 - Pro Tools | HD system supports 96kHz and 192kHz HD audio; Mbox and Digi 002 (March and September); 2003 - Pro Tools | HD Accel system with additional DSP capabilities; Pro Tools Users group founded in Los Angeles; 2005 - VENUE Pro Tools for live sound; Mbox 2; Pro Tools M-Powered (August); Pro Tools 7.0 (November), 7.1 (supports Apple's PCIe G5) (December); 2006 - Pro Tools 7.2 (August) and 7.3 (December); Pro Tools LE and HD support Intel-based Mac (May and September, respectively); Mbox 2 Pro; Mbox 2 Mini; 2007 - 003 and 003 Rack (February); Mbox Micro (October); Pro Tools 7.4 (November) (Elastic Audio); PRO TOOLS HD HARDWARE: HD 1/2/3 Core Systems (PCI); HD 1/2/3 Accel Systems (PCI-e); 192 I/O (8 analog + 8 digital input; 8 analog + 8 digital output 44.1, 48, 88.2, 96, 176.4, 192KHz interface); 192 Digital I/O (16 digital input; 16 digital output 44.1, 48, 88.2, 96, 176.4, 192KHz interface); 96 I/O (8 analog + 8 digital input; 8 analog + 8 digital output 44.1, 48, 88.2, 96KHz interface); 96i I/O (16 analog input; 2 analog output 44.1, 48, 88.2, 96KHz interface); Pre I/O (8ch microphone pre-amp); SYNC I/O (Time Code Synchronizer); MIDI I/O (10in-10out MIDI Interface); PRO TOOLS LE HARDWARE: 003; 003 Rack; Digi 002; Digi 002 Rack; Digi 001 only compatible with Pro Tools LE 5.0-6.4; Mbox 2; Mbox 2 Pro; Mbox 2 Mini; Mbox 2 Micro; Mbox; PRO TOOLS M-POWERED HARDWARE: M-Audio Interfaces; Black Box; Ozone; MobilePre USB; Ozonic; ProjectMix I/O; NRV10; Transit; Jamlab; KeyStudio 49i; Audiophile 2496; Audiophile 192; Delta 44; Delta 66; Delta 1010LT; Delta 1010; Fast Track Pro; Track USB; Fast Track Ultra; FireWire 410; FireWire 1814; FireWire Solo;

ProFire Lightbridge; ProFire 2626; Torq Xponent; Torq Connectiv; HARDWARE FOR CONTROL SURFACES: VENUE live sound console; ICON D-Command and D-Control, current flagship control surfaces; ProControl, former flagship control surface; Control|24, 24 fader control surface with 16 built in Focusrite "A" Class Mic Preamps; C|24, successor to the Control|24; Command|8, small 8 fader control surface; Tascam - FW-1082, HUI emulation; Euphonix MC MIX , MC Control, Eucon system, but functions via HUI emulation; JL Cooper Mc3000, HUI. SYSTEM SPECS: Macintosh; Windows.

Pro Tools Plug-ins Web Page (www.digidesign.com/index.cfm?navid=115&langid=1 00&mkt=all): Links to many Digidesign and third party plug-ins that can be used with Pro Tools. SYSTEM SPECS: Macintosh; Windows.

Pro Tools Virtual Instruments (www.digidesign.com): Digidesign Advanced Instrument Research (A.I.R.) group; developed from the ground up specifically for Pro Tools; combines innovative plug-in engine technologies with cutting-edge sounds and interface designs; TRANSFUSER: innovative, real-time loop, phrase, and groove creation workstation for Pro Tools; create, manipulate, and perform loop- and rhythm-based music on the fly; STRUCTURE: features three powerful RTAS instruments; each offers a tailored set of features for playing and modifying sound samples; STRIKE: plug-in that makes it easy to create professional drum performances in Pro Tools with realism and human feel; VELVET: realistic emulations of electric pianos; HYBRID: combines the warmth of classic analog waveforms with digital wavetables; recreate sounds you remember or create something new; XPAND!: Free Sample-Playback/Synthesis Workstation for songwriters, film composers, DJs, electronic musicians, music producers, and sound designers; provides fast ways to access and manipulate thousands of high-quality sounds. SYSTEM SPECS: Macintosh; Windows.

Professional Microphone Techniques (www.halleonard.com): Microphone usage for dozens of different instruments as well as vocals, amplifiers, Leslie cabinets, and more; audio CD to hear different effects of microphone placement techniques in real time. SYSTEM SPECS: Book and Audio CD.

Propellerhead Reason (www.propellerheads.se): Virtual studio rack with all the tools and instruments; set of synths and effects; complete music system; synthesizers, samplers, drum machine, REX file loop player, professional mastering tools, mixer, vocoder, world class effects, pattern sequencer, and more; expandable all-in-one music production environment, complete with its own realtime sequencer; flexible music system; sophisticated tools such as the MClass mastering suite, the Combinator device, and the Thor synth; choose a synth, a drum machine, a loop player or any device from the Create menu, and it will instantly appear in rack, logically patched into the signal chain; can repeat the process; eleven samplers and ten compressors; if create more machines than mixer channels, can create another mixer; all controls work as their real life counterparts; each unit in Reason's virtual rack is edited from its own on-screen front panel; all the sliders, knobs, buttons, and functions are in front of user, ready to be tweaked, turned, and twisted in absolute real-time; all front panel actions including filter adjustments, pitch bending, gain riding, or panning can be recorded and automated in the Reason sequencer; radical routing; will never run out of rack space; single keypress will turn Reason's rack around; most audio connections are made automatically; when a new device is created, it appears immediately below the currently selected device, and Reason patches it into the system in the most logical way; Repatch by dragging the patch cord plug to the desired connector, or make a pop-up menu choice; most devices have one or more parameters controlled by Gate and/or CV; all instrument devices have several Gate or CV output options; easy, transparent patching; Thor synthesizer is a multi-synthesis synthesizer with six oscillator types, four different filters, a step sequencer, and a modulation matrix; fully routable, fully automatable; RPG-8 monophonic arpeggiator with multiple play modes, an insert function and a pattern section; Sequencer features multiple track lanes, vector automation, dedicated device tracks, clips, count-in, and more; ReGroove realtime, 32-channel timing and groove handling mixer; applies non-destructive, freely editable grooves to Reason's sequencer tracks. SYSTEM SPECS: Macintosh; Windows.

Propellerhead Reason Adapted (www.propellerheads.se): Slimmed-down version of Reason; powerful package of versatile sound tools; not as powerful as Reason. SYSTEM SPECS: Macintosh; Windows.

Propellerhead ReCycle (www.propellerheads.se): Software capable of more than timestretching and tempo-fitting; suite of programs that gives full creative loop control; lets user do with sampled loops what can be done with beats programmed from individual drum sounds such as alter the tempo or replace sounds and process them individually; start out with a regular audio file or sample, preferably one of a rhythmic nature; load the groove into ReCycle, and the program will look at the groove, analyze it, and break it up into its rhythmic components; each part is called a slice; process itself is fully automated; once the slices are there, they are there to move, audition, or delete, using the programs on-screen tools and controls; other tools allow user to set the length, attack, and decay of the slices, and to change

grooves' overall tempo or pitch, without one affecting the other. SYSTEM SPECS: Macintosh; Windows.

Propellerhead ReFills (www.propellerheads.se): Reason Electric Bass ReFill puts eight electric bass guitars into the Reason rack; Jason McGerr Sessions ReFill is a drum kit and loop library from Jason McGerr, drummer for Death Cab for Cutie; Abbey Road Keyboards ReFill is a collection of vintage keyboards from legendary Abbey Road Studios; The Salazar Brothers Reggaeton ReFill is the sound of Bomba-Reggae-Hiphop; and more. SYSTEM SPECS: Macintosh; Windows.

Propellerhead Reload (www.propellerheads.se): Converts AKAI S1000 and S3000 formatted media into formats that can be used with Reason, ReCycle and other audio applications. SYSTEM SPECS: Macintosh; Windows.

Propellerhead ReWire (www.propellerheads.se): The audio cable of the virtual studio; lets user connect virtual instruments to each other. SYSTEM SPECS: Macintosh; Windows.

PSP Plug-ins (www.pspaudioware.com): Develops high-quality audio processors and effects plug-ins; supportive tool during mixing or mastering; PSP VINTAGEWARMER: digital simulation of analog-style, multi-band compressor-limiter. LEXICON PSP 42: digital stereo delay and phrase sampler. PSP VINTAGEMETER: provides professional VU and PPM metering for mono and stereo tracks; PSP MIXPACK: to add rich, detailed, warm, lively, and punchy sound to tracks. PSP STEREOPACK: plug-ins designed for creating, expanding, improving, controlling, and analyzing quality of stereo audio signals. PSP PIANOVERB: reproduces special kind of reverberation originally provided by piano strings; PSP 608 MULTIDELAY: full-features delay plug-in; PSP MASTERQ: high quality parametric equalizer; PSP XENON: full band precision limiter; PSP NITRO: multimode filter plug-in; PSP MASTERCOMP: high fidelity single band stereo mastering compressor with distinctive sound and extra linking features; PSP NEON: linear phase precison equalizer; PSP EASYVERB: reverb effect plug-in with nine high quality algorithms. SYSTEM SPECS: Macintosh; Windows.

PSP 84 (www.pspaudioware.com): High-quality processor, capable of producing a wide variety of delay-based effects; two independent delay lines operating with variable sampling rate and precise tape saturation algorithm with adjustable gain; allows for convincingly sounding simulation of tape delay, including effects resulting from tape speed instability; filtration section consisting of three second order switchable resonant filter types can be used to process input, feedback, or wet signal adjustable slope of filter ranges from a gentle curve; useful for simulating high-frequency absorption typical for tape delay and wet signal equalization to an extremely steep curve with a high cutoff frequency peak; all wah-wah and resonance effects easily available; delay line sampling rate and filter cutoff can be modulated by any of the 5 LFO waveforms that are automatically synchronized to the sequencer tempo or envelope follower with adjustable sensitivity and attack/release; contains fully functional reverb unit with simplified settings tuned to exactly reproduce the sound of classic spring and plate reverberators. SYSTEM SPECS: Macintosh; Windows.

QSound (www.qsound.com): Global supplier of audio software technology for mobile devices, headphones, Bluetooth headsets, televisions, stereo PC multimedia equipment, and other consumer electronics; proprietary audio algorithms truly deliver a fuller, more natural and immersive audio experience; QSound's sonic technologies, algorithms and special effects include: polyphonic wavetable synthesizers, 3D (three dimensional) audio, multi-speaker system surround synthesis, virtual surround sound capability, 3D sound stage expansion, 3D positional audio, low/mid/high frequency spectral enhancement, reverberation, dynamic range control, equalization, and anti-saturation among others; becoming a standard in the mobile and handheld device marketplace; enable the phone to ring using microQ's mQSynthTM; enhance the music listening experience with microQ's digital audio effects mQFX; interactive gaming with mQ3D; microQ is the leading mobile audio solution; technologies have also been used to enhance CDs, DVDs, video games, movies, television programs, streaming Internet audio, MP3s and more; 3D positional audio and virtual surround sound technologies power the QSound branded products QSurround, QHD, QMSS, and Q3D Interactive; newer and more innovative consumer products require increasingly advanced audio technologies. SYSTEM SPECS: Macintosh; Windows.

Quick Start Series (www.musicsales.com): Understand home recording, MIDI, Reason, Cubase, audio mastering, CD burning, music publishing online, and more; illustrated, easy-to-understand books answer questions about a variety of music topics; valuable tips and troubleshooting skills; audio examples, demo songs, MIDI software, MP3 software, and more. SYSTEM SPECS: Book and Hybrid CD-ROM.

Record Producer Series (www.turtlebeach.com): Includes *Record Producer, Record Producer MIDI*, and *Record Producer Deluxe;* turns MIDI-equipped PC into a desktop music production studio; record song using MIDI and digital audio tracks, edit, and play back; compose multitrack songs with MIDI keyboard and live instruments; add lead vocals, background harmony; process with professional sounding effects; for creating demos or fully mastered CD quality recordings; layer guitars, drums, and other instruments; dozens of digital audio tracks to record drums, guitars, keyboards, bass guitars, sound effects, and more; wide variety of audio and MIDI files; drum loops, keyboard riffs, guitar leads, etc.; MIDI composition tools; play back. SYSTEM SPECS: Windows.

Roxio RecordNow Music Lab 10 Premier (www.roxio.com): Collect, organize and enjoy your music; software tool for people who want to collect, organize, and enjoy their digital music; collect music from disc, iPod, Internet radio, and LPs; automatically rename music by artist, title, and album; copy music to disc or portable player; create DVD Music Discs with up to fifty hours of music; smart navigation by title, artist, album, etc.; ability to write to M4A format; professionally designed menu themes or the tools to make own. SYSTEM SPECS: Windows.

Roxio Toast Titanium (www.roxio.com): Catalog and burn all files across multiple CD, DVD, and Blu-ray discs formatted for both Mac and PC; schedule backups with the Get Backup application; import and create high-def video from TiVo, EyeTV, AVCHD camcorders and burn to Blu-ray and standard DVD discs; watch movies and TV shows over WiFi on iPhone or any net connected Mac or PC; expand music library by recording streaming audio directly from the Internet; use new audio fingerprinting technology to identify songs and tag with titles, artists, album, and more; create mixes for burning to CD or create music DVDs; create Director's Cuts of favorite TV shows and movies; fit 9GB of dual-layer DVD video onto a single standard DVD; use time saving batch DVD-Video compression/conversion; single click copy of CDs. SYSTEM SPECS: Macintosh.

Samplitude (www.samplitude.com): Products of the Sequoia/Samplitude family; professionally edit audio from its recording to mastering; comprehensive range of applications; sound based on 100% sound neutrality as well as object-orientated editing; Sequoia 10 high-end digital audio workstation; Samplitude 10 available as Pro or Master version; solution for digital audio editing; VST Plug-ins: Analogue Modelling Suite, Vintage Effects Suite, and VariVerb Pro; high quality plug-ins for studio production. SYSTEM SPECS: Windows.

Shaping Your Sound (www.halleonard.com): Two-DVD set; by Tom Lubin; Shaping Your Sound with Signal Processors teaches how to understand compressors and gates and how to use them to shape the dynamics of any instrument by emphasizing or diminishing the attack, sustain, or release of each note; learn how to create custom flanging, delay, phasing, echo, and chorusing effects, when to use them and when not to use them in recordings; learn to use EQ to open up the sound of recordings and make room for each instrumental texture while discovering various types of EQ curves and devices with the techniques professional engineers use to shape the space where the sound happens; Shaping Your Sound with Microphones, Mixers and Multitrack Recording teaches how to best mike, record, and mix drums, guitars, pianos, horns, vocals, strings, and more; professionally build a song, step by step, through the tracking and overdubbing process with dozens of musical examples and demonstrations; learn fundamental characteristics of analog tape and professional multitrack recorders and the techniques to make top quality recordings; explore the inside of the recording console and learn to route signals through mixer to get the best sound. SYSTEM SPECS: Instructional DVD.

Software Synthesizers—The Definitive Guide to Virtual Musical Instruments (www.halleonard.com): By Jim Aiken; CD-ROM; authoritative guide; concise explanations of sound synthesis techniques; Reason, Reaktor, Kantos, Absynth, Attack, Live, Fruityloops, and more than two dozen other applications; physical modeling and FM synthesis, filters and envelope generators, using MIDI, sampled loop libraries, and more. SYSTEM SPECS: Hybrid CD-ROM.

Sonic Timeworks (www.sonictimeworks.com): DirectX Plug-ins for recording and mixing: DR4081L Digital Reverberator; ReverbX; CompressorX; Timeworks Delay 6022; Timeworks Reverb 4080L; Timeworks Phazer Model 88; for mastering: Timeworks Equalizer V1; Timeworks Equalizer V1-LP for DirectX; Timeworks Mastering Compressor; Pro Tools/RTAS plug-ins: ReverbX RTAS; ChannelX RTAS; CompressorX RTAS; Pulsar/Scope plug-ins: Pulsar/Scope Pro Reverb; Pulsar/Scope VintagEQ Series; Pulsar/Scope CompressorX; Mastering Compressor's for Scope/Pulsar; SharcOne for Scope/Pulsar; P-100 Classic Plate Reverb; A-100 w/I-100 Reverbs. SYSTEM SPECS: Macintosh; Windows.

Sony Sound Series: Loops and Samples (www.sonycreativesoftware.com): PREMIUM COLLECTION: 2CD, 24-bit, highly specialized collections; titles include: arhythmiA: Drums & Drones, Volume One; arhythmiA: Drums & Drones, Volume Two; arhythmiA: Free ACID Projects; Bill Laswell: Volume IV Covert Diaspora; Cinemascape: Free ACID Projects; Cinemascape: Soundtrack Construction Elements; Dr. Fink's Funk Factory; Drums from the Big Room: The Mixes; Matt Fink: StarVu Session Keys; Metal: The Ultimate Construction Kit; Parthenon Huxley's Six-String Orchestra; Songwriter's Acoustic Guitar Companion; Sonic Excursions for Acoustic Guitar; Sonic Excursions: Free ACID Projects; The Electronic Music Manuscript: A Richard Devine Collection; Tony Franklin: Not Just Another Pretty Bass; Vital Drums: The Vitale Collection. STANDARD COLLECTION: Bedrock libraries of the series; full-on construction kits, single instrument libraries, and multi-genre volumes

suited for multimedia work; titles include: ACID Techno Expander Pack; Afterhours EDM: Electronic Dance Music; American Piano; Aural E: Eclectic Electronica; Available Light: Free ACID Projects; Available Light: Natural Music for Cinema; Bass Taster; Bill Laswell: Volume I False Encryptions; Bill Laswell: Volume II Undocument; Bill Laswell: Volume III Letter of Law; Black Paint: Indie Rock Anthems; Blip: Glitch Electronica; Bradley Fish: High Strung; Bradley Fish: Restrung; Bradley Fish: Unstrung; Bunker 8: Extremely Abrasive Synths; Bunker 8: Nu Groove Pop; Caliente: Reggaeton Construction Kit; Chicago Fire: Deep House; Chicago Fire: Drum 'n' Bass; Chicago Fire: Electro; Chicago Fire: Old School; Chicago Fire: Progressive; Cinematic Funk: Urban Tone Poems; Cinematix Volume 1; Cinematix Volume 2; Designer Dance Tools; Diamond Cuts: Hip-Hop Gems; Discrete Drums: Volume I; Discrete Drums: Volume II; Downtempo Beats; Drum Tools; Either/Or Electronica; Electro Lounge; The Electro Set; The Electro Set: Free ACID Projects; Electronic Point-Blank; Esoterik Beatz; Essential Sounds III; Euro Techno; Flammable: Club Joints & Street Anthems; Flow & Function: The Hip-Hop Playbook; George Pendergast: alt.rockdrums; Global Groove: International Hip-Hop Flavor; Groove Spectrum R&B Drums; Headstrong Grooves; Horncraft for R&B; Hydroponic Hip-Hop; Iced: Minimalist Electronica; ILONA! Universal Female Vocal Toolkit; Jade Hill: Rock/Pop Guitars; Jade Hill: Total Spanish Guitar; James Johnson: Slow Silhouette; James Johnson: Spectral Minimalism; Jazz Trap Kit; Joe Vitale: Organ Donor; Loop Noir: Paranormal Sound Design; Ma Ja Lé: Ethereal Textures; Mac Money: Electro Hip-Hop; Mac Money: R&B 101; Machine Language; Machine Language II; Mellow Jazz/Funk Elements; Mick Fleetwood: Total Drumming; Modular Electronica featuring Test Shot Starfish; New Roots Reggae; New York Dance; Nigel Ayers: Myths of Technology; Numina I: Emotional Peak Sounds for Cinema; Numina II: More Peak Sounds for Cinema; On The Jazz Tip; Orchestral 1: Classical; Orchestral 2: Modern; Orchestral 3: Cinematic; Orchestral 4: Rock & Pop; Platinum Theory Hip-Hop; Platinum Theory Hip-Hop: Free ACID Projects; Pocket Diva: World Class Vocal Samples; Poptronica; Prototechno; Randy Jackson's Producer's Pack 2: Dance Explosion; Randy Jackson's Producer's Pack 3: Radio Ready Synth Pop; Randy Jackson's Producer's Pack 4: Heavy Hitters; Randy Jackson's Producer's Pack 5: Super Soul; Rhythmicronics: Processed Percussion; Robert Rich: Ambient Atmospheres & Rhythms; Rondo Brothers: Trip-Hop Loops & Samples; Rudy Sarzo: Workingman's Bass; Siggi Baldursson: Zero-Gravity Beats; Soul Jazz Experience; Steve Tibbetts: Friendly Fire; Structure/Capture: Future Retro Dance

Excursions; Stylus Pressure: Urban Grooves On Digital Wax; Sweet & Low Bass; Synchro-Funk; Synchro-Funk: Free ACID Projects; Techno Club Grooves; The Best of Siggi Baldursson: The Drum Loops; Tony Brock: Rock Drummer; TOYZ; Trance NRG; Troy Klontz: Rhythm & Twang; Ugly Remnants: Volume One; Ugly Remnants: Volume Two; Underground Soundlab; Underground: UK House & Electro; Vintage Analog Synths; Westside Underground. CLASSIC COLLECTION: Staples in any studio; titles include: ACID DJ Expander Pack; ACID Rock; Ambient Grooves; Bass X; Bunker 8: Extremely Abrasive Beats; David Torn: SPLaTTeRCeLL; Electro-World Percussion; Electrocution; Fluid Dynamics: Computational Drum 'n' Bass; Futurist Drum 'n' Bass; George Pendergast: Essential Percussion; Joe Vitale: Latin Percussion; Knutrix Drum 'n' Bass; Ma Ja Lé: Electronic Imprints and Astrobeats; Mac Money: Hip-Hop/R&B Vocals; Metarock Visions; Methods of Mayhem: Industrial Toolkit; Nashville Wire: Pedal Steel Guitar; Paul Black: Blues Guitar; Siggi Baldursson: Drumsugar; Vince Andrews: Jazz Solos and Sections; World Percussion; World Pop. SOUND EFFECTS: titles include: 1,001 Sound Effects; Sony Pictures Sound Effects Series Volumes 1-10: Sony Pictures master set; ten-disc package contains over 2,300 effects in a wide assortment of categories; Sony Pictures Sound Effects Series Volumes 1-5: five-disc collection of the best recorded materials and effects, handpicked from the Sony Pictures sound editorial vault; Sony Pictures Sound Effects Series Volumes 6-10: second installment focuses on high-end sound design, period effects, and otherworldly noises. SYSTEM SPECS: Windows.

Sound Advice on Compressors, Limiters, Expanders & Gates (www.halleonard.com): Compressors, limiters, gates, expanders, and other dynamics processors for creating recordings that sound professional; step-by-step instruction; audio examples. SYSTEM SPECS: Book and Audio CD.

Sound Advice on Developing Your Home Studio (www.halleonard.com): Equipment connection, selection, and placement; cables; patch bay; monitors; acoustics. SYSTEM SPECS: Book and Audio CD.

Sound Advice on Equalizers, Reverbs & Delays (www.halleonard.com): Techniques and examples designed to help mixes come alive; understand how the controls on equalizers and effects processors work; step-by-step equalization guidelines for recording and mixing guitars, bass, drums, keys, vocals, and other popular instruments; learn how to use reverbs and delays to set music in a controlled, blended, and dimensional space; how to craft and shape each sound. SYSTEM SPECS: Book and Audio CD.

Sound Advice on Microphone Techniques (www.halleonard.com): Microphone selection and technique; how the three most common microphone designs work and how to use them; which microphones are recommended for different instruments and voices and why. SYSTEM SPECS: Book and Audio CD.

Sound Advice on MIDI Production (www.halleonard.com): MIDI sequencing; supporting acoustic recording; synchronizing equipment; practical applications of MIDI keyboards, sound modules, effect processors, recorders, mixers, triggers, and controllers. SYSTEM SPECS: Book and Audio CD.

Sound Advice on Mixing (www.halleonard.com): Mixing techniques; audio examples; build a mix from the ground up; how to set up a mix. SYSTEM SPECS: Book and Audio CD.

Sound Forge (www.sonycreativesoftware.com): Professional digital audio production suite; create and edit stereo and multichannel audio files; analyze, record and edit audio; digitize and restore old recordings; model acoustic environments; design sound for multimedia; master replication-ready CDs; MP3 editor, wave editor, audio recording software; includes tools for sound design and mastering; includes CD Architect software for designing, mastering, and burning Red Book audio CDs, Noise Reduction plug-ins to fix common audio problems such as tape hiss, camera hum, clicks, and pops, and the Mastering Effects Bundle powered by iZotope, a collection of four professional audio plug-ins; stereo and multichannel recording; complete set of tools for recording audio; record straight into sound card or use the Record Timer to begin and end a session at a specific time and date; can start recording when a certain audio threshold is reached with Threshold Record Triggering; record and edit multichannel audio files as easily as stereo files; precise audio editing; edit stereo and native multichannel audio files down to the sample level in real time; use familiar Windows commands to cut, copy, paste, mix, and crossfade audio; drag and drop to edit between channels, and work on one file while processing others in the background; supports full resolution 24-bit and 32-bit/64-bit float 192 kHz files; effects processing; apply over forty professional studio effects and processes including Normalize, EQ, Delay, Chorus, Volume, Dynamics, Noise Gate, Pitch Shift, Flange, and Vibrato; chain multiple effects together and apply them to selections or entire files using the Plug-in Chainer; supports DirectX and VST effects, including parameter automation; Audio-for-Video; supports multiple video formats including AVI, WMV, and MPEG-1 and MPEG-2; synchronize audio and video frame by frame; import Flash (SWF) files to visually synchronize audio to project; includes MPEG-2 templates for writing HDV-compliant files at both 720p and 1080i resolutions; templates for encoding WMV 720p and 1080p; ActionScripting, motion video, and audio not supported; Dolby Digital AC-3 export; export multichannel files in surround AC-3 format using the included Dolby Digital AC-3 plug-in. SYSTEM SPECS: Windows.

Sound Forge Audio Studio (www.sonycreativesoftware.com): Home recording studio for audio production; audio editing and mastering professional-quality audio on home computer; record live instruments and vocals, edit and restore audio, apply studio-quality audio effects, and convert files; create karaoke tracks with included vocal remover software, Vocal Eraser; basic commands such as cut, copy, and paste; music editor, vocal remover, audio production and music production software; capture and record music; edit audio; share and save audio productions; import music from CDs and MP3s, record live performances, capture audio from vinyl, cassettes, and more; plug in microphone, instrument, or playback device; edit and mix; pro-level control over audio editing and effects processing; mix audio tracks, apply effects, restore damaged recordings, remove vocals, and synchronize audio with video; encoding tools for saving audio and video in popular formats including MP3, WAV, WMV, and QuickTime; multiple export options make it possible to burn CDs, export audio to MP3 player, or upload songs to the web; to record live audio, plug a microphone or instrument into computer's sound card and click Record; capture instruments, vocals, keyboards, and more; import audio from CDs and MP3s, or use the Vinyl Recording and Restoration tool to record audio from LPs and cassettes; enhance audio with effects; customize projects with more than thirty built-in audio effects such as EQ, delay, chorus, and reverb, as well as 1,001 sound effect; DirectX and VST support expands the number of effects that can be applied and increases mastering flexibility.; effects processing; make karaoke tracks with the Vocal Eraser plug-in; remove vocals from most recordings or isolate vocals; can also use this plug-in to extract vocals from songs for remixing; Vocal Eraser plug-in contains presets for various recording situations; drag and drop to balance sound levels, trim unwanted sections, and synchronize audio with video; create music loops and samples to use with ACID Music Studio software; recording and editing; integrated CD burning; create professional-sounding CDs; burn one track at a time or choose disc-at-once (DAO) to burn a disc with full control over the pauses between tracks; encode audio and video; convert audio files to MP3, WAV, WMA, and other formats including QuickTime and RealMedia for the web; create podcasts and streaming media or export audio to MP3 players and other portable devices; encoding and sharing; Show Me How tutorials include text dialogue boxes, pointers, and guides. SYSTEM SPECS: Windows.

Sound Studio (www.freeverse.com): Mac OS X application for recording and editing audio digitally on computer; digitize tapes and vinyl records, record professional-sounding podcasts, record live performances, create own mixes with crossfades, tweak the levels and EQ, apply digital effects and save in all major file formats; between more expensive programs with steep learning curves, and far less robust apps; app for recording voiceovers, tweaking audio, or creating sound effects. In fact, Freeverse has used it for years to create all the dialog and sound effects in its games; multi-track support: layer stereo sounds and save in interleaved format; Audio Unit plug-in effect support; saves in MPEG-4 AAC (advanced audio coding) m4a format; saves in MP3 when the LAME framework is installed; automator support; New Mono Document command for creating a monophonic document; 24-bit/96 kHz sample quality, in stereo or mono; low latency monitoring, using Core Audio; automatic recording starting and stopping based on timers or audio levels; sample-accurate edits; markers with text labels; time ruler with units for video and film; copy-and-paste editing; basic mixing edits; AppleScript and Automator support; effects; supports Audio Units; Dynamics: Compressor, Expander, and Noise Gate; Equalization: Graphic EQ, Low Pass Filter, and High Pass Filter; Delay: Chorus, Flanger, Echo, and Reverb; Volume: Amplify, Fade In/Out/Special, and Normalize; Repair: Interpolate, Silence, DC Offset, and Swap Channels; repair clicks and pops by interpolating samples or silencing; tone, FM and noise generators; pitch adjustment; Backwards/Reverse Audio; AIF and AIFF-C with compression including IMA 4:1; AAC and MP3 (importing only); Sound Designer II; Wave (.wav, PCM only); tab-delimited text (export only). SYSTEM SPECS: Macintosh.

Steinberg Cubase (www.steinberg.net): Advanced Music Production System; digital audio workstations; designed for professionals; intuitive handling; advanced audio and MIDI tools for composition, recording, editing, and mixing; state-of-the-art Audio + MIDI Recording/Editing/Mixing; complete new set of VST3 virtual instruments and effects; real multi-channel 5.1 surround sound; SoundFrame Universal Sound Manage; Control Room integration within outboard studio environment; seamless integration of external audio and MIDI hardware; 32-bit floating point audio engine; professional music notation and score printing; cross-Platform: Windows and Mac OS X Universal Binary; compatible with PPC- and Intel-based Macintosh computers; new VST3 plug-in set and four new integrated software instruments with more than 1000 sounds; SoundFrame is combination of Track Presets, Instrument Tracks, and MediaBay database, to help organize all sounds from every instrument, both software VSTi and hardware; mixer offers a flexible Control Room section and up to four independent studio mixes; enhanced score editor; redesigned user interface with many new features speeds up workflow; Sidechain input for VST3 Plug-ins; free routing and recording from summing objects; redesigned sample editor; track quick controls; advanced MediaBay options; a Global Transpose Track; advanced Arranger Track; Logical Editor; Sequel project import and content compatibility; Music XML support; VST Plug-in Bridge; QuickTime support; drum editing enhancements; load projects inactive; remote control extensions; Apple remote support; MIDI file playback using HALionOne; new file type: MIDI Loop; over 400 presets for Embracer, Prologue, Spector, and Mystic; Control Room; new virtual instruments; Score Editor enhancements; user interface redesign. SYSTEM SPECS: Macintosh; Windows.

Steinberg Cubase Essential (www.steinberg.net): Personal Music Production System; tools for composing, recording, editing, and mixing; entry-level version of Cubase; same user interface and Audio Engine as Steinberg's Cubase; sequencer for home recording studio or a multi-track recorder for the band rehearsal room; Audio + MIDI Recording and Mixing; VST3 Plug-In Set including HALion One and Guitar Amp Simulator; 32-bit Audio Engine, 24-bit/96-kHz Recording; editors for MIDI and audio processing; Media Bay database for sound management; AudioWarp realtime time stretching/pitch shifting; cross-platform: Windows and Mac OS X Universal Binary; compatible with PPC- and Intel-based Macintosh computers; formerly Cubase SE product line; new set of plug-in effects; HALion One Sample Player instrument; guitar amp and more than sixty other new features and improvements; Arranger Track; linear and pattern-style arranging is seamlessly integrated; AudioWarp realtime time stretching and pitch shifting for working with loops and tempo-based audio. SYSTEM SPECS: Macintosh; Windows.

Steinberg Cubase Studio (www.steinberg.net): New workstation tailored to project studios and creative musicians; based on the same core technologies as Steinberg's Cubase Advanced Music Production System; streamlined Cubase Studio offers professional tools for composition, recording, editing, and mixing; new capabilities such as SoundFrame, full notation features, and brand new VST3 instruments and effects; Audio + MIDI Recording/Editing/Mixing; new VST3 virtual instruments and effects; SoundFrame Sound Management System; 32-bit Audio Engine; full scoring features; streamlined feature set tailored for project studios, musicians, and composers; cross platform: Windows and Mac OS X Universal Binary; compatible with PPC- and Intel-based Macintosh computers; brand new plug-in set based on the new VST3 standard; two software instruments with hundreds of ready-to-play sounds; SoundFrame system with Track Presets, Instrument Tracks, and MediaBay database to manage

and access media files and presets; professional scoring and notation printing feature set; interface and workflow enhancements; Sidechaining for VST3 Plug-ins; free routing; a Global Transpose Track; Music XML support, and more. SYSTEM SPECS: Macintosh; Windows.

Steinberg Nuendo (www.steinberg.net): Advanced Audio and Post Production System; next-generation audio production environment for audio post, studio production, and live recording; for audio professionals in media, recording, and film industries; provides scalable, cross-platform systems that integrate easily and fully with premiere components by industry-leading plug-in and hardware manufacturers; state-of-the-art digital audio production environment; 32-bit audio engine with full surround throughout; faster, more efficient workflow with dedicated tools, options, and features; complete set of next-generation VST3 surround effect plug-ins; utilizes best available audio and computer hardware and plug-ins; advanced new automation system for full control; Control Room integrates into any monitoring setup; Network Collaboration for multi-seat projects via LAN or WAN; full project exchange with other leading audio and video editing systems; cross platform for latest Windows and Macintosh operating systems; state-of-the-art automation system; combines with new recording functionality and Track Preset management features to speed up audio production workflows; next-generation VST3 effect plug-in suite; MediaBay database; new editing commands; Track Quick Controls. SYSTEM SPECS: Macintosh; Windows.

Steinberg Sequel (www.steinberg.net): Music Creation and Performance; affordable and easy-to-use music studio designed for first-time computer music enthusiasts; combines intuitive tools to record, edit, mix, and perform music with loops, instruments, and effects; first step into music production and performance; runs on both PCs and Macs; state-of-the-art audio engine; all-in-one package ready-to-use straight out of the box; record, edit, and mix music in any popular style; more than 5000 loops from world-class producers included, covering popular styles like Hip-Hop, R&B, Dance, Electronic, Pop, Metal, World, and many more; more than 600 ready-to-play instrument sounds including more than 60 drum kits for various styles; live performance mode for remixing/recombining songs on the fly; linear and pattern based arranging; audio and instrument parts follow tempo and key in realtime; built-in studio-quality audio effects, including EQ and Dynamics in every channel; more than fifty Audio Track Presets for various instrument types, as well as vocals; cross-Platform: Windows and Mac OS X Universal Binary; plug into Sequel with almost any hardware controller or keyboard; Controller Learn feature; live control of performances using a MIDI keyboard or external hardware controller; play melodies and chords without MIDI keyboard using the keyboard or mouse; Track Icons to label tracks visually; Track Freeze for more CPU power; MediaBay handling and overview; Sample Editor with Free Warp and Audio Reverse; set project tempo by tapping it on a PC or MIDI keyboard; low latency on Windows Vista even with no ASIO sound device with Windows Vista Core Audio; Sequel Content Sets available with thousands of additional loops. SYSTEM SPECS: Macintosh; Windows.

Steinberg Sequel Content Sets (www.steinberg.net): Hundreds of outstanding audio loops from top producers; organized into easy-to-use construction kits; demo songs are included; for Sequel or Cubase owners; Industrial: Elektro, Industrial, and Drum'n'Bass; Hip Hop: Hip Hop and R&B; Rock: College Rock, Punk, Grunge, and Alternative. SYSTEM SPECS: Macintosh; Windows.

Steinberg VST Instruments (www.steinberg.net): GROOVE AGENT 3: more sounds, kits, and drummers; new version of Steinberg's virtual drummer VST instrument; Special Agent and Percussion Agent modules in addition to the Classic Groove Agent module; new player technologies extend the functionality, including user sample import, Dual Mode, a new FX section, and more; HALION SYMPHONIC ORCHESTRA: full symphonic orchestra; scores, arrangements, accompaniments; for composition, production, pre-production in music, TV and film scoring, and game sound; HALION 3: software sampler; over fifty new features; virtual sampling technology; HALION PLAYER: sample player; based on HALion 3 technology; same content as the full HALion 3 version; can load every one of the hundreds of libraries available for the HALion platform. SYSTEM SPECS: Macintosh; Windows.

Steinberg V-Stack (www.steinberg.net): Virtual VST-Rack; VST instrument rack that can power up to sixteen VST instruments; for live use on stage or extending existing VST System Link network without requiring an additional sequencer program; extends the power of Cubase and Nuendo systems by integrating the CPU power of another computer that processes VST additional instruments; as a standalone application works as a performance rack for VSTi's, providing a CPU efficient platform for integrating the power of VST instruments on stage; quick access to master keyboard functions like Transpose, Layer, and Splitting of VSTi's; up to five insert effects, up to eight send effects per audio channel, and up to four EQ bands per channel and up to four subgroups; remote control; for VST System Link users; Cubase and Nuendo systems can be extended by adding more computer processing power; using V-STACK, CPU intensive VST instruments can be triggered and played in V-STACK

from another computer with sample accuracy; ReWire 2 support: audio channels can be sent from a ReWire-compatible application to V-STACK for effects and EQ processing. SYSTEM SPECS: Macintosh; Windows.

Steinberg WaveLab (www.steinberg.net): Audio Editing and Mastering Suite; solution for professional mastering, high resolution multi-channel audio editing, audio restoration, sample design, and radio broadcast work; complete CD/DVD-A production; standard application for digital audio editing and processing; sample accurate audio editing in stereo and surround; sample rates up to 384 kHz, 32-bit floating point resolution; Audio Montage for simultaneous editing across several tracks; Red Book-compatible CD mastering and DVD-A authoring; comprehensive suite of real-time metering and analysis tools; EQs, dynamics, and effects, with optional VST effect plug-in integration; audio restoration tools; support for all standard audio formats including WAV, AIFF, AU, MP3, MP2 (M.U.S.I.C.A.M.), RAW, Windows Media 9, AES-31 Import und Export plus many more; support for all common bit-rates 8-, 16-, 20-, 24-bit at up to 384 kHz; over 120 new features and enhancements; highlights in new version include the Spectrum Editor, the seamless integration of external effect hardware, support for MIDI remote controllers, the SmartBypass system with automatic loudness compensation, DIRAC time-stretching and pitch-shifting, support for Bob Katz' K-System metering, and much more. SYSTEM SPECS: Windows.

Steinberg WaveLab Essential (www.steinberg.net): Personal Audio Editing System; suite of audio editing tools tailored to the needs of musicians, smaller recording environments, and podcast authors; streamlined editing and CD/DVD burning capabilities; integrated podcast tools combine professional editing, restoration, and mastering capabilities with full internet audio publishing features; application for recording, editing, CD burning, and online publication via podcast; extension to both Sequel and Cubase; Podcast creation and publishing; Redbook compatible CD burning with CD-Text; stereo non-destructive editing with versatile clip grouping over multiple lanes; real-time engine with integration of clip-based and global effect plug-ins; audio processors; video track for sample accurate alignment of audio and video; sample accurate audio editor with audio processing at up to 96 kHz and 32 bit floating point resolution. SYSTEM SPECS: Windows.

Steinberg WaveLab Studio (www.steinberg.net): Audio Editing and Mastering Suite; state-of-the-art audio technology; streamlined workflow and editing and mastering features targeted at project studios and aspiring musicians; sample accurate 32-bit audio engine; advanced tools; sample accurate audio editor with audio processing at up to 192 kHz and 32 bit floating point resolution; stereo and multi-channel non-destructive editing with versatile clip grouping over multiple lanes; video track for sample accurate alignment of audio and video; real-time engine with integration of clip-based, track-based, and global effect plug-ins; audio processors including DIRAC time stretch and pitch shift algorithms; state-of-the-art audio plug-ins for EQ, Resampling, Declicking, Denoising, and many more; Redbook compatible PQ editing including Audio-in-Pause, CD-Text, and track sheet export Extended audio file handling and manipulation system including files sizes > 2 GB; sonogram-style Spectrum View for quick overview of the frequency structure of the audio file with simultaneous aligned use of Wave- and Spectrum View; batch processing and scripting features. SYSTEM SPECS: Windows.

TC Electronic PowerCore Plug-ins (www.tcelectronic.com): Range of plug-ins that can be used in any VST or AU compatible audio system, on PC or Mac, with Logic, Cubase, Nuendo, ProTools (using a wrapper), Live, Digital Performer, Bias, and many more; integrates with any VST or AU based digital audio workstation; range of plug-ins cover any need from basic tools like reverbs, EQs, compressors, expanders, choruses, and delays, over plug-ins that are dedicated to the voice, sporting pitch correction and Voice Modeling, to the best VST or AU compatible tools on the market, like the Restoration Suite and the System 6000 for PowerCore tool, the MD3 Stereo Mastering package; includes synths like the V-Station from Novation and the Virus|PowerCore by Access; depending on the hardware chosen, may get plug-ins included with the package; others are optional and can be bought in music stores and on the Internet; one hardware choice comes without any plug-ins; to run the PowerCore plug-ins, a piece of PowerCore hardware is needed; this hardware will make sure that the plug-ins won't strain the host CPU. SYSTEM SPECS: Macintosh; Windows.

TC Electronic Pro Tolls HD Plug-ins (www.tcelectronic.com): Products include: LM5 Loudness Radar Meters; Tube-Tech CL1B TDM; TC Helicon - Harmony4 TDM; VSS3 Stereo Source Reverb TDM; DVR2 TDM; NonLin2 TDM; MD3 TDM; Unwrap TDM; MasterX3 TDM; System 6000 Bundles for TDM. SYSTEM SPECS: Macintosh; Windows.

The AudioPro Home Recording Course Volumes I, II and III (www.halleonard.com): Includes everything necessary to start recording; basics on mixer, signal processing, and microphones; detailed information on recording guitars, drums, and percussion; illustrations and audio examples; wiring, impedance, and stereo imaging; recording bass guitars, vocals, pianos, and synths; digital hard disk recording, MIDI sequencing, mastering with computers, CD-R

technology and more; glossary of common terms used in recording; two CDs of audio examples. SYSTEM SPECS: Book and Audio CD.

TrackNotes (www.virtualstudiosystems.com): Track management software; custom studio configuration; supports up to sixty-four multitracks, plus 2,048 virtual tracks; signal path tracking; digital image viewer; artist, musician, musical instrument, and audio equipment documentation; studio asset tracking and valuation; printed reports, including several versions of Track Sheets. SYSTEM SPECS: Windows.

Tune 1000 (www.halleonard.com): General MIDI files; sound-alike arrangements; songs of top artists; lyrics display; backup vocal parts; 157 titles in catalog. SYSTEM SPECS: General MIDI-compatible keyboard.

Twiddly Bits (www.keyfax.com): Standard MIDI files; hundreds of riffs, runs, patterns, grooves, and licks; sequences can be cut and pasted; drums, keyboard, guitar, horn section, and more. SYSTEM SPECS: Macintosh; Windows.

UltimateSoundBank Virtual Instruments (www.ultimatesoundbank.com): Virtual Instruments include: PlugSoundPro; Retro Organs; Synths Anthology; Xtreme FX; Mayhem of Loops; Retro Keyboards; over sixty-one volumes of SoundScan Samples; UVI Engine. SYSTEM SPECS: Macintosh; Windows.

Universal Audio Powered Plug-ins (www.uaudio.com): Product headings include: Chorus and Delay; Equalizers; Compressors and Limiters; Special Processing; Channel Strip; Reverbs. SYSTEM SPECS: Macintosh; Windows.

USB Music Studio Kit (www.turtlebeach.com): Play songs on music keyboard; mix and edit on PC; Plug-N-Play capabilities and convenience of USB; USB MIDI Cable; overdub additional instruments; edit; mix; print sheet music; Setup Utility; includes Record Producer Music Software; hundreds of music loops; MIDI music files; musical templates to quickly create songs by providing drum patterns, instrument melodies, and more; paste together to create background patterns of bass lines, drum beats, and melodic loops; variety of styles, including rock, funk, dance, techno, blues, and more; bonus software. SYSTEM SPECS: Windows.

VAZ Modular (www.software-technology.com): Can run sixteen separate synths at once, each with up to sixteen-note polyphony and up to 255 modules; includes sample-playback module, several types of filters, support for DirectX, VST, and ASIO, and arpeggiator, pattern sequencer, MIDI control of on-screen sliders and delay, chorus, phaser, flanger, and reverb effects. SYSTEM SPECS: Windows.

Vegas Pro (www.sonycreativesoftware.com): Professional HD video editing, audio editing, and DVD authoring software; Vegas Pro collection combines Vegas Pro, DVD Architect Pro, and Dolby Digital AC-

3 encoding software; integrated environment for all phases of professional video, audio, DVD, and broadcast production; edit and process DV, AVCHD, HDV, SD/HD-SDI, and all XDCAM formats in real time; fine-tune audio with precision; author surround sound, dual-layer DVDs; offers h.264 codec for video compression built in; edit SD or HD video with drag-and-drop functionality, mouse and keyboard trimming, and ripple editing; includes ProType Titling technology, multicamera editing tools, 32-bit floating point video processing, customizable window layouts, color-coded snapping, improved HDV/SDI/XDCAM support, Cinescore plug-in support, A/V synchronization detection and repair, and auto-frame quantization; interface provides a fully customizable workspace for accomplishing a wide range of production requirements; dock multiple windows across multiple monitors; save layouts to fit specific editing tasks; nest Vegas projects within the timeline, customize and save keyboard commands, and use application scripting to automate repetitive tasks; system-wide media management; network rendering saves time by using multiple computers and networked drive arrays to render complex projects; supports 24p, HD, and HDV editing; use unlimited tracks, 24-bit/192 kHz audio, punch-in recording, 5.1 surround mixing, effects automation, and time compress/expand; apply customizable, real-time audio effects like EQ, Reverb, Delay, and more; expand audio processing and mixing options with supported third-party DirectX and VST audio plug-ins; mixing console; DVD and Blu-ray Disc Authoring Tools; burn Blu-ray discs directly from the timeline; create standard DVDs with multiple video angles, subtitles, multiple languages, and running commentary; apply Brightness and Contrast, Auto Levels, Crop, and Anti-Flicker filters; set CSS and Macrovision copy-protection flags for masters; DVD Architect Pro software supports the latest devices, including dual-layer DVD burners; DVD Architect Pro software with Blu-ray Disc authoring is free to registered DVD Architect Pro users; comprehensive help system, as well as detailed interactive tutorials that provide walk-through demonstrations of common features and functionality; tutorials provide an easy step-by-step method of learning the product and the workflow necessary to complete most common tasks. SYSTEM SPECS: Windows.

VS Pro (www.datasonics.com.au/): Graphical control interface for the Roland VS Digital Audio Workstations via MIDI; supports VS880, VS880VX, VSR880, VS890, VS1680, VS1880 & VS1824CD in any and all configurations; controls operations such as recording, audio cut and paste, automated mixing, and FX control. SYSTEM SPECS: Windows.

VSampler (www.maz-sound.com): Transforms PC into a 255 voice polyphonic software sampler that is able to use any recorded sound as a musical instrument; provides all of the classical sampler features in excellent sound quality; plays XXL instruments without being limited to the RAM size; extensive editing abilities; drag and drop actions and context menus allow quick access to all functions and provide for a smooth workflow; can operate either as a plug-in (VSTi, DXi) in sequencer or as an independent program (ReWire, MIDI); uses up to thirty-two separate audio outputs (ASIO, DirectSound); included "virtual MIDI-cable" connects VSampler to any MIDI-file player or classical MIDI sequencer. SYSTEM SPECS: Windows.

WaveArts (http://wavearts.com): Plug-in products include: Power Suite 5; Master Restoration: Professional Audio Recording Cleanup; TrackPlug 5; MasterVerb 5; FinalPlug 5; MultiDynamics 5; Panorama 5; MR Noise; MR Click; MR Hum; MR Gate; Master Restoration; TrackPlug 4; MasterVerb 4. SYSTEM SPECS: Macintosh; Windows.

Waves Plug-ins (www.waves.com): COMPRESSORS, GATES, AND DEESSERS: API 2500; AudioTrack; C1 Parametric Compander; C4 Multiband; DeEsser; Linear Phase Multiband; MaxxVolume; PuigChild 670/660; Renaissance Axx; Renaissance Channel; Renaissance Compressor; Renaissance DeEsser; Renaissance Vox; SSL E-Channel; SSL G-Master Buss Compressor; V-Comp; DeBreath; TransX; SSL G-Channel. LIMITERS: L1 Ultramaximizer; L2 Ultramaximizer; L3 Multimaximizer; L3 Ultramaximizer; L3-16 Multimaximizer; L3-LL Multimaximizer; L3-LL Ultramaximizer. EQUALIZERS: API 550A; API 550B; API 560; Q10 Equalizer; Linear Phase Equalizer; PuigTec EQP-1A; PuigTec MEQ-5; Q-Clone; Renaissance Channel; Renaissance Equalizer; SSL E-Channel; SSL G-Equalizer; V-EQ3; V-EQ4; AudioTrack; SSL G-Channel. REVERBS: IR-1; IR-L; IR-360; Renaissance Reverb; TrueVerb. MODULATION EFFECTS: Doubler; Enigma; MetaFlanger; MondoMod; Doppler; SuperTap; Morphoder. SURROUND: S360° Surround Panner; S360° Surround Imager; IDR360° Bit Re-quantizer; LFE360° Low-Pass Filter; L360° Surround Limiter; C360° Surround Compressor; R360° Surround Reverb; M360° Surround Manager; M360° Surround Mixdown; IR-360. RESTORATION: Z-Noise; X-Click; X-Crackle; X-Hum; X-Noise. PITCH AND TIME: Waves Tune; Waves Tune LT; SoundShifter; UltraPitch. STEREO IMAGING: S1 Stereo Imager; PAZ Analyzer; Doppler; PS22 Stereo Maker. MAXXBASS: MaxxBass; Renaissance Bass. SYSTEM SPECS: Macintosh; Windows.

XFX 1 (www.sonycreativesoftware.com): Six classic plug-in effects: Simple Delay, Multitap Delay, Reverb, Chorus, Pitch Shift (maintaining correct tempo or speed), and Time Compression (maintaining correct pitch); create multieffects within Sound Forge; with real-time previewing. SYSTEM SPECS: Windows.

XFX 2 (www.sonycreativesoftware.com): Six essential mastering plug-in effects: Graphic Equalizer (ten-band), Parametric Equalizer (four Filter Modes), Paragraphic Equalizer, Graphic Compressor, Multiband Limiter, and Noise Gate; hear results as screen setting change; for mastering and CD preparation. SYSTEM SPECS: Windows.

XFX 3 (www.sonycreativesoftware.com): Six eclectic plug-in effects include Amplitude Modulation, Gapper-Snipper, Flange-Wah-Wah, Vibrato, Distortion, and Smooth-Enhance; optimizes editing time by allowing real-time previews; as parameters for an effect are modified, the result is heard immediately; use with any Windows audio editor that fully supports DirectX Audio plug-ins, including Sound Forge. SYSTEM SPECS: Windows.

Digital Audio Recording and MIDI— Computer Music Software and Electronics Web Sites

---

A & S Case Company, Inc. www.ascase.com A&S Kriz-Kraft, A&S Fortress Cases, A&S Fly Weight, The A&S Axe Box, the A&S Nest, A Kriz-Kraft Plasma/LCD Lift Case, A&S Studio & Road Rack.

ABC2Win abc2win.com Integrated shareware music notation program; supports writing and editing of tunes, file management, and playback; view tunes as publication-quality music; registration enables printing.

Acoustica, Inc. www.acoustica.com Mixcraft 3.0, Spin It Again, CD Label Maker, Beatcraft, Gold Bundle, Musician's Bundle.

Akai www.akai.com Consumer electronics; founded in 1929 in Tokyo, Japan; quality home entertainment products specializing in the audio and video arenas.

AKG Acoustics www.akg.com Microphones; headphones; sound processing equipment; mixers; news; distributors; links.

AKoff Sound Labs www.akoff.com *Music Composer* is music recognition software which performs Wave to MIDI conversion; recognizes polyphonic music from microphone (other Wave input or file) and converts it into MIDI sequences.

Alesis www.alesis.com ADAT and recorders; performance FX tools; power amplifiers; studio mixers; electronic drums; signal processors; synthesizers; studio monitors; new products.

Algorithmix www.algorithmix.com *Sound Laundry* and *Easy Tools* software for cleaning and mastering old recordings; download demos; *AlgoRec* is an add-on program to all CD recording programs.

Alien Apparatus Company, Inc. www.alienapparatus.com Alien Apparatus, Solo.

Allegro Multimedia, Inc. www.musicwizard.com Piano Wizard, Music Wizard Academy, Wizard Tunes, Guitar Wizard.

Almateq SRL www.overloud.com Overloud.

AMG www.amguk.co.uk Longest established producer of sample CDs in the UK; preview studio.

Analog Modular Systems, Inc. www.analogsynths.com Supplier of vintage analog instruments; synthesizer service and restoration.

Analog Samples www.analogsamples.com Samples online.

Antex Electronics www.antex.com Digital audio products; audio for digital broadcast; satellite receivers.

Anvil Studio www.anvilstudio.com Windows freeware program to multitrack record, compose, and edit with audio and MIDI.

Aphex www.aphex.com Microphone preamplifiers; aural exciters; dynamics processors; effects pedals; modular products; audio interfaces.

Apogee Electronics Corp. www.apogeedigital.com *Master Tools; Session Tools;* developer of digital audio software and hardware; product information; download manuals; updates; news.

Apple, Inc. www.apple.com News; hardware; software; education; pro; support; where to buy; iTunes Music Store; iPod; iPhone; iMac, and more.

Art Vista Productions www.artvista.net Cool Vibes, Malmsjo Acoustic Grand, Malmsjo GVI, Virtual Grand Piano 2.

ASK Video www.askvideo.com ASK Video Music Tutorial DVDs.

Association of Shareware Professionals www.asp-shareware.org Trade organization for independent software developers and vendors.

Audible Magic www.audiblemagic.com Provides innovative technology, applications, and information services to traditional and digital media industries.

Audix www.audixusa.com Vocal microphones; professional instrument microphones.

AuReality midiworld.com/AuReality/index.htm Building Blocks; QE and QE; Kai'cku; AIM (Automated Instrumental Musician); Reaktor Library.

Bose www.bose.com Speaker manufacturer; sound technologies; product information; sound reproduction; car audio systems; new developments.

Byte www.byte.com Online magazine about hardware and computer technology.

Celemony Software www.celemony.com *Melodyne;* news; support.

Chicken Systems, Inc. www.chickensys.com Translator, SampleManage, Constructor, Kontakt Assistant, Millennium, ZoeOS, Ensoniq, MIDI-Disk Tools, Ensoniq Disk Tools, Ensoniq ASR-X Tools, SamplerZone, GigaStudio.org, Kontakt.org, EmulatorX.com, EAVES.

Chonwoo Corp. www.chonwoo.co.kr Chonwoo, Baxus, Baxus-Pro, Bamboo Country, Turtle, Cover the World.

Cinram www.cinram.com Media duplicator; design templates.

Cipex International www.roadreadycases.com Road Ready Cases, Gigskinz Bags, Intellistage Portable Stages.

Circuit City www.circuitcity.com Electronics retailer.

Clavia www.clavia.com Digital musical instruments; Nord Lead Synthesizer; Nord Rack; Nord Modular; ddrum4; Nord Electro; downloads; brochures; manuals; press; awards; history; FAQs.

CNET news.com.com Technology news Web site.

CNet Shareware.Com shareware.cnet.com Source of shareware for all computer platforms; not music specific.

CNMAT Home Page Center www.cnmat.berkeley.edu Center for New Music and Audio Technologies; at the University of California, Berkeley; showcases creative interaction between music and technology.

Computers and Music www.computersandmusic.com Retailer of audio hardware and software.

Creative www.americas.creative.com *Sound Blaster*; MP3 players; speaker systems; music and PC keyboards and more.

Crown International www.crownaudio.com Amplifiers; microphones.

CrusherX-Live www.crusher-x.de Vapor algorithm enables creating very complex waves; can be used as a synthesizer or as a versatile effect unit; creates unusual sounds with oscillators, WAV files, and real-time inputs.

Cybercorder skyhawktech.com Provides VCR-like recording for radio shows or any audio input.

Cycling '74 www.cycling74.com Max, MSP, Jitter, Pluggo, Mode, Hipno, Radial, UpMix, Octirama, Cycles.

Dbx www.dbxpro.com Signal processing; equalizers; pre-amps; online resources.

Deepsound Sample Calculators deepsound.net/calculation.html Sample calculators to help sampler users deal with time-stretching, pitch-shifting, delay times, etc.

Denon www.denon.com Speakers and car stereo systems; home audio CD and DVD players; pro audio products; news; links; FAQs; dealers.

Depopper www.droidinfo.com/software/depopper Software to get near CD quality from vinyl disks; minimizes clicks, scratches, and noise without removing treble sounds.

Digigram www.digigram.com Digital audio solutions for public address and pro sound installations, and broadcast and media production companies worldwide; innovative networked audio devices, computer sound cards, and audio management software.

Digital Music Corp. www.voodoolab.com *Voodoo Lab Pedal Effects; Ground Control System.*

Digital Sound Works www.digitalsoundworks.com Digital Sound Works, Drums on Demand.

Digitech www.digitech.com Guitar and studio effects; resources; artist pages; sound community; FAQs.

Dissidents www.dissidents.com Develops software for audio, music, and multimedia applications.

Dod www.dod.com Products; manuals; FX pedals; multieffects; signal processors; graphic equalizers; effects processors; press; outlet stores; FAQs.

Dolby Laboratories www.dolby.com Develops audio signal processing systems; manufactures professional equipment to implement technologies in the motion picture, broadcasting, and music recording industries; invented noise reduction; site includes new information, press releases, Dolby news, statistics, cassettes, technical information, movies and cinema, home theatre, multimedia, cinema products, professional products, literature, Dolby digital, DVD, company information, people, career opportunities, and trademark information.

Download.com www.download.com Freeware; shareware.

Dramastic Audio Corp. www.dramasticaudio.com Dramastic Audio, Obsidian, Retrophonix, TXIO.

Drawmer www.drawmer.com Dynamic signal processing; leading digital platforms.

DVCPRO Errorchecker www.errorchecker.de Software tool to report the OnTape error rate of DVCPRO and DV tapes.

East West Communications, Inc. www.soundsonline.com Sampled sounds superstore; search by category or format; downloads.

Eblitz Audio Labs www.eblitzaudiolabs.com BodyGlove, Fxpansion.

Eccentric www.eccentricsoftware.com *A Zillion Kajillion Rhymes and Cliches.*

Echo Corp. www.echoaudio.com Products; sales; support; downloads.

Echo Digital Audio www.echoaudio.com AudioFire, Indigo, Layla.

Edirol www.edirol.com Media production tools.

Electronic Music Foundation (EMF) www.emf.org Materials and information for understanding the history and development of music technology.

Electronic Musical Instruments 1870-1990
www.obsolete.com/120_years Vintage electronic
music instruments; links.

Electronisounds.com www.electronisounds.com Loops
and samples.

Emu Systems www.emu.com Samplers; sound modules;
command stations; keyboards; digital audio;
support; digital audio systems; software
instruments.

ESI Audiotechnik GmbH www.esi-audio.com ESI,
AUDIOTRAK, Luxonix, SKYLIFE, Shaman.

ESI www.esi-audio.com Professional audio products.

Etcetera www.etcetera.co.uk UK source for computer
music products.

EveryMac www.everymac.com Complete guide to
every Macintosh, Mac Compatible, and upgrade
card in the world; technical, configuration, and
pricing details.

FL Studio www.flstudio.com Image Line BVBA.

Fostex www.fostex.com Hard disk recording systems;
multitrack recorders; digital effects; product
information; FAQ and Tips; distributors.

Frontier Design Group www.frontierdesign.com
AlphaTrack, TranzPort, Dakota, Wave Center PCI,
Apache.

Fruityloops www.fruityloops.net Loop creating tool;
started as a drumloop creator; evolved into a
complete loop and song creating package; can hold
an unlimited number of samples and channels; play
stand-alone or by triggering MIDI equipment.

Future Loops www.futureloops.com Royalty free
samples, loops, and beats; sample CD.

FXpansion Audio UK Ltd www.fxpansion.com BFD,
BFD Expansion Packs, Guru, D-Cam Synth Pack,
Platinum Samples.

Gallo Engineering www.studiodevil.com Studio Devil.

Garritan www.garritan.com Authorized Steinway
Virtual Piano, Personal Orchestra, Jazz and Big
Band, Concert and Marching Band.

Gator Cases, Inc. www.gatorcases.com Gator, G-Tour.

GCI Technologies www.gci-technologies.com Gemini,
cortex, iKEY.

GForce Software LTD www.gforcesoftware.com M-
Tron, Oddity, Imposcar, Minimonsta, VSM.

Gigskinz www.gigskinz.com Cipex International.

Glyph Technologies www.glyphtech.com GT Series,
Net Drives, PortaGIG, TRIP, GPM-216.

GoldWave www.goldwave.com Digital audio editor for
Windows; Multiple Document Interface for editing
dozens of files in one session; large file editing, up
to 1 GB in size; configurable RAM; real-time
oscilloscopes.

Greytsounds www.greytsounds.com CD-ROMs, floppy
disks, synth patches, and audio CDs; electronic
delivery for some synth patches with Internet

orders; over 2,000 Sampling and MI products for
over 70 different keyboards.

Groove Maker www.groovemaker.com Groovemaker;
Loops.

Grundorf Corporation www.grundorf.com Grundorf,
Grund Audio Design (GAD), Road Runner,
Mighty Light, Altar Clarity, GALA.

Guillemot www.guillemot.com Sound cards; speakers;
support; links.

*GZ Foreign Economic Development Company For
Nansha E&T Zone* www.asunwell.com Sunwell.

Hands-on-MIDI www.hands-on-midi.com MIDI and
MIDI Karaoke files; MP3 backing tracks; band
arrangements; digital sheet music.

HeadKase www.headkase.com Headkase.

Heavyocity Media www.heavyocity.com Heavyocity
Media.

High Criteria www.highcriteria.com *Total Recorder*
recording and sound editing software.

Hitsquad.com Software Titles
www.hitsquad.com/smm/alphabetic/a/ or
www.hitsquad.comsmm/ Large list of music
software titles listed alphabetically; information,
system requirements, and downloads; freeware;
shareware; commercial titles.

Hobbes Internet Timeline
www.zakon.org/robert/internet/timeline/ Trace the
history of the Internet.

Hosa Technology, Inc. www.hosatech.com Cables and
adapters.

Humes & Berg Mfg. Co., Inc. www.humes-berg.com
Stonelined Mutes, Colorfold Stands, Kardova
Wooden Stands, Custom Fibre Cases, Econoline
Cases, Enduro Molded Cases, Enduro Pro Molded
Cases, Road Boss Cases, Galaxy Riggid Plush Line
Cases, tuxedo Padded Bags, DrumSeeker Bags,
Energy Savers, E-Z Fold Risers, Tuff Saxophone
Straps, Music Folio's, Music Room Equipment.

Hyperreal Music Machines
www.hyperreal.org/music/machines/ General
music; MIDI and equipment sites; manufacturer
sites; publications; retailers; dealers.

I/O MUG www.iomug.org Internet Only Macintosh
Users Group; links to Macintosh Web sites,
companies, and software.

Icon Digital Corporation www.icon-global.com ICON,
Nexkon.

IK Multimedia Production SRL www.ikmultimedia.com
SampleTank, Sonik Synth,Miroslav Philharmonik,
AmpliTube, T-Racks, Stealth, Stomp.

iKEY Audio www.ikey-audio.com GCI Technologies.

ILIO Entertainments www.ilio.com Virtual
instruments; Synthogy, Vienna Symphonic
Library, Applied Acoustics Systems,
Spectrasonics, Overloud, Vital Arts, Samplebase.

IntelliScore www.intelliscore.net Convert MP3 and WAV files to MIDI; convert music from a CD to a MIDI file; MIDI-enable any musical instrument, even voice; helps remove vocals.

International Music Software Trade Association (IMSTA) www.imsta.org Home page.

Iomega www.iomega.com Zip drives; data storage; online storage.

JBL www.jbl.com Speaker manufacturer.

Kaysound Imports, Inc. www.kaysound.com SMPro Audio, Violet Audio, XP Sound, Adagio Pianos, Hercules, Mixvibes, CME, SAC, Kaysound, Gateway Audio.

Keyfax Software www.keyfax.com *Twiddly.Bits* MIDI sample series; *Phat Boy;* demos.

Kid Nepro www.kidnepro.com Developer of sounds for many instruments; catalog; soundlists; synth patches; digital samples.

Korg USA, Inc. www.korg.com Korg, Marshall, Vox.

Lamb Productions www.casextreme.com CASEXtreme, Fly It Safe Case, Clam Case.

Lexicon www.lexicon.com Digital effects; multiprocessor effects; MIDI reverberators; power amps; demos; downloads; upgrades; support.

Line 6 www.lipeguitars.com POD, Spider III, Spider Jam, Spider Valve, TonePort, LowDown, FlexTone III, Vetta II, Stompbox Modeleres, ToneCore, Guitarport, HD147, FBV.

Lintronics www.lintronics.de Specialist for analog synthesizers; MIDI interfaces and modification upgrades; repairs for Moog, ARP, SC, etc.

Little Labs www.littlelabs.com LMNOpre, Multi Z PIP, REDEYE, IB P, IBP Jr., STD, IBPJRTX.

Logic Users www.logicuser.net/group Home of the world wide group.

Looper's Delight www.loopers-delight.com/loop.html Information on making and using loops.

LoopMasters www.loopmasters.com LoopMasters.

Lynx Studio Technology, Inc. www.lynxstudio.com Lynx, Aurora, LynxOne, LynxTwo, L22.

Mac Music www.macmusic.org/home/?lang=EN&vRmtQjpAz nOhM=1 Music on the Macintosh; large set of links; freeware; shareware; downloads; resources.

Mackie www.mackie.com Mixers; Desktop Studio Tools; studio monitors; recorders; speakers; amplifiers.

macProVideo www.macProVideo.com www.macprovideo.com Multimedia software video tutorials, training, and forums.

Macware macware.erehwon.org/Audio-Midi.html Downloadable shareware and freeware.

Magix Entertainment Corp. www.magix.net Products for music, video, media, and more.

Magix www.magix.com Samphitude, Sequoia, Music Makes, Music Studio, MP3 Maker.

Magma www.magma.com PCI Expansion products; products for OEMS.

Making Waves www.makingwavesaudio.co.uk/ Original music production software.

ManyMIDI www.manymidi.com Synthesizer sound libraries.

Master Bits www.masterbits.com CD-ROMS; sample data.

M-Audio www.m-audio.com M-Audio EX Series Studio Monitors, Studiophile Reference Monitors, Keystation Keyboard Controllers, Axiom Advanced Keyboard Controllers, ProFire FireWire Audio/MIDI Interfaces, ProjectMix I/O Control Surface, MicroTrack Mobile Recorder, USB MIDISPORT Interfaces, ProKeys Digital Stage Pianos, Torq Xponent and Torq Conectiv DJ Systems, Fast Track USB Interfaces, Black Box Guitar Performance Recording System, Delta Audio Cards, Sputnik Microphone, Octane and Tampa Preamps, Trigger Finger Drum Control.

Maz Sound Tools www.maz-sound.com Large collection of MOD/S3M/XM/IT tracking software; *Mazzive Injection* sample CDs; free samples in .WAV format; downloads; links; software synthesizers; MP3 players and encoders.

McDSP www.mcdsp.com Software for Pro Tools.

MDA-VST www.mda-vst.com Digital audio freeware.

Mechanical Music Corporation www.pro-activesoftware.com Pro-Active Software, Cutting-Edge Solutions, InterNetWork, ShowCase, Stick Handler, Tastee-Reeds, Advantage, Pro-Caddy Rax, Rhino, Area 51.

MediaMation, Inc. www.mediamat.com Entertainment systems integrator; designs and implements creative solutions for complex interactive shows, rides, exhibits and theaters; software and hardware products.

MetaSynth www.uisoftware.com Synthesis and sound design software; downloads.

Microboards Technology, LLC www.microboards.com Disc publishers, duplicators, printers.

MIDI Farm www.midifarm.com MIDI and music site; news; audio recording; press releases; free MIDI files; music software; FTP site; connection to MIDI and digital audio sites on the Internet; product updates; demos.

MIDI Hits www.midi-hits.com Large catalog; MIDI, MP3, and Audio CD formats; medleys, current hits, and piano only; pay for downloads.

MIDI Loops www.midiloops.com/copyrite.htm Site licensing MIDI files for use on the Internet; information about copyright and MIDI music; use of MIDI music under copyright; permission to use files, MIDI files, and shareware.

MIDI Manufacturers Association (MMA) www.midi.org Source for information on MIDI technology; up to date MIDI specifications; issues unique manufacturer IDs; licenses logos that identify MMA standards.

MIDI Mark www.midimark.com Sounds and samples.

MIDI Solutions www.midisolutions.com Pedal Controller; MIDI-powered products.

MIDI Workshop www.midiworkshop.com Music technology workshops and information; information about music software.

MIDI World midiworld.com Collection of MIDI and music-related information; basics; synthesizers; software; sounds; links; files; lab; marketplace; PC and Macintosh; downloads; archive of MIDI files; links to music software and hardware companies.

MIDI-OX MidiOx.com MIDI utility; free downloads.

MidiSyn planeta.clix.pt/acesteves/MidiSyn/MSynMain.htm MIDI to WAVE file converter.

Millennium Music Software www.millennium-music.biz/home/?res=800&actualres=800&ref= Online UK retailer of audio technology.

MiniDisc.org www.MiniDisc.org Community portal.

Minimusic www.minimusic.com/index.html Music software and hardware for Palm.

Minnetonka Audio Software www.minnetonkaaudio.com Surround Sound authoring tools.

Mixman www.mixman.com *Mixman Studio;* demos; support.

Mixmeister Technology LLC www.mixmeister.com Mixmeister Fusion, Mixmeister Studio.

MODARTT www.pianoteq.com Pianoteq.

Moog Music www.moogmusic.com Robert Moog is one of the original synthesizer developers; information on current products, including the Minimoog and modular synths; archive of older, classic instruments; products; support; dealers.

MOTU-MAC Mailing List www.unicornation.com Mailing list and forum for users.

Mu Technologies www.mu-technologies.com MU Voice.

Muse Research www.museresearch.com Receptor, Receptor Pro, Receptor with Komplete Inside.

Music Loops www.MusicLoops.com Royalty-free music loops and sound effects.

Music Marketing, Inc. www.musicmarketing.ca Celemony, Music XPC, Brainwerks, Image-Line, Wave Arts, Sontronics, Modartt, Virsyn, TL Audio, EKS.

Music Software at Harmony-Central www.harmony-central.com/Software Online listing of music software products by platform; downloads.

Navigator Systems www.hiretrack.com Developer of software for use by entertainment industry equipment rental companies.

Needle Doctor www.needledoctor.com Large selection of needles cartridges, turntables, and phono accessories.

Newtronic www.newtronic.com High-end tools for MIDI programmers; dance and electronic music; MIDI files; sample CDs; MIDI programming books, software, and synthesizer sounds.

Northstar Productions www.northstarsamples.com Digital sample CD-ROMs.

Numark www.numark.com Numark, CUE, MixMeister, Virtual Vinyl.

Ocean Way Recording, Inc. www.oceanwayrecording.com Ocean Way Audio, Ocean Way Drums, Ocean Way Monitors.

Odyssey Innovative Designs www.odysseygear.com Krom, Flight Zone, L Stand, Vulcan.

Omnirax www.omnirax.com Professional studio furniture.

Overloud www.overloud.com Almateq SRL.

Patchman Music www.patchmanmusic.com Over 787 sound banks.

Peavey Electronics www.peavey.com Musical instruments manufacturer; guitars, amps, drums, and keyboards; product information.

Penn-Elcom, Inc. www.penn-elcom.com Cases, racks, computer holders, and more.

Percussa www.percussa.com Percussa, Audiocubes.

Peterson Electro-Musical Products, Inc. www.petersontuners.com StroboStomp, StroboFlip, AutoStrobe, StroboTuner.

Phantom 5 Music Group, Inc. www.p5audio.com P5 Audio.

Polyhedric Software www.polyhedric.com/software ACE of WAV; WAVmaker; Gsound 22; Virtual Sampler SDK; Mellosoftron; MIDInight Express.

Power Technology www.dspfx.com Developer of *DSP/FX* digital audio DirectX plug-ins for PC; information about effects; magazine reviews; user comments; press releases; download a demo.

PRO TEC www.protecmusic.com PRO PAC Cases, iPAC Cases, MAX Cases, Thumbfort Thumb Rest, Quick Note Stamps.

Professional Sound Projects www.psp.l.pl Audio processors and effects plug-ins.

Pro-Rec www.pro-rec.com Synthesizer sounds; sample CDs; MIDI files.

Prosoniq www.prosoniq.com Developer of *SonicWorx* software for Macintosh and digital audio plug-ins for *Cubase VST.*

ProSound Web www.prosoundWeb.com Pro audio community; forums; news.

Puremagnetik www.puremagnetik.com Micropak Catalog, PM Videos.

Purple Audio www.purpleaudio.com Audio equipment manufacturer.

Q Up Arts www.quparts.com/cgi-bin/cp-app.cgi Sample collections for computers and samplers.

Q-Sound Labs www.qsound.com Supplier of 3D audio solutions for the Internet, PC/multimedia, consumer electronics, and health care marketplaces.

QuickShot www.quickshot.com Developer of peripherals for electronic/multimedia entertainment.

Radikal Technologies www.radikaltechnologies.com SAC-2K Software Assigned Controller.

Radio Shack www.radioshack.com Audio equipment; batteries, parts, accessories; phones; keyboards.

Radix Services www.radix.co.uk/radsamp *Radsamp* PC Sample Player; supports vari-speed, looping, and volume for each channel; demo for download.

Rapco.com www.rapco.com Electronics.

Realitone www.realitone.net Realivox Vocal Palette, Latin Rhythm Machine.

Rebeat Digital GmbH www.rebeat.com Digital software.

Redmatica www.redmatica.com State of the art in sampling tools.

Remixer www.remixer.com Source for digital audio information.

Road Ready Cases www.roadreadycases.com Cipex International.

Røde Microphones, LLC www.rodemic.com Podcaster, K2, NT2-A, VideoMic, NTK, Classic II, NT1A, NTG-2, NT55, NT5, NT6, NT3, NT4, NT1000, NT2000, NTG1, S1, Broadcaster, NT450, M3.

Roland www.rolandus.com Electronics manufacturer; keyboards; digital pianos; synthesizers; studio workstations; sound modules; and more.

Royal Case Co. www.royalcase.com Products; capabilities.

Rubber Chicken Software Co. www.chickensys.com *Translator* sample converter.

SampleTank www.sampletank.com Software sound module; combines sampler/synth engine with multisampled sounds into a VST instrument; for Cubase, Logic, or any VST compatible MIDI sequencer; natural and synthesized sounds.

Samson Technologies Corp. www.samsontech.com Samson Audio, Wireless, Hartke, Zoom; Equalizers; loudspeakers; headphones; microphones.

Selenium Loudspeakers www.selenium.com.br Warm Music, Appotek, Loudvox, Midnight, Maveria.

Sennheiser Electronic Corp. www.sennheiserusa.com Microphones; headphones; wireless solutions.

Serato Audio Research www.serato.com Serato Scratch LIVE, Pitch n' Time.

Shadow Pickups www.shadow-pickups.com Pickups; pre-amps.

Shareware Music Machine www.SharewareMusicMachine.com or www.hitsquad.com/smm Over 4,400 music software titles available to download; world's largest music software site; software categories include: audio editors, audio players, audio recording, audio restoration, business application, SCD burner, SCD player, SCD rippers, collecting and cataloging, computer-aided music, CSound drums and percussion, ear training, effects, format converters, guitar, jukebox and multiformat karaoke, label printing, metronomes, MIDI players and utilities, MIDI sequencers, miscellaneous, mod trackers and players, MP3, MPEG, multitrack recording, music calculators, music tuition, notation, oscilloscopes, patch editors and librarians, plug-ins, radio production, remixing and DJ software, samplers, software synthesizers, sound cards, device drivers, sound fonts, spectrum analyzers, streaming audio, media, tuners, video and multimedia, and wavetable emulators.

SIMS America, LLC www.simsamerica.com JamMate, Infrasonic.

SKB Corporation www.skbcases.com SKB Cases.

Software Publishers Association www.spa.org Software and Information Industry Association.

Sonic Emulations www.sonicemulations.com Digital audio content.

Sonic Network, Inc. www.sonivoxmi.com Sonivox, Sonic Implants, Fable Sounds, Scarbee, Hand-Held Sound.

Sonic Reality, Inc. www.sonicreality.com Reason Refills, Sonik Capsules, Expansion Tanks, Instrument Plug-ins, Individual Libraries.

Sonic State www.sonicstate.com News; views; events; links to synthesizer sites; Macintosh and PC software to download; chat.

Sonic Timeworks www.sonictimeworks.com Digital audio software.

Sonivox MI www.sonivoxmi.com Sound libraries, virtual instruments; *Sonic Implants*.

Sonnox, Ltd. www.sonnoxplug-ins.com Sonnox, Oxford Plug-ins.

Sonomic www.sonomic.com Sample and sound effects downloads.

Sony Electronics, Inc. www.sony.com/professional All electronic products offered by Sony.

Sound Blaster www.soundblaster.com Software, gaming, music and movies.

Sound Central www.soundcentral.com Computer audio samples; MIDI files; freeware; shareware.

Sounder www.sounder.com Software for creating interactive music.

Sounds Logical www.soundslogical.com *WaveWarp;* products; news; store.

SoundToys, Inc. www.soundtoys.com SoundToys Native Effects, SoundToys TDM Effects, SoundToys EchoBoy.

Spectrasonics www.spectrasonics.net Virtual instruments.

Speedsoft Vsampler www.vsampler.com Audio software.

SRS Labs www.srswowcast.com/demonstrations.asp Invents technologies and audio techniques that make products sound better.

Stage Research, Inc. www.stageresearch.com Developer of SFX; to aid the sound designer and the sound technician in creating, maintaining, and executing sound effects, music, and show control for a live entertainment environment.

Studio Devil www.studiodevil.com Studio Devil, British Valve Custom, Studio Devil BVC, Virtual Guitar Amp, Studio Devil VA.

Studio Electronics www.studioelectronics.com Synth products; support; downloads.

Summit Audio www.summitaudio.com Pre-amps; compressors; Eqs.

Super Loops www.SuperLoops.com Drum loops and samples on CD.

Sweetwater Sound www.sweetwater.com Music technology supplier and retailer.

Swiftkick Productions www.swiftkick.com Developer of the *Environment Toolkit* book and disk; tools for customizing Logic Environment to MIDI studio; descriptions of advanced features; *ET4* quarterly electronic journal.

Synchro Arts www.SynchroArts.co.uk *VocALign Project; ProTools* plug-ins; information; downloadable demos.

Synful www.synful.com Synful Orchestra.

Synth Museum www.synthmuseum.com Vintage synth resource.

Synth Zone www.synthzone.com Synthesizer resources on the Internet; links to manufacturer and user group sites; music and audio software; MIDI, synthesizer, and electronic music; electronic keyboards and effects.

Synthax, Inc. www.synthax.com RME, Alva, Tronical, Terratec.

Synthogy www.synthogy.com Ivory, Italian Grand.

Tascam www.tascam.com Multitrack reel-to-reel recorders; data storage products; consumer audio equipment; mixers; DATs; product information; FAQs; technical support; list of repair centers; pro audio division of TEAC Corporation; PortaStudio, GigaStudio, X48, GVI.

TC – Helicon www.tc-helicon.com VoiceSolo VSM Personal Vocal Monitors, PowerCore Plug-ins, ProTools TDM Plug-ins, Voiceworks Plus, VoiceDoubler, Voice Pro.

Terzoid www.terzoid.com *NoiZe* for Windows universal MIDI patch editor/librarian.

TG Tools tgtools.de Finale plug-ins.

The Center for Computer Research in Music and Acoustics (CCRMA) ccrma-www.stanford.edu/ News and events; information; overview.

The Freddy LLC www.the-freddy.com Muse Research, Fxpansion.

The Online Directory of Electronic Music members.tripod.com~emusic/index.html Links to electronic music sites.

The Sonic Spot www.sonicspot.com Comprehensive library of computer music and audio resources.

Thinkware www.thinkware.com Audio, MIDI, and video solutions; distributor of computer music hardware and software.

Time and Space www.timespace.com Sample CDs, CD-ROMs, virtual instruments, and software.

Tobybear Productions www.tobybear.de/ Extensive list of links relating to digital audio recording and other audio related web sites.

Total Recorder www.highcriteria.com/products.htm Universal sound recording tool; captures sound being played by other sound players, either from a file or from the Internet; records audio from CD, microphone, line-in; converts any sound formats to WAVE.

T-RackS 24 www.t-racks.com IK Multimedia; analog modeled, stand-alone software dedicated to audio mastering; built with actual physical models of tube circuitry; updated to support 24-bit file processing; complete workstation made of four discrete processors; state-of-the-art six band parametric EQ; classic stereo tube compressor/leveler; multiband master stereo limiter; soft-clipping adjustable output stage.

Tran Tracks www.trantracks.com MIDI files; rhythm, groove, and style disks.

Tune 1000 www.midi-classics.com/tune1000.htm General MIDI sequences.

U&I Software www.uisoftware.com Unique music software products.

Ueberschall www.ueberschall.com Sample CDs; sound libraries.

Unitec Products Corp. www.unitecproducts.com Case manufacturer; racks.

Universal Audio, Inc. www.uaudioi.com UAD-1, UAD-1e, UAD-Xpander, 1176, LA-2A, 2-610, 6176, LA-610, 8110, 4110, 2-1176, 2192, LA-3A, Solo/110, Solo/610, 2-LA-2, DCS Remote Pre Amp.

VAZ Modular www.software-technology.com Synthesizer sounds.

Vestax www.vestax.co.uk Mixers; turntables; merchandise.

Vintage Synth www.vintagesynth.com Links to over 500 vintage and new synthesizers.

Vinyl to CDR Processing Software www.wavecor.co.uk/ganymede.html Support for Wave Corrector; application for removing vinyl clicks, ticks, and plops from wave recordings of vinyl records prior to transfer to CD.

Voicecrystal www.voicecrystal.com Developer of sounds and voices for synthesizers on floppy disk, CD, and RAM cards; sample CDs and music software; product information; sound clips to download; mailing list.

Wave Distribution www.wavedistribution.com High-end audio processing.

Wave Mechanics, Inc. www.wavemechanics.com *UltraTools; Sound Blender; Speed; Pitch Doctor; Pure Pitch;* designs and manufactures DSP plug-ins for audio professionals.

Way Out Ware, Inc. www.wayoutware.com TimewARP 2600, KikAXXE.

Wexler Music Co. (David Wexler & Co.) www.wexlermusic.com Amati, Blitz, Buckle-Gard, Creepnomore, Demand Silk Swabs, Downbeat Bags, Bobby Dukoff, E.A.R. Noise Filters, French American Reeds, Kafko, Kazoo, King David, Mike Balter, Modular/MTS, Original Swab, Pacific Trends, Strunai, Wabash/Whitehall, Windy City Mutes, Woodstock Music Collection.

World Wide Woodshed www.worldwidewoodshed.com *Slow Gold; Slow Blast!*

X-Tempo Designs LLC www.x-tempozone.com Poki.

Yamaha Corporation of America www.yamaha.com Music manufacturer of keyboards, drums, guitars, Clavinovas, Disklaviers, receivers, stereos, tuners, pro-audio, mixers, brass, woodwind, recorders, and software.

Yamaha Music Soft www.yamahamusicsoft.com Yamaha music software products.

Record Label Web Sites

All Record Labels allrecordlabels.com Links to record labels worldwide; over 10,400 record label sites.

Association of Independent Record Labels www.air.org.au National Association of Australian Owned Independent Record Labels.

Atlantic Records www.atlantic-records.com Label Web site; artists; news; events; tours.

Blue Note Records www.bluenote.com Jazz; information; artists; catalog; shopping; new releases; FAQ; history of the company.

Capitol Records www.hollywoodandvine.com Current releases; tours; chances to win; listen to album extracts; join the monthly newsletter; information about Capitol Studios and gear.

Classical Music Record Companies on the Web www.search-beat.com/labels.htm The Classical Music Beat; classical music history Internet links; classical music history time lines; composer history resources.

Columbia Records www.columbiarecords.com Record label; video channel; artist biographies and schedules; reviews; links.

Cooking Vinyl www.cookingvinyl.com Eclectic roster.

Curb Records www.curb.com Record label; artist information; new releases.

Del-FI Records www.del-fi.com Rock 'n' roll legends; blues.

Deutsche Grammophon www.dgclassics.com Classical music record label; new releases; tour dates; new studio.

Dirty Linen's Record Label List www.dirtynelson.com/linen/special/label.html Extensive alphabetical listing.

Discogs www.discogs.com Database of recorded music; 14,583 labels; 153,950 releases; 100,813 artists;100% user-built.

Edel www.edel.com/index_js.html German company.

EMI Music www.emimusic.ca Record label; artist information; new releases.

EMI Records www.emirecords.co.uk Label Web site.

Epic Records www.epicrecords.com Record label; artist information; new releases.

Geffen Records www.geffen.com Record label; tours; new releases; artist links.

Hollywood Records www.hollywoodrec.com Artists; soundtracks; pictures; tracks; videos; tours.

Hyperion www.hyperion-records.co.uk British classical music label.

Info for Artists and Labels www.racerrecords.com/ArtistsAndLabels.html Believe in sharing information and in supporting other folks who are trying to make music available.

Interscope Records www.interscope.com/ Links to artist sites; news; tours; merchandise; information, including how to submit a demo; jobs at A&M; tracking down old records.

Island Def Jam www.islanddefjam.com Label site.

J Records www.jrecords.com/ Information on artists; audio and video clips.

Jive www.jiverecords.com Label Web site.

MCA Nashville www.mca-nashville.com Record label Web site.

Mercury Records www.mercuryrecords.com Record label; artist information; links.

Motown www.motown.com Information; music; featured artists; games and trivia.

MusicMoz musicmoz.org/Record_Labels/Major_Labels/ Major record label links.

National Association of Record Industry Professionals (NARIP) www.narip.com Membership; events; industry jobs; news.

Naxos www.naxos.com Classical music label.

Polydor www.polydor.co.uk Label Web site.

RCA Victor www.rcavictor.com Information; artists.

Record Labels and Companies Guide www.record-labels-companies-guide.com Resource for record label and other music company contacts, articles, news, tips, and more.

Reprise Records www.RepriseRec.com Record label; artists; audio files.

Rhino www.rhino.com United States reissue label.

Rounder Records www.rounder.com Independent record label; Massachusetts based; folk; roots; ethnic; children's.

Sony BMG Entertainment www.bmg.com Browse music by genre; own over 200 record labels; music club site; order CDs online.

Sun Records www.sunstudio.com Where rock and roll began; label for Elvis Presley, Jerry Lee Lewis, Johnny Cash, B. B. King, Roy Orbison, and others from the Golden Age; history of Sun's development; information on major artists.

TAXI: Major Record Labels www.taxi.com/members/links-labels.html Independent A&R Vehicle that connects unsigned artists, bands, and songwriters with major record labels, publishers, and film and TV music supervisors.

Universal Classics www.universalclassics.com Rosters of classical labels; artist bios.

Universal Music Nashville www.umgnashville.com/ Label Web site; artists and more.

Verve Records www.vervemusicgroup.com/verve/ Great jazz artists.

Virgin Records www.virginrecords.com Music information; technical questions; who to send demo tapes to; artists.

Walt Disney Records www.disney.com or www.disney.com/DisneyRecords/index.html Information; pictures; new releases; audio and video downloads.

Warner Bros. Records www.wbr.com or www.warnermusic.ca or www.music.warnerbros.com Feature artists; company's artists; new releases; job opportunities; Newswire; artists' message board; tour dates and information; FAQ; subscribe to the mailing list; audio and video clips.

Worldwide Internet Music Resources www.music.indiana.edu/music_resources/recind.html Record labels, record producers, studios.

Worldwide List of Record Labels spraci.cia.com.au/labels/labelsw.htm Alphabetical list of links to information about record labels around the world.

Yahoo Directory: Labels dir.yahoo.com/Business_and_Economy/Shopping_and_Services/Music/Labels/ Links to record labels.

Recording Web Sites

4-Track Recording Tips members.tripod.com~PROPAC/4track.htm Tutorial; tips on recording; EQ; links to recording equipment manufacturers.

Absolute Sound www.theabsolutesound.com Journal of Audio and Music; articles.

Analog Tape Recorders arts.ucsc.edu/ems/music/equipment/analog_recorders/Analog_Recorders.html FAQ.

Association of Professional Recording Services (APRS) www.aprs.co.uk UK-based professional audio organization; traditional music studios; project studios; post-production; broadcast; live sound; film soundtracks; duplication; training; leading force within the British music industry; concerned with standards, training, technical, and legal issues; Board of Directors is elected by members; studios can become members; list of associated studios.

Audio Amigo www.audioamigo.com Audio recording; digital home studio equipment; digital; resources; multitrack digital recording software; articles on promotion, home recording, and audio mastering.

Audio Engineering Society (AES) www.aes.org Professional society devoted exclusively to audio technology; membership includes leading engineers, scientists, and other authorities; membership information; members in forty-seven concentrated geographic areas throughout the world; conferences; links to other audio-related links including audio education and research; audio equipment; audio-related usenet newsgroups; computers and audio; electronic music and MIDI; magazines and publications; music; musical instruments; professional audio companies; professional organizations; radio and broadcast; search the World Wide Web; test and measurement; submit an audio-related URL.

Audio Forums www.AudioForums.com Audio-related forums.

Audio Institute of America www.audioinstitute.com Train to be a recording engineer.

Audio Recording Center www.audio-recording-center.com Resource for analog, digital, home demo, sound software, studios, and more.

Audio Revolution www.audiorevolution.com Reviews; Audio Video Marketplace.

Audio Web www.audioweb.com Auction and classified Web site; reviews.

Audio World www.audioworld.com Digital music news; articles; industry news.

Azalea Music Group www.azaleamusic.com/ Recording services through Azalea Productions and independent music producer Fett; music business-related education through courses, consulting, critiques, and various products; artist promotion and record label services for contemporary folk/rock, singer-songwriter Nancy Moran.

Blue Danube Music Production www.bluedanubemusicproduction.com Web site for Los Angeles-based producer, songwriter, and multi-instrumentalist Peter Roberts; has produced and/or written songs for George Benson, La Toya Jackson, Irene Cara, Daechelle, The Beu Sisters, his smooth jazz duo The Roberts Bros., and many others; songs and soundtracks for film and TV; contact info; audio samples; collaborators; gallery.

Denny Martin Music www.dennymartinmusic.com Web site for Nashville-based producer and songwriter Denny Martin; song demos; full-length album projects; client list; gear list; studio photos; musicians; testimonials; tips; samples.

Digital Domain www.digido.com Site to help audio engineers and musicians make compact disks and CD-ROMs; CD and CD-ROM mastering.

Disc Makers www.discmakers.com Audio duplication company; tutorials; CD promotion; pocket guides; newsletter.

Doctor Audio www.DoctorAudio.com Recording Web site.

Electronic Musician www.emusician.com Recording magazine; product reviews; articles; features; resource for musicians interested in personal music production; direct access to music industry and article databases; download past features and reviews.

EQ Weekly www.eqweekly.com Online magazine featuring articles for music producers.

EQ www.eqmag.com Recording magazine.

Harmony Central: Recording www.harmony-central.com/Recording/ Links to information resources.

Home Recording www.homerecording.com Equipment reviews; MP3; digital music recording on CDs or hard disks; tutorial for beginners; mailing list; articles on recording and mixing; FAQs on how to get started; active forum; detailed glossary; numerous tutorials.

Keyboard Magazine www.keyboardmag.com Recording information; product reviews; articles; columns.

Live-Audio.com www.Live-Audio.com Recording; study hall; forums.

Matthew Dela Pola www.mattdp.com Matt DP has excelled in virtually every area of music production; he has done work for film studios such as Warner Bros. Pictures, Walt Disney Studios, 20th Century Fox, Universal Pictures, Paramount Pictures, IMAX Films, RTVE Espana, all four national broadcast television networks, MTV, PBS, major cable networks, many major recording labels as well as hundreds of live shows; he has worked as music director, conductor, arranger and/or done production for artists such as Andrea Bocelli, Barbra Streisand, Kenny G, Celine Dion, Josh Groban, David Foster, Alejandro Sanz, Elton John, as well as many other international artists; he continues to work with record producer David Foster and with some of the top musicians in Los Angles on CDs and live shows; he is currently producing music from Alicante, Spain.

Mix Online www.mixonline.com Pro audio, live sound, music recording, and live post for audio pros.

Music Producers Guild mpg.org.uk Information; for professionals.

Musician's Tech Central www.musicianstechcentral.com/library.html Technical information; links.

Muzique.com www.muzique.com Bibliography of books on musical electronics.

National Academy of Recording Arts and Sciences (NARAS) www.grammy.com Organization of recording professionals; presents the Grammy Awards; organizes educational programs; member services and benefits; forum; MusiCares; LARAS; Master Track; Media Center; features; daily news; Grammy winners; Grammy store; Grammy Foundation; chapter updates.

National Association of Recording Merchandisers (NARM) www.narm.com Official Web site; about; members and membership.

Oasis CD & Cassette Duplication www.oasisCD.com Audio duplication company.

Pro Audio Music www.ProAudioMusic.com Audio equipment retailer.

Pro Audio.net www.soundwave.com News; information; discussion groups.

Pro Studio Edition www.discmakers.com/pse Studio newsletter; interviews with engineers; tips.

Prorec.com www.prorec.com Introductory and advanced technology; online music magazine; site index which can be viewed by title, company, product, author, or topic; bookstore; classified ads; active discussion board.

Recording Career www.recordingcareer.com Los Angeles Recording Workshop; recording engineer school; newsletter; scholarships; jobs.

Recording Connection www.recordingconnection.com Training for engineers.

Recording Industry Association of America (RIAA) www.riaa.com Current copyright infringement and piracy issues; censorship; information; resources.

Recording Workshop www.recordingworkshop.com Learn the art of recording.

Recording www.recordingmag.com Recording magazine; TAXI newsletter included.

Recording.org www.recording.org Composed of world-class Grammy award-winning producers, engineers and music business enthusiasts from around the world; how to record music, how to master music, what type of recording tools to use, etc.

Remix Magazine www.remixmag.com Artists; production; performance; gear; mixed media.

Rod Hui www.rodhui.com A multi-platinum engineer and one of the early pioneers of hip-hop and rap recording; discography; filmography; services.

Session Players www.sessionplayers.com Find top musicians for recording sessions.

SongMaker Productions www.songmakerpro.com Web site for Tracey James Marino and Vance Marino; professional musicians, songwriters, composers and arrangers; Pro-Tools studio; San Diego-based; music for film, TV, and media projects.

Sound on Sound www.soundonsound.com UK high-tech recording magazine; articles and reviews.

Studio Buddy www.studiobuddy.com Home Recording Helper; self-contained, easy to use database of recording tips for people with home studios; free download.

Studio Finder www.studiofinder.com Over 5,000 studios by location, equipment, and experience.

Studio Menu www.studiomenu.com Recording site.

Sun Studio www.sunstudio.com Virtual tour of the legendary studio; artist bios; who recorded there.

The Association of Professional Recording Services www.aprs.co.uk For producers and engineers.

The Educational Recording Agency www.era.org.uk/ Recording for educational purposes.

The Encyclopedia of Record Producers www.mojavemusic.com Database of producers.

The Home Recording Web Ring homerecording.com/webring.html Recording, mixing, and more.

The Recording Institute of Detroit www.recordinginstitute.com Licensed recording arts trade school featuring online training.

The Recording Web Site www.recordingwebsite.com Online music recording and production forum.

The Stereo Shop www.thestereoshop.com/links.htm Large collection of links to manufacturer sites.

Total Recording www.kiqproductions.com Book; Golden Ears Audio Eartraining course for musicians, engineers, and producers.

Track Star Studios www.trackstarstudios.com Producer Josquin des Pres; all aspects of music production; recording; mixing; mastering; composing; arranging; recording classes; artist development; music career consulting; audio post productions; La Mesa, CA.

We Make Tapes www.wemaketapes.com Nashville-based duplicating service.

World Wide Pro Audio Directory www.audiodirectory.nl Over 10,000 manufacturers and dealers listed; search by subject.

Yahoo Directory: Recording dir.yahoo.com/Entertainment/Music/Recording Information on recording; links to recording related web sites.

16
Music on the Internet

Music Magazines—E-Zines—Webzines— Newspaper Web Sites

Alternative Press Magazine
www.alternativepress.com News; reviews; features; interviews; sound clips.

Bards Crier www.bardscrier.com Weekly guerrilla music marketing and promotion e-zine for the working musician.

BerkleePress www.berkleepress.com Publisher of music instructional materials; interviews.

Billboard www.billboard.com Industry news; interviews; features; reviews; Radio Charts: Hot 100 Singles, Billboard Top 200 Albums, Pop, Country, Hits of the World, Contemporary Christian, Gospel, R & B, Rap, Dance Music, Latin, Blues, Reggae, World Music, Internet and Indie Charts and more; Top Videos; Fun and Games; The Power Book guide to radio and record promotion; online store.

Canadian Magazine Publishers Association www.cmpa.ca Official Web site.

Canadian Musician www.canadianmusician.com Music of Canada; news; articles; reviews; industry information.

CCM www.ccmcom.com American lifestyle and music magazine.

Chicago Tribune www.chicagotribune.com Newspaper.

CNN Interactive www.cnn.comSHOWBIZ/Music Music information; celebrities.

Collegiate Presswire www.cpwire.com Press release and newswire service.

Crawdaddy www.cdaddy.com United States classic rock magazine; interviews; features.

Direct Contact PR www.directcontactpr.com/ Press release and newswire service.

Dotmusic www.dotmusic.co.uk Guide to music; news.

Editor & Publisher www.mediainfo.com *International Year Book:* United States Dailies, United States Weeklies, and Special Newspapers, Canadian Newspapers, Foreign Newspapers, News, Picture and Syndicated Services; database available on disk or labels.

Entertainment Weekly Online www.pathfinder.com/ew Online version of the entertainment magazine.

Eworldwire www.eworldwire.com Press release and newswire service.

E-zineZ.com www.E-zinez.com Handbook of e-zine publishing.

Fast Forward www.discmakers.com/ffwd Interviews; articles.

Gale Directory of Publication and Broadcast Media www.gale.com Annual Guide listing newspapers, magazines, journals, radio stations, television stations, and cable systems; sold as a three-volume set: *Newsletters in Print, Encyclopedia of Associations, International Associations.*

Gebbie Press www.gebbieinc.com Publication search engine.

Harp Magazine www.harpmagazine.com For those passionate about their music.

Internet News Bureau www.newsbureau.com Online press release service.

Internet Professional Publishers Association www.ippa.org Association of over 10,500 professionals involved in New Media and the Internet.

Jam! www.canoe.ca/Jam Offbeat entertainment and cultural news.

Life www.life.com/Life/ Photographs; past features.

Live Magazine www.livemagazine.com Online magazine.

Live Sound! International Magazine www.livesoundint.com Webzine.

Los Angeles Times www.latimes.com Newspaper.

MediaFinder www.mediafinder.com Publication search engine.

MediaMagnet www.mediamagnetpro.com Press release utility.

Mix Magazine www.mixmag.com Music industry resources.

MTV Online www.mtv.com Industry news; bands; celebrity news; music videos; charts.

Music Alive Magazine www.musicalive.com Educational resource magazine; music education for today's generation.

Music for the Love of It www.musicfortheloveofit.com Bimonthly newsletter for people who love making music; musically literate forum in which amateur and professional musicians share stimulating ideas, up-to-date technical information, and heartfelt enthusiasm for music-making.

Music Information www.musicinformation.com E-mail subscription service; artist information; new releases; tour dates; TV appearances.

Music Industry News Network—Music Dish www.Mi2n.com Webzine; industry newsletter; links; newswire service for music professionals featuring band and record label announcements, tour and event dates, digital music news, and new releases.

Music Maker Publications Inc. www.recordingmag.com *Recording; Musico Pro; Playback Platinum.*

Musician www.musicianmag.com *The Musician's Guide to Touring and Promotion.*

New List new-list.com/ E-mail newsletter directory.

New Music Weekly www.newmusicweekly.com Covers the Radio and Music industry; over twenty-four pages; weekly magazine; Web site; mail and fax services; built by radio stations who "break" the hits first; standard for tracking radio airplay nationwide.

New Musical Express www.nme.com Music news and gossip.

NewsDirectory.com www.newsd.com Publication search engine.

Newshub www.newshub.com Search news archives.

Newspaper Association of America www.newspaperlinks.com Publication search engine.

NME www.nme.com UK Webzine; indie news; reviews; rock quotes; directory.

Old Farmer's Almanac www.almanac.com Trivia; folk wisdom.

Parrot Media Network www.parrotmedia.com United States TV Station Directory: printed quarterly; United States Cable TV Directory: printed semiannually; Newspaper Directory: printed semiannually; Radio Directory: printed semiannually; directories priced per issue or per year; subscriptions available for online use; directories updated daily.

Poets & Writers Magazine www.pw.org Webzine.

Pollstar www.pollstar.com Industry news; tour schedules; box office reports; albums sales; radio plays.

PR News Wire www.prnewswire.com Press release and newswire service.

Pro Audio Review www.imaspub.com *Pro Audio Review; Radio World.*

Publishers Weekly www.publishersweekly.com Online version of the industry magazine.

PubList www.publist.com Publication search engine.

Q www.qonline.co.uk Pop music culture in England; archives.

Radio & Records Online www.radioandrecords.com/RRWebSite/ Industry newspaper; information; facts and figures; links to a wide range of sources including record labels and industry sites; industry news; radio news; reviews; radio charts.

Rolling Stone www.rollingstone.com Features; CD reviews; music news; e-mail newsletter; MP3 and music video Pick of the Day; message board and more.

Salon www.salon.com Music news.

Sonic State www.sonicstate.com Industry news.

Spin www.spin.com Music news and information.

Stereophile www.stereophile.com Online magazine.

The New York Times www.nytimes.com Newspaper.

The World's Greatest Music Magazine Online www.qonline.co.uk From the UK's biggest selling music magazine; latest music news and reviews; Gig Guide; quizzes; competitions; chat; database of 17,000 Q reviews.

Time time.com News coverage.

United States News & World Report Online www.usnews.com News magazine.

URL Wire www.urlwire.com Press release and newswire service.

USA Today Life www.usatoday.com/life/lfront.htm Entertainment section.

USA Today www.usatoday.com Newspaper.

Virgin.Net www.virgin.net News; reviews.

Viva Music www.vivamusic.com Music business reports.

Wired www.wired.com Webzine.

World Press and Media Finder www.escapeartist.com/media/media.htm Publication search engine.

Yahoo! Entertainment Summary www.yahoo.com/headlines/ Entertainment industry headlines.

ZDNet Music News music.zdnet.com Music news service; technology update; white papers; downloads; reviews and prices; wired and wireless; software infrastructure; hardware upgrades.

Music on the Internet—Legal MP3s and Ringtones—MP3 Software and Hardware—Mobile Providers—Streaming Audio and Video Web Sites

---

7 Digital www.7digital.com MP3 music downloads.

9squared www.9squared.com Independent mobile content provider.

Alltel Wireless www.alltel.com Cell phones.

Artist Direct www.artistdirect.com Major label and indie artists.

AT&T www.att.com Wireless; cellphones; digital content; iPhone.

Audible.com www.audible.com Download audio books and more.

Audio Galaxy www.audiogalaxy.com Download site; MP3; free Web site hosting; indie artists; MP3 search engine; chat.

AudioLunchbox www.audiolunchbox.com Unrestricted indie music.

Audion www.panic.com For Macintosh; MP3s; audio CDs; streaming Web audio.

AudioRequest Home MP3 Player www.request.com/us/ Digital music services.

Audiosparx www.audiosparx.com Sound effects; royalty-free music; artists, songwriters, and publishers can upload tracks to license.

Axialis AX-CDPlayer www.axialis.com/axcdplayer CDDB compatible CD player for Windows; automatically get disk and track titles accessing CDDB worldwide database through the Internet.

Beatnik www.beatnik.com Audio software solutions.

Bell Mobility www.bell.ca Canadian provider of cell phones and mobile entertainment.

Berkeley Multimedia Research Center bmrc.berkeley.edu/projects/mpeg MPEG information.

BeSonic www.besonic.com Music; radio; search; shop; news; community.

Bitmunk www.bitmunk.com Indie music; news; downloads.

Black Diamond Sound Systems www.blackdiamondsound.com Turn computer into a virtual recording studio with music software, including the audio file editing and MP3 encoding program *TsunamiPro*.

Blackberry http://na.blackberry.com/eng/ Smartphones; products; software; support.

Blue Frog www.bluefrog.com Mobile content.

BuyMusic www.buymusic.com Music downloads; news and reviews.

BuyMusic.com www.buymusic.com Music downloads; top selling singles.

CD Wow! www.cdwow.com Online music store.

CDBaby www.cdbaby.com Since 1998; site for independent artists to sell CDs and digital downloads; digital distribution; founded by Derek Sivers; articles; album art; editor's picks; new arrivals; web hosting.

CDON www.cdon.com Music, DVDs, and more; Scandinavia.

Chello Musiczone www.chello.at/Musik/ Austrian music site.

Click Music www.clickmusic.co.uk Music downloads; links; news; celebrities; features; interviews.

CNet Download.com http://music.download.com/ Music downloads.

COMPO10 http://compo10.com?musicHosts.htm Compare attributes of many sites hosting and distributing music.

Creative Technology MP3 Players www.creative.com/products/mp3/ MP3 hardware player manufacturers.

Daily MP3 www.dailymp3.com/ Updated daily; everything MP3.

Destra www.destra.com Australian digital media.

DFX www.fxsound.com Audio enhancer; audio adaptor.

Dimension Music www.dimensionmusic.com MP3 Web site; artist information; industry news; links; forums; chat.

Djuice www.djuice.com Digital PC and mobile provider.

Eircom Net Music http://music.eircom.net/ Music downloads, reviews, news, and more.

eMusic www.emusic.com Downloadable music site; listen to song samples before purchasing.

Epitonic www.epitonic.com Source for MP3 recordings; reviewed and selected indie MP3 music; download site.

EvO:R www.Evor.com Interactive music site for the Indie community.

EZ-Mixer www.ez-mixer.com IK Multimedia; multifunctional MP3 player/encoder; live remixing tool which emulates a two-track DJ mixer with all necessary features to produce compilation or live remix; like a DJ in a club; supports the import/export of other audio formats including Wav, Aiff, QDesign, QuickTime.

Fnac.com www.fnac.com French mobile entertainment.

Fraunhofer, Developer of the MP3 Format
www.iis.fhg.de/amm/techinf MP3 reference site;
audio and multimedia technology; licensing;
industry news.

Free Record Shop www.freerecordshop.com Music,
movies, games, and more.

Getmusic.com www.getmusic.com Links to all
genres.

GiantDisk giantdisc.org/ Organize an audio jukebox
with MP3 files.

Gigabeat http://explore.toshiba.com/gigabeat Find
your song.

Grace Note www.gracenote.com Digital media
technology.

GreatIndieMusic www.greatindiemusic.com Indie
artists; MP3 digital downloads.

GroupieTunes www.groupietunes.com Downloads
and ringtones of indie music.

HDtracks.com www.hdtracks.com High resolution
audiophile music downloads.

Helio www.helio.com Mobile phones.

HMV Downloads
https://digital.hmv.com/HMV.Digital.WebStore.
Portal/ Digital PC and mobile provider.

ID3.org www.id3.org ID3 tag standard; audio file
tagging format.

iMusica www.iMusica.com MP3 players and
downloads.

Inprodicon www.inprodicon.com Independent
provider of digital content.

Into Music www.intomusic.co.uk/ Features hand-
picked free download music from independent
musicians, all files are checked to ensure they are
virus free and of good sound quality.

iPhone www.apple.com/iphone/ Phone and media
player by Apple, Inc.

iPod Touch www.apple.com/ipodtouch/ Touch screen
iPod; media player.

iSound www.isound.com Artists; MP3s; videos.

iTunes www.apple.com/itunes/ Music Store with
legal downloads; iPod; import CDs; Smart
Playlists; sync with iPod; play audio CDs on
Macintosh; convert files on CDs to MP3 format;
manage songs collected; create playlists; tune in
to Internet radio stations; create music CDs.

JukeBytes www.jukebytes.00go.com Jukebox
simulator for PC.

Karstadt www.karstadt.de/ Sells multimedia.

Lala www.lala.com Digital music made easy.

LaMusica www.lamusica.com/ Spanish music web
portal.

Liquid Digital Media www.liquiddigitalmedia.com
Solutions for Internet media delivery.

LullaPets www.lullapets.com The musical
companions.

Media Wizard www.cdhnow.com/mw.html Powerful
and complete multimedia solution supporting all
popular audio and video formats.

Media World Compra Online
http://compraonline.mediaworld.it/ Phones,
audio, and more.

Messaggeriedigitali.it www.messaggeriedigitali.it/
Music downloads.

MidiRunner www.midirunner.com Integrated Play
Center for MIDI, MP3, Wave, CD-Audio files,
and all other WindowsMedia supported sound
files; can also be used to create, edit, and load
playlists.

Mobilestreams www.mobilestreams.com Mobile
video, games, and music.

Moderati www.moderati.com Mobile content.

Moviestar www.moviestar.ie/ Movie downloads.

MP3 Audio Player www.yukudr.com/mp3player
EasyPEG3; simple freeware application which
allows user to play MP3 audio.

MP3 Newswire www.mp3newswire.net MP3 news.

MP3 Shopping www.mp3shopping.com
MP3 players; news; software; site map; products;
links; music; search.

MP3Machine.com www.mp3machine.com/database
MP3 technology.

MP3tunes www.mp3tunes.com Player, locker,
downloads, support.

MPEG www.mpeg.org MPEG and MP3 reference
site; FAQs; links.

MPEGX.com www.mpegx.com Large guide to MP3
software programs and other related material;
listing of various MP3 programs with ratings.

Mpg123 www.mpg123.de Fast, free MP3 audio
player for Linux, FreeBSD, Solaris, Hpux, and
near all other UNIX systems; decodes MP1 and
MP2 files.

MSN Music http://music.msn.com/ Entertainment;
music; movies; television.

MTV Italy www.mtv.it Italian music downloads.

MTV www.mtv.com/music/downloads/ Music
downloads; join; search.

MTV Soundtrack http://soundtrack.mtv.com Listen to
music by new artists.

Music Choice UK www.musicchoice.co.uk Up to
fifty CD quality genre specific audio channels;
no ads or DJs; available twenty-four hours a day.

Music Choice www.musicchoice.com Commercial-
free, professionally programmed music channels
and digital downloads available on one site.

Music Exchange www.musicex.com Safe sales and
licensing of music on the Internet.

Music Net www.musicnet.com Widely distributed
digital music service; legal downloads; large
catalog; variety of genres; FAQ; stream.

Musician MP3 www.musicianmp3.com Music downloads.

MusicIsHere www.musicishere.com Music downloads; choose file size and type.

Musicload www.musicload.com MP3 downloads since 1999.

Muze.com www.muze.com Entertainment product information.

MuzicMan www.muzicman.com MP3 player and organizer; designed for converting a large CD collection to a PC-based stereo system.

MyCokeMusic www.music.coca-cola.com/home_index Discover and share new music.

Napster www.napster.com Legal music downloads; large digital music library.

Nareos www.nareos.com Digital content.

Nokia www.nokia.com/ Mobile provider; cell phones; support and software.

NTT www.ntt.com Communications.

Nullsoft www.nullsoft.com *WinAmp* and other product downloads.

Ogg Vorbis www.vorbis.com Open, patent-free, professional audio encoding and streaming technology.

One Source onesource.pan.com Distribution system for e-CDs; buy whole CDs or individual tracks; PAN's patent-pending anti-piracy platform Digital Interactive Fingerprinting.

Orange www.orange.com Information and entertainment services on mobile, including music, video, games, information and sports content plus access to other mobile Internet sites.

Panasonic www.panasonic.com Phones and more.

PassAlong www.passalong.com MP3 music store.

Passionato www.passionato.com Classical music downloads.

PayPlay http://payplay.fm/ Large MP3 store.

Planet Music Stream http://movie-stream-planet-music-search-lyrics.kohit.net/_/ MP3 downloads; lyrics.

PlayIndies www.playindies.com Private log-in.

Prefueled www.prefueled.com Online entertainment; Scandinavia.

Puretracks www.puretracks.com MP3; e-singles.

QuickTime www.quicktime.com or quicktime.apple.com Streaming audio and video format; free download.

Real Tones www.realtones.com/ Find service provider and download ringtones.

RealNetworks UK www.real.co.uk Delivers streamed data from Web to computer in real time; information about the technology; samples; free plug-ins download.

RealNetworks www.real.com The Web's first streaming media introduced in April 1995; first to stream audio to the masses; RealPlayer; RealAudio stations.

Resort Records www.resortrecords.com Downloadable music retail; affiliate program.

Rhapsody www.rhapsody.com Streaming audio; downloads; videos; lyrics; photos.

Rhythm Net www.rhythmnet.com Gain exposure and industry recognition; sell songs; international distribution; sell recordings.

Rioport www.rioport.com Ecast is the largest broadband touchscreen media network in the United States, providing digital music to over 10,000 bars and nightclubs across the country.

Ruckus www.ruckus.com/ruckus/home.do Downloadable content aimed at college students.

rVibe www.rvibe.com Share music; make friends.

Rykodisk www.rykodisc.com Download site; MP3.

Samsung www.samsung.com/us/ Mobile phones and more.

SendMe Mobile www.sendmemobile.com/ Songs, ringtones, and games for phones.

Sight Sound www.sightsound.com Digital distribution.

slotMusic www.slotmusic.org New physical format sold by all four major labels; high quality, DRM-free MP3 music on microSD cards; can be played on mobile phones or MP3 players; any computer with a USB connector and a growing number of in-car sound systems will be able to play slotMusic cards.

Sonic Net www.sonicnet.com News; reviews; events; downloads; videos; music directory; contests; radio; artist database.

Sound Click www.soundclick.com Download site; MP3 and streaming audio; free membership.

Sprint www.sprint.com Cell phones; TV and music phones.

StompinGround.com www.stompinground.com Song distribution resource; download site; MP3; unsigned band promotion.

Stream Box www.streambox.com Streambox provides a single software-based platform for live and file-based video transport and acquisition over IP.

Tactile 12000 www.tactile12000.com MP3 DJ program.

TDC http://tdc.com/ Unlimited music to customers.

Telenor www.telenor.com Mobile communications services across twelve countries in Europe and Asia; Fixed-line and Broadcast services in the Nordic region.

TextAloud MP3 www.nextuptech.com/TextAloud Converts any text into voice and to MP3; listen to text, e-mail and Web pages on computer or portable MP3 player.

Tiscali Music Downloads www.tiscali.com Italy and UK; leading alternative telecommunications operators in Europe.

TMobile www.tmobile.com Mobile provider.

Tradebit www.tradebit.com The digital outlet.

U.S. Cellular www.uscellular.com Phones; downloads.

UltraPlayer www.ultraplayer.com Free Windows audio tool; plays MP3s, WAVs, and CDs; features playing and recording of streaming MP3 broadcasts; visual plug-ins and skins.

USEN www.usen.com Media contents company.

Verizon V-Cast http://products.vzw.com//index.aspx?id=music_v cast Cell phones; high speed internet; music from Rhapsody.

Virgin Mobile www.virginmobile.com Mobile provider.

VirginMega.fr www.virginmega.fr/accueil.htm Music downloads.

Virtual Turntables carrot.prohosting.com/vtt_overview.shtml Play and mix MP3s; options, effects and tools to aid in mixing of music; DJ software.

Virtuosa Gold www.mp3-converter.com/virtuosa.htm MP3 player and encoder software.

Vodafone www.vodafone.com Didital PC and mobile provider.

Vortex Technology www.vortex.comav.html Streaming audio and video.

Vtap www.vtap.com/index.html Search for videos.

Wal-Mart Downloads http://downloads.walmart.com/swap/ Download music.

Web Tunes www.webtunes.com Download site; MP3.

Winamp Player for Windows www.winamp.com MP3 player and encoder software; from Nullsoft; high-fidelity music player for Windows; supports MP3, CD, and other audio formats; the original Windows MP3 player.

Windows Media Player www.microsoft.com/windows/products/winfamil y/mediaplayer/default.mspx Microsoft audio/video; handles MP3 files and many other audio and streaming formats.

Xaudio www.xaudio.com Cross-platform MP3 players; Xaudio Player for Unix.

XMMS www.xmms.org X Multimedia System; open-source MP3 player for Linux and UNIX; MP3 player and encoder software.

Yahoo Music new.music.yahoo.com/ Music downloads; music videos; music news; Internet radio.

Zebox.com www.zebox.com Indie music.

ZuKool www.zukool.com Personalized music recommendations.

Music Resources—Directories— Portals Web Sites

About.com Music home.about.com/entertainment Directory of music categories; links.

Amazon www.amazon.com/music or www.amazon.co.uk/music Leading Internet retail site; reference database.

America's Shrine to Music Museum www.usd.edu/smm Home page; index; musical instrument museum and research center located in South Dakota.

AMG All Music Guide www.allmusic.com Database of all recorded music; search by album, artist, or song name; key artists; key albums; music styles; music glossary; music maps; new releases; featured albums.

ArtNet www.artnet.com Samples of art exhibitions around the world.

Basic Music www.basicmusic.net Directory of links to many music categories.

Berklee School of Music Library library.berklee.edu/ Cross-referenced recordings.

Biography www.biography.com Based on the popular A&E television series; includes profiles of composers and musicians.

Britannica Online www.eb.com Online version of the Encyclopedia Britannica; articles on music topics.

Cyber Alert www.cyberalert.com Clipping service for hire; compile information daily on topics of interest; use search engines, forums, and online databases.

Encarta Online www.encarta.msn.com Online encyclopedia.

Encarta Online Music Links encarta.msn.com/encnet/refpages/SRPage.aspx?s earch=music&x=19&y=14 Links to music topics.

FAQ Archives www.faqs.org Frequently asked questions.

Harmony Central www.harmony-central.com Information on many musical topics; major collection of resources for the musician; news; communities; software; MIDI; computer music.

Indiana University Library www.music.indiana.edu/muslib.html William and Gayle Cook Music Library; access to important library catalogs for music in the United States and abroad.

Library of Congress www.lcWeb.loc.gov/homepage/ Largest library in the United States.

Music Business Solutions www.mbsolutions.com Resource directory; consulting; articles; books; links.

Music Database www.roadkill.com/MDB/ Search by album title and artist; listeners' reviews and links.

Music Information Resources www.library.ucsb.edu/subj/music.html Links to music educational sites, directories, and more.

Music Library Association www.musiclibraryassoc.org Placement service for music librarians and more.

Music Yellow Pages www.musicyellowpages.com Phone numbers for any music-related company.

Music.com www.music.com Music videos.

Musical Quotes www.cybernation.com/victory/quotations/subjects/quotes_music.html Famous quotations.

Musical Web Connections www.columbia.edu/~hauben/music/web-music.html Large list of music links.

MusicSearch.com www.musicsearch.com Search engine for music only; links to artists, events, industry news, reviews, radio stations, and music publishers.

Music-Sites.net www.music-sites.net Music links directory; music community.

Musreview www.musreview.com Music charts; radio stations; artists; labels; country artists; country music links; record labels; disk jockeys; booking and talent; jazz; links and directories; rock artists; bands; blues; music publishers; Christian and gospel music; recording studios; managers; rap; R&B bands; music stores; musical instruments; music promotion; music news; radio stations; music charts; graphic design; production; MP3/MIDI; classical; songwriters.

Open Directory—Arts: Music www.dmoz.orgArts/Music/ Music-related links.

PC Webopaedia www.pcwebopaedia.com Encyclopedia of computer and Internet information.

Showbiz Data www.showbizdata.com The entertainment search engine.

The American Music Center www.amc.net Resource for musicians and producers; grant information; music directories; artist information and publications.

The Instrument Encyclopedia www.si.umich.edu/chico/instrument/ More than 140 artifacts from the Stearns Collection at the University of Michigan; features musical instruments from around the world.

The Names of Instruments and Voices in Foreign Languages www.library.yale.edu/cataloging/music/instname.htm English, French, German, Italian, Russian, and Spanish.

UCLA Music Library www.library.ucla.edu/libraries/music University of California at Los Angeles music library.

Virtual Museums www.icom.org/vlmp Links to hundreds of museum exhibits around the world; Smithsonian, Louvre, and more.

Voice of the Shuttle vos.ucsb.edu/browse.asp?id=2722 Music and dance resources.

Web Sites for Music Research www.lib.unc.edu/music/research/ Compiled by the University of North Carolina; links.

Webring.org dir.webring.com/rw?d=Music Music-related links.

World of Mechanical Music Museum www.mechanicalmusic.co.uk Self-playing musical instruments; antique musical boxes.

World Wide Arts Resources www.wwar.com Comprehensive directory of the arts on the Internet.

Worldwide Internet Music Resources www.music.indiana.edu/music_resources/ Informational links.

Yahoo Directory Music Links www.yahoo.com/entertainment/music Links to music sites on the Internet.

Music Retailer Web Sites

123Posters www.123posters.com Buy music-related posters online.

Alexander Publishing www.alexanderpublishing.com Self-paced problem/solution instruction; Alexander University Campus Music Store.

Allegro Music www.allegro-music.com Classical, jazz, world, pop, blues, etc.

Amazingcds.com www.amazingcds.com Independent music artists' CDs from around the world; online music store that is listening to original music and accepting all styles of music; see Submission Information page.

Amazon www.amazon.com Music; books; software; reviews; links; Advantage Program for independent publishers and artists.

American Musical Supply www.americanmusical.com Online retailer.

Backstage Commerce www.backstagecommerce.com/ Independent CDs; artist web pages.

Backtrack Records www.backtrackrecords.com Hard-to-find music; independent; imports.

Barnes and Noble www.barnesandnoble.com/ Music; books; software; reviews; links.

Blockbuster Online www.blockbuster.com Movie music and video shopping; online store.

BMG Music Service www.bmgmusicservice.com Music club; membership.

Borders www.borders.com Online books and music retailer.

Buy.com www.buy.com Online electronics retailer.

Carvin www.carvin.com Factory-direct music store.

CD Access www.cdaccess.com CD-ROM titles; educational.

CD Baby www.cdbaby.com Most successful online retailer of independent CDs; downloads.

CD Warehouse www.cdwarehouse.com Retailer.

Crotchet Web Store www.crotchet.co.uk Ten departments dedicated to classical music, jazz, film soundtracks, and world music; browse latest releases; online database.

Encore Music Company, Inc. www.encoremusic.com Sheet music; music books; accessories; gifts.

Everything English www.everythingenglish.com New and used CDs; English paraphanalia.

Forced Exposure www.forcedexposure.com Online store; reviews of new releases.

Forever Vinyl www.forevervinyl.com Buy and sell vinyl; large inventory.

Friendship House www.friendshiphouse.com Music teaching aids; gifts; novelties; trophies; software; books; CDs.

Global Electronic Music Marketplace (GEMM) www.gemm.com Large catalog of music; combines catalogs of 2,000 discounters, importers, collectors, labels and artists; new, used, hard-to-find, and out-of-print albums.

HMV www.hmv.com Canadian retailer.

Horizon Records www.horizonrecords.net Folk, jazz, blues, world beat, classical, regional, Jewish, Celtic, vintage vinyl.

Independent Distribution Network www.idnmusic.com/index.html Rare items.

K-TEL www.ktel.com Compilations; online retailer; digital downloads.

La Jolla Music www.lajollamusic.com La Jolla, CA; lessons; sheet music; band instruments.

Music 123 www.music123.com Online music retailer.

Music and Arts Online CD Catalog www.musicandarts.com Contemporary and historic classical, jazz, and world music recordings.

Music Books Plus musicbooksplus.com/ Thousands of titles; Canadian.

Music Box World www.musicboxworld.com Specializes in custom music boxes, carousels, fine Italian inlaids, dolls, ballerinas, and children's boxes; choose a tune from alphabetical list of hundreds; virtual museum.

Music Dispatch www.musicdispatch.com Online retailer of products distributed by Hal Leonard.

Music for a Song www.musicforasong.com Over 15,000 selections, including out-of-print, cutout, hard-to-find CDs and cassettes; Gold Disks and imports.

Music Gear OnLine musicgearonline.com Large guide to musical equipment including music software, soundware, MIDI, MIDI controllers, effects, signal processors, synthesizers, samplers, recorders, accessories, and more.

Music in Motion www.musicmotion.com Music education and gift catalog for all ages; music books, videos, audios, awards, teaching aids, posters, bulletin board aids, gifts, software, creative dramatics, multicultural resources.

Music Jackpot www.musicjackpot.com Online connection to online music stores; CDs, tapes, music videos, laser discs, video games, sheet music, and more.

Music Mart www.musicmart.com Online music retailer.

Music Room www.musicroom.com Online retailer of sheet music.

Music123 www.music123.com Online musical instrument store.

Musichotbid.com www.musichotbid.com Online music auction site.

Musician Store www.musicianstore.com Sheet music; software; musician's gear.

Musician's Friend www.musiciansfriend.com Order all types of music equipment online; music software; clearance sales.

MusicYo.com www.MusicYo.com Wholesaler of brand names.

Norwalk Music www.norwalkmusic.com Online musical instrument store; links to manufacturers' Web sites; index for every instrument.

Other Music www.othermusic.com Independent record store; New York City; downloads.

Parasol www.parasol.com Indie CDs and vinyl; new and used; catalog.

Past Perfect www.pastperfect.com Remastered songs from the 1920s to 1940s.

Preferred Music Retailers www.allmusic.com/com/amg/music.html Links to retailers.

Pro Audio www.proaudiomusic.com Equipment retailer; links.

Pro Music Find www.promusicfind.com Worldwide marketplace for musicians; instruments; music; downloadable sheet music and files.

Pulse Music www.pulseonline.com Equipment and instruments.

Rockabilia www.rockabilia.com Purchase rock music collectibles online.

Rough Trade Shop www.roughtrade.com Alternative music; used CDs; vinyl; concert listings; tickets; search engine.

Sam Ash Music www.SamAshMusic.com or www.samash.com Online music retailer; equipment.

Second Spin www.secondspin.com Buy and sell used CDs.

Sold Out www.soldout.com Purchase tickets online.

SongCast www.songcastmusic.com Music distribution.

Sonicrec.com www.sonicrec.com Collectible vinyl.

Stagepass.com www.stagepass.com Instructional books, videos, software, and MIDI files collections.

Tempest Music www.tempestmusic.com.au/ Sheet music; print music; online store and catalog; music; stringed; bowed; woodwind; brass; piano; percussion instruments; vocal music; novelty; accessories; strings; reeds.

The Federal Trade Commission www.ftc.gov Information on consumer e-commerce protection.

The Music House www.themusichouse.com Online music retailer.

The Music Resource www.themusicresource.com Home page; resources; links.

The Sound Professionals www.soundpros.com Stereo equipment.

Ticket Web www.ticketweb.com Purchase tickets online.

Ticketmaster Online www.ticketmaster.com Buy tickets to events online.

Ticketmaster UK www.ticketmaster.co.uk UK tickets online.

Tickets.com www.tickets.com Ticketing software.

Tower www.tower.com Online music and book retailer; track listings; audio samples.

Vintage Vinyl www.vvinyl.com 100,000-item inventory; all genres; 1950s, 1960s; imports.

Virgin Megastore www.virginmega.com Online music retailer.

West L.A. Music www.westlamusic.com Pro gear.

West Music www.westmusic.com Online music retailer.

Wherehouse Music www.wherehousemusic.com Music retailer.

World Music Store www.worldmusicstore.com CDs from around the world; multicultural media.

World of Music Boxes www.worldofmusicboxes.com Music box designs and mechanical movements imported from Switzerland, Italy, Germany, and the Orient; classic and children's collectibles; jewelry boxes; handcrafted gifts.

Yahoo Directories: Music Retailers dir.yahoo.com/Business_and_Economy/Shoppin g_and_Services/Music/Instruments_and_Equipm ent/Retailers/ Sellers of instruments and equipment.

Yestermusic www.yestermusic.com Oldies; all genres and decades.

Zzounds www.zzounds.com Online music gear and accessories retailer.

Musical E-Greetings—Singing Telegrams Web Sites

1001 Postcards www.postcards.org Large collection of free virtual postcards; cartoons; special occasions; scenic; comedy.

Abby's Good Stuff for Free www.abbys-good-stuff.com/greeting.html Free e-greetings.

American Greetings www.americangreetings.com Personalized greeting cards, printed and electronic.

Animated Greeting Cards with Music www.animatedfun.com/holiday.htm Holiday cards with animation and music.

Blue Mountain www.bluemountain.com Variety of e-greetings with music; printed greeting cards; poetry books.

CanWebCards www.canwebcards.com Personalized musical electronic greeting cards by e-mail.

Care2 E-Cards www.care2.com/send/categories Free animated and musical greetings that help save wildlife; over 25,000 greetings.

Compufield www.compufield.net/cards/ E-cards; musical greetings.

Egreetings.com www.egreetings.com Hosts free E-cards.

Greet2K www.greet2k.com Free greetings for the millennium.

Greeting-Cards.com www.greeting-cards.com/index.jsp?affiliate_id=01640 Electronic greetings.

Hallmark www.hallmark.com Electronic greetings for e-mail friends.

Happy Birthday to You www.happybirthdaytoyou.com Singing birthday cards; personalized, professionally recorded versions; all styles.

P.S. I Love You! www.personal-ads-network.comPersonalSongs.shtml Personalized songs on CD or cassette.

Singing Phonegrams www.singingphonegrams.com Sent anywhere in the world with ten-second recorded greeting included.

Singing Telegrams Inc. www.singingtelegrams.com.au Delivering gifts, poems, balloons, and breakfasts; Sydney, Australia.

Singing Valentines www.singingvalentines.com
Saying "I love you" with a song; available in all
regions.

The E-Greetings Portal
www.theegreetingsportal.com Links to e-
greetings Web sites.

Yahoo Greetings greetings.yahoo.com Send a free
greeting.

Networking—Blogs—Chat—Forums— Career Information—Indie Music Promotion Web Sites

1212.com-Internet Music Production Guide
www.1212.com Search Engine for music sites
dedicated to professional musicians, singers,
recording studios, sound engineer, and
composers around the world.

411 Music www.411-music.com Stringed
instruments; artists and bands concert schedules;
DJ services; duplicating; bookstore.

A&R Online www.aandronline.com Connect with
A&R reps.

Acid Planet www.acidplanet.com Site for music,
video, and unique artists; online community of
individual digital musicians and videographers;
create and upload music and videos; listen to
music created by others; check out popular
videos; enter contests where contestants remix
music by major artists and score music videos;
get discovered by label reps and studios.

Acoustic Friends www.acousticfriends.com Music-
related social networking site.

AIMusic www.aimusic.org Advancing independent
music; blogs; forum; for all members of the
independent music community.

Allindie.com www.allindie.com Indie artists and
labels.

American Idol www.americanidol.com Audition
dates and locations; contestants; winners; photos;
community; downloads; show guide; videos.

*Applause Music Production and Performance
Careers* www.cnvi.com/applause Tips, tricks,
and secrets for a show business, performance, or
production career; links.

Ariel Publicity www.arielpublicity.com Publicity at
the grassroots level.

Artist Development www.artistdevelopment.com
Duplication; design services; promotion.

Artist Direct www.artistdirect.com Artist Web sites;
links; search site; superstore; music downloads;
music community.

Artist Launch www.artistlaunch.com Sell indie
music; all styles.

Artist Server www.artistserver.com/ Online
community; music; downloads; MP3s.

Association for Family Interactive Media
www.afim.org Information for families about
video games, rating systems, and more.

Association of Independent Music
www.musicindie.com AIM; Resources and
contacts for independent musicians.

AudioPyro www.audiopyro.com Music-related social
networking site.

Badoo http://badoo.com/ London-based social
networking site.

Band Name www.bandname.com Worldwide band
name registry.

Band Radio www.bandradio.com Unsigned band
resource.

Band Store www.bandstore.com Independent music
store.

Band Wear www.bandwear.com Custom screen
printing and embroidery.

Bandit A&R Newsletter www.banditnewsletter.com
New music companies seeking acts, songs, and
masters every month; available in United States
and worldwide editions; sample current issue;
success stories file; introductory subscriptions.

Bandsintown www.bandsintown.com Music-related
social networking site.

Be the Movie Star www.bethemoviestar.com/ Social
networking site for actors and filmmakers;
casting calls.

Berklee Music
www.berkleemusic.com/school/courses Online
courses; Pro Tools; songwriting; lyric writing.

Big Meteor Publishing www.bigmeteor.com *The
Indie Music Bible;* free exposure for music-
related site or service; indie link exchange; indie
resource land; submit site.

Blogger www.blogger.com Create a free blog.

Broadcaster www.broadcaster.com Social
networking site; video sharing; music.

Broadjam www.broadjam.com Artist web pages;
upload songs, photos; peer reviews; pitch
opportunites; contests.

Bryan Farrish Radio Promotion www.radio-
media.com Song/album promotion; syndicated
program promotion; radio interview promotion;
internships.

Buy Indie Music www.buyindiemusic.com
Independent artist's music and merchandise.

Buzznet www.buzznet.com Music-related social
networking site.

*Canadian Independent Record Production
Association* www.cirpa.ca Canadian indies;
resources; links.

Careers in Music
spider.georgetowncollege.edu/music/Careers/car

eers.html Professional areas representing a number of career possibilities in music.

Careers.org www.careers.org The Internet's Directory of Career Directories; access to over 7,500 links sorted by topic and region.

CD Sonic www.cdsonic.com CD-Audio and CD-ROM duplication.

CD Stands www.cdstands.com Display CD and CD cover like a trophy.

Clinko www.clinko.com Music-related social networking site.

Coalition of Independent Music Stores www.cimsmusic.com/index.html Indie music.

College Board Online www.collegeboard.org Help with exams.

CollegeNET www.collegenet.com Search for colleges using different criteria.

Community Musician www.CommunityMusician.com Local listings for United States cities.

Cool Site of the Day www.coolsiteoftheday.com Cool picks are archived; links.

Crack the Whip Promotions www.crackthewhippromotions.com Promotion for independent artists; news; bands; events.

Creative Musicians Coalition www.aimcmc.com International organization representing independent artists and independent record labels; albums and videos available for purchase; ongoing dialogue with artists; showcases.

Cybergrrl.com www.cybergrrl.com Entertainment and informational site to celebrate and inspire women; technology, music, travel, and books; focus on profiles of women and women's personal essays; started by Aliza Sherman who wrote the book *Cybergrrl: A Woman's Guide to the World Wide Web.*

Dmusic.com www.dmusic.com Online indie distribution venue.

Do It Yourself Convention www.diyconvention.com Contests for film, music, and books; events in Los Angeles, Nashville, and New York; news; features; reviews.

Duck Music www.duckmusic.com Artists services; Web sites; online consignment CD sales; online tools.

Earbuzz.com www.earbuzz.com Online indie store; 100 percent of profits to the artist.

Female Musicians and Artists Network www.femmuse.com Shows; calendar; musicians; links; reviews.

FemaleMusician.com www.femalemusician.com Music industry education for young women; indie music company.

Femina.com www.femina.com Searchable directory of exclusively sites for, by, and about women with a special section of sites for girls.

FinAid www.finaid.org How to borrow money for education.

FineTune www.finetune.com Music-related social networking site.

Flixster www.flixster.com Share movie reviews and movie ratings with friends.

Flotones www.flotones.com Music-related social networking site.

Focus Marketing www.focusmarketing.us For independent artists; solutions; resources.

Free Music Classifieds www.freemusicclassifieds.com Home page.

Garage Band www.garageband.com Indie music company; online community created by musicians for musicians.

Gather www.gather.com Social networking site; share videos and more.

GetSigned.com www.getsigned.com Music biz advice from leading experts in the industry; indie tools; artist interviews; books; tour booking; interviews; home recording tips; gear reviews; music law; legal issues; press kits; management tips; playing live; promotion.

Girlmusician.com www.girlmusician.com Designed with the female singer/songwriter in mind; emphasis on the independent recording artist.

Girls Rock 'n' Roll Camp www.girlsrockcamp.org Day camp for girls, ages eight-eighteen, to learn basics of creating and playing rock 'n' roll music on their instrument of choice.

Go Girls Music www.gogirlsmusic.com Promoting women in music; reviews; new releases; join lists; regional festivals.

Great Music Sites www.greatmusicsites.com Links to featured artists; MP3 stations; genre listings; music reviews; gig alert; open forum.

Groove House www.groovehouse.com CD replication.

Groove Shark www.grooveshark.com Music-related social networking site.

Gruvr www.gruvr.com Music-related social networking site.

GuitarGirls.com www.guitargirls.com Resource and support site for female artists who write, sing, and play guitar; audio files; contest showcases and promotes independent female talent.

Haystack www.haystack.com Music-related social networking site.

Honky-Tonkin www.HonkyTonkin.com No charge to be added to online site; catalog of titles goes out worldwide to wholesale and retail account base; pay per transaction; no returns; no contracts.

Hostbaby.com www.hostbaby.com Web hosting for independent musicians.

I Seek You (ICQ) www.icq.com Chat in real time; free program download.

Ijigg www.Ijigg.com Music-related social networking site.

Ilike www.Ilike.com Music-related social networking site.

imeem www.imeem.com Social networking site; share music, videos, and more; playlists.

Independent Bands www.independentbands.com Indie band listings.

Independent Distribution Network www.idnmusic.com/index.html Global indie network; CD catalog.

Indie Artists Alliance www.indieartistsalliance.com Resources for independent musicians.

Indie Pool www.indiepool.com Canadian independent recording artists.

Indie Pro www.indiepro.com Indie music promotion.

Indie Rhythm www.indierhythm.com Indie store.

IndieGate www.indiegate.com Indie music Web site; buy CDs.

IndieGirl www.indiegrrl.com Forum for information, networking, and conversation in the realm of independent music from a female perspective; welcomes all female musicians, singers, songwriters, and others in indie music; men supportive of women in music are welcome.

Indie-Music.com www.indie-music.com Musician's resources; links; Internet primer; bands; education; labels; radio; reviews; studios; tour guide; venues; add URL; mailing list; CDs; mailing list; e-mail; ads; shop; journal; tips.

IndiePromo.com IndiePromo.com Information for independent musicians; resources; links; networking; e-zines; Internet radio; promotion; Web site design; tutorials; reviews; publications.

Indierec.com www.indierec.com Indie music company.

Indiespace www.indiespace.com Indie music promotion since 1994 founded by Jeannie Novak; consulting and development for indie artists; new media arts and entertainment.

InHance www.InHance.com Music-related social networking site.

Intermixx www.InterMixx.com/webzine Webzine for independent artists and musicians.

Internet Relay Chat www.ircle.com (Macintosh) or www.mirc.com (Windows); IRC channels.

ItBreaks www.ItBreaks.com Music-related social networking site.

Jamendo www.jamendo.com Music-related social networking site.

Jamnow www.jamnow.com Music-related social networking site.

JobStar-Specific Career Information www.jobsmart.org/tools/career/ Public library sponsored guide to information for the job search; 1,000 job hotlines; calendar of job and career events; career centers; libraries and more.

Jukeboxalive www.jukeboxalive.com Music-related social networking site.

KindWeb.com www.kindweb.com Music resources; band links.

Kompoz www.kompoz.com Music-related social networking site.

Kweevak.com www.kweevak.com Music promotion services; classic rock MP3 downloads.

La Costa Music Business Consultants www.lacostamusic.com Music business advice; songwriting; publishing; artist management; publicity; production; record promotion.

LA Music Awards www.lamusicawards.com LA area awards.

LAMN (Los Angeles Music Network) www.lamn.com News; FAQs; created to promote career advancement, continued education and good will among music industry professionals.

Last.fm www.last.fm The social music revolution; music; videos; radio.

Live Nation www.livenation.com Concert tickets and tour dates.

Master Merchant Systems www.mmscom.net Point of Sale; Barcoding.

Media Omaha www.mediaomaha.com CD duplication.

Meet New Players www.meetnewplayers.com Indie music company.

Meetyourband www.meetyourband.com Music-related social networking site.

Midomi www.midomi.com Music-related social networking site.

Modern Postcard www.modernpostcard.com Postcard printing.

MOG http://mog.com/ *Discover people through music and music through people.*

Monster.com www.monsterboard.com Search jobs; resume builder.

Music Biz Academy www.musicbizacademy.com Resources and books for indie musicians.

Music Builder www.MusicBuilder.com Upload music; statistics.

Music Business Software www.musicbusinessstore.com Professional Music Business Contracts: 100 music industry contracts; Record Company in a Box: complete record company management software; Tour Manager: manage gigs and complete tours, financial reports, and itineraries; Macintosh; Windows.

Music Connection www.musicconnection.com Magazine for musicians; music marketplace; free classifieds; find pro players; exclusive directories; detailed industry reference guide in every issue.

Music Dish www.musicdish.com Indie music resource; music industry e-newsletter; links; career tips; Online Music Industry Showcase Award; Music Industry Survey.

Music Distribution www.musicdistribution.com Promote and sell music.

Music for People www.MusicForPeople.org Music workshops.

Music Industry Career Center www.music-careers.com Sponsored by Sweetwater Sound; music industry companies list position openings; potential employees post resumes; free service.

Music Jobs www.music-jobs.com Job seekers; employers; bands; upload resume, picture, MP3s; jobs board; message board.

Music Makes Friends www.musicmakesfriends.com Music-related social networking site.

Music Network USA www.mnusa.com Resources for musicians and bands; musicians seeking bands; bands seeking musicians; recording artists; songwriters; music publishers; recording studios; talent agencies; producers and more.

Music Pro Insurance www.musicproinsurance.com Insurance for the musician; instruments; equipment; vehicle; life.

Music Promotion Tips www.musicpromotiontips.com Tips on selling CDs and more.

Music Registry www.musicregistry.com Industry contact listings available in digital format.

MusicCareers.net www.musiccareers.net/index.php In the studio; on the road; songwriting; education; reviews; interviews; links.

Musicians Atlas www.musiciansatlas.com Resource for musicians including clubs, venues, and more.

Musicians Contact Service www.musicianscontact.com Contact other musicians; find paying jobs.

Musicians Institute www.mi.edu Career development center for musicians located in Hollywood, CA; classes; workshops; private lessons; 500-seat concert hall.

MusiciansPage.com www.musicianspage.com Home page; resources.

Musicplayer.com www.musicplayer.com Resources; networking opportunities; lessons; forums.

Musicpromotion.net musicpromotion.net/ Resources for independent musicians; publications; tutorials; articles; links; newsletter; Web site design; online ordering.

Musocity www.musocity.com Music-related social networking site.

My Music Job www.mymusicjob.com Listing of music industry jobs and internships.

My Music Source www.mymusicsource.com Production music for film, TV, and advertising.

MySpace www.myspace.com Join as a band or musician; upload pictures, videos, and songs; blog; add friends; add comments; send messages; calendar; sell music.

MyStrands www.mystrands.com Music-related social networking site.

National Band Name Registry www.bandreg.com Database of names and band information; find out if a band name is in use; free; legal advice for bands; information about CDs by unsigned bands; site's magazine, *GIG*, features music industry news and reviews of unsigned bands.

New-List www.new-list.com Mail lists and discussion groups.

Outer Sound www.outersound.com Indie music community; articles; links; reviews; forums.

Overseas Jobs Express www.overseasjobs.com International job openings and links.

Pandora www.pandora.com Music-related social networking site.

Peoplesound www.peoplesound.com A&R involvement for emerging bands.

Petersons.com www.petersons.com Online college and career guides.

Postcard Mania www.postcardmania.com Postcard printing service.

Postcard Press www.postcardpress.com Bizcards; postcards.

Power Chord Academy www.powerchordacademy.com Rock 'n Roll Music Camp; brochure; registration; dates and locations.

ProjectOpus www.projectopus.com Music-related social networking site.

Promote Yourself www.promoteyourself.com Musician's guide to the Zen of hype.

Punk Bands www.punkbands.com Indie music company.

Purevolume www.purevolume.com Music-related social networking site.

Qloud www.qloud.com Music-related social networking site.

Quarterlife www.quarterlife.com A community for artists, thinkers, and doers.

Rainbo Records www.rainborecords.com Custom CDs, cassettes, and vinyl.

Rainmaker Publicity www.rainmakerpublicity.com Indie music promotion company.

Reverb Nation www.reverbnation.com Music-related social networking site.

Sellaband www.sellaband.com Music-related social networking site.

Show Biz Jobs www.showbizjobs.com Entertainment professional's network; employers; job seekers.

Skype www.skype.com Make calls from a computer; free to other people on Skype; great rates to phones and mobiles across the world.

Slacker www.slacker.com Music-related social networking site.

SliceThePie www.slicethepie.com Music-related social networking site.

Small Publishers Association of North America www.spannet.org Resource for book-selling ideas and money-making strategies for independent presses and self-publishers.

SoGrimey www.sogrimey.com Music-related social networking site.

SongRamp www.songramp.com Online music community for songwriters and fans; artists and songwriters can upload songs; Open Mic; Artist of the Month; artist web pages; charts.

Sonicbids www.sonicbids.com Electronic press kits; subscription fee; drop box; online submissions; for independent artists; upload songs, photos, bios, videos; submit to opportunity listings.

Sonific www.sonific.com Music-related social networking site.

Sound Click www.soundclick.com Charts, genres, bands; independent music.

Sound Generator www.soundgenerator.com UK music site; charts; artists; industry; education.

Sound Unwound www.soundunwound.com Music site from IMDB and Amazon.

SoundFlavor www.soundflavor.com Music-related social networking site.

Soundpedia www.soundpedia.com Music-related social networking site.

Star Polish www.starpolish.com Store; advice; community; label management; artist development; features; resources; Velvet Rope.

Taco Truffles Media www.tacotruffles.com Indie music promotion by John Dawes; Web site design; resources; tutorials; links.

Taltopia www.taltopia.com Online artistic community.

Telephone Directories on the Web www.infobel.com/teldir/ Links to Yellow Pages, White Pages, business directories, e-mail address directories, and fax numbers.

The Buzz Factor www.thebuzzfactor.com Music marketing tips by Bob Baker; indie music marketing resources; tips and tools to help indie musicians market their music on a budget.

The Indie Contact Bible www.bigmeteor.com/icb Resources for indie musicians; large international list organized by genre and location; links; sell CDs; available on disk; lists

publications that review CDs and radio stations that play indie music; all genres.

The Local Scene www.thelocalscene.com Alternative; indie Web site.

The Music Business Registry www.musicregistry.com Up-to-date music industry contact information; available as hard copies and downloads; Record XPress.

The Velvet Rope www.velvetrope.com Music industry information.

The Wonderwall www.beat.co.uk/wonderwall.html Links to artists.

Tile.Net www.tile.net Mail lists and discussion groups; comprehensive lists of newsgroups.

Tim Sweeney & Associates www.tsamusic.com Independent artist development company; promotion; publicity; retail marketing; distribution network; Internet promotion; workshops; publications.

Topica http://lists.topica.com/ Discussion groups.

TSI CD Manufacturing www.cdmanufacturing.com CD manufacturing.

Tunester www.tunester.com Music-related social networking site.

Ultimate Band List (UBL) www.ubl.com Artist directory; band Web sites and CDs; resources; information; music industry-related links.

Virb www.virb.com Music-related social networking site.

Vision Music USA www.visionmusicusa.com Booking, management, and promotion consulting services for independent musicians.

Webgrrls.com www.webgrrls.com Hub for nearly one hundred Web sites for Webgrrls chapters around the world; local chapters have gatherings where women meet face to face to talk about the Internet and new media.

Women in Music www.womeninmusic.com Nonprofit membership organization dedicated to promoting the advancement and recognition of women in the music industry; mentoring.

World Replication Group www.worldreplication.com CD replication; fulfillment; graphics; packaging; video duplication; digital audiocassettes.

World Wired Productions www.wwpro.com Promotion and positive representation of artists, bands, labels, agencies, and management on every level.

Writers Net www.writers.net Resources for writers, editors, publishers, and agents.

Writers Online Workshops www.writersonlineworkshops.com Introductory, intermediate, and advanced workshops in a variety of genres; writing tips.

XFM www.xfm.co.uk Alternative; indie Web site.

YouTube www.youtube.com Upload videos; view videos; featured videos; search.

Zebra Music www.zebramusic.com Music career development; information; tips; links; free monthly e-newsletter.

Radio—Internet Radio—Television Web Sites

650 WSM (Grand Ole Opry) www.650wsm.com The Grand Ole Opry's very own and first radio station, WSM-AM 650, is now live on the Internet; "Opry Star Spotlight" show with host Matthew Gillian offers songwriters an opportunity to play their songs on the air.

A&E www.aetv.com Arts and Entertainment; program listings and previews.

ABC www.abc.com American Broadcasting Company.

Academy of Television Arts & Sciences www.emmys.org Information on the Emmy awards.

Action Radio www.chez.com/actionradio International Internet radio.

American Movie Classics www.amctv.com Classic films.

American Music Channel www.americanmusicchannel.com Internet broadcast network devoted to country music.

Audiences Unlimited www.audiencesunlimited.com Free tickets to TV show tapings.

Austin City Limits www.pbs.org/klru/austin/ Program featuring original music.

Beatlock Technology djmixpro.com/beatlock.html DJ *Mix Pro* DJ mixing program for parties and nightclubs or background music; design mixes on headphones while music is playing on speakers.

Black Channel www.blackchannel.de Radio station.

Bravo Cable Network www.bravotv.com Cable TV.

Broadcast Science www.broadcastscience.nl Advanced software for the broadcast industry; automation systems, cart replacement software, and transmission line protection software.

Burli Software, Inc. www.burli.com *Newsroom System* integrates newswires, audio feeds, faxes, e-mail, Web access, and more in an intuitive drag-and-drop editing interface.

CBC Television and Radio www.cbc.ca Television and radio Web site.

CBS www.cbs.com Central Broadcasting System.

Cherry Moon www.cherrymoon.com Radio station.

Choice Radio www.choiceradio.com Radio Web site.

Comedy Central www.comcentral.com Humor.

Country Music Television (CMT) www.country.com Country music videos.

DigAS www.david-gmbh.de Digital audio system for broadcast professionals; system modules are a complete package of programs for working with audio material in radio stations.

Disney Channel www.disney.com/disneychannel Family entertainment; Disney movies.

DJ Jukebox www.gammadyne.com/jukebox.htm Playlist generator and MP3 organizer; supports remote control through a LAN; rate each song to ensure favorites are played often.

DJ Mix Pro djmixpro.com/djmixpro/djmixpro.html MP3 player and mixer; performs fully automatic quality DJ mixes, including cross-fading and beat matching between songs; screenshots.

DJjmixed.com www.djmixed.com News; reviews; downloads.

DMX Music www.dmxmusic.com Digital Music Express (DMX) provides digital music by subscription to businesses and consumers via cable, satellite, and disc.

DRS--DigiTrax Services www.drs-digitrax.com Producers of video software; teleprompter, video, and video broadcast software.

E! Entertainment Television www.eonline.com Entertainment news.

Fast Channel Network www.fastchannel.com/fastchannel/default.asp Creative channel; traffic channel; asset channel.

FOLK DJ-L www.folkradio.org Lists folk stations; shows; DJs and playlists.

FOX www.fox.com FOX Television Network.

GLR www.bbc.co.uk/london/ Radio Web site; London station.

Hamfests www.arrl.org/hamfests.html Calendar of events run by ham radio operators.

HBO www.hbo.com HBO Web site.

House of Blues www.hob.com Internet radio site that accepts submissions.

Intercollegiate Broadcasting System (IBS) www.frontiernet.net/~ibs/ibshome.html College radio.

Internet Radio Linking Project www.irlp.net/ Commercial-free radio.

Jazz 88 Radio www.jazz88.org World music; jazz.

KCRW www.kcrw.org Eclectic music.

LesBiGay Radio Chicago www.lesbigayradio.com AM 1240 and 1470; daily show aimed at the gay, lesbian, transgender, and bisexual population.

Live Radio www.live-radio.net/ Extensive radio station list.

Live Radio and Television from Asia broadcast-live.com/asia.html Live television and radio broadcasts from China, India, Japan, Korea,

Singapore, Thailand, and elsewhere in Asia; music, news, and sports.

Live Radio and Television from Europe broadcast-live.com/europe.html Watch television and listen to radio broadcasts; music; news and sports.

Live Television from Around the World broadcast-live.com/television Live television broadcasts are available from a number of countries including Belgium, Croatia, Canada, France, Germany, United States, and the UK from this site.

Live365 www.live365.com/index.live Create an Internet radio station for free.

MediaBureau.com www.mediabureau.com Live and direct Web casts and original content.

Mic Check Radio www.miccheckradio.com Hip-hop radio Web site.

Much Music www.muchmusic.com Streaming audio and video.

Music Television (MTV) www.mtv.com Music videos; features.

National Public Radio www.npr.org Home page of NPR.

NBC www.nbc.com National Broadcast Network.

Nick at Nite & TV Land nick-at-nite.com Games; vintage TV.

Nickelodeon www.nick.com Entertainment for kids.

One World Radio TV oneworldradiotv.com Twenty-four-hour world and reggae music; Internet radio; live shows Monday through Saturday.

Onradio.com www.onradio.com Find US radio stations.

PBS www.pbs.org Public Broadcasting Station.

Pirate Radio www.pirateradio.com PC-based Internet broadcasting software.

Pseudo.com www.pseudo.com Internet radio; audio; video; chat; message boards.

Radio 1 www.bbc.co.uk/radio1 Radio Web site; RealAudio streams.

Radio 2 www.bbc.co.uk/radio2 Radio Web site; jazz; folk; country.

Radio 3 www.bbc.co.uk/radio3 Radio Web site; classical.

Radio Connection www.radioconnection.com Train for a career in the music industry; on-the-job training in local major recording studios, radio, and TV stations.

Radio Margaritaville www.margaritaville.com Jimmy Buffet's Internet radio Web site.

Radio Moi www.radiomoi.com Radio Web site; MP3 format; create own station; stations; music library; facts.

Radio Tower www.radiotower.com Internet radio directory.

Radio X www.radiox.com Information about Internet radio shows.

Radiojock.com www.radiojock.com/labels.html Web site for professional broadcasters; production and equipment sources; music; charts; show prep; mix jocks; links to related Web sites.

Radio-Locator www.radio-locator.com Lists U.S., Canadian, European, and other international stations; stations that broadcast on the Internet.

RadioTV www.radiotv.com Internet radio site that accepts submissions.

RealGuide www.realguide.real.com Comprehensive directory of RealAudio and RealVideo broadcast sites.

Relax Online College Radio Directory www.relaxonline.com/radio State-by-state listing of college radio stations.

Sci-Fi Channel: Dominion www.scifi.com Science fiction.

SHOUTcast www.shoutcast.com Free Internet radio.

Spank Radio www.spankradio.com Underground music twenty-four hours.

Special TV Resources www.specialweb.com/tv Directory of television Web sites.

Spinner www.spinner.com Internet radio site; channels in all genres; free Spinner player; over one hundred stations; artist information.

Streaming Media World www.streamingmediaworld.com Submissions; subscribers.

Sunday Morning Klezmer & Other Jewish Music www.angelfire.com/nj/WBZCFMsndymrnngklzmr An Internet and radio exploration of Jewish music, art, and culture.

Tactile12000 MP3 DJ www.tactile12000.com 3D interactive simulation of a DJ setup; allows users to cross-fade, backspin, and change the speed of full-length WAV and MP3 files.

Talk Radio News www.talkradionews.com Radio Web site; online version; news from Washington, DC.

The History Channel www.HistoryChannel.com History channel.

The Paley Center for Media www.mtr.org Exhibitions; seminars; radio broadcasts; members; education; information.

Totally Radio www.totallyradio.com New material on the radio.

TV Guide Online www.tvguide.com Online version of TV Guide.

V Tuner www.vtuner.com Information about Internet radio shows.

VH1 www.vh1.com Online version of the cable channel; video hits; popular music; original movies.

Virgin Radio www.virginradio.com Radio Web site.

Virtue TV www.virtuetv.com Live Internet video broadcasts.

Visual Radio www.visualradio.com Online multimedia service.

Women on Air www.womenonair.com Weekly one-hour radio series; eclectic mix of female artists from around the world.

World Radio Network www.wrn.org Live international newscasts.

Yesterday USA www.yesterdayusa.com Radio Web site; radio shows from 1920s to 1950s.

Search Engine Web Sites

About.com www.about.com Information on hundreds of topics.

Alexa www.alexa.com Web traffic and rankings.

All the Web www.alltheweb.com Search engine.

AltaVista www.altavista.com Search engine.

AOL.com www.aol.com Web guide; sites for many subjects and interests.

Ask Jeeves www.askjeeves.com Ask questions; replies with a list of answers about where to find related material.

Beaucoup www.beaucoup.com Specialty search engine; find music-related search engines.

Blinx www.blinkx.com/ Search engine for video and audio content.

Cuil www.cuil.com/ Large web search engine.

Dogpile www.dogpile.com Multisearch engine; lists up to twenty-four search engines; specify order in which to search.

Euroseek www.euroseek.net European-based search engine; can search in any country, in any language.

Excite www.excite.com Concept-based searches narrow search to relevant sites.

Excite UK excite.co.uk/ Searches UK and European sites.

FinderSeeker www.finderseeker.com Specialty search engine; find music-related search engines.

Find Sounds www.findsounds.com/ Search for sounds on the web.

GenieKnows www.genieknows.com/ Games search engine.

Google www.google.com The best search engine; fast and effective.

HotBot www.hotbot.com Search engine.

Infospace www.infospace.com Many categories including Yellow Pages, White Pages, business listings, personal e-mail addresses, links.

Live Search www.live.com/ Search engine; formerly MSN Search.

Lycos www.lycos.com Lycos network; search.

Mamma.com www.mamma.com "The mother" of all search engines.

MetaCrawler www.metacrawler.com Meta search engine; search multiple engines.

MetaSearch metasearch.com Six search engines.

PicSearch www.picsearch.com/ Image, video, and audio search engine.

Podscope www.podscope.com/ Audio and video search engine; find podcasts.

Search Engine Guide www.searchengineguide.com Guide to general and subject-specific search engines, portals, and directories; search the resources by keyword or browse by category.

Search Engine Watch searchenginewatch.com Information about search engines; links to major search engines; how to use search engines.

Search.Com www.search.com Search in a range of categories and topics; over one hundred specialty searches listed alphabetically; music entries.

Seeqpod www.seeqpod.com/ Find audio, video, and podcasts.

The Free Encyclopedia www.encyclopedia.com Over 17,000 articles from *The Concise Columbia Electronic Encyclopedia.*

The Internet Sleuth www.isleuth.com Select up to six databases such as news, business, software, Web directories; list of twenty-one categories.

The Open Directory www.dmoz.org Human-driven search engine.

TracerLock www.tracerlock.com Automated service that monitors URL search engine placement.

UK Index www.ukindex.co.uk List of UK sites; search by category.

WebCrawler www.webcrawler.com Search by topic; create personalized search pages; UK site link goes to *Excite UK.*

Yahoo www.yahoo.com First search engine and directory on the Internet; list of categories; several search methods.

Yahoo UK www.yahoo.co.uk Search UK and Ireland sites.

Bibliography

Aczon, Michael, Esq. *The Professional Musician's Legal Companion.* Milwaukee, WI: Hal Leonard Publishing Corp., 2005.

Althouse, Jay. *Copyright: The Complete Guide for Music Educators.* Van Nuys, CA: Alfred Publishing Co, Inc., 1997.

Anderton, Craig. *Home Recording for Musicians.* New York: Amsco Publications, 2004.

Aschmann, Lisa. *1000 Songwriting Ideas.* Milwaukee, WI: Hal Leonard Publishing Corp., 2008.

Avalon, Moses. *Confessions of a Record Producer: How to Survive the Scams and Shams of the Music Business.* Milwaukee, WI: Hal Leonard Publishing Corp., 3rd ed., 2006.

———. *Secrets of Negotiating a Record Contract: The Musician's Guide to Understanding and Avoiding Sneaky Lawyer Tricks.* Milwaukee, WI: Hal Leonard Publishing Corp., 2001.

Baker, Bob. *Guerilla Music Marketing Handbook.* Saint Louis, MO: Spotlight Publications, 2005.

———. *MySpace Music Marketing: How To Promote & Sell Your Music on the Worlds Biggest Networking Site.* Download at www.thebuzzfactor.com, 2006.

Bartlett, Bruce. *Practical Recording Techniques.* Burlington, MA: Focal Press, 5th ed., 2008.

Bates, Jefferson D. *Writing with Precision.* New York: Penguin Books, 2000.

Beall, Eric. *Making Music Make Money: An Insider's Guide to Becoming Your Own Music Publisher.* Boston, MA: Berklee Press, 2003.

Besenjak, Cheryl. *Copyright Plain and Simple.* Franklin Lakes, NJ: Career Press, 1997.

Billboard's International Buyer's Guide. Annual. New York: Billboard Books.

Blesh, Rudi. "Scott Joplin: Black American Classicist" in *Scott Joplin Collected Piano Works.* Van Nuys, CA: Alfred Publishing, Inc., 1971.

Blume, Jason. *Six Steps to Songwriting Success—The Comprehensive Guide to Writing and Marketing Hit Songs.* New York: Billboard Books, 2008.

———. *This Business of Songwriting.* New York: Billboard Books, 2006.

Bond, Sherry. *The Songwriter's and Musician's Guide to Nashville.* New York: Allworth Press, 3rd ed., 2004.

Borg, Bobby. *The Musician's Handbook: A Practical Guide to Understanding the Music Business.* New York: Watson-Guptill Publications, 2003.

Bove, Tony. *iPod & iTunes for Dummies.* Foster City, CA: IDG Books Worldwide, 2008.

Brabec, Jeffrey, and Todd Brabec. *Music, Money, and Success.* New York: Schirmer Books, 5th ed., 2006.

Braheny, John. *The Craft and Business of Songwriting.* Cincinnati, OH: Writers Digest Books, 3rd ed., 2006.

Buchmam, Dian Dincin, and Seli Groves. *The Writers Digest Guide to Manuscript Formats.* Cincinnati, OH: Writers Digest Books, 1987.

Burt, George. *The Art of Film Music.* Boston: Northeastern University Press, 1994.

Buskin, Richard. *Inside Tracks – A First-Hand History of Popular Music from the World's Greatest Record Producers and Engineers.* New York: Avon Books, 1999.

Bye, Dean. *You Can Teach Yourself about Music.* Pacific, MO: Mel Bay Publications, 1989.

Cameron, Julia. *The Artist's Way: A Spiritual Path to Higher Creativity.* Los Angeles: Perigee, 2002.

Cann, Simon. *Building a Successful 21st Century Music Career.* Milwaukee, WI: Hal Leonard Publishing Corp., 2007.

Carter, Walter. *The Songwriter's Guide to Collaboration.* Milwaukee, WI: Hal Leonard Publishing Corp., 2nd ed., 1997.

Chapman, Robert L., and Barbara Ann Kipfer, eds. *The Dictionary of American Slang.* New York: Harper Collins, 3rd ed., 1998.

Childs, G. W. *Creating Music and Sound for Games.* Boston, MA: Course Technology, 2006.

Churchill, Sharal. *The Indie Guide Book to Music Supervision for Films.* Los Angeles, CA: Filmic Press, LLC, 2000.

Clark, Andrew. *Composing Music for Video Games.* Hingham, MA: Charles River Media, 2005.

Clark, Rick. *The Expert Encyclopedia of Recording.* Milwaukee, WI: Hal Leonard Publishing Corp., 2001.

Collins, Karen. *Game Sound: An Introduction to the History, Theory, and Practice of Video Game Music and Sound Design.* Cambridge, MA: MIT Press, 2008.

——. *From Pac-Man to Pop Music: Interactive Audio in Games and New Media.* Hampshire, UK: Ashgate Publishing, 2008.

Collins, Mike. *A Professional Guide to Audio Plug-ins and Virtual Instruments.* Burlington, MA: Focal Press, 2003.

——. *Choosing and Using Audio and Music Software – A Guide to the Major Software Applications for Mac and PC.* Burlington, MA: Focal Press, 2004.

Cook, Perry. *Real Sound Synthesis for Interactive Applications (Book and CD-ROM).* AK Peters, Ltd., 2002.

Cool, Lisa Collier. *How to Write Irresistible Query Letters.* Cincinnati, OH: Writers Digest Books, 1987.

Cooper, Helen. *The Basic Guide to How to Read Music.* New York: AMSCO Publications, 1986.

Coryat, Karl. *Guerilla Home Recording: How to Get Great Sound from Any Studio.* Milwaukee, WI: Hal Leonard Publishing Corp., 2005.

Crouch, Tanya. *100 Careers in the Music Business.* Hauppauge, NY: Barron's, 2nd ed., 2008.

——. *100 Careers in Film and Television.* Hauppauge, NY: Barron's, 2002.

Cupit, Jerry. *Nashville Songwriting.* Nashville, TN: Cupit Music, 1995.

Curtis, Richard. *How to Be Your Own Literary Agent.* Boston: Houghton Mifflin Company, 1984.

Davis, Richard. *Complete Guide to Film Scoring: The Art and Business of Writing Music for Movies and TV.* Boston, MA: Berklee Press, 2000.

Davis, Sheila. *Successful Lyric Writing.* Cincinnati, OH: Writer's Digest Books, 1988.

——. *The Craft of Lyric Writing.* Cincinnati, OH: Writers Digest Books, 1985.

——. *The Songwriters Idea Book: 40 Strategies to Excite Your Imagination, Help You Design Dis-tinctive Songs, and Keep Your Creative Flow.* Cincinnati, OH: Writer's Digest Books, 1996.

Dawes, John, and Tim Sweeney. *The Complete Guide to Internet Promotion for Artists, Musicians, and Songwriters.* Temecula, CA: Tim Sweeney and Associates, 2000.

Dearing, James W. *Making Money Making Music (No Matter Where You Live).* Cincinnati, OH: Writers Digest Books, 1982.

Delton, Judy. *The Twenty-Nine Most Common Writing Mistakes and How to Avoid Them.* Cincinnati, OH: Writers Digest Books, 1985.

Dolan, Michael J. *Mastering Show Biz. . . From the Heart: 10 Timeless Principles.* Studio City, CA: Mulholland Pacific, 1998.

Downing, Douglas, and Michael Covington. *Dictionary of Computer Terms.* Hauppauge, NY: Barron's Educational Series, Inc., 1992.

Editors of *Songwriter's Market. The Songwriter's Market Guide to Song and Demo Submission Formats.* Cincinnati, OH: Writers Digest Books, 1994.

Eiche, Jon, and Emile Menasche. *What's MIDI? - Making Musical Instruments Work Together.* Milwaukee, WI: Hal Leonard Publishing Corporation, 2nd ed., 2001.

Fisher, Jeffrey P. *Cash Tracks: Compose, Produce and Sell Your Original Soundtrack Music and Jingles.* Milwaukee, WI: Hal Leonard Publishing Corp., 2nd ed., 2005.

——. *Ruthless Self-Promotiion in the Music Industry.* Milwaukee, WI: Hal Leonard Publishing Corp., 2nd ed., 2005.

Frankel, Aaron. *Writing the Broadway Musical.* Cambridge, MA: Da Capo Press, 2000.

Franz, David. *Producing in the Home Studio with Pro Tools* Boston, MA: Berklee Press, 2nd ed., 2005.

——. *Recording and Producing in the Home Studio: A Complete Guide.* Boston, MA: Berklee Press, 2005.

Fries, Bruce, with Marty Fries. *The MP3 and Internet Audio Handbook—Your Guide to the Digital Music Revolution.* Burtonsville, MD: TeamCom Books, 2000.

Gavenda, Victor. *GarageBand 2 for Mac OS X.* Berkeley, CA: Peachpit Press, 2005.

Gerou, Tom, and Linda Lusk. *Essential Dictionary of Music Notation.* Van Nuys, CA: Alfred Publishing Company, Inc., 1996.

Gibson, James. *How You Can Make $30,000 a Year as a Musician without a Record Contract.* Cincinnati, OH: Writers Digest Books, 1986.

Goldberg, Natalie. *Writing Down the Bones: Freeing the Writer Within.* Boston: Shambhala, 2006.

Goldstein, Jeri. *How to Be Your Own Booking Agent.* Charlottesville, VA: The New Music Times, Inc., 1998.

Gordon, Steve. *The Future of the Music Business: How to Succeed with the New Digital Technologies.* Milwaukee, WI: Hal Leonard Publishing Corp., 2005.

Green, Stanley. *The World of Musical Comedy.* Cambridge. MA: Da Capo Press, 4th ed., 1980.

Guiheen, Annamarie, and Marie-Reine A. Pafik. *The Sheet Music Reference and Price Guide.* Paducah, KY: Collector Books, 1995.

Halloran, Mark, ed. *The Musician's Business and Legal Guide.* Beverly Hills Bar Association Committee for the Arts, Englewood Cliffs, N.J.: Prentice-Hall, 3rd ed., 2001.

Hamm, Charles. *Music in the New World.* New York: W. W. Norton and Company, 1983.

Harnsberger, Lindsey C. *Essential Dictionary of Music.* Van Nuys, CA: Alfred Publishing, Inc., 1976.

Harris, James F. *Philosophy at 33-1/3 RPM—Themes of Classic Rock Music.* Chicago, IL: Open Court, 1993.

Hatschek, Keith. *How to Get a Job in the Music Industry.* Boston, MA: Berklee Press, 2007.

Higgins, William R. *A Resource Guide to Computer Applications in Music Education.* Grantham, PA: Messiah College, 1994.

Hill, Brad. *Internet Directory for Dummies.* Foster City, CA: IDG Books Worldwide, 1999.

Hill, Dave. *Designer Boys and Material Girls.* New York: Landford Press, 1986.

Hoffert, Paul. *Music for New Media: Composing for Videogames, Web Sites, Presentations and Other Interactive Media (Book & CD).* Boston, MA: Berklee Press, 2007.

Huber, David Miles, and Robert E. Runstein. *Modern Recording Techniques.* Burlington, MA: Focal Press, 6th ed., 2005.

Hustwit, Gary. *The Musician's Guide to the Internet.* San Diego, CA: Rockpress Publishing, 1997.
——. *Websites for Musicians.* San Diego, CA: Rockpress Publishing, 2000.

Irvine, Demar. *Writing about Music.* Seattle: University of Washington Press, 1979.

Jamsa, Kris. *Welcome to Personal Computers.* New York: MIS Press, 1992.

Jones, Tom. *Making Musicals: An Informal Introduction to the World of Musical Theatre.* New York: Limelight Editions, 1998.

Jordan, Barbara L. *Songwriters Playground: Innovative Exercises in Creative Songwriting.* Pacific, MO: Mel Bay Publications, 1995.

Josefs, Jai. *Writing Music for Hit Songs.* New York: Schirmer Books, 2000.

Kasha, Al, and Joel Hirschorn. *If They Ask You, You Can Write a Song.* New York: Simon & Schuster, 1989.

Kimpel, Dan. *Networking Strategies for the New Music Business.* Vallejo, CA. Milwaukee, WI: Hal Leonard Publishing Corp., 2005.

Klavens, Kent J. *Protecting Your Songs and Yourself.* Cincinnati, OH: Writers Digest Books, 1989.

Kohn, Al, and Bob Kohn. *Kohn on Music Licensing.* Frederick, MD: Aspen Publishers, 3rd ed., 2002.

Kompanic, Sonny. *From Score to Screen: Sequencers, Scores, and Second Thoughts: The New Film Scoring Process.* New York: Schirmer Books, 2004.

Krasilovsky, M. William, and Sidney Shemel. *This Business of Music: The Definitive Guide to the Music Industry.* New York: Billboard Books, 10th ed., 2007.

Kusek, Dave. *The Future of Music: Manifesto for the Digital Music Revolution.* Boston, MA: Berklee Press, 2005.

Kushner, David. *Music Online for Dummies.* Foster City, CA: IDG Books Worldwide, 2000.

Larsen, Michael. *How to Write a Book Proposal.* Cincinnati, OH: Writers Digest Books, 1985.

Lathrop, Tad. *This Business of Music Marketing and Promotion.* New York: Billboard Books, Revised and updated edition, 2003.

Lees, Gene. *The Modern Rhyming Dictionary.* Cherry Lane Music, revised edition, 1987.

Levine, John R., Carol Baroudi, and Margaret Levine Young. *The Internet for Dummies.* Foster City, CA: IDG Books Worldwide, 1997.

Levine, Michael. *The Music Business Address Book.* New York: Harper and Row, 1989.

Levinson, Jay Conrad, Mitch Meyerson, and Mary Eule Scarborough. *Guerilla Marketing on the Internet: The Definitive Guide from the Father of Guerilla Marketing.* Irvine, CA: Entrepreneur Press, 2008.

Levitin, Dan. *From Demo Tape to Record Deal.* Van Nuys, CA: Alfred Publishing Company, Inc., 1992.

Lewin, Esther, and Albert E. Lewin. *The Thesaurus of Slang.* Hertfordshire, UK: Wordsworth Editions, 1998.

Linderman, Hank. *Hot Tips for the Home Recording Studio.* Cincinnati, OH: Writer's Digest Books, 1994.

Livingston, Robert Allen. *Music Business Reference.* Cardiff-by-the-Sea, CA: La Costa Music Business Consultants, 1988.

Luboff, Pat, and Pete Luboff. *101 Songwriting Wrongs and How to Right Them: How to Craft and Sell Your Songs.* Cincinnati, OH: Writers Digest Books, 2007.

Maran, Richard. *Creating Web Pages Simplified.* Foster City, CA: IDG Books Worldwide, Inc., 1996.

Maran, Ruth and Paul Whitehead. *Internet and World Wide Web Simplified.* Foster City, CA: IDG Books Worldwide, Inc., 1997.

Marks, Aaron. *The Complete Guide to Game Audio: For Composers, Musicians, Sound Designers, and Game Developers.* Burlington, MA: Focal Press, 2nd ed., 2008.

Mash, David. *Computers and the Music Educator.* Melville, NY: SoundTree, 1996.

———. *Musicians and Computers.* Van Nuys, CA: Alfred Publishing, Inc., 1998.

———. *Musicians and Multimedia.* Van Nuys, CA: Alfred Publishing, Inc., 1998.

———. *Musicians and the Internet.* Van Nuys, CA: Alfred Publishing, Inc., 1998.

Mash, David, C. Floyd Richmond, and Stefani Langol. *Basic Skills in Music Technology: Technology Assisted Learning Software and Multimedia.* Wyn, PA: TI:ME, 2005.

McCormick, Scott. *The Musician's Guide to the Web.* Pennsauken, NJ: Disc Makers, 2000.

McGraw Hill's Dictionary Of American Slang And Colloquial Usage. New York: McGraw-Hill, 4th ed., 2005.

MENC. *Growing Up Complete—The Imperative for Music Education.* Reston, VA: MENC, 1991.

———. *National Standards for Arts Education.* Reston, VA: MENC, 1994.

———. *The School Music Program: Description and Standards.* Reston, VA: MENC, 1986.

Metter, Ellen. *Facts in a Flash—A Resource Guide for Writers from Cruising the Stacks to Surfing the Net.* Cincinnati, OH: Writers Digest Books, 1999.

Mewton, Conrad. *All You Need to Know About Music & the Internet Revolution.* London: Sanctuary Publishing, 2005.

Middleton, Chris. *Creating Digital Music and Sound: An Inspirational Introduction for Musicians, Web Designers, Animators, Videomakers, and Game Designers.* Burlington, MA: Focal Press, 2006.

Miller, Lisa Annee, and Mark Northam. *Film and Television Composer's Resource Guide: The Complete Guide to Organizing and Building Your Business.* Milwaukee, WI: Hal Leonard Publishing Corp., 1998.

Mills-Huber, David and Philip Williams. *Professional Microphone Techniques.* Milwaukee, WI: Hal Leonard Publishing Corp., 1999.

Milstead, Ben. *Home Recording Power.* Cincinnati, OH: Muska & Lipman, 2004.

Mitchell, Kevin. *Hip-Hop Rhyming Dictionary.* Van Nuys, CA: Alfred Publishing, Inc., 2003.

Monaco, Bob, and James Riordan. *Platinum Rainbow.* Sherman Oaks, CA: Swordsman Press, 1980.

Moser, David. *Moser on Music Copyright.* Milwaukee, WI: Hal Leonard Publishing Corp., 2006.

———. *Music Copyright for the New Millenium.* Milwaukee, WI: Hal Leonard Publishing Corp., 2001.

Muench, Teri, and Susan Pomerantz. *Attention A & R.* Van Nuys, CA: Alfred Publishing, Inc., 1988.

Murrow, Don. *Sequencing Basics.* Van Nuys, CA: Alfred Publishing, Inc., 1998.

Nackid, Terri, ed. *The MTNA Guide to Music Instruction Software.* Cincinnati: OH: Music Teachers National Association, 1996.

NAMM. *International Music Market Show Directory.* Carlsbad, CA: NAMM, 2008.

Nashville Songwriters Association International. *The Essential Songwriter's Contract Handbook.* Nashville, TN: NSAI, 1994.

Nevue, David. *How to Promote Your Music Successfully on the Internet.* The Music Biz Academy, Download at www.musicbizacademy.com.

Newer, Hank. *How to Write Like an Expert about Anything.* Cincinnati, OH: Writers Digest Books, 1995.

Noad, Frederick. *The Virtual Guitarist - Hardware, Software, and Web Sites for the Guitar.* New York: Schirmer Books, 1998.

Novak, Jeannie. *Game Development Essentials – An Introduction.* Florence, KY: Cengage Learning, Inc., 2nd ed., 2007.

Oland, Pamela Phillips. *The Art of Writing Great Lyrics.* New York: Allworth Press, 2001.

———. *The Art of Writing Love Songs.* New York: Allworth Press, 2003.

———. *You Can Write Great Lyrics.* Cincinnati, OH: Writers Digest Books, 1989.

Passman, Donald S. *All You Need to Know About the Music Business.* Free Press, 6th ed., 2006.

Patterson, Jeff, and Ryan Melcher. *Audio on the Web - The Official IUMA Guide.* Berkeley, CA: Peachpit Press, 1998.

Pattison, Pat. *Songwriting: Essential Guide to Rhyming.* Boston, MA: Berklee Press, 1991.

———. *Songwriting: Essential Guide to Lyric Form and Structure.* Boston, MA: Berklee Press, 1991.

———. *Writing Better Lyrics.* Cincinnati, OH: Writers Digest Books, 2001.

Perricone, Jack. *Melody in Songwriting: Tools and Techniques for Writing Hit Songs.* Boston, MA: Berklee Press, 2000.

Pickow, Peter, and Amy Appleby. *The Billboard Book of Songwriting.* New York: Billboard Publications, 1988.

Poe, Randy. *New Songwriter's Guide to Music Publishing: Everything You Need to Know to Make the Best Publishing Deals for Your Songs.* Cincinnati, OH: Writer's Digest Books, 2005.

Pogue, David. *GarageBand 2 – The Missing Manual.* Sebastopol, CA: O'Reilly Media, Inc., 2005.

Prendergast, Roy M. *Film Music - A Neglected Art.* New York: W. W. Norton Company, Inc., 1977.

Purse, Bill. *The Finale NotePad Primer.* San Francisco, CA: Milwaukee, WI: Hal Leonard Publishing Corp., 2003.

——. *The Finale Primer.* San Francisco, CA: Milwaukee, WI: Hal Leonard Publishing Corp., 2004.

——. *The PrintMusic Primer,* San Francisco, CA: Milwaukee, WI: Hal Leonard Publishing Corp., 2003.

——. *Home Recording Basics.* Van Nuys, CA: Alfred Publishing, Inc., 1998.

Rabin, Carol Price. *The Complete Guide to Music Festivals in America.* Great Barrington, MA: Berkshire House, 1990.

Rachlin, Harvey. *The Songwriter's and Musician's Guide to Making Great Demos.* Cincinnati, OH: Writers Digest Books, 1988.

——. *The Songwriter's Handbook.* New York: Funk and Wagnells, 1977.

Randall, Robin, and Janice Peterson. *The Lead Sheet Bible.* Milwaukee, WI: Hal Leonard Publishing Corp., 1997.

Randel, Don. *The Harvard Dictionary of Music.* Cambridge, MA: Belknap Press of Harvard University Press, 4th ed., 2003.

Rapaport, Diane S. *How to Make and Sell Your Own Recording.* Englewood Cliffs, NJ: Prentice Hall, 1999.

——. *Music Business Primer.* Englewood Cliffs, NJ: Prentice Hall, 2002.

Reese, S., K. McCord, and K. Walls. *Strategies for Teaching: Music Technology.* Reston, VA: MENC, 2001.

Richmond, F. ed. *Technology Strategies for Music Education.* Wyncote, PA: TI:ME, 2nd ed., 2005.

Rona, Jeff. *The Reel World: Scoring for Pictures.* Milwaukee, WI: Hal Leonard Publishing Corp., 2000.

Rooksby, Rikki. *The Songwriting Sourcebook: How to Turn Chords into Great Songs.* Milwaukee, WI: Hal Leonard Publishing Corp., 2003.

——. *Arranging Songs.* Milwaukee, WI: Hal Leonard Publishing Corp., 2008.

——. *Chord Master: How to Choose and Play the Right Guitar Chords.* Milwaukee, WI: Hal Leonard Publishing Corp., 2004.

——. *How to Write Songs on Guitar: A Guitar-Playing and Songwriting Course.* Milwaukee, WI: Hal Leonard Publishing Corp., 2000.

——. *How to Write Songs on Keyboards: A Complete Course to Help You Write Better Songs.* Milwaukee, WI: Hal Leonard Publishing Corp., 2005.

——. *Inside Classic Rock Tracks: Songwriting and Recording Secrets of 100+ Great Songs.* Milwaukee, WI: Hal Leonard Publishing Corp., 2001.

——. *Lyrics: Writing Better Words for Your Songs.* Milwaukee, WI: Hal Leonard Publishing Corp., 2006.

——. *Melody: How to Write Great Tunes.* Milwaukee, WI: Hal Leonard Publishing Corp., 2004.

Rudolph, Thomas and Vincent Leonard. *Finale: An Easy Guide to Music Notation.* Boston, MA: Berklee Press, 2nd ed., 2005.

——. *Recording in the Digital World: Complete Guide to Studio Gear and Software.* Boston, MA: Berklee Press, 2001.

Rudolph, Thomas, Floyd Richmond, David Mash, and David Williams. *Technology Strategies for Music Education.* Wyncote, PA: Technology Institute for Music Educators, 1997.

Rudolph, Thomas. *General Music Curriculum.* New York: SoundTree, 1995.

——. *Teaching Music with Technology.* Chicago, IL: GIA Publications, 2nd ed., 2005.

Rumsey, Frances, and Tim McCormick. *Sound and Recording, An Introduction.* Burlington, MA: Focal Press, 5th ed., 2005.

Russell, William. "Notes on Boogie Woogie" in *Frontiers of Jazz,* ed. by Ralph de Toledano. New York: Ungar Pub., 1962.

Schock, Harriet. *Becoming Remarkable for Songwriters and Those Who Love Songs.* Nevada City, CA: Blue Dolphin Publishing, Inc., 1998.

Schulenberg, Richard. *Legal Aspects of the Music Industry: An Insider's View of the Legal and Practical Aspects of the Music Business.* New York: Watson-Guptil Publications, 2005.

Schuller, Gunther. "The Future of Form in Jazz" in *Saturday Review,* January 12, 1957, 62.

Schwartz, Daylle Deanna. *Start and Run Your Own Record Label.* New York: Billboard Books, Revised and Expanded Edition, 2003.

Scott, Richard J. *Money Chords: A Songwriter's Sourcebook of Popular Chord Progressions.* Writer's Club Press, 2000.

Sexton, Jamie. *Music, Sound and Multimedia: From the Live to The Virtual.* Edinburgh: Edinburgh University Press, 2007.

Sharp, J. D. *Home Recording Techniques.* Van Nuys, CA: Alfred Publishing, Inc., 1992.

Short, Marion, and Roy Short. *The Gold in Your Piano Bench: Collectible Sheet Music - Tearjerkers, Black Songs, Rags, & Blues.* Atglen, PA: Schiffer Publishing, 2000.

——. *More Gold in Your Piano Bench: Collectible Sheet Music - Inventions, Wars & Disasters.* Atglen, PA: Schiffer Publishing, 2000.

——. *Covers of Gold: Collectible Sheet Music - Sports, Fashion, Illustration, & Dance.* Atglen, PA: Schiffer Publishing, 2000.

——. *Collectible Sheet Music: From Footlights to The Flickers - Broadway Shows and Silent Movies.* Atglen, PA: Schiffer Publishing, 2000.

——. *Collectible Sheet Music - Hollywood Movie Songs.* Atglen, PA: Schiffer Publishing, 2000.

Skolnik, Peter L. *Fads.* New York: Thomas Y. Crowell Company, 1978.

Songwriter's Market. Annual. Cincinnati, OH: Writer's Digest Books.

Sparrow, Andrew. *Music Distribution and the Internet: A Legal Guide for the Music Business.* Hampshire, UK: Gower Technical Press, 2006.

Spears, Richard A. *NTC's American Idioms Dictionary: The Most Practical References for the Everyday Expressions of Contemporary American English.* New York: McGraw-Hill, 3rd ed., 2000.

Spellman, Peter. *CD Marketing Plan.* Boston, MA: Music Business Solutions, 2005.

——. *Indie Marketing Power: The Resource Guide for Maximizing Your Music Marketing.* Boston, MA: Music Business Solutions, 2006.

——. *The Musician's Internet: Online Strategies for Success in the Music Industry.* Boston, MA: Berklee Press, 2002.

——. *The Self-Promoting Musician: Strategies for Independent Music Success.* Milwaukee, WI: Hal Leonard Publishing Corp., 2008.

Stanfield, Jana. *The Musicians Guide to Making and Selling Your Own CDs and Cassettes.* Cincinnati, OH: Writers Digest Books, 1997.

Stangl, Jean. *How to Get Your Teaching Ideas Published.* New York: Walker and Co., 1994.

Starr, Greg R. *What's a Sequencer? - A Basic Guide to Their Features and Use.* Milwaukee, WI: Hal Leonard Publishing Corp., 2nd ed., 2001.

Stern, Jane, and Michael Stern. *Encyclopedia of Pop Culture.* New York: Harper Perennial, 1992.

Stewart, Dave. *The Musician's Guide to Reading and Writing Music.* San Francisco, CA: Miller Freeman Books, 1999.

Sweeney, Tim, and John Dawes. *Using Email Effectively as an Artist or Songwriter (Audio CD).* San Diego, CA: Taco Truffles Media, 2004.

TI:ME. *Technology Guide for Music Educators.* Milwaukee, WI: Hal Leonard Publishing Corp., 2005.

——. *Technology Integration in the Elementary Music Classroom.* Milwaukee, WI: Hal Leonard Publishing Corp., 2008.

Trubitt, David. *Managing MIDI.* Van Nuys, CA: Alfred Publishing Company, Inc., 1992.

Truesdell, Cliff. *Mastering Digital Audio Production – The Professional Music Workflow with Mac OS X.* Indianapolis, IN: Wiley Publishing, Inc., 2007.

Tucker, Susan. *The Secrets of Songwriting: Leading Songwriters Reveal How to Find Inspiration and Success.* New York: Allworth Press, 2003.

Tucker, Susan, and Linda Lee Strother. *The Soul of a Writer: Intimate Interviews with Successful Songwriters.* Nashville, TN: Journey Publishing, 1996.

Turcan, Peter, and Mike Wasson. *Fundamentals of Audio and Video Programming for Games.* Microsoft Press, 2003.

Underhill, Rod, and Nat Gertler. *The Complete Idiot's Guide to MP3: Music on the Internet.* Indianapolis, IN: Que Corporation, 2000.

Uscher, Nancy. *Your Own Way in Music - A Career and Resource Guide.* New York: St. Martin's Press, 1990.

Vincent, Frances. *MySpace for Musicians.* Boston, MA: Course Technology, 2007.

Volanski, John. *Sound Recording Advice.* San Diego, CA: Pacific Beach Publishing, 2002.

Waterman, Guy. "Ragtime" in *Jazz,* ed. by Nat Hentoff and Albert McCarthy. New York: Rinehart & Co., Inc., 1959.

Waugh, Ian. *Music on the Internet (and Where to Find It).* Kent, UK: PC Publishing, 1998.

Webb, Jimmy. *Tunesmith - Inside the Art of Songwriting.* New York: Hyperion, 1998.

Westin, Helen. *Introducing the Song Sheet.* Nashville, TN: Thomas Nelson, Inc., 1976.

Whitmore, Lee. *MIDI Basics.* Van Nuys, CA: Alfred Publishing, Inc., 1998.

Whitsett, Tim, and James Stroud. *Music Publishing: The Real Road to Music Business Success.* Mix Books, 5th ed., 2001.

Wilde, Martin. *Audio Programming for Interactive Games.* Burlington, MA: Focal Press, 2004.

Wilkerson, Scott, and Steve Oppenheimer. *Anatomy of a Home Studio: How Everything Really Works, From Microphones to MIDI.* Emerysville: EM Books, 1998.

Williams, David and Peter Webster. *Experiencing Music Technology*. New York: Schirmer Books, 3rd ed., 2005.

Williams, Robin. *The Little Mac Book*. Berkeley, CA: Peachpit Press, 1993.

———. *Cool Mac Apps*. Berkeley, CA: Peachpit Press, 3rd ed., 2008.

Wills, Dominic, and Ben Wardle. *The Virgin Internet Music Guide Version 1.0*. London: Virgin Publishing Ltd., 2000.

Wixen, Randall. *The Plain and Simple Guide to Music Publishing*. Milwaukee, WI: Hal Leonard, Publishing Corp., 2005.

Zager, Michael. *Writing Music for Television and Radio Commercials and More*. Lanham, MD: Scarecrow Press, Inc., 2008.

———. *Music Production: A Manual for Producers, Composers, Arrangers, and Students*. Lanham, MD: Scarecrow Press, Inc., 2006.

Zollo, Paul. *Songwriters on Songwriting*. Cambridge, MA: Da Capo Press, 4th ed., 2008.

About the Author

Elizabeth C. Axford (B.A., Music, University of Illinois, Urbana-Champaign; M.A., Musicology, San Diego State University) is an independent piano instructor and freelance writer living in Del Mar, California. She is an active member of the Nashville Songwriters Association International (NSAI), having served as regional workshop coordinator in Miami, FL (1990-1992) and San Diego, CA (1992-present). She is also a member of the Music Teachers' Association of California (MTAC), California Association of Professional Music Teachers (CAPMT), an affiliate of the Music Teachers National Association (MTNA), ASCAP, NARAS (voting member), TI:ME, CMA, TAXI, and SCBWI.

Ms. Axford has been teaching piano, keyboard, music theory, and voice to students of all ages, levels, and backgrounds since 1984.

She has attended or produced over one hundred and fifty songwriting, music industry, and piano pedagogy seminars and conferences in San Diego, Los Angeles, Nashville, Miami, Dallas, and Orlando.

Ms. Axford is a published songwriter and arranger of piano music as well as a published poet. Her original songs and arrangements have been heard on the radio, on television including CNN, PBS, and in TV infomercials, in short films, as sound chips in greeting cards, and on the Internet. She has recorded and produced many products for teachers and students through her company, Piano Press.

She is the author of Keyboard Chops articles written for www.Indie-Music.com, and her column "Songwriting and the Web" appeared in the NSAI Newswire. Other publications by Ms. Axford include *Traditional World Music Influences in Contemporary Solo Piano Literature* (Scarecrow Press, 1997), *Merry Christmas Happy Hanukkah—A Multilingual Songbook and CD* (Piano Press, 1999), *My Christmas Fun Books* (Piano Press, 2006), and *My Halloween Fun Books* (Piano Press, 2008).

Born in Van Nuys, CA in 1958, Ms. Axford has lived in six different states, including California, Texas, Illinois, New Mexico, Kansas, and Florida.